Buddha Śākyamuni

Guru Padmasambhava

Longchen Rabjam Drimé Özer

༄། །རྒྱལ་བ་ཀློང་ཆེན་རབ་འབྱམས་ཀྱིས་མཛད་པའི་
ཆོས་དབྱིངས་རིན་པོ་ཆེའི་མཛོད་ཀྱི་རྩ་བ་དང་
ཁང་སར་རིན་པོ་ཆེ་བསྟན་པའི་དབང་ཕྱུག་གིས་མཛད་པའི་
འབྲུ་འགྲེལ་འོད་གསལ་ཐིག་ལེ་ཉག་གཅིག་
བཞུགས་སོ། །

པདྨ་ཀཱ་རའི་སྒྲ་བསྒྱུར་མཐུན་ཚོགས་ནས་
སྒྲ་བསྒྱུར་ཞུས།

The Padmakara Translation Group gratefully acknowledges the generous support of the Tsadra Foundation in sponsoring the translation and preparation of this book.

KHANGSAR TENPA'I WANGCHUK'S COLLECTED WORKS

The Precious Treasury of the Dharmadhātu

Longchenpa

WITH A COMMENTARY BY

Khangsar Tenpa'i Wangchuk

TRANSLATED BY THE

Padmakara Translation Group

SHAMBHALA

Shambhala Publications, Inc.
2129 13th Street
Boulder, Colorado 80302
www.shambhala.com

Cover design: Meredith Jarrett

9 8 7 6 5 4 3 2 1

Printed in the United States of America

Shambhala Publications makes every effort to print on acid-free, recycled paper.
Shambhala Publications is distributed worldwide by
Penguin Random House, Inc., and its subsidiaries.

LIBRARY OF CONGRESS CATALOGING-IN-PUBLICATION DATA
Names: Bstan-pa'i-dbang-phyug, Khang-sar Rin-po-che Dbon-sprul, 1938–, author | Klong-chen-pa Dri-med-'od-zer, 1308–1363. Chos dbyings rin po che'i mdzod. English. | Comité de traduction Padmakara, translator
Title: The precious treasury of the dharmadhātu / Longchenpa; with a commentary by Khangsar Tenpa'i Wangchuk; translated by Padmakara Translation Group.
Other titles: Chos dbyings rin po che'i mdzod kyi 'Bru 'grel 'od gsal thig le nyag gcig. English. | Chos dbyings rin po che'i mdzod
Description: Boulder: Shambhala, 2026. | Series: Khangsar Tenpa'i Wangchuk's collected works | Includes bibliographical references and index.
Identifiers: LCCN 2024053729 | ISBN 9781645473718 (hardback)
Subjects: LCSH: Klong-chen-pa Dri-med-'od-zer, 1308–1363. Chos dbyings rin po che'i mdzod. | Rnying-ma-pa (Sect)—Doctrines. | Rdzogs-chen.
Classification: LCC BQ7950.K667 B8713 2025 | DDC 294.3/923—dc23 /eng/20250911
LC record available at https://lccn.loc.gov/2024053729

The authorized representative in the EU for product safety and compliance is eucomply OÜ, Pärnu mnt 139b-14, 11317 Tallinn, Estonia, hello@eucompliancepartner.com.

Contents

Foreword

Everyone knows that among the great works of the Omniscient Longchenpa, the Seven Treasuries hold a special place and that among those seven great works *The Treasury of the Dharmadhātu* is particularly revered.

It is hard for people like ourselves to find the words to speak adequately of *The Treasury of the Dharmadhātu*, for it is so much more than an ordinary book. In his famous exhortation to read the Seven Treasuries, Patrul Rinpoche tells us that *The Precious Treasury of the Dharmadhātu* is the very image (*'dra 'bag*) of the realization of Longchenpa. It represents, and in a sense embodies, the state of complete and perfect enlightenment that he has attained. Although it is written in language and words and is addressed to us, it speaks of something that is completely beyond the world, utterly beyond the ordinary mind. It is, Patrul Rinpoche says, the actual dharmakāya appearing in the form of a text. It reveals directly the wisdom of the Victorious Ones and carries within it the quintessence of the Three Jewels of Buddha, Dharma, and Sangha. To hear a single word of it is enough to tear samsara to shreds. To see, hear, or remember it brings liberation.

Even more remarkably, speaking of *The Precious Treasury of the Dharmadhātu* in terms of a treasure text, Patrul Rinpoche says that sealed within its words and preserved for future generations is the fresh, unspoiled blessing power of Longchenpa's wisdom. To discover this text, he says, is like being in the presence of the omniscient master himself. Even if one is unable to appreciate fully the meaning of the words, if one has genuine devotion, to meet with this text is like receiving the precious word empowerment. It is the empowerment of the creative power of awareness, an introduction to the nature of the mind.

Now if this is true, what greater benefit could there be for us than to have a trustworthy introduction to the actual meaning of Longchenpa's precious teaching? Here we have a translation of the wonderful commentary of the great Khangsar Tenpa'i Wangchuk Rinpoche, in which he explains every syllable of Longchenpa's text. During his many long years in a concentration camp and in a situation of great duress, he had the great good fortune to meet his root teacher, Akyong Togden Lodrö Gyatso, an incarnation of Vairotsana himself, and it was from him that he received in secret the transmission of this and many other profound teachings. Years later, while in solitary retreat, he composed this unique and completely unprecedented commentary, based on his own vast erudition and profound realization, and assisted, we are told, in the interpretation of particularly difficult passages, by the wisdom protectress mamo Ekajaṭī herself and other dharma protectors. I think, therefore, that we can be quite sure of the accuracy and authenticity of this incomparable commentary.

When I first heard of Khangsar Tenpa'i Wangchuk Rinpoche, I felt a great and joyful aspiration to receive his teachings, especially his commentary on *The Precious Treasury of the Dharmadhātu*. Unfortunately, I did not have the merit to meet this great master in person. Nevertheless, thanks to the intervention of Yingrik Drubpa Rinpoche and my brother Taklung Tsetrul Pema Wangyal Rinpoche, it became possible for Tenpa'i Wangchuk Rinpoche's spiritual heir and nephew, Tsultrim Zangpo Rinpoche, the abbot of Taklung Monastery in Golok, to travel all the way to Dordogne in France in order to give us the empowerments and textual transmissions of all Tenpa'i Wangchuk's works that have been so far published.

Translating this text has been an arduous enterprise, and no doubt it contains many imperfections, but we hope that it will be useful nevertheless and be of benefit to devoted practitioners in the West. I am grateful to our sponsor and publisher and all who have contributed to the production of this book.

Jigme Khyentse Rinpoche
Dordogne, France
Autumn 2024

Series Introduction

The Collected Works of Khangsar Tenpa'i Wangchuk (1938–2014) bears eloquent testimony to the continuance in Tibet, despite the immense difficulties endured since the Chinese invasion in the 1950s, of the literary tradition of original texts and commentaries composed by Tibetan masters over the past fourteen centuries. The writings of this great contemporary scholar are all the more remarkable for including not only works on Indian and Tibetan classics but also unprecedented commentaries on two of Kunkhyen Longchenpa's Seven Treasuries.

A detailed biography of the author is included in the first volume of his Collected Works. For the present purposes, that of introducing the series generally, the salient details of his remarkable life may be briefly reviewed as follows. Khangsar Khenpo Tenpa'i Wangchuk was born in the Akyong Khangsar district of Golok, a remote region of Eastern Tibet now included in the Chinese administrative province of Qinghai. Not long after his birth, he was recognized by important lamas of different schools as the rebirth of Panak Öntrul Rigdzin Dorje, an emanation of Yudra Nyingpo, a disciple of the great eighth-century translator Vairotsana, and one of the twenty-five principal disciples of Guru Padmasambhava. He received his first monastic ordination in 1952 at the age of fourteen from Akyong Khenpo Lozang Dorje of the Payul tradition. Affiliated as he therefore was to the Nyingma school, in the years that followed, Tenpa'i Wangchuk received a rigorous education that was strongly marked by the nonsectarian spirit of the rimé movement, which was inaugurated toward the end of the nineteenth century in Kham and had done so much to preserve and invigorate the teachings of all Tibetan schools. Consequently, in addition to his fundamental training in the Nyingma tradition, which included the complete transmission of the teachings of Mipham Rinpoche, Tenpa'i Wangchuk devoted two years to the study of logic and epistemology in the Geluk tradition at the monastery of Amchok Tsenyi in Amdo. And his training was further enriched by the reception of teachings on Prajñāpāramitā and Madhyamaka according to the tradition of the celebrated Jonang master Bamda Thubten Gelek. Furthermore, it is said that inasmuch as Tenpa'i Wangchuk was an incarnation of Yudra Nyingpo and thus directly connected with the yogic power of Guru Rinpoche, when propitious circumstances appeared, his potential as a *tertön*, or "treasure revealer," awakened, and he was able to reveal a number of spiritual treasures.

This broadly based training was put to the test, and indeed perfected, in the course of the decades that followed, when, like so many other masters, Tenpa'i Wangchuk had to endure the horrors of the Cultural Revolution and the social changes inflicted by the communist regime. At the age of thirty-one, he was sentenced to twelve years' imprisonment in various gulags. Yet despite these dreadful circumstances—which were intended to be, and might well have proved, the final destruction of Tibet's cultural and spiritual patrimony—the light of the teachings was not extinguished. Indeed, it was during the years of his captivity that Tenpa'i Wangchuk met his most important teachers, prisoners like himself, who, thanks to their previous training of many years, their undimmed faculties, and their great spiritual realization, were able to transmit to him from memory, and in situations of great peril, many priceless teachings and pith instructions.

Following his release from imprisonment, and taking advantage of the somewhat more favorable social situation, Tenpa'i Wangchuk single-mindedly devoted the rest of his life to the preservation of the Buddhist teachings. He rebuilt and founded monasteries and places of study, where the tradition could be rekindled. He tirelessly guided multitudes of disciples, both Tibetan and Chinese, and composed for them important commentaries and much needed texts of instruction.

In the autumn of 2019, several years after Tenpa'i Wangchuk's death, his nephew and lineage holder, Tsultrim Zangpo Rinpoche, the abbot of Khangsar Taklung Monastery, visited Dordogne in France where he bestowed the full transmission of Tenpa'i Wangchuk's Collected Works, his treasure texts and doctrinal compositions, requesting and thereby inaugurating the present project of translating his published writings into English and subsequently into other Western languages.

The Collected Works

A tireless and skillful teacher, Tenpa'i Wangchuk was also a prolific writer and produced a series of important and fascinating writings, some of which are still being edited. At the moment of writing, the collection comes to eight Tibetan pecha volumes or five Western-style books. In the enormous efforts made to rekindle the Buddhist teachings in Tibet—and to save many teachings that might otherwise have been lost, preserving them for future generations of practitioners both inside and outside Tibet—Tenpa'i Wangchuk committed to writing in clear and accessible form many essential instructions pertaining to both the sutras and tantras, and most especially to teachings of the Great Perfection. These include his, as yet unpublished, expositions of Jigme Lingpa's *Highest Wisdom* (*Ye shes bla ma*) and Mipham Rinpoche's *Beacon of Certainty* (*Nge shes gron me*) and—perhaps most extraordinary of all—his important and completely unprecedented commentaries on two of Longchenpa's Seven Treasuries: a medium-length commentary on *The Precious Treasury of the Fundamental Nature* and a long and detailed commentary on *The Precious Treasury of the Dharmadhātu*, which is translated in the present volume.

Of the five volumes of Tenpa'i Wangchuk's writings currently available, the first begins with Tenpa'i Wangchuk's biography and is followed by a collection of some thirty poems, twenty-six spiritual songs and counsels related to the Great Perfection, and over forty prayers and short practice texts. Many of these are only three or four pages long.

The second volume contains a number of more substantial works related to the sutra vehicle: a commentary on Gyalse Thogme's celebrated *Thirty-Seven Practices of a Bodhisattva* (*rGyal sras lag len*), autocommentaries on two of Tenpa'i Wangchuk's own poems in the first volume, an instructional text on the four thoughts that turn the mind to the Dharma (*bLo ldog rnam bzhi*), and commentaries on three well-known prayers of aspiration—Kunkhyen Jigme Lingpa's *Prayer to Be Reborn in the Copper-Colored Mountain* (*Zangs mdog dpal ri'i smon lam*), Karma Chakme's *Prayer to Be Reborn in Sukhāvatī* (*Chags med bde smon*), and Samantabhadra's *Prayer of Good Action* (*bZang spyod smon lam*).

The remaining three volumes are devoted to several texts related to the Great Perfection. The third volume contains a commentary on *The Cloudless Sky* (*Nam mkha' sprin bral*), a detailed exposition, in the form of a poem, of the practice of *trekchö* by his teacher Togden Lodrö Gyatso; *Notes on An Instruction That Points Out the Nature of the Mind according to the Way of Old and Realized Yogis* (*Sems ngo mdzub tshugs*) and on Garab Dorje's well-known *Three Statements That Strike Upon the Vital Points* (*Tshig gsum gnad brdeg*); an outline of Shabkar Tsokdruk Rangdröl's *Flight of the Garuḍa* (*mKha' lding gshog rlabs*); *Notes Explaining the Words of Inner Lama Sādhana* from Jigme Lingpa's *Heart Essence of the Vast Expanse* (*kLong chen snying thig*), *The Assembly of Vidyādharas* (*Nang sgrub rig 'dzin 'dus pa*); and *Notes on Mipham's Prayer to Mañjuśrī, the Great Perfection* (*'Jam dpal rdzogs pa chen po'i smon lam*).

In the fourth volume we find Tenpa'i Wangchuk's unique commentary on Kunkhyen Longchenpa's *Precious Treasury of the Fundamental Nature* (*gNas lugs rin po che'i mdzod*). This is followed by a commentary (*The Light of Wisdom*) on a tantra discovered by the treasure revealer Deshek Lingpa, which is a complete guide to the practice of the Great Perfection titled *The Natural Openness and Freedom of the Mind* (*Sems nyid rang grol*). Finally, there is a commentary on a pith instruction text of the Great Perfection.

The fifth and final volume is entirely taken up with Tenpa'i Wangchuk's extraordinary commentary on Kunkhyen Longchenpa's *Precious Treasury of the Dharmadhātu* (*Chos dbyings rin po che'i mdzod*), which is the content of this present book.

Translators' Introduction

Longchen Rabjam (1308–1363) was, by all accounts, an author of astonishing productivity. While at Tharpa Ling in Bhutan—and therefore sometime in the six years between 1353, when that temple hermitage was built, and 1360, when he returned to Tibet—he composed a partial catalog of all his works.[1] This list was incorporated, with a number of additions, in the biography composed by his disciple Chödrak Zangpo and numbers no fewer than 271 compositions.[2] Nyoshul Khen Rinpoche, again basing himself on Longchenpa's catalog, raises this figure to 307.[3] Admittedly, many of these texts appear to have been short incidental pieces: poems, prayers, essential instructions, and so on. Moreover, the greatest portion has been lost and there are several stories of catastrophic accidents in the course of Longchenpa's travels when pack animals carrying his library were swept away by rivers, fell into ravines, and so on. Despite these adversities, many of Longchenpa's important works have survived—profound compositions, some of great length: the Seven Treasuries, the Four Parts of Heart Essence, the numerous texts belonging to the cycles known as the Trilogy of Rest, the Trilogy of Natural Openness and Freedom, the Trilogy on Dispelling Darkness, and so on. Dealing with the whole range of Buddhist teachings, but mainly the tantras and particularly the Great Perfection, these writings have come to form a cornerstone of the teachings of the Nyingma tradition.

In his catalog, Longchenpa mentions all but one of the Seven Treasuries, listing them in a rather disconnected fashion and without associating them together. This has led to the idea that, in Longchenpa's mind at least, the Seven Treasuries were composed as stand-alone texts and not as a coordinated series. While this is perfectly plausible, it is nevertheless the case that, owing no doubt to the similarity of their titles and the overall trajectory of their contents, the Seven Treasuries have come to be regarded in the Tibetan tradition as a single integrated collection and, as such, one of Longchenpa's greatest masterpieces.

Interest in them has been particularly marked in modern times. It is said for instance that Khenpo Jigme Phuntsok (1933–2004), the founder of the immense monastic complex of Larung Gar in Serta in the east of Tibet, devised an entire teaching curriculum based on the Seven Treasuries.[4] Perhaps inspired by Patrul Rinpoche's celebrated exhortation to read these texts,[5] and no doubt following the order laid down by Mipham Rinpoche in his prefatory essay and catalog composed to mark the printing of the Seven Treasuries in Derge in 1908,[6] Jigme Phuntsok followed what he considered to be the natural expository order of the collection, beginning with the exoteric sutra topics and progressing to the texts that focus exclusively on the Great Perfection. He would therefore start with *The Treasury of Wish-Fulfilling Jewels* and *The Treasury of Tenet Systems*.[7] Taken together, these two texts describe, comprehensively and in great detail, the nature of the Buddhist path of learning and practice. On this firm basis, *The Treasury of Essential Instructions*[8] would then be studied. This extraordinary text, consisting of 413 stanzas of different length but each expounding six points, is addressed to practitioners, beginners or advanced yogis, guiding them on the path—informing, correcting, encouraging, and cajoling—from the most elementary precepts of the sutra vehicle to the most refined and advanced teachings of the Great Perfection.

The cumulative effect of *The Treasury of Essential Instructions* is to bring into focus the nature and importance of the doctrine of the Great Perfection. It is at this point that Jigme Phuntsok's students would be brought into direct and inspiring contact with these teachings in their most essential form through the study of two beautiful and poetic works: *The Treasury of the Dharmadhātu* and *The Treasury of the Fundamental Nature*.[9] Both these texts expound the intrinsic nature of the mind: awareness, the vast expanse of the dharmadhātu, as the basis and medium of the endless and unlimited display of phenomenal existence, of both samsara and nirvana. They do this according to the approach of *trekchö*, the practice that "cuts through" the tough deposit of conceptual fabrication and habitual tendencies, accumulated from beginningless time, which obscures the original, unimpaired, and ever-present purity of the mind's nature, the sugatagarbha.

Finally, Jigme Phuntsok's curriculum of study would culminate with the reading and explanation of *The Treasury of the Supreme Vehicle* and *The Treasury of Words and Meanings*,[10] profound and systematic expositions in prose, which provide, with scholastic precision, the theoretical basis of the Great Perfection teachings, covering the approaches of both the trekchö and *thögal* practices.

It should be noted that the time and order of composition of Longchenpa's works is notoriously difficult, indeed impossible, to establish with certainty. Although, in the colophons to his writings, Longchenpa often indicates the place of composition, he rarely, if ever, specifies a date. Of the Seven Treasuries, four are clearly stated to have been written in Kangri Thökar, Longchenpa's hermitage high in the mountains above the valley of the Khyichu river, and it is tempting to imagine that the other three were also composed there or elsewhere in Tibet. There is, nevertheless, a tradition stating that the Seven Treasuries, along with other substantial works, were all composed during Longchenpa's seven-year exile in Bhutan and that, during a river crossing in the course of his journey home, they were lost and had to be "recomposed" in Kangri Thökar on his return. There are, however, fairly solid reasons for doubting the veracity of this implausible legend. It is far more likely that most if not all the Seven Treasuries were composed before 1350 when Longchenpa left for Bhutan at the age of forty-two—a mere thirteen years before his early death in 1363 at the age of fifty-five. This means that all Longchenpa's major works were composed while he was still a young man—attesting to the fact that he was a scholar of a truly astonishing range and precocity. One suggested date that we do have is from Tulku Thondup, who says that Longchenpa composed *The Treasury of the Supreme Vehicle* to fulfill the dying wishes of Kumaradza, his root master, who passed away in 1343 when Longchenpa was in his early thirties.[11] Moving on from these historical details, we must now consider the character and contents of the texts translated here.

The Commentary

The present volume is in large measure a rendering of *The One Sole Sphere of Luminosity*, Khangsar Tenpa'i Wangchuk's commentary on *The Precious Treasury of the Dharmadhātu*. The work of a Tibetan master, a holder of an authentic lineage of the Great Perfection teachings, and a master of immense learning and widely acknowledged realization, Tenpa'i Wangchuk's commentary is unprecedented. Completed in 1996, it is the first extensive and detailed commentary ever to be produced on Longchenpa's work, excepting of course the author's own autocommentary.

Whereas the orally transmitted explanation lineage of Longchenpa's texts was never lost, despite the lapse of time and the catastrophic events that overtook Tibet in the course of the twentieth century, it is a fact that—perhaps out of reverence for the towering figure of the author himself, perhaps out of fear of censure—no Tibetan scholar ever composed extensive written commentaries on Longchenpa's works. This situation has now changed. In response to the needs of the time and perhaps especially in view of the sheer fragility of the tradition, as demonstrated by the traumatic experience of his early years, Tenpa'i Wangchuk composed remarkable commentaries on two of the Seven Treasuries: *The Treasury of the Dharmadhātu*, translated here, and *The Treasury of the Fundamental Nature*, which now also exists in translation. Happily, he was not alone in this endeavor, and it is a matter of great good fortune that there now exists, for instance, a full-length commentary on *The Treasury of Essential Instructions* composed by Tenpa'i

Wangchuk's contemporary, Jamyang Drubpa'i Lodrö, a disciple of Khenpo Jigme Phuntsok.

In contrast with the general "meaning commentary" composed by Longchenpa himself, which explains the sense of the root text in broad strokes, supporting it with many scriptural citations, Tenpa'i Wangchuk's *One Sole Sphere of Luminosity* is a "word commentary" in which both the words and syntax of the root text are painstakingly elucidated, thereby giving clear guidance and insight into the intentions of the author. Such an assistance has proved to be of crucial significance for the reader and most especially for the translators. *The Treasury of the Dharmadhātu* is the expression of the realization of an enlightened being. Taken alone, it conveys a message, the meaning of which is barely to be glimpsed by the unassisted reader. Moreover, as the work of a subtle and accomplished poet, it is couched in language that is frequently difficult to construe, being allusive and elliptical to a truly hermetic degree. Without the assistance of a skilled commentator, the translation of *The Treasury of the Dharmadhātu* would indeed be a hazardous enterprise.

Tenpa'i Wangchuk explains the root text following the divisions already established by Longchenpa in the autocommentary, embedding it in his own work in the traditional manner. Consequently, a translation of the commentary automatically called for a new rendering of the root text, closely aligned with Tenpa'i Wangchuk's own interpretation.[12] In order to supply the reader with an overall vision of Longchenpa's verses in their entirety, and to facilitate their recitation should that be desired, we have extracted them from the commentary and placed them, with all due diffidence, as a complete text at the beginning of the book.

The composition of *The One Sole Sphere of Luminosity*, which must rank as one of Tenpa'i Wangchuk's great masterpieces, was no easy task even for a scholar of such a high caliber. To begin with, he received the transmission and explanation of the text in secret from his teacher, Akyong Togden Lodrö Gyatso, when both master and disciple were under close surveillance in a communist gulag.

Such are the mysterious workings of karma that it was only in these circumstances of extreme hardship and peril that Lodrö Gyatso (the revered incarnation of the great Tibetan translator Vairotsana) and Tenpa'i Wangchuk (the incarnation of Yudra Nyingpo, Vairotsana's chief disciple) were able once again to encounter each other. And so it was that Tenpa'i Wangchuk received from his long lost master, and in the most unlikely of circumstances, the transmission of many texts and instructions, thus ensuring their preservation from almost certain destruction—to the great good fortune of his disciples East and West.

Released from prison in 1981, Tenpa'i Wangchuk became an indefatigable teacher, the founder and restorer of numerous monasteries and places of learning. Revered for his erudition and profound realization, he was recognized by Jigme Phuntsok himself as a bodhisattva residing on the grounds of realization. Eventually, after over fifteen years of meditative practice following the reception of the teachings from his master, Tenpa'i Wangchuk composed his commentary on *The Treasury of the Dharmadhātu* in the course of a long retreat in solitude, writing it down, as he tells us, in the periods between meditation sessions. Long reflection and practice had no doubt given rise to profound realization, but even then there were moments when it was only thanks to explanations received in direct visionary encounters with Ekajaṭī and other dharma protectors that Tenpa'i Wangchuk was able to elucidate Longchenpa's meaning.

The Treasury of the Dharmadhātu

In view of the sublimity and subtlety of the teachings of the Great Perfection, the exclusive sphere of practitioners well advanced on the path of the Vajrayāna, and given also the presence of a detailed commentary by an acknowledged master, it is scarcely the role of the present translators to hazard any kind of introductory explanation. However, for the sake of readers like ourselves, ordinary practitioners of the Buddhist path who have a deep respect for the root and lineage masters and the teachings of the Great Perfection, there are several interesting aspects of *The Treasury of the Dharmadhātu* that we would like briefly to point out.

First of all, there is some disagreement regarding the position of *The Treasury of the Dharmadhātu* within the general classification of the Great Perfection teachings. The evident emphasis on awareness as the "enlightened mind," as well as the alignment of much of the text's contents with the teachings of *The All-Creating King* and other tantras, might lead to the conclusion that *The Treasury of the Dharmadhātu* belongs to the mind class of the Great Perfection. By contrast, certain other scholars, such as Shechen Rabjam[13] and Nyoshul Khenpo Jamyang Dorje,[14] consider that it belongs to the space class. Tenpa'i Wangchuk, following Mipham Rinpoche's more general view,[15] considers *The Treasury of the Dharmadhātu* to be a general synopsis of all three classes of the Great Perfection teachings, bringing together, moreover, all the crucial points of the tantras and pith instructions. It is, he says, the very quintessence of all the Seven Treasuries, through which the practitioner is brought to the direct and naked realization of awareness, the dharmatā, the vast, primordially pure nature of the mind.

On the intellectual level, *The Treasury of the Dharmadhātu* is a scripture of profound import, filled with information concerning the Great Perfection, as well as key instructions for the practice. Nevertheless, its most remarkable quality derives not so much from its scholarly character as from the fact that it is said to constitute a medium, a form of words, through which a completely ineffable reality is revealed from within the depths of the transcendent wisdom that is Longchenpa's own direct and personal experience. He is resting perfectly and definitively in the state of awareness, having reached the point in which phenomenal appearance is exhausted in the expanse of primordial purity, the ultimate fundamental nature itself. As he himself declares in the twenty-first stanza of the ninth chapter,

Within the vast expanse, the vast expanse,
Within the great and vast expanse,
I, Longchen Rabjam, am immersed in the expanse,
The great abyss of luminosity.
I dwell within the one, nondual immensity—
Immensity of bliss.
I, Natsok Rangdröl, have attained the dharmatā,
The state of the exhaustion of phenomena,
Unchanging, present of itself,
The summit of all perfect aspiration.[16]

With reference to this stanza, Tenpa'i Wangchuk comments,

> Not abandoned, samsara is primordially pure for him. Not accomplished, nirvana is entirely present for him. He is immersed in the view of the vast abyss of luminosity, uncontrived, self-arisen, and spontaneously present. He has realized that all the phenomena of samsara and nirvana have a single, nondual savor in the one expanse of awareness. He dwells within the space of primordial wisdom of great bliss. . . . In this very life, he reached the state of dharmakāya beyond the ordinary mind. Thus for him, the vast ocean of manifold phenomenal appearances subsided, open and free, in awareness—the open, unimpeded, and naked state of primordial purity. His realization of the dharmatā, the state of phenomenal exhaustion, has reached its consummation. In his very life, he captured the unchanging, spontaneously present, everlasting kingdom of the sovereign dharmakāya and completely accomplished the summit of all perfect aspiration.[17]

It is significant that Longchenpa attained this supreme realization, enlightenment itself, while *in his very life.* Having become a buddha, he remained present in the world. He continued to teach and compose his texts. With the possible exception of yogis who had been successfully introduced to the nature of their minds, who had attained the path of seeing and were residing on the bodhisattva grounds, the majority of Longchenpa's disciples were presumably ordinary beings like ourselves.

Ordinary beings are those who have not yet attained the path of seeing. They understand the Dharma through the medium of mental images, for they do not have the direct vision of the ultimate truth. They do not *know* awareness, the nature of the mind; they only know about it. Beings like ourselves are entirely immersed in the conventional truth and in terms of direct experience, we know nothing else. Our conscious life is entirely bound by the dualistic, subject-object mechanism of discursive thought and language. We cannot function in any other way. Our knowledge is exclusively "on this side" (*tshur mthong gi shes pa*) of the divide between ordinary dualistic thought and the nondual, primordial wisdom of superior beings. And although the teachings repeatedly inform us that there is an ultimate reality that transcends our perceptions, that our present experiences are dreamlike and deluded, and that there is a manner of knowing that is completely beyond the duality of subject and object, we are nevertheless as incapable of envisaging such a state as a fish is able to imagine life on dry land. However much we may try, we cannot attain such knowledge by means of ordinary mental processes. It is impossible for the discursive reasoning of the ordinary mind to lay hold of the nondual state. As Longchenpa says repeatedly, no amount of cogitation, no amount of effortful, conceptually based practice will lead to the realization of the primordial fundamental state. An entirely different approach is called for. Mental elaborations must be brought to a state of stillness and silence, and the way laid open for the transmission of blessing from the lineage of enlightened masters.

In addressing his disciples, Longchenpa summons them, as it were, across the great divide into the state that he himself is experiencing, and since he is addressing ordinary beings, he must of necessity make use of language. He must in some sense speak *about* the goal and reveal a path whereby it may be attained. In so doing he is obliged to elaborate and employ concepts and words. Languages, all languages, including Tibetan (however one may theorize about its special qualities deriving from its non–Indo-European character) are intrinsically a matter of dualistic mind. As Tenpa'i Wangchuk remarks,

> If there is a notion that the ultimate view is such and such a thing—if there are such opinions and ideas—it follows that this same view is a phenomenon endowed with attributes. According to the Great Perfection, however, there are no phenomena endowed with attributes, for of necessity they are free and open of themselves right where they stand. If self-arisen awareness is verbally expressed, this expression is a conventionality and has never existed from the very first. Moreover, classifications of existence and nonexistence are the extremes of existence and nonexistence only on the conventional level. And none of these has any validity whatsoever in the actual, true reality of the fundamental nature. Here there is just the state of equality, primordially open and free, devoid of all views marked by conceptual elaboration.[18]

All this points to the extraordinary, paradoxical nature of *The Treasury of the Dharmadhātu*. In itself, it is a poetic work, a finely woven, beautifully composed expression of Great Perfection teaching, as intellectually fascinating as it is aesthetically inspiring. In being the presentation of awareness, the nature of the mind, on the part of a yogi immersed in the direct experience of it, *The Treasury of the Dharmadhātu* is declaratory and descriptive. It is not a work of analytical reasoning as one finds for instance in the great texts of Madhyamaka. It is the revelation of Longchenpa's own realization. And though, for the reasons just mentioned, it is necessarily expressed in human language, it constantly points beyond itself to something that words, even Longchenpa's words, are powerless to express but can only suggest. As one struggles to read and understand the text itself—for Longchenpa's language is often difficult—one is constantly made aware that he is speaking of something that is unknown to those of us who are still on the path, something that seems always to lie beyond the horizon, beyond the limits of experience. This is the essential paradox of this text: although expressed in words, its meaning is ineffable, beyond the reach of thought and language.

It is for this reason that, as the vehicle of a teaching coming from a transcendent source, *The Treasury of the Dharmadhātu* assumes an importance that is in some sense independent of the intellectual content of the text itself. In his *Exhortation to Read Longchenpa's Seven Treasuries*, Patrul Rinpoche says that among all of them, *The Treasury of the Dharmadhātu* is the most profound. It is the dharmakāya appearing in the form of a text. It directly reveals, Patrul Rinpoche says, the wisdom teaching of the Conqueror such that even if one were to meet the Buddha himself, one would find nothing more than what is here. It embodies the unsurpassable path trodden by all enlightened beings. It is the image of the realization of the omniscient master himself. For those who truly encounter it, Patrul Rinpoche says, this is their last life in samsara.

For those who are so inclined, *The Treasury of the Dharmadhātu* is indeed a considerable object of study, replete with the profound and subtle teachings of the Great Perfection. But in itself, it is, as Patrul Rinpoche repeatedly says, the quintessence of the Dharma, a vehicle of blessings of irresistible power—even for those who are incapable of understanding the literal meaning of its words. One is brought to liberation simply by seeing, hearing, or remembering it. All who make a connection with it, he says, will become a buddha in the future. Those who truly penetrate its enlightened meaning are buddhas already.

The best way for practitioners to connect with *The Treasury of the Dharmadhātu* and to receive the transmission of the wisdom power that it conveys is not so much through an intellectual study of the text itself but rather through the attitude of humility, faith, and openness that is the genuine character of devotion. This is the avenue through which the transmission of the blessing power of the lineage occurs—not through one's ability to understand the text in rational terms. It makes no difference, Patrul Rinpoche says, whether one understands or does not understand the text itself, whether one realizes its meaning or not. For, as Longchenpa declares even more forcefully, all mental states—whether of understanding or the absence of understanding, of realization or the lack of realization—are all the same in being the manifestations of awareness, the nature of the mind. If one has devotion, Patrul Rinpoche says, the mere reading of the text will act as a vehicle for the transmission of the blessing power of the lineage, and this is not different from the introduction to the nature of the mind received in the course of the word empowerment or the empowerment of the power of awareness.

One is therefore encouraged to read *The Treasury of the Dharmadhātu*, and to keep reading it, regardless of one's level of understanding. For it constitutes a spur and support for meditation, bringing practitioners ever closer to the recognition of the nature of the mind. Those who are able to read Tibetan are often encouraged to recite the original text as much as possible, even though the meaning may be beyond their immediate grasp. One is encouraged to read it in an attitude of trust and then simply to sit, resting in the nature of the mind. Once again, *The Treasury of the Dharmadhātu* has a sacramental power, a power of blessing beyond the actual meaning of its words. And this is why, in the Nyingma tradition, this wonderful text is used as a *tödröl* (*thos grol*), a scripture that liberates by hearing, and is read to the dying or the recently dead as a means of aiding them in the after-death state.

In conclusion, *The Treasury of the Dharmadhātu* is what might be called an efficacious sign. It depicts and describes the ultimate, enlightened state of awareness, and charged with the power of Longchenpa's blessing, it is itself a tool and means whereby that same state may be attained. Tenpa'i Wangchuk summaries the matter thus:

> [Longchenpa] rests in the fundamental stratum of his own primordial nature, unmoving in the unaltered naked dharmakāya. He has himself recognized the dharmatā, spontaneously present of itself, which is the subject matter of this treatise and is what is to be realized. His text constitutes an empowering blessing. It creates the auspicious circumstance whereby the uncontrived, original purity, the ultimate primordial wisdom, which is beyond delimitation and falls to no extreme, arises in the minds of fortunate beings who implement it.[19]

Implementation is of course the operative word. Given the above description, one might wonder why it is even necessary to go to the trouble of studying this text and its demanding commentary—and why indeed one should go to the immense labor of trying to translate it. But as the reader will discover, to work through Tenpa'i Wangchuk's long and reflective exposition, to examine the root text and to bring it as much as possible into one's understanding, only serves to deepen one's appreciation of Longchenpa's marvelous work. It brings confidence, inspires devotion, and powerfully contributes to one's growing certainty of the truth of the teachings of the Buddhadharma generally and of the Great Perfection in particular.

The Treasury of the Dharmadhātu and the Woes of Translators

When Pema Wangyal Rinpoche received the request that Padmakara translate the works of Tenpa'i Wangchuk, he agreed to it on condition that the necessary transmissions would be conferred. In response to this counter request, Tenpa'i Wangchuk's own nephew and spiritual heir, the venerable Khenpo Tsultrim Zangpo Rinpoche, accompanied by Yingrik Drubpa Rinpoche and a party of other disciples, came all the way from Golok to Dordogne in Southwest France and, for several weeks in the autumn of 2019, bestowed all the necessary teachings and empowerments. One day in the course of that memorable event, Khenpo Tsultrim Zangpo was giving the transmission of the commentary on *The Treasury of the Dharmadhātu*. Suddenly he paused and, as we learned later, said quite unexpectedly, "But how can they translate these texts? They haven't seen the nature of their minds!"

This devastating remark was indeed true. The Padmakara translators had completed traditional three-year retreats in Chanteloube, or elsewhere, and had been trying to practice the teachings for many years. None of them, however, would have claimed that they had reached such a level of attainment; and if they had made such a claim, it is certain that their teachers would have been quick to puncture such bubbles of pretension.

One can of course agree that the best possible translation of a work of this kind, in which every point and nuance of meaning is perfectly reproduced, would require a translator of high realization, perhaps equal to that of Longchenpa himself. Maybe in the future such a set of circumstances will arise. In the meantime, one must work with what one has. And one might argue that while there is no possibility of placing oneself at the level of the author—as one might in the translation for instance of a work of modern fiction—the translators can at least place themselves in the position of those of Longchenpa's Tibetan readers who were not, and are not, enlightened. As a means of reaching his disciples, Longchenpa employed words; and it is an axiom of translation that whatever is heard and read in one language may be interpreted and understood in another. Even then, of course, the task of translating *The Treasury of the Dharmadhātu* is a very steep prospect. As we have said, Longchenpa is a difficult writer and it would indeed be the height of folly to attempt a rendering of his text without considerable assistance from qualified authorities. And so our line of defense is to say that our attempted translation is based closely on the explanation of Tenpa'i Wangchuk, a master who surely did recognize the nature of his mind.

Technical Details

The translation of the works of both Longchenpa and Tenpa'i Wangchuk has required, for important key terms, a number of word choices that reflect our understanding of their meaning as well as our own predilections. It would be surprising if they met with the approval of all our readers. We have endeavored to be as consistent as possible and have supplied a glossary at the end of the book so that the original Tibetan terms can be easily identified. Be that as it may, a number of particularly important terms perhaps call for a more lengthy explanation.

First of all, Longchenpa frequently uses the term *changchub ki sem* (*byang chub kyi sems*), which under usual circumstances would be regarded as the Tibetan translation of the Sanskrit word *bodhicitta*. This same expression is used constantly in *The All-Creating King*, a text quoted very extensively by Tenpa'i Wangchuk. Here the term is clearly used to refer to awareness, Samantabhadra. It is important to understand that it is not the equivalent of *bodhicitta* as understood in the Mahāyāna context—namely, the wish to achieve buddhahood for the sake of all beings. It is rather to be interpreted etymologically according to the different elements of the Tibetan expression, where, by strict equivalence, *chang* (*byang*) means "pure," *chub* means "all-encompassing," and *sem* (*sems*) means "mind." The pure, all-encompassing mind (corresponding to ultimate bodhicitta on the Mahāyāna level) is a synonym for awareness, *rigpa*. In order to avoid confusion, we have consistently refrained from using the term *bodhicitta*, which might be misleading for those who are more familiar with the term in the Mahāyāna context, preferring "enlightened mind" instead.

The Great Perfection teachings frequently make use of an important threefold expression: *ngowo* (*ngo bo*), *rangzhin* (*rang bzhin*), and *tukje* (*thugs rje*). Outside the context of the Great Perfection, *ngowo* and *rangzhin*, rendered here by "nature" and "character," are practically synonymous. But since in the Great Perfection, they refer respectively to the emptiness and luminosity aspects of the mind's nature, we have for sake of clarity consistently rendered *ngowo* as "ultimate nature" and *rangzhin* as "luminous character," even in the cases when these qualifications are not explicitly mentioned. The element *tukje* has been rendered as "cognizant power or potency" and not as "compassion," which, although a valid rendering in other contexts, is not intended here and would be misleading.[20]

In *The Treasury of the Dharmadhātu* and Tenpa'i Wangchuk's commentary, *drölwa* (*grol ba*) is a term of particular importance and occurs constantly. As we have tried to explain on other occasions, this Tibetan verb, which is classified as "nonseparative" or intransitive (*tha mi dad pa*), is frequently, but in our view unadvisedly, translated into English as "to liberate," no doubt through a confusion with the similar but transitive verbs *drölwa* (*'grol ba*) and *drölwa* (*sgrol ba*), which have a similar pronunciation but different spelling. This is not a satisfactory solution and leads in the end to confusion and to such unfortunate—that is to say, meaningless—"Buddhist-hybrid English" terms as *self-liberate* and *self-liberation*.[21] In the attempt to capture the real sense of the Tibetan expression, we have translated *drölwa* (*grol ba*) as "to subside" or "to be open and free" and sometimes by both these expressions together. For example, we find the following passage in Tenpa'i Wangchuk:

> Phenomena, therefore, have never existed, which means that primordially, they have never been phenomena. From the very first, they are devoid of the status of phenomena. This is what is meant when it is said that phenomena subside primordially or that they are primordially open and free (*grol ba*).[22]

In no sense does *drölwa* mean that phenomena cease to appear or that they are somehow annihilated. In another passage, in which Tenpa'i Wangchuk follows Longchenpa's autocommentary, we find the following:

> Regarding awareness as the state in which phenomena are open and free or as the state in which they subside (*grol ba*), the meaning is that when bare awareness is directly and nakedly realized, phenomena are released, or vanish, into a state in which they are no longer objects of reference, and there manifests only awareness stripped to its nakedness. This, however, does not mean that there is nothing to be seen, that phenomena actually go away, or that they actually disappear into the state of awareness, like objects sinking into a lake. For all things (phenomena and awareness) are by their very nature groundless and rootless.[23]

Finally, we have, in all our translations, consistently rendered *rigpa* as "awareness." Inasmuch as this English word, in ordinary parlance, refers to a state of consciousness that is limpid and contentless, it may serve, so it seems to us, as a sufficient, if approximate, appellation for the nondual, knowing but empty, aspect of the mind—that is, *rigpa* as understood in the Great Perfection. There is no need, in our view, for additional qualifications.

In the case of *yeshe* (*ye shes*), the Tibetan equivalent of the Sanskrit *jñāna*, we have consistently followed the nuance of the Tibetan term *ye ne shepa* (*ye nas shes pa*): "wisdom from the beginning" or "primordial wisdom." We have at all times avoided the Greek word *gnosis*, which, despite its etymological connection with *jñāna*, simply means subject-object knowledge in the ordinary sense. It has nothing to do with nondual wisdom and has assumed, in the history of Western ideas, the connotation of esoteric secrecy, which in this Buddhist context is not intended.

On a more bibliographical level, Longchenpa's root text, as cited by

Tenpa'i Wangchuk, follows the Dodrupchen version of the Adzom Chögar edition except on four particular occasions. In the first two cases (chapter 1, stanza 9 and chapter 5, stanza 7), the discrepancies appear to be merely scribal errors since the text quoted in the commentary on both occasions corresponds to the above mentioned edition. However, in the last two cases (chapter 7, stanza 2 and chapter 10, stanza 3d), both the root and commentary are worded differently. In other words, unless Tenpa'i Wangchuk was using an edition unknown to us, his reading of the root text on these two occasions, diverging as it does from the earlier edition, must spring from his own interpretation.

As the reader will discover, Tenpa'i Wangchuk's commentary contains numerous textual notes. These are the work not of Tenpa'i Wangchuk himself but of his disciples Khenpo Kelsang Namdren of Taklung Monastery in Golok and the scholar and polymath Abu Karlo, both of whom acted as editors of the text.[24]

Acknowledgments

When the request to translate the complete works of Tenpa'i Wangchuk was received, the commentary on *The Treasury of the Dharmadhātu* was first allotted to our friend and esteemed colleague Gyurme Dorje. He began to work on it immediately and with enthusiasm but did not get far before he was overtaken by serious illness and, alas, died in 2020. When our own work on *The Treasury of the Fundamental Nature* was completed, we were asked to take up the task where he had left off. However, given differences of style, vocabulary and so on, it seemed best to start again from the beginning.

As always, our first thanks go to our teachers, Taklung Tsetrul Pema Wangyal Rinpoche and Jigme Khyentse Rinpoche, who have, over all these years, been our constant inspiration and mainstay. We dedicate this work to their long life, excellent health, and the fulfillment of all their wishes. We also thank, with the deepest sincerity, Khenchen Pema Sherab of the monastery of Namdroling in

India, who has accompanied us from the very beginning, patiently answering our interminable questions. Without his learned direction and inestimable kindness over many years, none of our translations, with few exceptions, could have been completed. May he live long in the best of health and remain as a compassionate presence among us. We are very grateful also to his faithful assistant and translator Khenpo Sonam Tsewang for his kind, patient, and ever-friendly help and to the Bhutanese Khenpo Gyurme Dorje (Jakar Khenpo) of Shechen, who assisted us on a number of occasions to negotiate difficult passages.

We would also like to express our profound gratitude to Eric and Andrea Colombel of the Tsadra Foundation for their immense generosity and for their long, unfailing friendship and support; to Nikko Odiseos of Shambhala Publications for his good-humored and benevolent encouragement; and to our kind, patient, long-suffering editor Anna Wolcott Johnson.

This book was translated by Helena Blankleder and Wulstan Fletcher of the Padmakara Translation Group, for whom this work on Longchenpa's sublime masterpiece has been the summit of their life's endeavors.

Dordogne, July 2024

A Caution for Readers

The Great Perfection, with its vast literature coupled with an unbroken, orally transmitted deposit of scholarly explanation, and above all with its lineage of empowering blessing transmitted by an uninterrupted succession of accomplished masters, is the most sublime and treasured patrimony of the Nyingma School of Tibetan Buddhism. In order to preserve the power, freshness, and efficacy of its teachings, tradition insists that they be introduced and encountered in the right circumstances and, perhaps even more importantly, at the right time—when aspiring students are ready and at their most receptive. This is why they are kept secret and their dissemination is restricted. As the work translated in this volume explains, this is not merely to protect the integrity of the tradition itself. It is also intended as a means of avoiding situations where the deep meaning of the Great Perfection is misunderstood, mistakenly applied, and even scorned and criticized—circumstances that will inescapably lead to negative karmic consequences for all concerned, teachers and disciples alike.

Whereas it is important that the works of authentic masters of the Buddhist teachings, including those of the Great Perfection, be translated and made accessible to the modern world, it is difficult to achieve this in our society without the publication and distribution of books in the usual manner. The traditional restriction remains, however, intact. This specifically states that those who wish to read and study such texts as *The Precious Treasury of the Dharmadhātu* should have received the necessary empowerment of Atiyoga (*dbang*), the oral transmission of the text itself (*lung*), and the guidance of a qualified teacher (*khrid*).

Until these proper conditions have been fulfilled, it is better to keep this book respectfully in a place of honor until such time as the necessary authorization to study has been obtained.

PART ONE

The Precious Treasury of the Dharmadhātu

Longchen Rabjam

In Sanskrit: *Dharmadhāturatnakośanāma*
In Tibetan: *Chos dbyings rin po che'i mdzod ces bya ba*

Homage to glorious Samantabhadra!

Marvelous wonder,
Present of itself from the beginning,
Primordial wisdom,
Luminous and self-arisen,
The enlightened mind!
This is the treasure mine from which arises
All phenomenal existence,
Samsara and nirvana,
The world and its inhabitants.
I bow in homage to this unmoving freedom
From conceptual elaboration.

The supreme peak, the Sumeru of all the vehicles,
The radiant expanse of sun and moon,
Luminous and present of itself—
This is the vast expanse of vajra essence.
Beyond all effort and all practice,
It is the vast expanse,
The natural state beyond all fabrication.
Listen to me now, for I shall tell you
Of this wondrous and primordial immensity.

1. Samsara and Nirvana Do Not Stir from the Ultimate Expanse

1. The vast space of spontaneous presence
Is the ground whence all arises.
Empty in its nature,
Luminous in character, unceasing,
It does not exist as anything at all,
Though anything at all arises from it.
Samsara and nirvana both emerge unbidden
In the space of the three kāyas.
Yet from this ultimate expanse they do not stray,
The field of blissful ultimate reality.

2. The vast expanse, the nature of the mind,
Is changeless like the sphere of space.
Indeterminate is its display:
The vast expanse of manifest appearance of cognizant power.
All things are inexistent
Except as ornaments upon the ultimate expanse.
The outer and the inner and the to and fro of consciousness
Are the creative power of the enlightened mind.
Not anything, yet giving rise to everything,
It is a marvelous prodigy, endowed with wonderful display.

3. The outer and the inner,
The world together with its beings,
All the things that manifest as forms
Are but adornments of the ultimate expanse,

Arising as the wheel of the enlightened body.
All reverberation, sounds and language,
As many as there are without exception,
Are but the adornments of the ultimate expanse,
Arising as the wheel of the enlightened speech.
Memories, awareness, mental movement,
Proliferation, no-thought—
All mental states in number past imagining—
Are but the adornments of the ultimate expanse,
Arising as the wheel of the enlightened mind.

4. Beings in the six migrations
And four ways of being born
Stray not a single atom from the sphere of ultimate reality.
Phenomenal existence—
Six objects, apprehended-apprehender—
All indeed appears.
It is a magical illusion in the dharmadhātu,
Perceived but not existing.
Unsupported, substanceless,
A vast expanse primordially empty,
It is luminosity itself,
Adornment of the dharmadhātu.

5. However things appear, however they resound
Within the vast and ultimate expanse,
They do not waver from spontaneous equality,
The dharmakāya, the enlightened mind—
The primordial natural state that, in and of itself,
Is empty and devoid of movement and of change.
No matter what appears, it is the dharmatā,
Primordial wisdom, self-arisen.
Free of effort, free of striving,
It is gathered in the one expanse of bliss.

6. Unwavering luminosity is the sambhogakāya.
Everything appearing, in the moment of appearing,
Is present of itself as luminous character.
Uncontrived, unchanging,
It is all-pervading and spontaneous equality.

7. Arising as a manifest display,
Appearing in distinct diversity,
The nirmāṇakāya is a self-arisen emanation,
Marvelous and illusory,
Beyond the scope of action,
Never stirring from Samantabhadra.

8. In the enlightened mind, free of pits and chasms,
The three kāyas are complete all by themselves,
Without the need for striving.
Not stirring from the ultimate expanse,
The kāyas, wisdoms, and enlightened action,
Spontaneous and unconditioned,
Are naturally complete therein.
They are the great accumulation,
Complete from the beginning
In the vast expanse primordially arisen.

9. From the outset present of itself—
Such is the buddha field free of change and movement.
The vision of the dharmatā within the dharmadhātu[25]
Is a knowledge unimpeded that adorns the ultimate expanse.
Not created, not achieved, but present from the first,
It is like the sun arising in the sky,
A wonderful and marvelous prodigy.

10. Within the womb of ultimate expanse,
Present of itself from the beginning,

Samsara is Samantabhadra,
Nirvana is Samantabhadra.
And therefore from the very first,
Within Samantabhadra's vast expanse,
There has never been samsara and nirvana.
Appearance is Samantabhadra,
Emptiness is Samantabhadra.
Therefore from the very first,
Within Samantabhadra's vast expanse,
There has never been appearance and emptiness.
Birth and death are both Samantabhadra,
Joy and pain are both Samantabhadra.
Therefore from the very first,
Within Samantabhadra's vast expanse,
Birth and death and joy and pain have never been.
Self and other are Samantabhadra,
Permanence, annihilation are Samantabhadra.
Therefore from the very first,
Within Samantabhadra's vast expanse,
No self and other, no permanence and no annihilation
Have there ever been.

11. To grasp existence in the nonexistent—
This is called delusion.
Samsara and nirvana
In their nature are like baseless dreams.
How strange to cling to them as real existent things!

12. All things are Samantabhadra,
Great, spontaneous presence.
There is no samsara
That is now, or has been, or will be, hallucinatory.
It is just a name; it is beyond
The extremes of both being and nonbeing.

No one anywhere has been deluded in the past,
No one is deluded now nor will be in the future.
Such is the primordial purity
Of the three worlds of existence.

13. Since there's no delusion,
There's no absence of delusion.
Vast awareness, self-arisen and supreme,
Is from the outset present of itself.
It never was, nor is, nor ever will be freed.
In a past that's just a name,
No one has been freed.
There will never be a state of freedom
Since there never was a state of bondage.
All is pure like space,
Unrestricted, unconfined—
The utter openness and freedom
Of primordial purity.

14. Briefly, in the womb of ultimate expanse,
Immense and present of itself,
Samsara or nirvana—
Whichever is displayed by the creative power—
Has no existence from the moment it arises.
Whatever happens in one's dreams
Through sleep's creative power—
None of it is real.
There is just awareness self-cognizing,
Blissful in its fundamental stratum,
An all-encompassing immensity
That's even, present of itself.

2. Phenomenal Existence Is a Pure Buddha Field

1. The ultimate expanse from the beginning
Is by nature present of itself.
Extending all-pervasively, it has no out or in.
It has no boundaries,
No zenith and no nadir,
And no directions main or intermediate.
It is neither wide nor narrow,
For it is awareness, pure and spacelike—
A vast expanse devoid of mind's elaboration,
Free of thought and points of reference.

2. Displays born in the unborn ultimate expanse
Are completely limitless and indeterminate.
They cannot be identified as this or that;
They are not substances with attributes.
Their nature is like space that spreads
Through infinite directions.
It is unborn spontaneous presence.
No past, no future does it have,
No ending, no beginning.

3. Samsara and nirvana
Are by nature the enlightened mind,
Unborn and without origin,
Indeterminate and present of itself.
It came from nowhere; nowhere does it go.

Free of past and future,
The expanse of the enlightened mind
Is free of one side or another.
Not going and not coming,
It is boundlessly pervasive.

4. Suchness, dharmatā, has no beginning.
It has no center and no limit.
In its purity it is like even, all-pervading space.
Without beginning, it is endless.
It transcends all objects of the past and future.
Unborn, unceasing,
It has neither attributes nor substance.
It neither comes nor goes
And cannot be defined as this or that.
Not accomplished through striving,
It is free of all activity.
The ground of suchness is without a center or directions.
With no objective reference or interruption,
It is the dimension of equality.

5. The nature of all things is dharmatā, equality itself.
Thus there's not a single thing
That does not rest in that equality,
And in this one equality all things are equal!
Such is the condition of enlightened mind.
Since it is the unborn state of all-pervading,
Spacelike, vast immensity,
This same equality is free of interruption.

6. Spontaneous, directionless,
This is the stronghold all-embracing.
Seamless, without high or low,
It is the stronghold of immensity.
Impartial, all-accommodating,

It is the stronghold of the unborn dharmakāya.
Immutable and present of itself,
It is the stronghold of the precious secret.
Phenomenal appearance, samsara and nirvana—
This is the primordial stronghold,
The stronghold of the one and only evenness.

7. Upon the all-pervading and all-spreading ground,
There stands the citadel of the enlightened mind
Impartially pervading all samsara and nirvana.
Its high imposing tower
Is the vast expanse of dharmatā.
Its central ward transcending all the four directions
Is the uncreated nature.
Its entrance gate is utterly immense,
The freedom from all gradual exertion.
Within that castle, adorned in rich array that's present of itself,
Is primal wisdom self-arisen,
The king upon his throne.
The cognizant acts of the creative power
Of primal wisdom are his ministers
Who hold the land in sway.
Immanent absorption is his sublime queen,
While qualities of realization,
Which manifest spontaneously,
Are like his heir apparent with the servants and attendants.
All are gathered in the vast space of great bliss,
The thought-free luminosity.

8. The mastery of all phenomenal existence,
The universe and its inhabitants,
Lies in the unmoving state
Beyond imagination and description,
The boundless vast domain of dharmadhātu.

9. If in that domain you stay,
All is dharmakāya,
Never stirring from the single, self-arisen primal wisdom,
Which, uncreated and possessed primordially,
Transcends all effortful endeavor.
Since this single sphere, free of edge or corner,
Is all-encompassing,
The natural state of things, just as it is,
Beyond all differentiation,
Is gathered in this single vast expanse.

10. The abodes of the six kinds of beings
Together with the buddha fields
Do not exist but in the spacious realm of dharmatā.
Within the luminous enlightened mind,
All are of a single taste.
Samsara and nirvana both
Are utterly encompassed by awareness.

11. In this treasury, the dharmadhātu, source of everything,
Nirvana is spontaneously present with no need for striving.
The changeless dharmakāya,
Free of all objective reference,
Is all-pervasive, present in all things.
Appearances both out and in,
The world and its inhabitants,
Are the sambhogakāya.
The self-arising of phenomena, reflection-like,
Is the nirmāṇakāya.
Therefore there are no phenomena
That are not perfectly subsumed
As the adornments of the triple kāya.
Everything that manifests is the display
Of the enlightened body, speech, and mind.
Even the unnumbered buddha fields

Of the sugatas, leaving none aside,
Arise from the same source:
The nature of the mind,
The vast expanse of the three kāyas.

12. The cities, also, of the six migrations,
Samsara in their nature,
Appear just like reflections in the dharmadhātu.
The various experiences of birth and death, of joy and sorrow
Are like images projected
In the space of the mind's nature.
They seem to be and yet are nonexistent.
Appearing, they are utterly unfounded.
Like clouds up in the sky, they're adventitious,
Arising merely through conditions.
Not existent and not nonexistent,
Their nature is beyond the ontological extremes.
They are utterly encompassed
By the sphere of freedom from elaboration.

13. The enlightened mind, the nature of the mind,
Is pure like space and therefore free
From birth and death, from joy and pain.
Without substance and not falling to one side or to another,
It is free of the phenomena of samsara and nirvana.
You cannot point to it as "this."
Utterly immense, just like the vast abyss of space,
Changeless, without movement,
It is present of itself and unconditioned.
It is the vajra heart of luminosity.
It is buddhahood itself.
All things are the field of self-arisen bliss,
Supreme enlightenment, spontaneous equality.

3. Metaphors for the Enlightened Mind

1. All things are subsumed within
The enlightened, all-subsuming mind.
Nothing is there other than enlightened mind.
By nature, all things are enlightened mind.

2a. The enlightened mind
Is metaphorically compared with space.
It has no cause. It has no place of birth.
It is not localized.
Transcending speech,
It lies beyond the reach of thought.
"The vast abyss of space"
Will merely indicate it metaphorically.
And since that which has been given as a metaphor
Is not a thing that can be pointed to as "this,"
How could that which is compared with it
Be thought or spoken of?
Understand: this metaphor refers
To its pure nature.

2b. That which is referred to
Is awareness, the enlightened mind,
Self-cognizing, vast as space.
Not within the reach of thought,
It cannot be described or pointed out.
Luminous, unmoving,

An immense expanse of luminosity,
It is uncreated, present of itself,
With neither height nor breadth—
The vast sphere of the dharmakāya,
The essence of enlightenment.

2c. The evidential sign is
That anything at all arises
Through the awareness's creative power.
But when arising happens,
There's no place for such arising
And nothing that in fact arises.
"Arising," thus, is just a word.
It is like space, when you examine it.
Everything is utterly contained
In seamless great equality—
An all-pervading space
Devoid of apprehending subject
And an object to be apprehended.

3. Self-arisen primordial wisdom, ultimate reality,
Is completely boundless.
This is clearly shown
By metaphor, by referent, and by sign.
This spacelike nature,
Wherein all is gathered without difference or exclusion,
Is established by these three great nails.
In the vast womb of the ultimate expanse,
The vast, supreme state of equality,
All is from the outset equal—
Neither earlier nor later, neither good nor bad.
Such is the wisdom mind
Of Samantabhadra-Vajrasattva.

4a. The enlightened mind is like the very essence of the sun,
Luminous intrinsically, unconditioned from the first.
There is nothing that might darken it.
It is open, unimpeded, present of itself,
Free of mind's elaboration,
Ultimate reality devoid of thought.

4b. Empty, it is dharmakāya;
Luminous, it is sambhogakāya;
Radiant, it is nirmāṇakāya.
These three kāyas are inseparable.
Since these qualities are from the outset present of themselves,
They have never been obscured
By the gloom of flaws and faults.
And in the past and future,
Through the course of time,
They are one in being free
Of movement and of change.
They are one in their pervasion
Of all buddhas and all beings.
They are what is called the self-arisen and enlightened mind.

5. Its creative power may arise as anything at all—
As realization or the absence of the same,
As phenomenal existence,
The world and all the beings it contains,
And as all the various experiences of living beings.

6. All such things occur,
And yet they lack intrinsic being.
They're like the water in a mirage,
Like dreams, like echoes, like emanated apparitions,
Or like images reflected in a glass,
Like cities of gandharvas, or like tricks of sight.
Clearly they appear and yet are nonexistent—

Groundless, unsupported,
They are mere appearances arising adventitiously.
Understand that they are fleeting in the present moment.

7. Within the nature of the enlightened mind,
Spontaneously present,
Samsara and nirvana manifest,
Unceasingly displayed in their array.
Understand that this display
Is utterly encompassed by the ultimate expanse
And never strays beyond this primal state.

8. There, all things are the enlightened mind—
One is perfectly contained,
All are perfectly contained,
The unconditioned too is perfectly contained.
Their nature is primordial wisdom,
Self-arisen, perfect of itself.

9. The enlightened mind does not exist
As manifest, unmanifest, samsara or nirvana,
As outer things or inner things.
Yet through the stirring of creative power
A various display arises naturally:
Phenomenal existence, samsara and nirvana.

10. In their moment of arising,
Things are by their nature empty forms.
Because there's no arising, they appear to arise.
Yet in their moment of appearing,
There is nothing that arises.
Because there's no cessation, they appear to cease.
And yet they do not cease;
They are illusions, empty forms.
While remaining, there is nothing that remains.

For what remains is groundless,
And it neither comes nor goes.
However things appear, they do not exist as such.
They are without intrinsic being.
They are no more than names.

11. These appearances moreover
Self-arise through the creative power.
Thus only figuratively are they said
To be dependently arisen by their nature.
In the very moment they appear
By virtue of creative power,
They do so in a manner free
From such divisions and extremes
As the arising and the absence of arising.
Creative power is also just a figurative label.
It too lacks all reality.
Nothing in the least stirs ever
From the enlightened mind,
Which is the state beyond all movement and all change.

4. The Nature of the Enlightened Mind

1. The nature of the all-encompassing enlightened mind
Does not appear, it transcends appearance.
It is not empty, it transcends emptiness.
It is not existent, it has no substance and no properties.
It is not nonexistent, it pervades samsara and nirvana.
Not existent and not nonexistent, present of itself and even,
It is the vast primordial expanse.
With no extremes, with no divisions,
It is groundless, rootless, and devoid of substance.

2. Unbroken in its continuity,
Awareness is enlightenment's expanse—
Changeless, motionless, the vast abyss of space,
Pervasive from the very first.
It is self-arisen primordial wisdom
From the very first without a peer.
Not arising and not ceasing,
Encompassed by the one sole sphere,
Indeterminate and all-pervading,
It is utterly beyond all limiting extremes.

3. Unwavering equality, present of itself—
Such is the lineage of the vajra essence.
This supreme and infinite expanse,
Which from beings is never separate,
Is not within the reach of verbal indication.

It is the bursting forth of wisdom—
The sphere of self-knowing awareness.
Yogis who are free from all activity
Of thought and word
Possess decisive certainty that this expanse
Transcends both indication and nonindication.
And finding neither meditation nor anything on which to meditate,
These yogis do not need to slay the foes
Of dullness, agitation, and discursive thought.

4. Within the dharmatā, which from the very first subsists
Immediate and unmediated,
There is no thought of self and other.
The three worlds, therefore, by their nature
Are a buddha field of evenness.

5. The Victorious Ones of the three times
Are awareness's pure self-experience.
Nothing is there to abandon, nothing to accept.
All is but the single state of evenness.
No achievement in the slightest
Is attained from somewhere else.
All phenomena are clearly present
In the vast expanse of the mind's nature.
They do not in the slightest waver from the nature of equality.

6. Free of out and in, arising and subsiding,
Free of all turbidity,
Dispeller of the gloom of all extreme positions—
Such is the enlightened mind, the root.
It does not relinquish anything,
And yet it naturally removes all deviation.

7. Although the various appearances of the world and beings,
And also the pure buddhas and primordial wisdoms—
A ceaseless play pervading the expanse of space—
Appear through awareness's creative power
(Through realization or the lack of realization),
In truth, within the dharmadhātu,
"Realize," "not to realize"—
These are simply names.
Thanks to realization,
There arise the pure perceptions of the sugata.
Through lack of realization, there occur, in their diversity,
Perceptions, which arise
Through ignorance and dualistic habit.
Yet none of this stirs from the ultimate expanse.

8a. The enlightened mind indeed
Is the actual ground of everything.
It arises ceaselessly in various array,
But this is but the radiance
Within the pure expanse of luminous dharmatā.
Without division or exclusion,
This is but the dance of unconfined awareness.

8b. Primal wisdom, open, unimpeded,
A self-arisen vast expanse,
Is unobstructed luminosity, free of out and in.
It is awareness self-cognizing,
The great light of the mirror of the mind.
It is the precious jewel of dharmadhātu
That brings forth all that one desires—
For all arises naturally
Without the need for striving.
Self-arisen primordial wisdom
Is the source of all that one might wish.

9. All the many great and wholesome qualities
Arising in the ultimate expanse
Are of that same expanse.
They ceaselessly occur
As supreme skillful means
And are spontaneously perfect in the vast unborn expanse.
Phenomena are therefore overwhelmed by emptiness,
The vast space of enlightenment.
And emptiness in turn is overwhelmed
By awareness self-cognizing,
The vast space of enlightenment.

10. There have never been appearances and emptiness
In the enlightened mind.
But do not grasp at "nonduality,"
For there is indeed an inconceivable display.
The no-time of the three times
Is the unborn dharmadhātu,
The vast space that is changeless, unconditioned, undivided.
It is the buddhas of the three times,
The ultimate expanse of self-cognizing primal wisdom.
The vast space of enlightenment,
Awareness self-cognizing,
Overwhelms the apprehending subject
And the object to be apprehended.
With no division, out or in,
Ultimate reality is vast and present of itself.

5. The Enlightened Mind Is beyond Effortful Striving and Causality

1. Within the nature of the mind—
Enlightened mind itself—
There is no view on which to meditate,
No action to perform and no result to gain.
There are no paths, no grounds to cross,
No mandala to visualize, no mantra to recite,
And no perfection stage.
No empowerment is there to grant and no samaya to observe.
In ultimate reality,
Primordially pure and present of itself,
All adventitious effort, step by step,
All causes and effects are utterly transcended.

2. These factors are enlightened mind itself.
Not obscured by darkness and by clouds,
The sun shines by its very nature in the sky.
It is not adventitiously produced.

3. Whatever has been taught
Concerning ten things grounded in exertion
Was given in relation to hallucinatory experiences
That through awareness's creative power
Adventitiously arise.
They are but skillful means for gradual engagement on the path
By beings who, according to their faculties,
Exert themselves in gradual stages.

For those who are authentically united
With Atiyoga's vajra essence,
They have not been taught.

4. For beings who progress by stages and by means of effort,
The gradual teachings are set forth
To guide them to the dharmatā's primordial expanse.
These are the three small vehicles
Of śrāvakas, pratyekabuddhas, bodhisattvas.
Then three tantras—Kriyā, Upa, Yoga—
Are naturally set forth as intermediate.

5. Then as the three great vehicles,
Mahā, Anu, Ati are primordially perceived.
Through the opening of the doors of Dharma
Of the causal and resultant vehicles,
The fortunate are led to the three levels of enlightenment.

6. All of them lead of necessity
To the supreme and marvelous secret of the ultimate—
The vajra essence, culmination of them all—
The highest and unchanging luminosity.
This is celebrated as the vehicle
Of the heart of manifest enlightenment.

7. There are indeed two kinds of Dharma,
One of which demands concerted effort
In adopting and rejecting.
It is set forth as a means of cleansing
Mind and mental factors and habitual tendencies,
Which naturally arise as the display
Of awareness's creative power.
In this approach, primordial wisdom
Is said to be more pure than ordinary mind.[26]

8. Beyond concerted effort and beyond accepting or rejecting,
Great dharmatā is self-arisen primordial wisdom,
The enlightened mind itself.
You actualize it when you do not waver
From direct and face-to-face experience.
There is no need to strive for it elsewhere.
It is within yourself. Do not look somewhere else.

9. It is likened to the sun itself.
It is said that when one rests within its natural state,
Its luminosity is motionless.
The other way is said to be
Like making a new sun
By striving to remove the obscuring clouds.
These two approaches are as different
As the earth is from the sky.

10. "Elephants," these days, who claim to practice Ati
Actually allege that thoughts that move and that proliferate
Are themselves the enlightened mind.
These fools are sunk in darkness,
Far from the Natural Great Perfection.
They fail to differentiate creative power
From that which issues forth from it—
Still less do they discern the enlightened mind itself.

11. For us the enlightened mind, primordially pure,
Is the ultimate expanse, the truth of dharmatā.
Transcending thought and word,
It is the wisdom that has gone beyond.
Naturally unmoving, its character is luminous;
It is primordially free of the elaboration
Of all moving and unfolding thought.
It is called "the nature" and is likened

To the sun's essential core.
Its creative power is ceaseless in its dawning.
Awareness open, unimpeded
Is free of both detecting and discerning.
Clearly present, it is free of apprehender and of apprehended.

12. Through its own creative power, awareness manifests
As the conceptually elaborating mind.
This generates duality of apprehender-apprehended
With all its various propensities.
Nonexistent things are taken as existent things,
And thus the five sense objects manifest.
Nonexistent self is taken as existent self,
And thus there come the five defilements.
All the false appearances
Of the world and its inhabitants,
Manifesting as samsara,
Occur through the creative power.
When you fail to understand this,
False perception manifests.

13. All things come from nowhere,
Nowhere do they go,
And nowhere do they stay.
All is but the vast expanse of dharmatā.
For those who realize this, there is
The "utter openness and freedom of the triple world."
This is the Ati teaching of the vajra essence present of itself,
Arising in Samantabhadra's vast expanse.

14. Within the utterly immaculate enlightened mind,
There is no view, no object of a view.
There is not the slightest trace
Of something to be viewed or someone viewing.
There is no mind that meditates,

Nor anything on which to meditate.
Neither is there action or a subject acting.
Because it is spontaneously present,
There is not the slightest trace of a result to gain.

15. In what is nonexistent
There are no grounds to be traversed
And therefore from the first,
There is no path to follow.
Luminosity, as the supreme sphere,
Is present from the first.
Thus there are no mandalas for thought to generate,
No mantras and no recitations,
No empowerments, and no samayas.
Since no gradual dissolution is observed,
There is no perfection stage.
For the kāyas and the wisdoms, present from the first,
There is no causal process
Based on adventitious and conditioned circumstances.
If such a thing there were,
Primordial wisdom, not being self-arisen,
Would have to be conditioned
And therefore subject to destruction.
How could it be defined
As unconditioned and spontaneous presence?

16. Therefore the ultimate expanse
Itself transcends causality.
The ten elements of tantra have no place therein.
This, I beg you, understand:
The nature of the mind,
True reality beyond all effort and all practice,
Is the stilling of conceptual elaborations
Of existence and of nonexistence.

6. All Is Subsumed within the Enlightened Mind

1. Just as light is gathered in the sun's essential core,
All things are gathered in their root, the enlightened mind.
Phenomenal existence, impure, hallucinatory—
The world and its inhabitants—
When its wellspring and support
And the space of its abiding are examined,
Is found to be completely gathered in the mind,
Groundless, free and open from the very first.
Delusion and the absence of delusion both
Are gathered in the nature of the mind,
The vast immensity of the primordial expanse,
Transcending names and entities.

2. The wonderful display,
Pure self-experience of awareness—
The buddhas and the buddha fields,
Primordial wisdoms and enlightened action—
This also is inseparably subsumed
Within the self-arisen state.
Samsara and nirvana, all phenomenal existence,
Are the unconditioned, all-encompassing
Enlightened mind,
Luminous and empty like the sun and sky.
Self-arisen from the first,
It is the vast, immense, primordial expanse.

3. The nature of the mind
Is an unchanging vast expanse,
A realm of space.
Its multifarious display
Is the enlightened mind's creative power.
Since it has samsara and nirvana
Along with all the vehicles within its power,
All things are subjected
To its one sole state beyond activity.
There is nothing that is separate from it,
Nothing that exceeds its boundary.
There is no moving from the dharmatā, enlightened mind.

4. Since all arises in Samantabhadra,
This one spontaneous presence,
All things are subsumed therein without exception.
Peerless and sublime, it is the greatest of the great.
Samantabhadra, the expanse of ultimate reality,
Is like a king who gathers all things to himself.
He rules samsara and nirvana,
And they never part from him.

5. All things are Samantabhadra;
Not one thing is there that is not Samantabhadra.
As Samantabhadra, all is one in being neither good nor bad.
All existent things, all nonexistent things
Are one within the ultimate expanse.
Not stirring from spontaneous presence,
All things are one in their equality.

6. This one state where all things without exception manifest
Is the ultimate expanse of dharmatā.
It is a state beyond all action;
It cannot be achieved or striven for.
Practice done with effort

Is not different from the ultimate expanse.
What goal is there to strive for?
Where could it be achieved?

7. It is not something to be sought,
And it is not seen in meditation.
It is not a state to be achieved;
It does not come from somewhere else.
It does not come; it does not go:
It is the state of evenness, the dharmakāya.
It is subsumed within the vast expanse
Of the great sphere spontaneously perfect.

8a. The teachings of the śrāvakas,
Of the pratyekabuddhas, and the bodhisattvas
Are decisive on the nonexistence
Of both "I" and "mine."
Their common realization is the spacelike state
Of freedom from elaboration.
The supremely secret Atiyoga teaching
Is that one should rest in true reality—
Self-arisen primal wisdom as it is—
Within the vast expanse
Where self and other cannot be distinguished.
The realizations gained in the small vehicles
Are thus subsumed in this supreme quintessence.

8b. The three classes of tantra—Kriyā, Upa, Yoga—
Are all the same in holding that accomplishments
Occur when body, speech, and mind are purified
Through self-visualization, through the deity,
Through concentration, and through making offerings.
According also to the sovereign
Secret teachings of the vajra peak,
Appearances and sounds are pure awareness,

The primordial deity.
When body, speech, and mind are fully cleansed,
Accomplishments will manifest.
The realizations of these tantras
Are thus subsumed in this supreme quintessence.

8c. There are also the three classes of Mahā, Anu, Ati.
[In Mahāyoga,] phenomenal existence,
The world and its inhabitants,
Is a pure field of male and female deities.
[In Anuyoga,] the inseparable union
Of primal wisdom and the ultimate expanse
Is said to be unmoving dharmatā,
Primordial wisdom self-arisen.
In the supreme and most secret [Atiyoga],
All phenomena are pure,
The unproduced, immeasurable
Primordial expanse, the field of bliss.
Within this all-pervading state,
Beyond both out and in,
There is nothing that is marked
By acceptance, by rejection, or by effortful exertion.
Everything is free and open in primordial infinity,
The vast expanse of dharmakāya.
All preceding realizations are subsumed
In this secret quintessence.

9. One is perfectly included,
All are perfectly included
In the vast expanse encompassing all things.
All is gathered and subsumed in great spontaneous presence,
Natural, primordial luminosity.

7. All Is Present Spontaneously and Primordially in the Enlightened Mind

1. The teachings on the enlightened mind,
By nature uncreated, present of itself,
Wherein all qualities subsist,
Are like the summit of the king of mountains,
High above all other teachings.
They are the sovereign supreme vehicle.

2. From the summit of the king of mountains,
Once it has been scaled,
The valleys down below can all be seen at once.
But from these valleys down below the peak cannot be seen.
So too, the vajra essence of the Atiyoga,
The highest peak of all the vehicles,
Surveys the goals of all these vehicles
But is to them invisible.
Spontaneous presence therefore is the peak,
The summit[27] of all vehicles.

3. It is like a mighty wish-fulfilling jewel,
Which, when people pray before it,
Lavishes upon them all that they might wish.
This is not the case with ordinary stones.
Since the vajra essence
Is the triple kāya present of itself,

When all is left just as it is,
Buddhahood is gained within the ultimate expanse.
This absence of exertion is itself
A sign of the superiority [of Ati teachings].
The lower vehicles are marked
By effort in accepting and rejecting,
And buddhahood is not achieved for many kalpas.
It is as though they are afflicted
By a strong debilitating sickness.

4a. Awareness, even and primordially spontaneous,
The enlightened mind,
The natural state just as it is,
Is the vast dharmatā.
By nature it is dharmakāya,
The vast primordial expanse of evenness.
Though present in all beings, it lies within the reach
Of only very few who have great fortune.
Left just as it is, it is achieved quite naturally
Within that very state.

4b. Its all-pervasive luminosity
Is the sambhogakāya, present of itself.
Although it is in everyone,
Only few can see it.
When without exertion
You leave appearances just as they are,
It manifests.

4c. Its display, which never ceases,
Is the all-pervading space of the nirmāṇakāya.
Present in all beings, it clearly manifests
In the arising of phenomena.
The array of wish-fulfilling qualities

And of enlightened action
Is the pure space of awareness self-cognizing.
It appears if, just like turbid water settling,
You rest within the natural limpid state.

5. Ultimate reality, primordially pure,
Is not found by searching.
The buddhas and the bodhisattvas
Dwell within this self-arisen vast expanse.
Since this is present from before,
There is no need to gain it now, anew.
This great indwelling state
Is the immense expanse of dharmatā.
Do not strive for what is changeless, present of itself.

6. The primal ground, the natural ground,
The ground of the quintessence of enlightenment
Never waver from the natural condition.
Therefore do not stray from your awareness,
The expanse of luminosity.

7. Attainment comes when all is left in this condition.
For the unchanging, all-pervading sovereign
Together with the five primordial wisdoms,
The five aspects of enlightened body,
The five aspects of enlightened speech,
The five aspects of enlightened mind,
The five enlightened qualities and activities
(In other words, primordial buddhahood)—
All are present of themselves
Within this endless and beginningless expanse.
Do not search for them elsewhere,
For in its luminous character
They are present from the very first.

8. Enlightenment itself,
The dharmakāya of the buddhas,
Is none other than immutable equality.
Since this is present of itself
Within the self-arisen state,
Do not search for it and do not try to gain it.
Just let go completely of your hopes and fears.

9. The self-arisen primal wisdom of all beings,
Uncreated, not achieved through effort,
Is present of itself as dharmakāya.
Therefore do not reach for it—
Accepting this, rejecting that.
Just rest in this expanse of ultimate reality.

10. Within the ultimate nature,
Even, present of itself,
Unwavering, devoid of thought,
There lies the ground's immense expanse
Where uncreated qualities are found.

11. This changeless, all-pervading sovereign
Of the kāyas and the wisdoms
Is the self-arisen, great, direct empowerment
In the manner of a king.
Therein phenomenal existence
(The world and all the beings it contains)
Is free and open from the first spontaneously.
There is no need for action or exertion—
By its nature it is present in and of itself.
Everything is present and unfolds
As great spontaneous presence.

8. There Is No Duality in the Enlightened Mind

1. Within the one expanse of self-arisen primal wisdom,
All things are nondual in their final way of being.
The duality that ceaselessly appears
Is the display of the creative power.
Appearances and the imputing mind
Are both nondual enlightened mind.

2. Samsara and nirvana, all phenomenal existence,
Arise within the enlightened mind,
Awareness changeless and unmoving.
They are not to be rejected or acquired.
For yogis who are free
From apprehended and from apprehender,
Phenomena, appearing while not existing,
Are a matter of amazement and of laughter.

3. Though nonexistent while appearing,
Phenomena arise in all their various forms.
Though nonexistent in their emptiness,
Things are present everywhere.
Although there are no subjects apprehending
And no objects to be apprehended,
Beings cling to "I" and to the self of things.
Although they have no ground or root,
The stream of lives flows on continuously.

Although there's nothing to accept and nothing to reject,
Beings opt for happiness and flee from pain.

4a. Observing beings, I find that their perceptions
Are extremely strange.
What is not true they think is true,
And true indeed it seems to them.
The undeluded they take as deluded,
And utterly deluded does it seem to them.
That which is unreal they take as real,
And extremely real does it appear to them.
What is not so they take as being so,
And so indeed does it appear to them.
That which is not tenable they take as tenable,
And tenable indeed it seems to them.
Thus their minds are pointlessly deceived
By various trivial objects of their senses.
Awareness has become for them
A stream of conscious instants,
And thus in days and months and years
Their lives are all consumed.
They take as dual what is nondual,
And thus these wanderers deceive themselves.

4b. Yogis with pure karma
Turn within and watch their minds.
Awareness, groundless, unsupported, is beyond all naming.
It is not seen through being pointed at or talked about.
View and meditation are a seamless continuity.
And in this state of evenness, relaxed, immensely vast,
"Practice" is unknown,
For there is no distinction "in or out of session."
At all times there is just the state
Of seamless, spacious evenness.

4c. There are no reference points:
Bodies, sense objects, or other things.
There is but the all-pervading evenness
Of the expanse of space.
The inner element, therefore,
Is not to be regarded as a self.

5. When outwardly [these yogis] turn their gaze
At objects of their senses manifesting in the outer world,
Everything is evanescent, weightless, and transparent,
Phantom-like, diaphanous, impossible to grasp.
They perceive, hear, recollect,
Know, taste, feel as never they had done before.
"What is this?" they ask. "Is this a dream?
Are these the visions of a lunatic?"
And they will simply laugh.

6. No notion is there now of friend or foe,
Of near or far, or of attachment or aversion.
There's no division into day and night
But just a single, equal, all-pervasive state of evenness.
Samsara with its apprehension
Of phenomena endowed with features is dispelled,
And this is called the state
Of self-arisen primordial wisdom.
Because there are no thoughts,
The meshes of accepting and rejecting,
Of things to be removed together with their antidotes,
Are now transcended.
Through such a realization,
Nondual wisdom is made manifest.
Self-arisen Samantabhadra's wisdom mind is reached.
The level of phenomenal exhaustion,
From which there is no possibility of falling back, is reached.

7. Without the realization of equality
Within the self-arisen state,
You may talk of nonduality,
Just clinging to the words,
And place your trust in mind's analysis
And in a blankness where there's nothing to be seen.
This is indeed the very essence of wrong understanding,
The dark abyss of ignorance.

8. And so, within that self-arisen state
Devoid of movement and of change,
Train yourself in sovereign nonduality,
Wherein all thoughts are worn away.
The three worlds thus will be completely free and open.
Samsara and nirvana will be indivisible.
The fortress of the dharmakāya, completely pure like space,
The nature that arises from within,
Surpassing all analogies, will manifest.

9. As long as you fixate on different entities,
Asserting "this" or "that,"
Remaining in duality,
You're trapped in the delusion of "yourself and others."
But when you're free of bias
And make no distinctions, saying "this" or "that,"
Everything is even in the state
Of an equality beyond all reference.
As Vajrasattva said,
This is to realize nonduality.

9. The Decisive Certainty That All Phenomena Are the Enlightened Mind

1. In the one expanse,
By nature a supreme immensity,
Is found the "nail" of the enlightened mind,
Commensurate with space itself.
Focus on its vital point and strip it to its essence.
It is the greatest of the great,
The vast mind of Samantabhadra,
By whose nature all is gathered
In the surge of its immense horizon.
And in this single vast expanse,
Realization and the lack of it,
Freedom and the lack of it
Are all a nondual great equality.

2. A garuda with its wings full grown
While still within the egg
Glides in the vault of heaven as soon as it is hatched.
It soars with mastery above the vast abyss
And overwhelms the nāgas.
Yogis graced by fortune
Realize perfectly the vajra essence,
Peak of all the vehicles.
They overwhelm the lower vehicles
And soar above samsara's vast abyss.

3. The openness and freedom of all things,
Their great state of equality,
Is unacceptable to those who strive
According to the law of cause and fruit.
But it makes sense to those who understand
The meaning of unwavering equality,
Expounded in the supreme vehicle.

4. Everything is supreme bliss,
The vast expanse of spacelike dharmakāya.
And in that vast expanse of dharmakāya,
There is nothing that's not free and open.
The self-arisen kāya of the vajra essence
Is the very nature of phenomena.
When in the yogis' bodies
(The product of habitual tendencies)
This essence has been mastered,
And when their bodies of existence
Are relinquished in the bardo states of life or death,
These yogis are inseparably united
With the single sole awareness,
Attaining thus the kingdom
Of the level of spontaneous presence.
Their emanations without limit then pour forth
And labor for all beings unimpeded.
This is the domain of yogis
Who are "carried without effort on the wind."
This makes no sense to those upon the lower vehicles.
Only Ati rightly sets it forth.
It is the crucial point of the result.

5. The display of birth occurs within the unborn state,
But the deluded mind ascribes to it
The character of causes and results.

The Ati teachings say that it is free of causes and conditions.
Though unacceptable to those who practice lower vehicles,
This is correct and is a crucial point.

6. The state of buddhas and the state of beings
Are indivisible.
To apprehend them differently
In terms of two realities, samsara and nirvana,
Is the attitude of the deluded mind.
The Atiyoga teaching that they are not two,
Though unacceptable to those who practice lower vehicles,
Is correct and is a crucial point.

7. Whether or not you realize it,
All is the state of openness and freedom.
To think that this arises through your realization
Is an enemy that hinders you.
Ati says that realization and the lack of realization
Are a single state of evenness.
Though unacceptable to those who practice lower vehicles,
This is correct and is a crucial point.

8. To claim that the inexpressible cannot be realized
Without special methods that reveal it
Is but the attitude of fools.
The Ati teachings show
That it is never separate from the ultimate.
Though unacceptable to those who practice lower vehicles,
This is correct and is a crucial point.

9. To say the state of great perfection—
Limitless, unfathomable,
All-pervading from the very first—cannot be reached
Is but the attitude of fools.

The Atiyoga teaching that it is both sharp and limitless,
Though not acceptable to those who practice lower vehicles,
Is correct and is a crucial point.

10. Because within the one sole sphere
The order is reversed,
There is no hope or fear regarding the result.
For there is just a vast expanse commensurate with space.
It is a great abyss, the mind of the Victorious Ones,
Immense as space itself.
There is nothing to reject and nothing to accomplish.
There is but the vast immensity, the one sole sphere,
Which, being free and open from the first,
Transcends both realization and the lack of it.
Upon this spacelike path devoid of action,
Yogis are at ease.

11. Primordially the state of buddhahood,
Awareness is devoid of all objective reference.
It does not wander in samsara;
It transcends the whole foundation of delusion.
No one is there who has been,
And no one is there who can be, deluded.
All things are the dharmadhātu's single, luminous expanse.
They are not different in the past or future.
They are a skylike vast expanse
Primordially uncontrived, spontaneously present.
Samsara from the very first is pure.

12. Do not opt for freedom or embrace nirvana.
In the changeless vast expanse,
There has never been samsara or nirvana
To be rejected or adopted, to be feared or hoped for.
They are the vast immensity
Of enlightenment's primordial ground.

They are but names and are, in truth,
Beyond both indication and description.
Clearly certain that samsara does not mean delusion,
That nirvana is not freedom,
Let no one strive, let no one change or alter anything.

13. Awareness without breadth or height
Is without limits, falls to no extreme.
And so hold back from aiming at it.
Awareness, free of agent and of action,
Free of coming and of going,
Entails no lapse of time, no remedy.
Therefore do not cling to it or strive.
If there is deliberate focus,
This will be the cause of bondage.
Therefore do not grasp at anything
But let it go in evenness.

14a. It makes no difference if phenomena
Are or are not free and open from the very first.
It makes no difference if the fundamental nature
Is or is not pure intrinsically.
It makes no difference if the mind itself
Is or is not free of all elaboration.
It makes no difference if, within the nature uncontrived,
There is or is not anything existent.

14b. It makes no difference if by nature samsara and nirvana
Are or are not a duality.
It makes no difference whether thoughts and words
Are or are not passed beyond.
It makes no difference if delusions of negation or assertion
Do or do not fall apart.
It makes no difference if the view that should be realized
Is or is not recognized.

14c. It makes no difference
If you do or do not meditate upon the dharmatā.
It makes no difference whether you examine it or not—
It is not something you can take or else reject.
It makes no difference whether you attain or not
The fundamental nature, the result.
It makes no difference whether you progress or not
Upon the grounds and paths.

14d. It makes no difference whether you are free or not
Of all your obscurations.
It makes no difference whether or not the dharmatā
Is gained through the generation and perfection stages.
It makes no difference whether you achieve or not
The fruit of liberation.
It makes no difference whether or not
You wander in the six migrations of samsara.

14e. It makes no difference whether or not
Your nature is spontaneously present.
It makes no difference whether or not
You're bound by dualistic clinging to permanence or to annihilation.
It makes no difference whether or not
You reach the realization of the dharmatā.
It makes no difference whether or not
You follow in the footsteps of the masters of the past.

15. No matter what may happen,
Though earth and heaven be upturned,
You experience nothing but the bare and open state
Of groundless openness, relaxed and even.
All things are unstable, hazy, evanescent, nebulous—
And like a lunatic you act without duality of hope and fear.
View and meditation—all are merged without division.

The asserting, purpose-driven mind collapses.
You are no longer trammeled by ambition,
There are no goals that you now strive to gain.

16. All that happens you allow to happen.
Whatever may appear, you allow it to appear.
Whatever may arise, you allow it to arise.
Whatever there may be, you allow it to exist.
If there's anything at all, you let it be;
And if there's nothing, you allow it not to be.

17. Unpredictable is your behavior
For awareness is preeminent.
You take no account of virtue or nonvirtue,
For you are in a bare and open state
Beyond the snare of philosophic doctrines.
Eating, walking, lying down, or sitting—by day and night,
You're in a state of all-pervading evenness,
Equality, the dharmatā.
No deities to worship, no spirits to drive out,
No Dharma to be meditated—
This is the simple, ordinary state.
You, a sovereign free of all contrivance and pretension,
Are in an all-embracing evenness.
Relaxing in equality, you now have found
The one and only state spontaneously present,
Not now achieved, because primordially accomplished.
How pleasant to be free of striving and exertion!

18. The view has no foundation and there is no meditation.
There is no action, no result to be achieved.
Since all are thus encompassed by the undivided equal state,
There is no need to strive.
Bliss lies in freedom from the wide and narrow.

19. When there is no wishing,
The notion of achievement ceases.
When there's nothing to abandon,
You go beyond the bondage of relying on an antidote.
All there is, whatever it may be,
Does not exist, nor does it not exist.
Whatever is perceived, no matter what arises,
All inescapably subsides.

20. There is nothing that's not free and open,
Free and open from the first, and of itself.
When certainty is reached
That all things, all together, are insubstantial,
They pass beyond the status of phenomena.

21. Within the vast expanse, the vast expanse,
Within the great and vast expanse,
I, Longchen Rabjam, am immersed in the expanse,
The great abyss of luminosity.
I dwell within the one, nondual immensity—
Immensity of bliss.
I, Natsok Rangdröl, have attained the dharmatā,
The state of the exhaustion of phenomena,
Unchanging, present of itself,
The summit of all perfect aspiration.

22. All you who follow after me
Bring everything together thus
In one immense, primordial, all-enveloping expanse.
And surely you will gain Samantabhadra's everlasting realm.

10. The Enlightened Mind Does Not Stir from the Dharmatā

1. The enlightened mind, by nature pure from the beginning,
Is dharmatā, which does not come or go
And is beyond acceptance and rejection.
The dharmatā is the expanse of space
And is not gained through effort.
When you settle in it naturally,
The sun and moon of luminosity arise.

2. If you do not block the objects of your senses,
If you do not hold your mind in check,
If you do not stray from the spontaneous equality
Of your natural condition, you will reach the wisdom
Of Samantabhadra, vast immensity.

3a. When thoughts do not unfold and dissipate,
There is a natural, pure limpidity—
It's like an ocean, limpid, smooth, unmoving.
It is the dharmatā, deep luminosity,
The state of self-arisen, primordial wisdom
In which you rest, where hope and fear
Do not arise and you are not caught up in them.

3b. Indescribable and free of mind's entanglement,
The plain and natural state is uncontrived and unalloyed.
It is the space where everything dissolves,

The dharmatā devoid of attributes.
There is neither meditation nor something to be meditated.
Therefore dullness, agitation both are dissipated naturally,
And the self-arisen state appears.

3c. Not eliminated through elimination,
Thoughts are themselves awareness's creative power.
There are no distinctions, differentiations, in the dharmatā.
The dharmatā is therefore not achieved through practice.
Arising as it does within the ultimate expanse of dharmatā,
Samsara is not spurned.
Rather, through the pure yoga
Linked with the creative power of this vast expanse,
You see samsara as primordial wisdom self-arisen.

3d. Appearances and mind are from the first
The natural state of dharmatā.
Unmoving concentration
Manifests in a continuous stream.
This is the vajra peak,
Samantabhadra's sublime mind.
Through meditation[28] on the fact that all things
Without any difference
Are the skylike supreme, spacious dharmatā,
The supreme, wondrous sovereign, primordially unlimited,
Is spontaneously discovered.

4a1. Within this state, where nothing is adopted or rejected,
The primordial stream of luminosity
Immediate and unmediated
Is present of itself.
This is the very nature of samsara and nirvana,
The supreme state of dharmadhātu.
This skylike vast expanse,

Unwavering and indescribable,
Is from the first and by its nature
Present in all beings.

4a2. Phenomena appearing separate from oneself
Are a delusion of the mind.
The will to meditate, to make an effort
Is a delusion of the mind.
All delusion is the natural state of dharmatā,
The purview of equality.
In this vast expanse
Of the unmoving nature pure from the beginning,
There's nothing to be done, no effort to be made;
There is no remaining and no not remaining
In the state of meditative evenness.

4b1. Unchanging dharmatā, spontaneously present,
Is free of object, thought, and agitation.
If you look at it repeatedly
With awareness self-cognizing,
You see that there is nothing to be viewed.
Awareness that cannot be viewed
Is the direct, unmediated view.

4b2. Not meditated on, awareness
Is devoid of anything to keep or to reject.
If repeatedly you meditate thereon,
You see that there is nothing to be meditated.
Awareness that cannot be meditated
Is direct, unmediated meditation.

4b3. The fundamental nature is nondual.
It is beyond acceptance and rejection.
If you act on it repeatedly,

You see that there is nothing to be acted on.
Awareness that you cannot act upon
Is direct, unmediated action.

4b4. Spontaneous presence, beyond all hope and fear,
Is of itself primordial.
When repeatedly you struggle to accomplish it,
You see that it is something
That can never be accomplished.
Awareness that can never be accomplished
Is the direct result unmediated.

4c. Within the state of evenness,
You do not conceive of objects.
You do not seize on them as mind.
Stilled are the arising and involvement with
Your hopes and fears.
Mind and objects stay within that state of evenness,
Not stirring from the vast expanse of dharmatā.
This is the direct, unmediated resting
In the absence of objective reference
With regard to things endowed with attributes.
Because of the unmediated directness
Of primordial and nondual awareness,
Samsara and nirvana are inseparable;
They are the state of great perfection
Where all things are encompassed
By the state of evenness,
Without some being taken, others spurned.

4d. Things and nonthings—both are equal
In the ultimate expanse.
Buddhas and beings—both are equal
In the ultimate expanse.

Relative and ultimate—both are equal
In the ultimate expanse.
Defects and good qualities—
All are equal in the ultimate expanse.
Zenith, nadir, main and intermediary directions—
All are equal in the ultimate expanse.
No matter what displays occur therefore
Within the self-arisen state,
All arises equal in the moment of arising,
Neither good nor bad.
What need is there to take some things and spurn the rest
Or alter them with antidotes?
In their remaining, all remain as equal,
Neither good nor bad.
Whatever now arises in your mind,
Relax within its natural disappearance.
In their subsiding, all subside as equal,
Neither good nor bad.
Don't run after thoughts, accepting some, rejecting others,
Promoting their proliferation.

5. Within the enlightened mind, the ground's expanse,
The way in which all things arise
As its creative power and its display
Is unpredictable.
Though things arise as equal, they yet arise
Within the vast primordial expanse.
Though they arise unequal, they yet arise
Within equality's ultimate expanse.
Though they remain as equal, they yet remain
Within the natural state of dharmatā.
Though they remain unequal, they yet remain
Within equality's ultimate expanse.
Though they subside as equal, they yet subside

Within the space of primal wisdom self-arisen.
Though they subside unequal, they yet subside
Within equality's ultimate expanse.

6a. All things are primordial equality,
Awareness self-arisen.
Therefore from the very first,
There's no arising and no nonarising
In the ultimate expanse.
From the very first,
There's no remaining and no nonremaining
In the ultimate expanse.
From the very first,
There is no freedom and no lack of freedom
In the ultimate expanse.

6b. Within awareness, the unwavering state of great equality,
When things arise, they arise quite naturally,
Keeping to their natural condition.
Remaining, they remain quite naturally,
Keeping to their natural condition.
Subsiding, they subside quite naturally,
Keeping to their natural condition.

6c. Within awareness, changeless,
Free of all conceptual movement,
All arising is primordial arising;
All remaining is primordial remaining;
All subsiding is primordial subsiding.
All is of a spacelike nature.

6d. Consciousness arises, stays, subsides—
It arises and subsides in seamless continuity.
Being seamless, it is not divided into cause and its effect.

Because there is no cause and no effect,
There is no chasm of samsara.
This being so, how can you go astray?

6e. Samantabhadra's vast expanse
Is primordially unchanging.
Vajrasattva's vast expanse
Is free of change and movement.
Buddhahood is but a name for just the recognition
Of the fundamental nature.

6f. If you realize this, there's nothing to adopt or spurn
And all things are encompassed by the single dharmatā.
As in a golden island, no distinctions can be made.
Things are untouched by conceptual extremes;
All deviations and all obscurations are resolved,
And thus there is no chasm of samsara.
Without exertion, without effort,
The three kāyas are spontaneously, completely present
In the enlightened mind.
To call them inconceivable, ineffable
Is nothing more than words.

6g. When appearances are left alone,
Awareness self-arisen is clearly present,
Unobscured and open,
Unimpeded, free of out or in.
If you stay without contrivance in this natural state,
It is clearly present as great dharmatā.
Relax your mind and body deeply
In a carefree state, at ease,
Serenely like a person who has nothing more to do.
Neither tense nor loose,
Let mind and body rest in comfort.

6h. However beings may be, they are within their nature.
However beings may stay, they stay within their nature.
However beings may move, they move within their nature.
In the vast space of enlightenment,
By nature, there's no going and no coming.
The bodies of victorious buddhas
Neither go nor come.

6i. However speech occurs, it occurs within its nature.
However expression occurs, it occurs within its nature.
The enlightened mind is, by its nature,
Free of speech and of expression.
The speech of the Victorious Ones, past, present, and to come,
Is free of speech and of expression.

6j. However reflection may occur, it does so in its nature.
However thoughts occur, they do so in their nature.
The enlightened mind is from the first
Without reflection, without thought.
The minds of all Victorious Ones, past, present, and to come,
Are free of thought and of reflection.

6k. Without existing, it appears as anything at all,
And thus it is nirmāṇakāya.
It enjoys itself,
And thus it is sambhogakāya.
It has no substantial ground,
And thus it is the dharmakāya.
It is the expanse, spontaneously present
Of the triple kāya, the result.

6l. Within the vast expanse
Of the enlightened mind,
No thoughts occur, no recollections.

When all such attributes of ordinary cognition
Do not stir within the mind,
This is the condition of the one sole buddhahood.

6m. The luminous character of the enlightened state
Is like the sky's immense expanse.
To be devoid of thoughts and recollections
Is the supreme meditation.
The luminous character of awareness in itself
Is without movement, free of all contrivance.
Free of thought and mental action,
The natural state, the dharmatā,
Throughout the three times is devoid
Of movement and of change.
If there are no moving and unfolding thoughts,
This is supreme meditation.

6n. That which dwells in suchness
Is the sublime state of mind,
The one sole state of buddhahood
Devoid of every attribute.
It is the unwavering dharmadhātu,
Which at once transcends fixating thought.
It is by nature the supremely vast expanse of wisdom
Of Victorious Ones.
When you abandon all contrivances
Whereby the mind and body are encumbered,
There comes a natural state of relaxation.
Thoughts and memories occur,
But if you do not waver
From the ground left as it is,
The state of dharmatā,
All is but a vast immensity,
The wisdom of Samantabhadra.

6o. Do not hold within; do not project outside.
Do not be tightly tense or loose.
Just as it is, the unrestricted natural state
Is of its own accord attained.
If within the vast expanse—
Unmoving, limitlessly spread, transcending measurement—
Self-arising thoughts and recollections naturally subside,
This is indeed the spacelike wisdom mind of Vajrasattva.

6p. If in the expanse devoid of all contrivance
You remain without distraction,
Though thoughts and memories engage with objects,
The state of dharmatā is there.
But if you try with vigorous purpose to contrive
The dharmatā, which in itself
Is free of thought and vast like space,
It will be trapped inside conceptual attributes.
And though you may spend day and night in practice,
All is an entangling obsession.
The Buddha said that it resembles
The samādhi of the gods.
And so it is important that,
Without distraction but without concerted effort,
Your mind rest naturally free
Of all exertion and fixation.

6q. Primordial wisdom self-arisen
Has no boundaries, no extremes.
And so you cannot point it out
With words like "It is this."
Within its nature, all elaborations cease.
So leave the mind's activity aside
And train yourself in what is meant
By groundless vast immensity.

6r. The one sole dharmatā, primordial wisdom self-arisen,
Is the one sole view devoid of all elaboration.
It is the one sole meditation free of keeping and rejecting,
Free of going, free of coming.
It is the one sole action free of all activity
Of taking and rejecting.
It is the one sole fruit devoid of the duality
Of spurning and acquiring.
These are the states of self-arisen spontaneous presence.

6s. Phenomenal existence, samsara and nirvana,
The world and all the beings it contains—
None of this has ever stirred
From the primordial state of dharmatā,
Primordial wisdom self-arisen.
Understand therefore that all things are the dharmatā,
The ground left as it is.

6t. Regarding all the things
Appearing as the objects of the senses,
Do not think "It's thus that on them I will settle."
Rest instead spontaneously in the natural state
Without your thoughts unfolding and dissolving.
You will naturally remain in the expanse
Of the equality of dharmatā.

6u. Neither drawing in your sense powers
Nor letting your eyes wander
To what appears as objects in their rich variety,
Not thinking of yourself,
Not having thoughts concerning others,
Stay in luminosity,
Within the even state, supremely vast.

6v. Within the state of primal self-arisen wisdom
Of the equality of all things,
Wherein there is no out or in and nothing in between,
A lofty and expansive mind
Devoid of thoughts unfolding and dissolving
Is experienced as though it merged with space.
There manifests a concentration that is free
Of all elaborations—bliss and luminosity.

7a. In the ground left as it is,
The state of the unmoving dharmatā,
There is no out, no in,
No conceptual elaboration
Of apprehender-apprehended.
There is no mind that fixes
On an object different from itself.
Thus there are no things to apprehend;
There is no clinging to the appearance
Of the world and beings.
There is no place within samsara
Where you might take birth,
For all is similar to space itself.
Inwardly, because you do not take your mind
As being your "self," there is no apprehender—
All samsaric thoughts are stilled.
That which causes birth within samsara is completely cut,
And all things then are similar to space.
Outwardly and inwardly,
No hallucinatory phenomena are found.
The state of dharmakāya is attained.
You reach the level of phenomenal exhaustion—
Going and coming are no more.
Everything is but an infinite expanse,
Samantabhadra's field.
You have attained the supreme palace of the dharmakāya.

7b. If awareness in the present moment
Does not wander from the ground,
And if you grow familiar with this,
Subsequent existence in samsara ceases.
You will be free of action and habitual tendencies
That cause rebirth.
You will have decisive certainty
Regarding causes and effects,
Proclaiming that samsara and nirvana are now equal.
You will reach the essence of enlightenment
That does not dwell in peace or in existence.
Therefore in the present moment,
It is vital to distinguish this awareness
From one-pointed calm abiding.
Such is the teaching of the Natural Great Perfection.

7c. When you stray from the awareness state,
Cogitation happens
And samsara with the law of cause and fruit occurs.
Without decisive certainty in its regard,
Beings, thus mistaken, wander ever lower.
The supremely secret Great Perfection therefore says
That if you do not wander from the ultimate expanse,
The appearances of its creative power
Sink back into the ground,
And without stirring from the dharmatā
You rest within equality.

7d. Within this state, there is no cause and no effect;
There is no effortful activity.
There is no view and so forth to be meditated.
There is no center, no periphery, and no duality.
All is thus negated.
But when creative power strays outward from awareness,
The manifold display of all phenomenal existence

Appears in every way.
So never say that there's no cause and no effect.
Conditioned things dependently arise,
They are past numbering and inconceivable.
The hallucinations of samsara
And even states of peace and bliss
Are countless and beyond the mind's imagining.
Everything dependently arises
From the gathering of causes and conditions.

7e. When you appraise the fundamental state of things,
There's nothing to be found.
When you use it as the path, not stirring from this state,
There's nothing to be seen.
This is regarded as the moment of the [dharmakāya] wisdom.
You have perfectly attained the fundamental state of things
And therefore are unstained by anything at all.

8. This great chasm of defilements, actions, and propensities
Has no support.
It is but a magical display of illusory appearances.
Free yourself from it, I beg you.
Be convinced regarding causes and results.
To this end, there's nothing greater than this teaching.
Therefore it is vital not to wander
From the state of dharmadhātu.
Vast and deep, this is a counsel from my heart.
"All is," "All is not," "All exists," "Nothing exists"—
It's so important to transcend them all.

11. All Experiences Are Pure Like Space

1. All things are the one enlightened mind,
Commensurate with space.
And yet, because of dualistic clinging,
You are deluded in samsara with its causes and results.
But such hallucinatory appearances have no support;
They are but magical illusions.
So disregard them when you meet with them,
Keeping to a state in which they leave no trace.

2. When something you don't want occurs,
You have the attitude of wanting to be rid of it.
You are angry and displeased.
You are jealous, irritated, spiteful.
You are weary and in anguish,
You have pain and discontent.
You are afraid of death, rebirth, and all the rest.
When all this happens, recognize it
As the display of awareness's creative power.
Do not reject it, do not try to cleanse it.
Do not transform it or accept it.
Do not watch it, do not meditate on it.
Stay rather without effort
In the one sole natural state of evenness,
Free of thoughts unfolding and dissolving.
It will vanish without trace, and from within,

The spacious, pure expanse of mind
Will sharply, clearly, limpidly appear.

3. When appearances are encountered
In unlimited awareness,
Beyond both being and nonbeing,
And without point of reference,
If you rest without contrivance
And do not grasp at such appearances,
Acceptance and rejection vanish,
Traceless in this state
Where there's no [thought of] openness and freedom.
An experience without clinging and fixation
Wells up from within.
This is the vast, primordial expanse:
Awareness as it is.

4. In just the same way,
When you have the joy
Of gaining what your heart desires,
Happiness is yours.
Companions, pleasant conversation, riches,
A delightful dwelling place and region—
When, through all such circumstances,
A joyful state of mind arises,
Recognize its nature. Rest freely in its natural state.
You will be within the uncontrived primordial expanse
Spontaneously present.

5. When, while sitting down or walking,
You are in a neutral, ordinary state,
Neither joyful nor depressed,
Do not indulge in it, do not reject it.
Recognize its nature in the moment it appears.
Not different from the natural state of dharmatā,

This is said to be an ignorance or dullness
That subsides into great luminosity.

6. At night or other times,
Though you be stupefied by sleep,
You lie within the natural condition,
Free of thoughts unfolding and dispersing.
Gross perceptions therefore disappear
And with them their perceiver.
Then subtle and extremely subtle thoughts subside
And also that which apprehends them.
The mind then rests aware within a state
Of evenness devoid of concepts.
It dwells within its nature—
Thoughts do not arise, and there is no engaging with them.
There is neither hope nor fear.
This is the point when all thoughts sink into the dharmadhātu.
Therefore it is called "subsiding of samsara in nirvana."

7. Even sleep itself is but the self-arisen
Primordial expanse.
Awareness's reative power is stilled,
Absorbed into the ground, the ultimate expanse.
All cognitions that lay hold of its display
Come naturally to stillness.
This is the state devoid of action,
The state of self-arisen primordial wisdom.

8. And therefore all your attitudes
Of wanting or not wanting or indifference,
As well as the three poisons that appear
Through awareness's creative power as its display—
All occur within the ultimate expanse,
All arise within the ultimate expanse.
Since they subsist within the ultimate expanse,

Not stirring from it in the slightest,
Do not fall into the meshes
Of contriving or transforming these same attitudes.
It is crucial that you recognize this ultimate expanse.
As soon as you are settled there,
These attitudes come naturally to stillness.
They naturally vanish and subside.

9. Even the defilements, actions, and habitual tendencies
Arise as a display through awareness's creative power.
Even antidotes and virtuous acts—the path of liberation—
Manifest as a display arising through creative power.
Both are a display primordially arising through creative power.
Recognize therefore their nature.
Rest within it uncontrivedly—this is indeed a crucial point.
Both are equal in rapidity and movement,
Equal in their stirring in the ground.
Occurring through conditions, they're compounded
And are not beyond dependent origin.
It is important thus to rest within the natural state,
To leave them as they are,
And to be certain with regard to cause and fruit.

10. This is the very summit of the supreme secret vehicle.
It is most secret. Do not speak of it to those of lesser mind.
For they will mar the quintessential teachings
By superimposition or depreciation.
Understanding falsely, they will wander from its view.
Those who breach the door of secrecy
Will fall to lower destinies that have no end.
Therefore the heritage of the most secret sovereign vehicle
Should be entrusted and revealed
To sublime beings of excellent good fortune.

11. In short, whatever circumstances may occur—
A sense object or state of mind—
Do not apply an antidote.
Do not strive to rid yourself of it.
For the key point of awareness is the natural state,
The unaltered state, the state left as it is.

12. All happiness and suffering
Are ways in which awareness manifests.
If you regard them dualistically,
As things to take or to reject,
Then you are bound within existence.
All objects that appear are equal—
They do no more than manifest to faculties of sense.
All mental states are equal—
They are no more than thoughts that in awareness leave no trace.
Both are equal in immediate presence—
They do no more than bind you in acceptance and rejection.
Truly in their final status they are equal—
They are no more than things appearing groundlessly.
In their distinctiveness the objects of the senses are all equal—
They are no more than traceless when they're broken down.
All mental states are equal in the way they are perceived—
They are no more than space when they're investigated.
Mind and objects are not two—
They're no more than the pure and intervening air.
Those who know this are the scions of Samantabhadra.
They are vidyādharas upon the highest ground,
The supreme heirs of the Victorious Ones.

13. Therefore all phenomena are equal—
Equal in existing, equal in their not existing,
Equal in appearing, equal in their emptiness,
Equal in their truth, and equal in their falsity.

Abandon therefore all fixation, all that fetters you—
Things to be abandoned, their counteracting antidotes,
And all concerted effort.
Grow, become commensurate with great equality,
Free of all objective reference.
Grow, become commensurate with great awareness,
Free of ordinary mind.
Grow, become commensurate with great equality and purity,
Free of any flaw.

12. Phenomena Are Primordially Open and Free within the Enlightened Mind

1a. Everything is free and open in the enlightened mind.
There are no phenomena that are not free and open.

1b. Samsara is free and open from the very first,
Free and open in primordial purity.
Nirvana is free and open from the very first,
Free and open in spontaneous perfection.
The appearing world is free and open from the very first,
Free and open in its groundlessness and rootlessness.
Living beings are free and open from the very first,
Free and open in the essence of enlightenment.
The elaborations of the mind are free and open from the very first,
Free and open in their lack of limits and extremes.
The absence of elaboration too is free and open from the very first,
Free and open in its unborn purity.

2. Happiness is free and open from the very first,
Free and open in the all-pervading dharmatā.
Suffering is free and open from the very first,
Free and open in the ground's immense equality.
Indifference is free and open from the very first,
Free and open in the spacelike dharmakāya.
Purity is free and open from the very first,

Free and open in the emptiness of the ground's purity.
Impurity is free and open from the very first,
Free and open in the supreme state of utter openness and
freedom.

3. The grounds and paths are free and open from the very first,
Free and open in transcending generation and perfection.
View and meditation are free and open from the very first,
Free and open in the absence of acceptance and rejection.
Action too is free and open from the very first,
Free and open in the vast space of Samantabhadra.
The result is free and open from the very first,
Free and open in transcending hope and fear.
Samaya too is free and open from the very first,
Free and open in great dharmatā.
Recitation, mantra repetition
Both are free and open from the very first,
Free and open in transcending all expression.
Concentration too is free and open from the very first,
Free and open in transcending the domain of contemplation.

4. Existence, nonexistence
Both are free and open from the very first,
Free and open in transcending such extremes.
Permanence, discontinuity
Both are free and open from the very first,
Free and open in their groundlessness and rootlessness.
Wholesomeness is free and open from the very first,
Free and open in transcending thought and aim.
Unwholesomeness is free and open from the very first,
Free and open in transcending thought and partiality.
Karmic deeds are free and open from the very first,
Free and open in not staining.
Defilements too are free and open from the very first,
Free and open in the absence both of bondage and of freedom.

Habitual tendencies are free and open from the very first,
Free and open in the absence of foundation.
The full ripening of acts is free and open from the very first,
Free and open in the absence of a basis of experience.

5. Antidotes are free and open from the very first,
Free and open in there being nothing to abandon.
Acceptance and rejection—neither has existence;
Both are free and open in a vast spacelike immensity.
Freedom too is free and open from the very first,
Free and open in there being no bondage.
Freedom's absence too is free and open from the very first,
Free and open in there being no freedom and no bondage.
Relaxation too is free and open from the very first,
Free and open in there being nothing to relax.
Leaving as it is is free and open from the very first,
Free and open in that there is nothing to leave as it is.

6. In brief, then, all things that appear or can appear
And all that is beyond such things and does not or cannot appear
Are free and open from the very first
Within the ultimate expanse.
No one therefore needs to strive
To make them free and open now.

7. Though you may strive therein, it is to no avail.
So do not do it! Do not do it!
Do not try with effort to achieve it!
Do not watch them! Do not watch them!
Do not watch your thoughts!
Do not meditate! Do not meditate!
Do not meditate on mind!
Do not investigate! Do not investigate!
Do not investigate the objects of the senses and the mind!
Do not labor! Do not labor!

Do not labor for the fruit with hope and fear!
Do not reject! Do not reject!
Do not reject defilements and activities!
Do not adopt! Do not adopt!
Do not adopt the pure phenomena!
Do not fetter! Do not fetter!
Do not fetter your own mind!

8. All things break down together;
No "object" is there found in anything.
There is no plan of action and there's nothing to be done.
No conceptual target is there to identify.
The ground breaks down, the path breaks down,
And the result breaks down.
Excellence and defects, deviation and decline—
The slightest trace of these cannot be found.
All is even, utterly without existence,
Nonexistent from the first—
Phenomenal existence is reduced to nothing.
Samsara and nirvana both break down.
They're nonexistent in the ultimate expanse.
So what is there and what is going on?
There is nothing to be pointed out by saying "It is this."
So what is "you" and where indeed is "I"?
These are but traces of a past that is no more.
And who is there who might do anything about it?
Ha ha! It's so amazing that it makes me laugh!

9. The delusion of phenomenal existence,
The world together with the beings it contains, breaks down.
Day and night clear naturally away, primordially away;
Into space, they clear away.
Days and dates are cleared away;
Years and months, whole kalpas, clear away.
One is cleared and all is cleared away;

Virtue and nonvirtue are all cleared away.
Samsara and nirvana, the basis of delusion,
Clear away into the ground's primordial, vast expanse.
And the so-called primordial expanse,
Convention of the ordinary mind, is likewise cleared away.
So what is to be done and what is there to strive for?
What purpose is there to pursue?
There are no ties of the desiring mind.
There is just space, a great and supreme wonder.
The nature [realized by] this beggar free of Dharma
Is like this and is nothing more!

10. The precious foundation is the citadel of space.
It is without support; it's free and open from the very first
And present of itself within awareness.
The three worlds of existence,
The world and all the beings it contains,
Are therefore open and free in that great state
That is devoid of all objective reference.

11. Those bound by taking sides where there are no such sides
Do not know the nature of phenomena
And by this they are damaged.
They are confused, they are deluded, they are so deluded!
Though there is no delusion,
These beings are deluded
And perceive [samsara's] great abyss.

12. Delusion and the absence of delusion
Are but the vast expanse of the enlightened mind.
From the very first, in the enlightened mind,
There never was delusion nor the freedom from delusion.
You are fettered by your clinging
To what arises as enlightened mind's display.
But since there is no bondage and no freedom,

There is neither mind nor object.
Do not be misled by taking for existent
What does not exist.

13a. Awareness, free and open,
Is the state of primal buddhahood.
Therefore do not snare it in the clinging and fixating
Of the trap of Dharma.
Pure in every way, it is the vast expanse
Devoid of objects of the senses from the very first.
It is the vast space of enlightenment,
The ground and root of great bliss, equal to the sky.
It is the primal nature where samsara is not possible.

13b. There are no edges and no corners in the one sole sphere.
To see identity or difference is the mind's delusion.
There are no causes and conditions that relate
To self-arisen primal wisdom.
To claim so is to go upon samsara's path:
It is a blockage to enlightenment.
Spontaneous presence is impartial and beyond extremes.
To think of it one-sidedly
In terms of ontological extremes
Is but the māra of conceit.
Unceasing emptiness is substanceless and has no features.
To label it existent, nonexistent, empty, or appearing
Is simply the distorted mind.
Forsake the snare, therefore, of your one-sided claims,
Knowing that spontaneous presence
Is like space; it has no partiality.

13c. Whatever may arise in the six consciousnesses—
Sights seen, sounds heard, and all the rest—
They are the vast expanse of luminosity,
Beyond all differentiation.

They are the vast expanse, primordially free and open, of equality.
Be utterly convinced of this!

13d. [Awareness] is the ultimate expanse,
For all appearances occur
Within this one state of equality.
It is the ground, for it gives rise to every excellence.
It is the vast expanse,
For in it all arises naturally
Free of differentiation.
It is the enlightened mind, for it arises
As the essence of everything that manifests.
Understand that, like space,
It is pure from the beginning.

13e. Primordial wisdom self-arisen,
The ground's immense expanse,
Is pure in being primordially unstained,
Untainted by samsara.
It is all-encompassing, for all its qualities
Are present of themselves therein,
Transcending causes and effects.
And it is mind—awareness self-cognizing,
The essence of pure luminosity.
In this mind that's pure and all-encompassing,
All things are gathered, all completely pure.

13f. When you realize the nature of phenomena
That arise as the display of the creative power,
There comes a sudden "re-enlightenment."
When there is no such realization, there is ignorance
And the arising of deluded consciousness.
From the universal ground unfold
Eight consciousnesses with their objects.
But no matter what display may manifest,

Of worlds and their inhabitants,
It does not stray beyond
The vast expanse of the enlightened mind.
Not stirring from this mind's expanse,
Samsara and nirvana are encompassed by equality.
They are free and open in the vast space of awareness.

14a. In the fundamental state,
Samsara and nirvana are impossible
Because this state is natural, free of fabrication.
Good and bad, adoption and rejection are impossible therein
Because this state is natural, free of fabrication.
Gain, rejection, apprehender, apprehended are impossible therein
Because this state is natural, free of fabrication.
Defilements of five poisons are impossible therein
Because this state is natural, free of fabrication.
Limits and extreme positions are impossible therein
Because this state is natural, free of fabrication.
Creative power and its display are impossible therein
Because this state is natural, free of fabrication.
But there is no negation of their simple labels,
Because this state is natural, free of fabrication.

14b. Self-arisen primordial wisdom
Is the exhaustion of phenomena,
Where even names do not exist.
Its creative power and all that is displayed
Are but a state of groundlessness.
No bondage is there and no freedom—
The fundamental nature of them both
Is but the natural state devoid of fabrication.
"Freedom" is no more than labeling
That simply fades away and leaves no trace.
"All are" and "all are not," as labels, are not contradictions,

For all is free and open from the very first.
And this is all that one can say.

15a. There is no differentiation—all is free and open
In the expanse of spontaneous presence.
There is no separation—all is free and open
In the expanse of the one sole sphere.
Anything may manifest—free and open
In the expanse free of all determination.

15b. All appearances perceived as forms
Are free and open in themselves.
All that resonates as sound
Is free and open in itself.
All that is perceived as smell
Is free and open in the ultimate expanse.
Experiences of taste and touch
Are free and open in themselves.
Thoughts and recollections, all perceptions
Are all free and open—groundless, rootless, and without support.

15c. All is free and open in the one sole sphere,
Free and open in the space of dharmatā.
Minds and objects are not two,
Free and open in equality.
Free and open is the self-arisen,
Free and open in the space of primal wisdom.
Free and open is spontaneous presence,
Free and open in the ground's immaculate expanse.

15d. Phenomena in their variety are free and open,
Free and open in the single sole expanse.
Without orientation, they are free and open,
Free and open in the vast space of spontaneous presence.

Everything is free and open,
Free and open in the vast expanse of the quintessence.

15e. Luminosity is free and open,
Free and open in the vast expanse of sun and moon.
Dharmatā is free and open,
Free and open in the vast expanse of space.
Phenomena are free and open,
Free and open in the ocean's vast expanse.
The immutable is free and open,
Free and open in Mount Meru's vast expanse.

15f. All is free and open from the very first,
Free and open in the unborn vast expanse.
All is free and open, all at once,
Free and open in the vast expanse primordially pure.
All is free and open in an utter openness and freedom,
Free and open in the vast expanse primordially in flower.

13. The Regaining of Buddhahood without Effortful Practice

1. If, with the crucial point of freedom from exertion,
You train in the spontaneous and enlightened essence of
phenomena,
Already buddha from the first, you will be buddha once again.
This is the summit of the vajra essence unsurpassed,
The heart of the nine gradual vehicles,
The vast expanse of the enlightened state.

2a1. Like mandalas of sun and moon
That clearly shine within the vault of heaven,
Enlightenment resides within, though it does not appear.
This quintessence is completely hidden
By great clouds: the lack of realization.

2a2. The great clouds that have gathered in the sky
Vanish into space all by themselves.
So too, when without effort
Clouds of causes and effects disperse,
There naturally appears, within the vault of heaven,
[The sun,] the essence of enlightenment.
To this end, different vehicles exist
According to the level of capacity.

2a3. Like the sun, awareness brightly shines
In the expanse of dharmadhātu.
And like the sun's rays, its creative power

Gives rise to everything without distinction.
As these rays fill with warmth the earth, the sea, and rivers,
The rising vapor forms the clouds' display
That veils the sun and its creative power.
Likewise the face of the quintessence
Is obscured by an impure display
Deriving from its own creative power:
An inconceivable hallucinatory array—
Appearances of phenomenal existence,
The world and its inhabitants.

2a4. Through the power of the sun's rays,
Winds are stirred that drive the clouds away.
So too when the nature of awareness has been realized,
Its display arises as its ornament.
Delusion, which is free and open from the first,
Then and there subsides.
Hallucinatory perceptions and appearances
Are not spurned but purified within the ultimate expanse,
And there's no knowing where they went.
The sun (the kāyas and the wisdoms
Present of themselves)
Shines in the unencumbered sky.
The kāyas and wisdoms
Are but the stainless self-experience of awareness.
They do not come from somewhere else.

2b. Within the egg, the twice-born's full-fledged wings
Cannot be seen, enveloped by the shell.
But when the shell is broken, the garuda soars
At once into the heart of space.
Likewise, if defilements and the false cognitions
Of an apprehending subject and an apprehended object
Have been previously exhausted,

When finally the shell of the residual form,
The product of defilement, breaks,
Awareness luminous by nature
Immediately arises present of itself.
The kāyas and the wisdoms fill the vast expanse of space.
When they recognize their nature,
Yogis come to freedom
In Samantabhadra's vast expanse.

2c1. The display of their cognizant power
Knows no bounds throughout the ten directions.
They send forth emanations that bring benefit to beings.
And till the emptying of samsara,
They perform enlightened deeds.
Within the natural fundamental state, all this is a display
Arising from cognizant potency's creative power,
Which manifests on every side
And brings abundant benefit to beings.

2c2. Even though the impure display
In all its aspects is completely quelled,
Emanations manifest for impure beings.
They manifest—as in the case of our own Teacher—
Through natural cognizant potency
And through the stainless acts and aspirations
Of wandering beings of pure, unsullied mind.

2c3. At that time, in all the buddha fields,
Unnumbered emanations
Lead beings without limit to enlightenment,
While never stirring from the ultimate expanse,
The Teacher's dharmakāya.
In the vast expanse of primal wisdom,
Not permanent or discontinuous, not falling to extremes,

The field of Dense Array arises by itself.
And here the inconceivable display of the sambhogakāya
Appears for the vidyādharas and ḍākinīs,
As also for the bodhisattvas who reside on the ten grounds.
It appears within the ultimate expanse
Through the cognizant power of the Teacher
Together with the virtue and the aspirations
Of beings to be guided.
It is the very face of the spontaneous presence.

3a. The dharmakāya
Is primordial wisdom self-arisen.
Primordial wisdom's oceanlike omniscience is its display,
Present as the one sole sphere
Within the ultimate original expanse.

3b. The sambhogakāya is the luminous character,
Spontaneously present.
Its display is the five families
Together with the five primordial wisdoms,
Which manifest and fill
The vast expanse of space.

3c. The nirmāṇakāya is cognizant potency,
The ground and basis for arising.
Its displays occur according to the needs
Of beings to be guided.
It has mastery of great enlightened action.

3d. These three kāyas are not gained
Through striving and in causal sequence.
They are present of themselves primordially
And manifest when all is left just as it is.
To those most adept in the supreme secret,

They manifest within this very life,
And also they appear to those
Who in the bardo state are not misled.
The vajra essence, summit of all vehicles,
Is thus exalted over all the causal and resultant vehicles.

Conclusion

1. This song of ultimate reality, the vajra essence,
Spacelike nature pure from the beginning,
Arose all by itself within the groundless,
Rootless, and unchanging place.
It is the play of what is free of movement and of change.

2. Its meaning is the vast state, all-pervasive,
Of primordial equality.
Without arriving anywhere,
I stay in my primordial nature—
The unmoving dharmatā, spontaneously present,
Limitless, not falling to extremes.

3. In themselves, these teachings
Are a vast immensity that equals space itself.
Here, unmoving is the sovereign
Of the self-arisen vast expanse.
Here, all manifold appearances subside just where they stand.
I have gone into the vast womb of the ultimate expanse,
Which is not to be pointed out by saying "this."

4. In the certainty of realization,
I, a yogi similar to space itself,
Set forth, in sum, my own experience
In concord with the scriptural tradition:
The twenty-one root scriptures of the mind class,
The three series of the space class,
And the four sections of the pith instruction class.

5. Through this virtue,
May all beings, leaving none aside,
Attain without exertion the primordial ground.
May they, upon Samantabhadra's level,
Free of movement and of change,
Be sovereigns of the Dharma,
Spontaneously accomplishing
The twofold goal.

6. In all directions may there be
Glory, wealth, and happiness,
And may all wishes, just as in a buddha field,
Be spontaneously fulfilled.
Through the sounding of the Dharma drum
May liberation's flag of victory be raised.
And, never waning, may the sacred teaching spread and flourish.

This completes *The Precious Treasury of the Dharmadhātu*, well composed upon the slopes of Kangri Thökar by Longchen Rabjam, a yogi of the supreme vehicle.

PART TWO

The One Sole Sphere of Luminosity

A Word Commentary on The Precious Treasury of the Dharmadhātu

Khangsar Tenpa'i Wangchuk

Khangsar Tenpa'i Wangchuk

Textual Outline

Preamble

To awareness, self-arisen,
The true face of the primordial sovereign lord,
Never parted from the mind of my own teacher,
I bow down in perfect faith.

Samantabhadra, Vajrasattva, Master Garab,
Śrīsiṃha, Padmasambhava, Vimalamitra,
The twenty-five disciples, king and court,
And holders of the long transmission and the treasures—
Who from mind-to-mind, through gestures,
Or by word of mouth have set the teachings forth—
To all this throng of teachers I bow down.

Within the field, primordial and indestructible,
Perfect, uncontrived,
You are a buddha; you personify
The kayas and primordial wisdoms.
Yet here, in this our land, in dancing manifested form,
You learnedly set forth the teaching so profound,
And as *Rays of Stainless Light*,
You reign supreme above my head.

Emanated dance of Vima and of Vairotsana,
Who in this chilly country of Tibet,
Have manifested willingly as our kind teacher,
Venerable king of Dharma, Matisāgara,
The dust beneath your feet I place upon my crown.

The primordial Lord, the Buddha Samantabhadra, is perfectly enlightened in the dharmadhātu, the vast expanse of primordial purity. In the buddha field that in ground and essence is adorned with flowers and is the spontaneously present display of cognizant power, the emanation of this same Samantabhadra appears spontaneously as the Buddha Vairocana Mahāsāgara. Within his body, various buddha fields appear in their diverse array, and there the emanations of this Teacher's body, speech, and mind appear as three bodhisattvas, guides of beings to be trained. Of these, Kumāra Sthiracakra [Mañjughoṣa] is the omniscient Longchen Rabjam in person.

Formerly, Longchenpa appeared in the form of the great paṇḍita Vimalamitra, as Virūpa, Mahāmutra[29] and others, paṇḍitas and accomplished masters of the Noble Land. Finally, for the sake of the Doctrine and beings, he willingly appeared in this world, the sublime good fortune of those whom he might guide, the wandering beings of this age of dregs.

Patrul Rinpoche, Orgyen Jigme Chökyi Dawa Palzangpo, once said,

> Paṇḍita Lord of Sakya, sunlight of the teachings of five sciences;
> Tsongkhapa, wellspring of fine discourse on the sutras and the tantras;
> Longchenpa, sovereign lord of all the teachings:
> All three were truly Mañjughoṣa in the Land of Snow.

As this text declares, the victorious Longchen Rabjam was one of the three emanations of Mañjughoṣa in the snowy land of Tibet. His treatise, *The Precious Treasury of the Dharmadhātu*, which establishes all phenomena as awareness (*rigpa*)—the single great expanse of dharmadhātu—is the quintessential teaching of his Seven Great Treasuries. And in order to compose some notes upon it, following the oral instructions of my supremely venerable teacher, Lodrö Gyatso, I implore the latter's permission as well as that of my yidam deity.

The precious Lama Mipham said that this treatise expresses the essential view of all the general commentaries on the mind, space, and pith instruction classes of the Great Perfection, but that, in particular, it clarifies the view of the secret pith instructions. It is generally said that *The Treasury of the Dharmadhātu* brings together all the crucial points of trekchö, the teachings on cutting through the resistance [of the ordinary mind] to primordial purity, as set forth in the works of Longchenpa.

These writings include the Seven Treasuries,[30] which expound the vast range of teachings according to the scholarly approach of paṇḍitas; the Four Parts of the Heart Essence,[31] the cycle of profound teachings devised for yogis; the Trilogy of Rest,[32] the great chariot of definitive teachings that convey completely and without error the essential meaning of the profound and vast doctrines; and finally, the Trilogy of Natural Openness Freedom,[33] and the Trilogy on Dispelling Darkness.[34]

It is consequently said that fortunate beings, endowed with a karmic inheritance enabling them to implement the teaching contained within this treatise, will attain without doubt the state of union in a single life and body. Even those who but see, hear, recall, or touch this text are accounted persons of perfect fortune. This may be understood from various sources, such as *The Music of the Wisdom Clouds*, a biographical prayer, which is addressed to the omniscient Gyalwa Longchen Rabjam Palzangpo by the vidyādhara Gyurme Dorje[35] and sheds light on the greatness of the author of this text.

The text is arranged in three parts: first, an introduction; second, a detailed explanation of the treatise itself; and third, the conclusion.

Introduction

The introduction is an explanation of three items: the title of the text, Longchenpa's homage, and his promise to compose.

The Title

In Sanskrit: *Dharmadhāturatnakośanāma*
In Tibetan: *Chos dbyings rin po che'i mdzod ces bya ba*

Rendered word for word, *dharmadhātu* (*chos dbyings*) means "the expanse of ultimate reality"; *ratna* (*rin po che*) means "precious"; *kośa* (*mdzod*) means "treasury"; *nāma* (*ces bya ba*) means "name" or "this is called."

Generally speaking, at the beginning of every translated text of Indian provenance, the Sanskrit title of the original is given, and this for three reasons. The first is to inspire the readers with confidence that the text in question is authentic, for the Indian sources of the Dharma are pure. The second reason is that in the common perception of beings to be guided, when the Buddha turned the wheel of the Dharma, he spoke in Sanskrit, the well-ordered language of India. This being so, if through the presence of the title, the readers acquire a proclivity for the Sanskrit tongue, their minds will be imbued with its empowering blessing. The third reason for supplying the Sanskrit title is to remind the reader of the kindness of the translators and paṇḍitas of old.

Now it should not be thought that since this is a Tibetan treatise, its Sanskrit title serves no purpose. For although this text was not composed in India, it surpasses other Tibetan treatises in its many qualities. It is indeed a marvelous scripture on a par with those of Indian provenance, with which, therefore, it may be justly compared. To be sure, the birdsfoot flower is not a bird's foot, but it is so called because it resembles one.

In general, most compositions are given names for three reasons, and the name of the present text fulfills them all. When beings of highest capacity see the title of this book, they will understand in a condensed manner the meaning of the text from beginning to end. They are like skilled physicians examining a pulse. Beings of moderate capacity will be able to tell from the title that in the general distinction between the great and small vehicles, this text belongs to the Mahāyāna. Then, in terms of the distinction between the sutra and mantra, they will discern that it belongs to the mantra vehicle, and further, in relation to the six classes of tantra, they will understand that it belongs to the inner tantras of Atiyoga. Such beings are like soldiers reviewing an inventory of their ammunition. Finally, for those of lowest capacity, it is thanks to the title that the text can be searched for and found, as one may locate a medicine thanks to the label on its jar.

Regarding the general manner in which texts are named, there are some whose titles are taken from their authors, as in the case of *The Buddhapālita*—that is, the commentary on Madhyamaka by the master of that name. Some texts take their names from their intended recipients, as in the case of *The Sūtra in Response to the Questions of a Tigress*, *The Sūtra in Response to the Questions of an Old Lady*, and *The Sūtra in Response to the Questions of Devaputra Suṣukla*. Some books are named according to their size, such as *The Prajñāpāramitā Sūtra in Eight Thousand Lines* or *The Prajñāpāramitā Sūtra in One Hundred Thousand Lines*. Some texts are labeled according to an associated place, such as *The Namtsing Vinaya*. The titles of many texts involve a combination of a metaphorical expression and an intended meaning, as in *The Beacon of Certainty*, while others simply express the subject matter of the texts concerned, as in *The Way of the Bodhisattva*.

In the present case, *The Precious Treasury of the Dharmadhātu* is a combination of metaphor and meaning. It should be understood that the dharmadhātu is the expanse of ultimate reality. It is self-arisen primordial wisdom, the intrinsically pure nature of the mind, the ultimate truth, awareness. Since it is through the recognition or nonrecognition of this dharmadhātu that all the phenomena of nirvana and samsara arise without exception, the dharmadhātu is itself likened to a precious treasury of wish-fulfilling jewels from which there comes all that may be desired. The title of this text is therefore constructed on the basis of a combination of a metaphorical element and an intended meaning.

The dharmadhātu, as we so name it, is also described as the original expanse, awareness, the *sugatagarbha*, or buddha-nature, the state of buddhahood that is naturally and spontaneously present. There is nothing prior to this—neither buddhas nor beings, neither nirvana nor samsara, neither freedom nor delusion, neither the world and its inhabitants nor the five elements, and so on.

The tantra *Awareness Self-Arisen* says,

> In some former age when I was not,
> There would have been no buddhas and no beings—
> How then a path, how then accomplishment?
> There is not a single thing that has not come from me—
> From me, who am great emptiness.
> From me are the five elements produced.

Moreover, the dharmadhātu, as we call it—that is, self-arisen primordial wisdom, the naturally pure sugatagarbha, spontaneously present buddhahood—is said to be the precursor and forebear of all the buddhas, for it precedes them. In *Awareness Self-Arisen* we find,

> I am the precursor of all buddhas.
> In some former age when I was not,
> Not even the name "buddha" could there be.

Therefore, if one realizes that to which the word *dharmadhātu* refers, one is free, one is a buddha. If, as a result of confusion, one fails to do so, one is a deluded being. Everything depends upon the realization or the lack of realization of the dharmadhātu. As *Awareness Self-Arisen* declares,

> I am the tomb of all the buddhas;
> In me they are all buried; I am their unchanging grave.
> I am the place where every being dwells.
> Their habitual tendencies appear as bodies.

And,

> Since I am no substantial thing,
> I am without defining features,
> I raise up beings from their grave.

These passages mean that just as a burial ground is a place where the bodies of human beings disintegrate after death, dissolving into their component atoms, in the same way, awareness, the dharmadhātu, is the final place of freedom in which the buddhas "subside." It is therefore referred to as a "grave." However, when the text says, "I raise up beings from their grave," the meaning is that when beings realize the fundamental nature of the dharmadhātu as it is, they are drawn forth from the great ocean of samsara, the place of suffering, the grave in which they are buried.

As for the expression "precious treasury," since all phenomena, of both samsara and nirvana, arise without exception from awareness, self-arisen primordial wisdom, the dharmadhātu, the latter may well be described as a treasury. There are of course numerous ways of commenting on this expression in greater detail. In the present case, however, I will explain it concisely in terms of the three vajra points of ground, path, and result.

The spontaneously accomplished qualities of enlightenment are all primordially present within the ground, the dharmadhātu, the fundamental luminous nature of the mind. Therefore the ground is indeed a precious treasury.

On the basis of the empowerment of the power of awareness, which brings beings to maturity on the path, and thanks to the liberating instructions of one's teacher, the fundamental nature of the excellent qualities [of enlightenment] is realized just as it is. For this reason, the luminosity of the path is also a precious treasury.

Similarly, as far as the result is concerned, stainless, self-cognizing awareness, the dharmakāya endowed with twofold purity, is also like an immaculate treasury. For it is the ground from which all the enlightened qualities of the dharmadhātu emerge. The sambhogakāya is also likened to a precious treasury because it has perfect mastery of enlightened qualities, which are present of themselves. Finally, the nirmāṇakāya with its enlightened activity is also like a precious treasury able to fulfill the hopes of beings to be guided. In all such ways, therefore, the dharmadhātu, as the result, is described as a precious treasury.

Longchenpa's Expression of Homage

The Brief Homage

Homage to glorious Samantabhadra!

The word "glorious" is used because the dharmakāya Samantabhadra, the primordial lord, actualized the state of the dharmakāya for his own benefit, and without stirring from this ultimate expanse, he appears in the rūpakāya for the benefit of others. Until the very emptying of samsara, he strives solely for the benefit of beings by means of noble, inconceivable activities that are constant, all-pervading, and spontaneous. He is described as glorious because he is endowed with the glory of the perfect qualities of elimination and realization.[36]

He is described as "Samantabhadra" because he is the primordial lord, the entirely good dharmakāya, appearing as the teacher of the whole of samsara and nirvana. Through his excellent and spontaneous activities, he is from the very beginning the sovereign, perfect teacher, the sublime guide who infallibly reveals the system of the grounds and paths of realization just as they are. This is why he is referred to as Samantabhadra, the "entirely good."

It is to him that Gyalwang Longchen Rabjam, the author of this text, pays homage with undivided faith. We should not think however that this homage is paid to Samantabhadra alone. For it is to be further understood that since all the buddhas of the three times attain enlightenment as Samantabhadra himself, homage is paid to them as well. And with the further understanding that all the phenomena of the ground, path, and result are the five aspects of Samantabhadra, they too are objects of homage. As to these five aspects of Samantabhadra, it is said in *The Mirror of Samantabhadra's Mind*,

> It should be understood that all phenomena have the nature of the five aspects of Samantabhadra. These are Samantabhadra as nature, Samantabhadra as ornament, Samantabhadra as teacher, Samantabhadra as awareness, and Samantabhadra as realization.

The meaning of this citation is as follows. First, Samantabhadra as nature or Samantabhadra as ground is the fundamental nature of phenomena, the state of suchness. Second, Samantabhadra as ornament refers to the fact that phenomenal appearance arises as the display of awareness. In other words, it is the adornment of awareness, the expanse of dharmatā, and never stirs from it. Third, Samantabhadra as teacher indicates that while the buddhas dwell in Akaniṣṭha[37] as the dharmakāya and sambhogakāya, they also manifest as nirmāṇakāya teachers who guide beings according to their need. Fourth, Samantabhadra as awareness refers to self-arisen primordial wisdom, the sugatagarbha. Fifth, Samantabhadra as realization or path refers to the attainment of the eye of liberation—in other words, the realization of awareness, the fundamental nature, which occurs thanks to the kindness of the teacher.

The Detailed Homage

Marvelous wonder,
Present of itself from the beginning,
Primordial wisdom,
Luminous and self-arisen,
The enlightened mind!
This is the treasure mine from which arises
All phenomenal existence,
Samsara and nirvana,
The world and its inhabitants.
I bow in homage to this unmoving freedom
From conceptual elaboration.

Awareness present as the ground, the dharmakāya, uncontrived, ultimate primordial wisdom, is the self-arisen primordial buddhahood of the ground. This primal buddhahood does not depend on newly arising causes and conditions. No one has created it; it is present of itself. It is suchness, the unmoving and unchanging dharmakāya. The perfect qualities of awareness, the dharmadhātu—in other words, all the attributes of the result, the four kāyas and five wisdoms and so on—are inseparably present from the very first in the vast reach of the marvelous wonder that is empty awareness. The dharmadhātu itself is uncontrived, self-arisen, primordial wisdom. Devoid of face or arms, devoid of characteristics, it is the mind's own luminous nature. It is therefore referred to as the ultimate enlightened mind.

When, through ignorance and delusion, this ultimate enlightened mind—the dharmadhātu, the fundamental nature, the primordial wisdom of great equality—is not realized as it is, it is apprehended as phenomenal existence, as the world and its inhabitants. The appearance of the three realms of samsara occurs. When, however, the actual fundamental nature is realized, the appearance of the kāyas and wisdoms of the peaceful state of nirvana occurs. Thus the appearance of samsara or nirvana depends on whether or not the ultimate enlightened mind, the dharmadhātu, is realized. This is why this same ultimate enlightened mind is said to be like a treasure mine.

Its fundamental nature is unwavering. For throughout the passage of the three times, it is free of movement and change. It is free of all the conceptual elaborations of existence, nonexistence, both, and neither, identity, difference, and so on. This spacelike enlightened mind—namely, uncontrived ultimate primordial wisdom (empty, luminous awareness, self-arisen and unceasing)—is the subject of this entire treatise and is moreover the object of homage. It is to the state of awareness that Longchenpa bows down in homage.

The Treasury of the Dharmadhātu is a general synopsis of the mind, space, and pith instruction classes of the Great Perfection. It has also been described as a treatise that subsumes all the key points of the tantras together with their commentaries and associated pith instructions. The view of the outer mind class is to regard all phenomena as resting in the enlightened mind—limpid, clear awareness. It is the view that the whole of samsara and nirvana is completely contained within the mind. According to the inner space class, it is decisively determined that the whole of phenomenal existence, everything in samsara and nirvana, is gathered within the vast space of the mind's nature. It rests in the vast expanse of the inseparability of mind and space. This is the view of the space class. According to the secret pith instruction class, when all phenomena are realized as being the sole creative power and display of awareness, and when the naked state of this same awareness (empty, luminous, and unceasing) is maintained, the face of awareness is seen. This vision is the view of the pith instruction class.

Longchenpa's Promise to Compose His Text

The supreme peak, the Sumeru of all the vehicles,
The radiant expanse of sun and moon,

Luminous and present of itself—
This is the vast expanse of vajra essence.
Beyond all effort and all practice,
It is the vast expanse,
The natural state beyond all fabrication.
Listen to me now, for I shall tell you
Of this wondrous and primordial immensity.

Regarding the expression "the supreme peak of all the vehicles," it may be said in general that until the end of all mental activity is reached, the number of vehicles is difficult to determine; it is inconceivable. As Ngari Paṇḍita has declared,

> As long as there's no ending to the operations of the mind,
> The vehicles are inconceivable beyond the reach of
> numbering.
> As staging posts upon the one and only path,
> They bring forth corresponding, ever higher, fruits.

Nevertheless, in reference to the system of nine vehicles, *The Great Array of Ati* says,

> There are three stages for beings of small capacity.
> The Dharma is attuned to their respective dispositions:
> For those defiled by thought, there is the way of śrāvakas;
> For those who have discernment, there's the way of the
> pratyekabuddhas;
> For those who emphasize reflection, there is the way of
> bodhisattvas.

As this text indicates, the Buddha set forth three expository causal vehicles for beings of lesser capacity and according to their varying dispositions. The śrāvakas attain the realization of a rough personal no-self, but they believe that the indivisible, infinitesimal particles of the objects of apprehension and the indivisible instants of consciousness are truly existent. For them, tainted as they are by discursive thought, the vehicle of the śrāvakas was set forth. For those who have discernment, who can meditate on the twelve links of dependent arising in both their forward and reverse directions, the path of the pratyekabuddhas was set forth. Finally, for those who emphasize reflection, meditating on the equality and exchange of self and other, on the cherishing of others more than oneself, and so on, the path of the bodhisattvas was set forth. These are referred to as the three small vehicles.

Then, with regard to the three intermediate vehicles, *The Great Array of Ati* declares,

> Of the teachings for the three that come between,
> Action is for those of least capacity,
> Conduct is for those of small capacity,
> And Yoga is for those who focus on the mind.

The Action tantras were taught for the sake of those who emphasize the practice of ablution and cleanliness, rather than meditation. Of the outer classes of the tantras of the Mantrayāna, these are of the least eminence. By contrast, the Conduct tantras were taught for those who, in their conduct of giving equal weight to the rituals of the Action tantras and the meditative practice of the Yoga tantras, regard the deities and themselves as relatives and friends, without any qualitative difference between them. Finally, the Yoga tantras were taught for those who emphasize inner yoga rather than outer action and conduct and who, thanks to an emphasis placed upon the mind, regard the deities and their own minds as equal and indivisible. These three vehicles are regarded as the three outer classes of tantra of the Mantrayāna.

The three vehicles of the inner classes of tantra are described as the three great vehicles. *The Great Array of Ati* declares,

> Regarding thus the three great stages,

> Generation is for those of boundless mind,
> Perfection is for those who have the essence of the mind,
> And Great Perfection is for those who have the supreme secret.

For those of boundless or inconceivable mind, who realize the infinite purity of phenomenal existence, as well as the inseparability of the deity and mind, the Mahāyoga, which focuses on the generation stage, was set forth. For those who consider meditation on the path of skillful means and the path of liberation to be "the essence of the mind," and who emphasize the union of primordial wisdom and the ultimate expanse, the vehicle of Anuyoga was perfectly expounded. Likewise, for those of the highest capacity, who are vessels for the supreme and greatly perfect secret, the short path of the luminous Great Perfection was set forth. Whichever of the nine vehicles one may enter, however, for the ultimate attainment of perfect buddhahood, there is no means of gaining freedom that does not entail the realization of the nature of the mind—in other words, self-arisen primordial wisdom.

Like the summit of Sumeru, the king of mountains, higher than all the mountains of the four continents, the vehicle of Atiyoga is the very pinnacle of the nine vehicles. Like the radiant expanse of the sun and moon, whose light scatters the darkness of the four continents, self-cognizing primordial wisdom instantaneously dispels the gloom of ignorance. And this expanse is vast indeed, for it embraces the whole of samsara and nirvana.

Similarly, the luminosity of the utterly pure nature of awareness (to which nothing can be added and from which there is nothing to be removed) is uncontrived, self-arisen, and spontaneous. And since this luminosity is unchanging, it is ultimate truth, the expanse of the vajra essence endowed with the seven attributes of vajra-like indestructibility. Beyond the reach of all effortful practice, and transcending the scope of intellectual exertion, it is the expanse of awareness, the natural state free of fabrication, the fundamental nature of the mind. Awareness, thoroughly encompassed by the state of great primordial purity and equality, is indeed the marvelous fundamental nature. In *Awareness Self-Arisen* we find,

> The very peak of all the views
> Has been explained as Ati, Great Perfection.
> Understand that it is like the sky—
> Immense expanse of unobstructed openness.
> And it is like the depth of a great ocean—
> Vast and deep and difficult to fathom.
> Know too that it is like the circle of the sun—
> A mass of brilliant rays of light.

For the sake of future generations of fortunate disciples, Longchenpa says that he will discourse upon this sovereign wonder, primordially immense, whose openness is like the sky, whose vastness and profundity is like an ocean, and whose light is like the sun and moon—in other words, awareness, the enlightened mind, the spacelike vajra essence of Ati. This constitutes his promise to compose his text and so saying, he calls upon worthy recipients to listen.

This completes an explanation of the introduction to the composition of the treatise.

A Detailed Explanation of the Treatise

Wherein Secret Sovereign Awareness Is Revealed in Thirteen Chapters

1. Samsara and Nirvana Do Not Stir from the Ultimate Expanse

The first chapter shows that samsara and nirvana do not stir from the ultimate expanse and that therefore all phenomena dwell without change or movement within the spacelike state of great perfection. This chapter is divided into fourteen sections, the first of which shows that although samsara and nirvana arise within the state of awareness, the great spontaneous presence of the three kāyas, they do not stir from this ultimate expanse.

1. The vast space of spontaneous presence
Is the ground whence all arises.
Empty in its nature,
Luminous in character, unceasing,
It does not exist as anything at all,
Though anything at all arises from it.
Samsara and nirvana both emerge unbidden
In the space of the three kāyas.
Yet from this ultimate expanse they do not stray,
The field of blissful ultimate reality.

The pure appearances of the Victorious Ones and the buddha fields, and the impure appearances of the three worlds and the six realms, all emerge within the vast expanse of the precious spontaneous presence that is awareness. This same awareness, this precious spontaneous presence, effortlessly subsists as the ground for the arising of all appearances both pure and impure. This great and unfailing treasury—also called the mandala of luminosity present within the ground—is present of itself as the very basis for the arising of all pure and impure appearances, and for this reason, it is referred to as the "precious spontaneous presence."

Now, this awareness, this spontaneous presence, is itself primordially pure, which means that it is empty by its very nature. It is thus the dharmakāya. Moreover, its emptiness is not a mere nothing, a mere void or absence implied by a nonaffirming negation. For its character is luminous, and this is the sambhogakāya. Finally, its cognizant power or potency is unceasing, and this is the nirmāṇakāya. These three kāyas are from the very beginning spontaneously and effortlessly present in awareness. As we find in *The All-Creating King*,

> In me, the all-creator, are the three kāyas all assembled.
> All phenomena, however they appear,
> Possess three aspects uncontrived:
> Ultimate nature, luminous character, cognizant power.
> These are the three kāyas, which as my nature are revealed.

And in *Awareness Self-Arisen*, it is said,

> The sun, awareness, rises in the state of emptiness.
> Within the mandala of this great treasure that will never set,
> There arise, all by themselves, the five unchanging kāyas.

Awareness is the very indivisibility of the three kāyas. Within the state of emptiness, awareness, which is empty, luminous, and unceasing, appears like the rising sun. It is the actual ground for the emergence of the entire phenomenal array of the kāyas and wisdoms, and throughout the three times it remains without any diminution. For this reason, awareness is described as the mandala of the great treasure.

This being so, whereas awareness does not in itself *exist* as anything—for like space it is empty—nevertheless, it may *arise* as anything, for it is an unimpeded openness in which anything can manifest. It is like a stainless mirror that is limpidly clear. Therefore, the whole array of phenomena of both nirvana and samsara (the pure self-experience of buddhas and the impure subjective experience of beings), spontaneously arises without ever stirring from the state of awareness, the expanse of the three kāyas. As it is said in *Awareness Self-Arisen*,

> Though not appearing on the pure ground,
> Five aggregates and various phenomenal appearances
> Are revealed.

As this text says, all the displays that are perceived as the aggregates, elements, and sense fields—in other words, the hallucinatory appearances of the five samsaric aggregates and so on—which do not manifest upon the perfectly pure ground, arise as the play of the ultimate expanse, the dharmatā. In the same way that all kinds of dream visions, good and bad, never stray from the state of sleep, all the pure and impure appearances that manifest within awareness, the dharmadhātu, do not stray from the ultimate expanse. They naturally arise and naturally subside within it. When this is understood, all things are seen to be the blissful field of ultimate reality.

* * *

The second section shows that for this reason, phenomenal existence, samsara and nirvana, is the display of the ultimate expanse.

> **2. The vast expanse, the nature of the mind,**
> **Is changeless like the sphere of space.**
> **Indeterminate is its display:**
> **The vast expanse of manifest appearance of**
> **cognizant power.**
> **All things are inexistent**
> **Except as ornaments upon the ultimate expanse.**

The outer and the inner and the to and fro of consciousness
Are the creative power of the enlightened mind.
Not anything, yet giving rise to everything,
It is a marvelous prodigy, endowed with wonderful display.

The fundamental nature of the mind, suchness, is a vast expanse, for it pervades the whole of samsara and nirvana. It is unchanging, for throughout the sequence of the three times, it neither moves nor alters. When it is assessed in terms of metaphor, referent, and evidential sign, it is likened to the sphere of space. As it is said in *The All-Creating King*,

All phenomena are the enlightened mind.
All things may be compared with space.
This too exemplifies the enlightened mind.
For in itself the latter has a skylike nature.

And,

Thus, phenomenal existence,
The world and all the beings it contains,
Does not dwell—has no dwelling place—
In somewhere other than the sphere of space.
Buddhas, beings, worlds and their inhabitants—
Everything subsists within the vast immensity
Of the enlightened mind.

As these texts declare, the appearances of the world and its inhabitants arise within the abyss of space, while the appearances of samsara and nirvana appear within the expanse of the enlightened mind. In reality, however, space and the appearances of the world and beings both transcend the concepts of identity, difference, existence, nonexistence and so on. In like manner, although the appearances of samsara and nirvana arise within the expanse of the enlightened mind, the truth is that neither the enlightened mind nor the phenomena of samsara and nirvana are beyond the state of groundlessness and rootlessness—primordial emptiness, the state of equality beyond all conceptual elaboration.

And just as the appearances of the world and beings manifest within the bosom of space, so too the appearances of nirvana and samsara, good or bad, pure or impure, arise as a creative power and indeterminate display, within the expanse of the mind's nature. They appear as the manifestation of the cognizant power of self-cognizing primordial wisdom and have therefore never stirred from the ultimate enlightened mind, awareness, the primordial expanse of great emptiness.

All things that arise as an unceasing manifestation within the unborn expanse are but the ornaments of that ultimate expanse in the same way that rainbow-colored clouds are ornaments of the sky and the reflections of the stars and planets are ornaments upon the surface of the sea. Other than that, they are devoid of the slightest existence down to the merest atom. As it is said,

> Awareness is traced back to skylike spaciousness.
> Therein the spectacle unfolds: samsara and nirvana.
> A perfect skill is gained where all is seen as its adornment.

As these words indicate, no matter what objects of the six consciousnesses appear, they manifest within the expanse of awareness. It is important to understand that they are simply the ornaments of this same awareness and do not exist in any other way. The outer world and its inner beings are simply the creative power of the ultimate enlightened mind. Moreover, all the subjects, the consciousnesses that arise and cease, that emerge and are drawn back, in the detection of their appearing objects (the world and its inhabitants) are also the creative power and display of the ultimate enlightened mind.

This enlightened mind is nothing at all in itself. It is not existent, nonexistent, both or neither. It does not exclude and it does not include; it is neither the same nor different. It is the state of equality—empty, and beyond the reach of conceptual elaboration. And yet without losing its empty nature, it is present of itself as that which gives rise to anything at all. This is what makes the enlightened mind such a wondrous thing. For though it appears, it has never existed. It is empty, and yet, though empty, it arises as a manifest display. The primordial wisdom of great equality—the union of appearance and emptiness, as well as the inseparability of awareness and emptiness—is indeed an astonishing and marvelous prodigy.

* * *

The third section shows in detail how the display manifests within the expanse of the enlightened mind.

> **3. The outer and the inner,**
> **The world together with its beings,**
> **All the things that manifest as forms**
> **Are but adornments of the ultimate expanse,**
> **Arising as the wheel of the enlightened body.**
> **All reverberation, sounds and language,**
> **As many as there are without exception,**
> **Are but the adornments of the ultimate expanse,**
> **Arising as the wheel of the enlightened speech.**
> **Memories, awareness, mental movement,**
> **Proliferation, no-thought—**
> **All mental states in number past imagining—**
> **Are but the adornments of the ultimate expanse,**
> **Arising as the wheel of the enlightened mind.**

The whole of phenomenal existence, the universe and the beings that inhabit it, samsara and nirvana, manifest within awareness, appearing in the manner of dreams, magical illusions and reflections of the moon in water. Aside from this, they have not the slightest existence, down to the merest atom. Thus the outer universe and the wandering beings that are its inner contents, all the things that manifest as forms within the experience of the six classes of beings, are but the adornments of awareness, the expanse of ultimate reality. They arise as the wheel of inexhaustible ornaments of the enlightened body, the mandala of the kāya of primordial wisdom. It is said in *The Prayer in Seven Chapters*,[38]

> The outer world, the beings living there—
> All that you perceive as objects of your sight—
> Leave them as they are,
> Not grasping at their real existence.
> Pure of dualistic clinging,
> They are the clear yet empty body of the deity.

The same is true for what one hears. All sounds and languages, loud or soft, however many they may be—resounding within the state of awareness and experienced by the beings of the different realms of the world—are all the adornments of awareness, the dharmadhātu. They arise as the wheel of inexhaustible ornaments of enlightened speech, which is primordial wisdom. As Guru Padmasambhava says,

> All sounds you hear, sweet or harsh,
> Resounding as the objects of your ears,
> Are empty sound.
> Just leave them as they are without a moment's thought.
> Empty yet resounding, with no origin or ending,
> Such is the speech of the Victorious Ones.

Likewise, all the unimaginably numerous, indeed limitless, states of mind that are the mental objects of beings of the six classes: memories of things and attitudes, as well as awareness, the ultimate nature of phenomena, movements of thought, the sudden occurrence of mental proliferation, as well as the absence of both the emergence and dissolution of thought, and so on—all are the adornments of awareness, the dharmadhātu. They arise as the wheel of inexhaustible ornaments of the enlightened mind, self-arisen primordial wisdom. As it is said in *The Seven Chapters*,

> Whatever thoughts arise defiled by the five poisons,
> Moving as the objects of your mind,
> Don't welcome them, don't follow them, don't alter them.
> Leave the mental movement where it is.
> It will subside into the dharmakāya.

So it is that all appearances, the objects of the six sense faculties, together with the defiled mental states that cling to them as being truly existent, have never stirred from the one mandala of self-arisen primordial wisdom.

* * *

The fourth section shows in conclusion that everything is a single display and explains how this is to be understood.

> **4. Beings in the six migrations**
> **And four ways of being born**
> **Stray not a single atom from the sphere of ultimate reality.**
> **Phenomenal existence—**
> **Six objects, apprehended-apprehender—**
> **All indeed appears.**
> **It is a magical illusion in the dharmadhātu,**
> **Perceived but not existing.**
> **Unsupported, substanceless,**
> **A vast expanse primordially empty,**
> **It is luminosity itself,**
> **Adornment of the dharmadhātu.**

The appearance of the six classes of beings of the three worlds, and their four ways of being born—womb birth, miraculous birth, birth from heat and moisture, and egg birth—do not, in the slightest way, stray from awareness, the expanse of ultimate reality, the dharmadhātu. They simply appear in the manner of a display that, nonexistent, is yet clearly perceived. It is just as when a magician casts a spell on a pebble or a wooden stick with the result that the bystanders experience and enjoy them as the actual appearing objects of the six consciousnesses—horses, elephants, and all manner of riches. But the truth is that in the very moment that the onlookers perceive them, all these objects are completely unreal—just empty forms appearing to them.

In the same way, phenomenal existence, the world and its inhabitants—the six sense objects of apprehension and the six sense consciousnesses that apprehend them—all appear. And yet, without exception, they are nonexistent appearances occurring within awareness, the dharmadhātu itself. They are like magical illusions subjectively perceived. In the same way, arising, abiding, and ceasing, in the very moment of their being perceived, have never at any time existed. They are like the visions of a dream or castles in the clouds. As it is said in *The Root Stanzas of the Middle Way*,

> Like a dream and like a mirage,
> Like a city of gandharvas,
> So arising and abiding
> And cessation have been taught.[39]

Similarly, awareness, the enlightened mind, manifests as forms, as [sounds,] as smells, as tastes, as textures. Apart from awareness, the objects of the senses—forms, sounds, smells, tastes, and textures—have not the slightest atom of existence. As we find in *The Unwritten Tantra*,

> Unceasing sights are manifestations of my body.
> Unceasing sounds are the resonance of my speech.
> Unceasing odor is the perfume of my scent.
> Unceasing savor is the flavor of my taste.
> Unceasing feeling is but the sensation of my mind.

If the meaning of this is realized, then no matter how the things of samsara and nirvana appear within the expanse of awareness, they are nothing more than a display, clearly appearing and yet nonexistent. From the first moment that they are perceived, they have no existence and are without support, without substance. They are groundless. They are the all-embracing dimension of awareness alone. They are the expression of awareness alone. They are the buoyant impetus of awareness alone. They are the workings of awareness alone. When one is clearly convinced of this, then whatever arises becomes insubstantial, weightless, and diaphanous. One realizes that it does not extend beyond the vast, all-encompassing, primordially empty sphere of dharmatā. It is then that it is understood that all appearances arise as the creative power and display of the luminosity of awareness. All things manifest like rainbows in the sky, like stars and planets reflected on the surface of the sea, and like images in a looking glass. They are the adornments of awareness, the dharmadhātu.

* * *

The fifth section shows that, since all phenomena are subsumed within self-arisen primordial wisdom, everything imputed as appearing extramentally is simply the self-experience of awareness. From the very moment that they arise, phenomena are wholly encompassed by the state of great equality free of all activity.

5. However things appear, however they resound
Within the vast and ultimate expanse,
They do not waver from spontaneous equality,
The dharmakāya, the enlightened mind—
The primordial natural state that, in and of itself,
Is empty and devoid of movement and of change.
No matter what appears, it is the dharmatā,
Primordial wisdom, self-arisen.
Free of effort, free of striving,
It is gathered in the one expanse of bliss.

All the objects of the six sense consciousnesses that we perceive—sights that appear, sounds that resound, odors detected, flavors tasted, and so on—have never stirred from the expanse of ultimate reality, the great state of equality beyond all conceptual elaboration. In the same way and in this very moment, they never stray from awareness, the spacious state of spontaneous equality. They remain constantly within it, and this is the fundamental way of being of the dharmakāya, the ultimate enlightened mind. This awareness, this primordial, uncontrived, natural state, is not established in any way in terms of identity or difference, existence or nonexistence, exclusion or inclusion. It is primordial emptiness, which, throughout the passage of time, is beyond all movement and change. But even though the expanse of primordial wisdom, the state of equality free from conceptual elaboration, has no existence whatsoever, it is from the very beginning spontaneously present as that which can arise as anything at all. Whatever phenomena may appear, whether of samsara or nirvana, if one realizes that they never stir from the dharmatā, self-arisen primordial wisdom—in other words, if the fundamental nature of these phenomena is realized just as it is—one will be free of the hopes and fears involved in the fabrication, in the effort and exertion of trying to achieve such a state as something new. For whatever appears is gathered, wholly immersed, in self-cognizing awareness, the state of great equality or all-pervasiveness, the one expanse of nondual bliss and emptiness. This is a crucial point of the greatest importance.

* * *

The sixth section shows that whereas the ultimate nature of self-arisen primordial wisdom, awareness beyond the reach of effortful action, is the dharmakāya beyond acceptance or rejection, the luminous character of awareness is the uncontrived sambhogakāya.

> **6. Unwavering luminosity is the sambhogakāya.**
> **Everything appearing, in the moment of appearing,**
> **Is present of itself as luminous character.**

Uncontrived, unchanging,
It is all-pervading and spontaneous equality.

The empty nature of awareness is the dharmakāya, the body of ultimate reality. Being empty, it nevertheless has the character of luminosity—a luminous aspect that does not fluctuate, in the sense of being sometimes present, sometimes absent. This luminous character is unwavering and unchanging throughout the passage of time. It is the sambhogakāya, the body of perfect enjoyment. The kāyas and wisdoms that appear within luminous awareness (the awareness in the present moment[40] introduced through the teacher's pith instructions) are uncontrived and spontaneously present as the luminous character of that same awareness. This is the sambhogakāya.

In the sutra vehicle of the Prajñāpāramitā, it is said that the buddhas are endowed with twenty-one kinds of immaculate knowledge—namely, the ten strengths, the four fearlessnesses, the eighteen distinct qualities, and so on.[41] According to the Great Perfection, on the other hand, even beginners in the practice may, right now in this present moment, behold directly and clearly the naked face of the nature of their minds—the mind of all the buddhas of the three times. It therefore follows that the ten strengths, the four fearlessnesses, and so on are simply the qualities, [the appearance of which] depends on the perfection or otherwise of one's skill in recognizing this nature. At the present time, the mind has not been freed from adventitious obscuration, with the result that these qualities are not manifest. Consequently, until this skill is perfected, the spontaneously present qualities of the ten strengths, four fearlessnesses, and so on cannot appear.

Therefore, the luminous character of awareness in the present moment has been described as "perfect enjoyment." This body of perfect enjoyment is not brought about by action. On the contrary, it is self-arisen primordial wisdom, awareness itself, uncontrived and unchanging. Its luminous character is unfabricated and self-arisen, the spacious state of all-pervasive, spontaneous equality. It is by nature changeless, empty luminosity.

* * *

The seventh section shows that the unceasing manifestation of awareness arises from the very first as the nirmāṇakāya.

> **7. Arising as a manifest display,**
> **Appearing in distinct diversity,**
> **The nirmāṇakāya is a self-arisen emanation,**
> **Marvelous and illusory,**
> **Beyond the scope of action,**
> **Never stirring from Samantabhadra.**

The empty nature of awareness is the dharmakāya, its luminous character is the sambhogakāya, and the endless arising of appearances of both samsara and nirvana within the state of awareness is the nirmāṇakāya. All the various appearances, pure and impure, which arise distinctly and unceasingly within awareness like rainbows in the sky and never stir from it, are the outward manifestation of the display of the creative power of awareness. Just as any kind of reflection can unimpededly arise upon the polished surface of a mirror without in any way staining it, in just the same way, any appearance, pure or impure, may arise as the creative power and display of awareness, without leaving the slightest stain on the face of awareness itself. It is in such a way that the nirmāṇakāya manifests, the self-arisen, wondrous, and illusory emanation. It is said in *The All-Creating King*,

> All phenomena, however they appear,
> Possess three aspects uncontrived:
> Ultimate nature, luminous character, cognizant power.
> These are the three kāyas, which as my nature are
> revealed.

Not only does this mean in general terms that the ground awareness is the perfect union of the three kāyas, it means also that when appearances arise within the ground, all phenomena (the manifestations of awareness) are themselves the union of the three kāyas. In brief, the oceanlike infinity of phenomenal appearance, arising as the display of the creative power of awareness, is in truth beyond the scope of all action and effort. For throughout the three times, it has never stirred, and will never stir, from the expanse of Samantabhadra, who, free of action, is the dharmadhātu, the space of primordial wisdom of great equality beyond the reach of all mental elaboration.

When it is explained that the kāyas and wisdoms of the ultimate expanse are [in this very moment] complete and spontaneously present, certain foolish people who have neither studied this matter nor reflected upon it strongly disparage this view. They say that although it would indeed be a fine thing if the kāyas and wisdoms of buddhahood were actually present now in sentient beings, this is impossible. One should not debate with such individuals, for they are like people who think that there is no sun when in fact it is merely hidden by dark clouds. It is as Dharmakīrti said, "Since there is no end to such mistaken paths, I will not speak about them here." On the other hand, there is no cause for perplexity. For if beings did not already possess these qualities, which are said to be naturally present within the buddha element, it would be impossible for them to arise anew from somewhere else when buddhahood is attained. In *The Commentary on Bodhicitta*, these qualities are said to be unconditioned and spontaneously present. And *The Two-Chapter Hevajra Tantra* also says,

> Sentient beings are truly buddhas
> But veiled by adventitious obscurations.
> When these are removed,
> Their buddhahood is manifest.

We do not claim that the qualities of the utterly pure nature, veiled as they are by adventitious obscurations, are manifest now. And for this reason, and for as long as beings are not freed from such obscurations, they are not called buddhas. We should aspire with determination and one-pointed intelligence to render the qualities of the utterly pure nature manifest.

* * *

The eighth section shows that the kāyas and wisdoms are inseparable from awareness, the enlightened mind.

> **8. In the enlightened mind, free of pits and chasms,**
> **The three kāyas are complete all by themselves,**
> **Without the need for striving.**
> **Not stirring from the ultimate expanse,**
> **The kāyas, wisdoms, and enlightened action,**
> **Spontaneous and unconditioned,**
> **Are naturally complete therein.**
> **They are the great accumulation,**
> **Complete from the beginning**
> **In the vast expanse primordially arisen.**

Thanks to the profound instructions of one's sublime teacher and through the transference of his blessings, one may rest in meditation in the ultimate enlightened mind, awareness, which from the very beginning dwells inseparably within one's mind. In this state, there are no frightening places, no fearful pits or chasms into which one might fall—as when one fares upon a dangerous path where one may make mistaken turns, deviate, and lose one's way—plunging into samsara and the lower realms. One simply keeps to the very nature of awareness and remains in that self-arisen state, where there is no need for striving, no need for exertion—as there is when one relies on paths that are contrived and effortful. It is then that primordial wisdom, awareness, in which the indivisible trikāya is spontaneously complete, will be actualized. All the kāyas and wisdoms are present without movement or change in awareness itself in the same way that light is present in the sun.

And yet, without stirring from the expanse of ultimate reality, they naturally arise—in a manner uncontrived, spontaneous, and unconditioned—as the body, speech, and mind of all the living creatures of the world. The latter are the creative power and display of awareness (the enlightened body, speech, and mind) manifesting outwardly. It is said in *The Lion's Perfect Power*,

> Within the endless world three thousandfold,
> However many mandalas there are of the enlightened body,
> All without exception are but manifest appearances.
> Within the endless world three thousandfold,
> However many mandalas there are of the enlightened speech,
> All without exception are but myriad sounds.
> Within the endless world three thousandfold,
> However many mandalas there are of the enlightened mind,
> All without exception are revealed as ordinary knowledge.
> From enlightened body, speech, and vajra mind unmanifest,
> All things are made manifest.
> The buddha bodies and the light of primal wisdom
> Are the appearing self-experience of awareness—
> Samantabhadra, awareness self-cognizing.

The primordially present enlightened body, speech, mind, qualities, and activities are naturally complete in self-arisen awareness. Apart from being the actualization of this awareness, they do not arise through effortful action in the way that the two accumulations are being gathered at the present moment. Indeed, it should be understood that in the nature of primordially self-arisen awareness, the great twofold accumulation [of merit and wisdom] is complete from the beginning. It is the fundamental nature that never deviates from the primordially arisen vast expanse.

* * *

The ninth section shows that because the kāyas and wisdoms are complete within the state of awareness, it follows that the buddha fields of infinite Victorious Ones, who have realized this awareness, as well as their spheres of knowledge, are also the display of awareness.

> **9. From the outset present of itself—**
> **Such is the buddha field free of change and movement.**
> **The vision of the dharmatā within the dharmadhātu[42]**
> **Is a knowledge unimpeded that adorns the ultimate expanse.**
> **Not created, not achieved, but present from the first,**
> **It is like the sun arising in the sky,**
> **A wonderful and marvelous prodigy.**

When enlightenment endowed with twofold purity is gained—that is, when, in addition to the buddhahood of the pure nature present primordially within oneself, the buddhahood that is the freedom of adventitious stains is also achieved—the dharmadhātu, primordially uncontrived and present of itself (unborn empty awareness beyond all movement and change) constitutes the ultimate buddha field of the fundamental nature. At that time, all the wisdoms and appearances of the dharmakaya, sambhogakāya, and nirmāṇakāya manifest as awareness, the state of buddhahood, the dharmadhātu, great emptiness, the expanse of the primordial wisdom of equality. They are none other than the self-experience of awareness.

The unimpeded vision of dharmatā within the dharmadhātu is an unobstructed knowledge that embraces, among other things, the instantaneous perception of all the hallucinatory experiences of happiness and suffering of the beings that pervade the whole of space. While never stirring from the dharmadhātu, all these experiences emerge as the adornments of the self-occurring, self-arisen ultimate expanse.

The appearances of the kāyas and wisdoms are not created or accomplished anew through the accumulations of merit and wisdom. The two accumulations are primordially perfect and complete as the appearing yet empty qualities of enlightenment and are thus described as spontaneous. The two accumulations are present from the very first within awareness, the ultimate enlightened mind. Consequently, the adventitiously gathered accumulations are but a conditioning factor whereby impurities are eliminated—on account of which, they are referred to as the two causal accumulations. It is just as when we say that to clean a dirty gemstone with a cloth and a cleansing agent is the cause whereby the gem itself is rendered visible.

Since the four kāyas and the five wisdoms and so on are included within awareness, awareness itself is the ground of their manifestation. When the sun rises in the sky, its light engulfs the four cosmic continents while yet remaining in the sun itself. The sun is the ground for the arising of all the light that pours forth from it. The same is true, analogously, for awareness and all the phenomena of the kāyas and wisdoms, which arise as its adornments and which are self-occurring, self-arising, and self-subsiding—the illusory display of dependent arising. *Emaho!* It is indeed a wondrous and a marvelous prodigy!

* * *

The tenth section shows that because all phenomena, in their natural appearing and arising, are contained within awareness, the enlightened mind, it follows that no matter how they appear, they are but a magical spectacle devoid of true existence.

> **10. Within the womb of ultimate expanse,**
> **Present of itself from the beginning,**
> **Samsara is Samantabhadra,**
> **Nirvana is Samantabhadra.**
> **And therefore from the very first,**

> **Within Samantabhadra's vast expanse,**
> **There has never been samsara and nirvana.**
> **Appearance is Samantabhadra,**
> **Emptiness is Samantabhadra.**
> **Therefore from the very first,**
> **Within Samantabhadra's vast expanse,**
> **There has never been appearance and emptiness.**
> **Birth and death are both Samantabhadra,**
> **Joy and pain are both Samantabhadra.**
> **Therefore from the very first,**
> **Within Samantabhadra's vast expanse,**
> **Birth and death and joy and pain have never been.**
> **Self and other are Samantabhadra,**
> **Permanence, annihilation are Samantabhadra.**
> **Therefore from the very first,**
> **Within Samantabhadra's vast expanse,**
> **No self and other, no permanence and no annihilation**
> **Have there ever been.**

All phenomena of both samsara and nirvana are like space. Therefore, from the very first they have never existed as anything at all. There is just the one sole sphere of awareness. Nevertheless, they appear unceasingly as awareness's creative power or display. Longchenpa says that in this vast womb of the ultimate expanse—the dharmatā present of itself and free of all conceptual elaboration—the phenomena of samsara are Samantabhadra, self-arisen awareness. Likewise, all the phenomena of nirvana, the appearances of the dharmakāya and the buddha fields, are Samantabhadra, self-arisen awareness. Generally speaking, Samantabhadra is to be understood as appearance, while [his consort] Samantabhadrī represents emptiness. Longsel Nyingpo has said,

> Appearance is the dharmakāya, Samantabhadra;
> Samantabhadrī, the mother, embodies emptiness.

And,

> Appearance is the father, emptiness the mother.

And Karma Lingpa has declared,

> The clear and unimpeded mind within this present moment
> Is the primal lord Samantabhadra.

So it is that phenomena in their appearing are Samantabhadra, while phenomena in their emptiness are Samantabhadrī. And the indivisible union of appearance and emptiness is depicted as the inseparable coition of Samantabhadra with his consort. Therefore, if samsara is Samantabhadra, its nonexistence is Samantabhadrī. If nirvana is Samantabhadra, its nonexistence is Samantabhadrī. And in the nondual union of Samantabhadra-Samantabhadrī, father-mother, even the terms *samsara* and *nirvana* have never, from the very beginning, existed. They are groundless and rootless. In no way do they exceed the unimpeded and open display that is devoid of objective reference.

Likewise, if appearances are Samantabhadra, their emptiness, their lack of existence, must be Samantabhadrī. Since awareness, the enlightened mind—like the very nature of space—has no existence as anything at all, then however samsara and nirvana, appearance and emptiness, may be perceived, they have no existence. They are but the state or creative power or display of awareness. They appear unceasingly, manifesting in and of themselves like magical illusions, dreams, or the reflection of the moon in water. They are without intrinsic being. From the very moment that they appear, samsara and nirvana are without existence. They have never stirred from the groundless state of Samantabhadra father-mother. As it is said in *The Mirror of Samantabhadra's Mind*,

> Not one thing is there that does not come from me;
> I am the source, Samantabhadra.

There is not one thing not taught by me;
I am the teacher, Samantabhadra.

The meaning of this text is that there is not a single phenomenon that does not arise from awareness, self-arisen primordial wisdom—that is, from Samantabhadra and his consort in union. Since he is the ground from which everything arises, he is called Samantabhadra the source. And since there is nothing that he does not reveal—for he teaches the nine gradual vehicles as well as all the instructions of the ground, path, and result and is himself the teacher of all the buddhas—he is called Samantabhadra the teacher.

So it is that, within the self-arisen awareness that is the expanse of Samantabhadra, so-called appearance and so-called emptiness have never in fact existed. They partake of the nondual primordial wisdom of equality. And since awareness, the ultimate enlightened mind, is like space and is not in any sense an existent thing, all the experiences of birth, old age, sickness, and death, and so on are Samantabhadra—while the emptiness of birth, death, and so on is Samantabhadrī. The experience of happiness and suffering is Samantabhadra, while the emptiness of happiness and suffering is Samantabhadrī. Therefore, within the expanse of Samantabhadra, self-arisen awareness, all the appearances of birth, death, happiness, and suffering have never existed. They are the nondual primordial wisdom of equality.

Similarly, within the nature of awareness, self-arisen primordial wisdom, all the extremes of existence and nonexistence, permanence and annihilation, identity and difference have no existence whatsoever. For this reason, the appearances of self and other are likewise empty and without intrinsic being. All appearances, which unceasingly manifest in and of themselves as the display of the creative power of awareness, are like castles in the clouds, tricks of sight, and emanated apparitions—they are destitute of intrinsic existence.

The appearance of self and other is Samantabhadra. Their emptiness (the nonduality of self and other) is Samantabhadrī. Therefore, in the expanse of Samantabhadra, the ultimate enlightened mind, there has never been any such thing as self and other, permanence and annihilation. They are the primordial wisdom of equality free of all such conceptual elaborations.

Generally speaking, all things in phenomenal existence, samsara and nirvana, are Samantabhadra father-mother. In other words, there is nothing at all that does not arise from the expanse of awareness, itself the indivisibility of appearance and emptiness. As it is said in *The Mirror of Samantabhadra's Mind*,

> Samantabhadra father-mother
> Is a single state of indivisibility.
> All beings are pervaded
> By the indivisibility of the father-mother.
> There is no apprehension, no progression
> In Samantabhadra, the enlightened mind.
> Samantabhadra's face beholds all ten directions.

The meaning of this is that Samantabhadra is the appearance aspect and Samantabhadrī is the emptiness aspect. This is the reason why the primordial wisdom of the indivisibility of appearance and emptiness is depicted as the state of union, the inseparability of father-mother Samantabhadra. And since there is nothing at all that is not pervaded by the primordial wisdom of appearance and emptiness inseparably united, the indivisibility of father-mother Samantabhadra pervades all beings. This Samantabhadra—the enlightened mind—which pervades the whole of samsara and nirvana, is beyond all conceptual elaboration, beyond any kind of mental apprehension, beyond any kind of progress on the path, beyond any attainment of the result.

This then is Samantabhadra, the all-good, enlightened mind—Samantabhadra, the self-arisen primordial wisdom whereby all phenomena are pervaded. And since all the cardinal and intermediate directions, zenith, nadir, center, and periphery are included within the one expanse of Samantabhadra's wisdom, it is said that his face sees all the ten directions.

* * *

The eleventh section shows that within the state of Samantabhadra, dreamlike hallucinatory appearances arise for all beings as the self-experience or projection of their own minds.

> **11. To grasp existence in the nonexistent—**
> **This is called delusion.**
> **Samsara and nirvana**
> **In their nature are like baseless dreams.**
> **How strange to cling to them as real existent things!**

The ultimate enlightened mind, awareness, precious spontaneous presence, is like clear and empty space. It has no existence whatsoever. Its nonexistence is coterminous with its nature of emptiness. But when the nature of awareness is not recognized, coemergent ignorance casts a veil of blank oblivion over the mind, while conceptual ignorance, taking nonexistent things to be existent, attaches names to them and clings to them as distinct. Through the simultaneous occurrence of these two kinds of ignorance, beings are dominated by the hallucination of apprehended things and apprehending mind. And grasping at all kinds of hallucinatory phenomena of samsara as real, they stray into the cage of delusion. Indeed, to take as real the endless appearances of the universe and its inhabitants, and the experiences of happiness and suffering, which form like waves upon a great ocean, is called wandering in delusion. These hallucinatory appearances are not true even though they are apprehended as being so. Though they do not exist, they are perceived as existent. Through the meeting of the consciousness of the universal ground with the two kinds of clinging to self—just as during baseless dreams, when an outer world and its inhabitants arise and are taken to be true—there is a powerful belief in the reality of the world and beings, the hallucinatory appearances of phenomenal existence. But even though they clearly appear, they are completely unreal. They do not exist in the slightest way as objects of the senses. The experiences of happiness and sorrow are just like the fear and panic that arise when a rope is taken for a snake. They have the nature of hallucinatory experiences. They are taken to exist even though, in reality, they have no existence. They are taken to be happiness and sorrow, even though they are not, and this is delusion. As it is said in *The Necklace of Pearls*,

> And so it is that manifold appearances
> Are like the snake seen in a rope.
> They are not what they seem though they are taken to be so—
> The outer world and inner beings thus are formed.

And as we find in *The Secret Essence Tantra*,

> *Emaho!* From the sugatagarbha,
> Everything arises through our thought's activity.

As these texts declare, when awareness, the sugatagarbha, itself appears as earth, water, fire, and wind, it is perceived as an external world together with the living beings that live in it. But this is a hallucination. The appearances of last night's dreams, which (at the time) we took to be true, and the appearances of phenomenal existence, the world and its inhabitants, samsara and nirvana—which today we assume to be so solid and real—are just as false as each other. There is no difference between them. How strange it is, therefore, that even though they have never existed in themselves, the hallucinations of happiness and sorrow are uninterruptedly experienced as if they really existed.

* * *

The twelfth section shows that from the very moment that hallucinatory appearances are perceived as samsara, the hallucination or delusion has never truly existed. It is like a dream.

> **12. All things are Samantabhadra,**
> **Great, spontaneous presence.**

There is no samsara
That is now, or has been, or will be, hallucinatory.
It is just a name; it is beyond
The extremes of both being and nonbeing.
No one anywhere has been deluded in the past,
No one is deluded now nor will be in the future.
Such is the primordial purity
Of the three worlds of existence.

The three worlds of the outer universe and the beings contained in it, all things in samsara and nirvana, have never stirred from awareness, Samantabhadra, uncontrived, self-arisen, spontaneous presence. No matter what hallucinatory appearances of samsara may appear and in whatever form they may arise, they have never—from the very moment of their arising—existed. They are nonexistent even though they clearly appear. But nonexistent things are not hallucinations. They cannot be delusive. Since samsara did not appear delusively in the past, it cannot appear delusively now, and it cannot do so in the future. So it is that the appearances of samsara are not in fact hallucinations! For example, a barren woman's son is completely empty of being born. [There is no such thing as a barren woman's son.] Thus the barren woman's son was never born to begin with, and therefore it is impossible for him to be a young man living now. And it is completely impossible for him to grow old and finally die.

In this way, the phenomena of the universe and its inhabitants cannot exist even in the sense of "mere perceived appearances" [as things that merely appear and are perceived]. Since this is impossible, it follows that not only do they not exist on the ultimate level but even conventionally they are beyond the extremes of existence and nonexistence—even down to their mere names. To illustrate this, we should consider that when a rope is mistaken for a snake and fear arises, and when it is demonstrated that there is no snake but only a rope, some people might think that when the perception of the snake is dissipated, the rope persists as a real thing. And yet, when the rope itself is examined and analyzed, each of its strands—right down to the infinitesimal partless particle—is found to be empty of existence.

Therefore, when, on the basis of hallucinatory appearances, deluded perceptions occur, it is thanks to the essential instructions of one's venerable teacher that one comes to the understanding that these deluded perceptions are empty. When this happens, the deluded perceptions are dissipated just like the perception of the snake. When that which is to be dissipated (namely, the deluded perception) and that which dissipates it (namely, the realization that the perception is unreal) are examined, both are found to be without any existence whatever. It is the same as when the rope that had acted as the basis for the perception of a snake is itself found to be without existence.

So it is that nowhere in the three worlds of samsara, from beginningless time until the present, is there anyone—anyone at all—who has ever been deluded in the past, is deluded now, or will ever be deluded in the future. A decisive certainty is consequently reached that the ultimate fundamental nature of all phenomena is a supreme state transcending all ontological extremes—a state where not even the names of phenomena exist. And this is referred to as the primordial purity of the three worlds. As it is said in *The Necklace of Pearls*, a tantra of the Innermost Heart Essence,

> When it is examined, this very rope,
> The world with its inhabitants,
> Is empty from the outset,
> This is its final truth.
> Yet relatively it has form.
> To see the snake is truth for sight.
> To see the rope is truth itself.

As was said above, when one is alarmed, having taken the rope to be a snake, someone else may demonstrate that [what one is afraid of] is in fact a rope. And when that happens, the perceived appearance of the snake is dissipated but not the perceived appearance of a rope. But then it may be established that the rope itself, down to its every strand, is empty of existence. And at that point, the perceived appearance of the rope is undermined. Now if the world and its inhabitants are investigated with the same kind of reasoning, one will come to understand that they too are empty from the very beginning. On the ultimate level, all the appearances endowed with form on the relative level, which manifest through the creative power of awareness, are empty. When the colored rope is seen as a snake, this is true visually for those who have not examined it more closely. When, however, the rope is seen, the thought that clings to the snake collapses and vanishes. When the rope is seen, moreover, the perception is in fact true. On the other hand, when [the true nature of] the rope is definitively established, the thought that clings to the rope also disappears. In just the same way, when [the nature] of the world and its inhabitants is properly established, one will realize that they are primordially empty and beyond conceptual elaboration. At that time, however, although it is realized that they do not exist on the ultimate level, the belief that they exist just on the conventional level is not yet reversed. If, however, these conventional appearances, taken as the basis of emptiness, are analyzed, one is able to realize that—just as with the apprehension of the rope—they do not exist even as mere perceived appearances. At that moment, there is the thought that the conventional also does not exist as a mere perceived appearance. But then, when this thought is also established as being nonexistent, even on the level of the indivisible instants of consciousness, all phenomena—not only those that are invalidated but also the states of mind that invalidate them—are equal. They are the state of equality beyond all conceptual elaboration. As it is said in *The Necklace of Pearls*,

> This, then, is the character of the two truths.
> They are like a bird perched on a rock.

The world is no more than the all-concealing relative
And unrelated to the ultimate.
Within the vast expanse of emptiness—
All within that state is free and open.

When a bird flies down upon a rock and perches there, both bird and rock are apprehended equally as being truly present. When the bird flies away, the perception of it ceases, while the perception of the rock persists. When the rock crumbles, however, the state of mind that perceived the rock also disappears. It is the same with the two truths. Not only is the relative truth deceptive but that which is referred to as the ultimate is also empty. Within the world, in whichever way the two truths are posited, they are never anything other than the relative—they are false. They are not related to each other even in the way suggested by such statements as "In the fundamental nature, authentic reality, the two truths have no existence; they exist merely as conventionalities." In the ultimate expanse of emptiness—awareness, the dharmatā—the whole of phenomenal existence, samsara and nirvana, is neither negative nor positive; it is neither to be eliminated nor upheld. In empty awareness, the state of great equality, all phenomena are naturally free and open. As it is said in *The Heap of Jewels Tantra*,

Delusion there has never been.
Therefore ignorance, even as an object unexamined,
Is nonexistent from the first.
Before [the recognition of awareness],
No one was there to experience it.
These rough, coarse elements—even they
Have vanished from the very first.
Beings have no dwelling places—
These are naturally pure.
Their bodies also from the first have no existence
Whether in the past or in the future—
Even in the present, they are but awareness.

When an estimate is made of the nature of primordial awareness, since it has never been deluded, there has never been ignorance—that is, absence of awareness. Even as an object unexamined, delusion has never existed. From the very beginning there has never been any such thing. For awareness has never been deluded. And even before awareness is recognized, there is no one to experience delusion. Neither have the coarse elements—earth, wind, fire, and water—ever existed. By their nature, they are intrinsically pure. One's body too has no reality, for from the very first it has never existed. Since there was no delusion in the past, there was no body in the past. Delusion is also impossible in the future with the result that there is neither a past body nor a future body. And even in the present moment, there is no body existing apart from awareness, the state of primordial wisdom.

Generally speaking, in the case of the mind that apprehends as real the nonexistent phenomena of samsara and nirvana, it is fairly easy to understand that such a mind is deluded. On the other hand, it is actually quite difficult to understand that even the mind that believes the subject and object of apprehension to be nonexistent is also deluded. [It is like the way one has to proceed in the analysis of the rope-snake. First,] the cognition that apprehends the rope is said to be valid, whereas the cognition that apprehends the snake is invalid—the two cognitions are posited in relation to each other. On the conventional level, the cognition that apprehends the rope is valid, whereas the cognition that apprehends the snake is invalid. Subsequently, [continued analysis shows that, first,] the cognition that apprehends the rope is invalid, while the cognition that apprehends its fibers is valid. Then, one sees that the cognition of the fibers is invalid as contrasted with the cognition of the partless particles, which is valid. And then it should be understood that even the cognition of the partless particles is also deluded. Regarding this interrelatedness, it is said,

> What for one is ultimate
> Is relative for someone else.

According to the systems of the expository, causal vehicle, that which is considered ultimate in the lower system is certainly regarded as relative in the higher. For example, both the Vaibhāṣikas and the Sautrāntikas accept that the partless particles of matter and the indivisible moments of consciousness are the ultimate truth, whereas the proponents of Cittamātra hold that they are relative, in contrast with the self-cognizing, self-illuminating mind, which they consider to be ultimate. Then the Svātantrika Madhyamikas consider the ultimate of the Cittamātra to be the relative and then go on to define the ultimate as the absence of true existence in the self-cognizing, self-illuminating mind. Finally, the Prāsaṅgika Mādhyamikas declare that all this is relative, whereas the ultimate is beyond the intellect. As it is said in *The Way of the Bodhisattva*,

> The ultimate is not within the reach of intellect,
> For intellect is said to be the relative.

So it is that the increasingly higher views are posited in dependence of those that are lower. The meaning of the final view is that, as long as awareness, the state free of all conceptual elaboration with regard to the subject and object of apprehension—the primordially pure dharmatā, the primordial wisdom of equality—has not been actualized, it is impossible to attain the truth of the fundamental nature.

As a general principle, each of the different tenet systems, according to its own distinctive scope, makes assertions about phenomena. Of the śrāvaka schools, the Vaibhāṣikas say that the relative truth is the coarsely appearing phenomena of the world and its inhabitants—which can be physically destroyed or are seen to dissipate when subjected to analysis. The ultimate truth corresponds to the above mentioned partless particles of matter and the indivisible moments of consciousness, which cannot be destroyed in the way just described.

For the most part, the Vaibhāṣika and Sautrāntika schools are the same except that the latter define the relative as that which is void of causal effectiveness and the ultimate as that which is causally effective. For the most part, the Sautrāntika position corresponds to the logico-epistemological tradition of *pramāṇa*. It is said,

> Whatever is effective causally
> Has ultimate existence,
> While the rest has a relative existence.
> This is due to their specific or else general character.

This is in fact the theory of the Sautrāntikas Following Reasoning. The Sautrāntikas Following Scripture make the same assertions as the Vaibhāṣikas.

The Cittamātra school speaks of phenomena in terms of the three natures: imputed, dependent, and actual. All appearances, both apprehensible phenomena and apprehending cognitions, belong to the imputed nature and are thus hallucinatory. The mind that is the ground of such appearances is the dependent nature. And this same mind, the dependent nature, empty of both objects and subjects of apprehension, is the ultimate truth, for it really exists. The omniscient master Longchenpa has said [speaking of the Cittamātra view], "Of the two aspects (the object to be apprehended and the apprehending subject), the apprehender is held to be truly existent." According to the Cittamātra system, if there is no object of apprehension, there is no apprehending cognition. Consequently, they say that the self-cognizing, self-illuminating mind, in which there is neither subject nor object of apprehension, is truly existent.

Longchenpa says that according to the Svātantrika Madhyamikas, the [phenomena] of the relative truth, which appear extramentally through the interconnectedness of cause and effect—in being merely perceived appearances—are like magical illusions or reflections seen in a mirror. The Prāsaṅgika Madhyamikas, for their part, say that phenomena are nonexistent yet clear appearances like the reflection of the moon in water or the black lines seen by people with an ocular malfunction. This may give rise to doubt since the two examples—magical illusions [for the Svātantrikas] and black lines [for the Prāsaṅgikas]—are alike. So one might well conclude that there is no difference between the Svātantrikas and the Prāsaṅgikas. This, however, is not correct. Longchenpa points out that the Svātantrikas say that phenomena are ratified by valid cognition on the conventional level but when they are examined with the reasoning aiming at the ultimate, they are found to be like magical illusions. The position of the Prāsaṅgikas, as presented by the glorious Candrakīrti, is that on the conventional level, phenomena are like illusions and dreams, whereas on the ultimate level, they are emptiness, the state of equality beyond all conceptual elaboration.

Practitioners of the mind class of the Great Perfection consider that phenomena are the mere display of the creative power of awareness, the enlightened mind. They therefore assert that phenomena are the outward arising of awareness. Practitioners of the space class say that since within the expanse of awareness, phenomena are the self-experience of that same awareness, they are an array of ornaments embellishing awareness. In other words, apart from saying that phenomena are simply the self-experience of awareness, they do not talk about phenomena as being the outward arising of awareness. According to the tradition of the pith instruction class, the whole of phenomenal existence manifests within the state of awareness; it is nonexistent but appears like a magical illusion. And since phenomena are posited as being empty forms that merely appear, they are neither the mind nor different from the mind. They are said to be simply the self-experience of awareness. The three worlds have never existed. They are like the reflections in a mirror; they are primordially pure. Consequently, if one is able to maintain the fundamental stratum of awareness, hallucinatory appearances will subside into it.

* * *

The thirteenth section shows that since delusion does not exist even nominally, there is no contrasting state of nondelusion.

13. Since there's no delusion,
There's no absence of delusion.
Vast awareness, self-arisen and supreme,
Is from the outset present of itself.
It never was, nor is, nor ever will be freed.
In a past that's just a name,
No one has been freed.
There will never be a state of freedom
Since there never was a state of bondage.
All is pure like space,
Unrestricted, unconfined—
The utter openness and freedom
Of primordial purity.

The fundamental nature of primordial great perfection consists in the fact that all things in phenomenal existence, samsara and nirvana, are groundless and rootless. They are a spacelike, open, unimpeded display devoid of objective reference. This is why even the names "samsara," "nirvana," "freedom," and "delusion" have never existed.

In a general sense, freedom and delusion are necessarily posited in dependence on each other. For example, delusion is contrasted with the absence of delusion and the absence of delusion is contrasted with delusion. Therefore, if the state of delusion (taken as the basis for the interdependent relation) is canceled out and does not exist, its counterpart, the absence of delusion, is also canceled and does not exist. Conversely, if the absence of delusion as the contrasting counterpart is annulled, there can be no delusion to act as the basis of the interdependent relation. This being so, samsara and nirvana respectively transcend the states of bondage and freedom. It is as *The All-Creating King* declares,

I do not even speak about some higher state
Referred to as the ultimate.
There is no delusion;

> There is no attainment reached
> By following the path to buddhahood.
> Self-arisen wisdom is itself
> Beyond the reach of words.

This nearer hill is contrasted with that more distant hill. If there were no distant hill, there would be no way to describe this hill as "nearer." In the same way, the ultimate must be posited in dependence on the relative.

But if there are no relative phenomena, it is impossible to discourse upon their ultimate condition, the dharmatā, their sublime, fundamental nature. There exists neither a so-called ground of delusion nor a so-called path to enlightenment consisting of a number of vehicles and points of access to it. If these do not exist, there can be no such thing as the attainment of buddhahood, which is the result of the accomplishment of such a path. And if this is so, then self-arisen primordial wisdom is also beyond the conceptual elaborations of existence, nonexistence, both, and neither—the state beyond arising and cessation.

From the very outset, the ground, the fundamental nature beyond bondage and freedom, is awareness—vast, self-arisen, and present of itself. It is the uncontrived state in which not even the names of freedom and delusion are found—an immensity free of all elaboration of the mind. It has never been freed in the past, it is not freed now, and it will never be freed at some point in the future. It is primordial wisdom free of movement and change throughout the three times. And this is not all. Apart from being a mere mental imputation, the "three times" have never existed. The past is just a name. It does not exist. And if there is no past, it goes without saying that no one was freed in the past. Likewise, if there is no delusion, there will be no freedom from delusion. This is because it is in the sense of being freed or not freed from delusion that one speaks of freedom and the absence of freedom.

Similarly, if there is no delusion, there has never been a state of bondage. And this is because bondage and the absence of bondage are necessarily distinguished in the sense of being bound or not bound by the state of delusion. It is said in *The Great Garuda*,

> There are no buddhas,
> For who was there to be ensnared in bondage?
> For whom were ignorance, delusion possible?
> Even as names they don't exist.
> Since from the first there's nothing to be freed from,
> No freedom is there later gained.
> Some say the path is groundless,
> Yet they speak of a result.
> By such an affirmation
> Is the path to freedom veiled.

When it is said that the ground is free of both bondage and freedom, this is a reference to primordial purity, the state of equality free from all mental elaboration. Therefore, there has never been a buddha freed from delusion from the very first. As the tantra says, "There are no buddhas." For if there were such a thing as an "undeluded buddha," this would mean a buddha who had been freed from the snare of bondage. But if no one is ensnared in bondage—there being no bondage—a "buddha freed from bondage" is an impossibility. Similarly, if there has never been delusion, and if there has never been ignorance, which is the basis of delusion, how is it possible for there to be beings who are deluded on that basis? Even the names "delusion" and "ignorance" have no reality. Consequently, the ground free from both bondage and freedom refers to the fact that since from the very first there has never been a state of bondage in the past, there can be no such thing as freedom from bondage in the present, for there is no bondage from which to be freed. And if there is no freedom now, there can be no freedom in the future. If the ground is free of delusion, there can be no talk of following a path that leads to it. And if there is no path to be followed, it is impossible to attain a result—namely, the level of buddhahood. If anyone considers the ground, path, and fruit to exist as three separate elements, this belief is itself a deluded state of mind by which the path to liberation and buddhahood is obscured.

Therefore, all the phenomena of both samsara and nirvana are beyond bondage and freedom. They are utterly pure like space, beyond limits and extremes. This is referred to as the utter openness and freedom of primordial purity.

* * *

The fourteenth section gives a survey of the first chapter, showing that samsara and nirvana have never existed. Instead, there is the great vastness of the ultimate expanse, spontaneous and equal.

14. Briefly, in the womb of ultimate expanse,
Immense and present of itself,
Samsara or nirvana—
Whichever is displayed by the creative power—
Has no existence from the moment it arises.
Whatever happens in one's dreams
Through sleep's creative power—
None of it is real.
There is just awareness self-cognizing,
Blissful in its fundamental stratum,
An all-encompassing immensity
That's even, present of itself.

In brief, the meaning of the first chapter is that phenomenal existence, samsara and nirvana, arising within the womb of the ultimate expanse—awareness, the enlightened mind, present of itself and supremely vast—is the unceasing manifestation of the display of the creative power of spontaneously present awareness.

No matter what arises in the whole of phenomenal existence (samsara and nirvana), from the very moment of its appearance, it has no existence. It is groundless and by nature the great state of equality—in just the same way that everything appearing in one's dreams through the creative power of sleep (an outer world and the beings it contains) is devoid of existence from the very moment of its appearing. It is groundless and rootless. It is said in *The Great Garuda Tantra*,

> To those for whom the mind,
> (Which from the first falls not to any side),
> Appears existent as samsara and the lower realms,
> To them I say, "These are untrue.
> They are but dreams and magical illusions
> And cities in the clouds.
> It is impossible for such false appearances
> To have the effectiveness of truth."

As this text declares, the ultimate enlightened mind, primordially free of limits and extremes, is mistakenly perceived as samsara and the lower destinies. The latter seem to be truly existent and yet they are untrue just like the ten examples of illusion. It is impossible for them to possess even a hair's breadth of true existence.

Dream visions arise through the creative power of sleep; the appearances of the three worlds arise through the display of awareness's creative power. In short, the appearances of the three worlds have no existence. They have never stirred from the fundamental stratum of blissful, self-knowing awareness—the state of equality that is free of all mental elaboration. There is just awareness, primordial purity, an all-encompassing great immensity that is even and present of itself.

* * *

This concludes the first chapter of *The Precious Treasury of the Dharmadhātu*, which shows that samsara and nirvana do not stir from the ultimate expanse.

2. Phenomenal Existence Is a Pure Buddha Field

Now that it has been established that the ultimate expanse is the ground for the arising of all things, there follows a detailed demonstration in thirteen sections showing that the appearances of the ultimate expanse manifest primordially and spontaneously as a buddha field. In the first section, the ultimate expanse, vastly pervasive and present of itself, is compared with space.

> **1. The ultimate expanse from the beginning**
> **Is by nature present of itself.**
> **Extending all-pervasively, it has no out or in.**
> **It has no boundaries,**
> **No zenith and no nadir,**
> **And no directions main or intermediate.**
> **It is neither wide nor narrow,**
> **For it is awareness, pure and spacelike—**
> **A vast expanse devoid of mind's elaboration,**
> **Free of thought and points of reference.**

The ultimate expanse, the dharmatā free of mental elaboration, is the enlightened mind and is as pervasive as space. It is by its very nature primordially pure and present of itself. Now since this expanse, the ultimate enlightened mind, is from the very first utterly pure, it has neither out nor in [neither an exterior nor an interior], neither zenith nor nadir, neither cardinal nor intermediate directions. It extends all-pervasively throughout samsara and nirvana and, being free of boundaries, is without center or periphery. It is devoid of identifiable features such as size and volume, zenith and nadir, main and intermediate directions, up and down. It is neither wide nor narrow. It is uncontrived, self-arisen awareness as pure as space. As it is said in *The All-Creating King*,

> The mind is the authentic, ultimate reality.
> It is great bliss, the perfect nonduality.
> Possessing every aspect, it is utterly devoid of them.
> Free of mind's elaboration,
> It is from the very first like space.
> Devoid of reference point or object,
> It cannot be described as "one."

The fundamental nature of the primordially empty mind, the spacelike primal wisdom of great bliss, nondual and free of mental elaboration, is not like the figurative emptiness, the [understanding of] emptiness that comes through analytical investigation. It is nonfigurative emptiness, the emptiness that is empty from the beginning. Since it is free of all objective reference and targets—since it transcends all mental objects—it is beyond all conceptual elaborations such as identity and difference, existence and nonexistence, both and neither. It is empty awareness, the all-pervading state of equality, which is never anything other than the condition of an immensely vast expanse.

* * *

The second section shows that samsara and nirvana manifest as empty forms within the expanse of empty awareness.

> **2. Displays born in the unborn ultimate expanse**
> **Are completely limitless and indeterminate.**
> **They cannot be identified as this or that;**
> **They are not substances with attributes.**
> **Their nature is like space that spreads**
> **Through infinite directions.**

It is unborn spontaneous presence.
No past, no future does it have,
No ending, no beginning.

Clouds gather in the sky, the lightning flashes, the thunder roars, hailstones fall, meteorites strike, and so on. And yet throughout all this, the sky itself never changes. In just the same way, whatever may be the oceanlike infinity of phenomenal appearance—whether of an outer world or of inner beings, samsara or nirvana—it arises as a display born within empty awareness, the dharmatā, the unborn, spacelike ultimate expanse. Without ever wavering from awareness, the dharmadhātu, all appearances—good and evil, happiness and sorrow, excellence and imperfection, hopes and fears—all are utterly indeterminate hallucinatory appearances, arising unceasingly and completely beyond the limits of expression. They are empty and do not in the slightest way impair or enhance awareness, the dharmadhātu itself. They are limitless and fall to no extremes. They cannot be identified as this or that, as existent, nonexistent, both or neither, as exclusive or inclusive, identical or different, and so on. They are not substances endowed with attributes.

Now since their nature, awareness, the dharmadhātu, pervades all world systems throughout the ten directions, it is omnipresent like space. Awareness, the fundamental nature, the dharmatā, is not altered or contrived to the slightest degree. Therefore, unborn, self-arisen awareness, the great spontaneous presence, is free from all conceptual extremes such as past and future, arising and ceasing, beginning and ending. It is what is referred to as the nondual primordial wisdom of great equality.

* * *

The third section shows that this spontaneous presence is a state beyond going and coming.

3. Samsara and nirvana
Are by nature the enlightened mind,

Unborn and without origin,
Indeterminate and present of itself.
It came from nowhere; nowhere does it go.
Free of past and future,
The expanse of the enlightened mind
Is free of one side or another.
Not going and not coming,
It is boundlessly pervasive.

Awareness, self-arisen primordial wisdom, this precious spontaneous presence, is beyond all mental elaboration. Therefore there is no destination to which it might go, nor any place of origin from which it might come. This is why it is said to exemplify the state beyond going and coming. The ultimate nature of the oceanlike infinity of phenomenal appearances, samsara or nirvana, can be briefly described as the dharmadhātu, empty awareness, the ultimate enlightened mind. Having no source, it is unoriginate; it is emptiness; it does not derive from anything in phenomenal existence, the world and its inhabitants. Moreover, it is unborn in the sense that it does not pass through any of the three stages of arising, enduring, and ceasing and because it has never arisen from any phenomenon, outer or inner. Similarly, the ultimate enlightened mind is indeterminate in terms of existence, nonexistence, both, and neither.

Spontaneously present of itself, this primordially self-arisen buddhahood does not come from anything at all—whether the world or its inhabitants, the four elements, things or nonthings. It is primordial wisdom, spontaneously perfect in and of itself, a state of equality free of mental elaboration. Likewise in the future and until the world itself is emptied, awareness, the enlightened mind, will go nowhere, for it has no destination, whether in outer or inner phenomena, the world and its inhabitants, subjects, objects, and so on. It is therefore referred to as the primordial wisdom of the ultimate nature that is pure from the beginning. Similarly, because primordial self-arisen buddhahood is free of past and future and is without arising or cessation, grasping, effort, and mental elaborationand because it is free of one side or another, it is a wide-open, infinite dimension of the vast expanse of all-pervading awareness. It is the enlightened mind in which there is no trace of the coming and going of the phenomena of samsara and nirvana. Being thus boundlessly pervasive, it is described as the primordial wisdom of great equality that pervades both samsara and nirvana. As *The All-Creating King* says,

> All things have one root in the enlightened mind.
> Phenomenal existence, buddhas, beings,
> Worlds and their inhabitants—
> Within the essence of the enlightened mind,
> The source whence everything arises—
> Are not one and yet they are past numbering.
> Likewise the three kāyas of the buddhas,
> The bodies and the speech of beings—
> All are the enlightened mind,
> Free of subject-object apprehension from the very first.

* * *

The fourth section speaks of the great nail of the vast skylike expanse.[43]

> **4. Suchness, dharmatā, has no beginning.**
> **It has no center and no limit.**
> **In its purity it is like even, all-pervading space.**
> **Without beginning, it is endless.**
> **It transcends all objects of the past and future.**
> **Unborn, unceasing,**
> **It has neither attributes nor substance.**
> **It neither comes nor goes**
> **And cannot be defined as this or that.**
> **Not accomplished through striving,**
> **It is free of all activity.**
> **The ground of suchness is without a center or directions.**

With no objective reference or interruption,
It is the dimension of equality.

Ultimate truth, self-arisen awareness, in being free of every extreme of conceptual elaboration, has neither a beginning nor an ending. It is the fundamental nature of phenomena, suchness itself, without center or limit. The term *suchness* refers to the dharmatā, which is motionless and unchanging throughout the three times. As we find in *The Six Expanses*,

It has no edge; it has no central point.
It has no aspect; it is objectless.
It has no *deva* and no mantra.
It has no entity.
Transcending every label,
It has neither friend nor foe.

Since the nature of awareness has neither center nor limit, and is without an apprehending aspect, neither is there an object of such an apprehending cognition. It is also without a deva or deity, to act as the object of practice, nor does it have a mantra as the means of practice. Likewise, it is without entity and is beyond all phenomenal labeling. And inasmuch as there is nothing incompatible with it, awareness has no foes—and also no allies or friends that might bring it benefit.

Within the expanse of this same awareness, the enlightened mind, there is neither good nor evil, neither hope nor fear, nothing that ought to be removed and nothing to be added. It is primordial wisdom, which evenly pervades all the phenomena of samsara and nirvana. In dimension it is wide-open and infinite. Primordially pure wisdom, similar to space itself, is by nature the state of great equality, empty from the very first and free of any kind of mental elaboration. There is no way that it can be qualified as "this" or "that." It cannot be described or indicated by examples. It is without beginning or end. Since, throughout the passage of time, it has never been deluded, awareness transcends all objects qualified as past, present, and future. And likewise, since there was never a moment in the past when it was born, there will never be a moment in the future when it will cease. This then is unconditioned primordial wisdom free of all mental elaboration and devoid of substance and attributes like beginning and end, past and future, arising and cessation.

Moreover, since self-arisen awareness is in itself devoid of the manifold webs of mental elaboration, it is likewise free of the slightest attributes of existence and nonexistence, permanence and impermanence, identity and difference, exclusion and inclusion, coming and going, and so on. In short, since it cannot be described as being "like this," it is beyond indication. Awareness, primordial wisdom, beyond the range of all effortful practice, is not something that can be newly produced through exertion. Because it is primordially free of object, agent, and action, it is the spontaneously perfect primordial wisdom of equality, empty awareness beyond any kind of activity.

In the same way, since uncontrived awareness, free of all conceptual attributes, cannot be appraised in terms of spatial orientation, there is no dividing it in terms of zenith and nadir or in relation to the cardinal and secondary directions with their midpoints and boundaries. As Shabkar has said,

> Look and see if emptiness
> Has either edge or center.
> If it has no edge or center,
> See—does it have an outside or an in?
> With neither out nor in, awareness is like pure space—
> Open, unimpeded,
> Directionless and free of limitation.

Self-arisen awareness is beyond all mentally contrived ascriptions such as beginning and end, birth and cessation, past and future, substance and attributes, center or boundary, outside or in. It is free of anything [that might serve as an] objective referent or target. Being of such an open and unimpeded spacelike condition, it is necessarily free of any kind of interruption. This great expanse of primordial emptiness and equality is described as the "great nail of the skylike expanse." This fourth stanza is a summary outline.

* * *

The fifth section shows that awareness is the state of natural purity and equality.[44]

> **5. The nature of all things is dharmatā, equality itself.**
> **Thus there's not a single thing**
> **That does not rest in that equality,**
> **And in this one equality all things are equal!**
> **Such is the condition of enlightened mind.**
> **Since it is the unborn state of all-pervading,**
> **Spacelike vast immensity,**
> **This same equality is free of interruption.**

Of all the appearances of samsara and nirvana, there is not one that at any time stirs from the dharmatā, which is awareness. Being in truth beyond origin, remaining, and cessation, these appearances never leave the dharmatā, the state of equality. There is not a single thing that does not abide in the expanse of equality, the dharmatā, unborn awareness. All things belonging to phenomenal existence, samsara and nirvana, are equal in not arising as different or separate from the state of awareness, the enlightened mind. They are equal in not remaining and equal in not ceasing. They are equal too in that they do not diverge even slightly from the state that is free of going and coming.

Each of the nine vehicles, arranged in ascending order, make various assertions concerning the view, meditation, action, and result. However, if the state of equality, the expanse of the one primordially pure awareness (the view of the final teaching of Atiyoga) is not realized, freedom cannot be achieved. For so it is that the enlightened mind is a single state of equality, in which the infinite phenomenal appearances of samsara and nirvana are equal. They can never extend beyond the state of the enlightened mind.

Phenomena have never in the past arisen, do not arise now, and will never arise in the future elsewhere than in the state of the enlightened mind. Therefore, this vast spacelike immensity of awareness evenly pervades the expanse of the equality of samsara and nirvana. And if the meaning of this is correctly grasped, one will understand why, uninterruptedly and from the very first, phenomena never stir from the great equality of dharmatā, the single taste of samsara and nirvana. It is of the utmost importance to understand this point correctly.

* * *

The sixth section shows that in light of what has just been said, this spontaneous presence of great equality is the single state of unmoving and unchanging dharmatā within the indestructible vajra buddha field, and therefore awareness is the stronghold of the vajra essence.

6. Spontaneous, directionless,
This is the stronghold all-embracing.
Seamless, without high or low,
It is the stronghold of immensity.
Impartial, all-accommodating,
It is the stronghold of the unborn dharmakāya.
Immutable and present of itself,
It is the stronghold of the precious secret.
Phenomenal appearance, samsara and nirvana—
This is the primordial stronghold,
The stronghold of the one and only evenness.

In order to prevail in war against a dangerous enemy, one must first set up a secure position, a well-fortified stronghold, in order to protect oneself. Likewise, as a means of prevailing in battle against the adversaries of defilement and hallucinatory appearance produced through ignorance and dualistic apprehension, one must take up a secure position within the stronghold of the indestructible vajra expanse. This is none other than the state of equality, primordial wisdom free of delusion and artifice. This same awareness, self-arisen primordial wisdom, which is uncontrived and present of itself, is the all-embracing stronghold, wherein there are neither primary nor secondary directions, neither zenith nor nadir. It embraces evenly both samsara and nirvana. This stronghold is indestructible and impregnable. No deluded thoughts or defilements can harm it. Instead, they vanish into it. Within its vast expanse, ignorance and all the appearances of a subject and object of apprehension dissolve as when ice melts into water.

Awareness, the enlightened mind, is free of all mental elaborations—of all concepts such as primary and secondary directions, high and low. Consequently, it is a seamless, primordially present vast expanse, self-arisen and uncontrived. It is called the stronghold of immensity because it contains within it the whole of samsara and nirvana. It is said to accommodate everything because all things in phenomenal existence, samsara and nirvana, are gathered without partiality and are completely subsumed within the single expanse of awareness. The secure position seized within the expanse of awareness, empty and unborn, is called the stronghold of the dharmakāya. It is as *The Lion's Perfect Power* declares,

> The enlightened mind, the vast abyss,
> Is changeless, inconceivable, beyond the reach of words.
> It is the vajra citadel,
> The stronghold indestructible, without a flaw.

The supreme immensity of empty awareness, the enlightened mind, is an unchanging, inconceivable, and inexpressible stronghold.

And this indestructible vajra citadel of ultimate reality, endowed with the seven unchanging attributes of a vajra, is erected in the expanse of the one sole sphere of empty awareness. It is referred to as the stronghold of the unchanging vajra.

Since all phenomena are primordially and spontaneously present in unchanging awareness, pure, self-arisen primordial wisdom, this same wisdom is a precious abode. It is the inconceivable secret of the mind of all the buddhas. It is the source of the four kāyas and five wisdoms and the rest of the twenty-five qualities of the resultant state. This is why awareness is referred to as the stronghold of the precious secret.

Again, since the whole of phenomenal existence, samsara and nirvana, is primordially and spontaneously present in the expanse of the one sole sphere of empty awareness, since it is self-arising and self-subsiding therein, one speaks of a primordial stronghold, a stronghold of the one sole evenness. One speaks in this way because all phenomena are primordially and evenly settled in the perfect state of buddhahood—the stronghold of equality set up within the indestructible vajra expanse.

* * *

The seventh section shows that the palace of the self-arisen essence is arrayed upon the ground, the dharmadhātu.[45]

7. Upon the all-pervading and all-spreading ground,
There stands the citadel of the enlightened mind
Impartially pervading all samsara and nirvana.
Its high imposing tower
Is the vast expanse of dharmatā.
Its central ward transcending all the four directions
Is the uncreated nature.
Its entrance gate is utterly immense,
The freedom from all gradual exertion.
Within that castle, adorned in rich array that's
present of itself,

Is primal wisdom self-arisen,
The king upon his throne.
The cognizant acts of the creative power
Of primal wisdom are his ministers
Who hold the land in sway.
Immanent absorption is his sublime queen,
While qualities of realization,
Which manifest spontaneously,
Are like his heir apparent with the servants and attendants.
All are gathered in the vast space of great bliss,
The thought-free luminosity.

Uncontrived, self-arisen awareness is unfabricated and unaltered. There is nothing to be added to it and nothing to be subtracted. It is the ultimate expanse, which all-pervasively extends everywhere, throughout samsara and nirvana. Since it is the foundation on which all outer and inner phenomena are based—namely, the world and its inhabitants—it is compared to the ground. Upon this ground, and compared to a royal palace or citadel, is the ultimate enlightened mind, awareness, free of all delimitations and extremes and impartially pervading both samsara and nirvana. The highest of all the views, which recognizes and takes the measure of the immense expanse of suchness, the dharmatā, is likened to the high tower of that citadel, lofty, imposing, and exhilarating. The nature [the dharmatā or suchness], primordially uncreated by any causal process and intentioned effort, is beyond permanence and annihilation, and the two remaining ontological extremes. It is the immense expanse of awareness and is likened to the castle ward, the space that utterly transcends the four directions. For this reason, the entrance gate, for those of the highest capacity, is primordially and naturally established as what is free of every kind of causal and gradual procedure. This then is the palace of the enlightened mind. So it is that when fortunate beings enter such a palace, they find its entrance to be immensely vast. Spontaneous, self-arisen awareness is resplendent with the riches of opulent wealth—all the qualities of the result, such as the kāyas and the wisdoms, which are inseparable from each other, are likened to the rich array of the adornments of the palace itself.

Awareness, the quintessence present of itself, self-arisen primordial wisdom, empty, luminous, and unceasing, the genuine and uncontrived fundamental nature—in other words, awareness stripped and in its naked state—is compared to the king seated upon his throne, which he never forsakes. And the creative power and display of primordial wisdom or awareness, namely, the cognitions that actively perceive objects, are like the royal ministers who govern, keeping watch over the land and protecting the king's vassals and subjects. The indwelling meditative absorption or stability, which abides intrinsically within awareness, is likened to the sublime queen, for it is never separate, and can never be separated, from awareness. From the standpoint of the path, when yogis are engaged in practice, their meditative evenness within the state of awareness is called "indwelling meditative absorption." From the standpoint of the ground, however, it is self-arisen primordial wisdom itself and is referred to as the indwelling expanse of ultimate reality. When awareness, the fundamental nature, is realized precisely as it is, all the experiences and qualities of realization develop exponentially and the signs of warmth and accomplishment spontaneously appear. These are compared to the heir apparent together with the servants and attendants.

When a king is required to protect his realm, he gathers around him his queen, his ministers, his heir, attendants, and servants, all of whom are his subjects. In like manner, when the luminosity of self-arisen awareness (the primordial wisdom pervading the whole of samsara and nirvana) is actualized, it includes within its scope the activity of the creative power of awareness, the immanent or indwelling meditative absorption, and the entire aggregate of all experiences and realizations, and so forth. These are all its ornaments. Longchenpa says[46] that if one fails to understand this correctly, all such assertions are no different from the deranged utterances of a complete lunatic. All such qualities are in fact contained within the one expanse of the great bliss of Samantabhadrī, the state of the primordial wisdom of equality free from mental elaboration. They are simply awareness—empty, ineffable, self-cognizing, and self-luminous—and apart from that, they cannot be distinguished and individually apprehended by thought.

Now self-arisen primordial knowing, primordial wisdom, is not to be confused with the primordial knowing that cognizes objects [dualistically].[47] *The All-Creating King* declares,

> Primordial wisdom knows primordially.
> Knowing from the very first,
> It is primordial wisdom self-arisen.
> Primordial knowing that cognizes objects
> Arises from those objects—thus it is not self-arisen,
> And when there are no objects, it does not appear.
> Primordial knowing that from the first is self-arisen—
> Primordial wisdom, knowing from the very first—
> Is what should be referred to as "primordial wisdom."

As this text says, primordial wisdom is spontaneously present awareness, immanent at all times and in all situations. It does not depend on, or follow, objects of cognition. This beginningless knowing is called primordial wisdom.

There is, on the other hand, a primordial state of knowing that is a cognizant creative power that knows objects. It arises in relation to such objects and is contingent on them. However, if its inner nature is recognized as being self-arisen, this same cognizant creative power will subside into the ground and a decisive conviction will arise regarding primordial purity, the state of the exhaustion of phenomena. When, on the other hand, there is no such recognition, the self-arisen nature becomes the indeterminate state, and when the cognizant creative power engages with objects, it perilously turns into ordinary thought processes that are contingent on circumstances. This is why it is said that there is an enormous difference between these two kinds of primordial knowing.

Now when the primordial knowing that is the cognizant creative power arises in relation to objects, and when its inner nature is recognized as self-arisen primordial wisdom, the meditative absorption of immanent primordial wisdom occurs, and within this state, it is impossible for habitual tendencies to accumulate. For the mind of all the buddhas resides within the primordial wisdom of equality. It is as we find in *The All-Creating King*,

> The dharmatā, devoid of latent tendencies,
> Is said to be the wisdom of the buddhas
> Past, present, and to come.
> The wisdom mind of all the buddhas of the triple
> time
> Abides primordially in evenness
> And objects it does not cognize [dualistically].

Within the self-cognizing primordial wisdom that does not cognize sense objects dualistically, indwelling meditative absorption is present, unfabricated, and spontaneous. This is a reference to the meditative absorption of a yogi. It is the meditative absorption of immanent primordial wisdom. When the primordial knowing that is a cognizant creative power arises in relation to the objects of sense, and when [its inner nature] is not recognized, this same cognizant creative power engages with these objects [and there may arise in the course of meditation] what is referred to as the meditative absorption of childish beings. Since it perceives the objects of the senses, it also accumulates karma and latent tendencies, and thus the cognition that arises in relation to objects is called the samsaric mind. For it arises in the aspect of the apprehended object and the apprehending subject. It is thus of crucial importance to distinguish between these two kinds of absorption.

* * *

The eighth section demonstrates that the ultimate expanse beyond movement and change is at all times the domain of awareness.

8. The mastery of all phenomenal existence,
The universe and its inhabitants,
Lies in the unmoving state
Beyond imagination and description,
The boundless vast domain of dharmadhātu.

The dharmadhātu, being motionless and unchanging throughout the lapse of time, is unmoving. It is like space. This unmoving, self-arisen, primordial wisdom, the indwelling ultimate expanse, is beyond the mind's imagination and words cannot express it. It is free of the webs of all such conceptual elaborations. The displayed appearances of phenomenal existence arise naturally and unceasingly within this primordially empty, infinitely pervasive state. They never stir from it. They constitute the entire oceanic expanse of the phenomenal field, the universe and the beings it contains, the objects of the six consciousnesses.

If, without eliminating some things and retaining others, one is able to stay relaxed in the dharmadhātu, the state of awareness, then it is just as when ice melts into water and waves sink back into the sea. Appearances spontaneously arise; they spontaneously clear and spontaneously subside. This is what is meant [in the root text] by the mastery that awareness, the dharmadhātu, has over all phenomena. On an island of gold, no ordinary earth and stones can be found. Likewise, when awareness, the dharmadhātu, empowers the whole of phenomenal existence as the dharmakāya buddha field, all that manifests becomes the pure, immense realm of the dharmadhātu, the vast unlimited display of buddhas and buddha fields. As it is said in *The Parting Testament*,

> This awareness, which is not established as existent,
> Arises unimpeded in its various self-display.
> All phenomenal existence therefore manifests
> As the field of dharmakāya.
> And this arising naturally subsides.

These are the very words of Garab Dorje, spoken amid a brilliant mass of rays of light as he was passing into nirvana, the expanse wherein no residue of the psychophysical aggregates remains. It was at this point too that Mañjuśrīmitra cried out his twenty-five anguished words beginning "Alas, alas, sorrow and sadness!" Garab Dorje's vajra words, known as his *Parting Testament*, bring together all the crucial points of the tantras and their commentaries, as well as the pith instructions of the Great Perfection. They are an expression of the quintessence of the realization of the vidyādharas. Their blessing power is swifter than that of any other speech. Mañjuśrīmitra absorbed the meaning of Garab Dorje's words, and the realization of master and disciple became inseparable. This he transmitted to Śrīsiṃha, from whom it was passed to Jñānasūtra, and from him to Vimalamitra.[48] The latter, having attained the rainbow body of great transformation, is dwelling even now at Wutaishan, the mountain of five peaks.

Now the meaning of the citation from Garab Dorje's *Parting Testament* is as follows. Awareness, primordial wisdom, has never been established as something that subsists in some specific way—in terms of existence, nonexistence, both, or neither, or in terms of identity and difference, permanence, impermanence, exclusion, or inclusion. And yet, although this self-cognizing awareness, free of mental elaboration, has no existence whatever, it may nevertheless spontaneously arise as anything at all. The manifestation of its self-display is utterly unimpeded. Since the whole of phenomenal existence arises through the creative power of the dharmakāya, all that appears in this way manifests exclusively as the kāyas and wisdoms—that is, the pure buddha field of the dharmakāya. And because all such manifestation is self-arising and self-subsiding, this means that manifestation subsides naturally in awareness.

* * *

The ninth section shows that all things are contained within the one expanse of bliss, the enlightened mind.

9. If in that domain you stay,
All is dharmakāya,
Never stirring from the single, self-arisen primal wisdom,
Which, uncreated and possessed primordially,
Transcends all effortful endeavor.
Since this single sphere, free of edge or corner,
Is all-encompassing,
The natural state of things, just as it is,
Beyond all differentiation,
Is gathered in this single vast expanse.

If awareness, the fundamental nature of the dharmakāya, is realized just as it is, one is free. One is a buddha. If, on the other hand, it is not realized, one is deluded, a sentient being. Everything depends on whether realization is gained or not, on recognition or lack of recognition. If awareness is not recognized, and one remains in delusion, the habitual tendencies, stored in the universal ground from time without beginning, are activated, and the hallucinatory experiences [of samsara] endlessly proliferate. This is the inescapable result. If, on the other hand, awareness is recognized, a certainty is gained that whatever objects of the sense consciousnesses may manifest within awareness, they occur through the creative power of the dharmakāya. They naturally arise and naturally subside—with the result that one understands that they are but the ornaments of the ultimate expanse, a buddha field of the appearances of the ultimate expanse.

If, therefore, one remains in the state of immaculate awareness, the one sole sphere of the dharmakāya, the result is that within this primordially present domain, all the appearances of the oceanlike infinity of phenomena are seen to be the dharmakāya itself and do not possess to the slightest degree any existence other than that. If one remains firmly in the state of awareness, the self-arisen primordial wisdom that from the very beginning has never existed, one will see that the whole of the phenomenal field, whether of samsara or nirvana, never moves from the state of awareness, the one self-arisen primordial wisdom. The latter is also referred to as the one expanse of primordial, great emptiness; emptiness endowed with supreme aspects; emptiness that is itself primordially empty; and the abyss of emptiness, the ancient and primeval mother. All these terms indicate primordial wisdom that is pure from the very beginning, that in its fundamental nature has never been defiled, and that transcends all objects, be they beneficial or harmful.

This self-arisen awareness lies beyond all striving and is beyond the reach of all imagining. It is uncreated and is perfectly possessed from the very beginning. It is primordial wisdom, which transcends all effortful action, mental elaboration, negation, affirmation, hope, and fear. In terms of its inner disposition, since it is all-embracing and never stirs from the expanse of the one sole sphere of the dharmakāya devoid of the edges and corners of thoughts, this fundamental nature of all phenomena—just as it is, free of any differentiation from the very beginning—is gathered in the expanse of this one sole, all-inclusive sphere and never strays from it. As it is said in *The Necklace of Pearls*,

> Since all arises in the ground, the dharmakāya,
> The root of the transmission lineage is cut.
> Since the wish-fulfilling state is present from the very first,
> All movements of the mind
> Are but a natural state without contrivance.
> Since the stream of breath is severed from the first,
> There is neither birth nor death primordially.
> Since every object of desire
> Has been exhausted from the first,
> There is no meditation focused on an object.
> Since, without a step, the destination has been reached,
> The path to tread has been traversed already.

As this text declares, since the ground for the manifestation of all phenomena of samsara and nirvana is itself the dharmakāya or awareness, it follows that the appearances, pure or impure, that arise within it, have themselves never moved from awareness—the dharmadhātu that is their ground of manifestation. The fundamental nature of awareness has never been stained by samsara or nirvana. It has never been affected by mental elaboration, by freedom, delusion, and so forth. For it is beyond every object, whether beneficial or harmful, in samsara and nirvana. So it is that within the fundamental nature of awareness, not one word of instruction has ever been transmitted by teachers. The root of the transmission lineage has thus been severed. Something called the tradition of the transmission lineage has never existed. The dharmadhātu is the mind of all the Victorious Ones. It is a state that, like a wish-fulfilling jewel, abides primordially as the fundamental nature of awareness. And since therein there is not even the name of "buddha" or "sentient being," all the thoughts occurring there are in their nature pure. They are the uncontrived state of great primordial wisdom. If there are no beings, their breath of life is primordially stopped and has never existed. And if there is no breath, then from the very first, there is no birth, no age, no sickness, and no death. Since all that appears to the six consciousnesses—all desirable objects of the senses—is completely exhausted from the very beginning, there is no meditation focused on the appearances of these six consciousnesses. In short, there are no sentient beings, there is no breath, there is neither birth nor death, and no desirable objects of the senses. From the very beginning, there are no steps to take, and therefore there is no arriving. Likewise, from the very beginning, there is no path to be traversed and therefore no traversing it. For everything dwells in the one sole sphere of awareness.

* * *

The tenth section shows that all things are of a single taste within awareness, the enlightened mind.

> **10. The abodes of the six kinds of beings**
> **Together with the buddha fields**
> **Do not exist but in the spacious realm of dharmatā.**

Within the luminous enlightened mind,
All are of a single taste.
Samsara and nirvana both
Are utterly encompassed by awareness.

The first chapter of Longchenpa's text demonstrated that all phenomena appear within the very nature of awareness. The second chapter shows that they are perfectly included[49] in it. On the side of samsara, the four ways of taking birth— and all the various abodes, bodies, and resources that appear to the deluded perceptions of the six classes of beings in the three worlds—are all perfectly encompassed within the expanse of awareness, ultimate reality. On the side of nirvana, all the qualities of the result, such as the pure fields, the five buddhas, the five primordial wisdoms, and so on do not have the slightest degree of existence apart from awareness, the ultimate enlightened mind. Just as all the visions of one's dreams are of a single taste within the state of sleep, all the appearances of the oceanlike infinity of phenomena are likewise of a single taste within the nature of awareness, the spacious realm of ultimate reality, the luminous, ultimate enlightened mind. As it is said in *The All-Creating King*,

The root of all phenomena
Is the enlightened, all-creating, mind.
However things arise, they share my nature,
However they occur, they are but my display.
And all the sounds and words that resonate
Are but myself in form of word and sound.
Buddhas, wisdoms, perfect qualities,
All beings with their bodies and habitual proclivities,
All gathered in phenomenal existence—
The universe together with the beings it contains—
Are from the outset the enlightened mind.

Thus the whole of phenomenal existence, everything subsumed

within samsara and nirvana, is fully encompassed by awareness, the changeless, all-creating enlightened mind.

* * *

The eleventh section shows that since all phenomena are perfectly included in this state, the qualities of nirvana also dwell therein. They are present of themselves and do not need to be striven for.

> **11. In this treasury, the dharmadhātu, source of everything,**
> **Nirvana is spontaneously present with no need for striving.**
> **The changeless dharmakāya,**
> **Free of all objective reference,**
> **Is all-pervasive, present in all things.**
> **Appearances both out and in,**
> **The world and its inhabitants,**
> **Are the sambhogakāya.**
> **The self-arising of phenomena, reflection-like,**
> **Is the nirmāṇakāya.**
> **Therefore there are no phenomena**
> **That are not perfectly subsumed**
> **As the adornments of the triple kāya.**
> **Everything that manifests is the display**
> **Of the enlightened body, speech, and mind.**
> **Even the unnumbered buddha fields**
> **Of the sugatas, leaving none aside,**
> **Arise from the same source:**
> **The nature of the mind,**
> **The vast expanse of the three kāyas.**

The source of all phenomena, whether of samsara or nirvana, is the dharmadhātu, self-arisen primordial wisdom, free of all mental elaboration. Just as a treasury of precious substances is the foundation that gives rise to all that is needed and wished for, likewise, the phenomena of samsara—the aggregates, elements, and sense fields—are all present of themselves within the dharmadhātu, with the result that there is no need to strive for them. And indeed, all the perfect qualities and wisdoms of the state of buddhahood, the peace of nirvana, are spontaneously present from the very beginning—again without the need for them to be striven for. In other words, the phenomena of both samsara and nirvana are themselves the primordial great emptiness, the dharmakāya, which does not move or fluctuate throughout the passage of time and is thus unchanging. This dharmakāya, which is free of all objective reference and is open and unimpeded, is all-pervasive and present in all things. It is thus that the empty, ultimate nature of phenomena is shown to be the dharmakāya.

And as for all the outer and inner appearances of the world and its inhabitants, these are not empty in the sense of being nothing at all. They are the appearances of the luminous character [of awareness], the sambhogakāya. And again, all phenomena arise unceasingly of themselves—like reflected images appearing clear and distinct in a mirror. They are spontaneously present as the nirmāṇakāya. As *The All-Creating King* declares,

> My ultimate nature, uncontrived, is dharmakāya;
> My luminous character, also uncontrived, is the
>   sambhogakāya;
> My manifest cognizant power is the nirmāṇakāya.[50]

And,

> All phenomena, however they appear,
> Possess three aspects uncontrived:
> Ultimate nature, luminous character, cognizant power.
> These are the three kāyas, which as my nature are revealed.

A phenomenon that is not perfectly included in the adornments of the three kāyas—that is, awareness, the all-creating king—cannot be found, however much one may search for it. Everything that appears as a form within the reaches of the world arises as the wheel of the inexhaustible adornments of the enlightened body, which is awareness. All resonating sounds arise as the wheel of the inexhaustible adornments of enlightened speech, which is awareness. All that appears in the mind arises as the wheel of the inexhaustible adornments of the enlightened mind, which is awareness. Even the countless pure fields of the sugatas of the ten directions, all without exception, have their source in this same awareness, the all-creating king. So it is that all pure and impure appearances, of nirvana and samsara, are perfectly contained within the vast expanse of the three kāyas, the nature of the mind, and can never stray beyond it.

* * *

The twelfth section shows that the realms of beings, which appear within the expanse of the enlightened mind, are themselves encompassed by the one sole sphere, which is free from mental elaboration.

> **12. The cities, also, of the six migrations,**
> **Samsara in their nature,**
> **Appear just like reflections in the dharmadhātu.**
> **The various experiences of birth and death, of joy and sorrow**
> **Are like images projected**
> **In the space of the mind's nature.**
> **They seem to be and yet are nonexistent.**
> **Appearing, they are utterly unfounded.**
> **Like clouds up in the sky, they're adventitious,**
> **Arising merely through conditions.**
> **Not existent and not nonexistent,**
> **Their nature is beyond the ontological extremes.**
> **They are utterly encompassed**
> **By the sphere of freedom from elaboration.**

Everything within phenomenal existence and especially the hallucinatory appearances of the cities of the six classes of beings (samsara by their very nature) appear, and yet, in truth, they never stir from awareness, the dharmadhātu, the state of great equality, which is primordially empty. They are like the things one sees reflected in a mirror. They appear, but they do not exist. They simply arise in and of themselves as empty forms. Other than that, they do not exist in the slightest way. The various experiences of birth and death, happiness and sorrow, which we at present undergo, are taken to be truly existent, and we react to them, rejecting some and accepting others, pushing some away and seizing upon others in states of hope and fear. By contrast, for yogis who have realized that birth and death, happiness and suffering have not the slightest reality in the expanse of the dharmadhātu, the nature of the mind, they are simply the appearances of what does not truly exist. For such yogis they are simply phantasmagoria—empty forms like the things that appear in dreams or magical emanations, tricks of sight conjured up by sorcery, or the vision of the earth being covered with gold, which is one of the effects of the drug datura. As it is said in *The All-Creating King*,

> What we call the six migrations—all are empty.
> They are simply labels that have been applied.

Therefore, all such things are nonexistent appearances, like the empty forms of a magical display. But for those who take them for real and who lose themselves in further delusion, they do indeed exist. But the truth is that they are hallucinatory visions. They are groundless, essenceless, without intrinsic being. It is said in *The Great Garuda*,

> Unclouded is the self-experience of awareness,
> Free from causes and conditions.
> Not contrived by anyone through effort,

> It is perfect from the very first.
> This essence is spontaneously present
> And is displayed in objects of the senses.

And,

> Both karmic ripening and latent tendencies
> Are groundless, for by what are they supported?
> Mind is not within the body—it too has no abode.
> It is like a flower suspended in the sky,
> Without support, without a place
> In which to grow or stay.
> Mind cannot be the basis of habitual tendencies.

As these texts say, all the appearances of the six kinds of beings are groundless. They are devoid of causes and conditions; they are beyond striving. There is neither karmic ripening nor latent tendencies. There is neither body nor mind in the same way that the empty sky is not a place in with a flower can grow. All things are encompassed within the one sole sphere of the dharmakāya and are nowhere else. The hallucinatory appearances of the three worlds have no existence; they appear adventitiously. It is like the sky, which in its actual nature is not obscured by clouds. The clouds obscure it only adventitiously owing to circumstantial conditions. Likewise, the dharmatā, awareness, has never been affected by delusion, it is not affected now, and it will not be affected in the future. So it is that nonexistent but clear appearances occur only adventitiously, circumstantially, and apart from this, they have not the slightest reality. It is said in *The Necklace of Pearls*,

> The five afflictions whereby beings are defiled
> In fact do not exist. They are like clouds,
> Which in the sky are adventitious
> And produced by circumstance.
> Arising from the sky, they sink back into it.

To know this is to know the so-called state
Of oneness, indivisibility.

And in *The Commentary on Valid Cognition*, it is said,

The nature of the mind is luminosity;
All stains are adventitious.

All things in both samsara and nirvana are simply phenomena that arise adventitiously, from conditions. Other than that, they have no existence. But neither are they nonexistent like empty space. For phenomena, in their vast oceanic spread, appear clearly with all their specific features. Since they have no intrinsic being whatsoever, whether in terms of existence, nonexistence, both, and neither, they transcend all ontological extremes. Samsara and nirvana are completely encompassed by self-arisen awareness, which is free from all extreme positions of conceptual elaboration and is the one sole all-encompassing sphere.

* * *

The thirteenth section gathers all the foregoing points into great equality, the ultimate vajra expanse.

13. The enlightened mind, the nature of the mind,
Is pure like space and therefore free
From birth and death, from joy and pain.
Without substance and not falling to one side or to another,
It is free of the phenomena of samsara and nirvana.
You cannot point to it as "this."
Utterly immense, just like the vast abyss of space,
Changeless, without movement,
It is present of itself and unconditioned.
It is the vajra heart of luminosity.
It is buddhahood itself.

All things are the field of self-arisen bliss,
Supreme enlightenment, spontaneous equality.

The nature of the mind—self-arisen primordial wisdom, the ultimate enlightened mind free of all conceptual extremes—is utterly pure like the immaculate sky free from the three defects. In itself, it has never been stained by obscuration. It is motionless and unchanging throughout the continuity of time. Open and free from the very first, it is primordial wisdom. It is without the slightest trace of birth and death, happiness and sorrow. It is not a substantial thing and does not fall to one side or another. Not established as anything at all, whether in terms of thing or non-thing, it is primordially free from the phenomena of samsara and nirvana. It is the state of great primordial openness and freedom, the state of utter openness and freedom. It is the fundamental nature just as it is, the primordial wisdom of suchness. There is nothing that stands apart from this ultimate, fundamental nature. Even if the buddhas themselves were to look for it, they would find nothing. As *The All-Creating King* says,

> Mind is suchness.[51]
> All phenomena are suchness.
> In suchness make no alteration—
> Accomplish nothing other than the nature in itself.
> For even if they searched for it,
> The Victors would find nothing
> But the ultimate expanse.

The ultimate enlightened mind is free from all mental elaboration. It cannot be pointed out as this or that by means of words and expressions. And being infinitely spacious, like the vast abyss of the sky, it is beyond all measurement in terms of size and direction. Unchanging and unmoving throughout the three times, it is immutable and thus spontaneously present and unconditioned through cause and circumstance. The nature of the mind is primordial buddhahood, which, in a manner beyond obtaining and eliminating, is the heart or essence endowed with the seven vajra attributes and has the character of luminosity. When their fundamental nature is appraised, the outer and inner worlds—the universe and the beings it contains, the entirety of phenomenal existence—are but the display of the kāyas and wisdoms. They are the field of bliss, primordially self-arisen. They are never outside this primordial, spontaneous equality, supreme enlightenment.

* * *

This concludes the second chapter of *The Precious Treasury of the Dharmadhātu*, which shows that phenomenal existence is a pure buddha field.

3. Metaphors for the Enlightened Mind

The third chapter is a presentation of the metaphorical expressions used to indicate the enlightened mind. It is divided into eleven sections. The first section explains that all phenomena are perfectly and completely subsumed within the state of awareness itself.

> **1. All things are subsumed within**
> **The enlightened, all-subsuming mind.**
> **Nothing is there other than enlightened mind.**
> **By nature, all things are enlightened mind.**

Just as the sweet taste of a small amount of molasses is understood to be the same sweet taste of all molasses, and just as the universe and its inhabitants are contained within the expanse of space, likewise, the minds of all the buddhas, the wisdom of the dharmadhātu, are primordially subsumed within awareness, the enlightened mind. *The All-Creating King* tells us,

> The wisdom of the buddhas of the triple time
> Is all subsumed within myself.
> Within my nature their enlightened body is subsumed;
> Subsumed also is their enlightened speech,
> Subsumed likewise is their enlightened mind.

If it is understood that now in this very moment, the minds of all the buddhas past, present, and to come—the wisdom of the dharmadhātu—are all gathered within the state of awareness, and if one rests in meditative evenness within that awareness, this itself is of greater benefit than to fill the entire world with stupas of gold. This the meaning of this text.

Samsara and nirvana are both subsumed within awareness, the all-creating enlightened mind. Awareness subsumes also all the wisdom qualities of all the buddhas and all the essential teachings of the nine vehicles. There is nothing apart from the enlightened mind—not even so much as an infinitesimal particle. In other words, there is no phenomenon that is not the ultimate enlightened mind. For example, it is important to understand that *The Precious Treasury of the Dharmadhātu*, which, if properly grasped, causes one to understand the crucial points of all nine vehicles, is also awareness, the ultimate enlightened mind, the all-creating king. All things, therefore, of both samsara and nirvana, are by their nature that same ultimate enlightened mind, that all-creating king.

* * *

The first part of the second section shows that of the three elements—namely, the metaphor, the referent [that to which the metaphor refers], and the evidential sign—it is first by way of metaphor that this enlightened mind is understood.

2a. The enlightened mind
Is metaphorically compared with space.
It has no cause. It has no place of birth.
It is not localized.
Transcending speech,
It lies beyond the reach of thought.
"The vast abyss of space"
Will merely indicate it metaphorically.
And since that which has been given as a metaphor
Is not a thing that can be pointed to as "this,"

How could that which is compared with it
Be thought or spoken of?
Understand: this metaphor refers
To its pure nature.

The metaphor used to exemplify the enlightened mind is space. In the same way that space has neither exterior nor interior, neither birth nor death, neither dark nor light, neither movement nor change, neither substance nor characteristics—the ultimate enlightened mind also has neither out nor in, neither birth nor death, neither light nor dark. It has neither substance nor characteristics. It is uncaused and is without a place of arising. It is empty, luminous, free of elaboration. It does not dwell anywhere. It cannot be described as such and such. And not being an object of reference, it lies beyond the reach of thought. This is why awareness, the enlightened mind, can only be indicated metaphorically as being a vast abyss of space—inasmuch as the latter is devoid of color, shape, and recognizable identity. As it is said in *The Lion's Perfect Power*,

> The wisdom mind of all the buddhas,
> The state of evenness, devoid of substance,
> Is primordial wisdom self-appearing, pure like space.
> It is awareness, free of mental movement
> And coterminous with space itself.

Awareness, the state of equality devoid of substance and characteristics—itself the wisdom mind of all the buddhas, self-appearing primordial wisdom, the dharmakāya—is said to be pure like space. And it is the emptiness aspect of the mind's nature that is likened to space. On the other hand, awareness is by nature self-aware, self-cognizing. It is an empty, luminous, unceasing state of knowing, whereas space is devoid of knowledge, and is a mere and total void. From this point of view, awareness and space are unalike. As Shabkar has said in this regard,

> Although the nature of the mind has been compared with space,
> The likeness is but partial.
> Only the mind's emptiness is thus exemplified.
> But the nature of the mind is knowing
> And, being empty, can arise as anything.
> But space has no awareness.
> It is nothing—blank—a total void.
> In this sense, mind is not exemplified by space.

As this text says, it is only in terms of its emptiness aspect that awareness is likened to space. And since that which is cited metaphorically (namely, the vast abyss of space) is itself unestablished—whether in terms of existence or nonexistence, exclusion or inclusion, identity or difference, permanence or impermanence, and so on—it is not something that can be pointed to as a specific entity, as "this" or "that." Likewise, that to which the metaphor refers (namely, awareness, the enlightened mind) is also inconceivable and inexpressible. It is a state of seamless equality, free of all mental elaboration, open and unimpeded. How could it be imagined or described? Furthermore, it should be understood that the space metaphor illustrates only the utterly pure [empty] nature of awareness, the nature of the mind, inasmuch as the latter has no existence whatever and is beyond indication. As it is said in *The All-Creating King*,

> All things have the character of space;
> And space itself has no intrinsic being.
> Space itself has no analogy,
> No measure whereby it may be encompassed.
> All things, leaving none aside,
> Should thus be understood.

With respect to the three elements whereby meaningful comparisons may be made (the metaphorical expression or example, that to which the metaphor refers, and the evidential sign), Longchenpa, in his *Finding Rest in the Nature of the Mind*, cites *The All-Creating King*, which says,

> The mind resembles space.
> That which is referred to is the unborn dharmatā.
> The evidence is the arising of diversity.

* * *

The second part of the second section focuses on what the metaphor refers to.

> **2b. That which is referred to**
> **Is awareness, the enlightened mind,**
> **Self-cognizing, vast as space.**
> **Not within the reach of thought,**
> **It cannot be described or pointed out.**
> **Luminous, unmoving,**
> **An immense expanse of luminosity,**
> **It is uncreated, present of itself,**
> **With neither height nor breadth—**
> **The vast sphere of the dharmakāya,**
> **The essence of enlightenment.**

As shown in the text just cited from *The All-Creating King*, the metaphor of space is applied to the enlightened mind and what is being referred to is the unborn dharmatā—that is, the ultimate reality of things. The evidence for this is that the mind is unceasing in its nature. Of these three elements, the present stanza deals with what is being referred to—namely, unborn, empty awareness. Self-cognizing awareness, the ultimate enlightened mind, is an immense, all-pervading expanse. It is like space, which is immeasurable in terms of the cardinal and intermediate directions, zenith, and nadir. This ultimate enlightened mind is not within the reach of thought. It cannot be encompassed by the ordinary mind, and in itself, it cannot be indicated by metaphors. Speech cannot express it. It is beyond all the elaborations of the mind. This awareness, great, primordial emptiness, is moreover an immense expanse of luminosity, in which all the attributes of the sambhogakāya (empty by nature but with the character of luminosity) are naturally present, primordially unwavering, and beyond all movement and change.

Since this self-arisen primordial wisdom is from the very beginning spontaneously present as the essence of the dharmakāya, it is referred to in the root text as uncreated and present of itself. Uncreated and spontaneously present, awareness has never stirred from the vast expanse, the all-embracing one sole sphere of the dharmakāya, the essence of enlightenment, which is free of the webs of conceptual elaboration in terms of height and breadth.

* * *

The third part of the second section discusses the reason for saying that the nature of awareness, the enlightened mind, is pure, vast, and without limits or extremes.

> **2c. The evidential sign is**
> **That anything at all arises**
> **Through the awareness's creative power.**
> **But when arising happens,**
> **There's no place for such arising**
> **And nothing that in fact arises.**
> **"Arising," thus, is just a word.**
> **It is like space, when you examine it.**
> **Everything is utterly contained**
> **In seamless great equality—**
> **An all-pervading space**
> **Devoid of apprehending subject**
> **And an object to be apprehended.**

Of the three aspects—metaphor, referent, and evidential sign—this stanza discusses the sign or reason. Awareness, the nature of the mind, which is likened to space, is taken as the subject, the basis of argument. That it is unborn is posited as the thesis to be established. The evidential sign given as a proof that the nature of the mind is unborn is that the ceaseless arising [of phenomena and the ordinary mind,] through the creative power of the mind's nature, is itself primordially empty and free from mental elaboration.

Therefore, the evidence that the nature of the mind is unborn is that through the creative power of the mind's nature (primordially empty and free from elaboration), anything at all may arise in unceasing manifestation. As with the images of things reflected in a mirror, or like the stars and planets appearing on the surface of the limpid sea—even though all such appearing things seem to arise ceaselessly in all their diversity—the truth is that in the very moment of their arising, there is neither a place for such things to arise nor are there any objects actually arising. Being empty, they arise. Arising, they are empty.

"Arising" is no more than a word, and when it is examined, one finds that, apart from merely appearing, it has no existence. It is groundless and rootless. It is just like space. This means that all the phenomena of samsara and nirvana in their oceanlike infinity are gathered and contained in the immense expanse of seamless great equality. They subside upon arising, vanishing into emptiness. Whatever arises is encompassed by—it does not change from—the ultimate, uncontrived luminosity, the one sole sphere of the dharmakāya, which is the infinite, all-pervading expanse devoid of subject and object of apprehension.

Therefore, the evidence that proves that spacelike ultimate reality is unborn is the reasoning that shows that all things that unceasingly arise are a state of seamless great equality. It is as Longchenpa says in the autocommentary,

> Conventionally, the subject, the nature of awareness, can be said to be unborn, spacelike, and beyond both thought and word. This is because the mind that arises as the creative power—in the state where both awareness

> and mind are of the same nature—cannot be identified and is like space, free of mental elaboration.

The All-Creating King also says,

> The sign is that imputed nature
> Is enlightened mind.

The proof that the nature of the mind is unborn is the fact that all the phenomena of the imputed nature, arising in all their diversity, are not outside the enlightened mind. This is how it is demonstrated. Moreover, it is said in *The Lion's Perfect Power,*

> In the sky of dharmatā without a name,
> The garuda soars, awareness in its self-display,
> Free of any object, free of features.
> Awareness, uncontrived and self-cognizing,
> Is the very taste of bliss.
> Within the ocean of the dharmatā,
> Self-arisen, free of mind's elaboration,
> Swim the golden fishes,
> Free of substance, free of features,
> Gathered in the single savor
> Of the self-display of dharmakāya.

This and many other texts indicate that when awareness arises as objects, and when these objects are purified through [the realization of] the seamlessness of their arising and subsiding, they are all seen to be completely encompassed by the dharmatā, which is likened in this quotation to the sky and ocean. Awareness in its unceasing aspect is indicated by the garuda and the golden fishes.

* * *

The third section summarizes the meaning of the three preceding points as the dharmatā beyond center and circumference.

3. Self-arisen primordial wisdom, ultimate reality,
Is completely boundless.
This is clearly shown
By metaphor, by referent, and by sign.
This spacelike nature,
Wherein all is gathered without difference or exclusion,
Is established by these three great nails.
In the vast womb of the ultimate expanse,
The vast, supreme state of equality,
All is from the outset equal—
Neither earlier nor later, neither good nor bad.
Such is the wisdom mind
Of Samantabhadra-Vajrasattva.

Because awareness, self-arisen primordial wisdom, ultimate reality—which transcends all ontological extremes, all thought and word—is free of every limitation and of falling in one direction or another, it is wide-open dharmatā, devoid of spatial reference. This is why it is said to be boundless. But since we need to understand correctly the fundamental nature of this self-arisen primordial wisdom, it is presented, as previously, using metaphor, referent, and evidential sign. In this way, self-cognizing primordial wisdom, just as it is, is clearly shown. As it is said in *The All-Creating King*,

> If you wish to understand this thing with certainty
> Adopt the metaphor of space.
> That which is referred to is the unborn dharmatā.
> The fact that mind is ceaseless is the evidential sign.
> Thus spacelike dharmatā is indicated
> By a metaphor that likens it to space.

As this text says, if one wishes to realize correctly what the metaphor refers to (namely, awareness) it is necessary to consider the metaphor itself whereby awareness is likened to space. In the same way that space has neither outside nor inside, neither change nor movement, neither birth nor death, neither clarity nor obscuration, the same is true of self-arisen awareness. It is also empty. This is the referent: unborn ultimate reality, empty, luminous, and unceasing, the primordial wisdom of equality free of mental elaboration. The evidential sign is that the ordinary discursive mind is itself impossible to identify in being itself free of elaboration like space. For it is of the same nature as unceasing awareness, the nature of the mind, and arises as its creative power. This is why the metaphor of space is applied to spacelike dharmatā. As for the previously mentioned evidential sign, it is said that one should understand that the unceasing appearances of the nature of the mind are inseparable from awareness itself.

The All-Creating King declares,

> Ultimate reality, which cannot be observed,
> Is revealed by calling it "the unobservable."
> For ultimate reality, which cannot be described in words,
> Must be referred to as "the indescribable,"
> Revealing thus its nature inconceivable.

Ultimate reality cannot be observed, and therefore, when one has to mention it, it is referred to as unobservable, free of extremes, beyond the ordinary mind, and so on. And although ultimate reality cannot be expressed in words, when labels are applied to it, it is qualified as ineffable, free of conceptual elaboration, and beyond the intellect.

The All-Creating King declares,

> That which is in brief revealed
> Elucidates the nature
> Of what is being referred to.
> This referent, myself, will thus be understood.
> You may with words discourse upon it all you wish,
> But you will not encounter me.

That which is briefly expounded here through metaphor, referent, and evidential sign (these being a way to understand awareness) actually elucidates, or comments on, what is being referred to—namely, the all-creating king himself. It is thus that one should understand it. But if through such metaphor, referent, and evidential sign, one fails to grasp it—namely, "myself, the all-creating king"—one may discourse upon it with all kinds of words and phrases, but one will never actually meet, or come to grips with, that which "all-creates." One will be powerless to understand its fundamental nature precisely as it is. It would be like placing an elephant in the middle of a group of blind people and asking them to describe its shape. They will all give different accounts. It is as *The All-Creating King* declares,

> You will stray from me, and I shall be obscured.
> You will never see the essence of phenomena.

So it is that if one wants to understand self-arisen awareness, the vast and all-pervading spacelike expanse, it must be indicated and understood by means of the three elements of metaphor, referent, and evidential sign. It must be comprehensively set forth and established through these three great nails of immutability. If their meaning is correctly grasped, all the phenomena of samsara and nirvana will be seen to be gathered within the expanse of the one awareness, the all-creating king. It will be possible to realize their fundamental nature just as it is. If one realizes it thus, one will see that everything in samsara and nirvana—all good and evil, all happiness and suffering, and so on, without any differentiation or exclusion—is perfectly and altogether included within the womb of the ultimate expanse, the supremely vast state of all-pervading equality, all-embracing empty awareness beyond ontological extremes. Therefore, all the phenomena of samsara and nirvana, without any of the distinctions of past and future, good and evil, are indicated through the metaphor of space. And the realization that they are beyond mental elaboration and that they transcend thought and word is the wisdom mind of Samantabhadra and Vajrasattva.

The realization, through the metaphor of space, that awareness is great emptiness is described as Samantabhadra, who embodies the emptiness aspect. From the point of view of its luminous character, however, it is described as Vajrasattva. And from the standpoint of the indivisibility of emptiness and luminosity, it is described as the ultimate wisdom of nondual Samantabhadra-Vajrasattva. As we find in *The All-Creating King*,

> The all-embracing wisdom of Samantabhadra
> Subsumes all things however they appear
> Without distinctions of acceptance or rejection, good or bad,
> Within the All-Creating One.
> Vajrasattva's all-embracing wisdom
> Subsumes all things within the state
> Beyond both birth and ceasing.

When all appearances, without the distinctions of good and bad, acceptance and rejection, manifest as all-creating awareness (the fundamental nature of great emptiness), this corresponds to the all-embracing wisdom of Samantabhadra. By contrast, the all-embracing wisdom of Vajrasattva is the luminous character of awareness beyond birth and cessation. *The All-Creating King* goes on to say,

> Śākyamuni and the six preceding buddhas,
> The one thousand and two buddhas,
> And other buddhas numerous as atoms,
> And all whose acts bring benefit
> Through body, speech, and mind—
> Arise through the enlightened body, speech, and mind.
> The ways of benefiting beings

Through the enlightened body, speech, and mind,
Are all intrinsically encompassed by the All-Creating One.

As this text says, of the seven enlightened beings in the line of the buddhas (Vipaśyin, Śikhin, Viśvabhuk, Krakuccandra, Kaṇakamuni, Kāśyapa, and Śākyamuni), and of the thousand and two buddhas of this fortunate kalpa, as well as of all other buddhas equal in number to all the atoms of the world, there is not a single one who is not gathered within awareness, the all-creating enlightened mind. It is therefore said that when one settles, if only for a single instant, in meditative evenness, in empty awareness free of all mental elaboration, in that unceasing state of empty luminosity, one is inseparably blended with the wisdom of all the buddhas just mentioned. Similarly, of all the sublime qualities of the enlightened body, speech, and mind, there is not a single one that is not encompassed by awareness, the all-creating enlightened mind.

* * *

The fourth section, which shows that awareness is like the essence of the sun, is divided into two parts: a brief description and a detailed explanation. The first part is as follows.

4a. The enlightened mind is like the very essence of the sun,
Luminous intrinsically, unconditioned from the first.
There is nothing that might darken it.
It is open, unimpeded, present of itself,
Free of mind's elaboration,
Ultimate reality devoid of thought.

This section shows that awareness is like the heart or essence of the sun. As we have seen previously, the ultimate nature of awareness is empty like space. In its luminous character, however, it is shown to be like the sun. In other words, although the ultimate nature of awareness is empty, this is not to be understood in the sense of a mere absence, as when one says that there is no tea or no water. Neither is it like the utterly nonexistent horns of a rabbit. It is not empty in the sense of being the blank nothingness of a nonaffirming negation. On the contrary, awareness is by character naturally luminous, and thus it is compared with the very essence of the sun.

Awareness, the enlightened mind, is by nature empty. But although it is like space, primordially void and beyond all mental elaboration, utterly without existence, nevertheless, the character of this emptiness is by nature luminous like the essence of the sun. And just as the sun is, of itself, intrinsically luminous, causing the darkness to vanish, the same is true of awareness, the enlightened mind. It too is luminous of itself and thanks to it, the darkness of ignorance that is to be eliminated vanishes into groundlessness. Awareness, therefore, is comparable to the sun.

Awareness, in which luminosity and emptiness are inseparable, is unconditioned from the very first. In its own nature, it has never been veiled by ignorance, action, defilement, and so on. And since there is within it nothing that could darken it, open and unimpeded awareness is, from the very beginning, spontaneously present of itself as inner and outwardly radiating luminosity, free of any obscuration. Since it is devoid of the four ontological extremes and so on, it is untouched by mental elaboration. It is primordial wisdom free of all discursive thought. It is said in brief to be the infinitely spreading, all-pervading ultimate expanse of great primordial emptiness, which is forever inseparable from the state of ultimate reality, empty, luminous, and unceasing. As it is said in *Awareness Self-Arisen*,

> The supreme dharmakāya, free from all the four extremes,
> Is, like pure crystal, stainless luminosity.
> The dharmakāya, free from all extremes,
> Is the kāya that drives away obscurity.
> It is immaculate and scatters darkness

Like the circle of the sun.
Dispelling the obscurity of all the four extremes,
It is, primordially, present of itself.

Because the supreme dharmakāya is empty of the four ontological extremes and is of a luminous character, its stainless luminosity is exemplified by a crystal. Moreover, this dharmakāya, which is likened to the circle of the sun, is shown to be spontaneously present as the dispeller of the ignorance that is to be eliminated.

* * *

The second part of the fourth section gives a detailed explanation of awareness, which is likened to the essence of the sun.

4b. Empty, it is dharmakāya;
Luminous, it is sambhogakāya;
Radiant, it is nirmāṇakāya.
These three kāyas are inseparable.
Since these qualities are from the outset present of themselves,
They have never been obscured
By the gloom of flaws and faults.
And in the past and future,
Through the course of time,
They are one in being free
Of movement and of change.
They are one in their pervasion
Of all buddhas and all beings.
They are what is called the self-arisen and enlightened mind.

Since the nature of the mind is free from all conceptual extremes and is therefore empty like space, it is, from this standpoint, said to be the dharmakāya. Since the character of its emptiness is luminous like the essence of the sun, it is accordingly said to be the sambhogakāya. And since it is radiant like the five-colored lights that emerge from a crystal when the sun shines on it, it is called (from the point of view of this ceaseless arising of diversity) the nirmāṇakāya. But though referred to by these different appellations, the three kāyas are not in fact separate and distinct. They are primordially inseparable. As it has been said,

> When the three kāyas are introduced,
> One speaks of them as different.
> And yet in truth they are a single ultimate expanse.
> Beloved children, do not wrongly think of them as
> different.

It is further said in *The King of Concentration Sūtra*,

> The sugatagarbha pervades all beings.

It has been said that it is correct and appropriate to cite the lower scriptures in support of higher teachings—like enthroning a commoner as a king. Indeed the sugatagarbha is regarded as the indivisibility of the three kāyas. When speaking of the ground, from the point of view of its ultimate nature, it is said to be empty. From the point of view of its luminous character, it is said to be the inseparable union of luminosity and emptiness. And from the point of view of its cognizant potency, it is the inseparable union of awareness and emptiness. Although the ultimate nature, luminous character, and cognizant potency are each described in different terms as the three kāyas, they are never separate from the one awareness itself. As it is said in *The All-Creating King*,

> I, the all-creating king, reveal
> How only in a manner of speech
> Do the three kāyas come
> From the three aspects uncontrived
> Of my own nature.

> In truth, by nature, the three kāyas
> Never stir from suchness.

As this text says, awareness, the all-creating enlightened mind, englobes the dharmakāya, which is the uncontrived ultimate nature; it englobes the sambhogakāya, which is the uncontrived luminous character; and it englobes the nirmāṇakāya, which is uncontrived cognizant potency. Although they are thus designated as three uncontrived aspects, they never in fact stir from awareness or suchness. Although they are individually designated, the three kāyas have never existed to the slightest degree as items that can be separately identified. They are primordially and spontaneously present as qualities of the dharmakāya, which is unwavering, beyond all movement and change throughout the whole of time. *The All-Creating King* says,

> Indeed the dharmakāya, just a name,
> Never stirs from suchness . . .
> Indeed the sambhogakāya
> Never stirs from suchness . . .
> And finally indeed the nirmāṇakāya
> Never stirs from suchness . . .

Awareness, the all-creating king—motionless and unchanging throughout the three times—has never been deluded, is not deluded now, and will never be deluded in the future. Therefore, it is not obscured by the gloom of the faults and flaws of the hallucinatory appearances of samsara. This primordial state of purity, which is free and open from the very beginning, can never be divided according to the three times. It has neither past nor future. From the beginning, it is without movement or change. Within the one sole sphere of awareness, the three kāyas are of one taste. Awareness, the all-creating king, in which the three kāyas are undivided, pervades all buddhas and all beings, samsara and nirvana, bringing them all together into a single taste. This all-pervading state of equality—namely, awareness—is itself called self-arisen primordial wisdom, the ultimate enlightened mind.

* * *

The fifth section shows that phenomenal existence manifests within the state of awareness.

> **5. Its creative power may arise as anything at all—**
> **As realization or the absence of the same,**
> **As phenomenal existence,**
> **The world and all the beings it contains,**
> **And as all the various experiences of living beings.**

Within the mirrorlike character of awareness, the all-creating enlightened mind, the creative power arises as anything at all in the manner of reflections, abiding within the ground. If one speaks in terms of ground, path, and result, then the ground awareness, the dharmatā, is the ultimate nature. The path consists in familiarizing oneself with this ground so that at the time of the result, the ground itself is actualized. And thus it is through the realization of that same ground awareness that the pure forms of the Victorious Ones and their buddha fields are actualized. If there is no realization and one strays into delusion, phenomenal existence manifests—the world and its inhabitants, along with the whole range of experiences that living beings, inconceivable in number, must undergo. But though they all arise, awareness itself remains primordially pure, beyond all movement and change. From the very beginning, it is untainted by all such arisings. It is like a mirror, which is unstained by whatever is reflected in it.

* * *

The sixth section shows that in the very moment of their occurrence, phenomena are without intrinsic being.

6. All such things occur,
And yet they lack intrinsic being.
They're like the water in a mirage,
Like dreams, like echoes, like emanated apparitions,
Or like images reflected in a glass,
Like cities of gandharvas, or like tricks of sight.
Clearly they appear and yet are nonexistent—
Groundless, unsupported,
They are mere appearances arising adventitiously.
Understand that they are fleeting in the present moment.

However the unceasing appearances of samsara and nirvana may arise through the creative power of awareness, none of them has the slightest existence apart from awareness, the enlightened mind. They have no being in themselves. They appear but are nonexistent, just like the water in a mirage, which is perceived [as water] but has no existence apart from the mirage. They are like the visions of a dream, which appear during sleep and have no existence apart from the state of sleep. They are like echoes, which have no existence apart from the cliff from which they resound. They are like the apparitions shown forth by masters of illusion and which have no existence apart from their conjurers. They are like the things reflected in a mirror from which they have no separate existence. They are like cities of the gandharvas, castles in the clouds, which appear above a plain in the light of the setting sun. They have no existence apart from such conditions. They are like tricks of sight, as when a single form appears as multiple when one presses one's eyes—multiple forms that are merely clear appearances with no existence separate from the original single form. They are in truth groundless, unsupported, merely adventitious appearances.

Take for example the things that appear in a dream. They had no existence in the past, before the occurrence of sleep, nor will they continue to exist when one has woken up. And yet, during the period of slumber, they appear. In just the same way, the hallucinatory appearances [of this present life] have no existence at the time of the primordial ground, prior to the emergence of buddhas (who are free) and sentient beings (who are deluded). Neither will they exist at the end, at the time of the result, in the state beyond suffering. On the other hand, they do indeed manifest, in this present but passing moment of time, to minds that are deluded. Even so, at the time of their appearance, it should be understood that these phenomena have no existence whatsoever. They are empty forms, nonexistent and yet appearing.

So it is that phenomena lack intrinsic being—they are unreal throughout all the three phases of arising, abiding, and cessation. It is as we find in *The Root Stanzas of the Middle Way*,

> Like a dream and like a mirage,
> Like a city of gandharvas,
> So arising and abiding
> And cessation have been taught.[52]

* * *

The seventh section shows that appearances do not stir from the ultimate state.

> **7. Within the nature of the enlightened mind,**
> **Spontaneously present,**
> **Samsara and nirvana manifest,**
> **Unceasingly displayed in their array.**
> **Understand that this display**
> **Is utterly encompassed by the ultimate expanse**
> **And never strays beyond this primal state.**

Awareness, the nature of the ultimate enlightened mind, primordially uncontrived, self-arisen, and present of itself, never transcends the state of great emptiness, which is like space and is beyond all mental elaboration. It does not exist as anything in itself and yet its ability to arise as anything at all is primordially complete. Therefore, the display of its creative power unfolds unceasingly as the diverse array of the conditioned existence of samsara and the peace of nirvana—like rainbows that appear in the sky or as the reflections of the stars and planets appearing in a watery surface.

All these manifestations, the diversity of outer and inner phenomena, samsara and nirvana, the world and its inhabitants, are fully encompassed by the expanse of awareness, the dharmatā. One should understand therefore that they never stir from the immense, all-pervading expanse of primordial emptiness. *The All-Creating King* says,

> The root of all phenomena
> Is the enlightened, all-creating mind.
> However things arise, they share my nature.
> However they occur, they are but my display.

All things in samsara and nirvana—from the very instant that they appear—never move from the enlightened mind itself.

* * *

The eighth section shows that since all things are perfectly contained in the ultimate expanse, they are a great perfection.

> **8. There, all things are the enlightened mind—**
> **One is perfectly contained,**
> **All are perfectly contained,**
> **The unconditioned too is perfectly contained.**
> **Their nature is primordial wisdom,**
> **Self-arisen, perfect of itself.**

There [within the ultimate expanse], all things of both samsara and nirvana are never outside awareness, the all-creating enlightened mind, the immense state of equality. Consequently, the one sole sphere of awareness is itself also perfectly, and from the very beginning, contained within the expanse of the all-creating enlightened mind—on account of which, it is said that "one is perfectly contained."

It is said in *The Unwritten Tantra*,

> Since I am neither one nor two,
> All things belonging to the one sole sphere
> Are perfectly and utterly contained in me.

And,

> Since I am neither self nor other,
> The aspects of awareness
> Are perfectly and utterly contained in me.

Likewise, all the phenomena of the ground, path, and result are perfectly included within great emptiness, the ultimate expanse. This refers to all the hallucinatory phenomena present at the time of the ground, such as the aggregates, the elements, and the sense fields. It also refers to the various vehicles, the inconceivable approaches to the path and the unimaginable attainments of the result, which are present at the time of the path. And finally, it refers to the twenty-five attributes of the result, such as the four kāyas and the five primordial wisdoms, which are present at the time of the result. Therefore, the root verse says that "all are perfectly contained."

It is not only conditioned phenomena that are perfectly contained within the expanse of great emptiness, the ultimate space. Unconditioned phenomena—that is, the profound aspects of the fundamental nature—are also perfectly contained in it. It is said in *The Unwritten Tantra*,

> Since I am free of bias and division,
> Secret primal wisdom is completely, perfectly,
> Contained in me.

And,

Since in me appearances are beyond cessation,
The three aspects of the ultimate expanse[53]
Are completely, perfectly, contained in me.

And,

Since I am free from birth and death,
Cessation is completely, perfectly, contained in me.
Since I am free of out and in,
Luminosity is completely, perfectly, contained in me.
Since I am free of emptiness and real existence,
Appearance is completely, perfectly, contained in me.
Since I am free of referential focus,
Visual form is utterly and perfectly contained in me.

The meaning of these texts is as follows. Since I, the all-creating king, am without true existence in terms of outer and inner, arising and cessation, all appearing phenomena—outer or inner, arising or ceasing—manifest without impediment. They are like reflections in a mirror. It is precisely because the forms reflected have no existence that they can appear to be *in* the mirror. If they existed as they appear, there would be no way for them to arise therein. And there would be no way for all the visual forms of the vast outer universe and its inner inhabitants to be accommodated within a tiny mirror—just as, on the conventional level, it is impossible for two atoms to coincide in the same place. So it is that anything at all may appear, provided that it does not truly exist. Conversely, if it does truly exist, it cannot appear at all. This is the basic import of the view of dependent arising, the emptiness of the Middle Way. As [Mipham Rinpoche remarks in his commentary] *The Adornment of the Middle Way*,

If of all things there were one existing truly,
Not one of them could ever manifest.
But since not even one has true existence,
The varied range of things is limitless.[54]

If among all objects of knowledge there were a single one that existed truly, not only would it be unable to manifest but nothing else could manifest either. But since of all phenomena there is not a single one that truly exists, the limitless appearances of samsara and nirvana are able to occur.

Therefore, the tantra says, "Since I, the all-creating king, neither arise nor cease, I appear to arise and cease." Thus the fundamental nature of all phenomena is self-arisen primordial wisdom, uncontrived and spontaneously perfect. Awareness is not a kind of voidness. It is referred to as great perfection because it perfectly includes all phenomena and their nature, the two truths and the three purities. As it is said in *The Secret Essence* in *The Illusory Net of Manifestation*,

> A single cause, the way of syllables,
> Empowering strength, direct perception—
> With these four understandings,
> All things are the great king, truly perfect.[55]

* * *

The ninth section shows that because awareness has no existence whatever and yet can manifest as anything, all things arise unceasingly in this unborn state.

> **9. The enlightened mind does not exist**
> **As manifest, unmanifest, samsara or nirvana,**
> **As outer things or inner things.**
> **Yet through the stirring of creative power**
> **A various display arises naturally:**
> **Phenomenal existence, samsara and nirvana.**

Awareness, the enlightened mind in itself, has no existence whatever. It is the primordially, utterly pure nature, the empty but luminous dharmakāya. It exists neither as manifest nor as unmanifest—that is, neither as samsara nor nirvana, neither as outer nor as inner phenomena. It is the ultimate nature, which is utterly free of all adventitious impurities. It is primordially pure emptiness endowed with supreme qualities. Nevertheless, through the stirring of the creative power of awareness, and depending on realization or the absence of realization, there naturally arises the various display of phenomenal existence, samsara or nirvana. It is like a sphere of crystal, which does not exist as anything other than a pure, transparent object but which, when it meets with favorable adventitious conditions like sunlight, sends out a brilliant array of five-colored light.

* * *

The tenth section shows that since awareness in itself does not exist as anything at all, it is beyond both appearance and emptiness and cannot be indicated or described. Consequently, whatever arises within it is a false appearance that has never existed.

> **10. In their moment of arising,**
> **Things are by their nature empty forms.**
> **Because there's no arising, they appear to arise.**
> **Yet in their moment of appearing,**
> **There is nothing that arises.**
> **Because there's no cessation, they appear to cease.**
> **And yet they do not cease;**
> **They are illusions, empty forms.**
> **While remaining, there is nothing that remains.**
> **For what remains is groundless,**
> **And it neither comes nor goes.**
> **However things appear, they do not exist as such.**
> **They are without intrinsic being.**
> **They are no more than names.**

One can take any appearing object of the six consciousnesses—a form that is the object of the eyes, a sound that is the object of the ears, and so on. From the very moment of their first arising, such objects are themselves nonexistent appearances. By their nature, they are empty forms arising externally. They appear to arise through the creative power of primordially pure unborn emptiness. If their arising were truly real, they would not be able to appear to arise, as was explained above:

> If of all things there were one existing truly,
> Not one of them could ever manifest.

Therefore, it is because there is no such thing as truly existent arising that phenomena appear to arise. For the sake of argument, take a vase placed on the ground in front of you. It has no arising precisely because it appears to arise. This must be so because if something appears to arise, its arising has to be without true existence. This is why the root text says, "Because there's no arising, they appear to arise." And in *The Scripture of the Summarized Wisdom of All the Buddhas*, it is said,

> *Emaho!* A wondrous and a marvelous thing,
> A secret all the perfect buddhas know!
> Because there is no birth are all things born.
> In the moment of their being born, they are unborn!

That is, because in truth they have no birth, all appearances are born unceasingly. Yet the fact is that in the very moment of their birth or arising, [phenomena] never experience birth. Therefore, as the text says, "they are unborn."

> *Emaho!* A wondrous and a marvelous thing,
> A secret all the perfect buddhas know!
> Because there's no cessation, all things cease.
> In the moment that they cease, they do not cease.

> *Emaho!* A wondrous and a marvelous thing,
> A secret all the perfect buddhas know!

Because there's no dwelling, all things dwell.
In the moment of their dwelling, they do not dwell.

That is, because in truth there is no dwelling, all things on the conventional level dwell. Yet the fact is that in the very moment of their dwelling, [phenomena] never experience dwelling. Therefore they do not remain.

Emaho! A wondrous and a marvelous thing,
A secret all the perfect buddhas know!
Because there is no going and coming, all things go and come.
In the moment that they go and come, they neither go nor come.

That is, because in truth there is no going and no coming, appearances go and come unceasingly. But in the very moment of their going and coming, phenomena neither go nor come. This matter is similarly explained in *The Scripture of the Gathering of the Great Assembly*.

So it is that all phenomena of both samsara and nirvana are unborn precisely because they appear to be born. They do not cease because they appear to cease. They do not remain because they appear to remain. They neither come nor go because they appear to come and go. This is the sufficient proof. When, however, this point is established in this way, it appears contradictory to those who are new to the subject. But it is not contradictory. For as Mipham says,

The sense of words that seem to contradict
Is vital for the path that's free of contradiction.
In the pith instructions on the view and action,
Check this secret point and taste its meaning![56]

It is because of the crucial point of being without birth or arising that phenomena seem to be born. And yet their actual nature is such that in the very moment that they appear, these same phenomena are groundless and rootless. They are free of objective reference; they are open and unimpeded. Therefore, nothing whatsoever is born. Likewise, because they have no cessation, things appear to cease. If cessation were truly existent, nothing could appear to cease. If things appear to cease, this is because cessation has no true existence. Consequently, since "unceasingness" (the absence of cessation) is the genuine fundamental nature of phenomena, things that conventionally appear to cease—like last night's dreams—are empty forms. They are like magical illusions, nonexistent appearances that are perceived. Similarly, in the very moment that things remain, there is no such thing as a truly existent remaining. And that which [apparently] remains is groundless, rootless, and without objective reference, free of going and coming, and never outside the state of equality, which is empty and free of mental elaboration.

All the phenomena of samsara and nirvana are without existence from the very first. From the beginning, they are empty by their nature and similar to space. No matter how they manifest, they do not exist as such. They are like the things reflected in a mirror, like rainbows in the sky, and like stars and planets reflected in the sea. So it is that, bereft of intrinsic being, they are in fact no more than names.

* * *

The eleventh section sums up the meaning of this chapter, explaining that no matter how things appear, they lack intrinsic being.

11. These appearances moreover
Self-arise through the creative power.
Thus only figuratively are they said
To be dependently arisen by their nature.
In the very moment they appear
By virtue of creative power,
They do so in a manner free
From such divisions and extremes

As the arising and the absence of arising.
Creative power is also just a figurative label.
It too lacks all reality.
Nothing in the least stirs ever
From the enlightened mind,
Which is the state beyond all movement and all change.

The pure and impure appearances of nirvana and samsara, which variously arise, are indeed awareness, the dharmadhātu. This is devoid of all intrinsic being and yet is the spontaneously present agent of whatever manifests. In other words, the different appearances of samsara and nirvana arise naturally and unceasingly through the creative power of awareness. All that occurs is like a magical illusion, like a dream. And as the root text says, it is nothing but an appearance that arises dependently. Phenomena are not established except as what arises within the sphere of emptiness. As it is said,

Except as what arises in dependence
There are no existent things.
Thus except for what is empty,
There are no existent things.[57]

All things are by their nature dependently arisen, and since this is so, appearance and emptiness being thus united, it is only figuratively that they are referred to as "conventional appearances." Otherwise, they have not the slightest degree of existence. In the very moment that the phenomena of samsara and nirvana appear, occurring through the creative power of awareness, these same phenomena, within awareness itself, are beyond extremes and distinctions such as the place of arising, the thing that arises, the arising, and the nonarising. Appearing, they are empty; empty, they appear. Appearance does not cancel the fact of emptiness and emptiness does not occlude appearance. It is important to understand that appearance and emptiness are not two; they are one and the same.

Whatever arises through creative power is indeed a dependent arising wherein appearance and emptiness are indivisible. As the root text says, it arises merely in a figurative, or metaphorical, sense. In awareness itself, it has no intrinsic being. It never at any time shifts from the state of the equality of the dharmatā. It never goes beyond the union of awareness and emptiness, which is forever motionless and unchanging. The stars and planets seem to arise, reflected, on the limpid surface of the sea, but in truth they do not arise there. There is nothing but the limpid ocean, the place of their arising. For stars and planets, as they appear, never move from the expanse of the firmament. And this meeting of the ocean with the stars and planets in the sky has never occurred in the sense of a real encounter of disparate entities. Other than being the appearance of just an empty reflection, it could never happen in truth. In the same way, the phenomena of samsara and nirvana have never in the slightest way moved from the expanse of the ultimate enlightened mind.

The homage at the beginning of Nāgārjuna's *Root Stanzas of the Middle Way* declares,

> To him who taught that things arise dependently,
> Not ceasing, not arising,
> Not annihilated nor yet permanent,
> Not coming and not going,
> Not different, not the same:
> The stilling of all thoughts, and perfect peace—
> To him, the best of teachers, perfect Buddha, I bow down.

This text actually comes from *The Jewel Mound Sūtra*,[58] and Nāgārjuna, regarding it as authoritative, used it as a verse of homage for his *Root Stanzas of the Middle Way*. He did so because it summarizes the entire meaning of his verses.

When the Buddha, our Teacher, set forth the Dharma, he taught the path of dependent arising. All phenomena are unceasing in the sense that they arise unceasingly within the expanse of awareness. Though they arise unceasingly, they have never in truth arisen. They are unborn. They are nonexistent from the very beginning. Yet this is not to say that they are nothing, like the horns of a rabbit. Neither are they discontinuous in the sense of the manifest impermanence of something that existed in the past but that ceases to exist at some later time. And they are not permanent in the sense of things that are said to be permanent, in that they do not change from past to future. And since they do not come from some other place and do not depart elsewhere, they neither come nor go. As it is said,

> In what is said to go and come there is no going.
> And in what does not go there is no going.
> Apart from going and not going,
> So-called going cannot be conceived.

Things are neither different from each other nor the same. The stilling of all thought is set forth as peace. And the one who set it forth was the one in whom the qualities of elimination and realization were complete— namely the Buddha, the best, the supreme of all the teachers of the world. It is to him that this homage is made. Beside him there are many in this world who have proclaimed their teachings—the gods, the nāgas, Brahmā, Śakra, and so on. But they are merely the proclaimers of opinions. Brahmā, for example, said that the four great elements originated in himself—regarding which it is said in *The Treasury of Abhidharma*, "Brahmā is a deceiver." It is said that once Brahmā requested teachings in the presence of the Buddha, and on that occasion, the noble Aśvajit asked him, "Who created the world and its inhabitants?" Brahmā said, "It was I, Brahmā, the great Brahmā." And yet it was as if he cast his deceitful words into the wind. Indeed, all such sayings are no more than windy words. By contrast, the Bhagavan Buddha is the supreme teacher, for he enjoys the four fearlessnesses.[59]

* * *

This concludes the commentary to the third chapter of *The Precious Treasury of the Dharmadhātu*, which speaks of the metaphors used to refer to the enlightened mind.

4. The Nature of the Enlightened Mind

This fourth chapter sets forth the nature of the enlightened mind. It is divided into ten sections. In the first section, awareness, the nature of the enlightened mind, is ascertained so that what has previously been revealed through the use of metaphor may now be thoroughly understood.

1. The nature of the all-encompassing enlightened mind
Does not appear, it transcends appearance.
It is not empty, it transcends emptiness.
It is not existent, it has no substance and no properties.
It is not nonexistent, it pervades samsara and nirvana.
Not existent and not nonexistent, present of itself and even,
It is the vast primordial expanse.
With no extremes, with no divisions,
It is groundless, rootless, and devoid of substance.

It is said in our tradition of the Great Perfection that throughout phenomenal existence, samsara and nirvana, there is nothing that is not encompassed by the expanse of awareness. It therefore follows that self-cognizing primordial wisdom pervades the whole of samsara and nirvana. As it is said,

> The sugatagarbha utterly pervades all beings.

In reference to this, certain people, beginners in the practice, who have not yet recognized awareness, may have the following doubt. According to the sutra teachings, they say, there is a difference between a pillar and the consciousness that apprehends the pillar. This suggests that although the sugatagarbha pervades all living beings, it does not pervade [inanimate objects like] earth, rocks, mountains, and cliffs. Although the sugatagarbha may be said to permeate the whole of samsara and nirvana in the sense of its being the dharmadhātu (as object), it does not do so in the sense of its being self-cognizing, self-knowing awareness (as subject). These people think that there is a difference between the ground [the dharmadhātu], which, recognized or not, is free from all ontological extremes, and self-cognizing awareness, which is introduced and recognized in the present moment.

According to our tradition, this position is untenable. The people just mentioned are assuming that the original common ground and awareness [introduced and recognized in the present moment] are one and the same. But they are not the same. The original common ground is neither samsara nor nirvana but is their source. By contrast, awareness in the present moment is beyond samsara and nirvana. The common ground is the ground prior to the rift between samsara and nirvana and as such it is a third, unspecified, neutral state, all-pervasive like space. It possesses the twin aspects of awareness and ignorance in the manner of a piece of gold that is covered with dirt. If awareness is actualized, one is free like Samantabhadra. If ignorance is actualized, one is deluded, as we are at present.

Although nowadays the majority of those who uphold the Great Perfection say that awareness at the time of the path and the original common ground [of samsara and nirvana] are one and the same, the difference between them is in fact as great as between heaven and earth! Although it resembles the original ground in completely pervading both samsara and nirvana, awareness in the present moment, at the time of the path, has not the slightest trace of ignorance.

It is consequently a mistake to think that the dharmadhātu (as object) is the same as the original common ground. The complaint of the persons just mentioned—to the effect that whereas the dharmadhātu as object permeates the whole of samsara and nirvana, awareness [as subject] in its self-aware, self-knowing aspect does not do so, and to think that the sugatagarbha does not pervade [inanimate objects like] earth and stones—cannot be sustained. For the truth is that the dharmadhātu as object and self-cognizing primordial wisdom as subject are inseparably one. These objectors fail to understand that *all* phenomena, pillars, vases, and so on are nothing but awareness. If they understood this, they would easily grasp that the sugatagarbha pervades everything: earth, stones, mountains, and cliffs. Their problem is that they fail to understand that all phenomena are the self-experience of awareness. They do not realize that all appearances are the groundless, rootless display of awareness alone. The ultimate fundamental nature of all phenomena is the luminous character of awareness. It is described as the clear vision, unerring and uncontrived, of the ultimate nature of the mind. It is naked, self-cognizing awareness. Generally speaking, the so-called ground is distinguished [from awareness] in being the object aspect, whereas awareness, self-cognizing primordial wisdom, is distinguished [from the ground] as being the subject aspect. When, however, this is considered by experienced practitioners, awareness is understood as being coterminous, in an inseparably nondual manner, with the expanse of the ground [the dharmadhātu]. It is said that when one has such a realization, no distinction is made between them.

By way of a slight digression and with reference to doctrinal terminology, it may be said that "awareness" and "self-arisen primordial wisdom" are expressions typical of the pith instruction class of the Great Perfection, whereas "all-creating king" and "enlightened mind" are typical of the mind class. By contrast, "uncontrived mind" is a Mantrayāna term. However, since the realization and meditative experience belonging to the mind, space, and pith instruction classes are one and the same, teachers use these terms without distinction. In his *Trilogy of the Uncontrived Mind*, Mipham Rinpoche refers to awareness as the uncontrived enlightened mind, whereas in the present text, the all-knowing Longchen Rabjam refers to awareness as the enlightened mind and the all-creating king. Although the view of *The Treasury of the Dharmadhātu* accords principally with the pith instruction class, many citations taken from the scriptures of the mind and space classes are adduced in support of it.

Let us now turn to the meaning of the root stanza. Because there is nothing in phenomenal existence, samsara and nirvana, that is not included in the expanse of awareness, the latter is described as the all-encompassing enlightened mind. What, however, is its nature? It is said to be beyond all ontological extremes, for it is neither appearance nor emptiness. It is not existent, nonexistent, both, or neither, and so on. Awareness is not appearance. For the appearing things that are the objects of the six consciousnesses, although perceived, have never existed from the very beginning. They never go beyond the confines of the primordial wisdom of equality, which from the beginning is empty and free of conceptual extremes. Thus, awareness transcends appearance. Now it might be asked that if awareness is not appearance, does that mean that it is emptiness? The answer is that the nature of the all-encompassing enlightened mind is not empty in the sense of being totally nonexistent, like a rabbit's horns. While being empty, awareness is primordially present of itself as that which gives rise unceasingly to the whole variety of phenomena. Therefore, awareness does not fall into the extreme of emptiness; it transcends emptiness. Similarly, it might be thought that the all-encompassing enlightened mind exists. But it does not. As it is said, "It does not exist, for even the victorious buddhas have not seen it," and also "It does not exist; it has no existence whatsoever." In other words, awareness in itself has neither substance nor characteristics, neither shape nor color, and so on. It is beyond all such mental elaborations. Therefore, its nature is empty; it is open and unimpeded and beyond all such elaborations. One might therefore conclude that it is nonexistent. But then Jigme Lingpa tells us, "It is not nonexistent; it is the ground of both samsara and nirvana." And Shabkar also says, "It is not nonexistent; it is radiant and vivid."

As we have said, awareness, the sugatagarbha, pervades the whole of samsara and nirvana—just as oil pervades a sesame seed. One may look for a place that is not pervaded by it, but not a single particle will be found. The all-encompassing enlightened mind is neither existent nor nonexistent, neither both nor neither. In short, it is the primordial expanse of great emptiness, which is spontaneous, even, and uncontrived, free of all ontological extremes—existence, nonexistence, both, and neither. It is beyond permanence and discontinuity, identity and difference, opposition and relation. It is not subject to extremes and divisions. It is a great, nondual equality; it is groundless, rootless primordial wisdom, wholly devoid of substance and characteristics. This then is the nature of the all-encompassing enlightened mind. It is said in the tantra *Awareness Self-Arisen*,

> It has no birth and therefore no cessation.
> Without fixation, it is free and open where it stands.
> Devoid of reference, it is free of mental movement.
> Not appearing through being made, it is omnipresent.
> It is the unconditioned, spotless, ultimate expanse,
> Free from all conventional phenomena to which there could be grasping.

As this text says, self-arisen awareness, the enlightened mind, is unborn like space. It is unobstructive like a rainbow. It is free of all fixation, and like a picture drawn on water, it is free and open right where it stands. Beyond all thought and reference, it is free of mental movement. It has not come into being, fabricated by causes and conditions. It is always present in the mind streams of all beings, like the oil that permeates a seed of sesame. It is the utterly pure ultimate expanse, the spacelike, unconditioned dharmatā, free of all conventional phenomena that are apprehended by way of their characteristics and as objects of mind.

In the same text, it is also said,

> It is all-pervading, the nature of the father.
> Giving rise to everything, it is the mother's vast expanse.
> In wisdom that is inexpressible,
> There lies a great instruction that cannot be taught.

Because awareness permeates the whole of samsara and nirvana, which themselves arise within its expanse, this same awareness is said to be the nature of the father principle. And since all appearances, both pure and impure, are brought forth within the expanse of awareness, the latter is likened to the vast expanse of the mother. It is within this ineffable, inconceivable, and indescribable wisdom that there lies the great teaching—the essence of the minds of the Victorious Ones—which cannot be taught through the medium of sound and words.

* * *

The second section shows that because awareness is naturally pure and all-pervasive, it is perfectly coterminous with the dharmatā.

> **2. Unbroken in its continuity,**
> **Awareness is enlightenment's expanse—**
> **Changeless, motionless, the vast abyss of space,**
> **Pervasive from the very first.**
> **It is self-arisen primordial wisdom**
> **From the very first without a peer.**
> **Not arising and not ceasing,**
> **Encompassed by the one sole sphere,**
> **Indeterminate and all-pervading,**
> **It is utterly beyond all limiting extremes.**

The ultimate expanse, self-arisen primordial wisdom, has never been separate from us—and this without any interruption not even for a moment. So it is that we are inseparable from coemergent primordial wisdom, the great expanse of awareness, the enlightened mind. Throughout the three times, this is free of movement and change, and it is as vast as space itself. In its own fundamental nature, it has never, from the very beginning, been polluted by stains. It is the primordial wisdom of the great pervasive equality of samsara and nirvana.

This self-arisen primordial wisdom, being free of mental elaboration, is beyond the reach of metaphorical indication. It is unborn, for it has never arisen on the basis of causes and conditions, and so forth. Thus it is unceasing, for that which in the past has never been born cannot now be subject to cessation. Not arising, not remaining, and not ceasing, it is encompassed by the one sole sphere that is free of mental elaboration. Arising in a manner that is indeterminate, this one sole sphere has no existence whatever, and yet it is from the very beginning present of itself as that which causes anything at all to manifest. Thus, in the same way that a royal treasury is the basis of everything that may be needed or wished for, this sole sphere is primordially the source of a wish-fulfilling treasure through which an infinite ocean of mandalas is displayed and absorbed. It is said in *The Array of Studded Jewels*,

> The one sole kāya is manifest for every being.
> The one sole kāya is the final goal of wanderers.
> The one sole kāya is everywhere displayed.
> The one sole kāya rests in no extreme.
> The vajra essence, kāya of primordial wisdom,
> Is the very essence of ineffable samādhi,
> Present as the very form of manifest enlightenment.

The empty ultimate nature of the one sole sphere of self-cognizing primordial wisdom is the dharmakāya. Its luminous character is the sambhogakāya. Its unceasing cognizant potency is the nirmāṇakāya. The union of the three kāyas is primordial wisdom. Therefore, it is within the expanse of the one sole supreme dharmakāya, empty self-cognizing primordial wisdom, that phenomenal existence, the display of the world and its inhabitants, manifests for every being. The one sole kāya is the final objective for all who, progressing to the state of buddhahood endowed with twofold purity, actualize the ultimate state of Akaniṣṭha endowed with fivefold certainty (the exclusive self-experience of the sambhogakāya). The one sole kāya is displayed everywhere. While never stirring from the dharmadhātu, it appears as the diverse and unceasing display of the nirmāṇakāya, which uninterruptedly performs enlightened deeds that are everlasting, all-pervading, and spontaneous. As it is said,

> [In all the realms of six impure migrations,]
> As kings, as merchants, laborers, or priests,
> As outcastes, women, children, monks,
> Wandering ascetics, those engaged in training,
> As those deep versed in Vedic teachings,
> As those who through their lineage are respected
> Or as those who are not so revered,
> As praised or as reviled,
> As sick or as religious teachers,
> As birds or beasts, as beggars in the towns—
> In various forms they are the guides of beings
> In accordance with the latter's needs.

The one sole kāya that does not dwell in the extremes either of samsara or nirvana is the svabhāvikakāya. This single kāya, the wisdom kāya, the ultimate quintessence endowed with the seven attributes of a vajra, is the immutable vajrakāya. In truth, this kāya has no existence apart from awareness, the enlightened mind, the quintessence of meditative absorption, which transcends all verbal expression. The same scripture also asserts that this is enlightenment in which the qualities of elimination and realization are complete. It is the actualization of the ultimate result, present as the very kāya of the one sole sphere of awareness. The text continues,

> Primordial wisdom is the "one thing that cuts through."
> It is free from dual appearance.
> The vajradharakāya is free of all activity.
> Not dwelling in the two extremes,
> It is the highest luminosity.
> The vajra seal is changeless.
> And the completely steadfast kāya
> Arising in this same unmoving vajra
> Is the central core itself.
> The different attributes of this sole sphere
> Are the riches of this kāya.
> The mandala endowed with all such riches
> Is the perfection of the triple kāya.

Awareness, the enlightened mind, which directly cuts through all hallucinatory appearances, is the expanse of the one, undeluded primordial wisdom. When it is actualized, one is free of the apprehension of dual appearance. Awareness is endowed with the seven attributes of an indestructible vajra and is therefore referred to as the vajradharakāya. And since it performs no function, it is said to be free of all activity. Awareness moreover does not dwell in the extremes either of samsara or nirvana. It is great self-cognizing and self-illuminating primordial wisdom. Awareness, sealed with the dharmadhātu and endowed with the seven attributes of a vajra, is unchanging. Awareness, arising within the unmoving mandala of the ultimate kāya, which is free from birth and death, destruction and annihilation, and is endowed with the attributes just mentioned, is like the very core of perfect and ultimate wisdom. It is thus described as the completely steadfast and unchanging kāya.

All the mandalas of the body, speech, and mind of the Victorious Ones are perfectly contained within the expanse of the one sole sphere of the dharmakāya. And the unfolding display of this one sole sphere—the qualities and activities of the Victorious Ones—is said to be the wealth of this same kāya. This is metaphorically indicated by the mention of its riches. This supreme mandala, endowed with such riches, is awareness, empty, luminous, and unceasing, the spontaneous perfection of the trikāya. It is the ultimate, fundamental nature.

In brief, although the manifestations of the one sole sphere of the dharmakāya are diverse and indeterminate, they never go beyond the sphere of awareness; they are never beyond the domain of primordial wisdom, which pervades the whole of samsara and nirvana and is utterly free of limiting extremes.

* * *

The third section shows that although the ultimate expanse is present in all beings, it is the province of only a few who are endowed with fortune.

3. Unwavering equality, present of itself—
Such is the lineage of the vajra essence.
This supreme and infinite expanse,
Which from beings is never separate,
Is not within the reach of verbal indication.
It is the bursting forth of wisdom—
The sphere of self-knowing awareness.
Yogis who are free from all activity
Of thought and word
Possess decisive certainty that this expanse
Transcends both indication and nonindication.
And finding neither meditation nor anything on which to meditate,
These yogis do not need to slay the foes
Of dullness, agitation, and discursive thought.

Those who never waver from the spontaneous equality of uncontrived awareness, and who recognize its natural state as the great spontaneous presence, are supreme in mind and are referred to as holders of the lineage of the vajra essence. When yogis who abide by the fundamental nature of the dharmatā rest in the state of nonaction, they never separate from the condition of awareness, the dharmadhātu. Their awareness is blended indivisibly with the supreme infinite expanse of the dharmatā, the mind of all the buddhas of the three times. These yogis experience the fundamental nature—namely, ultimate primordial wisdom. This is not something that words can indicate and is not within the scope of intellectuals and scholars, who can only talk about it, as it were, from outside. Who therefore has the capacity for it? Only those who are qualified: those who possess extremely sharp faculties and who are supreme in mind. For them—as soon as they recognize awareness—all objects arise as the dharmatā. The fundamental nature is the sphere of self-cognizing primordial wisdom experienced by yogis in whom the wisdom of the simultaneous view and meditation bursts forth from deep within themselves. But what are such people like? *The Great Garuda* has this to say:

> Let thought-free primal wisdom,
> Through which delusion ceases,
> Be practiced by those who are of blissful mind,
> Strong in their simplicity, devoid of all activity,
> Whose minds are spacious, free of thought's
>   elaboration.

Such fortunate people have a natural way of behaving. They have a dark complexion and are of steady gaze. They walk with relaxed poise. They say whatever comes into their minds. Their speech is disconnected and there is an artless simplicity about them. Their minds are relaxed and they have few thoughts, and their behavior is uncomplicated and carefree. It is further said in *The Word-Transcending Tantra*,

> Again, they are relaxed and patient;
> They are simple, easygoing in their ways.
> They are serene and have few thoughts;
> They are unflustered in their words and deeds.
> They are wise and therefore may uphold it.

When such yogis are in the state that is free of conceptual and verbal activity, they remain in the sphere of self-cognizing awareness to which they have been introduced, and it is thus and at that moment that the nature of awareness, the dharmatā, is actualized. When they are at rest within the awareness state, no matter what occurs—stillness or the movement of thoughts, dullness or a state of agitation, and so on—there is only self-arisen primordial wisdom together with its display. There are no deviations or obscurations to be dispelled. For awareness, the primordial and supreme dharmakāya free from action, is now manifest. And just as ordinary earth and stones cannot be found on an island of gold, even if one looks for them, nothing that manifests for such yogis is outside the display of the supreme dharmakāya. Such a state of awareness is exclusively the domain of self-cognizing primordial wisdom. It is beyond the reach of thought and word. As we find in *The Wondrous King*,

> The enlightened mind, the dharmatā beyond conceiving,
> Is not established through reflection and description.

And *The Vajra Cutter* says,

> The dharmatā is not an object to be known;
> It is incapable of being known.

It is thus explained that the dharmatā is not something that can be known by the dualistic discursive mind. It is known only by self-knowing primordial wisdom. If yogis—those in whom this knowledge has burst forth from deep within—remain relaxed in their three doors of body, speech, and mind, they will experience a natural, spontaneous meditative absorption that is like a flowing stream without any need to cultivate it. And they will be utterly sure that, apart from maintaining this state, there is nothing that they should indicate or refrain from indicating. Since when this pure authentic state is reached, there is no mental effort to be found, whether in terms of meditation or something on which to meditate, there can be no altering of, no stirring from, the relaxed and natural state. This is the fundamental nature itself. It is said in *The All-Creating King*,

> When you abide within this nature,
> The unmoving state is gained spontaneously.
> Since it is a natural abiding,
> It is not contrived by anyone.
> Not seeking anything, but naturally remaining, free of action,
> This is to rely upon the supreme action.

If one is able to discover a meditative absorption that is natural and unwavering, that is beyond both indication and nonindication, beyond both meditation and nonmeditation—a concentration, in other words, that flows like a river without the need for cultivation—it will be realized that whatever manifests is but the display of the dharmatā. This being so, there will be no need to slay the enemies of dullness, agitation, and discursive thought. All such distractions are but the display of the dharmatā, which is beyond distraction or freedom from distraction. Nothing can possibly lie outside it. And so, even if one were to search for such so-called enemies (dullness, agitation, and discursive thought) that are not the display of the dharmatā, one would find nothing.

On the other hand, if one is enmeshed in the kind of meditative concentration enjoyed by childish beings, in which body, speech, and mind are tensely focused, one will be firmly anchored in the formless samādhis of samsara. The great, all-knowing Longchen Rabjam has said,

> If you try with vigorous purpose to contrive
> The dharmatā, which in itself
> Is free of thought and vast like space,
> It will be trapped inside conceptual attributes.
> And though you may spend day and night in practice,
> All is an entangling obsession.
> The Buddha said that it resembles
> The samādhi of the gods.[60]

* * *

The fourth section shows that since phenomenal existence is a buddha field, there is nothing to be either rejected or accepted. There is nothing either good or bad.

> **4. Within the dharmatā, which from the very first subsists**
> **Immediate and unmediated,**
> **There is no thought of self and other.**
> **The three worlds, therefore, by their nature**
> **Are a buddha field of evenness.**

In general, samsara and nirvana are one and the same in their ultimate nature, the dharmatā. This single dharmatā—while having no existence whatsoever—is able to appear as anything at all. Therefore, whatever different phenomena may arise, pure or impure according to their mode of appearance, they are, in their ultimate mode of being, nothing but infinite purity. The Tibetan expression *chiluk* (*spyi blugs*, "immediate and unmediated") is to be understood as referring to something that is instantaneous and direct.[61] The expression "direct empowerment granted in the manner of a king"[62] is to be understood as referring to the empowerment in which awareness is instantaneously or abruptly introduced. In the present context also, all the phenomena of samsara and nirvana are introduced in a single moment, instantaneously and in a very direct manner as being primordially the one sole buddha field of self-arisen primordial wisdom. And when one rests in this state of dharmatā, in which one has the realization that the world and its inhabitants are a single pure buddha field, there are no deluded concepts of self and other. Everything naturally manifests as being, from the very first, the buddha field of self-arisen primordial wisdom. So it is that the three worlds themselves have never been impure. On the contrary, they constitute the mandala of all the buddhas—the buddha field of equality, which according to the Great Perfection, is by its very nature the vajra expanse, the vajradhātu, or dharmatā. The whole of phenomenal existence is infinite purity, the mandala of the three perfect seats. The psychophysical aggregates and the elements are the seat of the male and female buddhas. The sense faculties and their objects are the seat of the male and female bodhisattvas. The body's limbs are the seat of the male and female wrathful deities. It is said in *The Secret Essence*,

> The components of the vajra aggregate
> Are known as the five perfect buddhas.
> The many sense fields and constituents
> Are the bodhisattvas by their nature.

Moreover, as Longsel Nyingpo has said,

> The aggregate of form is white Vairocana.
> The aggregate of consciousness is Vajrasattva blue in color.
> The aggregate of feeling is yellow Ratnasambhava.
> Perception is red Amitābha.
> Conditioning factors are green Amoghasiddhi.
> The five elements are the female buddhas
> Joined with male buddhas, never to be parted.

The Secret Essence also says,

> Earth is Buddhalocanā and water Māmakī,
> Fire is Pāndaravāsinī and wind Samayatārā,
> While space is Dhātīśvarī.
> All things that belong, without exception,
> To the three planes of existence—
> All are but a buddha field.
> Things extraneous to the buddhas
> Have by the buddhas never been discovered.

The appearances of the six classes of beings and indeed the three worlds are primordially the buddha field of self-arisen primordial wisdom. This shows that in truth all appearances are from the very first the state of buddhahood in the vajra expanse (the vajradhātu), the fundamental nature that is the highest dharmatā.[63] It is said in *The Word-Transcending Tantra*,

> Indeed through various circumstances
> Various beings arise.
> There is not one of them that is not buddha.
> Beings and buddhas are the same—
> They are primordial wisdom's self-display.
> There has never been samsara;
> Every being is a buddha.

It is because of the primary cause, the fact that deluded beings cling to self, and through the secondary condition—namely, their thoughts—that hallucinatory appearances manifest without interruption. And yet in truth, buddhas and beings are equal, the same in being the one self-display or experience of self-cognizing primordial wisdom. Beings are, by their very nature, the kāyas and wisdoms of awareness. This is their fundamental condition. Aside from this, one may search for beings that are actually—truly—deluded, but none will be found. Therefore on the understanding that beings are equal to the buddhas, the teachings declare that they *are* buddhas. On the other hand, if one does not understand how this equality is established, it is said that to speak in such a way is like laughing as one throws oneself into the abyss or like the ravings of a madman. As it is said in *The Word-Transcending Tantra*,

> To be born is to have realization.
> Resting in the womb is resting in the dharmadhātu.
> By the joining of the mind and body,
> Awareness is connected with the ultimate expanse.
> Dwelling in a body is the triple kāya.
> With age, hallucinatory appearance ceases in the
> dharmatā.
> Through illness are phenomena experienced.
> Through death comes emptiness, impossible to grasp.
> So it is that beings are truly buddhas.

The appearance of being born is compared here with the realization of the profound fundamental nature, when self-cognizing primordial wisdom is introduced. Remaining in the mother's womb is compared with the primordial abiding in the dharmadhātu without ever separating from it. The joining of the body and mind in the womb is compared with the union of awareness and the ultimate expanse. Following conception in the mother's womb, the remaining of consciousness within the body is compared with awareness residing in the three kāyas. Then, of the four rivers of suffering—birth, age, sickness, and death—the experience of the suffering of aging is compared with the exhaustion of phenomenal appearances in the expanse of the dharmatā, the cessation of all impure appearances. The torment of sickness, when the phenomena of the six gatherings make contact with the six sense consciousnesses, is compared with the experience of the fundamental nature of phenomena. Finally, death is likened to the realization of emptiness, the supreme absence of mental elaboration, which is impossible to grasp.

* * *

The fifth section shows that just like samsara, which manifests as the self-experience of awareness or primordial buddhahood, nirvana also is nothing other than the pure self-experience of buddhahood.

> **5. The Victorious Ones of the three times**
> **Are awareness's pure self-experience.**
> **Nothing is there to abandon, nothing to accept.**
> **All is but the single state of evenness.**
> **No achievement in the slightest**
> **Is attained from somewhere else.**
> **All phenomena are clearly present**
> **In the vast expanse of the mind's nature.**
> **They do not in the slightest waver from the nature of equality.**

Although it is not possible for the sun in the sky to be affected by the clouds, nevertheless, when the sky is overcast, it seems that the sun is darkened by the clouds and when there are no clouds, the sun shines brightly. In the same way, although awareness is never in itself occluded by stains, it is only when adventitious hallucinatory appearances are purified, there where they stand, that one is said to be a buddha, whereas when awareness is hidden by impure hallucinatory appearances, one is said to be a sentient being. There are no buddhas or beings apart from this. The Victorious Ones of the three times—all the buddhas of the past, present, and future—are said to have attained enlightenment through the actualization of awareness, the self-arisen primordial wisdom, which is itself beyond all causes, conditions, and striving. And this occurs on the basis of the removal of the adventitious stains that are themselves the self-display or experience of this same awareness. Other than this, there is no such thing as "buddhas" existing in and of themselves.

Thus the buddhas too are the inherently pure self-experience of awareness. They are awareness, the enlightened mind. And when, in the present moment, one's body, speech, and mind settle evenly in the uncontrived state, there is nothing for the mind to do in terms of rejecting or adopting, removing or adding. Empty, clear, lucid, vivid, and open awareness—the fourth state that is free from the other three [namely, thoughts related to the past, present, and future]—appears in its nakedness. In this state and at that moment, all phenomena are but a single evenness, without any distinctions of good or bad. And although phenomena continue to occur unceasingly, they are like the stars and planets appearing reflected in a lake. They manifest and yet never stir from the dharmatā, the primordial great emptiness that is free of all mental elaboration. It is said that when this is realized, one is a buddha. Aside from this, a state of buddhahood lying extraneously elsewhere, in the sphere of the five sense faculties, cannot in the slightest be attained. As it is said in *The Secret Essence*,

> There is no perfect buddha
> In any of the four times and the ten directions.
> The nature of the mind is perfect buddha—
> Do not look for buddhahood elsewhere!
> Even if the Victors were themselves to look,
> They would find nothing.

This text shows that no matter where one searches, whether in the ten directions (the cardinal and intermediate directions, zenith and nadir), throughout the three times, and even in the fourth time of timeless equality, no state of buddhahood will be found apart from awareness, the enlightened mind.

When one settles in the immense expanse of the nature of the mind, the dimension of all-pervading space, one finds that even though phenomena appear clearly, distinctly, and without ceasing—like the stars and planets appearing reflected in a lake—the truth is that they never stir to the slightest degree from the spontaneous, perfect, and immense state of equality. It is said in *The All-Creating King*,

All things present in phenomenal existence,
Together with the enlightened mind, which is not manifest,
Come from the suchness of the mind,
And they are this suchness.
When you fail to understand them thus,
They are perceived as separate entities.
Were they to seek for suchness in the ultimate expanse,
Even the Victorious Ones past, present, and to come
Would fail to find it.

As the text says, all phenomena both manifest and unmanifest come from awareness or suchness. And this same awareness or suchness is not separate and distinct from the dharmadhātu.

* * *

The sixth section shows that when the nature of awareness itself is realized, deviations and obscurations automatically dissipate.

6. Free of out and in, arising and subsiding,
Free of all turbidity,
Dispeller of the gloom of all extreme positions—
Such is the enlightened mind, the root.
It does not relinquish anything,
And yet it naturally removes all deviation.

When the very nature of awareness is correctly realized as it is, it is seen to be without distinctions such as outside and in. There is no source for its first arising and no place in which it might finally subside. It is limpidly clear, free of the turbidity of deluded thoughts. In short, within awareness there is no zenith and no nadir, no center or periphery, no main or intermediate directions. It is beyond the four conceptual extremes of existence, nonexistence, both, and neither. At once dispelling all the gloom of the ontological extremes, it is the bare freedom from conceptual elaboration. This foundation or root—namely, awareness—the fundamental mode of being, is at all times the ultimate enlightened mind itself. *The All-Creating King* declares,

> This nature, the enlightened mind,
> Is the essence of all things without exception.
> Pure, it is unborn and unobscured.
> Free from any path to tread, there is no deviation.

As this text says, awareness, the enlightened mind, is the essence of all phenomena. Being unborn, it is pure, and it is unstained by any deviation and obscuration. It does not exist as anything, and it does not dwell in anything.

Awareness, the enlightened mind, is beyond the reach of adoption and rejection; it is beyond all effortful striving. Without relinquishing defilement and defect, it is primordially pure in itself. Quite naturally it removes the deviations of bliss, luminosity, and no-thought, as well as drowsiness, agitation, and dullness, or the wild activity of thoughts. It is consequently said to be naturally free from the fettering shackles of the six active consciousnesses. It is said in *The All-Creating King*,

> Already present from the outset,
> It is not something to be striven for.
> The essence of all things
> Is the one enlightened mind.
> Now when this one sole state is sundered into aspects,
> Deviations, obscurations, all ensue.
> Within it there is no progression.
> And efforts to progress will lead to deviation.

Awareness in itself is, from the very beginning, self-arisen. In other words, it is spontaneously present of itself. It is something from which we are never separate. There is therefore no need to strive for it anew. All phenomena are awareness, the one sole enlightened mind. They are nothing other than this. Therefore, if through clinging to duality, one fragments this one sole state, deviations and obscurations will follow through all the many aspects or categories that emerge. Through the failure to understand that awareness is the primordial kingdom that cannot be reached by journeying, one may have the impression that one must traverse the grounds and paths—but this is a deviation.

* * *

The seventh section shows that everything that appears within awareness never wavers from the ultimate expanse.

> **7. Although the various appearances of the world and beings,**
> **And also the pure buddhas and primordial wisdoms—**
> **A ceaseless play pervading the expanse of space—**
> **Appear through awareness's creative power**
> **(Through realization or the lack of realization),**
> **In truth, within the dharmadhātu,**
> **"Realize," "not to realize"—**
> **These are simply names.**
> **Thanks to realization,**
> **There arise the pure perceptions of the sugata.**
> **Through lack of realization, there occur, in their diversity,**
> **Perceptions, which arise**
> **Through ignorance and dualistic habit.**
> **Yet none of this stirs from the ultimate expanse.**

When awareness or self-arisen primordial wisdom is not recognized, good and evil, happiness and sorrow—all the various indeterminate appearances and perceptions of the six classes of beings—manifest through the power of delusion and are taken to be truly existent. It is thus that there arises the whole array of the three worlds of the outer universe wherein these hallucinatory appearances and perceptions continue in their courses.

By contrast, when awareness or self-arisen primordial wisdom is recognized, all phenomena appear as pure buddha fields and the buddhas and primordial wisdoms. Phenomenal existence is perceived as nothing but infinite purity. These two ways of manifestation—of phenomenal existence and of infinite purity—are the ceaseless display arising through the creative power of awareness according to the realization or lack of realization of the fundamental nature of the ultimate expanse, self-arisen primordial wisdom. The appearances of samsara and nirvana in all their diversity, good or bad, inexhaustibly pervade the entire expanse of space to its very limits. Those who recognize the nature of all that appears, and who realize the one sole nature of the mind, are called buddhas. Those who fail to realize it are described as sentient beings. And yet within the dharmadhātu, not even the words "realization" and "lack of realization" are found. The appearances of the buddhas and buddha fields, and the appearances of earth, rocks, mountains, and cliffs are in themselves without the slightest trace of good or bad. They are awareness, self-arisen primordial wisdom, the state of equality. *The All-Creating King* declares,

> Everything contained within phenomenal existence,
> Within the universe and beings,
> All that is accounted for in buddhas and in beings
> Is made by me, the enlightened, all-creating mind.
> So everything is the enlightened mind.
> From the outset there was never something "other."
> All is thus revealed as the enlightened mind.

Through the true realization of the profound fundamental nature, the pure perceptions and appearances of the sugatas arise, whereas through the lack of realization, diverse perceptions and appearances, pure and impure, occur through ignorance and dualistic habit. In whichever way they appear, however, the truth is that irrespective of whether their nature is recognized or not, they are, without any distinction, awareness, self-arisen primordial wisdom. And since awareness has never in itself been deluded, these same appearances are likened to buddhas. It is as when a prince assumed the demeanor of an orphaned beggar and wandered to the ends of the earth. All who did not know him took him for a young beggar. Later, when he was enthroned, they realized that he had been a prince and thought to themselves, "We did not recognize him. He was a prince all along!" For so it was. Recognized or not, he was a prince. We find this example in the pith instructions of *The Secret Essence*. Therefore, whether or not the profound fundamental nature is realized, all appearances are indeed awareness, self-arisen primordial wisdom. However appearances may manifest—good or bad, pure or impure—they do not stray from the dharmadhātu, the expanse of ultimate reality.

* * *

The eighth section demonstrates that awareness is both empty and luminous. There are two parts: a short and then a detailed account. The short explanation is as follows.

8a. The enlightened mind indeed
Is the actual ground of everything.
It arises ceaselessly in various array,
But this is but the radiance
Within the pure expanse of luminous dharmatā.
Without division or exclusion,
This is but the dance of unconfined awareness.

The ultimate enlightened mind is the actual ground, the supreme dharmatā, of all things without end belonging to samsara and nirvana. This enlightened mind, which is like a sphere of immaculate crystal, is unborn. It is primordial great emptiness, the expanse of the ultimate reality of samsara and nirvana. It does not exist as anything at all, and yet since it is spontaneously present as that through which any display of its creative power might occur, it arises in an unceasing manifestation of an array of different pure and impure appearances. In truth, however, since the luminous character of awareness, the dharmatā—which is like a stainless mirror—has never been sullied by the two obscuring veils and their associated propensities, the result is that within the naturally pure expanse of dharmatā, the outwardly radiating luminosity has never stirred from inner luminosity. We find in *Awareness Self-Arisen*,

> It does not fall into extremes, it is without delimitation.
> Neither out nor in, it is a great immensity.
> Of unstained purity, it is like an orb of crystal.
> It's said that it appears and yet has no intrinsic being.

There is no delimitation in the fundamental nature of phenomena. There is no falling into extreme positions. This fundamental nature has neither out nor in. It is dimensionless and has neither center nor periphery. It transcends all spatial measurement. It is unstained by any obscuration or habitual propensity. It is like an orb of crystal. Without the differentiations of good, bad, samsara, and nirvana, all things without division or exception are simply awareness, the three kāyas. In whatever way phenomena may appear, they are in truth groundless and rootless. They are devoid of objective reference. They are an open, unimpeded dimension, the simple dance of unconfined awareness free of all fixation. However much one may look, one finds nothing but this. This is the meaning of the text just quoted.

When the root text says, "It arises ceaselessly in various array," it is referring to the diverse and unceasing manifestations of the nirmāṇakāya. When the text says, "This is but the radiance within the pure expanse of luminous dharmatā," it is referring to the sambhogakāya. Finally, when the text says, "Without division or exclusion, this is but the dance of unconfined awareness," it shows that the empty nature of both the sambhogakāya and the nirmāṇakāya is the dharmakāya. It is thus that awareness is shown to be the three kāyas, meaning that it is empty, luminous, and unceasing.

* * *

The second part of the eighth section explains in detail that awareness is empty and luminous.

> **8b. Primal wisdom, open, unimpeded,**
> **A self-arisen vast expanse,**
> **Is unobstructed luminosity, free of out and in.**
> **It is awareness self-cognizing,**
> **The great light of the mirror of the mind.**
> **It is the precious jewel of dharmadhātu**
> **That brings forth all that one desires—**
> **For all arises naturally**
> **Without the need for striving.**
> **Self-arisen primordial wisdom**
> **Is the source of all that one might wish.**

Self-cognizing primordial wisdom has neither out nor in; it has neither zenith nor nadir, neither center nor periphery, neither cardinal nor intermediate directions. This wisdom, open, unimpeded, empty, luminous, and unceasing, depends neither on causes nor conditions. From the very beginning, it is uncontrived, self-arisen, and present of itself. It is a vast expanse of awareness, an all-pervading spacelike dimension that permeates the whole of samsara and nirvana. Unobstructed by concrete objects—earth, stones, mountains, cliffs, and so on—it is without the distinction of "out" or "in." It is the luminous, self-cognizing primordial wisdom of inner luminosity, which radiates outwardly and is like the very essence of the sun. Self-cognizing awareness is thus like the stainless mirror of the mind, the immaculate radiance of which pervades the whole of samsara and nirvana, and which is therefore described as a great light. It is also compared to a precious wish-fulfilling jewel that supplies all one's wants and desires. For it is the dharmadhātu within which are all the supreme attributes of enlightenment, the kāyas and wisdoms, for example, which arise naturally and spontaneously without their having to be intentionally striven for. So it is that self-arisen, self-cognizing primordial wisdom is compared to a precious and glorious jewel, the king of wish-fulfilling gems, the source of all that one could wish.

Some texts say that awareness generally has three aspects. One may speak of the awareness that is luminous primordial wisdom, awareness that is a creative power, and awareness that arises as the display of its creative power. In the first case, when awareness is correctly recognized, and when one settles in this state, one will realize that by its very nature, awareness does not exist as anything at all and yet it is naturally present as that through which anything at all may arise. This is awareness in the sense of luminous primordial wisdom. Regarding the second aspect, although a diversity of phenomena arises within the nature of awareness, when consciousness does not stray into its object, this nakedly knowing aspect is referred to as awareness that is a creative power. Finally, regarding the third aspect, when, thanks to the creative power of awareness, there unfolds the display of the appearances of the six consciousnesses, and when these consciousnesses stray into them, apprehending them as their objects, this is described as awareness that arises as the display of its own creative power. Of these three aspects, the first and second are both considered to be awareness itself. In the third case, when there is no apprehension of [no straying into] an object, this too is awareness. By contrast, if there is the apprehension of an object, the third aspect, the display, is awareness only in name. In point of fact, it is a delusive state, the discursive mind.

* * *

The ninth section reveals that awareness is the immense expanse of enlightenment.

9. All the many great and wholesome qualities
Arising in the ultimate expanse

Are of that same expanse.
They ceaselessly occur
As supreme skillful means
And are spontaneously perfect in the vast unborn expanse.
Phenomena are therefore overwhelmed by emptiness,
The vast space of enlightenment.
And emptiness in turn is overwhelmed
By awareness self-cognizing,
The vast space of enlightenment.

Since it is wholly impossible for there to be something that is not encompassed by the expanse of the one dharmadhātu, all appearances of the billion worlds of the trichiliocosm are completely gathered within it. Therefore all the many great and wholesome qualities of all pure and impure phenomena gathered within the single dharmadhātu arise within this ultimate expanse. There is not a single thing that does not occur within it.

At the time of the ground, however many great qualities (virtuous roots, defiled or undefiled) occur within the minds of beings who apprehend as a self the psychophysical aggregates, elements, and sense fields, they all arise within the ultimate expanse. At the time of the path, however many great qualities there are in the minds of those who have embarked upon the path (virtuous roots such as the five fields of learning, the three collections of teachings, the view, meditation, and action proper to each of the nine vehicles and so on), these too arise or manifest within the ultimate expanse. Likewise, at the time of the result, all the many great qualities of the twenty-one classes of immaculate knowledge (the ten strengths, the four fearlessnesses, the eighteen distinctive qualities, and so on, as well as the pure buddhas and buddha fields), these too arise or manifest within the ultimate expanse. Thus the dharmadhātu ceaselessly arises as supreme skillful means [the qualities] in the manner of a magical illusion, like the reflection of the moon in water, like a mirage. Although these qualities appear, they are all perfectly contained in an uncontrived, self-arisen, and spontaneous manner within the unborn ultimate expanse, empty, open, and unimpeded. It is said in *Awareness Self-Arisen*,

> Like a mirage, magical illusion,
> Or the moon reflected in the water,
> It is not simply nonexistent,
> Nor yet is it existent.
> It lies beyond existence and the absence of existence.
> The nature of awareness is unborn;
> Unceasing is its character of luminosity.
> Awareness's display is without substance.
> Awareness's result is uncontrived.
> Awareness has the nature of the triple kāya,
> So the teachings say.

Even though phenomena manifest as the creative power and display of awareness—in the manner of magical illusions, reflections of the moon in water, or mirages—the truth is that they are empty. They have never really existed. Yet their emptiness does not fall into the extreme of nothingness, bare nonexistence. For they manifest in an unceasing process of dependent arising. And though they arise, they do not become existing phenomena, for their nature lies within the primordial great emptiness.

In short, because awareness is by its nature a state of equality beyond conceptual elaboration that transcends both existence and nonexistence, its nature is unborn and empty. Its unceasing luminous character is the union of appearance and emptiness. The display or manifestation of awareness is without substance whether in terms of existence, nonexistence, both, or neither. And the fruit that is awareness is the uncontrived indivisibility of the three kāyas.

Therefore, when the hallucinatory phenomena and perceptions of the three worlds (brought about through the duality of apprehender and apprehended) are all overwhelmed by the great primordial wisdom of emptiness (undeluded, primordially pure, open, and unimpeded), one will have the ability to realize directly that appearances have never stirred from the condition of emptiness, the vast space of great enlightenment. And in a similar fashion, when the self-cognizing primordial wisdom of the union of appearance and emptiness expounded in Atiyoga overwhelms the incorrect view of emptiness—the error of the mere nothingness of a nonaffirming negation (as when one says there is no tea or no water)—one will capture the citadel, the expanse of self-cognizing awareness, the ultimate enlightened mind, the summit of all views. It is like a snow lion that, becoming the lord of the snowy peaks, overwhelms all the other beasts.

* * *

The tenth section brings into focus all the preceding points as being the great immensity of the expanse of space.

10. There have never been appearances and emptiness
In the enlightened mind.
But do not grasp at "nonduality,"
For there is indeed an inconceivable display.
The no-time of the three times
Is the unborn dharmadhātu,
The vast space that is changeless, unconditioned, undivided.
It is the buddhas of the three times,
The ultimate expanse of self-cognizing primal wisdom.
The vast space of enlightenment,
Awareness self-cognizing,
Overwhelms the apprehending subject
And the object to be apprehended.
With no division, out or in,
Ultimate reality is vast and present of itself.

Awareness, the fundamental nature of the enlightened mind, has never been marred by the slightest corner or edge of conceptual elaboration. It never falls outside the one sole all-encompassing sphere, which is free of both appearance and emptiness, of existence, nonexistence, both, and neither, of permanence and impermanence, and of identity and difference. It exists neither as appearance nor as emptiness. If it were established as an appearance, this would be a conceptual elaboration. And if it were taken to be emptiness, this too would be a conceptual elaboration. And thus from the very first, awareness is not, to the slightest extent, either appearance or emptiness.

It does not however follow that if it does not exist as either appearance or emptiness, it must perforce exist as a nonduality of appearance and emptiness. One should not grasp at awareness as a fixed reference, thinking that it is the nonduality of appearance and emptiness. Instead one should *recognize* the fundamental nature, ineffable, inconceivable, and indescribable. If one fails to do so, the fixed idea of the nonduality of appearance and emptiness is just another concept.

Although the enlightened mind, being nothing whatsoever, is a state of great equality beyond all mental elaboration, it may yet arise as anything whatsoever. The inconceivably various and illusory display of samsara and nirvana arises without ceasing. As it is said in *Awareness Self-Arisen*,

> The appearances of awareness
> Ceaselessly arise as anything at all.
> Unending is awareness's display—
> As anything at all does it arise.
> Equality, the wisdom mind beyond all mental movement,
> Is awareness where there is no subject and no object.
> It is the buddhas of the triple time.

Just as appearance and emptiness and so on have never existed within awareness itself, likewise there has never existed the chronological sequence of the three times. Because there is no such thing as time past, there have never been buddhas who gained their freedom in former ages, nor have there been deluded beings of the six classes. Similarly, since the present time has no existence, samsara and nirvana, good and bad, joy and sorrow have no existence in the present. And if the present time does not exist, there is no need to say that the future does not exist either. It is also nonexistent, with the result that there cannot be such a thing as the formation, duration, destruction, and intervening void of universal systems. Consequently, the primordial wisdom of equality, the fourth time (or rather the timelessness of the three times) is unchanging. It is the unborn dharmadhātu, which is invincible and endowed with the seven indestructible attributes of a vajra. It is also indivisible in terms of a separate and distinct samsara and nirvana, good and bad, happiness and suffering. It is the vast space of awareness, the enlightened mind, not produced through causes and conditions. It is referred to as the buddhas of the three times and as the ultimate expanse of self-cognizing primordial wisdom.

The dharmadhātu, the primordial wisdom of the great and spontaneously perfect state of equality, overwhelms all hallucinatory and impure appearances of apprehending subjects and objects to be apprehended. It is self-cognizing awareness beyond all delusion. It is the expanse of enlightenment, beyond out and in, zenith and nadir, center and periphery. It is the primordial wisdom of the dharmadhātu, the mind of the Victorious Ones of the three times. And within this expanse of the dharmatā, spontaneous, even, and vast, all the appearances of samsara and nirvana merge inseparably in a single taste, like water mixed with water. It is important to understand this correctly. So it is that the meaning of this chapter is summarized in terms of the supreme immensity of the expanse of space.

* * *

This concludes the commentary on the fourth chapter of *The Precious Treasury of the Dharmadhātu*, which shows the nature of the enlightened mind.

5. The Enlightened Mind Is beyond Effortful Striving and Causality

The fifth chapter shows that the enlightened mind transcends all effortful striving and the law of cause and effect. It is divided into sixteen sections, of which the first section shows that the nature of the enlightened mind is beyond causality and exertion.

> **1. Within the nature of the mind—**
> **Enlightened mind itself—**
> **There is no view on which to meditate,**
> **No action to perform and no result to gain.**
> **There are no paths, no grounds to cross,**
> **No mandala to visualize, no mantra to recite,**
> **And no perfection stage.**
> **No empowerment is there to grant and no samaya to observe.**
> **In ultimate reality,**
> **Primordially pure and present of itself,**
> **All adventitious effort, step by step,**
> **All causes and effects, are utterly transcended.**

Suchness, the fundamental nature of the mind—the ultimate enlightened mind—is in itself free from all mental elaboration. It is empty from the very beginning. It is motionless and unchanging throughout the three times. It lies beyond the reach of the mind's exertion, beyond all reference and all fixation. Therefore, from its own standpoint, [the standpoint of the fundamental nature of the mind,] there is no view "to be viewed." Indeed, empty, unborn awareness, free of an object to be viewed and of a subject that views, is itself the sovereign view. There is no other view but this. There is no meditation to be practiced. For meditation is said to be the actualization of the luminosity of awareness—a luminosity that is free of an object of meditation and of a meditating mind. Aside from this, there is nothing on which conceptual meditation may be brought to bear. And likewise there is no action to be performed. In other words, simply to rest in a relaxed state, free of all effortful striving, and in a manner uncontrived and free of clinging—this is the very quintessence of action. Aside from this, there is no action to be performed and no agent to perform it. Neither is there a result to achieve. As it is said,

> By seeking it you will not find it,
> Abandon hope for a result . . .

And,

> To rest naturally without hope or expectation
> Is the supreme result.

From the very beginning, awareness is naturally endowed with the four kāyas and the five wisdoms. There is no need to strive for them. It is moreover the summit of all results, and beyond it there is no other result to be attained. There are no grounds and paths to be traversed, for all the grounds and paths are simultaneously and perfectly included in the expanse of awareness, the dharmadhātu. Aside from this, there is no such thing as the ten grounds of the causal path that are to be traversed. There are no mandalas to visualize. The uncontrived self-arisen mandala is awareness, the self-arisen primordial wisdom that from the very first has never been separate from oneself. Other than that, there are no mandalas to be constructed or visualized through mental concentration. Neither are there any recitations of mantra to be accomplished for the approach phase. All sounds, which arise through the creative power of awareness, are naturally and from the very beginning, the mandala of enlightened speech. Other than that, there is no recitation to be performed. Neither is there a perfection stage. For that which is so designated is simply the exhaustion within the ground (empty awareness alone) of all phenomena of samsara and nirvana. Aside from this, there is no perfection stage achieved through the fabrication and concentration of the mind. Likewise, there are no empowerments to be granted. For the ultimate self-arisen empowerment, beyond both granting and receiving, is self-cognizing primordial wisdom itself. There is no other, mentally elaborated, empowerment. There are no samayas to be observed. For the "samayas of nothing to observe" refer to the realization that self-cognizing primordial wisdom is itself nonexistent, even, spontaneously present, and a single nature.[64] Other than this there are no samayas to observe.

These ten items—view, meditation, action, grounds and paths, result, the visualization of mandalas, the recitation of mantra, the perfection stage, empowerment, and samaya—are known as the ten elements of tantra. In the Secret Mantra, these ten elements or ten essential factors are set forth as a method of explanation and as the great methods of practice. Nevertheless, according to Atiyoga, the tradition of great nondual equality, it is said that, apart from awareness itself, there is no such thing as the ten elements of tantra. As *The All-Creating King* tells us,

> Like space is the enlightened mind.
> Within the spacelike nature of the mind, the dharmatā,
> There is no view on which to meditate,
> And no samaya to observe,
> No activity in which to strive,
> And no primordial wisdom to obtain.
> There are no grounds or paths on which to train,
> No paths to be traversed.

And the Great Omniscient Master himself has said [in the third stanza of the present chapter],

> Whatever has been taught
> Concerning ten things grounded in exertion
> Was given in relation to hallucinatory experiences
> That through awareness's creative power
> Adventitiously arise.
> They are but skillful means for gradual engagement on the path
> By beings who, according to their faculties,
> Exert themselves in gradual stages.
> For those who are authentically united
> With Atiyoga's vajra essence,
> They have not been taught.

These ten well-known elements of tantra are set forth—according to varying capacities, modes of access to the path, and categories of the different vehicles—as methods for finally accomplishing the single taste of Atiyoga. But when the all-pervading state of equality is realized, the ten elements of tantra and so on all merge evenly and without distinction with the expanse of the one sole dharmakāya.

So it is that the primordially pure dharmatā, uncontrived, spontaneously present, empty and devoid of self—awareness that cannot be described or pointed out—transcends all adventitious gradual effort and causality, such as these ten elements of tantra.

* * *

The second section gives an example of this state, which is beyond striving and beyond acceptance and rejection.

> **2. These factors are enlightened mind itself.**
> **Not obscured by darkness and by clouds,**
> **The sun shines by its very nature in the sky.**
> **It is not adventitiously produced.**

As was explained earlier, [awareness] cannot be produced by the ten elements of tantra and so forth. For these same factors, which are beyond the conceptual elaborations of appearance and emptiness, existence and nonexistence, both and neither, identity and difference, and so on, can never, by their very nature, contrive or alter the ultimate enlightened mind. The nature of awareness has never been obscured by adventitious defilement, deluded thought, causes and effects.

The sun as it appears in the sky is at all times luminous by its very nature. In itself, it is unobscured, and can never be obscured, by adventitious clouds and darkness. From our point of view, however, it may well look as if the sun is hidden by clouds, and we may think to ourselves that the sun itself is darkened. This is however no more than our mistaken perception, for the sun and the clouds are separated by a distance of many leagues.

In like manner, the mind has the character of being at all times luminous. In itself, it has never been obscured by ignorance, by deluded thought and defilement. And yet, from the standpoint of deluded thought, it seems that awareness is darkened, that it has to be purified, and that enlightened qualities are to be developed. This is a real and genuine delusion. From the very beginning, the fundamental condition of awareness has never been darkened. Consequently, even if one does not engage in any adventitious activity marked by hope or fear, rejecting or adopting, or effortful practice as a means to removing obscurations, the fact is that within the expanse of dharmatā, awareness possesses the character of luminosity from the very beginning. Being intrinsically luminous, it cannot be obscured by any circumstances. It is said in *The Ornament of Clear Realization*,

> Therein is nothing to remove
> And thereto not the slightest thing to add.

And we find in *The Great Mother*,

> As for the mind, there is no mind;
> The nature of the mind is luminosity.

These quotations belong to the expository causal vehicle. They are not, however, of provisional meaning but pertain solely to the definitive meaning.

Generally speaking, the Lord Buddha set forth three successive turnings of the Dharma wheel. These are distinguished differently in terms of their provisional or definitive status by the upholders of the tenet systems of the four great fountainheads of the Dharma in the Snowy Land of Tibet. All agree that the first turning of the Dharma wheel pertains to the provisional meaning. There is however one tradition that states that, whereas the teachings of the first turning assert the existence of phenomena, and are therefore of provisional meaning, the teachings of the second turning deny the existence of phenomena. They do this as an antidote and as a means to averting attachment to existence. This implies that they too are of provisional meaning. By contrast, while the teachings of both the first turning and the second or intermediate turning are considered provisional, it is stated in this tradition that the teachings of the final turning of the Dharma wheel set forth the fundamental nature just as it is. Consequently, all the scriptures [belonging to the final turning], which speak of the sugatagarbha, are said to be definitive in meaning.

There are others, however, who say that the extensive, medium, and abridged versions of *The Mother* (*Prajñāpāramitā*), as set forth in the intermediate turning, are of definitive meaning and that it is rather the teachings of the final turning that are provisional. This tradition therefore regards the teachings of the first and third turnings to be provisional.

According to the old translation tradition, as upheld by the two omniscient masters, Rongzom and Longchenpa, it goes without saying that the second turning of the Dharma wheel belongs to the teachings of definitive meaning. For it expressly teaches the fourfold and eightfold emptiness of all phenomena—from form to omniscience—according to the view of the extensive, medium, and abridged versions of *The Mother.* By contrast, the final turning of the Dharma wheel is part provisional and part definitive. Some scriptures, such as the *The Sutra of the Visit to Laṇkā* and the *The Sutra Decisively Revealing the Wisdom Intention*, are partly provisional and partly definitive in meaning, while the ten sutras that expound the sugatagarbha—*The Sutra of the Questions of the Girl Ratna*, the *The Sutra of Śrīmālādevī*, and others—are [wholly] definitive.

In the present context, and according to our own tradition, the text quoted from *The Great Mother* (a sutra of the second turning of the Dharma wheel)—namely, "As for the mind, there is no mind"—teaches that all things, from form to omniscience, are without intrinsic being. By contrast, the words "The nature of the mind is luminosity" set forth the luminous character of the nature of the mind according to the view of the ten sutras of the third turning of the Dharma wheel, which set forth the doctrine of the sugatagarbha.

There are many texts that comment on both these topics. The most important scriptures that establish the view of the second turning are the five texts of reasoning on Madhyamaka that accompany *The Root Stanzas of the Middle Way*, composed by the glorious lord, the noble Nāgārjuna. By contrast, *The Sublime Continuum* and other texts of the regent Maitreya establish the view of the ten sutras that, as the teachings of the third turning of the Dharma wheel, set forth the doctrine of the sugatagarbha. Consequently, in our tradition, all these texts must be given a position of primary importance. Indeed, this tradition of ours, that of the old translations, stresses the union of emptiness and luminosity and sets forth correctly and without error the views of the second and third turnings of the Dharma wheel. The second turning clearly reveals the ultimate nature of emptiness, while the third turning reveals the [mind's] luminous character. And this is in accordance with the views of the two omniscient masters, Rongzom and Longchenpa, as well as of Lama Mipham Rinpoche.

The Ornament of Clear Realization declares,

> Therein is nothing to remove,
> And thereto not the slightest thing to add.
> The perfect truth viewed perfectly
> And perfectly beheld is liberation.

Although the meaning of this text is principally explained according to the sutras of the expository vehicle of causality, in the present instance, the first two lines are considered to refer to the ground, the third to the path, and the fourth to the result. In other words, this text chiefly refers to the union of emptiness and luminosity.

In our tradition, the union of emptiness and luminosity is considered to be present already at the time of the ground. If this were not so, it would follow that it is to be attained by extraneous means during the stages of the path and the result. And this would lead to the false consequence that the union of emptiness and luminosity is not intrinsic or self-arisen but arises through the agency of something else. Consequently, if the fundamental nature of the union of emptiness and luminosity—the final view of the Secret Mantra—is correctly understood in harmony with the union of emptiness and luminosity spoken of in the sutras of the vehicle of transcendent wisdom, one will be able to understand that all the sutras and tantras express the same insight—like a hundred streams passing beneath a single bridge.

* * *

The third section shows that because the nature of awareness is as it has just been described, the ten elements of tantra set forth for those of lesser capacity should be regarded as deviations and obscurations by practitioners of Atiyoga.

> **3. Whatever has been taught**
> **Concerning ten things grounded in exertion**
> **Was given in relation to hallucinatory experiences**

That through awareness's creative power
Adventitiously arise.
They are but skillful means for gradual engagement
on the path
By beings who, according to their faculties,
Exert themselves in gradual stages.
For those who are authentically united
With Atiyoga's vajra essence,
They have not been taught.

As we have seen earlier, the ten things grounded in exertion are the ten essential factors of the practice pursued in Mahāyoga: view, meditation, action, result, the grounds and paths, mandalas, the recitation of mantra, the perfection stage, empowerment, and samaya. These are the so-called ten elements, the great methods of explanation and practice of tantra. Now all the teachings on these ten essential factors are given as means to avert impure apprehension and clinging to characteristics—which manifest adventitiously in relation to the hallucinatory appearances that occur through the creative power, and as the display, of awareness. The effortful practices of the ten essential factors are set forth as skillful means for practitioners of basic to moderate acumen, who need a progressive approach allowing them to engage in the various stages of the path laid out according to the inconceivable classifications of the different vehicles. They are not taught for those who are genuinely able to unite with the indestructible vajra essence of Atiyoga, the fundamental nature that is free from mental elaboration. It is said in *The All-Creating King*,

Rest in the primordial view, on which there is no
meditating.
Rest in the primordial samaya, which cannot be observed.
Rest in the primordial action, not to be performed through
effort.
If so you rest, with suchness you will be in genuine union.

This authentic union or yoga is of four kinds: first, the union of the courageous mind (corresponding to the three outer tantras); second, the great union of Mahāyoga; third, the thoroughly engaged union of Anuyoga; and fourth, the highest union of Atiyoga. Of these, the yoga of the courageous mind, the great yoga, and the thoroughly engaged yoga all lack the self-arisen primordial wisdom of Atiyoga. They set forth a path on which one must train and that is to be traversed. They set forth the ten elements of tantra, such as the training on the grounds and paths, the keeping of samaya, view, meditation, action, and so on—all of which are to be strenuously cultivated. These yogas set forth their respective views and practices, the lower ones displaying defects in respect of the higher ones, which surpass them. By contrast, Atiyoga, the highest yoga, is free of all such contrived and elaborate views and actions.

* * *

The fourth section speaks of the first six of the nine vehicles, together with their views.

> **4. For beings who progress by stages and by means of effort,**
> **The gradual teachings are set forth**
> **To guide them to the dharmatā's primordial expanse.**
> **These are the three small vehicles**
> **Of śrāvakas, pratyekabuddhas, bodhisattvas.**
> **Then three tantras—Kriyā, Upa, Yoga—**
> **Are naturally set forth as intermediate.**

As a preparatory method or means of entry into the unsurpassed Atiyoga, the victorious buddhas, great in their compassion and skilled in means, set forth eight vehicles. These are like the rungs of a ladder and act as gradual stages suited for beings of varying acumen. Ngari Panchen has said,

For śrāvakas, pratyekabuddhas, bodhisattvas,
Three vehicles are expounded, causal and expository.
Then three outer tantras, Kriyā, Upa, Yoga,
Are followed by the father tantras of the Mahāyoga,
The mother tantras of the Anuyoga,
And last, the nondual tantras known as Atiyoga.
The latter are the unsurpassed three inner tantras.
All the teachings thus are gathered
In the nine successive vehicles.

Depending on whether the state of the primordial lord, the dharmakāya Samantabhadra, is attained in this very life, these vehicles may be described relative to each other, as paths that are long, fairly short, short, extremely short, and so on. When individuals who progress gradually and with strenuous effort are guided to the one and only path of Atiyoga, the lower vehicles are regarded as staging posts and resting places. On the basis of each of them, the particular result of each path is attained. However, in order to reach the final goal, it is certainly necessary to rely on the path of Atiyoga. As Ngari Panchen also says,

As staging posts upon the one and only path,
They bring forth corresponding, ever higher, fruits.
But since they do not constitute the one and only path,
How could the goal be gained through them?

The teachings of the eight lower vehicles are given so that beings who progress gradually may be guided to the primordial expanse of the dharmatā according to the sole vehicle of Atiyoga. The two lower vehicles of the śrāvakas and pratyekabuddhas, together with the great vehicle of the bodhisattvas—all belonging to the expository vehicle of causality—constitute the three sutra vehicles. Their gradual teachings are described as small in relation to the Secret Mantra, which conversely is regarded as great. And within the context of Mantra itself, the three tantras of Action, Conduct, and Union (namely, Kriyā, Upa, and Yoga) are described as small when compared with a higher and shorter path. Conversely, from the superior viewpoint of the vehicle of the Great Perfection, the view and meditation of these tantras do not lead to the experience of awareness itself. And in their activities, distinctions are made between clean and unclean. They are like vehicles devised for children. On the other hand, when viewed from the standpoint of the three causal vehicles, the vehicles of the three outer tantras are considered great since they are superior to them. In other words, it is within the context of what is superior and inferior to them that the outer tantras are naturally set forth as the three intermediate vehicles.

* * *

The fifth section discusses the three classes of the inner Mantra.

> **5. Then as the three great vehicles,**
> **Mahā, Anu, Ati are primordially perceived.**
> **Through the opening of the doors of Dharma**
> **Of the causal and resultant vehicles,**
> **The fortunate are led to the three levels of**
> **enlightenment.**

The three stages of Mahāyoga, Anuyoga, and Atiyoga are the three classes of inner tantra. Mipham Rinpoche said, "The Mahāyoga principally teaches the generation stage; the Anuyoga, the perfection stage; and the Atiyoga, their union."

With regard to the view and meditation of Mahāyoga, it may be said that—based on the three concentrations (the causal concentration on suchness, the all-illuminating concentration that is like a magical illusion, and the heroic concentration on the cause), the five procedures,[65] the four phases of approach and accomplishment and so on—emphasis is placed on the infinite purity of phenomenal existence. This means that in order to purify the habitual propensities of four ways of being born (which at the present moment are impure), the outer universe and its inhabitants are visualized as an immeasurable palace and deities. It is by means of such effortful practice that one meditates on the mind as being a deity. This means that self-cognizing awareness, the actual fundamental nature of action-free Atiyoga, is not seen.

Similarly, with regard to the view and meditation of Anuyoga, Jigme Lingpa said,

> Within the measureless array,
> The palace of your body,
> Is found the rainbow light dimension
> Of three channels and five chakras.
> These are awareness's display,
> The union of primordial wisdom and the ultimate expanse,
> The mandala of Anuyoga.

As this text says, the view of Anuyoga refers to the meditation on the inseparability of primordial wisdom and the ultimate expanse, based on either the path of skillful means or the path of liberation (whichever is appropriate), as a means to releasing the knots on the three channels and the five chakras of one's body. Since this focuses on a method whereby the knots on the channels are released through concentrated effort, it cannot lead to the actual state of great perfection, which is the primordial openness and freedom of the mind.

In the case of Atiyoga, when the natural, uncontrived view (the genuine fundamental condition) is maintained, all phenomenal appearance is exhausted in the expanse of primordial purity, the dharmatā, the ultimate fundamental nature itself. This is the final destiny of all vehicles, the sacred innermost wellspring of freedom, in the same way that the final destiny of all rivers is the mighty sea.

So it is that compared with the lower vehicles, it is said that Mahāyoga, Anuyoga, and Atiyoga are primordially perceived as the three great or superior vehicles—self-arisen and unmade by anyone. If briefly told, all the inconceivable approaches—openings of the doors of the Dharma—belonging to both the causal and resultant vehicles have many categories. As Ngari Panchen has said,

> The vehicles are inconceivable, beyond the reach of
> numbering.

There are also countless fortunate beings who practice these vehicles in all their different classes. But in the end, they all lead them on the path to the great, medium, and small levels of enlightenment. It is for this reason that the nine vehicles were set forth.

* * *

The sixth section shows that all these vehicles are doors of entry to the vajra essence.

> **6. All of them lead of necessity**
> **To the supreme and marvelous secret of the**
> **ultimate—**
> **The vajra essence, culmination of them all—**
> **The highest and unchanging luminosity.**
> **This is celebrated as the vehicle**
> **Of the heart of manifest enlightenment.**

The eight gradual vehicles and so on are taught as stages on the path, devised according to the differing mental capacity of beings who are unable to accept the language of the Great Perfection when it is directly set forth. This is found not only in the many tantras of the old translation school but is also referred to in the following verses taken from the *Hevajra Tantra*, which is a scripture of the new translations.

> First, ten topics of the training are set forth.
> Later, on the basis of the vows
> Of bhikṣu, śrāmaṇera, and upāsaka,

> As well as of the stages of the Mantra,
> Hevajra is revealed.

Accordingly, the lower vehicles are set forth in relation to the mental faculties of beings. But in the end, there is no way to achieve buddhahood without relying on the path of Atiyoga. In general, there are three ways in which a person on the sutra path may engage in the path of mantra: at the stage of the ground, at the stage of the path, and at the stage of the result.

Based on the text "They possess the great strength of the four bases of miraculous power," there is a tradition according to which beings may engage in the practice of Mantra while still on the path of joining, whereas, beyond this point, there is no difference between the views of both the sutras and the tantras. Another tradition, based on the text "Within seven days, they too become manifest and perfect buddhas," states that beings on the sutra path may engage in the path of Mantra on the first bodhisattva ground of realization. For without the extraordinary means and wisdom of the Secret Mantra, it is impossible to complete the practice of a countless great kalpa within the space of seven days. Yet another tradition states that it is only after the attainment of the eleventh ground of Universal Light that one is able to enter the path of Mantra. So it is that this topic has been assessed in numerous different ways.

Likewise in the old translation tradition, Ngari Panchen and certain other authorities say that the Mantra path is entered at the stage of the result [the path of seeing], whereas others consider that it may be followed while on the path of joining.

On the other hand, Lama Mipham Rinpoche said that on the first ground of realization, the dharmatā, Samantabhadra, is realized. This being so, there is no view higher than this even in the tantras. For whereas the purity and equality of all things in phenomenal existence, together with awareness—namely, self-arisen primordial wisdom—are not directly taught in the sutras, they are nevertheless implicitly established [at this stage]. When the first ground is achieved, the pure buddha fields and the primordial wisdom of the equality of samsara and nirvana and so on are actualized through the cultivation of the path. Mipham Rinpoche also said that this is the point when the purity and equality of phenomenal existence according to the mantra teachings, and the self-arisen, self-cognizing primordial wisdom spoken of in the Great Perfection both manifest. This means that the moment when self-cognizing primordial wisdom is recognized coincides with the first ground of realization mentioned in the sutras. Mipham also said that in contrast with this [experience], the understanding of this wisdom in terms of a mental image may occur at any stage.

In short, the eight gradual vehicles, as was explained, are set forth by way of remedial teachings for beings of lesser acumen, while the vehicle of Atiyoga is taught to fortunate beings of highest capacity. Even though, in awareness itself, there are no vehicles at all, nevertheless, as a means to realizing this same awareness, the many categories of the vehicles are set forth. In the end, they merge into one and progress toward the supreme immensity of Ati, the direct revelation of awareness. Therefore, the final destination of all these many categories of the vehicles is the ultimate vehicle of the vajra essence of the luminous Great Perfection. Of necessity, they all lead into this path of the marvelous, supreme secret.

If, on the other hand, the view of the Great Perfection is not yet realized, the way to accomplish it, from the first till the sixteenth ground—namely, Wisdom Unsurpassed, the culmination of all vehicles—is extensively elucidated in the tantra *Awareness Self-Arisen*. Although in the Great Perfection tradition, there is no effortful practice of training on, and traversing, the grounds and paths, one speaks nevertheless of distinct grounds corresponding to specific levels of actualization of the indwelling primordial wisdom and its associated qualities. Generally speaking, the eleventh ground, Universal Light, is so called because of the boundless emanations that occur. The twelfth ground, Lotus Free of All Desire, is so named owing to the boundless light associated with it. The thirteenth ground is called Great Wheel of Collections Free of Syllables[66] because of its boundless primordial wisdom. These three grounds correspond to the classification found in the tantras up to and including Anuyoga. The uncommon grounds belonging to the Great Perfection are the fourteenth ground of Supreme Concentration, the fifteenth ground of Vajra Holder, and the sixteenth ground of Wisdom Unsurpassed.

The manner in which these sixteen grounds are correlated with the sixteen emptinesses and the sixteen joys and so on is explained by Jamgön Kongtrul in his *Treasury of Knowledge*, while the ways in which they are completed in the course of the maturing empowerments are explained in *The Heart Essence of Chetsun* by Drodul Pawo Dorje, Adzom Drukpa Rinpoche. In the latter case, at the time of the vase empowerment, the eighth ground is reached and the five aspects of the enlightened body are consequently gained. At the time of the unelaborate secret empowerment, the eleventh ground is reached and the five aspects of enlightened speech are gained. At the time of the extremely unelaborate wisdom empowerment, the thirteenth ground is reached and the five aspects of enlightened mind are gained. At the time of the supremely unelaborate word empowerment of primordial purity, the sixteenth ground is reached and the five aspects of enlightened qualities and the five aspects of enlightened activities are gained. It is thus that in the tradition of the Great Perfection, the completion of the twenty-five resultant attributes is correlated with the sixteen grounds.

Without these realizations, it is not possible to progress to the ground of supreme luminosity, the self-arisen one sole sphere. This final vehicle moreover is renowned as the vehicle of the heart or essence of manifest enlightenment. In the tantra *The Seed of Secret Activity*, otherwise known as the tantra of *The Only Child of the Self-Arisen Teachings*, it is said,

> All who reach the fruit of buddhahood perceive it.
> Not a single buddha of the past or future fails to see it.

All who wish to gain the fruit of perfect buddhahood must behold the only child of the self-arisen teaching—namely, self-arisen awareness. For unless it is seen, there is absolutely no way to attain the enlightened state. It has never happened in the past nor will it ever happen in the future.

Moreover, it is said in the same scripture,

> Vajradharas beyond numbering
> All possess this one awareness,
> The bursting forth of their sole wisdom mind.

As this text indicates, the teaching that spontaneously and without contrivance bursts forth from the expanse of the dharmatā, the wisdom mind of the thousand and two buddhas of this fortunate kalpa and so on, the victorious Vajradharas beyond numbering, is precisely the tantra of *The Only Child of the Teachings*. It is awareness, the only meaning of the one sole sphere.

* * *

The seventh section concerns the stages of practice that require exertion.

> **7. There are indeed two kinds of Dharma,**
> **One of which demands concerted effort**
> **In adopting and rejecting.**
> **It is expounded as a means of cleansing**
> **Mind and mental factors and habitual tendencies,**
> **Which naturally arise as the display**
> **Of awareness's creative power.**
> **In this approach, primordial wisdom**
> **Is said to be more pure than ordinary mind.**[67]

There are two kinds of Dharma. One appears in the eight successive vehicles where the ordinary mind is taken as the path and the result is accomplished through concerted effort in adopting and rejecting. Contrasted with this is the Great Perfection, in which primordial wisdom, unstained by the ordinary mind, is taken as the path. It is said in *The Lion's Perfect Power*,

> Primordial wisdom is untouched by the habitual tendencies.
> All these various tendencies belong to ordinary mind.
> If mind is not distinguished from primordial wisdom,
> The root of the appearing objects of the senses is not cut.
> Pure dharmatā free from all conditions will be hard to realize.

The ordinary mind is a consciousness that apprehends the objects of the senses; it is a consciousness that accumulates various propensities. Primordial wisdom, awareness itself, is by contrast a state in which throughout the three times, there are no sense objects. It is a state that is beyond the elaborations of thought and word. Now primordial wisdom is the root of the ordinary mind. In other words, when one examines the mind, it is not the root of ordinary mind that is found; it is primordial wisdom. And since the radiance or creative power of primordial wisdom can be watched within the midst of the mind, it is only when one rests in primordial wisdom that the nature of the mind is recognized. In all eight gradual vehicles, the support for the ground, path, and result is located within the ordinary mind alone—and this, from the lofty viewpoint of Atiyoga, which takes primordial wisdom as its only path, is described as a deviation from the Great Perfection. In other words, the six vehicles (the first three causal vehicles taken together as one, followed by the three outer tantras together with Mahāyoga and Anuyoga) are all deviations from the Great Perfection. As it is said in *The All-Creating King*,

> Six vehicles for attaining certainty
> Are shown as deviations from the Great Perfection.

All of the lower vehicles, which take the ordinary mind as the path, being based on methods that, of their nature, are manifestations of the display of awareness' creative power, were set forth as a means of cleansing this same mind, its mental factors, and manifold habitual tendencies. For according to these eight gradual vehicles, it is considered that pure primordial wisdom is actualized when the mind and its habitual tendencies are cleared away. By contrast, the tradition of Atiyoga states that without relying on an object and subject of purification (an object and subject of cleansing), the mind and mental factors are, in their very nature and in this very instant, the primordial wisdom that dwells within them.

* * *

The eighth section reveals the exalted meaning of Atiyoga.

8. Beyond concerted effort and beyond accepting or rejecting,
Great dharmatā is self-arisen primordial wisdom,
The enlightened mind itself.
You actualize it when you do not waver
From direct and face-to-face experience.
There is no need to strive for it elsewhere.
It is within yourself. Do not look somewhere else.

There is no difference between nirvana that is to be adopted and samsara that is to be rejected. Both arise as the illusory display of awareness and are indeed a state of equality. When one is dreaming, one may encounter gold and all sorts of precious gems. One may also encounter earth and ordinary stones. All of them are but the illusory display of the dream, neither good nor bad. In the same way, the impure appearances of the present time and the appearances of the buddhas and buddha fields are in themselves neither good nor bad. They are the manifested display of awareness. They are all the same in appearing to be different and separate from awareness, and they are all the same in never stirring from it.

Beyond the concerted effort of accepting or rejecting, the dharmatā, the great perfection, is self-arisen, self-cognizing primordial wisdom, the ultimate enlightened mind itself. To rest without stirring from the direct face-to-face experience of this spontaneously present vajra essence, without altering this empty, naked awareness in the slightest way, is to actualize the dharmakāya, the "buddhahood of the ground." There is no need to strive with effort for an enlightenment somewhere else. Indeed, if one were to do so, one would find nothing. It is said in *The Necklace of Pearls*,

> Awareness self-cognizing is the perfect buddha.

And as we find [in *The Great Garuda*],

> Unclouded is the self-experience of awareness,
> Free from causes and conditions.
> Not contrived by anyone through exertion,
> It is perfect from the very first.
> This essence is spontaneously present
> And is displayed in objects of the senses.

And as *The All-Creating King* tells us,

> Do not look for buddhahood
> But investigate the mind beyond all action.
> Examined, it has no existence—
> There is but awareness self-cognizing,
> Primordially luminous.

As this text says, buddhahood, as we call it, has no existence apart from self-arisen awareness. This is indeed the distinctive and unique feature of Atiyoga, the resultant vehicle. In the sutras and other tantras, there are similar statements to the effect that there is no enlightenment apart from one's own mind. On the side of the sutras, it is said in *The Sutra of Wisdom at the Hour of Death* that one should cultivate the attitude of thinking that buddhahood is not to be looked for elsewhere. Moreover, in *The Vajra Cutter Sutra* it is said,

> Those who see me as a form
> And those who know me as a sound
> Have taken a wrong path.
> These beings do not see me.

And in the mantra teachings we find the saying,

> The nature of the mind is perfect buddha.
> Do not look for buddhahood elsewhere.

These [non-Atiyoga] texts, however, presuppose that if one generates devotion and confidence now, perfecting the accumulations and purifying obscurations, the result will eventually come. According to the sutras, it is understood that such statements [to the effect that buddhahood is not different from one's own mind] are made with reference to the later time of the result. In the context of the father tantras, it is said,

> Now meditate on emptiness. Then perform the concentrations on compassion and the cause. In that state, meditate on the syllable *āḥ*, or *hūṃ* and so on, which then transforms into a deity. Meditate on this deity, clearly perceiving it. Subsequently, as you meditate on the elaborate array of the deity belonging to one of the five or hundred enlightened families, you will one day actualize the perfect result. Then, as you progress on the four vidyādhara levels, the stage of perfection is accomplished. And it is at that time that the words "The nature of the mind is perfect buddha; do not look for buddhahood elsewhere" come true.

Also according to the Anuyoga tradition, when the channels, essence-drops, and winds are mastered by relying on the path of skillful means and the path of liberation, the stage of perfection is actualized without difficulty and without having to wait for a long time. It is then that the words "The nature of the mind is the perfect buddha; do not look for buddhahood elsewhere" come true.

By contrast in the tradition of Atiyoga, it is said that everything that manifests at the present time—the aggregates, elements, and sense fields, all of which belong to samsara—is awareness alone, without any change occurring in form or color. It is the one sole buddhahood. Therefore, if whatever manifests is left in the state of awareness, and uncontrived awareness is actualized, the whole of samsara and nirvana, without any division, is seen to be the dharmakāya, the buddhahood of the ground. Other than that, one should not look elsewhere for some buddha with a face, arms, and other features.

* * *

The ninth section discusses the difference between the two kinds of vehicle.[68]

> **9. It is likened to the sun itself.**
> **It is said that when one rests within its natural state,**
> **Its luminosity is motionless.**
> **The other way is said to be**
> **Like making a new sun**
> **By striving to remove the obscuring clouds.**
> **These two approaches are as different**
> **As the earth is from the sky.**

According to the tradition of the luminous Great Perfection of the old translation school, spontaneously present awareness, the vajra essence, is present already, in this very instant, as buddhahood. It is like the sun that is already there, risen in the sky. Whether recognized or not, awareness is buddhahood. Whether or not it is hidden by the clouds, the sun is never in itself obscured. In the same way, the dharmatā, suchness, buddhahood itself, is like the sun that is already there. Therefore, when one rests in the natural state of awareness, self-arisen primordial wisdom, a spacelike, flawless luminosity automatically occurs. If one remains unwavering within it, this is said to be the actualization of primordial buddhahood. As it is said in the formula,

> Beings are enlightened from the very first,
> Knowing thus that they are so . . .

According to the other account, buddhahood is achieved through elaborate and effortful practice. But this is like creating a new sun by strenuously removing the obscuring clouds even though the sun was never, in itself, obscured [or absent]. It is said that buddhahood is not now present but will be at length attained after engaging in effortful practice linked with the various causes and conditions that remove the two kinds of obscuration together with their habitual tendencies. As it is said,

> It is claimed in the expository causal vehicle
> That beings are the causal source of buddhas.
> In the vajra vehicle of Secret Mantra,
> It's said that beings are buddhas in themselves.

In the tradition of the Great Perfection, it is said that awareness, self-arisen primordial wisdom, is buddha in this very instant, self-arisen and spontaneously appearing. In the lower vehicles by contrast, buddhahood must be achieved anew in dependence on effortful practice that works upon its causes and conditions. The difference between these two approaches, therefore, is like the difference between heaven and earth.

Generally, the Buddha, the Victorious One, skilled in means and endowed with great compassion, set forth many gradual vehicles according to the capacities, temperaments, and aspirations of beings to be guided. The higher vehicles surpass the lower ones and, in particular, the three classes of the inner tantras possess many features that render them superior to the three classes of the outer tantras. And the sovereign culmination of the nine vehicles is Atiyoga itself. For in comparison with Atiyoga, in both Mahāyoga and Anuyoga, even at the moment when the ground is established, the immanent primordial wisdom of the ground cannot be actualized. Then, when [the ground awareness] is cultivated through meditation, it is necessary to appeal to the conditions of the paths of skillful means and liberation. Finally, when the result is explained, this is what the Great Perfection defines as the "awareness of the path" endowed with the nature of the dharmakāya, sambhogakāya, and nirmāṇakāya. This means that [in Mahāyoga and Anuyoga] the fundamental nature of the one sole sphere, the ultimate result of the Great Perfection, is not reached—that this realization is not present. Such is the difference between Mahāyoga and Anuyoga on the one hand and Atiyoga on the other.

In Mahāyoga and Anuyoga it is said that the appearances of the sambhogakāya and the nirmāṇakāya are pure—as compared with the impure appearances of earth, stones, mountains, and rocks. But in Atiyoga it is said that there is, in truth, no difference between the pure form body of the nirmāṇakāya Buddha Śākyamuni, endowed with the major and minor marks, and the impure aggregates, elements, and sense fields of Devadatta. For to pure perception, even the body of Devadatta appears as a form luminous and perfect and endowed with the major and minor marks of enlightenment. Therefore, the appearances of the path and the phenomenal appearances of the creative power [of awareness] are not awareness as such. For the nature of awareness is a state of equality devoid of mental elaboration. It is for this reason that the view, meditation, action, and result of the Great Perfection are utterly superior to those of the lower vehicles.

For ordinary perception on the level of conventional truth, there is a great difference in terms of beauty and ugliness between the body of the Buddha—which, being luminous and endowed with the major and minor marks, is a vision of harmony—and the impure body of Devadatta, which is itself a truth of suffering. And in terms of beauty and ugliness also, there is a great difference between the body of Devadatta and the body of a *preta*, or hungry ghost. This difference is the difference between the purity and impurity of perception based on past karma. It is similar to the way in which people with a bile disorder perceive a white conch as yellow, whereas those who are free of such a disorder perceive it as white. But when examined, both these perceptions are on a level in lacking true existence. When coarse phenomena are analytically divided into smaller parts, and these smaller parts are reduced to particles, and the particles are reduced to partless atoms, and when these (so-called) atoms are proven to be emptiness, [it is shown that] nothing at all exists. Consequently, both the aforementioned perceptions [of purity and impurity] are shown to be ephemeral.

* * *

The tenth section removes the error of failing to distinguish self-arisen primordial wisdom from thoughts arising through extraneous causes.

> **10. "Elephants," these days, who claim to practice Ati**
> **Actually allege that thoughts that move and that**
> **proliferate**
> **Are themselves the enlightened mind.**
> **These fools are sunk in darkness,**
> **Far from the Natural Great Perfection.**
> **They fail to differentiate creative power**
> **From that which issues forth from it—**
> **Still less do they discern the enlightened mind itself.**

Nowadays, [Longchenpa says], there are some who claim to be practitioners of Ati. Such pretentious people can do no more than aspire to this vehicle, bereft as they are of the correctly seeing eyes of true intelligence. This is why Longchenpa compares them to elephants. For just as elephants are puffed up with pride, thinking themselves to be the first among the beasts, such practitioners adopt an arrogant demeanor through their insouciant folly and deck themselves out with jealous envy and misjudgments, like elephants with their faces decorated with tassels. Such people have minds filled with the ambition to appear learned. In fact, through ignorance and defilement, they have strayed onto false paths and lead astray those who wish for liberation but are of feeble merit. As it is said,

> Many who wish for freedom are deceived by demons.

Such deceivers, brigands and thieves of this same vehicle, actually allege[69] that all thoughts, moving and proliferating, are the ultimate enlightened mind. But the moving and proliferating thoughts are a *display* arising through the creative power [of awareness]. It is the kind of cognition that strays into—loses itself in—the objects of the senses. How could this possibly be awareness? Awareness is a state of naked knowing. It does not stray into the cognitions that are displayed through its creative power—which for their part *do* stray into the objects of the senses. This is what has to be recognized, for the distinction between the two is precisely the difference between freedom and delusion—which are as wide apart as heaven and earth. These foolish beings, who think that awareness and the display of its creative power, which [as ordinary cognition] strays into objects, are one and the same, wander into the darkness of ignorance. There is no chance of their ever gaining liberation. They are as far away from the Natural Great Perfection as the sky is from the earth. And chronologically speaking, their enlightenment is very far—many kalpas—away. These people do not even understand the difference between the creative power of awareness and its manifested display. Still less do they discern the enlightened mind.

The difference between the creative power of awareness and the display that arises therefrom is as follows. When an appearing object manifests in awareness—like an image reflected in a mirror—and when thoughts do not unfold in its regard, it is at that point that naked awareness, empty and limpid, is the creative power of cognizant potency. Therefore, although "creative power" and "awareness" are different designations, they refer [in this instance] to the same thing. Creative power cannot be detached from naked awareness, for they are one. It is from the standpoint of the objects appearing in awareness that this same awareness is designated as "creative power."

When appearing objects occur in awareness, the naked, limpid aspect of knowing that is primordial wisdom [and does not stray into these objects] *is* the very nature of creative power. And this is what should be maintained. On the other hand, a cognition that does stray into the object is a *display* arising from that same creative power. Thus there is a great difference between the two: [creative power on the one hand, and its display on the other].[70]

It is said that when the five sense doors are all evenly operational, the five corresponding objects all appear unceasingly. Similarly, when one rests in awareness, and the five sense doors are all operational, the five sense objects manifest unceasingly. But though they arise, awareness is not impaired by them. The nonconceptual consciousnesses should not be arrested. It is not necessary to arrest them. For example, the arising of a form, limpid and vivid for the eyes to see, or a sound clear for the ears to hear, should not be halted. For they do not impair naked, limpidly empty awareness to the slightest degree. As Longchenpa says, "It is not the appearance of the mountain that is to be halted but the thought 'This is a mountain.'" And Jigme Lingpa also says, "It is unnecessary to block the nonconceptual consciousnesses. It is rather the conceptual consciousness that should be halted." Similarly, *The Word-Transcending Tantra* says,

> When the concept of the object does not manifest,
> This is the wisdom of Victorious Ones past, present, and to come.

So it is that the creative power does not stir from the state of luminous awareness. By contrast, the cognitions that manifest through the creative power and stray into the objects of the senses do apprehend their objects, fixating on them and following them. The two cases are quite different.

It is said in *The All-Creating King*,

> Knowing from the very first,
> It is primordial wisdom self-arisen.
> Primordial knowing that cognizes objects
> Arises from these objects—thus it is not self-arisen.

Awareness, self-arisen primordial wisdom, is the state of knowing that is beginningless. It is the uncontrived awareness—clear, limpidly empty, and naked—of the dharmakāya, the primordial state of buddhahood from which we have never been parted. It does not engage in objects; it does not apprehend them or unfold in their direction. By contrast, the display that manifests through [awareness's] creative power is the stirring of the creative power of cognizant potency from self-arisen primordial wisdom. It is the cognition that moves out and strays into its objects. This is what is called "the display that manifests through the creative power." Although it is designated as primordial wisdom that is not object-cognizing, it is not the actual self-arisen primordial wisdom. [It is self-arisen primordial wisdom only in name.][71] For it is a cognition that unfolds prompted by an object, and in the absence of an object it is impossible for it to do so. Therefore, given that the occurrence of this cognition depends upon the presence or absence of an object, it follows that if it is dealt with skillfully at the moment that it unfolds in dependence on an object—by letting whatever arises to subside naturally—it is possible for this same cognition to turn once more into awareness. If, on the other hand, this cognition is not skillfully handled, it will generate karma and defilement—it will not be self-arisen primordial wisdom but will turn into thoughts that manifest because of the objects of the senses. Moreover, as [Jñānagarbha] says in *Distinguishing the Two Truths*,

> Mind and mental factors are cognitions
> That mistakenly ascribe existence to the triple world.

And Dignāga said,

> Thoughts are ignorance;
> They cause a fall into the ocean of samsara.

If one follows one's thoughts, various unwholesome actions are performed and, sunk in the darkness of ignorance, one falls into the sea of suffering that is samsara, from which it is hard to free oneself.

* * *

The eleventh section is a clear explanation of self-arisen primordial wisdom.

> **11. For us the enlightened mind, primordially pure,**
> **Is the ultimate expanse, the truth of dharmatā.**
> **Transcending thought and word,**
> **It is the wisdom that has gone beyond.**
> **Naturally unmoving, its character is luminous;**
> **It is primordially free of the elaboration**
> **Of all moving and unfolding thought.**
> **It is called "the nature" and is likened**
> **To the sun's essential core.**
> **Its creative power is ceaseless in its dawning.**
> **Awareness open, unimpeded**
> **Is free of both detecting and discerning.**
> **Clearly present, it is free of apprehender and of apprehended.**

According to the old translation tradition, the fundamental nature in the luminous Great Perfection is awareness, self-arisen primordial wisdom—the enlightened mind in which all stains are primordially and inherently pure. This is referred to as the truth of dharmatā, the ultimate expanse. It is luminosity, empty and unceasing, like a globe of stainless crystal. And since it transcends all elaborations of thought and word, it is also called the Great Mother, the transcendent perfection of wisdom.

It is naked knowing, the aspect of empty luminosity, the naked, empty awareness that does not examine appearing objects, though they manifest unceasingly. It is the ground for the arising of the manifold array of different things, and yet from its own point of view, there is neither arising nor nonarising. If one does not stray beyond this open, unimpeded, limpid emptiness, and never moves from it, primordial wisdom will manifest, luminous in character—wherein luminosity and emptiness are never parted. This is why it is also referred to as luminous primordial wisdom, ultimate truth, the dharmakāya open and free from the beginning, awareness, the enlightened mind.

In brief, if empty awareness, primordially pure, open, and unimpeded, is realized, it may be described in various ways—such as the cutting through of solidity, the naked state, the open and unimpeded condition, or primordial openness and freedom. Yet in truth these are just different names for the one sole sphere of awareness. This is indeed the ultimate realization of the Heart Essence teachings. Even amid the movement of thoughts, there is, within this state, neither movement nor absence of movement. Even as movement unfolds, primordial wisdom, free from mental elaboration from the very beginning, is recognized. It is the fourth state free from the other three, [free from thoughts related to the three times]. Being free of object-apprehending cognition, this naked, knowing aspect subsists as primordial wisdom. We may refer to it as the uncontrived nature, awareness itself. Like the essential core of the sun, it is luminous by its very nature and within it, the ignorance to be removed simply vanishes without trace. It is said in *Awareness Self-Arisen*,

> In awareness free of all elaboration,
> How could there be ignorance, delusion?
> In primordial wisdom free of ordinary mind,
> How could there be habits and impurities?

And [in *The Word-Transcending Tantra*] it is also said,

> Awareness is by nature luminous but empty.
> It has a luminosity that does not merge with anything.
> Therein there is no apprehended object and no
> apprehending subject.
> Pure in itself, it is the dharmatā.

The dawning of the creative power within awareness, the enlightened mind, is unceasing. When its display arises, one should not discern it outwardly, nor examine it inwardly, nor leave it somewhere in between. One should instead rest in a state of open, unimpeded awareness, naked and limpidly empty, in a state that is free of detecting and discerning cognitions—in other words, free from the cognition of the apprehender. This is the ultimate enlightened mind, the unerring fundamental nature devoid of the slightest contrivance and alteration.

When this uncontrived fundamental nature—the state of naked, clear, limpidly empty awareness—is maintained, different appearances are unceasingly and clearly present. And yet if these appearances are left, as it were, unstained, completely untroubled by ordinary consciousness and the duality of apprehender and apprehended, and if this naked, clear awareness is left unaltered, all that appears through the ceaseless arising of the cognizant potency of awareness will be recognized as great primordial wisdom. Moreover, the creative power will be seen to be nakedly present within self-arisen primordial wisdom. It is important to see that awareness and the creative power of awareness are inseparable, that they are a single sole sphere.

Regarding this point, certain people make a difference between awareness and its creative power, saying that the ultimate nature of awareness is the stillness aspect while the creative power is exclusively the manifestation aspect. They say that they settle in the ultimate nature of awareness that is free of thought, and that they maintain a state in which the creative power self-subsides. So saying, they divide the practice into two parts. However, Longchenpa says in the autocommentary that this comes from a failure to understand the key points of the instructions and from the fact that such people do not recognize awareness itself. In our tradition, even though the ultimate nature and its creative power are separately designated, the ultimate nature is nevertheless simply awareness as such and the creative power is naked, limpidly empty cognition that, free of unfolding thoughts, does not attend to the objects manifesting within awareness. Although they are designated with different terms, since the creative power refers to the unceasing manifestation of objects in awareness itself—like the appearance of reflections in a mirror—this same creative power is said to share the same substance and nature as awareness itself. This is why Longchenpa says in the autocommentary that we should understand that this so-called creative power is not something distinct from naked awareness.

When thoughts unfold toward objects, a state of naked awareness should be maintained, and the thoughts should not be followed. When one rests in awareness, everything that manifests within its ceaseless radiance is unimpeded, just like reflections in a mirror. The ordinary, dualistic knowing that is present from the very beginning and the primordial wisdom that is self-arisen are not separate; they are not two different things. For neither of them is outside the one sole sphere of primordial purity, which is naked and limpidly empty.

* * *

The twelfth section shows how the creative power of cognizant potency is different from the cognitions of the apprehender and the apprehended.

> **12. Through its own creative power, awareness manifests**
> **As the conceptually elaborating mind.**
> **This generates duality of apprehender-apprehended**
> **With all its various propensities.**
> **Nonexistent things are taken as existent things,**
> **And thus the five sense objects manifest.**
> **Nonexistent self is taken as existent self,**
> **And thus there come the five defilements.**
> **All the false appearances**
> **Of the world and its inhabitants,**
> **Manifesting as samsara,**
> **Occur through the creative power.**
> **When you fail to understand this,**
> **False perception manifests.**

Speaking generally, the ultimate nature of awareness is empty, its character is luminous and its cognizant potency is unceasing. Awareness in itself is open and unimpeded; it is naked and naturally clear like a spotless mirror. And just as reflections arise in a mirror, appearances arise in awareness, the ground of all manifestation, thanks to the creative power of its cognizant potency. Whatever may appear, when cognition does not stray into its object—that is, when it does not stir from naked, clear awareness—this is precisely what is called the creative power of cognizant potency. Now awareness and its creative power are one and the same. Therefore, when awareness appears as objects, if these objects are not apprehended conceptually, and if they are recognized as bare, limpid awareness, they are primordial wisdom. On the other hand, when objects are apprehended conceptually, they are the ordinary mind.

When, in the manner of unceasing reflected forms, the creative power of cognizant potency manifests within the spotless mirror of awareness (the ground of all manifestation), and when cognition strays into its objects, the conceptually elaborating mind—which is its display—manifests and fixates on objects, apprehends objects, focuses on them, and so on. It generates the duality of apprehender-apprehended, together with its various deluded propensities. The eighty-four thousand defilements and so on unfold, and hallucinatory appearance is present everywhere.

The difference between these two kinds of cognition—that which strays into objects and that which does not stray—is as we have already mentioned. When appearing objects manifest within awareness, like reflections in a mirror, and when naked, limpidly empty cognition does not unfold toward them in the form of thought, this is the creative power of cognizant potency, the ground of manifestation. But when, in ignorance, cognition unfolds in the form of concepts related to these objects, thoughts of the subject and object of apprehension supervene. Because of this, outer objects, hallucinatory appearances that are totally bereft of real existence, are taken as existent things, and consequently the five sense objects of form, sound, smell, taste, and touch all come into being. And though the self, cognitively apprehended as the inner mind, is unreal—for it is groundless and rootless—it is nevertheless taken to be an existent self, and this results in the proliferation of the five defilements or poisons. Consequently, all the hallucinatory appearances of the three-thousandfold universe—the outer world and its inhabitants, all that is stable and everything that moves, the various karmic perceptions of the six classes of beings—arise.

When luminous awareness does not stir from its fundamental stratum, this is called buddhahood, but when the display of its creative power strays into objects, the phenomena of beings and samsara arise, and one is endlessly deluded. For so it is that when there is no knowledge of the crucial skillful means, thanks to which the display of the creative power naturally arises and subsides within the expanse of naked and empty awareness, the self-experience of awareness is mistakenly perceived as something distinct and separate. And on this basis, the hallucinatory appearances of the three worlds unfold.

* * *

The thirteenth section shows that yogis with realization are unaffected by the unfolding movement of thoughts and appearing objects, which are for them no more than a magical display.

> **13. All things come from nowhere,**
> **Nowhere do they go,**
> **And nowhere do they stay.**
> **All is but the vast expanse of dharmatā.**
> **For those who realize this, there is**
> **The "utter openness and freedom of the triple world."**
> **This is the Ati teaching of the vajra essence present of itself,**
> **Arising in Samantabhadra's vast expanse.**

The mind and the phenomenal field, the self-experience and display of the mind, simply arise without possessing the slightest degree of existence as objects. If one searches for the place where they first arise, nothing is found. They are empty of a place of origin. Coming from nowhere, they are the state of equality, awareness, open and unimpeded. Likewise, if one tries to find where the mind and appearing objects finally go, again one finds nothing. They are empty of a destination; they go nowhere. They are simply the state of equality, the state of freedom from mental elaboration. And again, if one tries to discover where they are at the present moment, the place where they are staying—or indeed anything that might conceivably stay there—nothing can be found. They aren't anywhere.

They do not stir beyond the vast expanse of the one sole sphere of primordial purity, the dharmatā. For yogis who realize this truth directly in a manner free from conceptual analysis, everything that occurs is quite evidently awareness—naked, open, and unimpeded. Although the appearances of the objects of the six consciousnesses manifest within awareness, the latter does not stray into them. This is so because there is no attachment or fixation, and there is neither affirmation nor negation regarding whatever appears. At that time, mastery of awareness is attained. Whatever is seen is pure in naked, unimpeded awareness. It is inseparable from the vast expanse of primordial purity. Cognitions of apprehender and apprehended, the very root of samsara, are emptied out. Phenomenal existence becomes a vast state of openness and freedom. It is the so-called utter openness and freedom of the three worlds.

It is at that moment that the final goal is attained: the realization of the teaching of the indestructible vajra essence, the ultimate truth, the uncontrived, spontaneously present primordial purity of the dharmakāya as set forth in Atiyoga. This realization manifests moreover within awareness, the vast expanse of Samantabhadra.

* * *

The fourteenth section shows that awareness itself is all-transcending like space.

14. Within the utterly immaculate enlightened mind,
There is no view, no object of a view.
There is not the slightest trace
Of something to be viewed or someone viewing.
There is no mind that meditates,
Nor anything on which to meditate.
Neither is there action or a subject acting.
Because it is spontaneously present,
There is not the slightest trace of a result to gain.

Within the enlightened mind, utterly pure of the conceptually elaborated view, meditation, action, and result—that is, within the state of equality devoid of conceptual elaboration—there is no object to be viewed. For this same enlightened mind is open, unimpeded, and devoid of conceptualization. And if there is no object to be viewed, there is not, and there has never been, any such thing as a view. There is not the slightest trace of something to be viewed and someone that views. From the very beginning, there has never been any such thing as an agent and object of the view. They do not exist. They are empty.

Likewise, within the utterly pure enlightened mind, there is no meditating mind. The cognition designated as the meditating mind, which is established as the indivisible instant [of knowing], is by nature an emptiness devoid of objective reference. And if the agent (namely, the cognition designated as the meditating mind) is nonexistent, it stands to reason that its object (that is, something to be meditated on) is equally nonexistent. It is none other than a groundless, rootless dimension of unimpeded openness devoid of objective reference.

Similarly, in the utterly pure enlightened mind, there is neither an object of action nor an agent (the consciousness of an active agent). For the enlightened mind is nondual, self-arisen primordial wisdom, uncontrived and spontaneously present. Thus by its nature it is unconditioned. And by the same token, since there is neither a result, an object to be attained, nor a consciousness, an agent that attains it, there is not the slightest trace of a result to be achieved.

Therefore, whereas—of necessity—view, meditation, action, and result have been [notionally] distinguished in relation to awareness, nevertheless, since awareness, being devoid of center and periphery, has no existence whatsoever and is emptiness, it follows that view, meditation, action, and result cannot [actually] be distinguished in relation to it. They are a state of equality beyond conceptual elaboration.

Moreover, a distinction between view, meditation, action, and result is necessarily made on the basis of a continuity of many instants. But phenomena cease at every instant; they do not endure for more than a moment. Therefore, since they last for only an infinitesimal point in time, there is no way for view, meditation, action, and result to be posited distinctly from each other.

In the same way, since self-cognizing awareness, the dharmakāya, is present primordially, there is no need for it to be produced anew. And if this is the case, it is pointless to set forth a scheme of view, meditation, action, and result as a means to attaining it. For awareness transcends view, meditation, action, and result. It is said in *The Lion's Perfect Power*,

> It's not by meditating that you find me,
> Awareness uncontrived, spontaneously present.
> It's not through acting that you see me,
> Unmade and self-arisen from the very first.
> It's not by view and viewing that you see me,
> The dharmakāya free of all extremes primordially.

From the very beginning, awareness is present in the manner of primordial meditation, and so there is no need now to engage in it again. Awareness, self-arisen primordial wisdom, is the perfection of uncontrived, self-arising action, which lies primordially beyond all effortful striving. In the present moment, there is no need to rely newly on the activities of adopting and rejecting. And since the dharmakāya is primordially free from all conceptual extremes, if now one tries to view it as something new, one will not succeed. It cannot be seen. For however much one may try to calculate the height and length of space, its shape and color, its cardinal and intermediate directions, one will achieve nothing but one's own fatigue. For space is beyond the mind's appraisal. In the same way, since awareness is free from all the conceptual ties of existence and nonexistence, permanence and impermanence, identity and difference, and so on, it cannot be compartmentalized or posited in terms of view, meditation, action, and result.

There are numerous texts from scripture that demonstrate on the basis of the three kinds of argument that the view, meditation, action, and result have no existence. In short, we may say, first of all, that since awareness in itself is free from all conceptual extremes, it follows that the view, meditation, action, and result are themselves without existence. Second, the view, meditation, action, and result are primordially present in awareness, and therefore, there is no need to practice them anew in the present moment. Third, since the view, meditation, action, and result implemented in the present are necessarily conditioned phenomena, it follows that they are like patches applied to awareness, which is unconditioned. It is impossible to posit them in this way, for conditioned and unconditioned are in direct contradiction.

* * *

The fifteenth section shows that it is necessary to understand that there are no grounds on which to train and so on [namely, the other elements of tantra].

> **15. In what is nonexistent**
> **There are no grounds to be traversed**
> **And therefore from the first,**
> **There is no path to follow.**
> **Luminosity, as the supreme sphere,**
> **Is present from the first.**
> **Thus there are no mandalas for thought to generate,**
> **No mantras and no recitations,**
> **No empowerments, and no samayas.**
> **Since no gradual dissolution is observed,**
> **There is no perfection stage.**
> **For the kāyas and the wisdoms, present from the first,**
> **There is no causal process**
> **Based on adventitious and conditioned**
> **circumstances.**
> **If such a thing there were,**

Primordial wisdom, not being self-arisen,
Would have to be conditioned
And therefore subject to destruction.
How could it be defined
As unconditioned and spontaneous presence?

Awareness, the enlightened mind, is primordially nonexistent. It is empty. It is a mistake to think of it as an existent thing. Unconditioned emptiness, the state of freedom from mental elaboration, and the conditioned entities associated with effortful practice are contradictory terms. It follows therefore that there are no paths or grounds of realization to be traversed. Neither is there any path to follow. It is like an empty space, open and unimpeded, in which the activity of progressing or following has no place.

Since awareness itself is, from the very first, present as changeless and unmoving luminosity, the supreme sphere free of the corners and edges of thoughts, there are no mandalas to be generated, no mantras to be recited, no prayers to be said, no empowerments to be bestowed, no samayas to be observed. For all these are grounded in concerted effort and rely on the conceptual procedures of the generation stage, the aspect of skillful means.

Since awareness is itself a nongenerated, self-arisen mandala, it is unnecessary to take the support of anything conceptual that is different from it—a mandala and so forth belonging to the generation stage. Since the concentration on the mantra of a deity is perfectly included within the creative power of awareness, there is no need to exert oneself in the recitation of mantras and prayers. And since the ultimate, self-arisen empowerment, beyond giving and receiving, is perfectly included within awareness itself, and since the samayas of nothing to keep also abide within it and not elsewhere, there is no need to take the support of the generation stage, the aspect of skillful means. As it is said in *The Lion's Perfect Power*,

Since at no time are you outside the unborn,
It's not the keeping of samaya

That will bring you to enlightenment.
Since the mandala is in you from the very first,
It is not a painted mandala
That causes you to see the deity.
Since the unchanging mudrā is within you from the very first,
Through mudrās made with effort, accomplishment will vanish.
The essential mantra is within you from the very first,
By recitation of essential mantras, the seed mantra decays.

In short, the ten elements or essential factors of tantric practice: the training on the grounds and progress on the paths, the visualization of mandalas, the giving of empowerments, meditation on the path, the keeping of samaya, and so on—none of this lies outside the state of unborn awareness. To think that buddhahood is gained through such conceptually elaborated means—rather than through awareness that is free of all such elaborations—is like sweeping dust from the earth while wanting to rid the sky of clouds. Within the fundamental nature of awareness, true reality itself, the ten essential factors of tantra have no existence at all. Indeed, it is said that if one were to regard them as existent, the fundamental nature would itself be misconstrued and buddhahood would not be gained, the deity would not be seen, and the seed mantra would be damaged. *The Lion's Perfect Power* says,

The measureless palace is primordially complete within you.
If you visualize it, it will dissipate
Awareness's own self-experience.
The light rays of cognizant power naturally arise.
If you meditate upon the deity's accoutrements,
This will undermine your own objective.
Perfection is spontaneous; it is not produced.
There is no need to visualize or invoke the deity.

> The deity is not pleased by praise and offerings made with effort.
> Open, unimpeded, dharmakāya cannot be grasped.
> It is not found through a conceptual meditation.

The mandala of the infinite purity of phenomenal existence (the measureless palace and so forth) is primordially complete within the vast expanse of awareness. If, failing to understand this, one strenuously meditates on mandalas endowed with characteristics—a measureless palace and so on—one will do no more than disperse the spontaneously present buddha field that is the self-experience of awareness. No benefit will come of this. If one does not recognize the fact that the light rays of the cognizant potency of awareness, the dharmakāya, manifest from the very beginning in the form of deities, and if one meditates instead on the accoutrements of the male and female deities endowed with characteristics, buddhahood will not be gained. One will fail of one's own objective. For the level of dharmakāya will not be achieved. Awareness subsists from the very beginning as the body of the deity, which is not generated but is self-arisen. To meditate now and, as it were, newly on the generation stage, inviting the deity and presenting offerings and praise, cannot in any way be pleasing to the non-generated, self-arisen deity. Because awareness, the dharmakāya, is ungraspable, free of mental elaboration, and open and unimpeded, it follows that the benefit of oneself and others is not achieved through effortful meditation involving something marked by conceptual attributes. For all these reasons, no generation stage (the aspect of skillful means) should be looked for anywhere else than in awareness.

Similarly, in the case of the perfection stage (the wisdom aspect), there is no concluding gradual dissolution—that is, the buddha field dissolving into the principal deity, which then dissolves into the wisdom deity, which then dissolves into the wheel of mantra syllables, which then melts into the concentration deity (namely, the seed syllable itself), which then disappears, melting into the dharmadhātu, the expanse of awareness. For that reason, there is no conceptual perfection stage.

Given, therefore, that all the qualities of the result, such as the kāyas and wisdoms, are present from the very first, inseparable from self-arisen awareness, there is no way to achieve buddhahood now, anew, by striving in the causal processes based on conditioned adventitious circumstances, such as the gatherings of the two accumulations, the purification of the two obscuring veils, meditation on deities, and the recitation of mantra. Indeed, if it *were* possible, it would mean that the qualities of the result would not be self-arisen primordial wisdom. For from the very first, this is free of all concerted effort. It is free of all acceptance and rejection, affirmation and negation. The appearance of the kāyas and wisdoms is naturally present within it, in a totally uncontrived manner, and from the very beginning. Just as heat is implicit in fire and moisture in water, [the kāyas and wisdoms] are inseparable from awareness. They rest in the state of equality free of mental elaboration, the one sole sphere of the dharmakāya, unconditioned spontaneous presence.

To achieve a buddhahood based on striving and through causes and conditions would be to achieve a conditioned buddhahood, which, in being conditioned, would be destructible and not beyond the law of impermanence. By contrast, awareness, unconditioned spontaneous presence, is naturally present as the ultimate truth, the indestructible vajra essence. This is why the difference between the two is indicated. The key point to be understood is that awareness is beyond all indication and description. This is the most important thing to understand. As this stanza demonstrates, awareness, in other words, self-arisen primordial wisdom, is beyond all training on the grounds and progression through the paths.

* * *

The sixteenth section summarizes the meaning of the previous stanzas—namely, that awareness transcends all effortful striving as well as the causal process itself.

16. Therefore the ultimate expanse
Itself transcends causality.
The ten elements of tantra have no place therein.
This, I beg you, understand:
The nature of the mind,
True reality beyond all effort and all practice,
Is the stilling of conceptual elaborations
Of existence and of nonexistence.

Indeed, for the reasons previously stated, the ultimate expanse, self-arisen primordial wisdom, is in itself neither damaged by the phenomena of samsara nor enhanced by the phenomena of nirvana. For it is self-arisen primordial wisdom free of mental elaboration. Since it lies beyond all concerted effort that partakes of the causal process, it is the fundamental nature, true reality, where view, action, samaya, empowerment, mandala, and all the other of the ten elements of tantra, have no place. It manifests for beings of the very highest capacity, faculties, and karmic fortune. As it is said in *The All-Creating King*,

> For yogis who have perfect karmic fortune
> Owing to their faith in me from countless ages past,
> In me, the all-creating and enlightened mind,
> There is no view on which to meditate,
> No samaya that they should observe,
> No striving in activities, no paths to be traversed.
> There is no training on the grounds, no causal law.

In light of the explanation just given, the sense of this citation is easy to understand.

And with regard to the nature of the mind, the true reality that lies beyond all effort and all practice, all that arises in the present moment in the aspects of enlightened body, speech, mind, qualities, and activities is not in the slightest way different from the one sole sphere of awareness. As we find in *Awareness Self-Arisen*,

All is perfect as my body;
All that is resounded is my speech;
All thoughts are realized as my mind;
Anything that manifests is my quality;
When not striven for, my activities are found.

The body is posited as what is visible to the eyes, speech as what is heard by the ears, and the mind as that which acts as the basis of these things. Nevertheless, it is generally said that whatever forms appear within awareness—namely, primordial wisdom itself—are all perfect as the enlightened body. Whatever sounds resound therein are the enlightened speech. Whatever thoughts arise, they are understood to be the enlightened mind. The appearances that are displayed are perfect as enlightened qualities and activities, which are present of themselves without any effort being made.

Similarly, view, meditation, action, result, samaya, empowerment, and so on [the ten elements of tantra] are none other than awareness, the enlightened mind. It is said in *Awareness Self-Arisen*,

My view is the kāya of the one sole sphere;
My meditation is free of intellect;
My action is beyond all objects.
My result is the one and unique state.
My samaya is "nothing to observe."
My empowerment is free of giving and receiving.

As this text says, "my" view—that is, the view of all-creating awareness—is the kāya of the one sole sphere, free from the corners and edges of ordinary cognition. Likewise, my meditation transcends the intellect with its concepts of existence, nonexistence, both, and neither. My action transcends all objects, whether positive or negative, to be accepted or rejected. My result is the one sole sphere beyond all hope and fear. My samaya is primordial wisdom—something that, from the first, is not to be observed. My empowerment is free of being given or received. As the same text says,

> If supreme empowerment were not within,
> What could be received by its bestowal?

And again,

> I am the supreme burial ground,
> The tomb of all the buddhas and of sentient beings.
> And through my supreme blessing power,
> All buddhas of the three times manifest.

When death arrives, the place where the body is left to disintegrate and disappear is called a burial ground. Accordingly, when non-abiding nirvana, the final place of freedom, is at length achieved, this expanse of the one sole sphere is referred to [figuratively] as a burial ground. For when awareness—that is, self-arisen primordial wisdom—is considered, it consists in the stilling of all concepts of existence, nonexistence, both and neither, identity and difference. Longchenpa requests us all to understand and realize this self-arisen primordial wisdom, true reality itself.

* * *

This concludes the commentary on the fifth chapter of *The Precious Treasury of the Dharmadhātu*, which shows that awareness is beyond concerted effort and causality.

6. All Is Subsumed within the Enlightened Mind

The sixth chapter, which shows that all phenomena are gathered within awareness, pure by its very nature, is divided into nine sections. The first section shows that all things—alike in their suchness, their ultimate nature—are subsumed within the unborn condition.[72]

1. Just as light is gathered in the sun's essential core,
All things are gathered in their root, the
enlightened mind.
Phenomenal existence, impure, hallucinatory—
The world and its inhabitants—
When its wellspring and support
And the space of its abiding are examined,
Is found to be completely gathered in the mind,
Groundless, free and open from the very first.
Delusion and the absence of delusion both
Are gathered in the nature of the mind,
The vast immensity of the primordial expanse,
Transcending names and entities.

That which drives the diffusion and absorption of all the rays of light that emanate from the sun's essential core is the sun itself. All the light that is diffused by it is gathered within it. In the same way, since all the appearances of the oceanlike infinity of phenomena unfold within awareness, the enlightened mind, they too are gathered in their root—awareness, the enlightened mind, the unborn expanse of equality. It is said in *The All-Creating King*,

> Because I gather in myself all things,
> However they may manifest,
> I am said to be their essence.
> Because I am the wellspring of all things,
> However they may manifest,
> I am said to be their seed.
> Because all things derive from me,
> However they may manifest,
> I am said to be their cause.
> Because from me come all the branches of phenomena,
> However they may manifest,
> I am said to be their trunk.
> Because all things abide in me,
> However they may manifest,
> I am said to be their ground.
> Because I am all things,
> However they may manifest,
> I am said to be their root.

Since all phenomena of samsara and nirvana are gathered within awareness itself, awareness is described as the essence of all phenomena. Since all phenomena arise within awareness, awareness is described as their seed. Since all phenomena emerge from awareness, awareness is described as their cause. Since all phenomena are like the branches of awareness, awareness itself is described as the branch-supporting trunk. Since all phenomena abide within awareness, awareness is described as the ground and root of all phenomena.

Consequently, no matter how manifold appearances belonging to impure, hallucinatory, phenomenal existence may manifest (the universe and its inhabitants), if all are well examined, it will be seen that they are no more real than last night's dreams. The things one dreamed about last night and the appearances of today, experienced in waking life, are similar in their duration, number, and verisimilitude. But if one examines the wellspring or source from which the dreamlike appearances of samsara and nirvana have arisen, one finds that it is nothing at all; it is simply emptiness. One then finds that the place where they remain is also nonexistent, simply emptiness. And finally, one finds that they go nowhere; they do not transcend the state of emptiness. They have no support; there is nothing to be supported. They do not remain; they have no abode. In themselves, there is no identifying them. They are all the single expanse of spacelike dharmatā. However much one may examine them, they are found to be nothing other than that. They are gathered within the ultimate enlightened mind—groundless, rootless, primordially open and free. *The All-Creating King* declares,

> Since all things are unborn,
> It's said that they are gathered in the unborn dharmatā.

And we find in *Awareness Self-Arisen*,

> All things by their nature
> Are beyond objective reference.
> The mind that looks for them has no existence either.
> All are gathered in the space of primal wisdom.

What need is there to say that when all phenomena are analyzed using the four great Madhyamaka arguments, they are shown to be devoid of any existence whatever? Even when they are left unexamined and unanalyzed, they are empty and without existence. They transcend thought and are ineffable. The all-knowing Longchenpa has said,

> When examined, they are groundless.
> When left unexamined, they have no existence.

When perfectly examined, they transcend
All word, all thought, and all expression.

In the same way that awareness is unborn, all phenomena are unborn. When one realizes that the nature of the mind, awareness, is unborn, one is able to realize that all phenomena are likewise unborn. This realization encompasses the realization of all Victorious Ones. If, therefore, it is realized that all appearing things mingle in a single taste within the great and vast immensity of the primordial expanse of the dharmatā, which is the state of awareness, empty and unborn, the deluded appearances of samsara and the undeluded appearances of nirvana can in no way be distinguished. When it is realized that they are beyond all mental elaboration and that not even their designations, the names and entities of samsara and nirvana, exist, all phenomena are seen to be subsumed within the expanse of supreme equality, the primordially empty nature of awareness.

* * *

The second section shows that no matter how phenomena appear, all are gathered within the state of awareness—in the same way that dreams are gathered within the state of sleep.

2. The wonderful display,
Pure self-experience of awareness—
The buddhas and the buddha fields,
Primordial wisdoms and enlightened action—
This also is inseparably subsumed
Within the self-arisen state.
Samsara and nirvana, all phenomenal existence,
Are the unconditioned, all-encompassing
Enlightened mind,
Luminous and empty like the sun and sky.
Self-arisen from the first,
It is the vast, immense, primordial expanse.

Also, the wondrous display of the pure self-experience of buddhahood—the buddhas, the buddha fields, the primordial wisdoms, enlightened activities, and so on—all is inseparably subsumed within the state of self-arisen awareness. Briefly, this display comprises the appearance of the twenty-five qualities of the result. These are the five aspects of the enlightened body—that is, the body, speech, mind, quality, and activity aspects of the enlightened body; the body, speech, mind, quality, and activity aspects of the enlightened speech; and similarly for the enlightened mind, qualities, and activity. It is said in *The All-Creating King*,

> The threefold kāya of the Teacher is my natural expression.
> The buddhas of the three times are my natural expression.
> The bodhisattvas are my natural expression.
> Four yogas are my natural expression.

The four yogas are the yoga of the courageous mind, the great yoga, the thorough yoga, and the supreme yoga.

The pure perceptions of the buddhas and the impure, hallucinatory perceptions of beings—that is, everything in phenomenal existence in both samsara and nirvana—are subsumed within the all-encompassing enlightened mind, leaving nothing aside. Awareness, the ultimate enlightened mind, which is luminous like the sun, is spontaneously present as that which dispels the darkness of ignorance. Not existing as anything at all, it is like the empty sky, devoid of self and spontaneously present. It is also spontaneously present primordially as unconditioned empty luminosity. All phenomena are accordingly encompassed from the very first by the vast and all-pervading expanse of primordial wisdom, self-arisen awareness.

Likewise, given that all phenomena manifest through the creative power of awareness, they are empty. Inasmuch as awareness is also empty and unborn, there is not a single phenomenon that is not encompassed by awareness. And also when appearances arise, when the six consciousnesses, the thoughts of the five poisons, and so on appear and are perceived—again, there is not even the slightest trace of anything that is not awareness. As previously stated, one posits a naked cognition that is the creative power of awareness and also a cognition that strays into sense objects, as well as the aspect of movement and the aspect of unimpeded openness. But this is only said to cater for beginners in the practice and to indicate the way that they are to maintain awareness itself. In truth however, from the point of view of the fundamental nature itself, the two aspects just mentioned (the two kinds of cognition) never stir from the sole expanse of empty, unborn awareness. All appearances are, from the very beginning, naturally open and free in the expanse of emptiness (this is the wisdom aspect). And, taking into account all the different kinds of emptiness, it is impossible for there to be a single thing that does not manifest as the unceasing display of dependent arising (this is the aspect of skillful means). It is as Mipham Rinpoche has said,

> Whatever appears is pervaded by emptiness.
> Whatever is empty is pervaded by appearance.
> If it appears, it cannot not be empty.
> If it is empty, it cannot not appear.

So it is that all appearances of the dharmatā are equal in the expanse of the unborn nature and all appearances of phenomena are the state of equality in that they never stir from the expanse of dharmatā. It is thus that all phenomena are encompassed by the expanse of awareness.

* * *

The third section shows that the nature of the mind is the vast expanse.

> **3. The nature of the mind**
> **Is an unchanging vast expanse,**
> **A realm of space.**

Its multifarious display
Is the enlightened mind's creative power.
Since it has samsara and nirvana
Along with all the vehicles within its power,
All things are subjected
To its one sole state beyond activity.
There is nothing that is separate from it,
Nothing that exceeds its boundary.
There is no moving from the dharmatā, enlightened mind.

Suchness, the fundamental nature of the mind, pervades the whole of samsara and nirvana. It is a vast expanse wherein all the phenomena of samsara and nirvana originate. Throughout the three times it is motionless and unchanging, an immensely vast expanse similar to the realm of space. Its multifarious display—all appearances, pure or impure, that manifest within the mind itself—is solely the creative power of the enlightened mind.

Since the abyss of space is the dimension and support of phenomenal existence, the world and its inhabitants, it contains them and has them in its power. Similarly, the vast, unchanging expanse of the mind's nature is the great space of all the phenomena of both samsara and nirvana; it is the ground for the arising of samsara and nirvana, and of all the vehicles. The whole of samsara and nirvana emanate from it, and into it they subside. It has them all within its sovereign power and therefore has the character, as it were, of a creator.

The dharmatā, the enlightened mind, is the spacious womb of the whole of samsara and nirvana. Before samsara and nirvana ever emerged, they were within the expanse of all-pervading dharmatā. This is described in *Awareness Self-Arisen*, which says,

Before space ever was,
Spaciousness was nonexistent from the very first.
Before there was the nature of phenomena,

> There were no names distinguishing their character.
> Before the buddhas were,
> There were primordially no attributes of beings.
> Before nirvana ever was,
> There was, primordially, nothing named "samsara."
> Thus I am the foremost,
> Of all the buddhas, the most venerable.

All the phenomena of samsara and nirvana arise, dwell, and subside, they are born, subsist, and cease, within the expanse of awareness. They never shift from it in any of these three moments, their beginning, their ending, and the time between these two. They never transcend it. This means that everything in phenomenal existence, samsara and nirvana, is subject to, or overridden by, the one sole state of awareness that transcends all effortful action and is the state of equality, free of mental elaboration. However much one may search for something extraneous to awareness, the enlightened mind—something that lies beyond its boundary—one will find nothing. All phenomena of samsara and nirvana are altogether gathered within the expanse of the one self-cognizing primordial wisdom. As it is said in *The All-Creating King*,

> Dharmatā, spontaneous presence,
> The essence of immensity,
> Has never moved, nor does it move,
> Nor ever will it move.
> The space of dharmatā,
> Encompassing phenomenal existence,
> The world and all its beings,
> Is present of itself and thus beyond all action.

The most crucial point, therefore, is to understand that phenomena never stand apart from the dharmatā, the enlightened mind—that they do not stir from the one expanse of awareness.

* * *

The fourth section illustrates the fact that everything is subsumed within awareness and never stirs from it.

> **4. Since all arises in Samantabhadra,**
> **This one spontaneous presence,**
> **All things are subsumed therein without exception.**
> **Peerless and sublime, it is the greatest of the great.**
> **Samantabhadra, the expanse of ultimate reality,**
> **Is like a king who gathers all things to himself.**
> **He rules samsara and nirvana,**
> **And they never part from him.**

Outer and inner phenomena, the world and its inhabitants, arise within Samantabhadra, the one expanse of spontaneous presence, uncontrived, self-arisen awareness. All phenomena of samsara and nirvana are without exception gathered in this expanse of awareness. Furthermore, since this awareness governs by natural capacity the whole of samsara and nirvana, it is a sublime and utterly peerless state.

All the buddhas, past, present, and to come, achieve their freedom on the basis of Samantabhadra. And the sentient beings of the three worlds have likewise no other way to accomplish liberation than in dependence upon Samantabhadra, which is awareness. So it is that Samantabhadra, awareness, is the greatest of the great, the essence of the essence, the more profound than the profound, the final point of all that is to be realized. Such is the expanse of ultimate reality, Samantabhadra.

Samantabhadra, awareness, the expanse of ultimate reality, is like a king, a universal ruler. For a king, without ever moving from his palace, holds all the peoples of his realm beneath his sway. Likewise, awareness, without ever stirring from the dharmadhātu, gathers within itself all things in samsara and nirvana. It is said in *The General Principle of Perfection*,

In the vast, skylike immensity of the enlightened mind,
All things are gathered, all without exception.
An equality unmoving that, ruling over all,
Is like a king. It is primordial wisdom self-arisen,
Changeless and unmoving from the very first.

All phenomena of samsara and nirvana arise within the expanse of awareness, Samantabhadra. Since they are brought about through Samantabhadra, samsara and nirvana lie entirely beneath his sway, for they never diverge from the display of awareness.

The world and its beings, the four elements and so on, appear *within* the expanse of space. Space is not the product of the elements. In just the same way, the phenomena of samsara and nirvana are created by awareness, the enlightened mind. They appear within it. But the mind itself has not been made by anyone. It is beyond all action. As *The All-Creating King* tells us,

The enlightened mind, the all-creator,
Is the one thing uncreated.
This all-creating and enlightened mind,
Creative by its nature,
Is uncreated—no need has it to be created.

All things are created by the ultimate enlightened mind. By contrast, the ultimate enlightened mind itself does not need to be created and is made by no one. Even if one wanted to make it, it would be impossible, for it is the state of equality free from all mental elaboration.

* * *

The fifth section shows that because the nature of phenomena is equality, phenomena are beyond concerted effort and are neither good nor bad in themselves.

5. All things are Samantabhadra;
Not one thing is there that is not Samantabhadra.

As Samantabhadra, all is one in being neither good nor bad.
All existent things, all nonexistent things
Are one within the ultimate expanse.
Not stirring from spontaneous presence,
All things are one in their equality.

All things, on the level of the ground, are neither good nor bad; on the level of the path, they are beyond effort; and on the level of the result, they are a state of equality. Therefore, everything in samsara and nirvana, the whole of phenomenal existence, is encompassed by the state of purity and equality, great primordial wisdom, the nature of Samantabhadra. There is not a single thing that is not Samantabhadra. And therefore, all phenomena of samsara and nirvana, in being Samantabhadra, are one and the same beyond any differentiation in terms of good and bad, and beyond adoption and rejection. All things perceived on the conventional level are the clear appearances of what does not exist; they are like a magical display. Equal in being neither good nor bad, they are beyond all concerted effort. Even the empty phenomena of the ultimate truth are like space, empty and equal, groundless and rootless. It is not that some things are good and others bad, to be adopted or rejected. They are a state of equality.

All existent things—the conditioned phenomena of form, sound, smell, taste, touch, and so on, and all nonexistent things (that is, the unconditioned phenomena of emptiness)—are one in the expanse of awareness, the enlightened mind, the unborn dharmatā. Appearances, in their oceanlike infinity, have never stirred, do not stir, and will never stir from the expanse of uncontrived awareness, self-arisen spontaneous presence. They are one, for they are all equally present in awareness, the enlightened mind.

* * *

The sixth section shows that since all appearances occur within the ultimate expanse, they transcend all effortful striving.

> **6. This one state where all things without exception manifest**
> **Is the ultimate expanse of dharmatā.**
> **It is a state beyond all action;**
> **It cannot be achieved or striven for.**
> **Practice done with effort**
> **Is not different from the ultimate expanse.**
> **What goal is there to strive for?**[73]
> **Where could it be achieved?**

All our present experiences of happiness and suffering, excellence, defects, good and bad appearances, have never existed. They are like dream experiences of joy and sorrow, which are taken to be truly real and which give rise to all one's exhausting and irksome efforts. It is as Candrakīrti says,[74]

> Just as a young woman dreaming
> That she has a son who later dies
> Rejoices at his birth and mourns his death—
> Understand that all things are like this.

The happiness and sorrow experienced in a dream do not stir from the state of sleep and in just the same way, hallucinatory appearances never stir from the state of awareness. However the things of phenomenal existence manifest within awareness, the one enlightened mind, not one of them ever stirs from the ultimate expanse of the dharmatā, empty awareness itself. No matter what efforts are made to implement the antidotes with regard to the things to be abandoned, they will achieve nothing except to render impossible one's release from the snare of delusion. They will not in the slightest way bring one closer to awareness, the dharmatā. One must simply rest in meditative evenness in the state of awareness beyond all action. For awareness can never be achieved through exhausting effort. It cannot be striven for by applying antidotes to the things that are to be abandoned, for the simple reason that it cannot be captured through action. The spacelike nature of the mind cannot be achieved through concerted effort and striving or through a transformation based on the law of cause and effect. Primordial wisdom self-arisen is the ground for the arising of all things, which manifest within it. It transcends both virtue and nonvirtue. One should rest naturally in the ultimate expanse of awareness. Effortful practice never achieves anything, for in fact it is not different from suchness, the dharmatā itself. This is something experienced only by disciples of the sharpest capacity, practitioners of the Great Perfection. If it is expounded openly to practitioners of the lower vehicles and to unqualified people of lesser scope, the result will be that they will find fault with it and this will cause them (and those who divulge it) to take rebirth in the lower destinies. As we find in *The Word-Transcending Tantra*,

> If this fundamental nature, the way things are,
> Is proclaimed to śrāvakas and to pratyekabuddhas,
> Overcome with fear, they will faint.
> It must therefore be utterly kept secret.

In the section of the Wisdom Chapter of *The Way of the Bodhisattva*—where the objections of ordinary people, the śrāvakas, and the Cittamātrins are answered, and just before the refutation of the śrāvaka position—it is first demonstrated that, with regard to the scriptures, the Mahāyāna is indeed the teaching of the Buddha and that with regard to the path, emptiness is proven to be the antidote. If the Mahāyāna teachings were not first demonstrated to be buddha-word, the śrāvakas would not accept them. On the other hand, when they state their own tradition, they set forth the phenomenal no-self as this is described in the *Stanzas of the Middle Way*,

> In his *Counsel to Kātyāyana*,
> The Lord, through understanding
> Both existent things and nonexistent things,
> Has rejected both the views "this is" and "this is not."[75]

According to their way of looking at things, the Buddha taught the phenomenal no-self by saying that gross extended phenomena are nonexistent, in contrast with the indivisible particles, which are *not* nonexistent. Accordingly, the śrāvakas assert only the coarse phenomenal no-self. They do not accept the four, eight, and eighteen aspects of emptiness as set forth in the Mahāyāna scriptures. On the contrary, they say that the emptiness taught in the Mahāyāna is a terrifying doctrine that flies in the face of conventional reality. They refuse to accept it as authentic scripture, saying that the Buddha never spoke in such a way. Consequently, if it is not first shown that the Mahāyāna scriptures are authentic, whenever a quotation is drawn from them as proof, the śrāvakas will reject them. For such scriptures are not, in their view, the buddha-word. One may understand from this that the teachings of the Great Perfection should be kept completely secret from unsuitable recipients such as these.

Given that awareness—as was explained earlier—is beyond the reach of effortful practice, what goal is there to strive for? There is no such thing. And where indeed could it be achieved? There is no place of achievement. For all is entirely contained *within* the display of open and unimpeded awareness.

* * *

The seventh section shows that for all these reasons, awareness is beyond the causal process. It is beyond the reach of effortful practice.

> **7. It is not something to be sought,**
> **It is not seen in meditation.**
> **It is not a state to be achieved;**
> **It does not come from somewhere else.**
> **It does not come; it does not go:**
> **It is the state of evenness, the dharmakāya.**
> **It is subsumed within the vast expanse**
> **Of the great sphere spontaneously perfect.**

One may use the ten elements of tantra to search for the nature of the mind, but one will find nothing. The nature of the mind is not an object to be sought. However much one may meditate on it—in the manner of a meditator meditating on an object of meditation—it will not be seen by such means. It is as Shabkar has said,

> It is beyond all seeking—
> What cannot be sought, cannot be found.
> It is beyond all meditation—
> It cannot be meditated; meditation ruins it.

And *The All-Creating King* says,

> The enlightened mind,
> The essence of all things,
> Is present of itself and from the very first.
> There is no need to look for it by means of the ten elements.
> There is no need to gain it.

The spacelike nature of the mind is not a state that can be achieved. It is all-pervading and unconditioned. If it were a state to be achieved, and if there were someone achieving it, it would be conditioned—and conditioned and unconditioned are incompatible. Three reasons show that the nature of the mind is not something that can be accomplished. First, the nature of the mind is not attained through the application of the ten elements of tantra. Second, the view, meditation, action, and result are all conditioned phenomena, whereas the nature of the mind is unconditioned. They are consequently incompatible. Third, the view, meditation, action, and result are primordially and naturally present within awareness itself. Therefore, there is no need for them to be achieved newly.

Awareness does not come from somewhere else. Indeed, it does not come and it does not go. It is the state of equality, the spacelike dharmakāya, which lies beyond the reach of effortful practice and the causal process. It is said in *The All-Creating King*,

My nature is like space,
The example that applies to everything.
In pure space there's no striving;
In pure space there is nothing to be striven for.
Space is utterly beyond all action, effort, and exertion.

And,

Wishing thus to see me and my nature—
It is like stepping out into thin air and falling down to
earth.
Trying to progress by means of the ten elements
Of tantra, they do not succeed.

When one tries to take space in one's hands, one finds that there is nothing to be grasped. In just the same way, it is impossible to realize awareness, the enlightened mind, through the effortful practice of the ten elements of tantra. If awareness is trammeled by fixation on what is to be adopted or rejected, on affirming and negating, it is just like stepping out into thin air and falling to the ground. One will only fall into the swamp of the hallucinatory appearances of samsara, and freedom becomes impossible.

In conclusion, therefore, all phenomena that are bound up with effortful practice—the view, meditation, action, and result—are themselves subsumed within awareness, the state of equality of the dharmakāya, the supreme expanse of the one sole spontaneously perfect sphere.

* * *

The eighth section shows that all the [nine] vehicles—understood in terms of great, intermediate, and small—are all subsumed within awareness, the enlightened mind. First, the manner in which the three small vehicles are subsumed is as follows.

8a. The teachings of the śrāvakas,
Of the pratyekabuddhas, and the bodhisattvas

Are decisive on the nonexistence
Of both "I" and "mine."
Their common realization is the spacelike state
Of freedom from elaboration.
The supremely secret Atiyoga teaching
Is that one should rest in true reality—
Self-arisen primal wisdom as it is—
Within the vast expanse
Where self and other cannot be distinguished.
The realizations gained in the small vehicles
Are thus subsumed in this supreme quintessence.

Rongzom Paṇḍita has said that all good meditative experiences and realizations of the lower vehicles occur in an enhanced form in the higher vehicles. The shortcomings of the lower (all the defects of incomprehension) are removed in the higher. The all-knowing Longchenpa concurs with Rongzom in saying that, according to the Atiyoga tradition, all the realizations and meditative experiences described in the vehicles of the śrāvakas, pratyekabuddhas, and bodhisattvas, as well as in the [tantra classes of] Kriyā, Upa, Yoga, Mahāyoga, and Anuyoga—which approximate more with the fundamental nature—are all present, enhanced, within the expanse of the view of Ati. In the case of the śrāvaka view, it is thanks to an understanding that the five psychophysical aggregates and the rest—as well as self and self-clinging—are empty like space, that the coarse, but not the subtle, aspects of the no-self of the person and phenomena are realized. Going further, the pratyekabuddhas realize the subtle aspect of the personal no-self but not the subtle aspect of the phenomenal no-self. By contrast, in the teachings of the bodhisattvas, both the coarse and subtle aspects of both the personal and the phenomenal no-self are well understood. So it is that the realizations of the first two views are subsumed and enhanced within the view of the third vehicle. Moreover, since the teaching of the third vehicle is decisive with regard to the nonexistence of the self and what belongs to it (of "I" and "mine"), all phenomena are understood to be a spacelike state free from elaboration. And if one rests in meditative evenness free from elaboration, the realizations [of the two lower vehicles] will be subsumed therein.

In the Great Perfection generally, awareness is set forth in various ways—as the primordial wisdom of luminous emptiness, as the primordial wisdom of empty luminosity, or as the primordial wisdom of empty awareness. It is said that awareness is posited as the primordial wisdom of luminous emptiness from the standpoint of its nature. It is spoken of as the primordial wisdom of empty luminosity from the standpoint of its character. And it is spoken of as the primordial wisdom of empty awareness from the standpoint of its being the unceasing ground of manifestation.

According to the nondual tantras of Atiyoga—that is, the teachings of the Great Perfection, the yoga of the supreme secret—when one rests in meditative evenness in the spacelike immensity of awareness, where the outer and inner phenomena of the universe and beings, self and other, and so on cannot be individually distinguished, one is resting in the state of true reality, self-arisen, self-cognizing primordial wisdom just as it is. Consequently, the realizations of these lower vehicles are all subsumed and enhanced in this supreme quintessence of the ultimate enlightened mind. It is said in *The All-Creating King*,

> Within the nature of enlightened, all-creating mind,
> The spacelike absence of the mind's elaboration,
> Everything without exception is subsumed.

* * *

The second part of the eighth section shows that the three intermediate vehicles are also subsumed within awareness.

> **8b. The three classes of tantra—Kriyā, Upa, Yoga—**
> **Are all the same in holding that accomplishments**
> **Occur when body, speech, and mind are purified**

Through self-visualization, through the deity,
Through concentration, and through making offerings.
According also to the sovereign
Secret teachings of the vajra peak,
Appearances and sounds are pure awareness,
The primordial deity.
When body, speech, and mind are fully cleansed,
Accomplishments will manifest.
The realizations of these tantras
Are thus subsumed in this supreme quintessence.

Kriyā, or Action, tantra; Upa, or Conduct, tantra; and Yoga, or Union, tantra are the three classes of the so-called outer tantras. In all of them, one meditates on oneself visualized as a deity—that is, the *samayasattva*, or commitment being. One meditates on the deity itself, the *jñānasattva*, or wisdom being. Finally, one meditates on the seed syllable in one's heart, the *samādhisattva*, or concentration being. Subsequently, one makes clouds of offerings and praise. These three kinds of tantra are all the same in holding that when the obscurations of body, speech, and mind are completely purified, the common and supreme accomplishments occur.

In the [special] Kriyā tantra tradition,[76] however, one meditates on oneself as a deity but in the role of a servant and on the actual deity, the jñānasattva, as being a lord or king. In other words, there is an inequality of rank between oneself and the deity. In the Upa tantra tradition, it is said that accomplishment is gained through visualizing the deity (the jñānasattva) in front of oneself in the form of a deity (samayasattva) in the manner of equals, like relatives or friends without any degree of difference, high or low. Finally, according to the Yoga tantra tradition, there is a separation between oneself and the deity during the preparatory section [of the sādhana] before the presence of the deity is invoked, as well as in the concluding section when the deity is requested to depart. During the main part of the practice, however, when the jñānasattva deity is invited into the mandala of oneself as the samayasattva, it dissolves into oneself like water poured into water. Jñānasattva and samayasattva become inseparable, mingling into a single taste. It is thus that accomplishment is gained.

Now the realizations of all these three tantra classes are subsumed within Atiyoga, and the manner in which this happens is described by the omniscient Longchenpa as follows.

> In any of the three outer classes of tantra, the supreme and common accomplishments are gained in dependence on the view, meditation, action, and result of their respective paths. But the state of the ultimate result that is their goal is entirely included, and its qualities enhanced, in the Great Perfection.

Furthermore, it should be understood that the master-servant relationship in Kriyā tantra; the friend-to-friend relationship in Caryā, or Upa, tantra; and the relation of identity in the main practice of Yoga tantra (excluding the preparatory and concluding sections) imply a progressive sublimity in the views of these tantras—to say nothing of the gradual enhancement of their qualities.

The main point to be understood, however, is that owing to the disparity in the profundity of their view of the fundamental nature, the qualities of the higher vehicles are enhanced in comparison with those of the lower ones. For example, the practitioners of Madhyamaka do not meditate on the deity, the jñānasattva, because they lack an understanding of the equality and purity of phenomenal existence. Practitioners of Kriyā tantra, on the other hand, gain an extraordinary certainty surpassing that of the Madhyamikas through meditation on the deity, the jñānasattva. Progressively, the Caryā tantra is much superior to Kriyā because the latter's characteristic assumption of a hierarchical difference between the practitioner and the deity is removed, and henceforth they are regarded as friends or relatives. And in the main practice of Yoga tantra, it is understood that the practitioner and the deity are indivisible and of a single taste, just as when iron is alchemically transmuted into gold. Yoga tantra is for this reason superior to Caryā tantra. For the latter presupposes a difference and separation between oneself and the deity. So it is that based on this progressive difference of views, the three outer tantras are considered superior to the lower vehicles.

Now in accordance with what Jamgön Sakya Paṇḍita has said (to the effect that if there is a view superior to that of Prajñāpāramitā, it must be a conceptual construct), although, apparently, there is a difference between the views of the Prajñāpāramitā and the tantra on the level of the relative truth, there is no difference between them on the level of ultimate truth. Again, he seems to imply that although there is a difference between them in terms of the view that considers phenomena and the view of self-cognizing awareness, there is nevertheless no difference between them when it comes to the view of the ultimate nature of phenomena.[77]

Although the majority of Nyingma scholars adopt the second interpretation, it is only because they do not dare to criticize such an august authority. Even so, according to the tradition of the old translations—and as Mipham Rinpoche clearly teaches in *The Beacon of Certainty* and in *The Essence of Luminosity*, his general overview of *Dispelling the Darkness in the Ten Directions*, [Longchenpa's] commentary on *The Secret Essence Tantra*, and elsewhere—there *is* a difference between them from the standpoint of the view that considers the ultimate nature of phenomena as well as the view that considers the self-cognizing awareness. I will not however enlarge on this matter here.

Moreover, according to the view of the profound and secret Atiyoga—the vajra peak of the tantras of the Vajrayāna and the king of all teachings—if it is understood that all phenomena (appearances and sounds) are primordially the utter purity of awareness, the pure and equal enlightened mind, one will come to the realization that the world and its contents are from the very beginning an infinite purity, a mandala of deities, the primordial state of buddhahood. And when the body, speech, and mind are thus completely purified, the resultant accomplishments will manifest. It is in this way too that the realizations produced by the three outer classes of tantra are also subsumed within the supreme quintessence, the luminous Great Perfection. It is said in *The All-Creating King*,

> If within the supreme mandala
> Of self-arisen essence,
> Your body, speech, and mind
> Rest in relaxation, in the natural state,
> The wisdom mind of me, the All-Creating One,
> Is present of itself.

If one's body, speech, and mind are left in a natural, relaxed, and uncontrived state, self-arisen, self-cognizing primordial wisdom, the mandala of the supreme quintessence, will manifest. And within its vast expanse, the realizations of all the other vehicles are naturally and spontaneously subsumed.

* * *

The third part of the eighth section shows how the three higher classes of tantra are perfectly subsumed within awareness.

> **8c. There are also the three classes of Mahā, Anu, Ati.**
> **[In Mahāyoga,] phenomenal existence,**
> **The world and its inhabitants,**
> **Is a pure field of male and female deities.**
> **[In Anuyoga,] the inseparable union**
> **Of primal wisdom and the ultimate expanse**
> **Is said to be unmoving dharmatā,**
> **Primordial wisdom self-arisen.**
> **In the supreme and most secret [Atiyoga],**
> **All phenomena are pure,**
> **The unproduced, immeasurable**
> **Primordial expanse, the field of bliss.**

Within this all-pervading state,
Beyond both out and in,
There is nothing that is marked
By acceptance, by rejection, or by effortful exertion.
Everything is free and open in primordial infinity,
The vast expanse of dharmakāya.
All preceding realizations are subsumed
In this secret quintessence.

The establishment of the ground as the purity and equality of phenomenal existence and the practice of the indivisibility of bliss and emptiness taken as the path are the foundations of both Mahāyoga and Anuyoga. But since their purpose is the direct realization of the state of ultimate, self-cognizing primordial wisdom, they are subsumed, and their qualities enhanced, within the Great Perfection.

The Mahāyoga, Anuyoga, and Atiyoga (respectively the father, mother, and nondual tantras) are the three classes of the inner tantras of the Mantrayāna. In the first of these, the Mahāyoga, which has to do with the generation stage practice, one has clearly in mind the ground mandala of awareness, and one visualizes the path mandala—namely the world and beings of phenomenal existence—as a field of male and female deities within a measureless palace. Considering that the world and its inhabitants are the display of the three mandalas, one recognizes that one's mind and the deity are inseparable, and one realizes the indivisibility of the superior two truths (of purity and equality). This constitutes the view of Mahāyoga.

Then, on the basis of the path of skillful means and the path of liberation, whereby the knots on the three channels and the five chakras are released, one practices the indivisibility of skillful means and wisdom—the utterly pure view of the inseparability of the ultimate expanse and primordial awareness. By this means, it is said that the unmoving dharmatā, the self-arisen, self-cognizing primordial wisdom is actualized. This is the view of Anuyoga. On this matter, the omniscient Longchenpa says,

> In brief, Mahāyoga emphasizes the ground: the view of the indivisibility of purity and equality. Anuyoga emphasizes the path: the indivisibility of bliss and emptiness. Atiyoga emphasizes the result: the indivisibility of awareness and emptiness.

According to the view of the supreme, unsurpassed secret, the Great Perfection, or Ati (the highest and final goal of all realizations), all things in phenomenal existence, both samsara and nirvana, are the utterly pure embodiments of the four kāyas and five primordial wisdoms. The outer universe and its living contents are not produced by causes and conditions. From the very beginning, they are perfectly subsumed in the mandala of buddhahood. As pure fields, immeasurable palaces, deities, wisdoms, and so on, they are present of themselves in the expanse of awareness—primordial, uncontrived great emptiness, the blissful, empty field of equality. Phenomena are not beyond all-pervading awareness—the open, unimpeded, empty luminosity that has neither out nor in. Phenomena are the expression of the one great emptiness. They are the all-embracing dimension of the one great emptiness. They are the buoyant impetus of the one great emptiness. Aside from that, dualistic phenomena, marked by acceptance, by rejection, and by effortful action, do not exist to the slightest degree. It is recognized that all things are the mandala of buddhahood from the very beginning. Without ever stirring from ultimate reality, they are from the beginning open and free in the expanse of the dharmakāya, the infinite, primordial state. Thus all the realizations and meditative experiences of the eight preceding vehicles are completely gathered and subsumed within this most secret quintessence, the Great Perfection.

* * *

The ninth section is the conclusion of the preceding stanzas and shows that everything is perfectly included and subsumed within the enlightened mind.

9. One is perfectly included,
All are perfectly included
In the vast expanse encompassing all things.
All is gathered and subsumed in great spontaneous presence,
Natural, primordial luminosity.

Longchenpa's words "One is perfectly included, all are perfectly included" are a reference to the teaching of *The All-Creating King*, which says,

> There is nothing not included perfectly in it—
> One is perfectly included, two are perfectly included,
> All are perfectly included.
> Sublime is its performance of all deeds.
> One included perfectly
> Means perfectly included in the enlightened mind.
> Two included perfectly
> Means that what enlightened mind produces
> Is also perfectly included.
> All included perfectly
> Means that abundant excellence is perfectly included.

The meaning of this quotation is as follows. "One included perfectly" indicates that awareness is itself actually and perfectly included in the ultimate enlightened mind. "Two included perfectly" indicates that the appearances of the world and its inhabitants—the creation of the ultimate enlightened mind—are perfectly contained within the vast expanse of the all-creating king. "All included perfectly" indicates that all the appearances of the abundant excellence created by both the ultimate enlightened mind and the ordinary mind are perfectly contained in the expanse of awareness, the all-creating king.

Since awareness, this all-creating king, is a vast expanse that encompasses all phenomena, it follows that everything in phenomenal existence is subsumed within awareness, the great spontaneous presence, primordially uncontrived natural luminosity. Again it is said in *The All-Creating King*,

> According to this teaching
> Of the one that's perfectly included,
> The wisdom of the buddhas dwells within it.
> Through this teaching that declares
> That all is perfectly included,
> Abundant excellence is produced.

If one is able to grasp the meaning of this teaching—that awareness is perfectly included within the ultimate enlightened mind—it will be understood also that the wisdom of all the buddhas dwells within awareness. A person who meditates on the teaching that all phenomena are perfectly included in the expanse of awareness, the all-creating king, will attain the level of all the buddhas. It is said, therefore, that this teaching is the creator of abundant excellence.

Yogis who have such realization are praised in texts such as *The Lion's Perfect Power*:

> One who sees the truth of buddhahood
> Becomes the child of the Victorious Ones.
> And when this realization is absorbed within oneself,
> One remains in bliss forever.

As this text says, when the truth of enlightenment—that is, awareness, self-arisen primordial wisdom—is seen, one is called the child of the Victorious Ones. One enters the path of the Great Perfection. Through practicing it, those of greatest capacity gain freedom in this very lifetime. Those of moderate capacity gain freedom at the moment of their deaths, while those of least capacity cannot but gain freedom in the bardo state. Indeed it is proclaimed in *The All-Creating King*,

> Those who dwell within the state devoid of action
> May have bodies human or divine,
> And yet their minds are dharmatā; they are enlightened.

All those who dwell in the view of the Great Perfection beyond all action may for the moment appear to have the body of a god or a human being. And yet, despite their physical appearance—for they are unable to transform their bodies into perfect, luminous forms endowed with the major and minor marks—their minds are the dharmatā, indivisibly blended with the wisdom minds of all the buddhas, supreme primordial wisdom.

* * *

This concludes the word commentary on the sixth chapter of *The Precious Treasury of the Dharmadhātu*, which shows that everything is subsumed within the enlightened mind.

7. All Is Present Spontaneously and Primordially in the Enlightened Mind

The seventh chapter, which shows that everything is naturally present in the enlightened mind from the very beginning, is divided into eleven sections. The first section shows that all the teachings are subsumed within the enlightened mind, present of itself.

> **1. The teachings on the enlightened mind,**
> **By nature uncreated, present of itself,**
> **Wherein all qualities subsist,**
> **Are like the summit of the king of mountains,**
> **High above all other teachings.**
> **They are the sovereign supreme vehicle.**

Awareness is, by its very nature, the uncontrived enlightened mind spontaneously present of itself. It is not created through effort by means of causes and conditions but is self-arisen, primordially present. And since awareness is naturally endowed, in this very instant, with the ultimate result: the four kāyas, five wisdoms, and so on, all qualities are already fully present within it. Just as the summit of Mount Meru, the king of mountains, is said to tower mightily above all the other mountains of the four cosmic continents and eight subcontinents, the teachings on awareness constitute the topmost vehicle of Atiyoga and are the pinnacle and king of all vehicles. They are supreme, the greatest of the great. As it is said in *Awareness Self-Arisen*,

The very highest peak of all the views
Is described as Ati, Great Perfection.

* * *

The second section shows that Atiyoga is the summit of all vehicles.

2. From the summit of the king of mountains,
Once it has been scaled,
The valleys down below can all be seen at once.
But from these valleys down below the peak cannot be seen.
So too, the vajra essence of the Atiyoga,
The highest peak of all the vehicles,
Surveys the goals of all these vehicles
But is to them invisible.
Spontaneous presence, therefore, is the peak,
The summit[78] of all vehicles.

According to the terms of the comparison, on reaching the summit of the king of mountains, one would be able to look down and see the valleys below clearly and in a single glance. On the other hand, someone looking up from deep down in the valley would be unable to catch sight of the summit. In the same way, since the vajra essence of Ati, the Great Perfection, is the highest summit of the system of nine vehicles, it can clearly and simultaneously take in all the objectives of the lower vehicles. By contrast, apart from achieving the realization of their own goals, the lower vehicles are unable to comprehend the realization of Atiyoga. For the higher and the lower are incommensurate. So it is that spontaneous presence, the vajra essence of Atiyoga, is the peak of all the vehicles. When it is realized, all the intellectually articulated tenets of the eight [lower] vehicles are strongly overpowered and completely eclipsed.

* * *

The third section explains in greater detail the vast difference between the higher and lower vehicles.

> **3. It is like a mighty wish-fulfilling jewel,**
> **Which, when people pray before it,**
> **Lavishes upon them all that they might wish.**
> **This is not the case with ordinary stones.**
> **Since the vajra essence**
> **Is the triple kāya present of itself,**
> **When all is left just as it is,**
> **Buddhahood is gained within the ultimate expanse.**
> **This absence of exertion is itself**
> **A sign of the superiority [of Ati teachings].**
> **The lower vehicles are marked**
> **By effort in accepting and rejecting,**
> **And buddhahood is not achieved for many kalpas.**
> **It is as though they are afflicted**
> **By a strong debilitating sickness.**

Only a few people chance upon a wish-fulfilling jewel and this is thanks to the merit they have accumulated in the course of previous good kalpas. People of lesser fortune fail to do so. In the same way, and again thanks to the accumulation of merit for many kalpas, only a few people realize awareness, self-arisen primordial wisdom. No one else can do so. Now if, in accordance with the example given, a wish-fulfilling gem is found, and if it is polished with great care and set upon the tip of a victory banner, it will lavish upon those who pray before it all that they may wish—whereas no matter how much they may pray before an ordinary stone, no riches will accrue.

Now awareness, self-arisen primordial wisdom, the ultimate and indestructible vajra essence, is the triple kāya, which is spontaneously present of itself. Therefore, when those endowed with a positive inheritance of past aspirations and actions leave their body, speech, and mind just as they are, relaxed and free of all contrivance and effort, it is then that through their being inseparable from awareness, the dharmadhātu, they are able to see that buddhahood is accomplished—clearly, vividly, nakedly, and without contrivance—in the very nature of awareness in the present moment. They are able to see it as the field of experience of self-arisen, self-cognizing primordial wisdom alone. This is not something that can be seen by engaging in effortful practice. Awareness cannot be attained through exertion. This is the superior, sublime quality of the ultimate enlightened mind.

Indeed, however much practitioners of the lower vehicles may exert themselves in accepting and rejecting, it is as though they were praying in the presence of an ordinary stone. The desired aim is not achieved. They may strive in this way for kalpas, but actual buddhahood, the fundamental nature, is not attained. Moreover, they are as though afflicted by a powerful, debilitating sickness, the fruit of all their wearying austerities. Not the slightest benefit will appear.

* * *

The fourth section, which shows that awareness beyond effortful action is the triple kāya, has three parts. The first of these concerns the natural state of the dharmakāya.

> **4a. Awareness, even and primordially**
> **spontaneous,**
> **The enlightened mind,**
> **The natural state just as it is,**
> **Is the vast dharmatā.**
> **By nature it is dharmakāya,**
> **The vast primordial expanse of evenness.**
> **Though present in all beings, it lies within the reach**
> **Of only very few who have great fortune.**
> **Left just as it is, it is achieved quite naturally**
> **Within that very state.**

Primordially spontaneous and even, awareness is the fundamental condition of the enlightened mind, the natural state of the ultimate mode of being just as it is, the immensity of the dharmatā. The latter is the primordial expanse of equality free from all mental elaboration, the empty, luminous dharmakāya, which is the very nature of awareness. It is present in the minds of all beings, pervading them like oil in a seed of sesame. As it is said, the sugatagarbha pervades all wandering beings. But although it is present in all, it lies within the reach of only a few fortunate beings—those who have a perfect karmic inheritance deriving from their aspirations and the two accumulations. It is not within the range of others. But when the fortunate rest in the natural state of awareness just as it is, leaving their three doors in a state of relaxed uncontrived simplicity, they actualize it naturally within that very state. It is said in *The Lion's Perfect Power*,

> When I, Samantabhadrī, dharmakāya,
> Free of ordinary cognition,
> Watch "over there" the clear and knowing dharmatā,
> I see awareness, free of all diversity, within myself.
> When I, awareness self-cognizing,
> Watch "over there" things in their multiplicity,
> I see within myself the dharmakāya free of ordinary
> cognition.

The meaning of this quotation is that "When I, unborn Samantabhadrī, the dharmakāya free of ordinary cognition, watch, as it were, separately—over there—the sphere of awareness, the empty, luminous dharmatā, I see awareness within myself, free of conceptual fixation and clinging, empty, luminous, clear, vivid, naked. And when, within the expanse of self-cognizing awareness free of mental elaboration, I watch, as it were, separately—over there—an oceanlike infinity of phenomenal appearances, objects in all their multiplicity, without considering some as good and some as bad, without taking some and leaving others, I find within myself the dharmakāya free of ordinary cognition, the great, self-arisen awareness."

* * *

The second part of the fourth section describes the natural state of the sambhogakāya.

> **4b. Its all-pervasive luminosity**
> **Is the sambhogakāya, present of itself.**
> **Although it is in everyone,**
> **Only few can see it.**
> **When, without exertion**
> **You leave appearances just as they are,**
> **It manifests.**

Awareness, self-arisen primordial wisdom, pervades the whole of samsara and nirvana. It is the great wisdom of the all-encompassing equality of conditioned existence and peace. Therefore, it is something that is all-pervading. It is an empty, all-pervading state. It is not mere emptiness, however—the emptiness of a nonaffirming negation. It is an emptiness that has a character of luminosity. And this luminosity is the spontaneously present sambhogakāya. The luminous character of the sambhogakāya is present in the minds of all, and yet it is only within the scope of a few beings who are very fortunate. It is beyond the perception of everyone else. When, in the present instant, awareness arises as objects, if one leaves these ceaselessly appearing objects just as they are, without fixating on them, remaining in a state that is free of any kind of exertion, this same clear, vivid luminosity will become manifest. And when this state is maintained, it is the natural state of the sambhogakāya.

* * *

The third part of the fourth section describes the state of the nirmāṇakāya.

4c. Its display, which never ceases,
Is the all-pervading space of the nirmāṇakāya.
Present in all beings, it clearly manifests
In the arising of phenomena.
The array of wish-fulfilling qualities
And of enlightened action
Is the pure space of awareness self-cognizing.
It appears if, just like turbid water settling,
You rest within the natural limpid state.

When through its unceasing creative power, the display of awareness unfolds as objects, and when the cognizing factor that arises does not chase after these objects, the ground of the arising of such endless appearances—namely, awareness open, unimpeded, and naked—is called the all-pervading space of the nirmāṇakāya. This is present in the minds of all beings, and yet only a few are able to recognize it. If one watches the very face of awareness when it manifests as objects, and if one does not chase after them, this same awareness, completely laid bare and naked, becomes clearly evident.

This awareness, the nirmāṇakāya, is the unceasing ground of manifestation. It is like a wish-fulfilling jewel, the source of everything that one might want. For so it is that the source of the multifarious array of qualities and enlightened action is simply awareness, the nirmāṇakāya. And it should be understood that these qualities and activities never stray beyond the pure expanse of self-cognizing awareness.

This state of awareness, free of anything to be adopted or rejected, free of any kind of exertion and action, is like limpidly clear water. If acceptance and rejection, effort and action occur—like water in a state of turbidity—the fundamental condition of awareness cannot manifest. But if one rests in the pristine, crystal clear limpidity of awareness, without adopting or rejecting, without effort or striving, the powers of vision, preternatural knowledge and other qualities will become clear and evident without obstruction within the expanse of awareness, like objects clearly reflected on the limpid surface of the water. *The All-Creating King* tells us why this is so:

> It is there from the beginning like the ocean
> And brings forth all things in their multiplicity.
> Its enlightened qualities extend
> To the very edges of the sky.
> All subsides, becoming insubstantial.
> In the instant of the essence of enlightenment,
> The sovereign concentration manifests.
> Phenomenal appearance, like [reflections on] an ocean,
> Is a state beyond the range of thought,
> Extending to the farthest reaches of the sky.

Awareness, self-arisen primordial wisdom, is motionless. It is like a still ocean and is present inseparably within us from the very beginning. When one rests in this state, the whole array of phenomena, the manifestation of awareness, arises like the reflection of the stars and planets on the surface of the sea. If, when this occurs, one preserves the naked state of awareness and does not fixate on these [appearances], they will subside in the moment of their arising and arise in the moment of their subsiding. Their arising and subsiding will occur inseparably. They will manifest simply as the adornments of awareness. And enlightened qualities will be equal to the very vastness of the sky.

In short, the crucial point of this passage is that no matter what display may manifest, if one does not attend to it but rests in the naked state of awareness, the occurrence will simply subside. When one rests in the essence of enlightenment, in other words, the state of awareness, every thought that manifests through the creative power of that same awareness immediately subsides right where it is. And the great, sovereign, meditative absorption—empty awareness, the self-arisen wisdom devoid of all mental elaboration—will supervene. No matter how great may be the diversity of appearances that manifest, like the reflections of the stars and planets on the surface of the ocean, they are simply awareness, beyond the range of thought, and this is as vast as the farthest reaches of the sky.

* * *

The fifth section shows that the state of the three kāyas is a single ultimate expanse beyond all action and exertion.

5. Ultimate reality, primordially pure,
Is not found by searching.
The buddhas and the bodhisattvas
Dwell within this self-arisen vast expanse.
Since this is present from before,
There is no need to gain it now, anew.
This great indwelling state
Is the immense expanse of dharmatā.
Do not strive for what is changeless, present of itself.

The nature of the mind, the dharmakāya, is our primordial birthright. If we neglect this fact, and if with effortful practice geared to its causes and conditions, we go off searching for it as if it were somewhere else, we will not discover it anew. Awareness has never been affected by obscuration. It is ultimate reality, primordially pure. The four kayas, the five primordial wisdoms, and so forth—in other words, buddhas in the state of the result and bodhisattvas in the present state of the path—dwell within the expanse of self-arisen awareness. Awareness is not something fabricated. It is naturally present already from before, and there is no need to achieve it anew by effortful training on the grounds and paths. Supreme awareness, the greatest of the great, the enlightened mind, the primordially indwelling state, never stirs from the expanse of the dharmatā. In accordance with its seven indestructible vajra attributes, it is unchanging, uncontrived, and spontaneously present.

Therefore, one should not engage in effortful action in order to achieve it.

* * *

The sixth section shows that awareness is the one immanent state.

> **6. The primal ground, the natural ground,**
> **The ground of the quintessence of enlightenment**
> **Never waver from the natural condition.**
> **Therefore do not stray from your awareness,**
> **The expanse of luminosity.**

The primordial ground here refers to the ultimate nature of awareness, the dharmakāya free from all mental elaboration—in other words, awareness that is present in the ground. The natural ground refers to the actualization of awareness, the dharmakāya—which happens only when one's three doors are left uncontrived in their natural state. The primordial ground (the ground awareness) and the natural ground (the path awareness) merge indivisibly and in one taste with the dharmadhātu, the mind of all the buddhas of the three times. This is referred to as the ground of the quintessence of enlightenment.[79]

Since these three aspects of the ground do not at all stir from the natural condition of empty awareness, the state of equality (the view of the primordial, natural state in which everything is left as it is), Longchenpa tells his future disciples not to stir from the luminous expanse of unmoving dharmatā—the state of open, unimpeded, and naked awareness—which, having no existence whatever in itself, is free of all unfolding and dissolving thoughts. For awareness, the unmoving dharmatā, is unconditioned, whereas the reverse is true of thoughts that move ever toward their objects. The two are incompatible.

* * *

The seventh section shows that all the qualities of the result are present within the expanse of awareness.

> **7. Attainment comes when all is left in this condition.**
> **For the unchanging, all-pervading sovereign**
> **Together with the five primordial wisdoms,**
> **The five aspects of enlightened body,**
> **The five aspects of enlightened speech,**
> **The five aspects of enlightened mind,**
> **The five enlightened qualities and activities**
> **(In other words, primordial buddhahood)—**
> **All are present of themselves**
> **Within this endless and beginningless expanse.**
> **Do not search for them elsewhere,**
> **For in its luminous character**
> **They are present from the very first.**

All things in phenomenal existence, the world and its inhabitants, samsara and nirvana, are present naturally in the expanse of awareness—awareness endowed with the four kāyas and five primordial wisdoms. Simply leaving them in this state, and meditating night and day, one will achieve the result. And the reason or evidence for saying this is as follows.

Since awareness is motionless and unchanging throughout the three times, it is immutable. And since it is primordial wisdom, omnipresent and all-pervading, it is the sovereign of the whole of samsara and nirvana. Since all the qualities of the result, such as the five primordial wisdoms, are naturally present in the expanse of uncontrived great bliss, awareness is indeed the five wisdoms. Because awareness is changeless, it is called Akṣobhyavajra, the "unmoving vajra." Because it is the wellspring of all supreme and common accomplishments, it is Ratnasambhava, the "source of gems." Because it is free of center and periphery, it is Amitābha, "infinite light." Because it achieves all aims, it is Amoghasiddhi, "accomplisher of meaningful action." And because it appears as anything whatever, it is Vairocana, the "source of manifestation." Therefore, awareness constitutes the five aspects of the enlightened body. Being inexpressible, it is the five aspects of enlightened speech: self-arisen enlightened speech and so on. Since awareness in itself is the primordial wisdom of equality and so on, self-arisen and free of all mental elaboration, it is the five aspects of the enlightened mind. Since awareness in itself is, like a wish-fulfilling jewel, the source of all that may be wished for, it is the five aspects of enlightened qualities. And since awareness in itself, the primordial wisdom of purity and equality, includes all enlightened deeds, such as the four activities, it is the five enlightened activities. Consequently, all the twenty-five qualities of the result are, from the very beginning, spontaneously present within the expanse of the primal buddha Samantabhadra, the ultimate enlightened mind without beginning or ending—awareness, the state of great equality. This is why the root verse admonishes us not to search for the qualities of the result elsewhere. For if one were to do so, they would not be found. From the very beginning, they are present in the luminous character of awareness. It is said in *The Secret Essence Tantra*,

> Perfect buddhahood will not be found
> In any of the four times or the ten directions.
> The nature of the mind itself is perfect buddhahood.
> Do not seek enlightenment elsewhere.
> Even if the Victors were to search for it,
> Nothing would they find.

* * *

The eighth section shows that since samsara and nirvana are established as awareness, they are none other than the dharmakāya, the nature of the mind.

8. Enlightenment itself,
The dharmakāya of the buddhas,
Is none other than immutable equality.
Since this is present of itself
Within the self-arisen state,
Do not search for it and do not try to gain it.
Just let go completely of your hopes and fears.

The attainment of enlightenment, the dharmakāya of all the buddhas, constitutes, so it is said, the mastery of the four kāyas and the five primordial wisdoms. It is none other than the immutable state of awareness itself, awareness that is forever beyond movement and change. It is in no way different—not even to the slightest degree—from the actual fundamental nature just as it is: the uncontrived state of equality devoid of mental elaboration. It is therefore referred to as the immutable state of equality. And since this is spontaneously present, uncontrived and self-arisen, within the state of self-arisen, empty, luminous, and unceasing awareness, we are told not to look for enlightenment elsewhere—for an external buddha endowed with face and hands—nor to attempt to gain a result that is different from awareness, the primordial wisdom that dwells within. Neither the state of buddhahood (the object of hope) nor the state of sentient beings (the object of fear) is found elsewhere. Longchenpa tells us simply [to let go and] settle in uncontrived state of spontaneous awareness.

* * *

The ninth section shows that since it is established that the samsaric mind is the dharmakāya, there is no need to reject it.

9. The self-arisen primal wisdom of all beings,
Uncreated, not achieved through effort,
Is present of itself as dharmakāya.
Therefore do not reach for it—

Accepting this, rejecting that.
Just rest in this expanse of ultimate reality.

If the body, speech, and mind of all beings were left uncontrived and in their natural state, it would be impossible for a single being to be without [the experience] in their mind stream of self-arisen primordial wisdom, empty, luminous, and unceasing. For so-called "sentient being" is none other than the state of awareness—awareness that is the inseparable union of samsara and nirvana. It is as we find stated in *The Lion's Perfect Power*,

Beings and buddhas—
Their awareness is not different.

And it is also said in *Awareness Self-Arisen*,

Sentient beings' awareness
Is buddhahood itself.

Awareness, the dharmakāya, is present within the mind streams of all beings. It is naturally present as primordially abiding luminosity, the dharmakāya, which is not produced through action nor achieved through effort. When this is understood, it should not be grasped at tensely with a mind full of hope and fear—accepting some things and rejecting others. One should rest in the state of equality, the all-pervasive expanse of ultimate reality, which is an immense and even vastness. It is said that it will then become manifest.

* * *

The tenth section shows that awareness transcends all movement and exertion.

10. Within the ultimate nature,
Even, present of itself,

Unwavering, devoid of thought,
There lies the ground's immense expanse
Where uncreated qualities are found.

Since awareness as such, the dharmakāya, is naturally present, it is unwavering, free of movement and change throughout the passage of time. Since it is devoid of all the extremes of conceptual elaboration—in word, thought, and expression—it is devoid of thought. Since all the kāyas and wisdoms are perfectly included within its self-arisen, spontaneous state of equality, awareness is referred to as the ultimate nature, even and present of itself.

Uncreated through causes, conditions, or concerted action, the four kāyas, the five primordial wisdoms, and so on are all perfectly included without any effort in the expanse of awareness. All these qualities are self-arisen. They are present without exertion in this all-pervading vast expanse of the ground, which is an immensity beyond all spatial measurement and contains the whole of samsara and nirvana. This is an astonishing thing concerning which *The Word-Transcending Tantra* says,

Primordial wisdom, wondrous and amazing,
Without past or future, free of origin,
Lies utterly beyond the reach of thought.
It is emptiness itself, beyond extremes.

* * *

The eleventh section shows that a spontaneously present stream of empowerment is perfectly included within awareness from the very beginning.

11. This changeless, all-pervading sovereign
Of the kāyas and the wisdoms
Is the self-arisen, great, direct empowerment
In the manner of a king.
Therein phenomenal existence

(The world and all the beings it contains)
Is free and open from the first spontaneously.
There is no need for action or exertion—
By its nature it is present in and of itself.
Everything is present and unfolds
As great spontaneous presence.

Awareness is immutable. It is free of movement and change throughout the continuity of time. It is omnipresent for it pervades all appearances both pure and impure. This same awareness, which is the owner or sovereign of the kāyas and wisdoms, moreover constitutes the direct empowerment granted in the manner of a king. Generally speaking, this empowerment is the instantaneous introduction to coemergent awareness, the indwelling primordial wisdom, which occurs in dependence on the reception of the blessing power of a sublime teacher. This shows that samsara and nirvana are totally encompassed by the single vast expanse of awareness. It is the ultimate, self-arisen, unelaborate empowerment that transcends both granting and receiving. It is an empowerment through which primordial wisdom itself becomes manifest and through which it is realized that phenomenal existence in its purity, and the world and beings in their equality, are primordially and spontaneously open and free. So it is that aside from awareness, there is nothing else to be referred to as empowerment.

The realization that the mandala of the three seats is completely and primordially present in the mandala of the pure vajra aggregate of one's body is referred to as the empowerment of the wheel of the inexhaustible ornaments of the enlightened body. Similarly, the realization that the wind energy of speech dwells, self-arisen from the very first, as the mandala of enlightened speech (the state in which all sounds are recognized as the sound of mantra) is referred to as the empowerment of the wheel of inexhaustible ornaments of secret enlightened speech. When unborn self-arisen awareness, the dharmakāya, is actualized, and when it is realized that samsara and nirvana embody the three kāyas perfectly and spontaneously—

that is, without any effort—this is the empowerment of the wheel of inexhaustible ornaments of the secret enlightened mind. Since all these empowerments are naturally and primordially present in awareness, no action or exertion is now called for. By their nature, they are present in and of themselves and are the ornaments of awareness. If this is fully realized, there is no need to rely on empowerments that employ symbolic substances and imply work and effort. It is said in *The Lion's Perfect Power*,

> The empowerment of the self-appearing, great primordial wisdom
> Rests likewise in the ground.

And *The All-Creating King* says further,

> When you have mastery
> Of the luminosity of sovereign awareness,
> You will not depend
> On empowerments of bliss through symbols.
> Realizing it, rest naturally in the state that's free of thought.

Since all empowerments are present in the expanse of awareness (self-arisen primordial wisdom), it follows that when awareness, the enlightened mind, manifests and unfolds as great spontaneous presence, one has a complete certainty that apart from this, there are no other empowerments, no generation and perfection stages. Right now in the present moment, it is important to have the settled conviction that samsara and nirvana, acceptance and rejection, activities, view, meditation, and so on are spacelike awareness devoid of objective reference.

In short, since awareness has no existence whatsoever, one should have a decisive certainty that it is primordially empty and spacelike. One must be convinced that everything that arises unceasingly within it is spontaneous presence (awareness itself). And since these dual aspects (of emptiness and appearance) come down to the same thing, it should be recognized that they are free of the extremes of existence and nonexistence. This indeed is the principal crucial point of our Great Perfection tradition: there is neither existence in appearance nor nonexistence in emptiness. They should both be understood in terms of great, nondual, spontaneous presence.

* * *

This concludes the word commentary on the seventh chapter of *The Precious Treasury of the Dharmadhātu*, which shows that all is primordially and spontaneously present in the enlightened mind.

8. There Is No Duality in the Enlightened Mind

The eighth chapter, which shows that in the enlightened mind there is no duality, consists of ten sections. The first shows that since phenomena arise within the single ultimate expanse, they are said to be nondual [that is, not different] in their very arising.

> **1. Within the one expanse of self-arisen primal wisdom,**
> **All things are nondual in their final way of being.**
> **The duality that ceaselessly appears**
> **Is the display of the creative power.**
> **Appearances and the imputing mind**
> **Are both nondual enlightened mind.**

All things in samsara and nirvana are devoid of any existence separate from the one expanse of ultimate reality. Consequently, whereas phenomena (subject and object, self and other, outer and inner, the world and the beings it contains) all appear variously within the one awareness—namely, self-arisen primordial wisdom; and although they seem to arise separate and distinct owing to deluded, dualistic perception, they are in truth nondual [that is, not different from each other] in that they do not lie outside the state of equality or awareness, which is their ultimate way of being.

Phenomena, devoid of separate, individual existence, are equal inasmuch as they subsist in empty awareness, primordial purity free of conceptual elaboration. They are equal on the level of appearance in that they arise unceasingly just like the forms of the moon reflected on the sea. They are also equal in that, from the point of view of our perceptions, they each have causal effectiveness on the level of mere perceived appearance. For example, fire is hot and burning, pillars support beams, vessels carry water, and so on. Furthermore, they are equal in that all appearances manifest simply as the display of dependent arising. For these four reasons, it should be understood that all phenomena partake of a state of nondual [undifferentiated] equality.

Although awareness in itself has no existence whatever, it is naturally present as the ground of manifestation. Therefore all things that unceasingly appear in terms of the duality of subject and object, apprehender and apprehended manifest in the manner of a display through the creative power of awareness, the enlightened mind. And yet in truth, these appearances, which arise as the display of the creative power, are not divided dualistically [in the sense of having two aspects]: appearances on the one hand and an imputing subject on the other. For they arise within the nondual enlightened mind.

In order to understand that all phenomena arise nondually in relation to the enlightened mind [in the sense of being undifferentiated from it], one must have recourse to three arguments. The first is that, just as everything reflected on the surface of a mirror is "nondual with," [or indivisible from,] the mirror itself, all phenomena manifesting within awareness are indivisible from this same awareness. Phenomena and awareness are "not two." The second argument is that just as all that one sees in a dream does not fall outside the state of sleep, likewise all the phenomena of samsara and nirvana manifest within the expanse of the same awareness. They do not fall outside the display of awareness alone. The third argument is that just as the waves that surge on the surface of the sea are not other than the sea itself, likewise no matter what phenomena emerge through the creative power of awareness, they are not different from the one dharmatā. They clearly appear and yet are nonexistent.

So it is that all the appearances of samsara and nirvana, which arise through the creative power of awareness, are indivisible from that same awareness. Awareness and appearances are "not two." Dream visions and the dreamer who sees them seem to be two different entities. In reality, however, they are not different. Although they simultaneously appear within the state of sleep, they are but nonexistent yet clear appearances, nothing more. It is said in *The Ornament of Clear Realization*,

> Just as dream and dreamer
> Are not seen as two,
> So likewise in a single instant
> Phenomena are seen to be "not two."

The sense objects, sense faculties, and their corresponding consciousnesses are also nonexistent but clear appearances. Indeed all things, the world and beings, outer and inner, are but nonexistent and yet clear appearances. Whatever appears—whether as identical or different, and so on—does not in the slightest way exist according to its characteristics. In truth, from the very moment that they appear, all things are groundless and empty. They do not fall outside the one sole sphere of equality free of mental elaboration. One may appeal to many scriptures in support of this point, but for fear of prolixity, I will not cite them here.

In this regard, there are some confused people today who thoughtlessly declare that, generally speaking, impure appearances are the [ordinary] mind, while pure appearances are the enlightened mind. In saying this, they are in fact propounding the view of the Cittamātra True Aspectarians. In our tradition, however, Longchenpa says, "These appearances are not the mind nor are they other than the mind." Accordingly, since appearances are neither the mind nor other than the mind, it is said that they are the array of the mind's creative power and display. The statement that appearances are the mind and the teaching that all appearances are one within the mind's expanse are as different from each other as the earth is from the sky. If appearances were the mind, an unwanted consequence would follow that, since appearances have color and shape, the same would be true of the mind as well. It would also follow conversely that when the mind moves or is still, appearances must follow suit. Moreover, if a pillar were the mind, it would follow that the mind would be causally effective in supporting a beam; if a vase were the mind, the mind would have a spout and a neck and bulbous shape. In our tradition, it is said that appearances occur because, owing to a failure to recognize their nature as the enlightened mind, inherent existence is ascribed to what is in fact the display of the latter's creative power. Appearances and the enlightened mind are said to have the same nature.

When the creative power of awareness arises as a display—that is, as an object—this same display may appear in two ways: either as the self-experience of awareness or as an object of the senses. These two kinds of appearing object are not the mind nor are they other than the mind. Although pillars and pots, and so forth, appear through the power of the mind, it must be admitted that they are not the mind. This is easy to understand in the light of the teachings of the Cittamātra and Prāsaṅgika Madhyamaka schools. The Cittamātrins say that phenomena are the mind. The Prāsaṅgikas say that although phenomena appear in the mind, they are not the mind. On the other hand, neither do they exist as objects external to the mind. For they are empty and beyond [the reach of] mental elaboration. This is similar to what is being said here. The omniscient Longchenpa has on several occasions refuted those who say that appearances are the mind. He does so, for instance, in his *Precious Treasury of Wish-Fulfilling Jewels*, in *The Treasury of Words and Meanings*, and in his autocommentaries to *The Treasury of the Dharmadhātu* and *The Treasury of the Fundamental Nature*, as well as in *Finding Rest in the Nature of the Mind*, and so on. From the standpoint of the ultimate view, to say that appearances are the mind is like saying that the rabbit's horns are the son of a barren woman. For appearances and the mind are both nonexistent.

Nowadays, for those who are beginners in the practice and who progress on the path gradually, appearances are introduced as the mind; the mind is introduced as being empty; and emptiness is introduced as being awareness. This method is set forth in most of the pith instructions of the Great Master of Oḍḍiyāna. His disciples, the many learned and accomplished masters of the Nyingma school, follow the same procedure, as do Marpa and Mila and the other masters of the Kagyu tradition.

The enlightened mind, the ground for the arising of all phenomena, has no existence whatever. It is empty like space. And since its creative power is likened, in its ceaseless arising, to the immaculate surface of a mirror, no division is made between this same creative power and awareness. They are not two. The display of the creative power arises as various phenomena in the manner of the eight examples of illusion. And since, from the standpoint of emptiness, these three factors—awareness, creative power, and display—have no existence whatever, there is no division (no "duality") between them. Nevertheless, on the level of appearance, they are distinct and therefore one speaks accordingly, referring to awareness, its creative power, and its display.

* * *

The second section shows that all phenomena manifesting within self-arisen primordial wisdom—where they are present in great undifferentiated equality—are seen by yogis as empty forms, nonexistent yet clearly appearing. The certainty that this is so, which arises in the realization of these yogis, is a matter for celebration.

> **2. Samsara and nirvana, all phenomenal existence,**
> **Arise within the enlightened mind,**
> **Awareness changeless and unmoving.**
> **They are not to be rejected or acquired.**

For yogis who are free
From apprehended and from apprehender,
Phenomena, appearing while not existing,
Are a matter of amazement and of laughter.

Yogis are utterly certain that all things in samsara and nirvana are, according to their ultimate nature, primordially nonexistent. They realize that both samsara and nirvana are pure and equal. They do not reject some things and strive to acquire others. For everything appears within the expanse of the enlightened mind—awareness changeless and unmoving. Nothing lies outside the all-pervading dimension of equality. No matter what arises for these yogis from within the sphere of phenomenal existence, samsara and nirvana, they take it as a nonexistent but appearing display. For they have established beforehand that all such things have no reality. For all such yogis, who are free of the assumption that things exist truly—an assumption produced by the duality of apprehended and apprehender—whatever manifests is simply a nonexistent appearance, empty by its nature. As this certainty is born within them, and as they realize that the empty forms that appear to them are but the unceasing manifestations of dependent arising, they simply laugh in amazement. They are like people who already understand the workings of a magic trick and who burst out laughing when they see that innocent onlookers, who are without this knowledge, believe that the magic horses, oxen, men, and women are truly real and react toward them with attachment or aversion.

Therefore, whatever appearances occur, whether of samsara or nirvana, they are but the particular instances of either the recognition or the failing to recognize the fundamental nature, awareness alone. They are nothing else. As it is said in *The Aspiration of Samantabhadra* taken from the tantra *The Unimpeded Openness of Samantabhadra's Wisdom*,

Ah
Samsara and nirvana, all phenomenal existence,

> Have a single ground, but there are two paths and two results,
> And these are the display of knowledge and of ignorance.

And it is said in *The Lion's Perfect Power*,

> Samsara and nirvana are perfectly included in but one awareness.
> Not reified, they are not ordinary things
> But are the self-experience of awareness.

Depending on whether one recognizes awareness or not, samsara or nirvana respectively appear. In truth, however, if they are not reified, they are just the self-experience of awareness and are thus free of the condition of things conceived in terms of existence, nonexistence, both, or neither.

* * *

The third section shows that in the very moment that they appear, all phenomena are without existence. They arise as no more than empty images, appearing yet not existing.

> **3. Though nonexistent while appearing,**
> **Phenomena arise in all their various forms.**
> **Though nonexistent in their emptiness,**
> **Things are present everywhere.**
> **Although there are no subjects apprehending**
> **And no objects to be apprehended,**
> **Beings cling to "I" and to the self of things.**
> **Although they have no ground or root,**
> **The stream of lives flows on continuously.**
> **Although there's nothing to accept and nothing to reject,**
> **Beings opt for happiness and flee from pain.**

When one reflects on the nature of phenomena, the fact that phenomena appear while being nonexistent is a source of amazement.

They arise as appearances within the expanse of awareness, the dharmatā, and they are perceived—even though they do not exist—as the multifarious array of samsara and nirvana, the universe and its inhabitants, enemies and friends, the desirable and the repulsive, good and bad. They are nonexistent but appearing empty forms, manifesting, in whichever way they do, within awareness.

Furthermore, phenomena that have never existed are perceived as empty. But they do not truly exist as empty, for they are infinitely spread everywhere from zenith to nadir, from center to periphery, in all the main and intermediate directions. In truth, phenomena do not fall into either extreme, whether of appearance or emptiness. They are beyond the extremes of existence and nonexistence.

In the same way, all phenomena, which appear in terms of apprehending subjects and objects to be apprehended, do not lie outside the groundless, rootless, open and unimpeded state devoid of objective reference. Nevertheless, this self-experience of awareness, devoid as it is of existence, is mistaken for something other, and then it is just as when one dreams about oneself and others, about pleasure and pain, wealth and possessions, good and bad, things to accept or to reject, past and future lives, and so on. Although they are nonexistent, the mind apprehends an "I," or personal self, as well as the self, or real existence, of things.

As the experience of subjects and objects of apprehension unfolds, there occurs a mistaken assumption of the real existence of the manifold phenomena of the three worlds of samsara. And yet, in truth, these hallucinatory appearances are groundless and rootless. Taking them as existent realities, the mind reacts to them in a manner conditioned by defilement. Investing these nonexistent appearances with a self-identity, one experiences the hallucinatory perceptions of them. The stream of lives flows on, filled with the continuous suffering of samsara.

There is nothing to accept and nothing to reject. All is empty. Everything is just open, unimpeded awareness. When, however, one fails to understand this, one embraces happiness and one recoils from pain. And yet these same experiences are but the appearing but nonexistent forms of emptiness manifesting within one's perceptions. As it is said in *The Sublime Sutra of the Precious Lamp*,

> Phenomena are like the buddhas gone in bliss,
> But those with minds of children seize upon their features.
> Thus they have experience of a world of nonexistent things.

Phenomena are similar to the sugata, the dharmakāya empty and aware, beyond the reach of mental elaboration. But confused beings with childish minds fail to understand this and, mistaking them for truly existent things, they seize upon their characteristics. And because of their deluded fixation to [what they think is] the reality of these things, beings experience a world of nonexistent and yet appearing things.

* * *

That which is not born from either outer or inner phenomena is pure and equal to space. The fourth section deals with the ascertainment of how this is realized. It has two parts. The first establishes that anything that appears as an external object is a groundless, illusory, empty form.

> **4a. Observing beings, I find that their perceptions**
> **Are extremely strange.**
> **What is not true they think is true,**
> **And true indeed it seems to them.**
> **The undeluded they take as deluded,**
> **And utterly deluded does it seem to them.**
> **That which is unreal they take as real,**
> **And extremely real does it appear to them.**
> **What is not so they take as being so,**
> **And so indeed does it appear to them.**
> **That which is not tenable they take as tenable,**
> **And tenable indeed it seems to them.**
> **Thus their minds are pointlessly deceived**

By various trivial objects of their senses.
Awareness has become for them
A stream of conscious instants,
And thus in days and months and years,
Their lives are all consumed.
They take as dual what is nondual,
And thus these wanderers deceive themselves.

Phenomena, outer and inner, do not extend beyond their original condition of primordial emptiness. Nevertheless, foolish beings do not realize that the empty forms that appear to them are like dreams and magical illusions, the products of dependent arising. Observing them, Longchenpa sees that they take as true what is not true, they believe the undeluded to be deluded, and what is untenable they believe to be tenable. The perceptions of these beings, he says, are very strange.

Generally speaking, the fundamental nature of phenomena is simply emptiness. The empty forms that appear to us are not true. They are deceptive, like magical illusions and dream visions. Yet childish beings, who are unaware of their fundamental nature, which is suchness, think that they are truly existent and take these hallucinatory appearances to be really true, really existent, and really present. And thus they are deluded in their endless samsara.

Similarly, although the ultimate, fundamental mode of being of awareness is the primordial wisdom of the equality of samsara and nirvana—in other words, primordially undeluded, aware emptiness, free of all mental elaboration—foolish beings, who have no understanding of this, assume that their state of dreamlike delusion is the truth. And for this reason, awareness, which is undeluded, appears to them as a state of utter delusion! So it is that hallucinatory appearances proliferate without end.

The pure surface of a mirror is the ground for the arising of all kinds of unreal images. Similarly, awareness is the ground for the arising of the whole of samsara and nirvana. All the various kinds of unreal appearance that arise thanks to awareness's creative power automatically subside and are, by their very nature, a state of great nondual equality. Nevertheless, beings in their ignorance are unaware of this. They take unreal appearances to be real entities, and these seem extremely real to them. Such is their delusion!

Awareness in itself is unconditioned, beyond all the conceptual elaborations of being something or not being something and indeed of existing or not existing. Those who do not know the fundamental nature of awareness take it as being something when it is not so. To those who are deluded and entangled in their clinging to its true existence, awareness really does appear to be something, and to exist. So it is that they strongly cling to their hallucinatory perceptions.

Likewise, all assertions about the existence or nonexistence of phenomena are wholly untenable. This includes propositions like "The things that appear to the mind are nonexistent because they are empty" and "They are not nonexistent because they unceasingly appear." On the other hand, confused beings fail to understand this and take statements about the existence or nonexistence of phenomena to be tenable. They take their stand on them and regard them as utterly tenable. Their heads spinning in confusion like a whirling firebrand within this state of samsara, they have the experience of hallucinatory appearance.

It is thus that for beings in samsara generally, but particularly in this decadent age, perceived appearances are crafty in deceiving them. The minds of beings are gullible, and they are quickly led astray by their thoughts, which recklessly follow whatever different phenomena arise. Beings are misled by the hallucinatory appearances of sense objects. And whereas there are no grounds for delusion, they are pointlessly deluded.

When awareness is recognized and when this recognition is maintained, all that arises through its creative power subsides—just as when a snake is tied in a knot, the knot comes undone all by itself. When awareness is not recognized, clinging to a self drives a wedge [between awareness and that which arises through its creative power], and hallucinatory perceptions endlessly proliferate.

The way this happens is as follows. When the nature of the very instant of consciousness is not recognized, the stream of multiple instants stretches out in a continuum, which is then mistaken for an hour of time. Many such hours follow one after the other, and by dint of continuous erroneous cognition, they are mistakenly regarded as an entire day. A succession of many days appears as a month. A succession of twelve months appears as a year. And the continuity of many years appears as an entire human life. People thus have an ongoing tendency to be deluded; and their time is spent in hallucinatory perceptions that follow one after the other in sequence.

In short, all phenomena in samsara and nirvana, according to their ultimate mode of being, are from the very beginning entirely gathered within the expanse of awareness, the ultimate enlightened mind. They are not at all outside the dimension of the one sole, open, and unimpeded sphere of nondual equality. When this is not recognized, and when nondual awareness is thus obscured by ignorance, phenomena are experienced dualistically in terms of apprehender and apprehended, self and other, subject and object. And in this way, the beings of the six realms are deceived. It is said in *The Necklace of Pearls*,

> All things are like the sky,
> They are obscured by clouds of adventitious thought.
> Even undeluded dharmatā
> Appears before the mind in a deluded guise—
> As momentary, produced by causes and conditions.

This means that before the seal of freedom and delusion of the original common ground was split asunder, samsara and nirvana were simply a vast expanse, skylike and all-pervading. But when awareness rose up from the ground and the appearances of precious spontaneous presence were not recognized as the self-experience of this self-same awareness, these same appearances were obscured, veiled by the clouds of thought arising from both coemergent ignorance and conceptual ignorance. For dualistic perception, awareness, the sublime dharmatā (which is free of delusion), consequently appears in a deluded manner and is mistaken for a self.

The hallucinatory appearances that ordinary beings perceive—phenomena that are assumed to exist by way of their specific characteristics—are perceived by yogis in the manner of a magical display and nothing else. This is because hallucinations are themselves groundless and rootless. When one realizes this, and when this realization is maintained steadfastly night and day, the time will come when the hallucinatory appearances of objects, the appearances of the ground, will dissolve into the expanse of the dharmatā—just as when the empty forms of a magical display simply vanish. Such a result is referred to as pure, spacelike yoga—a union with the natural condition of things—wherein not even the name of samsara remains.

Thanks to the text of the present stanza [4a] it may be understood that outer objects have no existence. And it is thus that spacelike dharmatā is established and made evident.

* * *

The second part of the fourth section establishes that the inner apprehender is also groundless, with nothing to support it.

> **4b. Yogis with pure karma**
> **Turn within and watch their minds.**
> **Awareness, groundless, unsupported, is beyond all naming.**
> **It is not seen through being pointed at or talked about.**
> **View and meditation are a seamless continuity.**
> **And in this state of evenness, relaxed, immensely vast,**
> **"Practice" is unknown,**
> **For there is no distinction "in or out of session."**
> **At all times there is just the state**

Of seamless, spacious evenness.

Thanks to their accumulations of wisdom and merit, the purification of their obscurations, and their many prayers of aspiration made in previous existences, beings with pure karma are now the fortunate vessels for the practice of the profound and secret teachings of Atiyoga. Yogis such as these turn inward and watch their minds. To begin with, they find that the mind has no source and is therefore empty. Then they find that it has no dwelling place and is therefore empty. Finally, they see that it has no place to go and is therefore empty. Free of origin, abiding, and ceasing, the mind has no support. It is groundless, rootless, unoriginate, devoid of objective reference, open and unimpeded, and free of all fixation and conceptual markers. The mind is empty, luminous, unceasing awareness. It is clear, limpid, naked, lucid, and sharp. It is beyond all identification. Being ineffable and indescribable, it is beyond all naming. It is as *The Word-Transcending Tantra* says,

> There is no place where the mind can be located.
> It is devoid of all existence
> And thus, regarding all appearing, empty things,
> There is no source for mindfulness and vigilance.

What we call the mind has no arising, dwelling, or ceasing. No contrivance or modificatory factor, such as mindfulness, vigilance, and mental focus, can affect it. It is like the sky free of the three defects [cloud, mist, and dust]. Accordingly, nothing can indicate self-arisen awareness, the enlightened mind. Speech cannot describe it. Through no amount of watching can it be seen. When one relaxes in the natural condition, the view, meditation, action, and result cannot be found as separate states. Within the natural flow of awareness, a riverlike stream of nonmeditation, they all blend into one. They become a single, seamless continuity, merging indivisibly. The image evoked here is that of a great river that flows on without interruption. This is what is described as a seamless continuity.

Within awareness, nothing falls outside the state of evenness, equality. If one remains relaxed in its uncontrived and natural flow, [one will find that] all the phenomena of samsara and nirvana are encompassed by it. In the expanse of this same awareness, which is like space itself by virtue of its vast immensity, there is not the slightest difference between them, in terms of good or bad, great or small. If one rests in meditative evenness in such an immense and all-pervasive vastness—since practice as such is unknown—there is no distinction between sessions of meditation and the periods between the sessions. At all times and in all situations, one remains in a state of nonreferential vastness and simply relaxes in this state of even immensity, blending seamlessly with the dimension of luminosity.

* * *

Awareness, which entails the realization of the nonduality of the subject and object of apprehension (as demonstrated in sections 4a and 4b), is now shown to be great, spontaneous presence devoid of all extremes.

4c. There are no reference points:
Bodies, sense objects, or other things.
There is but the all-pervading evenness
Of the expanse of space.
The inner element, therefore,
Is not to be regarded as a self.

The ocean-vast infinity of phenomena: bodies, the objects of the six consciousnesses, and other appearing things—all of which arise within the expanse of all-pervading, self-arisen awareness beyond all mental elaboration—in truth has never existed. Totally beyond conception and reference, phenomena have never stirred from the state of equality, the freedom from mental elaboration. Moreover, awareness itself does not in any way exist. It is immensely vast like the expanse of space and evenly pervades both samsara and nirvana. Empty, luminous, and unceasing awareness—lucid and without support—is referred to as primordial wisdom, the enlightened mind, the dharmakāya, the supreme and spontaneously present ultimate expanse, luminous and naked awareness, and so on. But these expressions are merely the labels of convention employed simply as a means to communicate. For in truth, there is no such thing as an "awareness" that might be the object of the conceptual mind. If there were, it would follow that awareness is not beyond the mind's elaboration. According to our tradition, awareness is beyond all conceptual constructs—of existence, nonexistence, both, and neither, identity, difference, and so on. This means that the inner element, the nature of the mind, the interior expanse called awareness, cannot be regarded as a self. For awareness is not located anywhere—in the main or intermediary directions, in the zenith or nadir. It is neither outside nor in.

Some say that the self-illuminating, self-cognizing awareness described in the Cittamātra system and the self-cognizing, self-illuminating awareness of which the Great Perfection speaks are the same. But this is not at all correct. For the Cittamātra says,

> When there is no object to be apprehended,
> We do not see an apprehending subject.
> Understanding fully that the three worlds are but
> consciousness,
> The bodhisattva who abides in wisdom
> Realizes that this too is but consciousness.

If there is no object of apprehension, there is no subject of apprehension. And the mind that is free of both has no location or support. This is what the Cittamātrins call the self-illuminating, self-cognizing mind, and it is to this that they ascribe true existence. This is something that we do not accept. According to our tradition, outwardly there are no appearing objects; inwardly there is no apprehending mind; and since there is neither an object nor a subject of apprehension, there is, secretly, no primordial wisdom, aware and empty, to act as a point of reference. There is no existent self-cognizing awareness or nature of the mind, for nothing exists either outside or in. There is no self-cognizing awareness because self and other do not exist. There is no awareness free of apprehended and apprehender, for neither of the latter exists. Finally, there is no self-cognizing, self-illuminating awareness, for if there is no self-cognition, there can be no self-illumination. The establishment of the first evidential sign—there is no self—shows that there is no *self*-cognizing awareness. The establishment of the second evidential sign—there is neither illumination nor absence of illumination—shows that there is no self-*illumination*. How could this in any way resemble the self-cognizing, self-illuminating mind of the Cittamātrins? It must be understood that the Great Perfection is a complete freedom from conceptual extremes.

Indeed, the way in which the Natural Great Perfection posits freedom from extremes and freedom from expression resembles for the most part that of the Prāsaṅgika Madhyamaka. The Madhyamikas, however, establish emptiness gradually, while the Great Perfection establishes it in an instant, emphasizing the emergence of naked awareness. This is the difference that lies between them. The Madhyamaka tradition, in saying that all the different kinds of emptiness are like space, asserts that both existent and nonexistent things, considered as being the basis of emptiness, are necessarily empty. As Mipham has said,

> Asserted as the basis of emptiness,
> Both things and nonthings
> Must themselves be empty.

By contrast, in our Great Perfection tradition, it is primordially pure awareness, limpid and pure, nonexistent yet unceasingly appearing, that is considered to be the basis of emptiness. It is this and the phenomena that arise within it that are established as being a spacelike freedom from extremes. And it is this spacelike freedom from extremes that is necessarily understood to be emptiness.

* * *

The fifth section shows that when yogis realize that both the outer object and the inner subject of apprehension have never existed and have the nature of space itself, all phenomena appear to them as the nonreferential state of complete openness and freedom. Therefore, as a sign that the inner apprehending subject has completely dissipated, this section shows that outer objects of apprehension subside into the infinity of space.

> **5. When outwardly [these yogis] turn their gaze**
> **At objects of their senses manifesting in the outer world,**
> **Everything is evanescent, weightless, and transparent,**
> **Phantom-like, diaphanous, impossible to grasp.**
> **They perceive, hear, recollect,**
> **Know, taste, feel as never they had done before.**
> **"What is this?" they ask. "Is this a dream?**
> **Are these the visions of a lunatic?"**
> **And they will simply laugh.**

Although they once looked upon the outer and inner appearances of the world as truly existent entities possessed of their own specific characteristics, and though the habits of such a tendency are deeply ingrained, yet through the kindness of their teachers, these yogis have been perfectly introduced to their own nature. They truly realize the fundamental nature of awareness just as it is, having in large measure attained the certainty of the view that comes with the full intensification of meditative experience. At that moment, their experience reaches such a pitch of intensity that whatever arises appears to them as if devoid of all solidity. And as a sign that mental fixation on true existence has now been overcome, when such yogis look at outwardly manifesting sense objects (forms, sounds, smells, tastes, textures, mountains, cliffs, houses), which have arisen through the creative power of awareness and as its very display—in other words, the very adornments of the wheel of primordial wisdom—these yogis will experience a deep conviction that all these things are simply nonexistent yet appearing empty forms occurring simply as the display of their awareness. And they will experience a sense of complete certainty.

It is as when people understand that magical apparitions are simply nothing. They not only realize that the magical images appearing to their perceptions are untrue, but they are able to infer that other people that have the same understanding as themselves are also not taken in by these same appearances, thinking that they are real. In just the same way, all phenomena are without real existence, like magical illusions, dreams, reflected images, tricks of sight and so on. They are false appearances, forms of emptiness. They are evanescent, weightless, undefined, and unimpeding. When the false assumption of true existence is shattered to its very foundation, all appearances become phantom-like, diaphanous, essenceless, and hollow like bubbles. These appearances are experienced like the forgeries of magic—things that might disintegrate and vanish from one moment to the next. The yogis will hesitate, wondering, "Are they real or not?" They are completely ungraspable. It is as when people who know that they are dreaming look upon the things that they are dreaming about. So it is that these yogis gain a clear conviction that whatever arises is none other than awareness, the state of dharmatā. It is as Shabkar has said,

> Appearances and mind are vague and undefined,
> Evanescent, weightless.
> If in the state of dharmatā you let them go,
> You will reach, within this infinite expanse,
> Samantabhadra's wisdom, there and then.

When that moment comes, nothing that the yogis perceive, hear, remember, know, experience, or feel is as it was before. Everything vanishes into emptiness. They will think that these appearances are but the fleeting projections of their minds, which are at that moment appearing. And though they may see these externally appearing phenomena, the latter seem to slip through their fingers and are ungraspable. As Shabkar says,

> Things will be for you just emptiness.
> You'll think the objects in the outer world cannot be
> grasped
> Even if you touched them with your hands.
> Truly, you will think, this is the view.
> And deep down, certainty will surely arise.
> That is when conviction in the view is born.

Furthermore, these yogis may have the feeling that the character and behavior of all other beings have changed, and they will wonder whether or not the view that they have realized is shared by anyone else. Moreover, when awareness has reached its full extent, and thoughts do not arise, they will wonder "What is all this? Where have all my thoughts gone?" When this happens, it means that thoughts have dissolved into their state of inherent purity. The yogis will wonder whether it is they who are mad or whether it is other people. They will wonder whether they are asleep and dreaming, or whether they are in the bardo. When perceptions are stripped to their utter nakedness, and open, unimpeded empty awareness supervenes, they will wonder (since it is impossible for awareness not to be present in all beings), "Why on earth do they not realize it too?" For it seems to them so obvious. What possible difficulty could there be?

Sometimes, when all their actions, and when all sounds and appearances become steadily insubstantial, open and without solidity, they will simply burst out laughing. And as they behave and do things in a manner unrestrained and free of all fixation, they may spontaneously wish to sing vajra songs on the spur of the moment. For when the state of awareness predominates, their behavior becomes unpredictable. They leave footprints in stone and pass unhindered through rocks, cliffs, and so on. At that time, when the conceived object of self-clinging is done away with, it is said that the dharmakāya, in which both the object and the subject of apprehension are naturally overthrown, arises from within. As it is said in *The Necklace of Pearls*,

> Since there's no impurity in things that naturally appear,
> The subtle and the gross are overthrown.
> Since there is no apprehended and no apprehender,
> Delusion now is overthrown.
> Since there is no movement, karmic wind is overthrown.
> Since everything is but a state of unimpeded openness,
> Entities are overthrown.
> And since there's luminosity,
> Emptiness is overthrown.

The meaning of this text is that since phenomena, which naturally appear, have never truly existed, the assumption that they do exist does not stain them. So it is that all thoughts, whether subtle or gross, are overthrown and are no more. Since there is no ordinary mind with its duality of apprehender and apprehended, the deluded mind is also overthrown. Since there is no movement of thought, the unfolding of the karmic wind energy is also overthrown. Since all appearing phenomena are the empty dimension of unobstructed openness, the solid and resistant appearances of earth, stones, and so on are now overthrown. And since self-cognizing awareness is naturally luminous, the unilateral emptiness of things, as well as the clinging to such an emptiness, are now overthrown. *The Necklace of Pearls* also says,

> It is perfect from the very first
> And so the generation stage is overthrown.

There is no effort, action thus is overthrown.
One rests without exertion,
Meditation thus is overthrown.
All subsides quite naturally,
Appearance thus is overthrown.
It is clearly manifest,
And thus the view is overthrown.
There are no sounds, no words.
Conventional expressions are therefore overthrown.

As this text declares, since within awareness, the ungenerated, self-arisen mandala is perfect from the very beginning, the elaborate practice of the generation stage endowed with characteristics is overthrown. Since all exertion is inherently pure in being without existence within awareness itself, effortful action is overthrown. Since one rests in the natural state of awareness free of striving, all effortful meditation is overthrown. Since all that arises within awareness subsides quite naturally, the perception of the solidity of what are hallucinatory experiences is overthrown. Since "it," the view that is free of all objects of viewing, is evidently manifest, the view that involves a duality of subject and object is overthrown. And since there are no sounds or words for ineffable and indescribable awareness, all conventional verbal expressions are overthrown. And so it is. There are many texts to this effect, but they cannot be cited here.

* * *

The sixth section further shows that this realization is an experience that arises from within and is without any point of reference.

6. No notion is there now of friend or foe,
Of near or far, or of attachment or aversion.
There's no division into day and night
But just a single, equal, all-pervasive state of evenness.
Samsara with its apprehension

Of phenomena endowed with features is dispelled,
And this is called the state
Of self-arisen primordial wisdom.
Because there are no thoughts,
The meshes of accepting and rejecting,
Of things to be removed together with their antidotes,
Are now transcended.
Through such a realization,
Nondual wisdom is made manifest.
Self-arisen Samantabhadra's wisdom mind is reached.
The level of phenomenal exhaustion,
From which there is no possibility of falling back, is reached.

When this moment comes, as a sign that all hallucinatory phenomenal appearances have reached the level of exhaustion in the expanse of the primordial purity of dharmatā, everything blends—without any distinction between night and day—in a single, all-pervading dimension of luminosity. As a sign that one is now free of any notion of friend or enemy, attachment or aversion, closeness or distance, the strong feeling of animosity toward hostile enemies evaporates, and all the thoughts that occur during the night are cleared away into the expanse of dharmatā. Since one has no further attachment to one's friends and relations, all deluded thoughts occurring during the day are likewise cleared away into the expanse of dharmatā. Since daytime luminosity and the luminosity of the night are uninterrupted by sleep, the kind of darkness that occurs for instance in the first period of slumber cannot occur, with the result that there is no division between day and night. One never stirs from an infinitely pervasive evenness, the great equality of primordially pure awareness free of mental elaboration. As a result, samsara, with its duality of apprehender and apprehended, its grasping at things with their features, is cleared away into the expanse of ultimate reality. Since there is no partiality with regard to enemies and friends, the veil of defilement naturally subsides.

Since one does not consider the antidotes to be superior, the conceptual veil also naturally subsides. This is referred to as "the gaining of freedom in the expanse of great primordial wisdom, the mind of Samantabhadra." It is the actualization of ultimate, nonconceptual primordial wisdom. By that point, one has gone beyond the meshes of acceptance and rejection, and of the factors to be eliminated together with the antidotes that are designed to eliminate them. Happiness and suffering are the same. Gold and filth are the same. The sky and the palm of one's hand are the same. Samsara and nirvana blend into the same taste, and one becomes a "glorious spacelike yogi" in the literal sense of the word.

With such a realization, the ultimate place of freedom, the primordial wisdom that is indivisible from the dharmadhātu, the mind of all the buddhas, is actualized. In a single taste, one merges with the wisdom mind of glorious Samantabhadra, the self-arisen king, and attains the level of Samantabhadra himself, the sovereign ruler of the kingdom of the dharmakāya. It is said that, at that point, phenomenal appearance is exhausted in the expanse of the dharmatā. And since there is no way that one could stir from the all-pervading state of great perfection, there is no possibility of falling back into the realms of samsara—in the same way that someone cured of smallpox can never succumb to it again. Just as in the morning when the sun has risen, there is no darkness to be found though one may search for it, once the apprehended and the apprehender have been dispersed into the openness and freedom of the ground,[80] they can never return, and one is freed of every fetter.[81] Those who attain this state are "yogis who are free of every fetter." And as the mighty yogi Dhekavajra said,

> For yogis free of every fetter,
> It is like the rising sun at dawn.
> *Emaho*—the vision of the dharmakāya!

Such yogis are said in the root verse to have attained the level of the exhaustion of phenomena.

Whether or not this has occurred in the course of the yogi's life may be assessed on the basis of the practices of trekchö and thögal. It must be determined whether the luminous appearances of thögal or the experience of fixation on emptiness of trekchö have been exhausted in the expanse of dharmatā. When all the appearances of deities and buddha fields of thögal vanish like clouds in the sky, this is referred to as the "exhaustion of luminous visions in the dharmatā." Since at that point, the inner defilements and all material, impure phenomena are exhausted, this is a sign that buddhahood has been reached in this very life.

When awareness, as experienced through the practice of trekchö, has been stripped to its naked primordial purity, its display—namely, all fixating thought—whether positive or negative, related with samsara and nirvana, is purified and is no more. Since defilements and thoughts are dissipated in the openness and freedom of the ground, they can never again recur—just like the darkness that is banished by the rising sun. Now at that time, it may seem in the eyes of others that yogis who have reached this level still have a few things to say and that they still have some defilements and thoughts. And they may clearly appear to be experiencing strong feelings. But this is simply a reflection of the impure and faulty mind of the observer. For from the standpoint of the yogis themselves, everything has become an unimpeded openness. And just as dust cannot adhere to space, defilement (for such yogis) simply vanishes into primordial purity. For they have actualized the ground, which is beyond bondage and freedom and transcends the extremes of virtue and nonvirtue. It is said in *The Necklace of Pearls*,

> Since it is all-pervading, extraneous production is negated.
> Since it is self-arising, darkness is dispelled.
> Since it is the essence, it pervades as dharmakāya.
> Since it is luminous, it blossoms as sambhogakāya.
> Since it is the meeting of the mother with her child, it arises as nirmāṇakāya.

As this text says, when the level of the exhaustion of phenomena is reached, one realizes that both samsara and nirvana manifest within awareness. It is understood that awareness pervades the whole of samsara and nirvana. The [theory of] extraneous production—which holds that phenomena arise from something other than awareness—is negated. Just as darkness is dispelled when the sun rises, when the radiance of self-arisen awareness manifests, the darkness of ignorance is cleansed away so that not even its name remains. Since this awareness is the heart or essence of all phenomena, all appearances, perfectly included within the dharmakāya, are pervaded by it. Since awareness luminously appears—for it is the great union of luminosity and emptiness—it blossoms as the field of the sambhogakāya endowed with the five certainties. When the luminosities of the ground and path meet, like a mother with her child, they mingle and become indivisible and of one taste. The unceasing creative power of awareness arises as the nirmāṇakāya, which brings forth the unlimited benefit of wandering beings.

Generally speaking, the level of exhaustion in the dharmatā is referred to, from the standpoint of thögal, as the exhaustion related to manifest luminosity. From the standpoint of trekchö, it is described as the exhaustion related to empty luminosity. As to the way in which this exhaustion happens, it is said in the context of thögal that beginning with the direct perception of dharmatā and until the completion of [the stage of] the culmination of awareness, there is a constantly intensifying manifestation of deities and primordial wisdoms. When the exhaustion of phenomena is reached, all these luminous appearances are consumed in the ultimate expanse of the primordial purity of the dharmatā. And this is referred to as buddhahood in the "ever-youthful vase body." When the yogis concerned pass into nirvana, their bodies and the space around them are suffused with light: rainbows, luminous disks of light, and the forms of deities. This is called the rainbow body of great transference.

From the trekchö perspective, when all impure appearances are purified where they stand, the stronghold of the primordially pure dharmatā is captured. One of the signs of this is that when yogis who have this realization pass into nirvana, the sky becomes utterly clear and devoid of clouds. Moreover, the freedom gained through the trekchö practice necessarily occurs either in the course of life or at the moment of death. When, just after death, the yogis concerned awake as if from a faint, and the ground luminosity manifests like an utterly limpid autumn sky, it is then that they gain freedom—in the luminosity of the moment of death. As for the way of gaining freedom in the bardo according to the thögal teachings, this refers to the freedom gained when the appearances of spontaneous presence—deities, wisdoms, and the threefold experience of sounds, lights, and rays—occur in the bardo of ultimate reality.

* * *

The seventh section shows that any kind of contrived, artificial semblance of such a realization is to be spurned.

> **7. Without the realization of equality**
> **Within the self-arisen state,**
> **You may talk of nonduality,**
> **Just clinging to the words,**
> **And place your trust in mind's analysis**
> **And in a blankness where there's nothing to be seen.**
> **This is indeed the very essence of wrong**
> **understanding,**
> **The dark abyss of ignorance.**

Generally speaking, and as it has been previously explained, it is on the basis of the pith instructions of one's teacher that one is able to realize uncontrived, self-arisen awareness nakedly, just as it is. Now because within this state, all phenomena and this same awareness are "not two" [they are indivisible], it is important that the authentic view of nondual equality be realized. If a person does not have such a realization and is without the pith instructions that elicit it, he or she can only repeat the words of others and makes statements like "Unborn awareness is like space and for this reason is neither improved by virtue nor damaged by negativity. It is beyond the karmic law, beyond action and reference. It cannot be observed. It cannot be grasped. It is a great, nondual equality." Having in no way integrated any of this into their own experience, such people may, like raving lunatics, spout these high-flown expressions, which are supposed to reveal the ultimate truth. Clinging strongly to the words, dry as dust, they may, in their own coarse behavior, ape the uncontrived yogic activities of the siddhas, wantonly indulging in tobacco, alcohol, sex, and the like. And they may place their trust in a stupid meditation wherein nothing at all is observed, or in views deriving from intellectual analysis. But such people do not even come close to the profound view and meditation of the Great Perfection. They are mostly the dupes of māra and the view in their minds is precisely the view of wrong understanding. In their subsequent lives, they will continue to wander in the darkness of ignorance, and it will be difficult for them to find the authentic view. And even though they may attract a following and have many disciples, they are false guides nevertheless and lead their charges to the lower realms. It is essential to dissociate oneself from them. As it is said in *Awareness Self-Arisen*,

> If things happen in this way and you are without [such experience], this is a sign that you have failed to gain profound realization and that your investigations go no further than the words in your mouth. And if you act like a lunatic, this is the work of obstacle-making demons. So you should make great gaṇacakra feast offerings and devote yourself to the practice.

As it is said, one should engage in virtue, abandon nonvirtue, gather the two accumulations, purify one's obscurations, and be convinced of the karmic law of cause and effect. It is of the greatest importance to train oneself in faith, devotion, loving-kindness, compassion, and so on, relying always on one's perfect teacher.

* * *

The eighth section admonishes fortunate beings that they should realize the nature of their minds as the vast expanse of the ground of perfect equality.

> **8. And so, within that self-arisen state**
> **Devoid of movement and of change,**
> **Train yourself in sovereign nonduality,**
> **Wherein all thoughts are worn away.**
> **The three worlds thus will be completely free and open.**
> **Samsara and nirvana will be indivisible.**
> **The fortress of the dharmakāya, completely pure like space,**
> **The nature that arises from within,**
> **Surpassing all analogies, will manifest.**

The self-arisen awareness of the ground, which throughout the sequence of the three times is beyond all movement and change, is said to be the primordially present dharmakāya; and this indicates the manner in which the ground is established. At the present moment, when one is meditating on the path, one trains in the sovereign view, the nonduality [the indivisibility] of arising and subsiding. By this means, all the wishes, recollections, and thoughts that arise in the mind are worn away in this nonduality of self-arising and self-subsiding. This indicates the manner in which meditation is practiced on the path. By such means, all the hallucinatory appearances of the three realms will be realized as being completely open and free, and the consequent inseparability of samsara and nirvana will become evident—and this indicates the manner in which the ultimate result is actualized. Thus the first six lines of the root stanza successively show that the ground is the dharmakāya, free from extremes, that the path is the self-subsiding of thoughts, and that the result is buddhahood itself. For the direct and indirect elucidation of the way in which the ground, path, and result are presented, it is important to consult the omniscient Longchenpa's autocommentary.

Despite the fact that the ground, path, and result are all dealt with separately, their nature is nevertheless one, and they cannot be divided. By training in them, yogis are able to realize this fact from within, through the strength of their practice. The spacelike realization that occurs is referred to here as the vajra-like indestructible fortress of the dharmakāya, which, it should be understood, is utterly pure and beyond the reach of all the analogies and expressions that are used to indicate it.

* * *

The ninth section shows that realization free from all clinging and fixation is subsumed within the one ultimate quintessence within the vast expanse of space.

> **9. As long as you fixate on different entities,**
> **Asserting "this" or "that,"**
> **Remaining in duality,**
> **You're trapped in the delusion of "yourself and others."**
> **But when you're free of bias**
> **And make no distinctions, saying "this" or "that,"**
> **Everything is even in the state**
> **Of an equality beyond all reference.**
> **As Vajrasattva said,**
> **This is to realize nonduality.**

Just as the purity or impurity of the sky is gauged in terms of the presence or absence of clouds, smoke, steam, and so on, a yogi's realization or lack of realization must be distinguished according to the presence or absence of clinging and fixation. As Sakya Paṇḍita said, "If there's clinging then there is no view." One can tell whether the view and meditation of the Great Perfection have hit the mark by the presence or absence of clinging and fixation. When, in one's view, one clings to existence or nonexistence; when, in one's meditation, one is caught up in the suppression of some things and the cultivation of others; when, in one's action, one makes judgments expressive of adoption and rejection, this means that one's view, meditation, and action have failed to hit the mark.

As long as one is not free from fixation on different entities ("this" or "that"), in other words, on self and other, subject and object, and so on, the result will be that when meditating on awareness, one's mind will be caught in duality owing to such clinging and fixation—rejecting factors that are to be eliminated and adopting their antidotes. And for as long as this lasts, one will be unable to avoid being trapped by the delusion of self and other. As the great paṇḍita Tilopa said to Naropa,

> Appearances don't bind you.
> You are bound by clinging.
> Cut your clinging Naropa!

And the mighty siddha Shabkar said,

> Dear son, not by appearances but by craving are you bound.
> Sever the delusion of your cravings and attachments.

And he also said,

> If you ask, "Is any deviation there?"
> The answer is that there is not a single error,

> Not a single deviation.
> But if there's craving and attachment,
> That's where there is deviation.

The Dharma Lord Kumaradza has said,

> Realization or the lack of realization of the fundamental nature is shown by whether you are free or not free of attachment.

And in the *Dohas*, the great siddha Saraha has said,

> Dissatisfactions small as just a husk of sesame
> Will never give you anything but suffering.

This means that if in one's mind there is even a tiny degree of clinging and fixation—as small as a husk of sesame—it has the power to cause the hallucination of suffering.

Therefore, if one must describe the yogis of the ultimate, secret Great Perfection, one could say that though, for ordinary perception, they may be skilled in distinguishing virtue from nonvirtue, and though they may be learned in an ocean of tenet systems, nevertheless, when resting in awareness, they are free of all clinging and fixation. They are free of even the slightest biased distinction, saying "this" or "that," as when one clings fixatedly to one's own or others' tenets, and to the view, meditation, and result. These yogis are without the slightest fixation and clinging to the expanse of equality, the dharmatā, where all phenomena are even and beyond all reference, self-arising and self-subsiding in the supreme state of openness and freedom. They thus have a genuine realization of the nondual fundamental nature of the state of great perfection, the primordial wisdom of equality. This is said by Vajrasattva himself.

So it is that when yogis are attached to the view and teaching of their tradition, or when they are attached to something else, their minds are fettered—regardless of whether the object in question is good or bad. As it is said in *The Treasury of the Fundamental Nature*,

> Just as ropes and golden chains bind equally,
> Virtuous and unvirtuous states
> Bind equally the ultimate, definitive quintessence.
> Clouds black and white enshroud the sky in equal measure.
> Likewise virtue and nonvirtue equally obscure awareness.

Moreover, *The Word-Transcending Tantra* says,

> Since sublime reality is free of ordinary mind,
> All at once the sense powers subside.
> And since you see it face to face,
> Your tenet system falls apart
> And you no longer cling to and fixate on it.
> You savor then the taste of ultimate reality.
> No further basis is there for a falling back
> Into the three worlds of samsara.
> For supreme yogis such as these,
> It is like space dissolving into space.

When supreme reality, the profound fundamental nature free of ordinary mind, is realized, everything that arises as the object of the senses immediately subsides in the expanse of awareness. The great equality of awareness is directly seen, and through this crucial fact, all fixation and clinging to tenet systems simply fall apart. Since there is no clinging and fixation with regard to awareness as such, freedom from mental elaboration occurs, and one relishes the taste of actual, profound dharmatā, the perfect fundamental nature. When one remains in this condition without ever parting from it, the three worlds of samsara subside naturally, all by themselves. Thus there is no further basis for a falling back into samsara. Like space dissolving into space, the supreme yogi is of one taste with nonduality.

* * *

This concludes the word commentary on the eighth chapter of *The Precious Treasury of the Dharmadhātu*, which shows that there is no duality in the enlightened mind.

9. The Decisive Certainty That All Phenomena Are the Enlightened Mind

This chapter reveals in twenty-two sections the decisive certainty that all phenomena lie within the expanse of the enlightened mind. In the first section, certainty is gained that the nondual enlightened mind is a skylike expanse that transcends ordinary cognition.

> **1. In the one expanse,**
> **By nature a supreme immensity,**
> **Is found the "nail" of the enlightened mind,**
> **Commensurate with space itself.**
> **Focus on its vital point and strip it to its essence.**
> **It is the greatest of the great,**
> **The vast mind of Samantabhadra,**
> **By whose nature all is gathered**
> **In the surge of its immense horizon.**
> **And in this single vast expanse,**
> **Realization and the lack of it,**
> **Freedom and the lack of it**
> **Are all a nondual great equality.**

A decisive certainty or conviction arises that in the single expanse of awareness, which by nature is a supreme immensity pervading both samsara and nirvana, all phenomena are nondually, spontaneously, and completely gathered. This awareness, which is itself nondual and does not fall into any extremes, is the "nail"—the unchanging mode of being—of the ultimate enlightened mind commensurate with space. This awareness, empty, luminous, and unceasing, free of the concept of self and of dualistic perception, is self-cognizing, self-illuminating primordial wisdom. The direct and instantaneous introduction to awareness stripped to its nakedness is expressed in the root verse with the words "Focus on its vital point and strip it to its essence." It is nothing other than that. It is the fundamental nature of all things, their ultimate point—more profound than the profound. It is the greatest of the great, the vast mind of Samantabhadra indivisible from primordial wisdom. Like the garuda, the king of birds, that soars in the heights of the heavens, the naked dharmakāya, unstained by the conceptual mind, gathers by its very nature within the "surge of its immense horizon" everything in both samsara and nirvana. To realize that all phenomena are primordially pure awareness, the great unimpeded openness of the dharmakāya, is to attain their ultimate fundamental nature. To reach the clear certainty or conviction that this is so is a crucial point.

There is no distinguishing realization from the lack of realization, freedom from the lack of freedom except in relation to the naked, uncontrived, and unadulterated recognition of this single vast expanse of awareness, the dharmakāya, and one's constant abiding in it. To come to a clear conviction that all phenomena are a single nondual state of equality—naked awareness in its unimpeded openness—is to reach an ultimate and decisive certainty in their regard. As it is said in *The Mirror of Vajrasattva's Heart*,

> Understand that all phenomena within awareness arise without there being any notion of their having a self. Understand that phenomena are unceasing. Understand that what is unceasing may manifest in any way. Understand that manifestation of any kind is unborn. Understand that unborn manifestation is beyond coming and going. Understand that all phenomena that are beyond such coming and going are nondual. Understand that their nonduality is their presence beyond

> extremes. Understand that they are a state beyond the thoughts of the ordinary mind. Understand the nature of phenomena clearly and without distraction.

This text means that primordial purity, the naked dharmakāya, in which phenomena are exhausted, marks the ultimate reach of these phenomena, the point at which they are transcended. If this is not understood, teachers may well explain that phenomena are unborn and transcend thought and word; and their listeners may well think as a result that phenomena are inconceivable and inexpressible. And it is in this way that what is beyond designation becomes a designation! One may say that phenomena are beyond thought and expression, but it is precisely in so saying that thought and expression arise in the mind. This is of no help at all. If the mind does not inwardly realize the state beyond thought and expression, and if thoughts about it spill outward, the nature of the mind cannot be realized. It is said in *Awareness Self-Arisen*,

> Not knowing that the dharmakāya is an unimpeded openness,
> You may declare that the perfection stage is without birth,
> But this is like pretending that a fox or monkey is a lion.

Now by way of a digression, but following the lead of the omniscient Longchenpa's autocommentary, I will explain the two ways in which awareness is directly introduced in a single instant: one that does not rely on crucial points and one that does.

The direct and instantaneous introduction to awareness without relying on crucial points is as follows. When the three doors are left relaxed and without any alteration, thoughts do not unfold outwardly, nor does one focus on anything inwardly, nor is one settled on anything in between. When, in short, the mind is left in its natural condition, without the slightest alteration or contrivance, there manifests a state that is free of arising, remaining, and ceasing. This is limpid, lucid, naked awareness. This is the way in which the nature of the mind is introduced through the transference of the master's blessing power.

Now with regard to the direct and instantaneous introduction to awareness that relies on crucial points, there are six methods.

First, there is the introduction to awareness based on the focused mind. Sitting cross-legged, breathing gently, leaving one's mind without thoughts, and remaining clearly and lucidly present, one will experience two states: luminosity and stillness. One should disregard them, for they are mere meditative experiences. By contrast, it is the naked aspect of awareness that should be introduced as the dharmakāya.

Second, awareness may be introduced on the basis of the stillness of the mind. When the mind is left unfocused, peacefully resting in its natural state, the aspect of stillness should be disregarded and the lucid, aware aspect should be introduced as the dharmakāya.

Third, awareness may also be introduced in the course of an investigation of the mind. When one examines the three limits of the mind (whence the mind arises, where it stays, and where it goes), nothing is found but a naked, lucid state. Then, the aspect of being devoid of thought should be disregarded, and the naked state of wakefulness that transcends sense objects and their designations should be introduced as the dharmakāya.

Fourth, awareness may be introduced by tracing things back [to their state of unreality]. When one's mind strays into objects, these same objects should be dispersed by mentally breaking them down into smaller and smaller parts. At the same time, one should investigate the mind, trying to see where it is. When one rests in the state of pure emptiness, which is inexpressible and in which neither mind nor objects are found, the aspect of stillness devoid of all mental activity should be disregarded and the nakedly aware, lucid aspect should be introduced as the dharmakāya.

Fifth, awareness may be introduced when the mind cognizes sense objects. Following the moment when one becomes conscious of an object and rests quietly without thinking about it, without adverting to an object "over there" and a cognizing mind "over here," there arises a seamless state of tranquility. This motionless state should be disregarded and the factor of wakeful, lucid awareness in its unimpeded openness should be introduced as the dharmakāya.

Sixth, awareness may be introduced by using distraction and dispersion. [The disciple] is allowed to remain for a moment in an ordinary state of mind, chatting and so on. When the mind is thus brought into a state of distraction, [the teacher] says, "What is the meaning of *hasaraki*? Tell me, tell me!" The mind of the disciple is reduced to a state that is alert and yet blank, for the disciple has nothing to say, nothing to comment on such a meaningless word. At that point, the aspect of blank stillness should be ignored, and the aspect of clear, naked awareness should be introduced as the dharmakāya. Or again, the disciple is told to leave but, on leaving, is immediately told to return. The procedure is repeated several times. The still aspect of the mind, when the disciple returns, should be ignored and the aware, naked aspect should be introduced as the dharmakāya.

In brief, awareness may be introduced by using methods that involve the subtle channels, winds, and essence-drops—or indeed any other appropriate means related to the mind in movement or the mind in stillness. The important thing is not to remain in either the exclusively luminous aspect or the exclusively empty aspect, but to strip awareness—which, like an orb of crystal, is simultaneously empty and luminous—to its sheer nakedness, devoid of ordinary mental processes. These methods of introduction are techniques for pointing out the view [of awareness directly and instantaneously], like the garuda swooping down to the ground.

In short, it is important to differentiate the experiences of luminosity, no-thought, and awareness. The experience of luminosity is the one-sided aspect of luminous stillness. The experience of no-thought is the one-sided aspect of emptiness devoid of thought. Awareness is neither the exclusive aspect of luminosity nor the exclusive aspect of stillness [emptiness]. It is like an orb of crystal. It is a naked state of wakefulness, open and unimpeded. [Enumerating these crucial points for introducing awareness,] *The Word-Transcending Tantra* says,

> To focus your mind, to let it rest;
> To analyze, to trace things back,
> To search the state where mind cognizes objects,
> And to induce distractions—this is what they are.

It is crucial to have decisive certainty concerning awareness in its unimpeded openness. According to our tradition, it must be acknowledged that awareness is free from birth, remaining, and cessation, that it is the great, ineffable, inconceivable, indescribable state. It is the exhaustion of phenomena (wherein not even their names remain), the great original purity, and so on. Awareness is not just luminosity nor is it a totally void emptiness.

The various methods for introducing awareness given in this text are not the same as those described in Mahāmudrā, or indeed in the outer mind class and the inner space class of the Great Perfection. They are the introductory methods proper to the secret class of pith instructions. Moreover, in the Madhyamaka teachings, phenomena are established as being empty, and it is in terms of this emptiness of phenomena that the nature of the mind is introduced. In our tradition, however, the nature of the mind is established in terms of awareness. These two methods are as different as heaven and earth. Now although the mind class and the space class make the introduction to awareness by evaluating the mind and the objects that appear to it as being neither existent nor nonexistent, they nevertheless present the great defect of slipping into the mere understanding and talk *about* everything being empty. Here, the approach is quite different and is very much the uncommon feature of the secret class of pith instructions.

* * *

The second section shows that for the yogis who have such a realization, and who abide in the riverlike stream of practice, samsara is dissipated so that not even its name remains.

> **2. A garuda with its wings full grown**
> **While still within the egg**
> **Glides in the vault of heaven as soon as it is hatched.**
> **It soars with mastery above the vast abyss**
> **And overwhelms the nāgas.**
> **Yogis graced by fortune**
> **Realize perfectly the vajra essence,**
> **Peak of all the vehicles.**
> **They overwhelm the lower vehicles**
> **And soar above samsara's vast abyss.**

Garudas, the kings of birds, have their wings fully developed even while they are chicks within the egg. In this way, they are different from every other bird. So it is that when their shells break open and the garudas hatch, no sooner are they freed from the shell than they take off and glide in the vault of heaven. It is different for the young of other birds. For the latter come forth from the egg, their feathers grow, their wings develop gradually, and only then can they take flight and soar in the sky. Garuda chicks are quite different. Moreover, garudas are the enemies of the nāgas. They subdue them and break their arrogance and pride. They overwhelm and terrify them. And since the strength of their wings and their soaring flight are very great, they soar with mastery above the vast abyss. Such are the extraordinary qualities of the garuda's young.

This is just like those fortunate yogis who have accurately realized the vajra essence of the luminous Great Perfection, the peak of all vehicles. Having gained an excellent understanding of awareness, the dharmakāya, introduced to them by their teachers, they diligently meditate day and night over a long period of time, with the result that they attain supreme realization. And even if they do not achieve the refinement of their bodies, so that the latter disappear into infinitesimal particles, the power of their realization is nevertheless perfected within their bodies (like chicks of the garuda with their wings fully developed while still in the egg). Therefore, as soon as the shell of their bodies breaks [in death], the inner expanse of their awareness blends indivisibly with the outer expanse of emptiness—the dharmatā, the mind of the Victorious Ones, past, present, and to come—and they attain buddhahood directly in the supreme openness and freedom of primordial purity. Until the emptying of samsara, while they never stir from the dharmakāya, their two form bodies accomplish the immense benefit of beings through their enlightened activities, which are constant, all-pervading, and spontaneous. These qualities of Atiyoga are not to be found in any of the lower vehicles. They are the uncommon preserve of the resultant vehicle. As Longchenpa has said,

> Mountain goats can scale a cliff with ease.
> A feat not possible for other beasts is possible for them.
> The Ati teachings, which decisively transcend extremes,
> Are not in harmony with lower vehicles
> And yet accord with self-arisen primordial wisdom.

Since the vehicle of Ati surpasses the lower vehicles and dominates the host of defilements, releasing the three worlds of samsara into primordial purity, it is said to "soar" above the vast abyss of samsara. As we find in *The All-Creating King*,

> It is like the great garuda soaring in the sky.
> There is no unfolding and no drawing in [of thought].

And it is said in *The Lion's Perfect Power*,

> Within the bodies of all sentient beings,
> Pure primordial wisdom rests,
> Unable to break through the shell.
> That which is concealed in womb or egg

Is hidden and invisible,
But when its strength is gathered, it bursts forth.
So too when yogis lay aside their bodies,
They reach the country of awareness that self-manifests.

The words "unable to break through the shell" indicate that while yogis remain confined within the shell of their bodies, they are unable to break free of it and experience directly the freedom of primordial purity.

* * *

The third section treats of the decisive certainty that, in itself, awareness is beyond the law of cause and effect.

3. The openness and freedom of all things,
Their great state of equality,
Is unacceptable to those who strive
According to the law of cause and fruit.
But it makes sense to those who understand
The meaning of unwavering equality,
Expounded in the supreme vehicle.

All phenomena, outer and inner, the world and the beings it contains, are from the very beginning open and free in the expanse of primordial purity, devoid of mental elaboration. Now the openness and freedom of all things—that is, their supreme state of equality—is beyond the understanding of those who belong to the lower vehicles and who strive in the practice of adopting and rejecting according to the law of cause and effect. Since it is beyond them, they should not be instructed in it. If practitioners of the lower vehicles hear the teaching of the twelve vajra laughters, the eight amazing sayings, and so on of the deep and secret Atiyoga, they will be bewildered, they will be frightened by it, and might even vomit blood and die. Alternatively, if they denigrate such a teaching, the complete ripening of such an action will be a fall into the lower realms; and for many kalpas, they will not encounter the profound instructions. Moreover, the teacher will incur the fault of betraying the secret and will be punished by the ḍākas and ḍākinīs. These teachings should therefore be kept hidden. On the other hand, they are appropriate and right for those fortunate yogis of the supreme vehicle of Atiyoga, who are able to realize the meaning of unwavering equality: empty awareness, free of all mental elaboration. As we find in *The All-Creating King*,

> Do not disclose these teachings,
> The lore of me, the All-Creating One.
> To followers of causal and resultant vehicles.
> For if it is shown openly to them,
> They will proclaim that actions good and bad
> Have causes and results.
> Denying or ascribing true existence
> To me, the true reality,
> For long ages they will not encounter me,
> Myself, the true reality.

At this point in his autocommentary, Longchenpa removes the doubts of those who have mistaken ideas. But since the purpose of the present account is to concentrate on an explanation of the words of the root text, I will not discuss this matter here.

* * *

The fourth section discusses the authentic signs that indicate the realization of awareness, which transcends exertion and causality.

> **4. Everything is supreme bliss,**
> **The vast expanse of spacelike dharmakāya.**
> **And in that vast expanse of dharmakāya,**
> **There is nothing that's not free and open.**
> **The self-arisen kāya of the vajra essence**
> **Is the very nature of phenomena.**

When in the yogis' bodies
(The product of habitual tendencies)
This essence has been mastered,
And when their bodies of existence
Are relinquished in the bardo states of life or death,
These yogis are inseparably united
With the single sole awareness,
Attaining thus the kingdom
Of the level of spontaneous presence.
Their emanations without limit then pour forth
And labor for all beings unimpeded.
This is the domain of yogis
Who are "carried without effort on the wind."
This makes no sense to those upon the lower vehicles.
Only Ati rightly sets it forth.
It is the crucial point of the result.

The outer and inner phenomena of the world and the beings it contains at no time fall outside the expanse of the dharmakāya Samantabhadra, which, equal to space, is measureless in its extent, the great bliss of empty awareness. And yet, despite the fact that they are already buddhas, deluded beings fail to recognize this and contrive all manner of assertions on the conventional level to the effect that, by perfecting the two accumulations and by purifying the two kinds of obscuration, the result of buddhahood is attained. In truth, however, there is no gaining of the freedom of the enlightened state apart from the actualization of indwelling primordial wisdom in the expanse of the dharmakāya or awareness. The ultimate place of freedom is the great primordial purity, which is itself the actual ultimate nature of hallucinatory phenomenal appearances. It is the kāya of the vajra essence, primordially self-arisen without dependence on causes, conditions, and concerted effort. In other words, it is the expanse of the ground of freedom of Samantabhadra. Now even when one is still caught within the impure material shell of one's body—the product of habitual tendencies—one can, through the kindness of one's teacher, recognize awareness, the dharmakāya. And if one is able to become completely familiar with it, this genuine vajra essence will be mastered even while one is still caught in the confines of one's bodily shell.

When practitioners of the highest diligence cast off the bodies of their conditioned existence in the bardo of the present life,[82] or in the bardo of the moment of death, they mingle completely, inseparably united in a single taste, with the expanse of the single sole awareness, which is the ground of freedom of samsara and nirvana. They find freedom on the level of spontaneous presence, the ever-youthful vase body. They gain the everlasting kingdom of the dharmakāya—in other words, buddhahood. Moreover, when enlightenment is attained in the original expanse of primordial purity, the activities for the sake of beings performed by the two form bodies become limitless and uninterrupted. Although there is no stirring from the dharmakāya, the emanations of the two form bodies work unceasingly for the benefit of beings according to their needs. This they do constantly, all-pervasively, and spontaneously, laboring without impediment for the happiness and welfare of all beings.

This is to say that these yogis gain freedom in the state of primordial purity, the dharmakāya, the expanse of emptiness, which is as immaculate as the sky in autumn. This primordial purity is naturally endowed with the appearances of spontaneous presence—namely, the buddhas and the buddha fields. It is just as when the sun's rays strike upon a ball of crystal. Lights of five colors naturally appear. Likewise, since awareness is the very nature of the kāyas and wisdoms, when the wind energy endowed with the network of the five lights generates the radiance of awareness—that is, the five primordial wisdoms, these yogis experience for their own sake all the kāyas and wisdoms complete, while for the sake of others, they uninterruptedly effect the welfare of beings according to need. This is what Longchenpa means when he speaks about the "domain of yogis who are carried without effort on the wind." This makes no sense to the minds of those who follow the lower vehicles, whereas it is rightly set forth in our tradition of Atiyoga. Indeed, it is a special key point of the resultant vehicle.

There are three ways of gaining ultimate freedom in the state of primordial purity. In the case of yogis of the greatest diligence and fortune, the strength of the four elements and so on ceases to manifest in this very life. All appearances are purified right where they stand and even the bodies of these yogis become an unimpeded openness. All delusion and subject-object perceptions are cleansed away, and the shell of their physical form simply dissolves like mist vanishing into space. Such yogis gain freedom or buddhahood within the vast expanse of the dharmakāya in this very life.

Practitioners of moderate diligence and karmic fortune familiarize themselves with [the experience of] awareness. Their bodies are like a vase, and their minds are like the space within it. When a vase is broken with a hammer, the space inside it mingles with the space outside. Similarly, when the shell of these yogis' bodies breaks apart at death, their awareness blends with the space of the dharmakāya of the ground and appears in all its nakedness. It is then that these yogis attain buddhahood, which is indivisible from the dharmatā.

The way in which practitioners of least capacity gain freedom may be compared to the setting and rising of the sun and moon on the fifteenth day of the lunar month. As the moon is setting in the west, the sun is rising in the east, and just as the sun is setting in the west, the moon is rising in the east. In similar fashion, yogis of this level of capacity are propelled at the moment of death by their perfect realization of naked awareness (like the setting sun on the fifteenth day) and are simultaneously welcomed by the primordial wisdom of the bardo of ultimate reality (which is like the rising moon). And without any intervening thoughts, and without ever departing from their realization of naked awareness, the dharmakāya, these yogis attain buddhahood. These three ways of attaining freedom are referred to respectively as the gaining of freedom in the manner of evaporating mist, as the gaining of freedom in the manner of space within a vase, and as the gaining of freedom in the manner of the moon on the fifteenth of the month.

In general, according to the profound pith instructions, when the inner breath ceases and consciousness is projected into space, primordial purity—luminous awareness—manifests, free of mental elaboration. Regarding the five wind energies, the earth wind, water wind, fire wind, and air wind dissolve into the space wind, which then merges with luminosity. Therefore, when the mind is on the point of leaving the body, the following instruction regarding the consciousness mounted on the wind is given. When the moment of death arrives, one should visualize one's consciousness in the form of the letter *hūṃ* or *āḥ* or as a sphere of light. Then, as one shouts *hik*, one's consciousness is projected up through the brahmā aperture, and as it dissolves into the expanse of the dharmakāya, one ascends directly and instantaneously to the state of freedom in that same expanse. This method, in which consciousness is mounted on the wind, is a way of gaining freedom in, a way of merging with, the expanse of primordial purity. It is based on the trekchö teachings and is a path that requires effort.

In order to merge with the kāyas and wisdoms, one should either sit in meditation posture with one's back straight or adopt the posture of a sleeping lion. As one rests, merging awareness with the outer expanse through the doorway of one's eyes, one attains buddhahood instantaneously and does not pass through the bardo state. This is said to be an extremely important essential instruction and is an uncommon feature of the Great Perfection, being the way of merging according to the path of thögal. The way to merge with the kāyas and wisdoms by transferring through one's eyes the awareness cultivated in trekchö is as follows. Awareness is the lamp of the utterly pure expanse. It is projected through the path of the eyes (the lamp of the far-catching water lasso) into the external space with which it merges.

Although the manner in which freedom is gained is the same, three levels of acumen (great, medium, and small) may be discerned according to the greater or lesser degree to which the yogi or yogini has become familiar with the practice in the course of his or her life. The way of merging just described is for practitioners of least acumen. For having just recognized the nature of their minds, they may be able, on the basis of this instruction, to gain freedom at the moment of death. The ability to gain freedom when the ground luminosity manifests belongs to yogis of moderate acumen, for it is only possible to attain freedom in this way if one has grown used over a long period to the luminosity of the path. This is according to the oral instructions of my most venerable and holy teacher Matisāra (Lodrö Gyatso). *The Union of the Sun and Moon* tantra says,

> With your body in the posture of a sleeping lion,
> Focus your awareness in your eyes
> And for a moment take the space before you as your path.
> If you do not alter your awareness and the ultimate expanse,
> Then, without passing through the bardo state,
> You will, without a doubt, accomplish buddhahood.

These three ways of gaining freedom refer to freedom in primordial purity. For one's own sake, one captures the everlasting realm of the sovereign dharmakāya within the secret dimension of the spontaneously present nature [the ground].[83] And in the same way that the moon, which cannot in any way detach itself from the sky, nevertheless appears reflected in every possible stretch of water all over the earth, one can work unimpeded throughout the world in the form body for the benefit of beings to be guided. It is thus that the benefit of oneself and others is spontaneously achieved. This is an extraordinary feature of the sovereign, supreme vehicle of the spontaneously present vajra essence. It is not to be found in the lower vehicles.

To this it may be added that the way of perfecting the four visions is described differently in trekchö and thögal. The four visions of trekchö occur in reverse order to those experienced in thögal. In trekchö, the exhaustion of phenomena in the dharmatā comes first.

This is followed by the climax of awareness, then the intensification of experience, and finally the direct perception of the dharmatā. In thögal, however, the forward order of the four visions occurs. First, there is the direct experience of the dharmatā, then the intensification of experience, then the climax of awareness, and finally the exhaustion of phenomena in the dharmatā.

As the omniscient Longchenpa explains, the progression of the four visions of trekchö is as follows. First of all, a perfect teacher introduces the disciple to awareness. This is the dharmatā, the final point in which all phenomena are exhausted. The recognition of awareness is the first vision of the dharmatā, the ultimate reality in which phenomena finally come to their exhaustion. As the disciple diligently maintains this awareness without ever parting from it, this same awareness, free from the extremes of one and many, reaches its full measure, becoming an unimpeded bare openness. This is called the climax of awareness. Then, as the yogi continues in the preservation of this state, and as defiled thoughts are automatically purified, unlimited experiences occur. Whatever arises subsides quite naturally. Because there is no clinging and fixation, there comes an unimpeded bare openness. Everything is experienced as insubstantial and vanishes without the yogi's being fettered thereby. This is the vision of the intensification of experience. As one continues in maintaining this state, there comes a point when passing experiences come to a halt and the original dharmakāya, great primordial purity, arises nakedly. Ultimate reality is beheld directly. This is the vision of the direct experience of the dharmatā. At that time, phenomena come to exhaustion, for which reason this experience is called the transcendence of phenomena. One then possesses unimpeded miraculous powers and preternatural knowledge. One has mastery over the four elements, with the result that one cannot be overwhelmed by the earth, carried away by water, burned by fire, or blown away by the wind. One can fly like a bird in the sky and swim unhindered like a fish in the water, and so on. One is like the eighty great siddhas of ancient India, the twenty-five Tibetan siddhas (the king and subjects), the hundred great meditators of Chuwori, the eighty great siddhas of Yerpa, the thirty tantrikas of Yangdzong, the fifty-five realized yogis of Sheldrak, the twenty-five ḍākinīs who attained the body of light, the seven ḍākinīs who accomplished pure celestial realms, and others. Since, at that time, one gains mastery over material objects, one is able to bring houses and distant mountains closer, and one is able to perceive one's own body as being as small as an atom. One gains the divine eye and possesses all manner of preternatural knowledge.

* * *

The fifth section shows that awareness is beyond causes and conditions.

> **5. The display of birth occurs within the unborn state,**
> **But the deluded mind ascribes to it**
> **The character of causes and results.**
> **The Ati teachings say that it is free of causes and conditions.**
> **Though unacceptable to those who practice lower vehicles,**
> **This is correct and is a crucial point.**

The actual condition of awareness does not extend beyond the spacelike, unborn nature. It is said in *The All-Creating King*,

> My nature is like space,
> The example that applies to everything.
> In pure space there's no striving;
> In pure space there is nothing to be striven for.
> Space is utterly beyond all action, effort, and exertion.

As the root text says, the nature of awareness is unborn like space and is beyond the scheme of cause and effect. Yet from within this very condition, there occurs, through its creative power, the display or manifestation of birth or origin. And by ascribing to it the character of causes and results, beings grasp at it in terms of acceptance and rejection, affirmation and negation, hope and fear. This is how the practitioners of the lower vehicles, with their deluded dualistic outlook, apprehend it. By contrast in the tradition of Ati, the very summit of the nine vehicles, it is taught that all phenomena are just empty forms. Nonexistent yet appearing, they manifest in the aspect of causes and conditions. But in truth, from the very beginning, they are without existence. They do not extend beyond the one sole sphere of awareness. Now if this doctrine is taught to people who uphold the tenets of the lower vehicles, they will decry it because their minds cannot adjust to it. This teaching, therefore, should not be given to them. Nevertheless, from the standpoint of Atiyoga, it is not only correct and just, it is a most profound and crucial point.

* * *

The sixth section expresses the decisive certainty that within awareness, samsara and nirvana are an inseparable state of perfect equality.

> **6. The state of buddhas and the state of beings**
> **Are indivisible.**
> **To apprehend them differently**
> **In terms of two realities, samsara and nirvana,**
> **Is the attitude of the deluded mind.**
> **The Atiyoga teaching that they are not two,**
> **Though unacceptable to those who practice lower vehicles,**
> **Is correct and is a crucial point.**

When one realizes the fundamental nature of awareness, primordially open and free, [one sees that] within this same awareness—this same great openness and freedom—the state of buddhas and the state of ordinary beings are indivisibly one and equal, transcending the extremes of acceptance and rejection, hope and fear. It is said in *The Lion's Perfect Power,*

> Samsara and nirvana are awareness self-cognizing.
> They are not two; they are not different.

Those, however, who do not understand this think that buddhas are higher and beings are lower, and accordingly consider dualistically that nirvana and samsara are respectively good and bad. But just as if one dreamed last night that nirvana was superior and samsara was inferior—and had hopes and fears accordingly—when one examines one's dreams today, one sees that neither the one nor the other had ever existed and one understands that both are equal in being the delusions of one's mind. The Ati teachings proclaim that samsara and nirvana are "not two," that they are indivisible. They are the one sole awareness. Although this is incorrect according to the followers of the lower vehicles, in our tradition it is correct and just and is indeed a crucial point.

* * *

The seventh section expresses the decisive certainty that realization and the absence of realization are both devoid of real existence.

> **7. Whether or not you realize it,**
> **All is the state of openness and freedom.**
> **To think that this arises through your realization**
> **Is an enemy that hinders you.**
> **Ati says that realization and the lack of realization**
> **Are a single state of evenness.**
> **Though unacceptable to those who practice lower vehicles,**
> **This is correct and is a crucial point.**

All phenomena are, from the very beginning, already open and free. They, therefore, have no need to be rendered so through one's realization in the present moment. If they were not already open and free from the start, no present realization could make them so. Being open and free from the very beginning, they have no need to be rendered so again. Since the ground transcends both bondage and freedom, it does not in itself depend on the presence or absence of realization. Consequently, even though it may seem that in this present moment, phenomena are open and free because one has realized them to be so, or that they appear in the manner of hallucinations because one lacks such a realization, the fact is that all phenomena are open and free from the very outset, regardless of realization or the absence of realization in their regard.

The belief that phenomena become newly open and free once their nature has been realized is a hindering, obstacle-producing enemy—an enemy that prevents one's understanding that the ground, beyond bondage and freedom, is a state of equality. To say that the appearances of the relative truth are good or bad [open and free or hallucinations] in dependence on one's realization or lack of realization is no more than a relative assertion on the conventional level. In truth, however, it is not possible for appearances to be improved through one's realization, or to be impaired through one's lack of it. Phenomena in other words are the state of equality. This means that for yogis in the state of meditative evenness, there is neither realization nor the lack of realization, for the dharmatā, the ultimate truth, transcends the ordinary mind. And in the post-meditation experience of these yogis, so-called realization is no more than a deluded notion on the relative level.

The Atiyoga teaching that realization and absence of realization (even as simple labels) have no existence and are the single state of equality—that is, awareness—is unacceptable to those who follow the lower vehicles, even though it is correct and is indeed a crucial point.

* * *

The eighth section expresses the decisive certainty that the realization of awareness is not based on the crucial points of skillful means and wisdom.[84]

8. To claim that the inexpressible cannot be realized
Without special methods that reveal it
Is but the attitude of fools.
The Ati teachings show
That it is never separate from the ultimate.
Though unacceptable to those who practice lower vehicles,
This is correct and is a crucial point.

According to all the lower vehicles, the ability to realize the nature of one's mind depends on the accumulation of merit and wisdom, the purification of obscurations, the control of the channels, winds, and essence-drops, and so on. It is therefore thought that—without these many skillful means that show it forth—awareness, the inexpressible fundamental nature, cannot be realized. This is a foolish attitude. According to the Ati tradition of the Great Perfection, awareness, inseparable from the ultimate truth, naked and unimpeded in its openness, is realized instantaneously through its being directly introduced without relying on anything else. This teaching is unacceptable to people who practice the lower vehicles. It is, however, correct and just and is a crucial point.

This stanza shows moreover that all the paths that employ effortful action confine and fetter the ultimate nature of phenomena. They are of no assistance whatever to its accomplishment. In *The Great Garuda* it is said,

Holding breath and closing eyes—
This just lays a fetter on the mind itself.
If you are not in the ungrounded state,
Uncontrived, dependent upon nothing,
Adopting postures fetters the experience
Of luminosity found only in the state of rest and ease.
If you do not have a mind that's free
Of all divisions and extremes,
Analysis and speculation simply fetter
The fundamental nature.

All practices involving the forceful holding and stopping of the breath through the control of the movement of the winds in the subtle channels, and the closing of one's eyes and the concentration on visualizations, as in the practice of the generation stage, merely hinder the ultimate nature of the mind as it rests in its natural state. When, on the other hand, one remains relaxed and at ease in a state that is uncontrived and free of any foothold, not dependent on conceptual assumptions, awareness will manifest. But if, on the contrary, one adopts certain specific physical postures, or indulges in other effortful practices, the experience of seeing luminous awareness within the natural state of comfort and ease will be obstructed. Awareness is the naked realization of the fundamental nature, free of extremes and dualistic divisions. Free of the discursive mind, it is free of all such impurities. Conceptual analysis and the speculations of the dualistic, one-sided intellect are said to hamper the genuine nature of the mind. The text just cited continues,

> If you have no trust in natural rest devoid of action,
> The state of primal openness and freedom,
> Your realization will be hampered
> By your wish for meditative experience.
> Without the key point of not striving, of leaving as it is,
> Awareness will be hampered by dependence
> On the teaching on causality.

If one wishes to behold awareness, which is open and free from the very beginning and is a natural state of rest beyond any action of the three doors, one must first have trust in it. For without this, the meditative experiences of bliss, luminosity, and no-thought, which one may well wish to have, will only hamper the realization of the uncontrived fundamental nature. If one wishes to experience the actual state of awareness, it is essential to rest naturally without making any effort. This is an important crucial point. If one fails in this respect and instead relies on the teachings that demand exertion according to the law of cause and effect, one's experience of awareness will be impeded.

* * *

The ninth section expresses a decisive certainty with regard to the inconceivable—beyond the merely limitless—state.

> **9. To say the state of great perfection—**
> **Limitless, unfathomable,**
> **All-pervading from the very first—cannot be reached**
> **Is but the attitude of fools.**
> **The Atiyoga teaching that it is both sharp and limitless,**
> **Though not acceptable to those who practice lower vehicles,**
> **Is correct and is a crucial point.**

Certain people who claim to be practitioners of the outer mind class and of the inner space class of the Great Perfection assert that since the state of great perfection is primordially all-pervading, unfathomable, and limitless, it is beyond the reach of knowledge. They say that if its depths and limits cannot be fathomed or attained, it follows that this so-called naked awareness cannot appear within the sphere of the yogi's mind. But this is a foolish attitude. The view of such people has slipped into a one-sided, endless, limitless voidness. It is a great mistake also with regard to the way one meditates on the view. Our tradition of Atiyoga proclaims that awareness is boundless and has neither center nor periphery, neither zenith nor nadir; it is beyond the cardinal and intermediate directions. And yet, the very face of empty, luminous, unceasing awareness can be seen vividly by way of self-illumination. Like a crystalline sphere, it is a naked state of knowing—open, unimpeded, and sharp. It transcends the domain of the dualistic mind and is therefore said to be unobservable. And yet it can be seen by self-cognizing primordial wisdom as lying within its sphere of knowing, though in a manner in which subject and object are not separate. How could awareness be beyond the sphere of knowledge?

Mind or intellect or consciousness, so-called, is what engages with, and apprehends, objects. It is the ordinary mind. Self-cognizing primordial wisdom on the other hand transcends objects of apprehension. This naked state of knowing is awareness. It is important to understand the difference between the two. The [ordinary] mind follows after objects: it apprehends things and engages with them. It is like a drop of water that falls into the dust. By contrast, awareness does not follow after objects, it does not apprehend or engage with them. It is like a drop of mercury that falls into the dust. In truth, the dharmadhātu, free of all mental elaboration, is the object of self-cognizing primordial wisdom, the subject. It is not, however, a specifically characterized object of dualistic perception.

The teaching that emphasizes this boundless, sharp, naked aspect of knowing is unacceptable to minds engaged in the lower vehicles as well as to those who, having deviated into a one-sided, limitless, and infinite void, nevertheless claim to be practitioners of the mind and space classes of the Great Perfection. By contrast, in our tradition, this teaching is a correct and crucial key point. It is said in *The Mirror of Samantabhadra's Mind*,

> The view that's uncontrived
> Is primordial wisdom, open, unimpeded.
> The meditation that is uncontrived
> Is the unchanging vast expanse of space.
> The action that is uncontrived
> Is naturally arising relaxation.
> The uncontrived result
> Is the awareness that appears quite naturally.

* * *

The tenth section expresses a decisive certainty regarding the naked dharmakāya, the one sole sphere.

> **10. Because within the one sole sphere**
> **The order is reversed,**
> **There is no hope or fear regarding the result.**
> **For there is just a vast expanse commensurate with space.**
> **It is a great abyss, the mind of the Victorious Ones,**
> **Immense as space itself.**
> **There is nothing to reject and nothing to accomplish.**
> **There is but the vast immensity, the one sole sphere,**
> **Which, being free and open from the first,**
> **Transcends both realization and the lack of it.**
> **Upon this spacelike path devoid of action,**
> **Yogis are at ease.**

All the outer and inner phenomena that make up the world and its inhabitants are established as the one sole sphere of awareness. All things in samsara and nirvana arise within its one expanse. In the beginning, they unfold within the expanse of awareness in progressive order. For this reason, when this order is reversed and phenomena are traced back to their place of origin, a decisive certainty is gained that their source is awareness alone. When it is understood that samsara and nirvana are but the manifestation of awareness, a clear certainty arises that there is no result, no state of buddhahood, other than awareness. Consequently apart from the capture of the stronghold of awareness, there is no nothing to be hoped for in the sense of the attainment of buddhahood. And since there is no samsara and no suffering in the lower realms apart from awareness, one has a clear conviction that if the stronghold of awareness is captured, samsara will subside in that same awareness. Therefore, there is no fall into samsara to be feared. For one understands that all the appearances of samsara and nirvana do not lie outside the spacelike vast expanse of empty awareness.

So it is that the whole of samsara and nirvana is the expression of the one great awareness, the buoyant impetus of the one great awareness, the all-embracing dimension of the one great awareness. Since awareness is an all-penetrating great expanse, equal to the immense reaches of space, Longchenpa calls it an abyss. And since all the appearances of samsara and nirvana are contained within the great expanse of the one awareness, he refers to this abyss as vast. And this great spacelike immensity of awareness, present in the ground, the dharmakāya, is called the mind of the victorious buddhas of the three times, the great dharmadhātu.

In the ground of primordial purity, supremely open and free from the very beginning, samsara is not something to be abandoned and nirvana is not something to be attained. For neither samsara nor nirvana ever extend beyond the expanse of the one sole sphere of equality. Referring to samsara and nirvana, the root text speaks of them as being open and free from the very first. It therefore shows that they are themselves the sublime state of openness and freedom and are utterly beyond the reach of names. For even the terms *freedom* and *delusion*, applied on the basis of the realization or nonrealization of the openness and freedom [of samsara and nirvana], are utterly unreal.

Yogis who understand this remain continuously, uninterruptedly, on the path of great spontaneous presence, devoid of action and exertion—awareness equal to space. They have certain knowledge of the sublime openness and freedom that is beyond all labels. Thus they are contented and at ease. It is said in *The Mirror of Samantabhadra's Mind*,

> The infinite expanse of the enlightened mind
> Is free from stain, immaculate.
> Buddhahood has no existence.
> Therefore even *buddha* as a term does not exist.
> There is no such thing as clinging.

Therefore even *sentient being* as a term does not exist.
There is no ordinary cognition.
Therefore there's no ignorance and no delusion.
There is no fixation,
Therefore there are neither thoughts nor objects of the same.

* * *

The eleventh section expresses a decisive certainty that delusion is the great state beyond all designations.

11. Primordially the state of buddhahood,
Awareness is devoid of all objective reference.
It does not wander in samsara;
It transcends the whole foundation of delusion.
No one is there who has been,
And no one is there who can be, deluded.
All things are the dharmadhātu's single, luminous expanse.
They are not different in the past or future.
They are a skylike vast expanse
Primordially uncontrived, spontaneously present.
Samsara from the very first is pure.

Because awareness is in itself the primordial state of buddhahood within the vast expanse that knows no delusion, there is no need for it to be enlightened again. Within awareness, the empty, objectless state of equality that is free of elaboration, the hallucinatory appearances of what we call samsara are like the visions of last night's dreams, nothing more. In the past, awareness has never wandered in samsara. It is not wandering in it now, and it is impossible for it to do so in the future. It utterly transcends the very basis of the illusion called samsara. It has never existed. Of all the beings of the three worlds, therefore, none has been deluded in the past, nor is there any possibility of their being so hereafter. For samsara has from the very first been open and free in the state of primordial purity. Dreams never move beyond the state of sleep, sleep itself never moves beyond the state of awareness, and awareness never moves beyond the state of dharmatā. In just the same way, nothing has ever moved beyond the one luminous expanse of the dharmadhātu. The appearances of samsara occur but are without intrinsic being—just like the visions of a dream that are recognized for what they are. They are nonexistent yet clearly appearing empty forms. Appearing to the mind, they are the mind's own self-experience and nothing more. In truth, these empty forms are groundless and rootless, and, therefore, they were not hallucinations in the past, they are not so in the present, and there will not be so in the future. Without differentiation into past or future, so-called samsara is by nature the one sole sphere of awareness, a vast, groundless immensity similar to space. So it is that within awareness, which is primordially uncontrived and present of itself and is a vast immensity free of all mental elaboration, what we call samsara is inherently pure from the very beginning.

* * *

The twelfth section expresses decisive certainty that samsara and nirvana are not two.

12. Do not opt for freedom or embrace nirvana.
In the changeless vast expanse,
There has never been samsara or nirvana
To be rejected or adopted, to be feared or hoped for.
They are the vast immensity
Of enlightenment's primordial ground.
They are but names and are, in truth,
Beyond both indication and description.
Clearly certain that samsara does not mean delusion,
That nirvana is not freedom,
Let no one strive, let no one change or alter anything.

Because beings are primordially awakened in the ground that is beyond both bondage and freedom, there is no need for them to be freed now. They could not *become* free even if they wanted to—and this is why the root text says, "Do not opt for freedom." Since primordially empty self-cognizing awareness is pure like space, and since it is beyond both the object and agent of bondage, this means that samsara is pure in its natural condition. And since awareness transcends the state of freedom, [release from bondage,] it follows that nirvana is also by nature the state of primordially open, unimpeded emptiness beyond the extremes of existence and nonexistence. And, therefore, since samsara is not something to be abandoned and nirvana is not something to be sought for, the root text says that the latter should not be embraced.

What we refer to as samsara and nirvana are already open and free from the very beginning within the space of all-embracing awareness, the changeless vast expanse that neither moves nor evolves throughout the passage of time. And it is for that reason that they have never existed as such. As we find in *The Unwritten Tantra*,

> There is no samsara; there is no nirvana.
> There's no bondage; there is no release.

This means that from the very beginning, samsara and nirvana are already free and open within awareness itself. They cannot be separated from awareness, which, as their ground, is neither hallucinatory appearance (samsara), nor the absence of delusion (nirvana). It therefore follows that the defining characteristics of both are in themselves pure [that is, nonexistent] and beyond conceptual elaboration. Because the ground primordially transcends both bondage and freedom, it is neither bound by the hallucinatory appearances of samsara nor freed anew in the undeluded state of nirvana.

Within this ground beyond bondage and freedom, there is neither hope for nirvana as something to be attained nor fear of samsara as something to be rejected. Both samsara and nirvana are from the very first the vast, immense expanse of the ground of enlightenment. They are already the state of buddhahood. "Samsara and nirvana," "good and evil," "freedom and delusion" are nothing more than conventional terms. In truth, they are beyond the reach of indication and description. They are simply primordially pure awareness, the state of equality. Since "liberated buddhas" and "deluded beings" have never existed, a clear confidence is reached that samsara and nirvana are both the primordially pure expanse of ultimate reality. To have a deep certainty that this is so is of the utmost importance. Therefore, yogis should make no effort in striving, in altering or changing, in adopting or rejecting, negating or affirming. When the actual condition of awareness is maintained and the three doors are left unaltered and relaxed, without any effortful activity, the state of awareness is made evident. Awareness is not something that can be contrived. If one tries to fabricate it with a tightly focused mind, the face of awareness will be veiled.

Generally speaking, according to the view of the Great Perfection, awareness itself is neither samsara nor nirvana. And yet, apart from awareness, the so-called phenomena of samsara and nirvana have absolutely no existence. As it is said,

> The hare's horns do not differ in the slightest
> From the barren woman's child.
> The barren woman's child does not in the slightest differ
> From the horns upon a hare.
> Between the two there's not the slightest difference.

These words are taken from a sutra and yet they support the view of the Great Perfection, which states that samsara and nirvana have never existed—just like the horns of a hare and the barren woman's child. The statement about the equality of samsara and nirvana is made on the basis of the one sole sphere of bare, unimpeded awareness. It is not made on the basis of earth, stones, mountains, and cliffs. It is not a matter of dry words, clever talk empty of meaning. Neither is it an explanation based on an understanding of the external evidence of sense objects, but rather one that depends on the inner state of awareness. It is as Mipham says,

> Far better than to scrutinize a hundred distant objects
> Is to look at one thing here, your mind.
> My dear child looking over there,
> Today you must look over here!

By contrast, according to the explanation on the sutra level, where the existence of both nirvana and samsara is taken as a basis for discussion, it is said that

> Nirvana does not differ
> Even slightly from samsara.[85]

Now, if this way of positing the equality of samsara and nirvana is appraised in the light of the explanation of the Great Perfection, it amounts to a simple contradiction. For if the matter is explained on the basis of the existence of samsara and nirvana—samsara being delusion and nirvana being the absence of delusion—and if one says that there is not the slightest difference between delusion and the absence of delusion, is this not a contradiction, as Khenchen Jigme Phuntsok Rinpoche has pointed out? He also said that the way of positing the equality of samsara and nirvana according to the sutras and the way of doing so according to the Great Perfection are as different as heaven and earth.

The Great Perfection is thus the summit of all vehicles, the ultimate wisdom mind of all the buddhas. Compared with the lower vehicles, it is utterly sublime.

* * *

The thirteenth section expresses the decisive certainty that freedom from conceptual extremes is the immense expanse.

13. Awareness without breadth or height
Is without limits, falls to no extreme.
And so hold back from aiming at it.
Awareness, free of agent and of action,
Free of coming and of going,
Entails no lapse of time, no remedy.
Therefore do not cling to it or strive.
If there is deliberate focus,
This will be the cause of bondage.
Therefore do not grasp at anything,
But let it go in evenness.

Awareness pervades the whole of samsara and nirvana and is devoid of mental elaboration. It has no breadth or height and is beyond all other conceptual constructs. It is free of delimitation and falls to no extreme, it subsists as the one sole sphere, open and unimpeded. It is not an object that can be taken hold of; it is not something that can be striven for. One should therefore hold back—meaning that one should refrain—from aiming at it. Awareness is self-arisen. In relation to it there is neither agent nor action, neither coming nor going. *The Unwritten Tantra* says,

Awareness in itself is ultimate.
It is unmade. What maker could it have?
It is uncontrived—there's no one to contrive it.

Since awareness does not require the use of antidotes or periods of time for its realization, one should let go of all clinging and striving. It is thus, Longchenpa says, that the primordial fundamental nature will become manifest. Awareness in itself has never been marred by such faults as clinging and fixation. It is like the vast and pure abyss of space. And so, if now, when watching awareness, there is a deliberate focusing on it as a target, the mind will fetter itself like a silkworm imprisoning itself with the threads of its own saliva. This will simply veil the face of awareness and will not be of the slightest help. Indeed it will be a cause of bondage. Therefore, without any grasping whatsoever, one should let go of everything in the vast state of evenness.

* * *

The fourteenth section expresses the decisive certainty (thanks to a realization as vast as space) that all phenomena partake of the great state of nonaction. This section has five parts. The first expresses a decisive certainty that, once their fundamental nature becomes manifest, phenomena are exhausted in the state beyond the ordinary mind.[86]

> **14a. It makes no difference if phenomena**
> **Are or are not free and open from the very first.**
> **It makes no difference if the fundamental nature**
> **Is or is not pure intrinsically.**
> **It makes no difference if the mind itself**
> **Is or is not free of all elaboration.**
> **It makes no difference if, within the nature uncontrived,**
> **There is or is not anything existent.**

It makes no difference whether or not phenomena are open and free from the very first. In the actual, genuine reality of the fundamental nature, there is no difference between being open and free and not being open and free. Consequently, when the uncontrived, open, unimpeded state of equality becomes manifest, openness and freedom and the lack of openness and freedom are the same.

Similarly, it makes no difference if the fundamental nature is intrinsically pure or not. Since the characteristics of purity and impurity have no existence in the fundamental nature of awareness, samsara and nirvana are both awareness. Awareness is the state of unimpeded openness. Unimpeded openness is the state of nakedness. Unconfined and even, awareness is seamless and unfettered.

It makes no difference whether the mind is free of mental elaboration or not. Once it is realized that, in itself, awareness is a perfect state of equality free of mental elaboration, there is no mind to think anything, no place in which to dwell, no path to tread, no view to be viewed, no object on which to meditate. Naturally open and free, awareness is bare and unimpeded. It is traceless like something drawn on water.

It makes no difference whether something exists in the uncontrived nature or not. Since awareness is open, unimpeded, and naked, samsara and nirvana are a seamless, uninterrupted expanse. The open, unimpeded state is traceless. Self-arising is without partiality. Self-subsiding is devoid of phenomena. In the exhaustion of phenomena, not even their names remain. There is never any stirring from the fundamental nature.

* * *

The second part of the fourteenth section expresses a decisive certainty regarding the great spaciousness of the blissful mind, thanks to the realization in which the states of hope and fear are transcended.

> **14b. It makes no difference if by nature samsara and nirvana**
> **Are or are not a duality.**
> **It makes no difference whether thoughts and words**
> **Are or are not passed beyond.**
> **It makes no difference if delusions of negation or assertion**
> **Do or do not fall apart.**
> **It makes no difference if the view that should be realized**
> **Is or is not recognized.**

It makes no difference whether samsara and nirvana are by nature a duality or not. In awareness, which is groundless and rootless, there are none of the characteristics of samsara or nirvana. Samsara is groundless, nirvana is primordially open and free. They are equal. All that arises subsides of itself. There is just a spacious, all-embracing state of naked, unimpeded openness.

It makes no difference whether thoughts and words are transcended, passed beyond or not. Free of conceptual elaboration, awareness is inconceivable and inexpressible. There is no mind to think anything, no speech to express anything, no path to be trod, no stains that obscure. This is the manifest state of the groundless, rootless, fundamental nature.

It makes no difference whether the delusions of negation or assertion fall apart or not. Within awareness itself, there are no phenomena either to deny or to assert. The bare, naked state of nonaction cannot be distorted thereby. There is nothing negative to reject and nothing positive to accomplish. There is no basis of delusion, no mind that is deluded, no delusion to be destroyed. Hallucinatory appearances and perceptions are open and free in the ultimate expanse. They do not stray beyond awareness, which is empty and free of mental elaboration—the great and perfect state of spontaneous equality.

It makes no difference whether the view that is to be realized is recognized or not. In the natural state of awareness, the fundamental nature, there are neither buddhas who have realization nor beings who are without it. There is no ground, no path, no result, no action, and no agent. There is neither clinging nor deviation, nothing to be rejected, nothing to be adopted. There is neither awareness nor ignorance. It is simply the unbounded state of the one sole sphere of primordial openness and freedom.

* * *

The third part of the fourteenth section expresses the decisive certainty that all conceptual processes, which unfold and dissipate, are themselves transcended through the realization that the mental consciousness is the great state of primordial exhaustion devoid of action.

14c. It makes no difference
If you do or do not meditate upon the dharmatā.
It makes no difference whether you examine it or
not—
It is not something you can take or else reject.
It makes no difference whether you attain or not
The fundamental nature, the result.
It makes no difference whether you progress or not
Upon the grounds and paths.

It makes no difference whether or not one meditates on ultimate reality, the dharmatā. When the true reality of the dharmatā is realized, awareness, the state of evenness and freedom from conceptual extremes, beyond delimitation and direction, simply manifests. It does not *become* free and open through meditative training. It is not found through searching. It is not seen through looking. It is not acquired through action. Awareness, in which phenomena are exhausted (to the extent that not even their names remain), is a state of freedom from all such fetters.

Since awareness is not something to be adopted or rejected, it makes no difference whether it is examined or not. One should simply recognize naked awareness itself, free from any mentally contrived effort or clinging. If, on the other hand, one does examine awareness, it will be just a concept. If one meditates on it, it will be just the ordinary mind. If one tries to express it, the result will be nothing more than words. If one watches it, there will just be a subject and object of apprehension. If one acts, there will just be samsara. For awareness is natural, primordial openness and freedom—an all-embracing space, a vastness without reference.

It makes no difference whether one attains the result, the fundamental nature, or not. Indeed, when the fundamental nature of primordial radiance is reached, there are neither accomplished buddhas nor unaccomplished beings. There is no hope for something good and no fear of something bad, and no indifference with regard to something in between. There is no movement within the seamless luminous awareness that is directly and instantly recognized.

It makes no difference if one traverses the grounds and paths or not. For in awareness, there is no training or progress. When the ultimate result, the fundamental nature, is actualized, there are no grounds to be attained, no paths to be traversed, and no destination to be reached. For the primordial ground, the everlasting kingdom of the dharmakāya, the primordial sovereign, has been captured.

* * *

The fourth part of the fourteenth section expresses the decisive certainty (through the realization of unobscured, bare, and open awareness) that there is nothing to eliminate and nothing to attain.

14d. It makes no difference whether you are free or not
Of all your obscurations.
It makes no difference whether or not the dharmatā
Is gained through the generation and perfection stages.
It makes no difference whether you achieve or not
The fruit of liberation.
It makes no difference whether or not
You wander in the six migrations of samsara.

It makes no difference whether one is free or not free of obscurations. When the dharmatā, spacelike pure awareness, manifests, there are no defilements that obscure and no one to be obscured. There is no karmic action to be purified and there is no antidote that purifies. There is no result to be attained and no path through which to attain it. There is nothing at all. For the ever-youthful vase body, the dharmakāya, the exhaustion of all phenomena in the state beyond the mind, is now manifest.

It makes no difference whether or not the generation and perfection stages accomplish the dharmatā. When the natural state of awareness, the dharmatā, the naked fundamental nature free of action, is manifest, there is no generation stage to be generated and no perfection stage on which to meditate. There is no teaching to reflect upon and there is no mind to be transformed. There is no past to be evoked, no future to be pursued, and no present to be seized upon. There is just open, unimpeded awareness, the carefree state of primordial wisdom—unconfined awareness that is the vast expanse beyond extremes.

It makes no difference whether or not the fruit of liberation is attained. For other than the actualization of awareness itself—the genuine fundamental nature, the dharmatā devoid of anything to be abandoned or acquired—there is no hope of gaining any other result or liberation. Whatever arises is awareness; whatever appears is the dharmakāya. It subsides in its very arising. It is empty in its very appearing. It vanishes in its very movement. One is never at any time parted from the meditative concentration that, in its nature, is like a river's ceaseless stream.

It makes no difference whether one wanders, or does not wander, through the six migrations of samsara. When the nature of awareness, beyond freedom and delusion, the state of phenomenal exhaustion beyond all action, is made manifest, there is no chasm of samsara. There is no place of fear and dread, no fear of lower destinies. There is no feeling of torment. If something is good, let it be good. If something is bad, let it be bad. When phenomena come to exhaustion in the state of no action, it is then that the fundamental nature manifests—ultimate reality in which there is no samsara to be rejected and no nirvana to be gained.

* * *

The fifth part of the fourteenth section expresses a decisive certainty regarding the carefree, unconfined state, thanks to the realization that the exhaustion of phenomena is the unfettered state of all-pervading evenness.

14e. It makes no difference whether or not
Your nature is spontaneously present.
It makes no difference whether or not
You're bound by dualistic clinging to permanence or to annihilation.
It makes no difference whether or not
You reach the realization of the dharmatā.
It makes no difference whether or not
You follow in the footsteps of the masters of the past.

It makes no difference whether one's nature is spontaneously present or not. If one has a clear certainty regarding awareness or self-arisen primordial wisdom, and if one is utterly convinced of the equality of samsara and nirvana, one's nature is neither spontaneously present nor is it not so. And even if it appears to be both or neither, it does not in fact fall into any of these positions. Even if it appears as happiness or suffering, it does not do so continually. Even if it is as pure as the dharmatā, the ordinary mind does not engage with it. Even if it is seamlessly open and free, its fundamental condition is not maintained.[87] Left to itself in its natural condition, the mind, impartial and unrestrained, will expand, free and relaxed, into the sublime dharmatā, the natural state of openness and freedom.

It makes no difference whether one is bound or not bound by dualistic clinging to permanence or to discontinuity. The uncontrived fundamental nature is free of all conceptual constructs of existence, nonexistence, both, and neither. It is free of both permanence and annihilation. Even if one meditates on it as existent, it cannot in itself become permanent. Even if one meditates on it as nonexistent, it is impossible for it to be annihilated. Even if it be viewed as both existent and nonexistent, it cannot fall to such an extreme. If it is existent, let it exist! If it is nonexistent, let it not exist! If it appears, let it appear! If it is empty, let it be empty! If it is this or that, let it be so! If it is not this or that, let it not be! In short, when there is no fixation on anything, permanence and annihilation are nothing but a natural display, open and free, within the vast expanse of dharmatā.

It makes no difference whether the realization of the dharmatā is attained or not. No matter what is observed, it does not fall outside the one sole vast expanse of primordial purity. Therefore, there is no hope of *attaining* the dharmatā, nor is there any fear of not doing so. There is no ground that is not open and free primordially. There is no path on which the nature is not recognized. There is no result that is not free and open by its very nature. There is no state or condition that is not the fundamental nature. Samsara and nirvana are therefore inseparable and never parted from the sublime and natural state of openness and freedom.

It makes no difference whether or not one follows in the footsteps of the masters of the past. Awareness in the present moment, empty, luminous, and unceasing (that is, self-aware, self-cognizing primordial wisdom) is inseparable from the mind of all the Victorious Ones, past, present, and to come—the great dharmadhātu, the expanse of ultimate reality. When a confident realization of this is achieved, one recognizes in truth the ultimate view of all the masters of the past. Apart from this, there is no need to follow in the footsteps of the masters who have gone before, there is no need to rely on a holy teacher, there is no need to search for essential instructions in some other place, and no need to meditate on profound precepts. Longchenpa says that, within the vast expanse of such awareness, we must attain buddhahood in the ever-youthful vase body, the primordial purity in which phenomena are exhausted.

* * *

The fifteenth section clearly explains the character of the realizations that have just been described.

15. No matter what may happen,
Though earth and heaven be upturned,

You experience nothing but the bare and open state
Of groundless openness, relaxed and even.
All things are unstable, hazy, evanescent,
nebulous—
And like a lunatic you act without duality of hope
and fear.
View and meditation—all are merged without
division.
The asserting, purpose-driven mind collapses.
You are no longer trammeled by ambition,
There are no goals that you now strive to gain.

No matter what may happen—even if heaven and earth were to change places—yogis who have realized the vision of the exhaustion of all hallucinatory appearances in the expanse of the primordial purity of the dharmatā are completely free of fear, alarm, and dread of anything. And since they have seen directly that all appearances are the display of awareness, they are quite certain that all such empty forms are the manifestation of its creative power. They understand that, other than being like reflections seen in a mirror, they have absolutely no existence. The minds of such yogis are immersed, even and relaxed, in the dharmatā, awareness—a bare state of groundless openness. They cannot stir from it. And at that time, all the various phenomena that appear to them seem unstable, weightless, vaporous, insubstantial, diaphanous, nebulous, evanescent. It is just as when one recognizes that one is dreaming or when someone watches an amazing spectacle, knowing it to be a magical illusion. These yogis are without the slightest hope or fear, without attachment or aversion. They are completely certain that appearances are none other than the dharmatā, spacelike pure awareness. And they act without any inhibition, like lunatics, neither accepting nor rejecting anything.

View, meditation, action, and result merge and blend together inseparably and beyond division. All ideas of the asserting, purpose-driven mind collapse into the ultimate expanse. Untrammeled by ambition, and without reference and bearings, these yogis no longer have goals to strive after. All appearances are for them nothing but a display of empty forms. All mental movement is naturally and primordially pure. Whatever arises disperses naturally without trace. All these are the signs of the freedom that these yogis have achieved in the state of phenomenal exhaustion, wherein not even names remain. It is said in *The Word-Transcending Tantra*,

> Since the self-arisen is not an object,
> Its "seeing" is not separate from awareness.
> Such seeing sinks into awareness.
> All subsides through understanding this one thing—
> There is no further count of two and three.
> There appears no object to which thought can cling.

This text means that within the expanse that is the union of awareness and emptiness, free of the conceptual elaborations of existence, nonexistence, both and neither, even self-arisen awareness itself is open and free. Therefore, by its nature, it is not an object; it is not something that can be seen. Although, conventionally, it is said that awareness is seen, in truth this seeing is not separate or distinct from the awareness wherein there is neither seen object nor seeing subject. Seeing and awareness blend together in a nondual unity. Similarly, when one speaks of "sinking," this too subsides into awareness. Other than that, there is no difference between the object and the agent of sinking. In reference to this awareness, it is said here that all subsides through the recognition of this one thing—of awareness alone. Therefore, it is thanks to the realization of awareness that all the eighty-four thousand mental states subside into it. So it is that all the appearances of samsara and nirvana are but the one sole sphere of awareness. Aside from this, the twin states of samsara and nirvana or the appearances of the three-thousandfold universe cannot be enumerated in the slightest. All are exhausted in the state of primordial purity, the expanse of the exhaustion of phenomena that is beyond the ordinary mind. Everything is therefore the one sole sphere of the dharmakāya in which nothing appears that thought might apprehend and examine.

* * *

The sixteenth section shows that when yogis experience the realization that occurs from within, everything that arises inescapably subsides, free and open in the dharmatā.

> **16. All that happens you allow to happen.**
> **Whatever may appear, you allow it to appear.**
> **Whatever may arise, you allow it to arise.**
> **Whatever there may be, you allow it to exist.**
> **If there's anything at all, you let it be;**
> **And if there's nothing, you allow it not to be.**

All the waves that surge upon the vast expanse of a single ocean do so as the display of that ocean's power and are not different from it. The ocean is the basis for the surging of the waves. Waves and ocean are identical and there is no qualitative difference, positive or negative, between them. All the waves naturally sink back into the ocean, and thus the two cannot be differentiated. Likewise, for yogis who have realized that everything is none other than the display of the dharmatā, all appearances, good and bad, that manifest within the expanse of awareness are not different. Since they all arise and manifest within the expanse of awareness, they are not different from awareness. Since the very ground for the arising of the creative power and display is awareness itself, yogis understand that awareness and its creative power are one and the same without any difference. Since they realize that this creative power together with the entire display of awareness is none other than awareness itself, they understand that there is no difference between a "good creative power" and a "bad creative power." And since the creative power and display naturally vanish in the expanse of awareness, yogis see no difference between them.

Those whose minds do not stir from the dharmatā, and for whom whatever arises naturally subsides, simply allow whatever happens to happen. Untroubled by the nature and circumstances of any event, even imminent death, they are without fear. They let whatever appears to appear. For appearances never stir from the single state of awareness; they are its creative power and display. As it has been explained above, such yogis allow whatever arises to arise. Whatever there may be, they let it be. If there is anything at all, they let it be; and if there is nothing at all, they let it not be. For within awareness, all such situations are without a hair of difference. No matter what arises, it arises within the state of awareness. And yet, since awareness itself is as unchanging as space, it is not in any way affected by the arising, or the nonarising, of anything. Whatever arises is none other than the creative power of awareness and as such is beyond the qualitative distinctions of good and bad. Since all that arises naturally subsides in the very moment that it arises, there is no difference between arising and nonarising. For yogis who allow anything at all to be and who allow nothing at all not to be, there is neither "is" nor "is not." All their recollections and thoughts naturally vanish and come to exhaustion, and consequently, there is for them nothing to choose, accepting some things and rejecting others. For the state in which phenomena are exhausted—in which nothing, not even their names, remains—is now made manifest.

* * *

The seventeenth section shows that although yogis who have realized the state of total openness and freedom devoid of reference points behave unpredictably, their experience of phenomena is quite ordinary and natural.

> **17. Unpredictable is your behavior**
> **For awareness is preeminent.**
> **You take no account of virtue or nonvirtue,**
> **For you are in a bare and open state**

Beyond the snare of philosophic doctrines.
Eating, walking, lying down, or sitting—by day and night,
You're in a state of all-pervading evenness,
Equality, the dharmatā.
No deities to worship, no spirits to drive out,
No Dharma to be meditated—
This is the simple, ordinary state.
You, a sovereign free of all contrivance and pretension,
Are in an all-embracing evenness.
Relaxing in equality, you now have found
The one and only state spontaneously present,
Not now achieved, because primordially accomplished.
How pleasant to be free of striving and exertion!

As the root text says, the conduct of yogis who have realized the state of total openness and freedom beyond all reference is unpredictable. It is referred to as the kind of behavior that interrupts the continuum of the city of samsara. For such yogis have no preferences at all in the way of food or clothing. The way they behave is completely free of dualistic clinging. They are without inhibition and do whatever comes into their minds. They say whatever words come into their mouths, and they display signs of the accomplishment of their yogic practice. These are all indications that, for them, awareness is predominant [over conduct].

Whereas ordinary people spend their time engaged in activities that have little to do with virtue, those who follow the path of Dharma are immersed in virtuous conduct. But yogis [of the kind just mentioned] take no account of what is virtuous and what is not virtuous, and neither adopt the former nor reject the latter. They understand that without being accomplished anew, virtue has already been achieved and there is no need to do it again. Since they are beyond virtue, all their virtuous activities are no more than natural, ordinary actions. All their mental fixations and clinging to objectives have been cleared away in the primordial purity devoid of action, and therefore, at all times and in all situations, however they may be, these yogis cannot move from the bare and open state that is free of all fixation—awareness stripped to its naked state. Since they have achieved the ultimate and unsurpassed objective of their own and others' tenets, such yogis are utterly beyond the snares of philosophical doctrines. Eating, walking, lying, sitting—day and night without any difference—they realize that everything is a state of all-pervading evenness. They never waver from the dharmatā, the state of equality.

For them, therefore, aside from self-cognizing awareness devoid of mental elaboration, there are no yidam deities to be worshipped. Aside from deluded dualistic thoughts, there are no spirits to exorcise. Aside from naked awareness, the all-pervasive primordial purity, which is free of meditating mind and meditated object, there is no Dharma on which to meditate. Understanding that the Dharma is already achieved, already accomplished, primordially, they leave it all behind. Being beyond Dharma, they have no "dharmic" activity at all. Contented in mind, they lie down happily in the normal ordinary state.

"But," some people may ask, "when yogis start acting in such a completely ordinary way, how can they not fall into delusion just like common people?" We will counter these doubts by answering as follows. Free of any purposeful activity of body, speech, or mind, these yogis remain unwavering in the primordial, natural state of the dharmatā. This being so, how could they possibly be deluded? When common appearances are cleared away, becoming the state of unimpeded openness, all bondage is gone. It is like when a hempen rope is burned, its ashes may still look like the rope. But a burned rope is unable to bind anything. Likewise, when the open, unimpeded nature of the mind manifests, it may seem that the ordinary mind of adopting and rejecting is still there, along with an attachment to food, clothing, possessions, and so on. And yet, when it is realized that these things are groundless—as when one realizes that one is dreaming—they have no power to bind. This is not the case for ordinary beings. For their minds are fettered by their belief in existence. Outer and inner phenomena are for them a matter of adoption or rejection, and they are bound by them—as by a rope that has not been burned! It is as the glorious Saraha has said,

> If you cling to something, throw it all away!
> If you realize it, it's everything!
> Apart from that, there's nothing to be understood by
> anyone!

And Tilopa said,

> Appearances don't bind you.
> You are bound by clinging.
> Cut your clinging, Naropa!

The minds of these sovereign yogis, who rest in the natural and uncontrived state, are completely free of the pretensions of mental elaboration and clinging thoughts. This [purity], like an immaculate autumn sky, is a state of all-embracing evenness. As these yogis settle, relaxed and natural, in this condition of equality, they spontaneously come, in this very life, to the realization of primordial wisdom, the exhaustion of phenomena beyond the ordinary mind. For everything now is clearly the one sole sphere of awareness.

These yogis do not gather the two accumulations in order to accomplish buddhahood. For them, the two accumulations are already complete, and there is no need for them to strive anew. From the very first, there is nothing for them to strive for. They have actualized primordial wisdom, the exhaustion of phenomena beyond the ordinary mind and so they can rest content with a sense of profound inner relaxation.

Some people object to this idea. For what is gained, they say, by remaining in the ordinary state? On the contrary, it is by the two accumulations and the purification of obscurations that yogis obtain again and again, in life after life, a divine or human birth, and in the end achieve enlightenment. What possible objection, they say, could there be to this position?

[In answer, it might be said that] to reject the view of the uncontrived state of nonaction and instead to cling to a teaching that involves concepts and exertion is like praying to an ordinary stone on the top of a victory banner instead of the wish-fulfilling jewel that one is holding in one's hand. There are many other ways of banishing such doubts, but I will not enlarge on them here.

* * *

The eighteenth section shows that the view and meditation are a state of spaciousness free of objective reference.

> **18. The view has no foundation and there is no meditation.**
> **There is no action, no result to be achieved.**
> **Since all are thus encompassed by the undivided equal state,**
> **There is no need to strive.**
> **Bliss lies in freedom from the wide and narrow.**

When awareness, open and unimpeded, is realized in its naked state, all phenomena come to exhaustion within it. When the exhaustion of phenomena beyond the ordinary mind manifests, then apart from that same naked awareness, there is no view, meditation, action, or result. When the final view is reached at the level of phenomenal exhaustion, it is not a state of primordial nonexistence—a mere, blank void. It transcends the ordinary mind, the sphere of thought. It is free of subject-object apprehension—beyond a subject that views and an object that is viewed. Since this is but the one sole naked awareness, empty, luminous, and ungraspable, the root text says that the view has no foundation.

In the same way, when the final meditation is reached at the level of phenomenal exhaustion, it is free of dullness and agitation, of drowsiness and lethargy. Whatever arises subsides of its own accord, without there being any clinging to anything. There is no adoption or rejection, the result of dualistic fixation. This is a state that is completely devoid of identity, completely free of the ordinary mind along with its conceptual bearings. The final meditation is nothing but naked, all-embracing awareness. And this is why the root text says that there is no meditation.

Again, when action or conduct is attained at the level of phenomenal exhaustion, it is no longer dictated by deluded habitual tendencies. It is consequently devoid of dualistic fixation and is beyond all action and exertion. It is uncontrived, devoid of grasping, and without any constraint being placed on the six consciousnesses. There is simply the state of openness and freedom, the dharmatā beyond all ontological extremes. Even if one were to look for action, one would not find it. Therefore, the root text says that there is no action.

When, at the level of exhaustion, the result is finally reached, there is neither adoption nor rejection, neither hope nor fear. For there is neither an expectation of gaining the result nor a dread of not gaining it. Aside from indwelling awareness, there is no other result. Moreover, this result does not have to be striven for, for it is spontaneously present from the very beginning. This is the state of phenomenal exhaustion, the ever-youthful body enclosed within a vase, the dharmakāya. No other result is there that could possibly be desired and this is why the root text says that there is no result to be achieved.

View, meditation, action, and result are all encompassed by the one, naked, unimpeded awareness, the one undivided state of equality. No striving is called for in relation to them. They are immersed in the one sole sphere of awareness free from wide and narrow [transcending all extension]. They are the primordial wisdom of supreme bliss. As it is said in *The Six Expanses*,

> I, Samantabhadra, have no view.
> Without a view, appearances all cease.

Neither have I any meditation,
And without meditation, there's no mindfulness.
I have no action to describe.
And since there's no activity,
The body's actions cease.

As this text says, Samantabhadra has no view to be viewed. Since he has no view, all phenomenal appearances cease in the expanse of the dharmatā, the exhaustion of the view. Samantabhadra does not have any meditation either. If he had meditation, he would have to maintain a state of mindfulness. But being without meditation, he is free of a meditated object and a [meditating] mind, and therefore mindfulness has ceased. Likewise, in relation to Samantabhadra (that is, awareness), no action can be described. He has reached the level of the exhaustion of action, and no further action can be performed. And so the body's various activities—going, sitting, eating, lying down, physical gestures, dance, and so on—all come to an end.

* * *

The nineteenth section shows that the openness and freedom of all things is a vast immensity.

19. When there is no wishing,
The notion of achievement ceases.
When there's nothing to abandon,
You go beyond the bondage of relying on an antidote.
All there is, whatever it may be,
Does not exist, nor does it not exist.
Whatever is perceived, no matter what arises,
All inescapably subsides.

When it is realized that all phenomena are the vast immensity of primordial openness and freedom, something that is not open and free will be impossible to find even if one searches for it. This is why the result—namely, buddhahood—is characterized by the absence of a wish [to achieve it]. The result is already achieved from the very beginning as the great primordial state of openness and freedom, and therefore one has no notion of achieving it anew. In other words, one has no expectation of a result.

Since hallucinatory appearances are brought to the state of exhaustion—with the result that there is nothing left to abandon—one has no thought that one must rely on an antidote (namely, undeluded awareness) as a means of discarding them. It is thus that the bondage of having to rely on antidotes is transcended—meaning that it too is brought to exhaustion.

At that point, one never stirs from the condition of dharmatā, whether in the past, present, or future. It therefore follows that in whatever situation one may find oneself, it is simply awareness. All the appearances of samsara and nirvana are awareness. They cannot be said to exist or not to exist. Whatever is perceived subsides as soon as it is perceived. Whatever arises subsides as soon as it arises. No matter what arises and is perceived, it inescapably subsides in the one sole sphere of awareness. It is impossible for there to be a phenomenon that does not subside. Generally speaking, the way of subsiding is very important. As Patrul Rinpoche has said,

> The way that thoughts occur is as before.
> The way that they subside however is a crucial point of great importance.
> Without this, meditation is but a deluded path.
> But with it, there is dharmakāya uncontrived.[88]

Since in awareness, adoption, rejection, and the state of being or not being [something] are not found, one gains confidence that appearances and mental states subside in four ways. As *The Word-Transcending Tantra* tells us,

> Since awareness self-cognizing is devoid of thought,
> There are four ways that thoughts subside.

Through confidence in these four crucial ways,
Samsara and nirvana are no more.
Not arisen and not made,
They have neither ground nor root.

Now with regard to these four ways of subsiding, there exists a general teaching as well as specific explanations corresponding to the practitioners' confidence of realization.

The general teaching explains, first, the subsiding [of appearances and mental states] into the state of naked awareness; second, the instantaneous subsiding [of thoughts]; third, the subsiding of appearances and mental states into the state of groundlessness; and fourth, the subsiding of phenomena into their self-emptiness. The explanation is as follows.

First, when one realizes that whatever arises has not the slightest existence separate from the one sole awareness, one becomes convinced that phenomenal appearances and mental states, which arise in a state of bare openness, sink back into the one sole awareness. This is the way of subsiding into naked awareness.

Second, all manifesting thoughts arise and subside simultaneously in the first instant. In the second instant, they are no more. They do not stay; and their [immediate] subsiding, without further extension, is referred to as instantaneous subsiding.

Third, because appearing objects together with the six sense consciousnesses that apprehend them are empty, groundless forms, it follows that when one leaves them just as they are and rests in the natural state of mind without any entangling fixation, they just subside. This is the subsiding of appearances and mental states into groundlessness.

Fourth, in general, when [certain] Madhyamikas investigate phenomena, using arguments such as the reasoning of "neither one nor many" and so on, they find that they are empty of something [a true existence] other than themselves. In the present context, however, the situation is quite different. For all phenomena are primordially empty of *themselves*. They are beyond all the effortful action and scope of the ordinary mind. To have confidence that they subside nakedly—that they vanish spontaneously into their own empty nature—is referred to as the subsiding of all phenomena into their self-emptiness.

The confidence that one gains regarding these four ways of subsiding is like the consummate certainty of the young garuda, king of birds, who with wings already fully developed, soars immediately in the sky across the vast abyss.

Now of the four specific explanations, given according to the yogi's confidence of realization, the first is primordial subsiding (in other words, the state of openness and freedom from the very first). The second is self-subsiding. The third is naked, or direct, subsiding. The fourth is complete subsiding.

In the first case, when yogis have the confidence of realizing that all phenomena subside primordially (that is, that they are free and open from the very first), these same yogis have no need in the present moment to render them free and open again, no need to settle in this truth again, no need to meditate on it again. For left in their natural condition, phenomena subside, they are open and free right where they stand.

Second, phenomena are self-subsiding—they are free and open in themselves. When yogis realize that everything that arises naturally subsides in the same way that a knot tied on a snake comes loose by itself, they have no need to rely on antidotes.

Third, when awareness is watched nakedly no matter what appears, the appearance itself subsides into—or is open and free in—this same awareness. This is referred to as naked or direct subsiding. Moreover, [when yogis realize that] whatever is seen subsides in the very place where it is seen, the seen object subsides so that there is nothing to see. This is subsiding on seeing.

Fourth, [when yogis realize that] there is not a single appearing phenomenon that does not subside in the vast and even state of awareness, [they do not need to strive and rest content].[89] This is complete subsiding.

It is said in *The Word-Transcending Tantra*,

Subsiding from the very first—there is no need for repetition.
Subsiding by themselves—there is no need for antidotes.
Subsiding nakedly—they vanish in the place where they are seen.
Subsiding utterly—there is no need for effort.

When all these key points are understood, the effort implied by antidotes collapses. Things to be abandoned are no more. Gone are the fetters of thoughts and memories. The fortress of adoption and rejection comes crashing down. And in the spacelike vast expanse, where phenomena and the ordinary mind are no more, the state of equality, the primordial purity free of mental elaboration—that is, the state of exhaustion—is reached. These are the special experiences of the practitioners of the Great Perfection.

It is then that primordial wisdom, free of a subject and object of apprehension, is actualized. Just as at dawn when the sun rises, the dark of night naturally departs—leaving no trace and going none knows where—when yogis achieve the perfect confident certainty of awareness, all impure hallucinatory appearances vanish. Not an atom of them is left behind.

* * *

The twentieth section leaves no room for doubt that the nonexistence of phenomena lies within the vast expanse that is like space.

20. There is nothing that's not free and open,
Free and open from the first, and of itself.
When certainty is reached
That all things, all together, are insubstantial,
They pass beyond the status of phenomena.

When one understands, and is utterly convinced, that all things are primordially equal and are completely open and free, one sees that of all the phenomena of samsara and nirvana, it is impossible for there to be even one that is not open and free. Moreover, it is not that phenomena become open and free when it is realized that they are so. For there is not a single thing that is not open and free from the very beginning. Neither is it the case that they are open and free in dependence on extraneous conditions. There is not a single phenomenon that is not open and free in its own right. Consequently, when one is utterly convinced that phenomena—all together and without exception—are insubstantial, that they are the one sole sphere of primordial purity free of all mental elaboration, one necessarily comes to the decisive conclusion that they transcend the state of being "phenomena," that they are primordially equal, free and open from the very beginning.

And yet, although it is said that one necessarily comes to a decisive conviction that phenomena are pure and equal primordially, the truth is that the three spheres [implied in such a conviction] have never existed. There has never been a state of conviction, never anything to be convinced about, and never anyone who is convinced. One therefore has a decisive certainty that, without the slightest conceptually characterized action, object, and agent, all is the expanse of awareness, the state of equality, the one great dharmadhātu. It is as we find in *The Natural Openness and Freedom of Awareness*,

> The fixed belief relating to the view
> Is not a thing endowed with attributes.
> It is free and open in itself.
> The "self-arisen" thus verbally contrived
> Is but a relative convention.
> All things belonging to the two conventionalities—
> The extremes of existence and of nonexistence—
> Are not observed in ultimate reality.

If there is a notion that the ultimate view is such and such a thing—if there are such opinions and ideas—it follows that this same view is a phenomenon endowed with attributes. According to the Great Perfection, however, there are no phenomena endowed with attributes, for of necessity they are free and open of themselves right where they stand. If self-arisen awareness is verbally expressed, this expression is a conventionality and has never existed from the very first. Moreover, classifications of existence and nonexistence are the extremes of existence and nonexistence only on the conventional level. And none of these has any validity whatever in the actual, true reality of the fundamental nature. Here there is just the state of equality, primordially open and free, devoid of all views marked by conceptual elaboration.

* * *

The twenty-first section summarizes the meaning of the preceding stanzas as the state in which Longchenpa's own benefit has been effortlessly accomplished.

> **21. Within the vast expanse, the vast expanse,**
> **Within the great and vast expanse,**
> **I, Longchen Rabjam, am immersed in the expanse,**
> **The great abyss of luminosity.**
> **I dwell within the one, nondual immensity—**
> **Immensity of bliss.**
> **I, Natsok Rangdröl, have attained the dharmatā,**
> **The state of the exhaustion of phenomena,**
> **Unchanging, present of itself,**
> **The summit of all perfect aspiration.**

The vast expanse of outer appearances is groundless, vast, primordial emptiness. The vast expanse of inner moving thoughts is intrinsically pure, a vast traceless state. The vast expanse of the secret ultimate enlightened mind is immersed in a great, vast, naked unimpededness. Outward appearances, the inner apprehending subject, and secret awareness—all these three are respectively groundless primordial emptiness, the intrinsically pure, traceless state, and the state of open, unimpeded nakedness. As for the person who spontaneously abides therein, this is the yogi of the supreme vehicle, Longchen Rabjam, who has realized it clearly and nakedly. Not abandoned, samsara is primordially pure for him. Not accomplished, nirvana is entirely present for him. He is immersed in the view of the vast abyss of luminosity, uncontrived, self-arisen and spontaneously present. He has realized that all the phenomena of samsara and nirvana have a single, nondual savor in the one expanse of awareness. He dwells within the space of primordial wisdom of great bliss. He is indeed the victorious Longchen Rabjam.

In his very life, he reached the state of dharmakāya beyond the ordinary mind. Thus for him, the vast ocean of manifold phenomenal appearances subsided, open and free, in awareness—the open, unimpeded, and naked state of primordial purity. His realization of the dharmatā, the state of phenomenal exhaustion, reached its consummation. In his very life, he captured the unchanging, spontaneously present, everlasting kingdom of the sovereign dharmakāya and completely accomplished the summit of all perfect aspiration. As it is said in *The Heap of Jewels*,

> All the key points of the Natural Great Perfection
> Are absorbed within the mind itself.
> Even thoughts that think "There is no object;
> There is nothing that appears"
> Are not cut off but disappear of themselves.
> Since there has never been delusion,
> The root of ignorance is cut primordially,
> Without investigation.

As this text says, when the dharmatā, the state of phenomenal exhaustion, is reached, all the profound key points of the Great Perfection are fully assimilated within the mind. The hallucinations of a subject and object of apprehension no longer occur. They vanish into the open and unimpeded state devoid of objective reference. Consequently, even the cognitions of apprehender and apprehended disappear and vanish right where they stand, without their being intentionally severed. Since the fundamental nature (which has never at any time been deluded) is realized in all its nakedness, the root of ignorance is cut out from the very outset, without any investigation being made.

* * *

The twenty-second section gives advice for the fortunate beings who will follow in Longchenpa's footsteps.

> **22. All you who follow after me**
> **Bring everything together thus**
> **In one immense, primordial, all-enveloping expanse.**
> **And surely you will gain Samantabhadra's**
> **everlasting realm.**

All who have a fortune equal to that of the Victorious Lord Longchenpa in being able to practice the profound path, and all fortunate disciples, fitting vessels who in generation after generation will follow in his footsteps, must embark upon this path. If they wish to practice according to these explanations—which bring all things together in one immense expanse of equality free of all mental elaboration (an all-enveloping state of primordial openness and freedom beyond all action)—they should, in support of their practice, study and imbibe the meaning of the commentaries and pith instructions. This includes all the works of Longchenpa himself: the Seven Treasuries, the Four Parts of Heart Essence, the Trilogy of Rest, the Trilogy of Natural Openness and Freedom, the Trilogy of the Three Chariots,[90] the Trilogy of the Secret Essence, and so on. And in their very lifetime, they will certainly attain the great, primordial citadel of the dharmakāya, the everlasting realm of Samantabhadra. It is said in *The All-Creating King*,

> *Kyéma!* Yogis who take this path and meditate on it,
> From that very moment, dwell upon the ground of victory.

And in *The Six Expanses* it is said,

> The fortunate who thus habituate themselves
> Have bodies but are free of thought.
> Possessing the same fortune as myself,
> They are my essence and my retinue.

Generally speaking, in the first eight chapters of *The Treasury of the Dharmadhātu*, the important points of the path and practice are explained in broad strokes, whereas from the ninth chapter onward, the practice of the path is explained in specific detail. Now whereas the fifth chapter of the text gives precise instructions on how to overcome the dangers of deviating, straying, and error, the ninth chapter expounds the way in which awareness is introduced according to the Great Perfection—along with numerous key points, essential outlines, principles, riveting nail-like instructions and so forth. For this reason, the great Khenpo Jigme Phuntsok described the fifth and ninth chapters as the heart and eyes of *The Treasury of the Dharmadhātu*. According to the oral teaching of Patrul Rinpoche, master of the Great Perfection, *The Precious Treasury of the Dharmadhātu* is the embodiment of the realization of the Great Omniscient Master himself. And in the biography of Khenpo Ngakchung, it is clearly stated that the view is explained from the first chapter till the ninth. The tenth chapter deals with meditation, and the eleventh sets forth the action or conduct. Finally, the twelfth chapter speaks of the result in the immediate term, while the thirteenth sets forth the result on the ultimate level.

* * *

This concludes the word commentary on the ninth chapter of *The Precious Treasury of the Dharmadhātu*, which shows with decisive certainty that all phenomena lie within the expanse of the enlightened mind.

10. The Enlightened Mind Does Not Stir from the Dharmatā

This chapter shows that awareness does not stir from the dharmatā. It has eight sections, and of those that teach that the fundamental nature (clearly established as awareness) is practiced in the state of natural meditative absorption, the first defines the nature of this same absorption in general terms.

> **1. The enlightened mind, by nature pure from the beginning,**
> **Is dharmatā, which does not come or go**
> **And is beyond acceptance and rejection.**
> **The dharmatā is the expanse of space**
> **And is not gained through effort.**
> **When you settle in it naturally,**
> **The sun and moon of luminosity arise.**

The nature of awareness is the pure, ultimate, enlightened mind. It is primordially free of delusion. Leaving one's body, speech, and mind relaxed and unaltered in this very moment, one should rest steadily in meditative evenness, in a state in which all deluded thoughts related to the three times neither come nor go, in which they are neither kept nor pushed away. If one does this, the dharmatā, which is one's very birthright, will clearly manifest. It is open, bare, naked awareness, the luminosity of the fourth state, free from the other three [namely, thoughts related to past, present, and future]. Now this is not achieved through deliberate effort—by strongly fixating on what one should or should not do, or on any other conceptual activity. All effort should be abandoned and one should simply rest naturally in the vast expanse of space that is the dharmatā. The luminosity of awareness will arise therein like the sun and moon. And just as darkness naturally vanishes when the sun and moon rise in the sky, in the same way, when self-arisen awareness clearly manifests, the darkness of ignorance naturally disappears.

At this point in the autocommentary, Longchenpa discusses three topics. First, he urges us to practice. Then he distinguishes the natural meditative absorption [of awareness] from meditative concentration. Finally, he explains how the actual practice should be implemented. Here, I shall summarize as follows. With regard to the first topic, it is said,

> The important thing is not to "meditate";
> It is to grow accustomed.
> When familiarity is perfectly achieved,
> That is supreme meditation.

And,

> Otherwise, although awareness may be recognized,
> If you have not grown used to it,
> You will still be carried off
> By thoughts, which are your enemy,
> Just like a baby on a battlefield.
> Unable to withstand both things and situations,
> You will be like an ordinary person.
> Experience will not grow
> For such a training bears no fruit.
> And yet Buddha did not say
> That without meditation
> Enlightenment can be attained.

Furthermore, it is said in *The Sutra of the Buddha's Ornaments*,

Deaf musicians, though they please their hearers,
Their own music do not hear.
Unmeditated Dharma is like that.

A skillful ferryman may carry
Many passengers across the stream
And yet may never disembark.
Unmeditated Dharma is like that.

Those tormented by their thirst
Who only see and hear of water
Fail to quench their thirst.
Unmeditated Dharma is like that.

As these texts imply, simply to recognize awareness does not take us very far. Longchenpa therefore urges us to become perfectly familiar with it. We should be like mothers nursing their babies so that in this very life, we may gain complete mastery of awareness and accomplish the exhaustion of phenomena in the dharmatā.

Longchenpa's second topic is the distinction between natural meditative absorption and meditative concentration. Here we should notice that the various methods for training in concentration spoken of in the lower vehicles (which here can be regarded as ways of leading beings of lower capacity to the path of Ati) may be condensed into two techniques: one in which the mind is focused on an [external] support and one in which it is not.

Concentration cultivated on the basis of such a support uses a piece of wood or stone, the letter *A*, the form of a deity, a hand emblem, and so on. Meditation without an external support focuses on a [visualized] mental object such as the channels, the essence-drops, the winds, a sphere of light, and so on.

In the kinds of concentration set forth in the common vehicles, the mind is focused undistractedly in a state of no-thought. In brief, all these ways of cultivating so-called meditative concentration have a target; their nature is a state of mental stillness; their purpose is to render the mind stable; and their function is to block the cognitions of apprehender and apprehended. It is said in *The Word-Transcending Tantra*,

> "Meditation" is the state of mental calm
> Where moving thoughts are severed,
> So to speak, from outside.
> Apprehender, apprehended both are stopped.

And,

> Focus on the key points of the body,
> On the channels, winds, and essence-drops,
> And focus upon emptiness—
> All this is "meditation."

The body is the support for the channels; the channels are the support for the winds; the winds are the support for the essence-drops. This being so, it is within this supporting structure of the channels, essence-drops, and winds that we have the means of pursuing the path of liberation, together with the methods of pursuing the path of skillful means, using the techniques of dripping, holding, reversing, and spreading. In short, the text is saying that one cultivates meditative concentration in dependence on the key points of the body, on mental focus, and on emptiness.

As for the purpose of these methods for cultivating meditative concentration, it may be said that thanks to the path through which the dualistic cognitions of apprehender and apprehended are forcefully arrested, these effortful methods will at length allow one to engage into the path of the ultimate, fundamental nature of the Great Perfection, which transcends all action. These techniques are referred to as "concentrations for the enjoyment of childish beings." It is nevertheless thanks to such childish concentrations that one will one day reach the state of awareness, the natural meditative absorption of the Great Perfection.

Longchenpa's third topic has to do with the actual practice of awareness—namely, natural meditative absorption. In this regard, it may be said in general that natural meditative absorption is a particular feature of the Great Perfection. Fire is suffused with heat. Water is suffused with wetness. In the same way, awareness (as spoken of in the Great Perfection) is at all times suffused with a natural meditative absorption, a meditative absorption that dwells within. If, after recognizing awareness, one remains at all times and in all situations within the natural meditative absorption that is proper to it, the states of bliss, luminosity, and no-thought will automatically arise without their being intentionally cultivated.

Moreover, the radiance of awareness is endowed with this natural meditative absorption even in the bardo state. From the radiance of awareness—namely, the mandala that encompasses the five quintessences—there arise in the bardo of ultimate reality, the forty-two peaceful deities and the fifty wrathful deities, together with the sounds, lights, rays, and so forth. They are naturally present within awareness and arise outwardly. Similarly, natural meditative absorption is intrinsically inseparable from awareness.

By way of a slight digression, I shall now contrast the ways in which the ordinary mind and the primordial wisdom of awareness are used as the path and then compare the state of no-thought of a great meditator with the thought-free awareness of a yogi [of the Great Perfection]. Finally, I will briefly explain the difference between the vivid clarity that dwells within the mind and the vivid clarity that is naturally immanent in awareness.

First, when using the ordinary mind as the path, when one practices mental stillness or calm abiding, the mind becomes still by dint of the effort with which one meditates, and when one stops meditating, this mental stillness disintegrates and ceases. When, however, self-cognizing primordial wisdom is used as the path, if one's three doors are left in a relaxed state, free of tightness or manipulation, awareness, stripped and in its naked state, becomes clearly manifest, and this is the natural state of meditative absorption. If this is preserved like a flowing stream, awareness becomes increasingly evident. When the ordinary mind is used as the path, and thoughts are eliminated by the use of an antidote, one's present thoughts simply vanish without trace. When, however, awareness is used as the path and becomes manifest, one is released from the shackles of thought. These two situations are similar inasmuch as thoughts and memories simply disappear. However, when the ordinary mind of no-thought is used as the path, awareness does not manifest and the root of the ordinary mind is not severed, with the result that reifying and fixating thoughts will haphazardly arise again. When this happens, one might well think that thoughts arise from an unborn source within the mind. This however is a mistake.

If, through using awareness as the path, awareness becomes naked and free of thought, all haphazard clinging and fixation vanishes. Thoughts do not arise. Neither is there anything that causes them to arise. Thus, the root of the ordinary mind is severed and the glow of the creative power of cognizant potency manifests unceasingly like a reflection in a mirror. The reflection simply manifests on the surface of the glass; it is not that the mirror itself unfolds as the reflection. Similarly, when an appearing object manifests in awareness, at that moment, primordial wisdom, knowing that such an object is intrinsically empty, perceives it as being like the rays of light that shine forth from the sun. There is therefore a considerable difference between using the ordinary mind as the path and using awareness as the path.

Now, when we compare the state of no-thought experienced by a great meditator and the awareness that occurs nakedly and free of thought as experienced by a yogi [of the Great Perfection], they are similar in the sense that no thoughts occur. However, the state of no-thought of a meditator occurs when the key points of bodily posture are maintained undisturbed. When they are disturbed, the state of no-thought is lost. This is because awareness has not been stripped to its naked state. The state of awareness free of thought, as experienced by yogis, does not depend on physical posture and so on. It is awareness nakedly manifest. The state of no-thought of the meditator and the thought-free awareness of the yogi are as different as heaven and earth.

Finally, the mind's indwelling vivid clarity and the naturally indwelling vivid clarity of awareness are again similar in their being clear and without thought. Nevertheless, since the ordinary mind is anchored in the dualistic cognition of apprehender and apprehended, it retains a strong clinging to the stillness aspect of the mind. Awareness, on the other hand, is seamless in its unimpeded openness. There is a considerable difference between the two.

The aspect of unceasing luminosity of appearing objects occurring within limpid awareness, and the cognition of the ordinary discursive mind unfolding outwardly to apprehend its object may be compared respectively to a drop of mercury and a drop of water falling into the dust. In the first case, appearing objects are not followed [engaged in], whereas in the second case, they are. There is therefore a great difference between the two cases. It is said in *The Six Expanses*,

> One's own mind free of all turbidity
> And awareness, self-cognizing, free of thought,
> Are so alike, the one might be mistaken for the other.

One's own mind, free of the turbidity of thought (the experience of no-thought occurring in the untroubled state of calm abiding) and self-cognizing, self-illuminating awareness free of thought and stripped to its nakedness are, from the point of view of the absence or presence of the awareness aspect, as different from each other as blindness is from sight. Nevertheless, because they are similar in being free of thought, it is possible to confuse them.

The Six Expanses also tells us,

> The vision of deep, unobscured luminosity
> And the stream of thoughts that beings grasp
> Are so alike, the one might be mistaken for the other.

The vision of the deep, unobscured luminosity of naked awareness and the continuous thought processes that beings seize upon, and which unfold toward the objects of the senses, are—from the point of view of the straying or not straying of cognition into the object—very different. Nevertheless, because they are similar in that both possess the aspect of luminosity, it is possible to confuse them.

The same text also says,

> Meditation that's a state of effortless repose
> And mind at rest because of winds and channels
> Are so alike, the one might be mistaken for the other.

The state of rest found in a meditation where one remains effortlessly in the natural state of awareness and the mental repose that comes from concentrating on the winds and channels are, on account of the respective absence or presence of effortful striving, completely different. But since they are similar from the point of view of actual rest, it is possible to confuse them.

In short, the meditation of a mind that is oriented toward an objective is the peg whereby the mind is tethered to a subject and object apprehension. By contrast, the natural meditative absorption of awareness is the natural and continuous flow of the dharmatā. Therefore, the difference between the two is very great. The first is the cause of the samsaric process and produces the mental states of the higher realms. The second joins one directly to the freedom of nirvana, whereby one dwells within the very state of buddhahood. It is said in *The Word-Transcending Tantra*,

> The fundamental nature
> Is a state of natural rest without contrivance.
> It never changes from this state.
> It is the wisdom mind of all the buddhas.

The view of Atiyoga, the Great Perfection, is in many ways vastly superior to the bodhisattva [sutra] path, the three outer tantras, and the Mahāyoga and Anuyoga. This superiority may be briefly expressed in terms of five sublime qualities, which are outlined in *The Word-Transcending Tantra* as follows:

> The Heart Essence may be summarized as follows.
> There is no difference between sharp and dull capacity.
> Assumptions, words—all such devices are exhausted;
> One sees it therefore with one's eyes, not with intelligence.
> The dharmatā is not perceived through words,
> And thus the common vehicles cannot attain to it.
> Since the three kāyas are seen while on the path,
> When they are seen, there's no regressing to the triple world.
> Since all phenomena, in evenness, are of a single taste,
> There's no relying on the ground, the path, and the result.

As this text declares, the path of the Heart Essence of the Great Perfection has many sublime and extraordinary qualities, which may be summarized in the following way. For the actual realization of open, unimpeded awareness, the sharpness or dullness of a person's faculties is of no consequence. Since verbal devices, assumptions and intellectual investigations are all exhausted, the Heart Essence is not realized through analytical intelligence. On the contrary, it is seen directly, in its unimpeded openness, by means of the [visual] faculty. Since the perception of the dharmatā, or true reality, does not occur thanks to verbal explanations, the vision of it is not achieved in the common vehicles. These are the key points of awareness, which is open, unimpeded, and beyond words. And since everything that appears is understood as the three kāyas perceived upon the path, it follows that when awareness is seen, it is impossible to regress to the three worlds. This is a key point for not falling back into samsara. And since within the evenness of the one awareness, all things are of the same taste, one relies neither on the view, meditation, action, and result nor on the ground, path, and result.

* * *

The second section of the tenth chapter describes how this extraordinary path is practiced.

> **2. If you do not block the objects of your senses,**
> **If you do not hold your mind in check,**
> **If you do not stray from the spontaneous equality**
> **Of your natural condition, you will reach the wisdom**
> **Of Samantabhadra, vast immensity.**

When one meditates according to the extraordinary path of the profound pith instructions, one leaves the three doors in a relaxed and natural state, neither blocking nor indulging in the appearing objects of the six consciousnesses. Whatever manifests, one leaves it alone, neither accepting it nor rejecting it. Neither does one hold one's mind in check by blocking the unfolding and subsiding of thoughts. Whatever manifests is simply left alone in a vast and even state, free of the mental fluctuation just mentioned. If one rests without straying from the spontaneous, intrinsic equality of the natural condition, free of all mental movement, one will reach the wisdom of Samantabhadra, the vast immensity. One will capture in this very life the ultimate and everlasting domain, the one sole sphere of phenomenal exhaustion beyond the ordinary mind. As it is said in *The Unwritten Tantra*,

> The self-arisen natural state, primordially uncontrived—
> Appearances do not change it nor does mind transform it.
> If you stay within the space of dharmatā,
> As awareness it will be revealed.

This text means that without straying from empty luminous awareness, open, unimpeded, and stripped to its naked state, one should not indulge in objects that appear in the outer world. Nor should the mind unfold inwardly. And in between these two, one should not constrict awareness with meditation on nonduality. Instead one should rest in the natural state, open and unimpeded.

* * *

The third section of the tenth chapter is a presentation of the four ways of leaving as it is and the three concentrations, which are methods for bringing awareness into one's unmistaken experience. The four ways of leaving as it is are as follows. The first is a leaving as it is that is mountainlike; the second is a leaving as it is that is oceanlike; the third consists in leaving awareness as it is; and the fourth consists in leaving appearances nakedly just as they are. The three concentrations are first, the great indwelling concentration; second, the great direct concentration; and third, the great sealing concentration. According to the gradual order of arising in the course of practice, the way of leaving as it is that is like an ocean is the one presented first.

> **3a. When thoughts do not unfold and dissipate,**
> **There is a natural, pure limpidity—**
> **It's like an ocean, limpid, smooth, unmoving.**
> **It is the dharmatā, deep luminosity,**
> **The state of self-arisen, primordial wisdom**
> **In which you rest, where hope and fear**
> **Do not arise and you are not caught up in them.**

In general, according to the wording of the tantras, the four ways of leaving as it is are given in the order first mentioned above. According to the pith instructions, however, and in the order in which they are experienced in the mind, the oceanlike way of leaving as it is comes first and is followed by the mountainlike way of leaving as it is. It is indeed a fact that beginners in the practice do not at first experience the mountainlike realization, free of change and movement.

Leaving the three doors in a natural state without contrivance, one should, with eyes wide-open, fix one's gaze into the space directly in front, just as if one were watching the ocean. With thoughts neither unfolding nor dissipating, one should simply rest in naked awareness, in its natural, pure, limpidity. In this way, one rests like a clear and limpid ocean, smooth and unruffled by the wind. One is free of the occurrence of, and involvement with, hope and fear. One rests in the state of open, unimpeded dharmatā, aware and profoundly luminous—the pristine, self-arisen primordial wisdom of equality that is naked awareness. This way of resting unwaveringly is called the oceanlike way of leaving as it is. By way of illustration, when the reflections of the stars and planets appear on the ocean's surface, even though they look like planets and stars, they do not stir from the water. In the same way, appearances arise unceasingly within the state of awareness, but they do not stir from this limpid state and thus have no existence apart from awareness. We read in *The Treasury of the Fundamental Nature,*

> Although the objects of the senses, ceaselessly appearing,
> Are vivid like the planets and the stars,
> If this is not impaired by the discursive mind,
> You will attain the state of highest wisdom,
> Awareness self-cognizing, free of ordinary cognition.[91]

And it is said in *The Unwritten Tantra,*

> The way of leaving as it is that's oceanlike
> Is not appearance; nor does it bring appearance forth.
> It is not emptiness; nor is it something that is empty.
> It is not luminosity; it is the sphere of supreme luminosity.

As this text tells us, this way of leaving as it is is not a phenomenal appearance. And since there is no fixation on any appearances that arise, it does not cause them to occur. It is not the state of emptiness, and since it has no existence in terms of a one-sided emptiness, it does not exist as something empty. This means that appearance and emptiness are inseparable. In the same way, [this way of leaving as it is] is not a one-sided luminosity. Luminosity and emptiness are inseparable, and therefore the oceanlike way of leaving as it is is said to be the sphere of supreme luminosity.

The Unwritten Tantra also says,

> When you're not fixated on the observed aspects
> Of the objects of the senses,
> Luminosity remains unceasing in this absence of fixation—
> Like the planets and the stars that seem
> To lie within the ocean's depths.
> The leaving as it is that's oceanlike is similar to this.

Some people say that the four ways of leaving as it is are methods of meditation peculiar to the practice of thögal. This merely demonstrates that they are unlearned in the meaning of the tantras. Although it is said in *The Blossoming Lotus*,[92] the commentary on *The Unwritten Tantra*, that these instructions apply only to the thögal practice, *The Instruction Concerning Precious Appearances*[93] states nevertheless that they are universally applicable. They must therefore apply to both thögal and trekchö.

Furthermore, *The Blossoming Lotus*, the commentary on *The Unwritten Tantra*, and *The Instruction Concerning Precious Appearances* are both "child" or subsidiary texts of the Heart Essence teachings. Generally speaking, the "mother" or main texts of the Heart Essence are the seventeen tantras,[94] to which are added many "child" texts. Each of the seventeen tantras possesses five such texts. Moreover, Śrīsiṃha, Mañjuśrīmitra, Jñānasūtra, Vimalamitra, and others composed commentaries on the seventeen tantras, all of which are regarded as subsidiary texts.

Whatever the practice may be, whether trekchö or thögal, the important thing is to strip awareness to its open, unimpeded nakedness. If one is ignorant of how to do this, then even if one meditates on trekchö, one will not rise above samsara; and even if one meditates on thögal, one will deviate into the realm of form. And as Longchenpa says, the reason for this is that one does not know how to maintain the state of naked awareness.

In general, for both trekchö and thögal, the four ways of leaving as it is are similar. It is through the mountainlike way of leaving as it is that the result is revealed. By the oceanlike way of leaving as it is, meditation is revealed. By leaving appearances as they are in their nakedness, action or conduct is revealed. By leaving awareness as it is, the view is revealed.

* * *

The second part of the third section discusses the way of leaving awareness as it is.

> **3b. Indescribable and free of mind's entanglement,**
> **The plain and natural state is uncontrived and unalloyed.**
> **It is the space where everything dissolves,**
> **The dharmatā devoid of attributes.**
> **There is neither meditation nor something to be meditated.**
> **Therefore dullness, agitation both are dissipated naturally,**
> **And the self-arisen state appears.**

According to the gradual way in which meditation unfolds, and experience and realization arise on the yogic path, it is necessarily on the basis of the oceanlike way of leaving as it is that the way of leaving awareness as it is is realized.

When planets and stars appear reflected on the surface of the sea, they look just like real planets and stars, and yet they do not stir from the water. Likewise, when all appearing objects, unceasingly occurring in awareness, do not stir from the latter's limpid state, this is referred to as the oceanlike way of leaving as it is. Now if, in addition to this, self-cognizing, self-knowing awareness is stripped to its very nakedness and brought to the fore, the seamless dharmatā, free of out and in, will manifest. And this is referred to as leaving awareness as it is.

In the context of the thögal practice, to settle in the radiance of awareness, the vajra chains, is also described in terms of leaving awareness as it is. In the present context, however, the instruction for the trekchö practice is to rest in naked awareness itself, open and unimpeded. When the three doors are left in a natural state without their being tampered with, there manifests a plain and natural state of mind that words cannot describe and that is free of the mental entanglement implicit in thought processes, apprehension, clinging, and effortful striving. When one simply relaxes in this state, awareness, uncontrived and unadulterated, appears, open and unimpeded in its nakedness. This is referred to as leaving awareness as it is. It is as we find in *The Unwritten Tantra*,

> The instruction for leaving awareness as it is
> Is where you touch the secret.

And also,

> Seek how to leave awareness as it is.
> This is the great secret of all secrets.

As these texts imply, leaving awareness as it is refers to actual awareness itself—open, unimpeded, and empty. This is the great perfection, the great secret of all secrets. On the level of the sutras, in the view of the Great Madhyamaka, there is no mention of naked awareness. It is the uncommon and special feature of the Great Perfection.

If, therefore, one maintains the condition of naked awareness, leaving awareness as it is; and if one gains complete familiarity with this, the day will come when all hallucinatory appearances dissolve into the expanse of the one sole sphere of awareness. The sign that this will happen is that when one rests in the expanse of naked awareness, all the many thoughts that arise now dissolve into it, and the dharmatā, which has neither dwelling place nor characteristics, which is beyond both object of meditation and the act of meditating, manifests. It is open, bare, naked awareness. Without their being intentionally arrested, the experiences of dullness, agitation, lethargy, drowsiness, and so on naturally dissipate in the expanse of naked awareness. And the state of self-arisen dharmakāya, which is never separate from oneself, manifests within that very state of leaving awareness as it is.

* * *

The third part of the third section discusses the way of leaving appearances as they are in their very nakedness.

> **3c. Not eliminated through elimination,**
> **Thoughts are themselves awareness's creative power.**
> **There are no distinctions, differentiations, in the dharmatā.**
> **The dharmatā is therefore not achieved through practice.**
> **Arising as it does within the ultimate expanse of dharmatā,**
> **Samsara is not spurned.**
> **Rather, through the pure yoga**
> **Linked with the creative power of this vast expanse,**
> **You see samsara as primordial wisdom self-arisen.**

The appearing objects, defilements, thoughts, and so forth, which arise through the creative power of awareness, are not eliminated by being discarded through the use of antidotes, as is the case in the sutra vehicle of the pāramitās. In the Great Perfection, all thoughts that manifest, be they good or bad, are recognized as the creative power of awareness—awareness being like a clear and limpid mirror. And all the things, good or bad, that are reflected in that mirror are without any separate existence. In the same way, whatever appearing objects occur, they arise in awareness as an unceasing creative power of cognizant potency. To let go of the arising aspect, and to watch naked awareness itself is referred to as leaving appearances as they are in their nakedness.

When one rests in the dharmatā, awareness, one perceives the objects of the senses manifesting clearly and unceasingly. But without making distinctions or differentiating them—rejecting some and accepting others—one must watch naked awareness directly. This naked awareness is not something that one reaches by making effort in the practice, but rather by relaxing in the state of leaving appearances as they are in all their nakedness. It is therefore important simply to rest naturally, without rejecting or accepting whatever appearances occur.

In just the same way, the five aggregates, which have arisen within the ultimate expanse of the dharmatā, are not rejected but instead are recognized as [the buddhas of] the five enlightened families. The five elements are not rejected but are recognized as the five female buddhas. The five poisons are not rejected but are recognized as the five primordial wisdoms. If this happens, samsara is not rejected but arises as primordial wisdom. Whatever appearances occur, arising through the creative power of the vast expanse of awareness, they manifest only as the pure, delightful vision of buddhas and buddha fields. Such are the perceptions of the practitioners of this pure yoga.

This then is an essential instruction on how to recall awareness in whatever may appear and in any of the circumstances that might occur. One leaves appearances as they are in their very nakedness. This is of great importance for beginners, for those who have made some progress, and for those who have gained some slight stability in the practice. Practitioners of great stability, by contrast, do not encounter any ordinary hallucinatory appearances, however hard they may look for them. As such, they have no need to recall awareness in every appearance and circumstance.

Generally, it is important to maintain open, unimpeded, naked awareness at all times and in all situations. But what *is* open, unimpeded awareness? From the standpoint of the mind's empty nature, it has no existence whatever, whether in the inner or extramental world or somewhere in between. It is like empty, indivisible space. Nevertheless, from the standpoint of the mind's unceasing luminous character, the very face of primordial wisdom free of all apprehension and fixation can be clearly seen. And this is referred to as awareness, open and unimpeded. As Mipham has said,

> In order to avert fixation upon emptiness,
> It is set forth in the Mantrayāna as great bliss.[95]

So it is that open, unimpeded awareness is also referred to as great bliss. The Madhyamikas establish all phenomena as being primordially empty and rootless, free of the ontological extremes of existence, nonexistence, both, and neither. This is their final view. According to the Great Perfection on the other hand, awareness is not established as being merely empty, for it is said,

> The character of emptiness is luminosity,
> And the cognizant potency of luminosity never ceases.

* * *

The fourth part of the third section discusses the mountainlike way of leaving as it is.

> **3d. Appearances and mind are from the first**
> **The natural state of dharmatā.**
> **Unmoving concentration**
> **Manifests in a continuous stream.**
> **This is the vajra peak,**
> **Samantabhadra's sublime mind.**
> **Through meditation[96] on the fact that all things**
> **Without any difference**
> **Are the skylike supreme spacious dharmatā,**
> **The supreme, wondrous sovereign, primordially unlimited,**
> **Is spontaneously discovered.**

When one has gained certainty that, from the very first, appearing objects and the apprehending mind do not stir from the uncontrived, natural state of the dharmatā, which is of the nature of awareness beyond all movement and change, and when one settles in meditative evenness within this very state, nothing can cause one's concentration to waver. It is like Sumeru, the unmoving king of mountains. Accordingly, since the dharmatā cannot be ruffled by thoughts regarding past, present, and future, nor by the objects of the senses, this way of resting is called the mountainlike way of leaving as it is. The resulting state of awareness manifests uninterruptedly like the flow of a great river. And when one has acquired a perfect confidence that one does not stir from it, the state of dharmatā or awareness manifests in every circumstance, no matter what appearances may occur. Indeed, the latter serve only to recall that same awareness. It is like adding fuel to the fire.

When all appearances become awareness (the result of the mountainlike way of leaving as it is), all moving thoughts and states of mind vanish of their own accord. As it is said in *The Unwritten Tantra*,

> Leaving as it is that's mountainlike constitutes the secret view.
> There is no doubt. It is immutable by nature.

When unmoving awareness, the result of the mountainlike way of leaving as it is, becomes evident, one attains the peak of the vajra vehicle of Secret Mantra, the sublime quintessence of the mind of Samantabhadra. All phenomena merge into a single indivisible taste in the supremely vast dharmatā, the great abyss of awareness, the evenness of Atiyoga. By meditating without differentiation on all the appearances that occur within this skylike vast expanse, in the mountainlike way of leaving as it is—which relates to unchanging spontaneous presence—the supreme result is accomplished. It does not matter what manifests. Whatever appears is from the very first present of itself as the state of evenness of empty awareness, the unlimited, marvelous sovereign wisdom of the supreme vehicle.

Although *The Unwritten Tantra* says that the mountainlike way of leaving as it is is a matter of the view, the omniscient Longchenpa says that, of the three ways of leaving as it is, the mountainlike way occurs quite naturally. And so saying, he applies it to the result.

Generally speaking, through the mountainlike way of leaving as it is, all movements of thought naturally subside, and finally, there manifests a state of awareness that is unwavering like a mountain, in which all discursive movement is actually impossible. This does not occur from the very beginning and will not arise unless one strives skillfully to render one's habituation to it ever more firm. When one tries to remain in awareness itself, one has to maintain a state in which the thoughts that naturally arise naturally subside.

In *The Father Teachings* and *The Son Teachings* of the Kadampa tradition, Drom asked Atiśa, "Lord, what should I do when thoughts arise?"

Atiśa answered, "Watch their nature and they will naturally subside."

"But," continued Drom, "what should I do, if they arise again?"

"If they arise again," replied Atiśa, "again just watch their nature. They will naturally subside. If a hundred thoughts arise in the course of a day, you will meet the awareness of the dharmakāya a hundred times. As my teacher Awadhuti used to say, 'As much as thoughts arise, so much is the dharmakāya, awareness, present.'"

In sum, when one settles in the oceanlike way of leaving as it is, all appearances are settled in the limpid state of awareness. In addition, the self-aware, self-knowing cognizance of the state of leaving awareness as it is lies stripped to its nakedness. Then, through the way of leaving appearances as they are in their nakedness, everything that arises is used as the path. In other words, while one watches appearances nakedly and directly, one maintains the state of awareness and trains oneself to see that the whole of phenomenal appearance is altogether pure as the five primordial wisdoms and so forth. And the unwavering preservation of this state is none other than the accomplishment of the mountainlike way of leaving as it is.

* * *

The fourth section of the tenth chapter speaks of the three kinds of concentration, which are here presented as a supplement to the four ways of leaving as it is. The first part of the fourth section is divided twofold. First, there is an explanation of the great sealing concentration, and second, an instruction on how to dispel hindrances to it.

> **421. Within this state, where nothing is adopted or rejected,**
> **The primordial stream of luminosity**
> **Immediate and unmediated**
> **Is present of itself.**
> **This is the very nature of samsara and nirvana,**
> **The supreme state of dharmadhātu.**
> **This skylike vast expanse,**
> **Unwavering and indescribable,**
> **Is from the first and by its nature**
> **Present in all beings.**

Samsara and nirvana are both sealed by awareness, and awareness is sealed by indwelling meditative absorption. We therefore speak of the great sealing concentration. When this is cultivated, one sits with legs crossed, gazing ahead into the sky with wide-open eyes. Free of reference points, and without the unfolding and dissipation of thought, the mind is settled in the indivisible union of awareness and the ultimate expanse. Following the teacher's immediate and unmediated—direct and instantaneous—introduction to indwelling primordial wisdom from which, from the very beginning, one has never in fact been parted, if one remains continually and uninterruptedly like a flowing stream within the luminosity that one has recognized—that is to say, the bare, clear, vivid state of awareness, the state in which nothing is adopted or rejected and in which there is no going or coming—the great sealing concentration is present of itself spontaneously and without contrivance. So it is that because samsara and nirvana are pervaded by awareness, and because awareness is itself pervaded by a natural meditative absorption, the supreme state of the dharmadhātu is achieved.

When the things that appear outwardly and the thoughts that move inwardly have been sealed by the great sealing concentration, the yogi follows neither the objects of the senses nor the states of mind that occur but remains within the unmoving, ineffable, sky-like, vast expanse of awareness, the indwelling primordial wisdom. It is as *The Six Expanses* describes,

> Those who wish to cultivate
> Great sealing concentration
> Should master the key point of changelessness:
> They should take support of physical posture
> And project their minds into the sky's expanse.
> With eyes held in the elephant gaze,
> They should watch the space in front
> And rest without intended mindfulness
> In the great sealing concentration.

The primordially indwelling meditative absorption—that is, the great sealing concentration—is from the very first naturally present in the minds of all beings and is never separate from them.

* * *

Second, the first part of the fourth section continues with an explanation of how the hindrances to the great sealing concentration are dispelled.

> **4a2. Phenomena appearing separate from oneself**
> **Are a delusion of the mind.**
> **The will to meditate, to make an effort**

Is a delusion of the mind.
All delusion is the natural state of dharmatā,
The purview of equality.
In this vast expanse
Of the unmoving nature pure from the beginning,
There's nothing to be done, no effort to be made.
There is no remaining and no not remaining
In the state of meditative evenness.

Deviation from the great sealing concentration happens when divisions are made as a result of dualistic apprehension, and when self and other are thought of as distinct and separate. When object and subject are divided, when there is good and bad, hope and fear, buddhas and beings, and so on, all such appearances are a delusion of the mind—a deviation from the great sealing concentration.

To consider the meditator, the object meditated upon, and the act of meditating as separate—willfully and powerfully striving in adopting and rejecting things—all this is also a delusion of the mind and constitutes a deviation from the great sealing concentration. In the expanse of the vajra essence, the natural state of dharmatā, all such delusions are never in fact beyond the nature of equality, wherein there is neither benefit nor harm. And it is in this purview of equality—this expanse of the ever unmoving primordially pure nature or uncontrived awareness—that one should settle naturally. Besides this, there is nothing to be done, nothing to be accomplished with effort. There is no remaining and no not remaining in the state of meditative evenness. When the nonduality, the oneness of all things, is realized, this constitutes the actual great sealing concentration. If one is able to distinguish this clearly, there will be neither hindrances nor deviations. As it is said in *Awareness Naturally Open and Free*,

For those who know the utterly pure nature
Awareness does not come through doer and through deed.
All clinging is the cause of deviation.

For yogis who know genuine and utterly pure awareness just as it is, awareness does not come through striving. For awareness is beyond both doer and deed. If one is bound by clinging and striving, this itself will be the cause of deviation.

* * *

The second part of the fourth section treats of the great indwelling concentration. It does so in four stages according to view, meditation, action, and result, which in fact transcend [what is usually referred to as] view, meditation, action, and result. The first stage refers to the view that, being beyond viewing, transcends the view.

> **4b1. Unchanging dharmatā, spontaneously present,**
> **Is free of object, thought, and agitation.**
> **If you look at it repeatedly**
> **With awareness self-cognizing,**
> **You see that there is nothing to be viewed.**
> **Awareness that cannot be viewed**
> **Is the direct, unmediated view.**

Beyond movement and change throughout the sequence of time, the unchanging dharmatā—present of itself as the uncontrived natural state of awareness (that is, self-arisen primordial wisdom)—is free of all mental objects of focus, all thoughts that unfold and dissipate, and all the agitation of adopting and rejecting. It is open and bare and is without mental elaboration. One may look repeatedly at self-cognizing awareness[97] according to the mechanism of someone who views and something that is viewed. But in fact there is nothing to be viewed. It is seen as an "emptiness" and other than this, there is nothing to be seen. The direct realization of "unviewable" awareness, immediate and clear-cut in its open, unimpeded nakedness, constitutes the view of awareness in its unmediated directness. As it is said in *The All-Creating King*,

If you understand the meaning
Of the view that is not to be cultivated,
You see that it is present of itself—
The sovereign state of uncontrived equality.

* * *

The second stage refers to a meditation that, being beyond meditation, is not meditation.

4b2. Not meditated on, awareness
Is devoid of anything to keep or to reject.
If repeatedly you meditate thereon,
You see that there is nothing to be meditated.
Awareness that cannot be meditated
Is direct, unmediated meditation.

Awareness, which is not meditated on, transcends both meditation and nonmeditation. It is free of the unfolding and dissipation of thought; it is free of anything to keep or to reject. If one meditates on it repeatedly according to the mechanism of meditator and object of meditation, it will be seen that there is nothing to meditate on—that it is empty—for there is neither meditating mind nor object of meditation. Other than this, there is nothing to be seen. Therefore, awareness that cannot be meditated on is meditation in unmediated directness. We can also explain this meditation in the sense that it completely gathers within itself awareness that transcends meditation. Indeed as *The All-Creating King* declares,

It is not found in meditation or nonmeditation.

This shows that, being beyond both meditation and nonmeditation, naked awareness is the meditation that transcends meditation. As *The All-Creating King* also says,

[To speak of] meditation and nonmeditation
Is like debating about space.

As this text says, however much one may debate about its existence or nonexistence, space remains inconceivable. Similarly, however much one may explain meditation or nonmeditation with regard to the self-arisen fundamental nature, the latter in truth lies beyond both meditation and nonmeditation. It is a state of equality beyond conceptual elaboration. It is said in *The Word-Transcending Tantra*,

The nature of meditation appears to be
The nature of awareness, luminous and empty,
Free of all identity whatever.
Therein the poles of apprehended-apprehender are no more.
It is the pure face of the dharmatā.

* * *

The third stage refers to the action or conduct that, being the luminous expanse of dharmatā, is beyond both object and agent of action.

4b3. The fundamental nature is nondual.
It is beyond acceptance and rejection.
If you act on it repeatedly,
You see that there is nothing to be acted on.
Awareness that you cannot act upon
Is direct, unmediated action.

When all things of samsara and nirvana are ascertained by all-perceiving wisdom, nothing is seen aside from the one sole sphere of awareness. Uncontrived awareness, naked, self-arisen primordial wisdom, is the ultimate nondual fundamental nature beyond both acceptance and rejection. One may act on it again and again in the manner of an agent and an object of action, but all one sees is that it is empty and cannot be acted upon. Other than that there is nothing to be seen. So it is that empty awareness, which cannot be acted upon in a subject-object manner, and which is simply the dimension of equality free of conceptual elaboration, is action in its unmediated directness.

* * *

The fourth stage refers to the result that, being primordially present of itself, is not something to be accomplished.

> **4b4. Spontaneous presence, beyond all hope and fear,**
> **Is of itself primordial.**
> **When repeatedly you struggle to accomplish it,**
> **You see that it is something**
> **That can never be accomplished.**
> **Awareness that can never be accomplished**
> **Is the direct result unmediated.**

In truth, all the qualities of the result—the four kāyas, the five primordial wisdoms, and so on—are, from the very first, present of themselves in the expanse of awareness without ever being produced. Therefore, the result is present now and is beyond the hope and fear of being newly attained or not attained. However much one may struggle, repeatedly and with mighty endeavor, to accomplish this great spontaneous presence (namely, uncontrived, self-arisen awareness) in the manner of a subject and object of achievement, one will see that the result, the very state of buddhahood itself, is not to be accomplished as something other than sheer, naked awareness, the state of equality beyond mental elaboration. This is the ultimate result. Wherefore, awareness that cannot be accomplished, the one sole sphere of the ever-youthful body of the dharmakāya, is the result in its unmediated directness.

* * *

The third part of the fourth section speaks of the great direct concentration.

4c. Within the state of evenness,
You do not conceive of objects.
You do not seize on them as mind.
Stilled are the arising and involvement with
Your hopes and fears.
Mind and objects stay within that state of evenness,
Not stirring from the vast expanse of dharmatā.
This is the direct, unmediated resting
In the absence of objective reference
With regard to things endowed with attributes.
Because of the unmediated directness
Of primordial and nondual awareness,
Samsara and nirvana are inseparable;
They are the state of great perfection
Where all things are encompassed
By the state of evenness,
Without some being taken, others spurned.

When one can remain in the state of equality (uncontrived awareness) without ever separating from it, one has attained the natural meditative absorption. At that time, all the phenomena, [the objects] of the six consciousnesses, arising in the guise of external things, vividly and unceasingly appear like the stars and planets reflected in a lake. However, because the apprehending cognition does not engage with them, the mind remains still, free of conceptual activity in their regard. And even though it is awareness that arises as these objects, they are not assumed to be, or apprehended as being, the inner mind. The arising of hope and fear, and one's involvement with them, is stilled. The mind remains in its natural state.

At that time, when the stillness aspect of concentration has been left aside, the most important thing is to recognize instantaneously and directly the awareness—nakedly clear and clearly naked—in the very moment when mind and objects are in a state of equality. This is the actual meaning of great direct concentration. It is this concentration that makes manifest the expanse of the dharmatā, awareness, the state from which one should never waver under any circumstances. And since, while in that state, one does not fixate on objects endowed with attributes—such as the stillness of concentration or the thoughts that move—it is said that great direct concentration corresponds to direct, unmediated rest, free of all objective reference.

This is the actual and unerring key point of the direct, unmediated nondual awareness that abides within us from the very beginning. If this is understood, samsara and nirvana are themselves the indivisible state of great perfection in which all phenomena—without some being taken and others spurned—are encompassed by the state of evenness. For they are inseparable from awareness, the great direct concentration.

* * *

The fourth part of the fourth section shows that, in their natural arising and abiding, phenomena are neither good nor bad.

> **4d. Things and nonthings—both are equal**
> **In the ultimate expanse.**
> **Buddhas and beings—both are equal**
> **In the ultimate expanse.**
> **Relative and ultimate—both are equal**
> **In the ultimate expanse.**
> **Defects and good qualities—**
> **All are equal in the ultimate expanse.**
> **Zenith, nadir, main and intermediary directions—**
> **All are equal in the ultimate expanse.**
> **No matter what displays occur therefore**
> **Within the self-arisen state,**
> **All arises equal in the moment of arising,**
> **Neither good nor bad.**
> **What need is there to take some things and spurn**
> **the rest**

> **Or alter them with antidotes?**
> **In their remaining, all remain as equal,**
> **Neither good nor bad.**
> **Whatever now arises in your mind,**
> **Relax within its natural disappearance.**
> **In their subsiding, all subside as equal,**
> **Neither good nor bad.**
> **Don't run after thoughts, accepting some, rejecting others,**
> **Promoting their proliferation.**

Existing things, the appearing phenomena of the relative level, and nonexistent nonthings, empty phenomena on the ultimate level, are equal and inseparable in the ultimate expanse of awareness, the great dharmatā. Likewise, deluded beings (as it were on the bad side) and the undeluded buddhas (on the good side)—so-called delusion and absence of delusion—are equal and inseparable in the ultimate expanse of awareness, the state of great enlightenment, primordially free and open. True phenomena on the ultimate level and false phenomena on the relative level—so-called true and false—are equal and inseparable in the ultimate expanse of awareness, great enlightenment, primordial and unbounded. Positive good qualities and negative defects—so-called good and bad—are equal and inseparable in the ultimate expanse of awareness, great dharmatā, equal and primordial. The zenith above and the nadir beneath and all directions main and intermediary are different only because they are misconceived. But in truth, they are equal in the ultimate expanse of awareness, empty and free of all directions, primordial purity free of mental elaboration.

Therefore, whatever creative power and display may manifest as good or bad within the state of self-arisen awareness, they are equal—just as the unmoving sea and the moving waves are equal in the expanse of the great ocean, without any distinction of better or worse. So it is that within the expanse of awareness, which is the great equality free of mental elaboration, all the phenomena of samsara and nirvana are equal in being unborn. Unborn, they are equal in their mere and ceaseless appearing. Appearing, they are likewise equal in being a display of clearly appearing but empty forms.

In the same way, whether from the point of view of its fundamental stratum or its arisings, awareness is neither good nor bad. When the natural luminosity of awareness becomes manifest, it is seen to be unwavering. When its creative power unfolds as objects, however, it only seems to arise, whereas in reality, it has not moved. It is as we find in *The Vajra Tent*,

> Thoughts as they unfold within the mind
> Have all the nature of the sovereign [awareness].
> Is there any difference between the water and the waves?

As this text says, inasmuch as thoughts unfold through the creative power of awareness, while never stirring from the dharmatā (the actual, ultimate, enlightened mind), they retain the nature of the sovereign—that is, the nature of awareness. Waves may seem to be different from the water, but in truth they never stir from it. So it is that if one does not stir from awareness, the creative power of awareness sinks back into it.

All appearances, pure and impure, in the very moment that they manifest as the display of the dharmadhātu or awareness, arise equal within the one expanse of that same awareness, without their being good or bad in the slightest degree. Therefore, what need is there to accept some and reject others—or to alter them through the application of antidotes? Therefore, whatever arises in vast and all-pervading awareness, one should simply leave it without tampering with it.

In the same way, when the pure and impure appearances that have arisen in the expanse of awareness persist, they all remain equal in this same expanse without there being some that are good and to be accepted and some that are bad and to be discarded. Since they are neither good nor bad to the slightest degree, whatever appearances—positive or negative, pure or impure—may now arise within the mind, one should simply leave them just as they are, without altering or manipulating them. And one should rest relaxed as they disappear naturally by themselves, just like salt dissolving in water.

At last, when good and bad appearances, which have arisen in the expanse of awareness, finally subside, if one remains without contrivance in that same expanse, they will all be equal in their subsiding, without some being in the slightest bit better or worse than the others. Without continuing in the process of proliferation, by accepting some thoughts and rejecting others, and without running after thoughts—welcoming those related to the past, and calling up those related to the future and so on—one should rest in the state of great equality, which is naturally open and free. In this way, thoughts will subside into the one sole nondual sphere. All fixation, all clinging, and all holding on to the states of meditation and nonmeditation should therefore be abandoned. It is as *The All-Creating King* declares,

> Spotless concentration, utterly unborn,
> Does not depend upon the circumstance
> Of meditation or nonmeditation.
> If all appearing things on which to meditate
> Are simply left just as they are
> Without exertion and without the methods
> Of when and how to meditate,
> That indeed is meditation.

As this text says, unfabricated, self-arisen meditation must have neither an object of meditation nor a meditating mind. And all mental elaborations, such as meditation and nonmeditation, should be laid aside.

* * *

The fifth section of the tenth chapter subsumes all the preceding topics into the great equality of the dharmatā.

> **5. Within the enlightened mind, the ground's**
> **expanse,**
> **The way in which all things arise**
> **As its creative power and its display**
> **Is unpredictable.**
> **Though things arise as equal, they yet arise**
> **Within the vast primordial expanse.**
> **Though they arise unequal, they yet arise**
> **Within equality's ultimate expanse.**
> **Though they remain as equal, they yet remain**
> **Within the natural state of dharmatā.**
> **Though they remain unequal, they yet remain**
> **Within equality's ultimate expanse.**
> **Though they subside as equal, they yet subside**
> **Within the space of primal wisdom self-arisen.**
> **Though they subside unequal, they yet subside**
> **Within equality's ultimate expanse.**

Though never stirring from the ultimate enlightened mind (the expanse of the ground awareness), phenomenal existence, everything in nirvana and samsara, good and bad, pure and impure, arises as an unceasing display through the creative power of cognizant potency. It does so in a manner that is quite unpredictable. When it is recognized that all things occurring in this way are the display of the great primordial wisdom of equality, [it is understood that] though they arise as equal, they arise within the expanse of awareness, the great primordial emptiness. They have no other existence apart from that. And though things arise as unequal, being taken for different and distinct, in truth they arise within the ultimate expanse of equality—namely, awareness—and therefore there is not a hair of difference between them.

Similarly, though the phenomena of nirvana (namely, the four kāyas, the five primordial wisdoms, and so on) and the phenomena of samsara (the five poisons and so on) all remain equal, they remain as equal within the vast and immense state of uncontrived dharmatā. And though they remain unequal, they do so without stirring from the ultimate expanse of equality of the vast and uncontrived dharmatā. In short, whether things arise in terms of good or bad or whether they do not arise in terms of good or bad, all things are alike; they are equal. And whether or not they remain as good or bad, they are nevertheless the equality of the dharmatā.

Likewise, though all things subside—it having been understood that they are equal in being neither good nor bad—they subside in the expanse of great equality, primordial wisdom self-arisen. And though they seem to subside as unequal, as being either good or bad, they also subside in the one unborn ultimate expanse of perfect equality—the vast palace of the dharmadhātu.

For example, all the visions of one's dreams are gathered and subsumed within the sole expanse of sleep. All the planets and stars aloft in the sky are gathered and subsumed within the sole expanse of space. All the reflections of the moon in water are gathered and subsumed within the sole expanse of water. And all the phenomena of samsara and nirvana are gathered and subsumed within the sole expanse of awareness. As it is said in *The Natural Openness and Freedom of Awareness*,

> Just as sun and moon are present in the empty sky,
> The manifold display of primal wisdom
> Is gathered in the palace of the dharmadhātu.
> Awareness, empty primal wisdom,
> Is gathered in the vast, pure, ultimate expanse.

This completes the explanation of the four ways of leaving as it is, together with the ancillary concentrations—all of which transcend meditation in the ordinary sense.

* * *

The sixth section of the tenth chapter clinches the essential import of the preceding topics and sets forth twenty-two key points that distill the essence.

The first key point distills the essence of phenomena in terms of the ultimate expanse, the primordial vast state of equality.

> **6a. All things are primordial equality,**
> **Awareness self-arisen.**
> **Therefore from the very first,**
> **There's no arising and no nonarising**
> **In the ultimate expanse.**
> **From the very first,**
> **There's no remaining and no nonremaining**
> **In the ultimate expanse.**
> **From the very first,**
> **There is no freedom and no lack of freedom**
> **In the ultimate expanse.**

Not a single phenomenon of samsara and nirvana has ever stirred from the state of primordial equality, the dharmadhātu, self-arisen awareness. Therefore, since from the very first, phenomena are essentialized as the state of awareness, there is in the present moment no difference between the arising and the nonarising of the phenomena, good or bad, of the six consciousnesses. From the very first, they neither arise nor do not arise within the dharmadhātu. They are neither existent nor nonexistent. Being undifferentiated in terms or arising or nonarising, existence or nonexistence and so on, they are, from the very first, essentialized as the state of great, nondual equality.

Likewise, awareness, the creative power of awareness, and the whole display of [external] phenomena and mental states transcend from the very first the concepts of existence, nonexistence, and so on. Therefore, just as in the case of arising and nonarising, they are not differentiated in terms of remaining or not remaining. From the very first, within awareness, the dharmadhātu, they neither remain nor do they not remain; they neither appear nor are they empty. They do not stray beyond primordial wisdom, which does not remain even in the state of great, perfect equality, free from mental elaboration.

And in the same way, there are neither buddhas who are free nor beings who are unfree. From the very first within awareness, the dharmadhātu, there has never been nirvana, there has never been samsara; there has never been freedom, there has never been delusion. They are primordially pure like groundless space. It is for this reason that awareness, the creative power of awareness, and the entire display of phenomenal appearances and mental states lie beyond the extremes of existence and nonexistence. Being thus encompassed by the state that is devoid of any mental activity whatsoever, they are the state of seamless equality, primordially and essentially expressed as the great exhaustion of phenomena.

* * *

The second key point distills the essence of phenomena in terms of the way in which they naturally subside and vanish—in the same way that a knot tied on a snake unties itself.

> **6b. Within awareness, the unwavering state of great equality,**
> **When things arise, they arise quite naturally,**
> **Keeping to their natural condition.**
> **Remaining, they remain quite naturally,**
> **Keeping to their natural condition.**
> **Subsiding, they subside quite naturally,**
> **Keeping to their natural condition.**

When anything, be it good or bad, arises within the expanse of naked awareness, the state of the great equality of samsara and nirvana (which is unwavering for it is without movement or change throughout the course of time), one should recognize that it arises within that same expanse. One should be decisively convinced that it is not different or separate from that same naked awareness. The result will be that one will neither accept nor reject whatever arises and one will remain in the state of naked awareness, the primordial purity of the expanse of dharmakāya. Moreover, given that phenomena naturally arise and naturally subside within this same expanse, without ever parting from it, they keep to their natural condition. From the very moment that they naturally arise, the distilled essence of their arising is, of necessity, their subsiding in awareness.

Likewise, when these same phenomena remain, one should recognize that they naturally remain within the expanse of naked awareness. One should be decisively convinced that in their remaining, phenomena are not separate from naked awareness. And in whatever way that phenomena persist, one will not accept some and reject others. Instead, one will rest in naked awareness, the primordial purity of the expanse of dharmakāya. Within this expanse, and without ever parting from it, phenomena naturally remain and naturally subside. It is thus that they keep to their natural condition. As they naturally remain, the essence of their remaining is distilled as naked awareness.

And again, when phenomena subside, one should recognize and be decisively convinced that they subside naturally in the expanse of naked awareness. In whatever manner that they subside, they subside naturally in naked awareness, the primordial purity of the expanse of dharmakāya, without ever parting from it. It is thus that they keep to their natural condition.

* * *

The third key point distills the essence of phenomena in terms of their rootlessness, their primordial subsiding, their primordial openness and freedom.

6c. Within awareness, changeless,
Free of all conceptual movement,
All arising is primordial arising;
All remaining is primordial remaining;
All subsiding is primordial subsiding.
All is of a spacelike nature.

Awareness neither moves nor changes throughout the three times; it is immutable. It is beyond the eight extremes, the conceptual elaborations of existence, nonexistence, both and neither, and so forth. Within awareness, arising, remaining, and subsiding have never, from the very first, occurred, even though they seem to do so in the present moment. They are like the mistaken perception of a mirage in which water now appears where, from the very first, it has never been. If the mirage is examined, one sees that despite appearances, the water has never existed—that there was never any water where water now seems to be. And just as from the very first there was never any water, in the same way, even though phenomena in their infinite, oceanlike array seem to us so real, their seeming existence is like the apparently real water of the mirage.

Phenomena, therefore, have never existed, which means that primordially, they have never been phenomena. From the very first, they are devoid of the status of phenomena. This is what is meant when it is said that phenomena subside primordially or that they are primordially open and free.

No appearances, whether of external things or inner mental states, have ever been born. They are empty of the cause of birth. Therefore, although they arise as though born, in fact they are never born. Indeed, one should come to the decisive conclusion that in fact they never arise, that they are but the great state of primordial openness and freedom.

Then, from the point of view of cognition, phenomena seem to remain. But since they are, from the very first, empty of the status of remaining phenomena, they in fact never remain. Since they are clear appearances of what is nonexistent, since they are not true but false, there is no question of their remaining.

Finally, although phenomena seem to cease and subside, the truth is that these ceasing and subsiding phenomena are from the very first empty of being such; they do not in fact subside. This being so, phenomena have never had an arising, a remaining, and a ceasing. Their essence is distilled as rootlessness—primordial openness and freedom. This may be illustrated as follows. The water in a mirage has never existed, and therefore, at the very outset, it cannot have arisen, it cannot remain, and it cannot cease. And since the mirage water is not water, it is empty of being water from the very first. In the same way, because all phenomena are primordially nonexistent, because primordially they are empty of being existent, and because primordially they are "existence-free," they have the nature of space, open and free from the very beginning.

Phenomena are open and free primordially. Therefore, they do not need to be made so anew through the application of antidotes. It is said in *The Necklace of Pearls*,

> They are not rendered free and open through exertion.
> They are free and open from the very first.

In practice, the essence of phenomena is distilled in the way described in *The Great Garuda*, which says,

> The primal purity of phenomenal attributes
> Is—without effort, without action—
> The basis of utter openness and freedom.
> The hindrances of the discursive mind are cleared
> Through the essential factor
> In the experience of the object of the threefold meeting.
> And this essential factor is distilled
> Within the meeting of the object with the mind,
> When one is not distracted by that which is arising.

Phenomena, which are seized upon and reified in function of their attributes or characteristics, are primordially pure. This primal purity is the ground or basis of the complete openness and freedom of phenomena. If one wishes to gain confidence in this great primordial openness and freedom, which is beyond the reach of [and therefore not to be attained by] effort and action, one must dispel the impediment to it—namely, the discursive mind that is at the moment clinging to the characteristics or attributes of things. But how is it to be dispelled? When the five inner sense consciousnesses arise as they meet with their corresponding outer sense objects, if one neither blocks the consciousness nor examines the object, then it is there, in the meeting of mind and object, that one may encounter awareness, open, unimpeded, naked, even, and limpid. This is how to distill the essential factor of the threefold meeting [of object, consciousness, and awareness]. In brief, when the outer object and the inner consciousness meet, and the object, mind, and awareness merge indivisibly in the state of naked awareness, it is then (provided there is no distraction) that the essential factor, which is awareness, is distilled in the meeting of the object with the mind. When consciousness arises regarding an object and one leaves them both as they are in their nakedness, the recognition of bare and open awareness manifesting in that meeting is a crucial point of very great importance.

* * *

The fourth key point distills the essence of phenomena as naked, direct subsiding—the great vanishing upon seeing.

> **6d. Consciousness arises, stays, subsides—**
> **It arises and subsides in seamless continuity.**
> **Being seamless, it is not divided into cause and its effect.**
> **Because there is no cause and no effect,**
> **There is no chasm of samsara.**
> **This being so, how can you go astray?**

When one rests in the state of unmoving awareness, great equality, which is uninterrupted like a river, and when its unceasing creative power—namely, consciousness—seems to perceive the objects of the senses, this consciousness cannot go beyond any of the three limits of its own arising, remaining, and subsiding. Whether it arises, remains, or subsides, consciousness, in the moment that it manifests, simultaneously subsides or vanishes into awareness. And it does so seamlessly as when one writes on water. In the first instance, it arises, and in the second, then and there, it has already vanished—into clear, limpid, naked awareness. Between these two instants, there is nowhere for delusion to occur. Since the arising and subsiding of consciousness occur seamlessly, there is no division between cause and effect, and naked awareness may be realized. Such a realization is known as the exhaustion of samsara's cause.

Since there is no causality, there is no further possibility for deviation and obscuration, which subside simultaneously with their arising. Deviation and obscuration vanish into the dharmatā. Since the cause, in the form of action (which is by definition deleterious), cannot be produced, the result—namely, delusion in the three worlds of samsara—is no longer possible. As the root text says, there is no chasm of samsara.

So it is that whatever appearing object arises within awareness, if one leaves it nakedly where it is, it subsides immediately and instantaneously. It vanishes naturally without leaving any trace. This is why one speaks of naked and direct subsiding—the great vanishing upon seeing. In general, whatever thought may arise relating to the three times, if one leaves it nakedly where it is, it is impossible for it not to vanish. And when it vanishes, one should ignore both the aspect of vividly present luminosity and the aspect of a thoughtless blank, which correspond respectively to movement and stillness, and one should simply recognize awareness open and unimpeded. This is the unsurpassed approach of our tradition. If this state is maintained, the chasm of samsara is no more, and so how can one go astray? It is impossible.

* * *

The fifth key point distills the essence of phenomena as freedom from extremes, transcending thought and description.

> **6e. Samantabhadra's vast expanse**
> **Is primordially unchanging.**
> **Vajrasattva's vast expanse**
> **Is free of change and movement.**
> **Buddhahood is but a name for just the recognition**
> **Of the fundamental nature.**

Awareness is unchanging from the very first. It is free of all conceptual elaboration and dwells in none of the extremes of existence, nonexistence, both, or neither. This ceaseless knowing in the present moment—clear, limpid, naked awareness—is described as the vast expanse of the wisdom of Samantabhadra, the primordial lord. As it is said in a treasure text,

> The clear and ceaseless knowing in the present moment
> Is Samantabhadra, the primordial lord himself.

In the same way, this awareness, free of movement and of change, and endowed with seven indestructible, vajra-like attributes, is described as the ultimate, indestructible vajra of awareness. It is referred to as the vast expanse of the wisdom of Buddha Vajrasattva. To put the matter briefly, there is no buddhahood other than one's own awareness. As *The Vajra Cutter Sutra* tells us,

> Those who see me as a form
> And those who know me as a sound
> Have taken a wrong path.
> These beings do not see me.

And it is said in *The Net of Illusory Manifestations*,

Perfect buddha is not found
In any of the ten directions and four times.
The nature of the mind is perfect buddha.
Do not look for buddhahood elsewhere.

And it is said in *The Noble Sutra on Wisdom at the Hour of Death*,

The nature of the mind is perfect buddha.
Do not look for buddhahood elsewhere.

As these texts say, buddhahood is the name given to the very recognition of true reality, the fundamental nature of the mind, unmarred by the slightest contrivance or adulteration. In other words, it is the very recognition of naked awareness itself.

Generally speaking, in Madhyamaka, phenomena are established as empty, and one rests in meditative evenness in that emptiness. By contrast, in the Great Perfection, one does not consider the objects of the outer world, nor does one reflect upon the mind within, nor does one rest, in between, upon the unborn nature. Instead, one recognizes directly one's open, unimpeded awareness and rests in its nakedness. In *The Unborn Precious Treasury* by Nāgārjuna, it is said,

Do not ponder anything; do not think of anything.
Do not contrive or alter anything, but rest naturally relaxed.
This freedom from contrivance is the precious, unborn treasury.
It is the way of all the buddhas, past, present, and to come.

* * *

The sixth key point consists in praising the dharmatā free of all extremes.

6f. If you realize this, there's nothing to adopt or spurn
And all things are encompassed by the single dharmatā.

> **As in an golden island, no distinctions can be made.**
> **Things are untouched by conceptual extremes;**
> **All deviations and all obscurations are resolved,**
> **And thus there is no chasm of samsara.**
> **Without exertion, without effort,**
> **The three kāyas are spontaneously, completely present**
> **In the enlightened mind.**
> **To call them inconceivable, ineffable**
> **Is nothing more than words.**

If one understands correctly that all phenomena are groundless and rootless like space, one will understand that there are neither good things to accept nor bad things to reject. One will see them as equal. And in that moment, one will realize that all things in samsara and nirvana are completely encompassed by the single, primordially pure dharmatā, which is awareness. If one were to go to an island made entirely of gold, everything would be gold, and one would be unable to find ordinary earth and stones even if one were to look for them. In the same way, all phenomena are encompassed by the one, sole, naked awareness—the state of great perfection free of all extremes. Therefore, one may search for impure, hallucinatory experiences, but they are impossible to find. Indistinguishable in terms of good or bad, all things are contained within the one sole awareness. Since phenomena are untouched by any of the impure, conceptual extremes—existence, nonexistence, both, and neither, identity and difference—all deviations and obscurations are automatically resolved. Because delusion, which is the cause, naturally subsides, the chasm of samsara, its result, is utterly without existence. Awareness, the enlightened mind, is made manifest. It is free of all causality and is beyond the concerted effort implied in the acceptance of some things and the rejection of others. Vast, even awareness, which has the nature of the three kāyas, is completely and spontaneously present of itself. Statements about its being inconceivable and ineffable are no more than verbal conventions.

In truth, when one has a decisive certainty that awareness is beyond expression and indication, there is just the spontaneously present experience of the great state beyond the ordinary mind. As we find in *The Openness and Freedom of Awareness*,

> It is beyond extremes; it is unstained.
> The impurity of all the four extremes
> Is cleansed all by itself.
> It is devoid of clinging to one side or to another.

* * *

Since there is nothing to compare with the one sole openness and freedom, the seventh key point distills its essence as the sheer, bare state of its nakedness.

> **6g. When appearances are left alone,**
> **Awareness self-arisen is clearly present,**
> **Unobscured and open,**
> **Unimpeded, free of out or in.**
> **If you stay without contrivance in this natural state,**
> **It is clearly present as great dharmatā.**
> **Relax your mind and body deeply**
> **In a carefree state, at ease,**
> **Serenely like a person who has nothing more to do.**
> **Neither tense nor loose,**
> **Let mind and body rest in comfort.**

The meaning of the expression "the one sole openness and freedom" is as follows. Beings do not possess an individual state of awareness proper to each one of them. The awareness of all beings is one. And this one awareness is the one sole sphere of the dharmakāya. If a person gains realization of this, he or she will surely achieve the state of openness and freedom. One therefore speaks in terms of the "one sole openness and freedom."

If, without fixation or clinging, one leaves appearances as they are, it is then that open, unimpeded awareness becomes manifest. When one rests naturally, without thinking in terms of object and subject—appearances and the mind—one discovers bare and open awareness, which is self-arisen and one. Recognizing that it is clearly present as the very face of the dharmatā, one settles in it. When one rests in this state, awareness itself is unobscured by circumstantial conditions. It is free of out or in; it is open and unimpeded. And if, without tampering with it, one rests in this natural state, the great dharmatā, awareness, the one sole openness and freedom, will be clearly present.

If at that moment one allows one's body and mind to relax deeply in a spacious, carefree state of ease, one will have the serenity of mind of someone who has completed some great task and has nothing more to do. When awareness, the one sole state of openness and freedom, is maintained, to leave one's body and mind in their state of rest, without being tense or loose, is a profound key point.

In practice, when consciousness arises in relation to an object—that is, when the three factors of object, sense faculty, and consciousness (the creative power of open, unimpeded awareness) coincide—if one can preserve the state of naked awareness, without adverting either to the object or to the consciousness that arises in its regard, it is as when the fastening peg of the tethering ropes is pulled out and the whole pack load is released. The three factors of object, sense faculty, and consciousness are purified into a state of groundless release: self-arisen primordial wisdom, the dharmatā in which the ordinary mind comes to exhaustion. The way in which this happens is described in *The Great Garuda*,

> Primal wisdom is beyond appearance and emptiness.
> Do not identify, do not dismiss, do not distort—
> Just leave it as it is.
> For those who with this one thing seal the other three,
> These three are clearly present,
> Neither false nor true.

As this text indicates, outer appearing objects have no existence. The mind, the inner apprehender, is empty. Naked, primordial wisdom is devoid of both object and subject of apprehension. One should not identify it as the inner mind, nor should one dismiss it as an outer object. One should not adulterate it with thoughts but should leave it in a fresh, natural state. Since this one awareness "seals the other three"—namely, the object, the sense faculty, and the consciousness—this means that as soon as one directly recognizes this same awareness, the object, the sense faculty, and the sense consciousness are seen to be neither true (for they are empty) nor false (for they appear), neither both nor neither. They are beheld as simply present within the one, naked awareness. In other words, neither samsara nor nirvana lie outside naked awareness, which is itself vividly present and free of ground and root.

* * *

The eighth key point establishes the validity of the one sole openness and freedom.

> **6h. However beings may be, they are within their nature.**
> **However beings may stay, they stay within their nature.**
> **However beings may move, they move within their nature.**
> **In the vast space of enlightenment,**
> **By nature, there's no going and no coming.**
> **The bodies of victorious buddhas**
> **Neither go nor come.**

Whatever happens in the course of a dream—walking, sitting, lying down, fighting against enemies, and protecting friends, together with all feelings of joy, sorrow, indifference, and so on—all these things appear within the one state of sleep. And in that sleep, they have no reality. Likewise, the whole of samsara and nirvana, all the things of phenomenal existence, manifesting as if they were really true, really existent, really present, all appear within awareness without ever existing. No matter how the beings of the hallucinatory worlds of the six migrations are, they are within the very nature of awareness and nowhere else. And awareness is itself free of beings and of any being that they may possess. It is but one sole openness and freedom.

No matter how outer and inner phenomena (the world and the beings it contains, samsara and nirvana) appear to persist or stay, they stay within the nature of awareness, the one sole state of openness and freedom. There is no other place for them to stay. The very nature of awareness is devoid of characteristics like staying and not staying, and it is impossible to differentiate within awareness a ground of staying and that which stays. Awareness is simply one sole openness and freedom.

Similarly, no matter how beings appear to walk or sit or move, they do so without ever leaving the nature of awareness. And although, on the level of their nonexistence yet clear appearance, they are perceived as walking or sitting, the truth is that all such actions are awareness, the one sole openness and freedom.

Therefore, whatever going or coming manifests within the expanse of the ultimate enlightened mind, it naturally vanishes—it is nonexistent—within the vast expanse of the great, luminous dharmatā, the perfect state of equality that is spontaneously present of itself. Awareness, the one sole openness and freedom, the dharmadhātu, is completely free of all characteristics such as going and coming. This is the fundamental stratum of the dharmakāya, the wisdom body of the Victorious Ones.

* * *

The ninth key point shows that since all speech and expression never stray beyond ineffable awareness, they have no existence [in themselves].

> **6i. However speech occurs, it occurs within its nature.**
> **However expression occurs, it occurs within its**
> **nature.**

The enlightened mind is, by its nature,
Free of speech and of expression.
The speech of the Victorious Ones, past, present,
and to come,
Is free of speech and of expression.

Whatever speech may arise between the people of this world, whether it be in pleasant or unpleasant words, it appears as the display of sound through awareness's creative power, and therefore it occurs within the nature of awareness, the one sole openness and freedom. It is the self-resonating sound of dharmatā.

Likewise, however people may express themselves, whether it be well or poorly, it too appears as the display of sound through awareness's creative power, and therefore it occurs within the nature of awareness and is the self-resonance of the dharmatā.

All sounds and verbalizations, all speech and expression, which arise within awareness, the enlightened mind, naturally vanish in the expanse of the primordial wisdom of equality, the dharmadhātu beyond all mental elaboration. They have no existence. Speech, expression, and the reverberation of all sounds within the world never move beyond awareness, the expanse of the dharmatā. Empty sound is the vajra speech of the Victorious Ones. Indeed, the wheel of the inexhaustible ornaments of the speech of the Victorious Ones is what appears to us as the appearance and perception of sound, speech, and expression. It is as the Great Master of Oḍḍiyāna has said,

All sounds you hear, sweet or harsh,
Resounding as the objects of your ears, are empty sound.
Just leave them as they are without a moment's thought.
Empty yet resounding, without birth or ending, such is the
speech of the Victorious Ones.

As this text says, the speech of the Victorious Ones is free of speech and of expression.

* * *

The tenth key point shows that since thoughts and recollections do not stray from the enlightened mind, they are in truth groundless and rootless. That which appears as thought and recollection has never existed.

> **6j. However reflection may occur, it does so in its nature.**
> **However thoughts occur, they do so in their nature.**
> **The enlightened mind is from the first**
> **Without reflection, without thought.**
> **The minds of all Victorious Ones, past, present, and to come,**
> **Are free of thought and of reflection.**

No matter how may be the cogitations of beings, they are like the thoughts and reflections experienced in last night's dreams. They have no existence. Since they do not stir beyond the nature of awareness, they occur as a display (through the creative power of awareness) manifesting in relation to objects. No matter how thoughts and recollections occur, they vanish within the nature of awareness, which is devoid of objective reference. It is as the *display* of awareness that thoughts stray into the object. If one understands them in this way, it is clear that since they are not different from awareness, and since this same awareness, the enlightened mind, is primordially free of reflection and thought, the latter are groundless and rootless. Naked awareness, free of reflection and thought, is thus the wheel of inexhaustible ornaments of the minds of the Victorious Ones, past, present, and to come. As the Great Master of Oḍḍiyāna has said,

> Whatever thoughts arise defiled by the five poisons,
> Moving as the objects of your mind,
> Don't welcome them, don't follow them, don't alter them.

Leave such movement where it is.
It will subside into the dharmakāya.

* * *

The eleventh key point shows that even the three kāyas and their pure fields are the one self-cognizing awareness.

6k. Without existing, it appears as anything at all,
And thus it is nirmāṇakāya.
It enjoys itself,
And thus it is sambhogakāya.
It has no substantial ground,
And thus it is the dharmakāya.
It is the expanse, spontaneously present
Of the triple kāya, the result.

In itself, awareness has no existence whatever and yet is spontaneously present as that which causes anything at all to arise. For this reason, anything may occur and things manifest unceasingly. The unceasing arising of cognizant potency, which is itself like a limpidly clear mirror free of stain, is the nirmāṇakāya, the body of manifestation. When awareness is realized as open and unimpeded, and not merely empty and void in a one-sided sense, [it is understood that] within its ultimate nature of emptiness, there is, present of itself, a luminous character, which is its fundamental stratum. And this is the object of its enjoyment. The ground of luminosity, the actual fundamental stratum of awareness, is the sambhogakāya, the body of perfect enjoyment. Finally, awareness in itself is free of all substance and characteristics. It is devoid of any basis for such verbal elaborations. And this is the dharmakāya, the body of ultimate reality, which is primordially empty like space. The three kāyas, the result, are spontaneously present within awareness. It is important to remain within its expanse without ever leaving it. It is said in *The Secret Magical Manifestation*,

The wondrous buddha fields and buddhas
Can nowhere else be found.
They are primordial wisdom self-arisen.

Therefore, Longchenpa says [in the autocommentary], "Samsara and nirvana do not stir from the one awareness. Therefore, if this sole awareness is open and free, the whole of samsara and nirvana is open and free. This reveals a profound key point."

The five ways of subsiding—that is, the five ways of being open and free—were mentioned above.[98] In accordance with what was said on that occasion, there is, first, no need for anything to be rendered open and free once again through the use of antidotes. All phenomena are primordially open and free, which is to say that they subside from the very beginning. This is their primordial state of openness and freedom, their primordial subsiding. Second, they subside quite naturally in the state of awareness, like a knot on a snake that unties itself. This is their self-subsiding, their natural openness and freedom. Third, whatever appearing objects arise in the bosom of awareness, when they are left in their nakedness, they subside immediately without leaving any trace. This is their naked or direct subsiding, their direct openness and freedom. In other words, this is the great vanishing on seeing. Fourth, phenomena are free of all ontological extremes, existence, nonexistence, both, and neither. This is the subsiding of extremes, the openness and freedom of extremes. Fifth, the awareness of all beings is one and cannot be differentiated. Therefore, any being that realizes the one sole sphere of awareness cannot but gain the state of openness and freedom. This is the one sole openness and freedom. It is as we find in *The Necklace of Pearls*,

It is primordial openness and freedom,
Thus it is exalted over all.
It is natural openness and freedom,
Therefore objects are exhausted.

It is naked openness and freedom,
Thus appearances are pure.
It is the openness and freedom from extremes,
And thus the four alternatives have ceased.
It is the one sole openness and freedom,
It is therefore empty of all multiplicity.

* * *

The twelfth key point distills the essence of the ultimate nature in terms of the spacelike state beyond thought and word.

61. Within the vast expanse
Of the enlightened mind,
No thoughts occur, no recollections.
When all such attributes of ordinary cognition
Do not stir within the mind,
This is the condition of the one sole buddhahood.

Awareness, the vast expanse of the ultimate enlightened mind, pervades the whole of samsara and nirvana. If one never departs from the inner radiance of awareness free of mental elaboration, which one has realized, all thoughts, recollections, and so on disappear into this same expanse never to reemerge. How so? When the attributes of ordinary cognition, such as fixation, clinging, and thoughts, no longer occur within the mind, an empty awareness supervenes that is free of the occurrence of, and involvement with, all hope and fear, the unfolding and dissolving movements of the mind. It is free of mental elaboration. It is a spacelike state that is inconceivable and ineffable. This very condition is the state of the one sole buddhahood, the empty dharmakāya. As *The Great Garuda* tells us,

Awareness self-cognizing is the state
Of resting without meditating.

It is the sphere beyond discursive mind and word.
What need is there therefore
To fabricate with thoughts this natural condition?

The natural, uncontrived state is not something to be meditated on with a tense, conceptual mind. On the contrary, if one possesses this method of resting without contrivance, awareness—self-cognizing and stripped to its very nakedness—will supervene beyond the reach of verbal expression, beyond the thought processes of the ordinary mind. It is therefore said to be beyond all delusion, and this shows that it is the undeluded, genuine, fundamental nature. So why, the text asks us, should we try to contrive this fresh nature of awareness by using the conceptual mind? If one rests naturally without contrivance, it will manifest all by itself.

Furthermore, it is said in *The All-Creating King*,

For dharmatā, enlightened mind,
Beyond adoption and rejection,
The spacelike mind and body
Are not to be contrived.

Of the three aspects of awareness—namely, ultimate nature, luminous character, and cognizant potency—this root stanza discusses the empty ultimate nature, the dharmakāya.

* * *

The thirteenth key point distills the essence of awareness as the great and luminous state of emptiness.

6m. The luminous character of the enlightened state
Is like the sky's immense expanse.
To be devoid of thoughts and recollections
Is the supreme meditation.
The luminous character of awareness in itself

Is without movement, free of all contrivance.
Free of thought and mental action,
The natural state, the dharmatā,
Throughout the three times is devoid
Of movement and of change.
If there are no moving and unfolding thoughts,
This is supreme meditation.

The luminous character of awareness, the ultimate enlightened mind, is like the sun and moon arising unobscured in the vast expanse of the sky. The nature of awareness is not a one-sided emptiness—a blank, void state devoid of luminosity. When one rests in its luminous character stripped to its nakedness, remaining in a state of lucidity devoid of the unfolding and dissolution of thoughts and memories, this is supreme meditation. Without stirring from the luminous character of awareness, one must know how to maintain naturally and without contrivance the state of undivided luminosity and emptiness. If one rests comfortably, relaxed and fresh, in a state that is free of any thoughts whatsoever—without any form of mental activity—it is then that one is necessarily resting in the natural state of the dharmatā. In other words, one is necessarily resting in the dharmatā's luminous character, which is primordially free of movement and change throughout the passage of time.

If, as one remains within this state, one disregards the inward movement of thoughts as well as any kind of unfolding toward outer things—in other words, if one rests in naked awareness—all thoughts will vanish naturally of their own accord, just as when one traces a design on the surface of the water. This indeed is the best of meditations.

This instruction, thanks to which thoughts naturally disappear, clearly shows the way in which the essence of awareness is distilled in terms of its character of luminous emptiness.

* * *

The fourteenth key point distills the essence [of the cognizant potency of awareness] in terms of naked, seamless subsiding in the moment of arising.

> **6n. That which dwells in suchness**
> **Is the sublime state of mind,**
> **The one sole state of buddhahood**
> **Devoid of every attribute.**
> **It is the unwavering dharmadhātu,**
> **Which at once transcends fixating thought.**
> **It is by nature the supremely vast expanse of wisdom**
> **Of Victorious Ones.**
> **When you abandon all contrivances**
> **Whereby the mind and body are encumbered,**
> **There comes a natural state of relaxation.**
> **Thoughts and memories occur,**
> **But if you do not waver**
> **From the ground left as it is,**
> **The state of dharmatā,**
> **All is but a vast immensity,**
> **The wisdom of Samantabhadra.**

Awareness, dharmatā, or suchness, is the ultimate, fundamental nature of all things. That which dwells in this condition, without ever parting from it, is the sublime state of mind of the one sole buddhahood. It is the exclusive domain of self-cognizing primordial wisdom, for it is free of every attribute that is the outcome of the dualistic, discursive mind. The dharmadhātu, which never wavers from this dharmatā or suchness, primordially and at once transcends all mental elaboration, all fixating thoughts. It is the wisdom expanse of the mind of the Victorious Ones past, present, and to come. It is the ultimate place of freedom—the ground of freedom, by nature supremely vast—of Samantabhadra.

If beginners wish now to rest in meditative evenness within this state, they must abandon all contrivances with which their minds and bodies are encumbered. They must leave their body, speech, and mind open and still in a natural state of relaxation. If they remain in this naturally relaxed state, they will come to realize unobscured self-cognizing primordial wisdom, clear and vast, like the sky when it is free of the three defects. Within this oceanlike awareness, the manifestation [of appearances] is unceasing like waves. Whatever thoughts and memories may stir (whether moving within the mind or reaching out to external objects), they are just like waves on the surface of the sea, neither good nor bad. If one disregards them, if one does not follow or watch them, one will recognize the ground left as it is—in other words, the dharmatā, the great state of equality of open, unimpeded awareness. And if one does not waver from this condition of limpid luminosity, bare, naked, immaculate, and uninterrupted, then whatever creative power may manifest, it will naturally subside, like waves that mingle indivisibly with the ocean when they sink back into it. Awareness, its creative power, and its display, without any difference between them, all merge indivisibly with the vast wisdom expanse of Samantabhadra, subsiding into it.

Given that, as one rests in awareness, all arising thoughts naturally vanish, one is not harmed by all such movement and arising, for they subside of their own accord. And since whatever arises simultaneously subsides, one speaks of awareness being the hidden flaw of moving thoughts. For the latter naturally vanish. It is thus that this stanza reveals the unceasing cognizant potency of awareness.

* * *

Now among the difficulties that are to be resolved in the vast abyss of dharmatā, the fifteenth key point resolves a difficulty implied in the unceasing manifestations of the creative power and display in terms of their being pure, equal, and beyond the ordinary mind.

> **60. Do not hold within; do not project outside.**
> **Do not be tightly tense or loose.**
> **Just as it is, the unrestricted natural state**

Is of its own accord attained.
If within the vast expanse—
Unmoving, limitlessly spread, transcending measurement—
Self-arising thoughts and recollections naturally subside,
This is indeed the spacelike wisdom mind of Vajrasattva.

If one rests, relaxed and free, in a state in which the mind is not held within, and thoughts are not projected outside—a state in which one is not restrained by a tightly focused attitude, and is neither tense nor loose—awareness will appear just as it is, naked and in its fundamental state, empty, luminous, and unceasing. If one remains undistractedly in this bare, plain, natural state, and the strength of awareness is not lost, no fault is incurred even if its creative power is left to unfold freely. It is as when one holds in one's hand an orb of crystal without dropping it. Even though the five-colored lights radiate in all directions, they make no impact on the crystal itself. In the same way, although the creative power unfolds freely, its self-arising also self-subsides and vanishes in awareness. It is therefore important at that moment to rest firmly in the state of naked awareness.

If one rests without distraction in the expanse of awareness, motionless, and infinitely spread, if one rests in this state of bare openness, equality beyond any kind of dimension, wide or narrow, high or low, all thoughts and memories that naturally arise within awareness (as the display of its creative power) naturally vanish and subside in it. The karmic wind energy dissipates. Awareness remains within its own nature. Its radiance is withdrawn within and its creative power sinks back into the ground. And if one does not part from the bare awareness gathered in the one sole sphere [of the dharmakāya], this is called the spacelike wisdom mind of Vajrasattva. It is said in *The All-Creating King*,

With the dharmadhātu they are one,
Therefore there is no progressing.
You keep company with the ultimate quintessence,
Therefore you are not distracted.
The one sole sphere is all-encompassing,
Therefore there is nowhere you can go.

As this text says, when phenomena subside within the dharmadhātu, they are no longer different from that same dharmadhātu, which is awareness. Therefore, there is no progressing to some other destination on the grounds and paths. Since from the very beginning, one keeps inseparable company with the ultimate quintessence, or fundamental nature (self-cognizing primordial wisdom), one is free of all distraction. And since the ultimate place of freedom is encompassed by the one sole sphere (of the dharmakāya), it follows that the fruit of buddhahood is attained within awareness. One gets nowhere by training on the grounds and paths.

Why does one speak of this in terms of resolving a difficulty implied by the creative power and display of awareness? The reason is that if the strength of awareness is not lost, no defect is implied by the free unfolding of its creative power. The difficulty in question is therefore said to be resolved.

* * *

Given that realization and the absence of realization are by nature the states of freedom and delusion respectively, the sixteenth key point resolves a difficulty [implied by deliberate meditation].

6p. If in the expanse devoid of all contrivance
You remain without distraction,
Though thoughts and memories engage with objects,
The state of dharmatā is there.
But if you try with vigorous purpose to contrive

The dharmatā, which in itself
Is free of thought and vast like space,
It will be trapped inside conceptual attributes.
And though you may spend day and night in practice,
All is an entangling obsession.
The Buddha said that it resembles
The samādhi of the gods.
And so it is important that,
Without distraction but without concerted effort,
Your mind rest naturally free
Of all exertion and fixation.

If one is able to remain at all times stable and undistracted in the expanse of limpid, clear, naked, uncontrived awareness, without ever parting from it, no problem is posed by the creative power and display of awareness, whether in the form of memories or in the form of the outflow of thoughts toward external objects of the senses. This is so because one does not stir from the state of the dharmatā, the awareness that is their root. The key point for this is that if one pays no attention to unfolding thoughts, and if naked awareness is not lost, these same thoughts will be deprived of any strength and will naturally subside as they arise. Otherwise, if one abandons naked awareness by vigorously engaging in deliberate contrivance and manipulation, by fixating on concepts and the experiences of bliss, luminosity, and no-thought, one will achieve nothing, for the dharmatā is by its very nature free from such delusion. Awareness is intrinsically free of discursiveness and is as vast as space. It is an emptiness free of all mental elaboration. And if this aspect of naked awareness is lost, the dharmatā falls into the trap of conceptual characteristics.

It is thus that one can spend days and nights meditating one-pointedly and with strong endeavor, but this is just the mind's entangling obsession. Such a meditation is like the samādhi of the gods, as the victorious and perfect Buddha declared in the chapter titled *The Supreme Collection of Meditative Concentrations.* This kind of meditation goes no further than the three worlds, it does not extend beyond what is called "the concentration enjoyed by childish beings." As it is said in this same text,

> The extremely stable concentration
> To which you strongly cling
> Is called "the enjoyment concentration of the childish."
> It will not lead beyond all sorrow.

Thus for yogis of the Great Perfection, there is but one important point. Although by virtue of the creative power of awareness, the consciousness of such yogis engages with sense objects, their minds, undistracted from awareness, and free of all concepts and intentional exertion, should remain in awareness, the natural state, never leaving the naked dharmatā, free of all fixation and effort. As it is said in *The All-Creating King,*

> Naturally rest, without distraction, in the view
> Of seeing thoughts as, in their nature, free and open.
> There's nothing to be done or striven for.
> All thoughts naturally arise and sink back where they stand.

If the naked nature of awareness is neglected, then however much one may deliberately meditate with the use of concepts, such a meditation presents a difficulty [regarding the dharmatā]. The present stanza explains how such a difficulty is to be resolved.

* * *

The seventeenth key point resolves a difficulty [that consists in trying to apprehend by means of thought] awareness, which lies beyond the ordinary mind, and ascertains that this same awareness is a state beyond the unfolding and dissipation of thoughts and memories.

6q. Primordial wisdom self-arisen
Has no boundaries, no extremes.
And so you cannot point it out
With words like "It is this."
Within its nature, all elaborations cease.
So leave the mind's activity aside
And train yourself in what is meant
By groundless vast immensity.

Awareness, primordial wisdom self-arisen, is free of all extremes and is without boundaries. It is beyond anything to be adopted or rejected and is beyond mental apprehension and effort. For all these reasons, it cannot be pointed out with examples and expressions such as "It is like this." It is inconceivable. Within the nature of awareness, all conceptual elaborations of existence, nonexistence, both and neither, of identity and difference and so on, completely cease. Awareness does not stir from the empty yet cognizant state that is beyond the ordinary mind, that is ineffable, bare, and open. One should therefore abandon all mental activity, all discursive thoughts and all clinging and fixation on things and concepts. One should not waver from awareness, naked, open, and unimpeded. This is of the greatest importance. Otherwise, although the ground in itself is free of mental elaboration and is beyond the reach of effort, if the stability of awareness is lost and meditation on the path is performed with effort, in terms of adopting and rejecting, the ground and the path will be in disaccord, and the result will never come. One must therefore train oneself in what is really meant by all-pervading, great immensity—the ground that is free of all conceptual elaborations. And one must bring such training to its full accomplishment.

In short, the meaning of this stanza is as follows. There is a difficulty involved in the attempt to apprehend bare, open awareness (which is beyond all mental elaboration and effort) by means of thoughts and mindfulness, and through affirmation and negation. This stanza therefore demonstrates how this difficulty is to be resolved and how one should settle in the natural, fundamental state.

* * *

The eighteenth key point resolves a difficulty regarding the use of different labels to refer to the one awareness, which is free of mental elaboration.

> **61. The one sole dharmatā, primordial wisdom self-arisen,**
> **Is the one sole view devoid of all elaboration.**
> **It is the one sole meditation free of keeping and rejecting,**
> **Free of going, free of coming.**
> **It is the one sole action free of all activity**
> **Of taking and rejecting.**
> **It is the one sole fruit devoid of the duality**
> **Of spurning and acquiring.**
> **These are the states of self-arisen spontaneous presence.**

The one sole dharmatā—that is, self-arisen primordial wisdom—is conventionally referred to in terms of view, meditation, action, and result. The ultimate view of the Great Perfection, the one sole self-arisen primordial wisdom, is devoid of all extreme conceptual elaborations. It is the state of great perfection beyond extremes, the one sole sphere of the dharmakāya. The one sole meditation is the state of natural relaxation in the naked state of awareness—a relaxation that is free of keeping and rejecting, coming and going. To preserve this empty, luminous, and unceasing condition is the one sole meditation on luminosity. The one sole action refers again to self-arisen awareness, which is free of the duality of taking and rejecting, good and bad. The natural freedom from taking and rejecting is the one sole, nondual action. Finally, because awareness is itself free from the duality of samsara and nirvana, the one sole result is likewise beyond the duality of something to be rejected (samsara) and something to be sought (nirvana). It is free of hope and fear. The result, therefore, is the one sole all-embracing sphere devoid of mental elaboration. The view, meditation, action, and result are, from the standpoint of their own nature, simply awareness. Nevertheless, on the conventional level and according to our tradition of the Great Perfection, all four of them, expressed in this way, are different states of spontaneous presence, which is uncontrived and self-arisen. It is said in *The Lion's Perfect Power*,

> Action is beyond duality and clinging;
> Meditation is beyond duality of keeping and rejecting;
> The view transcends positioning and taking sides;
> And the result is free of two extremes of spurning and
> acquiring.

* * *

The nineteenth key point resolves a difficulty implied by the fact that all things are primordial wisdom[99] by subsuming them within the vast equality of the ground.

> **65. Phenomenal existence, samsara and nirvana,**
> **The world and all the beings it contains—**
> **None of this has ever stirred**
> **From the primordial state of dharmatā,**
> **Primordial wisdom self-arisen.**
> **Understand therefore that all things are the dharmatā,**
> **The ground left as it is.**

All the things that appeared in last night's dreams—be it the oceanlike infinity of phenomenal existence, the world and its inhabitants, samsara and nirvana—seemed to be long-lasting and as real as the appearances of waking life experienced during the following day. Various feelings were experienced in their regard. There was hope and expectation in relation to what seemed good; there was dread in relation to what seemed bad, and indifference toward what seemed to be neither. But if these experiences are examined in the light of day, one sees that they appeared entirely within the state of sleep—they never existed. In the same way, the whole of phenomenal existence, the world and its inhabitants, samsara and nirvana, which appear in the common experience of everyone, seem to exist over a protracted span of time and to manifest continually and without interruption. Likewise, the whole universe and the beings it contains seem to exist for many kalpas, passing through the stages of formation, duration, destruction, and the void. Yet they are just like last night's dreams. In truth, they have never existed. In the past, they have never stirred from the primal state of the dharmatā, self-arisen, self-cognizing primordial wisdom. They do not stir from it now, and they will never stir from it in the future. Therefore, no matter what appears, it should be understood that everything is the dharmatā, the ground left as it is, the expanse of the enlightened mind of Samantabhadra, the primordial sovereign, the one sole sphere of primal purity. It is said in *The Exposition of the Utterly Perfect Qualities of Great Creative Power*,

> All phenomenal existence, samsara and nirvana,
> Has never stirred from primordial, self-arisen wisdom.
> All is its creative power, spontaneously perfect.
> Devoid of substance, it is emptiness's self-display.

* * *

The twentieth key point is to hold one's ground in the great, unmoving equality. This is the first of two ways of achieving decisive certainty with regard to clear luminosity, limpid like an ocean.

> **6t. Regarding all the things**
> **Appearing as the objects of the senses,**
> **Do not think "It's thus that on them I will settle."**
> **Rest instead spontaneously in the natural state**
> **Without your thoughts unfolding and dissolving.**

You will naturally remain in the expanse
Of the equality of dharmatā.

If one wishes to see the reflection of the moon in a limpid pool, it appears most clearly when the pool is left undisturbed, without any kind of agitation. In the same way, when one wishes to see the face of awareness, one should neither indulge in, nor reject, the phenomena that manifest through the creative power of awareness and that appear as the various objects of the senses (forms, sound, smells, tastes, and textures). One should not think that one will settle one's consciousness (the subject) on them in this way or that. One should not examine them or think about them. Instead, one should just leave one's body, speech, and mind relaxed in their natural condition. Without one's thoughts arising and dissolving, one should just rest comfortably in a state of naked relaxation, the condition of self-arisen, spontaneous awareness. Awareness—the fourth state devoid of the other three [thoughts related to the three times]—will manifest. Quite naturally, one will remain within the expanse of the equality of the dharmatā beyond all mental elaboration, never parting from it.

* * *

The twenty-first key point is to hold one's ground in open, unimpeded, naked luminosity. [This is the second of the two ways of achieving decisive certainty with regard to clear luminosity.]

6u. Neither drawing in your sense powers
Nor letting your eyes wander
To what appears as objects in their rich variety,
Not thinking of yourself,
Not having thoughts concerning others,
Stay in luminosity,
Within the even state, supremely vast.

One should neither indulge in nor reject anything that appears as objects of the six consciousnesses—the various forms that are objects of the visual consciousness, the sounds (pleasant or unpleasant) that are the objects of the auditive consciousness, the smooth and rough textures that are the objects of the tactile consciousness, and so on. One should just leave them as they are, like forms reflected on the limpid surface of the sea. One should not draw one's senses inward. One should simply gaze ahead and not allow one's eyes to stray in the direction of anything. Without blocking out the objects of the senses, one should simply leave them in all their vividness. One should neither think about oneself nor have thoughts about others. Free of thoughts arising and dissolving, one should simply rest in the open, unimpeded luminosity of awareness, the supremely vast and even state. If one does this, it will be impossible not to actualize the naked condition of awareness clearly. It is said in *The Array of Studded Jewels*,

> The image used to illustrate
> The ceaseless, unimpeded dwelling in awareness
> Is the reflection of the stars and planets
> Appearing on the surface of a limpid sea.
> Latent poisons disappear,
> Phenomena rest open,
> Unimpeded in their manifold variety.

The image used to exemplify the presence of the ceaseless, unimpeded cognizant potency within awareness, empty by its nature and luminous by its character, is that of the appearance of the planets and stars reflected on the limpid surface of the sea. Accordingly, if one maintains nakedly the nature of awareness, while staying relaxed in a state where various phenomena arise vividly and unceasingly, not only will the more obvious thoughts vanish, but even subtle and latent poisons will disappear. And appearances in all their variety will simply arise and remain in an open and unimpeded state.

* * *

The twenty-second key point refers to the elevation of one's mind into a vast, all-pervasive state of unconfined freedom.

> **6v. Within the state of primal self-arisen wisdom**
> **Of the equality of all things,**
> **Wherein there is no out or in and nothing in between,**
> **A lofty and expansive mind**
> **Devoid of thoughts unfolding and dissolving**
> **Is experienced as though it merged with space.**
> **There manifests a concentration that is free**
> **Of all elaborations—bliss and luminosity.**

Going to the top of a high mountain with a vast and open view, one should sit up with one's body straight and gaze into the sky. Allowing one's awareness to expand, one should lift up one's heart. Without the unfolding and dissolving of mental states, one should leave the mind free of thoughts and words and the five senses natural and relaxed. As one does this, all the phenomena of samsara and nirvana merge inseparably with the state of universal equality, self-arisen primordial wisdom. In that state there is no gap between out and in. It is a bare, naked, all-pervading state without directions main and intermediate, zenith and nadir. An experience then occurs in which it seems that one's body, speech, and mind are blended inseparably with space. A concentration comes to birth that is devoid of the elaborations of bliss, luminosity, no-thought, and so on.

There thus arises an experience of open, unimpeded, naked awareness—an experience in which all appearances are weightless and diaphanous and look as if they are about to dissolve and dissipate. One has the impression that one's mind is open and unimpeded like the traceless flight of a bird; and one is clearly certain that everything is empty and unconfined. The impression comes that anything can arise in that state of complete nonexistence. One feels that even if one were to look for thoughts, they could not be found, and one asks, "Why does everyone keep talking about thoughts?" In brief, there occurs an ineffable experience of unimpeded openness. As it is said in *The Lion's Perfect Power*,

> To dwell naturally within awareness
> Is concentration in its natural state.
> The insubstantial self-experience of awareness
> Is the chief of all the mandalas.
> Naturally purified in the unchanging state,
> All things are the field of dharmatā.
> Self-experience of awareness is clearly present
> In the simple absence of mentation
> And is beyond discerning thoughts.
> This is the ultimate conclusion of the Secret Mantra.

When one dwells naturally and without movement in awareness, the state of dharmatā, this is concentration in its natural condition. When the mind that apprehends phenomena as existent and endowed with characteristics vanishes where it stands, and when one realizes that whereas awareness is insubstantial and completely nonexistent, it may, as its own self-experience, arise as anything at all, this constitutes the chief of all mandalas. Since all things are naturally purified in unchanging awareness (ultimate, indestructible primordial wisdom), they constitute a field, open and free, that is in great nondual union with the dharmatā. Although the entire self-experience of awareness is present vividly, clearly, and distinctly in the one sole state of primordial wisdom beyond ordinary cognition—in other words, naked awareness—there are no thoughts that individually discern it. It is said that this is the crucial, profound, and final conclusion of Secret Mantra.

* * *

The seventh section has five parts corresponding to five great clarificatory distinctions designed to remove doubts. The first part shows the distinction that clarifies the method for purifying the hallucinatory perceptions of samsara by resting in self-arisen awareness.

> **7a. In the ground left as it is,**
> **The state of the unmoving dharmatā,**
> **There is no out, no in,**
> **No conceptual elaboration**
> **Of apprehender-apprehended.**
> **There is no mind that fixes**
> **On an object different from itself.**
> **Thus there are no things to apprehend;**
> **There is no clinging to the appearance**
> **Of the world and beings.**
> **There is no place within samsara**
> **Where you might take birth,**
> **For all is similar to space itself.**
> **Inwardly, because you do not take your mind**
> **As being your "self," there is no apprehender—**
> **All samsaric thoughts are stilled.**
> **That which causes birth within samsara is**
> **completely cut,**
> **And all things then are similar to space.**
> **Outwardly and inwardly,**
> **No hallucinatory phenomena are found.**
> **The state of dharmakāya is attained.**
> **You reach the level of phenomenal exhaustion—**
> **Going and coming are no more.**
> **Everything is but an infinite expanse,**
> **Samantabhadra's field.**
> **You have attained the supreme palace of the dharmakāya.**

When one rests in the spacelike ground awareness, the dharmatā, free of all mental elaboration, the state of this same unmoving dharmatā is without center or circumference. In it there is neither out nor in. There is neither zenith nor nadir, no primary and secondary directions. It is devoid of all concepts of subject and object of apprehension. There are no sense objects apprehended as different [from the mind], as when one thinks about the object over there. There is no fixating mind, as when one thinks about the subject, the mind, over here. In self-cognizing awareness, empty like space, there are no phenomena to be apprehended. And whatever display of awareness's creative power may arise, if the mind does not stray into these objects through fixated clinging, all appearances that manifest as the display of creative power leave not the slightest stain upon awareness. In itself, awareness remains naked, open and unimpeded.

Since the inner mind does not fixate on any of the appearances of the world and its inhabitants occurring within awareness, samsara decays and disintegrates, and thus there is nowhere for birth to take place. Wherever one looks, there is nothing but the vast expanse of spacelike primordial purity. When yogis realize that all appearing phenomena that manifest as a display through the creative power of awareness are naturally open and free, the mind that fixes on a supposed self naturally vanishes. And at that point there is, inwardly, nothing to cling to as being the mind. When yogis relax in a carefree, natural, thought-free state, there is no apprehender. All clinging to appearances and the mind subsides. Hallucinatory appearances, together with deluded perceptions, are rendered completely void. All samsaric thoughts are stilled. Since the delusion of apprehender and apprehended collapses, that which brings about birth in samsara is completely eradicated. Awareness—naked, open, and unimpeded—manifests, and in that moment all phenomena are [experienced as] empty like the vast abyss of space. Within primordial wisdom, outer and inner hallucinatory phenomena are nowhere to be found. The state of Samantabhadra is reached—meaning that yogis merge inseparably with it. For they have reached the level in which all phenomenal appearances are exhausted in the expanse of the dharmatā. They have arrived at the exhaustion of phenomena and the dharmakāya, the ever-youthful vase body, manifests. At that time, there is but the one sole sphere of dharmakāya wherein there is no further going and coming of appearances. The whole of samsara and nirvana is perceived as an unbounded expanse, Samantabhadra's field. And as these yogis reach the supreme palace of the dharmakāya, they take possession of its everlasting domain.

When awareness is released from the ordinary mind, all the hallucinatory perceptions of that mind cease. There is nowhere else to go than buddhahood alone. Awareness is primordial wisdom devoid of both the subject and the object of apprehension. By contrast, the ordinary mind is characterized by an object and subject of apprehension and by dualistic perception. When awareness is actualized, the mind, divested of all impure perceptions, is transformed into awareness itself.

In brief, when the nature of awareness is recognized, there is just awareness. When it is not recognized, thoughts have free rein and there is just the ordinary mind. The mind is the ground where all habitual tendencies are stored. It is the intellect that dualistically apprehends both subject and objects. In truth, since sense objects have no existence, the five appearances of forms, sounds, smells, tastes, and textures are all hallucinatory. And since the mind has no existence, the appearances of the five poisons or defilements are hallucinations likewise.

In our tradition, self-cognizing primordial wisdom, free of ordinary mind, is taken as the path, thanks to which, the dharmakāya, free of ordinary mind, is accomplished in this very life. In other traditions, up to and including Mahāmudrā, when one meditates, one takes the ordinary mind as the path, and therefore the time taken to achieve the result is necessarily longer.

Now at this point, certain people might object. Do the practitioners of the Great Perfection not halt the arisings of the mind? Do they not use as their path the subsiding of arising thoughts—namely, the aspect of cognizant potency? The answer to this is that practitioners of the Great Perfection do not use the arisings of the ordinary mind as the path. For if these are simply disregarded, and if awareness is maintained in its nakedness, these arisings naturally subside of their own accord. This point is made repeatedly. How has it not been understood?

* * *

The second part of the seventh section shows the distinction between the fundamental stratum of awareness and the state of one-pointed calm abiding.

> **7b. If awareness in the present moment**
> **Does not wander from the ground,**
> **And if you grow familiar with this,**
> **Subsequent existence in samsara ceases.**
> **You will be free of action and habitual tendencies**
> **That cause rebirth.**
> **You will have decisive certainty**
> **Regarding causes and effects,**
> **Proclaiming that samsara and nirvana are now equal.**
> **You will reach the essence of enlightenment**
> **That does not dwell in peace or in existence.**
> **Therefore in the present moment,**
> **It is vital to distinguish this awareness**
> **From one-pointed calm abiding.**
> **Such is the teaching of the Natural Great Perfection.**

In this stanza, a distinction is made between calm abiding and awareness. Generally speaking, however much one practices and becomes habituated to one-pointed calm abiding, one does not rise above the three worlds. By contrast, if—having correctly recognized it—one takes a definitive stand on awareness in the present moment, free of the dualistic apprehensions of the ordinary mind, and if one settles immovably in this fundamental nature of the ground, which is the fourth state devoid of the other three [namely, the thoughts related to the three times], the results will be as follows. Thanks to a constantly maintained familiarization with awareness, the result of a diligence that, like a bowstring, is neither too tight nor too loose, one will, in the best case, gain freedom in this very life. In the second case, it will lead to freedom at the moment of death, while, in the least case, freedom will be definitively attained in the bardo of ultimate reality without the need to pass through the bardo of becoming. There will be no subsequent existence in samsara, for one will be free of the karmic action and habitual tendencies that give rise to the taking of rebirth. When there is no cause, there will be no result. And since samsara and nirvana manifest as the appearances of the ground, the display of the creative power of awareness, they are nothing other than the ground awareness itself. They are just clear appearances devoid of any existence. Therefore, if one has decisive certainty that causes and effects, beings and buddhas, good and evil, happiness and sorrow, have no existence apart from the one awareness, one will proclaim that nirvana and samsara are a great nondual state of equality, where the one is not good and the other bad. As it is said in *The Lion's Perfect Power*,

> Nirvana and samsara—
> How can it be said that they are two?

And we find also in *The Commentary on Bodhicitta*,

> Between samsara and nirvana
> There is not the slightest difference.

When familiarization with awareness is brought to perfection, one reaches the essence of enlightenment that dwells neither in conditioned existence nor in the state of peace. It is an achievement that comes with the cessation of the ordinary mind, thanks to which, the final result is made manifest.

Therefore, in this present moment, it is vital that one-pointed calm abiding be distinguished from awareness. This is of the greatest importance. Whereas one-pointed calm abiding is simply stillness (the state in which thoughts do not proliferate), awareness must be described as a naked, self-knowing, self-aware cognizance. The difference between them is like not having eyes and having eyes. In his *Distinction of the Three Crucial Points*, Jigme Lingpa says,

> Calm abiding is likened to a man deprived of sense powers,
> It is stagnant and obscured, unclear and dark—
> Consciousness is stilled and focused on a target.
> Deep insight is likened to a man possessed of all his
> faculties.
> It knows its own face and beholds its very nature.

Distinguished in this way, calm abiding and awareness are as different from each other as the earth and the sky. This is the teaching of the Great Perfection.

* * *

The third part of the seventh section shows the distinction between the universal ground and the dharmakāya.

> **7c. When you stray from the awareness state,**
> **Cogitation happens**
> **And samsara with the law of cause and fruit occurs.**
> **Without decisive certainty in its regard,**
> **Beings, thus mistaken, wander ever lower.**
> **The supremely secret Great Perfection therefore says**
> **That if you do not wander from the ultimate expanse,**
> **The appearances of its creative power**
> **Sink back into the ground,**
> **And without stirring from the dharmatā**
> **You rest within equality.**

Although the most important point of the present stanza is the distinction between awareness and the universal ground, Longchenpa gives, in his autocommentary, a clear explanation of the consciousness of the universal ground and the six consciousnesses—namely, the five sense consciousnesses and the mental consciousness—that arise in relation to objects.

The ultimate nature of awareness is empty, its character is luminous, and its cognizant power is unceasing. The nature of awareness is empty like a mirror. Its creative power is like the mirror's limpid [reflective] sheen. Its display arises unimpeded, but in itself, the nature of awareness, stripped to its nakedness, is a self-knowing, self-aware cognizance, bare, open, and unimpeded.

The universal ground on the other hand is a murky, indeterminate state, devoid of active cognition, in which there is no realization of bare awareness. It is a blank, oblivious state, in which there is no movement of thought. As Jigme Lingpa says,

> The universal ground resembles turbid water.
> Clouded by an ingrained ignorance,
> Primordial wisdom, clear awareness, is concealed.

And,

> The dharmakāya is like water cleared of all turbidity.
> Marked by the elimination of adventitious obscuration,
> By nature it has all the qualities of utter freedom.
> It is primordial wisdom that knows no subsequent delusion.
> Like water when contrasted with its muddiness,
> It is the contrary of the indeterminate condition.
> Seize the stronghold of awareness self-cognizing
> Within the space of dharmakāya!

If one remains in the universal ground, this is called "the obscuration induced by samādhi whereby the karma productive of the higher realms is accumulated." When, from within this state, the consciousness of the universal ground, together with the six gatherings—that is, the five sense consciousnesses together with the mental consciousness—arise in relation to objects, the ordinary actions of samsara are performed. Neither of these two [the universal ground and the consciousness of the universal ground] is able to rise above samsara, for the universal ground is the basis of samsaric phenomena. Therefore, if one fails to understand the difference between the universal ground and the dharmakāya, every action undertaken will prolong the state of samsara.

The consciousness of the universal ground is the limpidly clear aspect of consciousness generally. Its fundamental condition—clarity but absence of specific discernment—is marked by a subtle clinging. As it is said in *The Distinction of the Three Crucial Points*,

> The consciousness of the ground of all
> Is like water filled with salt.
> Clinging permeates its fundamental state.
> Attached to apprehensible phenomena, it is generally
> deceptive.

The consciousness of the universal ground is the ground for the arising of the sense consciousnesses. Just as from within awareness, cognizant potency arises in relation to objects, the six object-apprehending consciousnesses unfold within the consciousness of the universal ground.

In brief, habituation to the state of the universal ground makes possible the delusions of the formless realm. Habituation with the consciousness of the universal ground makes possible the delusions of the form realm. And the six consciousnesses themselves make possible the delusions of the desire realm: the human state, the six levels of the desire realm gods, the beings in hell, and so on.

Therefore, if at all times one holds one's ground in the dharmakāya—bare, open, and unimpeded awareness stripped to its nakedness—one will not fall into a state of blank calm abiding, and thus one will not fall into the delusion of the universal ground.

On the other hand, by not straying one-sidedly into the aspect of limpid clarity, one will not fall into the delusion of the consciousness of the universal ground. And through not taking as one's path the cognitions that arise in reaction to outer stimuli, one will not stray into the six consciousnesses.

Consequently, the so-called understanding of the empty, luminous, and ineffable nature (that is, self-aware, self-knowing cognizance) and the so-called recognition of one's own nature—all these constitute the one eye of wisdom that eradicates all deviation.

When one strays from awareness (the bare, open, unimpeded state of naked dharmakāya) to the objects of the senses (the display of the creative power of awareness) and follows after them, a proliferation of fixating thoughts, cogitations, and so on arise. And by straying into the power of acceptance and rejection, affirmation and denial, taking and spurning, one is deluded in the three worlds of samsara. If one does not hold one's ground in the dharmakāya, awareness, one is deluded in the state of the universal ground, the consciousness of the universal ground, and the six consciousnesses. And thus one performs the actions, and accumulates the habitual tendencies, of samsara.

If on the other hand one does hold one's ground in the ultimate mode of being or dharmakāya, one will realize that cause and effect, samsara and nirvana, freedom and delusion, and so on have no existence. By contrast, from the standpoint of deluded conventional perceptions of the mode of appearance, it is impossible to reach the decisive certainty or conviction that cause and effect, samsara and nirvana, good and evil, freedom and delusion are utterly unreal. The reason for this is that until dualistic perception subsides, from the point of view of deluded conventional perception, the causal principle is forever infallible. If one touches fire, it burns. When one touches water, it feels cold. If one is struck by an arrow, wounded by a spear, beaten with a stick, one is hurt with lasting pain. All who, without having realized the profound fundamental nature, say that there is no such thing as causality, are denying the truth of karma. And because of their mistake, they will sink lower and lower, migrating endlessly in the evil destinies. Longchenpa therefore warns us to take care.

Therefore, the ultimate teaching of the supremely secret Great Perfection—for it is indeed extremely deep and secret, a supreme pith instruction more profound than the profound—is as follows. If one maintains naked awareness without ever straying from it—that is, from the expanse of ultimate reality—then however the creative power may manifest, all such manifestations will resolve, self-arising and self-subsiding, into the ground, the state of awareness. And without ever stirring from the dharmatā, one will be able to remain in great equality, primordial purity free of mental elaboration—bare, open, and unimpeded.

* * *

The fourth part of the seventh section reveals a distinction, already implied in the foregoing stanzas, regarding the ascertainment of the law of cause and effect.

> **7d. Within this state, there is no cause and no effect;**
> **There is no effortful activity.**
> **There is no view and so forth to be meditated.**
> **There is no center, no periphery, and no duality.**
> **All is thus negated.**
> **But when creative power strays outward from awareness,**
> **The manifold display of all phenomenal existence**
> **Appears in every way.**
> **So never say that there's no cause and no effect.**
> **Conditioned things dependently arise,**
> **They are past numbering and inconceivable.**
> **The hallucinations of samsara**
> **And even states of peace and bliss**
> **Are countless and beyond the mind's imagining.**
> **Everything dependently arises**
> **From the gathering of causes and conditions.**

From the standpoint of the ultimate truth, the realization of the final view of the Great Perfection, the naked state of the bare, open, unimpeded primordial wisdom of the dharmakāya, there is indeed no cause and no effect. There is nothing to be adopted or rejected, and no effortful activity. All is like space. Therefore, there is no view to be viewed, no meditation to be meditated, no deed to be done, no samaya to be kept, no mandala to be generated, no result to be accomplished. Indeed, the ultimate truth is not something that one can achieve through the ten elements or essential factors of tantric practice. For from the standpoint of the ultimate truth, phenomena have neither high nor low, neither center nor periphery. They are neither existent nor nonexistent, neither both nor neither. On the ultimate level, all such hallucinatory appearances of dualistic perception are negated. They have no reality.

Nevertheless, for as long as the profound fundamental nature is not realized, it is mistaken for the universal ground and the consciousness of the universal ground. Similarly, the display of the fundamental nature is misperceived as the array of various appearances. Cognition strays outward from the state of awareness toward the objects of the six consciousnesses and fixates upon the manifold display that arises through awareness's creative power. It is thus that the whole array of phenomenal existence and thoughts manifests, appearing to the senses in every possible way. Therefore, one should never deny the law of cause and effect. For if one does, one will fall into a nihilistic view such as that of the Carvakas. One should understand that all such conventional hallucinatory appearances are phenomena dependently arising, like dreams and magical illusions. Therefore, as it is said in *The Root Stanzas of the Middle Way*,

> Because there's nothing that is not
> Dependently arisen,
> There is nothing
> That's not empty.[100]

As this text says, all phenomena are dependently based appearances that arise in connection with something else. What is the cause on which they are based? They are based on the ground: empty awareness beyond all mental elaboration, which though it does not exist, may manifest as anything. And what are the things dependently connected? They are awareness (the dharmatā) on the one hand and the appearances of samsara and nirvana on the other. They are inseparably connected. Finally, what is it that arises? The appearances of samsara and nirvana, which seem to exist though they do not. So it is that conditioned appearances, innumerable and inconceivable, manifest through the dependent links of causes and conditions. The hallucinatory appearances of samsara—the impure fields, the six classes of beings and their sufferings—are inconceivable. Then there are the pure fields, the buddhas, wisdoms, and so forth, the states of peace and bliss, all countless and beyond the mind's imagining, equal to the vast expanse of space. All these things manifest on the conventional level in the form of dependently produced appearances, arising through the coming together of their respective causes and conditions. Although awareness has no existence as anything and is emptiness, this same emptiness can arise as anything at all. Its unobstructed openness that allows for the arising of phenomena is like a clear mirror free of all impurity. Through the power of the dharmatā, anything at all may manifest. Therefore, the various array of things has arisen, and arises, through the sole power of interdependence, in the same way that in dependence on a certain substance and a magical enchantment, horses, oxen, and various riches are perceived.

If causes, effects, effortful actions, and so forth are all examined from the standpoint of the view, they have no existence whatever. But until the view is perfectly realized, the law of cause and effect, and the mechanism of adopting and rejecting all exist infallibly. It is very important to understand that, according to the view, causes and effects are nonexistent. Nevertheless, from the standpoint of meditation and action, they do indeed exist. Yogis who have captured the stronghold of meditation within the expanse of the view are indeed unstained by both virtue and nonvirtue. But beginners in the practice only have an intellectual understanding of the fundamental nature of the view. Until the realization that comes from meditative experience is perfected, to say that there is no such thing as cause and effect is wrong view. It is crucial to understand this. As it is said in *The King of Concentration Sutra*,

> Actions undertaken never come to nothing.
> They ripen in samsara as results both white and black.

And in *The Jewel Mound* it is said,

> From virtuous deeds come happiness
> And the sight of endless buddha fields.
> From evil deeds comes suffering,
> The experience of burning in the lower destinies.

* * *

The fifth part of the seventh section concerns a distinction regarding the decisive certainty that the law of causes and effects [is transcended].

> **7e. When you appraise the fundamental state of things,**
> **There's nothing to be found.**
> **When you use it as the path, not stirring from this state,**
> **There's nothing to be seen.**
> **This is regarded as the moment of the [dharmakāya] wisdom.**
> **You have perfectly attained the fundamental state of things**
> **And therefore are unstained by anything at all.**

When you encounter (appraise) the fundamental condition of all things, the dharmatā or ultimate primordial wisdom, nothing is found. There is no samsara or nirvana, no causes or effects. This state is the one sole sphere of the dharmakāya, free from all conceptual extremes. And also, when through meditation one takes as the path the state of undeluded awareness in the present moment (which has now been recognized), everything manifests at all times, during the four daily activities and so on, as the radiance of awareness. And as one does not stir from the dharmatā, the fundamental nature, one does not observe or see any conceptual characteristics such as existence, nonexistence, both or neither, identity, difference, and so on. Since the firm stability of the fundamental nature is not lost, this is regarded as the moment of staying in the wisdom of dharmakāya Samantabhadra. If one is able to remain in this fundamental condition without ever stirring from it—thereby perfectly attaining it—this is what is referred to as "the state beyond virtue and nonvirtue, the state beyond cause and effect." It is also said to be "the clear convinced understanding of the law of cause and effect as the state of great perfection." And since defilements and so on thus become a state of openness and freedom, one cannot be stained by karma and defilement.

So it is that until one takes possession of the everlasting domain [of the dharmakāya], it is imperative that awareness be unaffected by adverse circumstances. As it is said in *The Necklace of Pearls*,

> This does not waver from the very nature
> Of the perfect buddhas.

If one does not stir from the fundamental condition of things, one remains in what is referred to as the great inseparable meditative absorption. As we find in *The Lion's Perfect Power*,

> Nonconceptual dharmakāya
> Is pure meditation not focused on an object.

When you realize it, it is
Great inseparable meditative absorption.

If, on the other hand, the stability of the fundamental condition is lost, the principle of cause and effect comes into play, and the sufferings of samsara and the lower realms, however unwanted they may be, arise. If a seed is planted when all the necessary conditions are present (soil, water, fertilizer, and warmth), the resultant shoot will emerge even if one does not want it to. Likewise, if one strays outward from the fundamental condition, it makes no difference whether one is a yogi or not. One enters a wrong path.

* * *

The eighth section summarizes the meaning of the preceding stanzas in terms of the dharmatā beyond cause and effect and effortful action.

8. This great chasm of defilements, actions, and propensities
Has no support.
It is but a magical display of illusory appearances.
Free yourself from it, I beg you.
Be convinced regarding causes and results.
To this end, there is nothing greater than this teaching.
Therefore it is vital not to wander
From the state of dharmadhātu.
Vast and deep, this is a counsel from my heart.
"All is," "All is not," "All exists," "Nothing exists"—
It's so important to transcend them all.

The great chasm of the three or five poisons, the eighty-four thousand defilements, actions, and habitual propensities, vast and long-lasting, are like the shoreless ocean on the rim of the world. But these hallucinatory phenomena, which appear to be objects of the senses together with the minds that perceive them, have never, from the very beginning, existed in truth. They are a groundless, rootless, bare, open, unimpeded display devoid of objective reference. They have no support, no basis. They are nonexistent yet appearing empty forms that we simply perceive. They are like a magical display of illusory appearance, like the visions of an outer world and its inhabitants that arose in last night's dreams. If we are to free ourselves from all such hallucinations, we must, Longchenpa tells us, gain certainty with regard to the law of cause and effect.

How are we to acquire such conviction regarding the nature of the causal law? To have certainty regarding cause and result means to be clearly convinced that the cause (action and defilement) has never, from the beginning, existed—that there is only awareness, only the primordial purity of the ground. The result derives from the presence or absence of the cause. If there is no fire in the hearth, there will be no smoke above the house. If there is no causal seed, no resultant shoot can come. In just the same way, if one is able to halt action and defilement, which are the cause, the sorrows of samsara and the lower destinies, which are the result, cannot come. As it is said,

> The cause of all things that derive from causes,
> This the Tathāgata has explained.
> Its cessation too he has explained . . .

As this text teaches, true suffering derives from a true cause, and the halting of this cause is true cessation, while that which brings cessation is the true path. In brief, this textual citation shows that if one is able to halt the cause, the result will not arise.

As the skillful means to halt the perception of the hallucinatory, false appearance of cause and effect, there is no teaching greater or more profound than the Great Perfection. For this very reason, never to stir from the fundamental condition of awareness, the dharmatā, is extremely important. It is the very essence of all crucial points. Therefore, never to stir, at any time or in any situation, from the state of the dharmatā is a vast and deep pith instruction, the distilled essence of the heart advice of the victorious Longchenpa, the composer of this text. It is the precious inheritance given by a loving father to his children. Those who follow in future generations should look upon it as the supreme instruction. They should acquire a clear conviction that there is nothing beside the one and only sphere of empty awareness, the fundamental nature of the dharmatā beyond all conceptual extremes. By contrast, it is a delusion simply to hold that everything exists—just as it is a delusion to think that nothing exists. To go beyond all concepts of existence, nonexistence, both, and neither, and with clear certainty never to stir from the state of dharmatā is the most valuable of instructions. It is a heart treasure.

* * *

This concludes what is just a brief word commentary on the tenth chapter of *The Precious Treasury of the Dharmadhātu*, which shows that awareness does not stir from the dharmatā.

11. All Experiences Are Pure Like Space

The eleventh chapter reveals that every kind of experience is pure like space. It comprises thirteen sections, the first of which speaks of the great nail whereby the meeting [of subject and object in sensorial experience] is inseparably fastened to its intrinsic openness and freedom, with which it is perfectly aligned.[101]

> **1. All things are the one enlightened mind,**
> **Commensurate with space.**
> **And yet, because of dualistic clinging,**
> **You are deluded in samsara with its causes and results.**
> **But such hallucinatory appearances have no support;**
> **They are but magical illusions.**
> **So disregard them when you meet with them,**
> **Keeping to a state in which they leave no trace.**

Generally speaking, the kind of meeting spoken of here is as when, for example, the visual consciousness meets with a physical object, such as a pillar. Now if, in the course of such an encounter, there is a realization of naked awareness, empty and luminous, it is as if the meeting of object and consciousness were "nailed to," and perfectly in line with, its intrinsic openness and freedom.

All the appearances of phenomenal existence, the universe and the beings it contains, are in truth entirely gathered within the expanse of the all-encompassing, one sole sphere of the enlightened mind, which is commensurate with space. But although these appearances do not lie outside this one sole all-encompassing sphere, deluded beings—not realizing the fundamental nature [of these appearances] just as it is—perceive the world and its inhabitants in terms of a dualistic polarity. Subject and object are two. Self and other are two. Apprehender and the object of apprehension are two. As a result, beings are deluded in samsaric existence, marked as it is by the ineluctable law of causes and results. Nevertheless, although the experiences of happiness and sorrow endlessly proliferate like ripples on water, the hallucinatory appearances of the three worlds are in reality but magical illusions destitute of any support. Although beings assume that they are real, they have no existence beyond this assumption.

Therefore, whenever there is a meeting between an appearing object and the consciousness that apprehends it, one should recognize the coming together of this meeting as naked, self-cognizing awareness. As has been said previously, when it is left just as it is, when it is left in its nakedness, when it is left uncontrived and free—in other words, when it is disregarded—this same meeting leaves no trace. The state of great openness and freedom, which is its very nature, becomes manifest. And this experience should be maintained. It is said in *The Necklace of Pearls*,

> The dharmatā, unchanging, is completely firm.
> In its domain the self-experience of awareness
> Naturally subsides. Its character
> Is but a pure intrinsic radiance.
> Leave it natural, leave it naked, leave it as it is!

As this text says, awareness, which is unchanging throughout the passage of time, is the dharmatā, the nature of phenomena. It is unbreakable, indestructible. It is therefore said to be completely firm. If all that arises within the expanse of awareness is left in its natural state, left in its nakedness, left just as it is, the self-display of awareness arises and subsides by itself. And the very place of awareness, its own domain, is directly captured. The character of all that appears is naturally pure within the expanse of awareness. It never extends beyond awareness's intrinsic radiance. This is what the exhortation "Leave it natural, leave it naked, leave it as it is" is intending to convey.

* * *

The second section speaks of the nail that fastens all circumstances to one's training in awareness with which they are perfectly aligned.

> **2. When something you don't want occurs,**
> **You have the attitude of wanting to be rid of it.**
> **You are angry and displeased.**
> **You are jealous, irritated, spiteful.**
> **You are weary and in anguish,**
> **You have pain and discontent.**
> **You are afraid of death, rebirth, and all the rest.**
> **When all this happens, recognize it**
> **As the display of awareness's creative power.**
> **Do not reject it, do not try to cleanse it.**
> **Do not transform it or accept it.**
> **Do not watch it, do not meditate on it.**
> **Stay rather without effort**
> **In the one sole natural state of evenness,**
> **Free of thoughts unfolding and dissolving.**
> **It will vanish without trace, and from within,**
> **The spacious, pure expanse of mind**
> **Will sharply, clearly, limpidly appear.**

When unwanted adversities occur, if without getting involved in them, one rests in the state of awareness, the empty, luminous, naked dharmatā, these same adversities will be powerless and one will not be overwhelmed. They will naturally subside as they arise.

This stanza therefore speaks of the nail that fastens such adversities to one's training in this method, bringing them perfectly into line.

When various and unwanted sufferings occur, one is alarmed and unable to tolerate them, wishing to rid oneself and to be free of them. When others show ingratitude, one becomes angry and displeased. Unable to tolerate the better fortune and advantages of others, one becomes jealous, irritated, and spiteful. One experiences weariness and anguish and all the various ills of physical pain and mental sorrow. Likewise, one is afraid of the suffering of death, rebirth, the pains of growing old, and so on. With regard to all these experiences, the discriminatory attitudes of accepting and rejecting, taking and refusing, arise. And yet, just like waves that, neither good nor bad, are but the play of the one same ocean, all these adversities manifest as the display of the one self-arisen awareness. They occur through its creative power. One should recognize them for what they are.

The creative power is beyond qualitive distinctions of good or bad. Therefore, one should be quite certain that all such adverse circumstances are none other than the display of a single awareness. One should not, like the śrāvakas, reject them. Nor should one purify them with antidotes as the bodhisattvas do, nor transform them into primordial wisdom, as in the case of the outer and inner tantras. One should not deliberately accept them like some practitioners of the mind class. One should not watch their nature as certain other practitioners do. Nor, like others, should one meditate on them. Instead one should rest without effort in the limpid, naked state of awareness, the uncontrived, natural, all-pervading state of evenness, which is unaltered by mental elaboration and the unfolding and dissolving of thoughts.

When one settles in naked awareness, all preceding circumstances vanish naturally and without trace like clouds melting away in the sky. At the same time, the pure, spacious expanse of the uncontrived mind—sharp, limpid, and clear—arises from within. So it is that primordial wisdom, awareness in its naked state, is realized. It is as *The Heap of Jewels Tantra* says,

The pain that wandering beings suffer
Appears quite naturally as my bliss.
Since pain and bliss are then not separate,
My excellence is complete therein.

This means that when one watches the nature of pain as it is experienced, it manifests as a bare, open, unimpeded, naked state. It manifests as "my"—that is, Samantabhadra's—bliss.

* * *

The third section speaks of the nail that fastens both the factors to be eliminated and their antidotes to the ground with which they are perfectly aligned and in which they are cleared away. It shows that all things are open and free in the moment of their being encountered.

3. When appearances are encountered
In unlimited awareness,
Beyond both being and nonbeing,
And without point of reference,
If you rest without contrivance
And do not grasp at such appearances,
Acceptance and rejection vanish,
Traceless in this state
Where there's no [thought of] openness and freedom.
An experience without clinging and fixation
Wells up from within.
This is the vast, primordial expanse:
Awareness as it is.

As it is said,

Understand the view
That "what exists" has no existence.

Experience in meditation
That "what does not exist" has no existence.

Limitless awareness in the present moment is beyond both being and nonbeing. It is not a point of reference and is not something that can be aimed at. When one rests naturally in this state of bare, naked, fresh awareness; and when, through the creative power of that same awareness, there arises a display in the form of sense objects; and when the apprehending consciousnesses meet with them—one should simply disregard these sense objects. One should rest, free of all contrivance, in awareness without holding on to them—one should not watch them, one should not meditate on them, one should not make effort in their regard. One should just let them be.

As one rests evenly in naked awareness, bare, open, and unimpeded, beyond the distinction of being or not being open and free, one sees that their bare nature is awareness. As a result, appearances subside. Since they are by nature primordially pure, they subside, open and free, primordially. Since they are by nature uncontrived, they subside, open and free, intrinsically. Since they vanish directly and nakedly, they subside, open and free in their very nakedness. Since they [all appearances] subside, open and free, their subsiding, their openness and freedom, is complete.

So it is that all acceptance or rejection of appearances simply vanishes without trace. There is no opportunity for clinging and fixating to occur. An experience wells up from within in which they subside, open and free, where they stand. In the first instant, appearances occur. In the second instant, they have subsided; they are open and free. This is known as "instantaneous subsiding" or "instantaneous openness and freedom." The fundamental condition of awareness—in its authentic state, just as it is—is made manifest, and one will never again move from the face of the dharmakāya, primordially uncontrived, unaltered, and immense.

Whatever situations may arise for yogis of the Natural Great

Perfection, if they understand the crucial point that these circumstances can do no harm to them, they acquire the decisive certainty that these same circumstances never diverge from the state of the dharmatā. As it is said in *The Word-Transcending Tantra*,

> I shall moreover now explain
> The nature of their openness and freedom.
> Through their openness and freedom—this crucial point—
> All effort and exertion fall away.
> They are free and open from the first—
> Therefore there's no need to make them so again.
> They are free and open naturally—
> Therefore there's no need for antidotes.
> They are free and open nakedly—
> They therefore vanish in the place where they are seen.
> They are free and open totally—
> Therefore they are by nature pure.
> They are free and open instantaneously—
> Therefore there's no need for training.
> Their openness and freedom is quite natural—
> Therefore for contrivance there's no need.

* * *

The fourth section speaks of the nail of the natural openness and freedom of great joy, which fastens the mind and phenomena to the state of bare and open unimpededness with which they are aligned.

> **4. In just the same way,**
> **When you have the joy**
> **Of gaining what your heart desires,**
> **Happiness is yours.**
> **Companions, pleasant conversation, riches,**
> **A delightful dwelling place and region—**
> **When, through all such circumstances,**

A joyful state of mind arises,
Recognize its nature. Rest freely in its natural state.
You will be within the uncontrived primordial expanse
Spontaneously present.

The meaning of the natural openness and freedom of great joy is as follows. When the praise and respect of others, the acquisition of wealth and good reputation and so on bring great joy to one's mind, and when at that time one rests in the state of awareness, this joy will subside there and then, open and free, and great primordial wisdom will be realized.

Just as it was previously explained, when in fulfillment of one's ambitions one gains the delightful objects of one's heart's desire—praise and respect, gain and reputation—all the things for which one has a powerful longing and indeed anything that brings joy to the mind, one is happy and content. A great deal of happiness derives from one's companions, close friends, marriage partner, and so on, from their pleasant talk and gifts, from the fact of living in a beautiful house in delightful countryside, in short, from everything that brings one pleasure. When this delightful state of mind, graced with joy, arises, one should simply disregard this vivid feeling of happiness, and one should recognize the ground from which it has arisen—awareness itself, bare, open, and unimpeded. Through the supreme method of resting freely, without contrivance, in the natural state of awareness, one will realize self-cognizing primordial wisdom, unaltered, self-arisen, and spontaneously present within the expanse of primordial great emptiness. All such appearances of joy and happiness will naturally arise and naturally subside.

* * *

The fifth section speaks of the nail that fastens the ordinary, unfolding and dissolving mind to the state of openness and freedom of the nondual dharmatā with which it is aligned.

5. When, while sitting down or walking,
You are in a neutral, ordinary state,
Neither joyful nor depressed,
Do not indulge in it, do not reject it.
Recognize its nature in the moment it appears.
Not different from the natural state of dharmatā,
This is said to be an ignorance or dullness
That subsides into great luminosity.

When one is in an ordinary everyday situation, just walking along, sitting, eating, lying down, and so on—actions that provoke thoughts that are neither positive nor negative—neutral feelings arise with regard to objects, feelings that are neither pleasant nor unpleasant. Without engaging with them as they occur, one should just recognize their nature: the primordially pure state of awareness, bare and naked, the ground from which these feelings arise. When, neither indulging in them nor suppressing them, one rests in the natural state of awareness, outer appearances, in the very act of their being perceived, subside, open and free, without being rejected. Likewise, inner mental movements subside, open and free, in the very act of their moving. All this occurs simultaneously. It is as when one unties a saddle strap, both saddlebags drop together. The neutral feelings subside, indistinguishable from their natural condition, the dharmatā. This is known as the subsiding of ignorance or dullness into empty luminosity.

In sum, when awareness is stripped to its nakedness, the display of its creative power cannot but subside into it. If the ordinary mind apprehends and clings to this display, the result is bondage. If it does not cling to it but lets it go, the result is freedom. And since awareness is beyond the object and location of openness and freedom, it transcends the extremes of bondage and of freedom.

* * *

The sixth section speaks of the nail that fastens dreams experienced in the ignorant state of sleep to the state of luminosity with which they are aligned.

> **6. At night or other times,**
> **Though you be stupefied by sleep,**
> **You lie within the natural condition,**
> **Free of thoughts unfolding and dispersing.**
> **Gross perceptions therefore disappear**
> **And with them their perceiver.**
> **Then subtle and extremely subtle thoughts subside**
> **And also that which apprehends them.**
> **The mind then rests aware within a state**
> **Of evenness devoid of concepts.**
> **It dwells within its nature—**
> **Thoughts do not arise, and there is no engaging with them.**
> **There is neither hope nor fear.**
> **This is the point when all thoughts sink into the dharmadhātu.**
> **Therefore it is called "subsiding of samsara in nirvana."**

Times of slumber, whether by night or day, are the ground for the ignorance of sleep. It is then that ignorance is very powerful. In the case of ordinary beings like ourselves, sleep is a state of stupefaction in which the operations of the six consciousnesses are withdrawn uncontrollably into the mind. The first period of sleep is a pitch-black state of complete unconsciousness. Following this, the consciousness of the universal ground unfolds in the luminous appearances of dream visions, which one takes to be just as true as the appearances of the waking state. So it is that one is deluded.

The profound pith instructions set forth various methods whereby the visions of one's dreams dissolve back into their natural condition. Such methods are to recognize one's dreams, to purify them, to transform them, to arrest them, and so on. In the present context, which is that of the trekchö practice, they are purified through the single crucial point of their ultimate nature, which is free of all mental activity.

When it is time to sleep, one should adopt the sleeping posture of a lion and rest in the state of awareness. One should lie down with one's mind in the natural state free of thoughts unfolding and dissolving, keeping to the nature of bare consciousness without straying from it. As one falls asleep, all one's gross perceptions—the thoughts that unfold toward outer objects, together with their corresponding apprehending consciousnesses, gradually dissipate and vanish. One's thoughts become more subtle. Then even subtle and extremely subtle thoughts, together with their apprehending consciousnesses, gradually disappear. The first period of sleep then follows. This is an experience of profound darkness, and from it there unfolds the state of luminosity. This is the moment when dreams occur. If one does not take these dreams as real, there manifests, within a nonconceptual state of evenness, a state of mind that is aware, naked, open, and unimpeded. Bare awareness, in which there is no arising of, and no engaging in, thoughts, and which is free of hope and fear, becomes manifest. To dwell within this state of awareness is described as the recognition of the luminosity of dreams.

Indeed, there exists a limited kind of vision of luminosity, which is marked by the discernment of what is seen. This is the luminosity of light sleep. By contrast, there is a vast vision marked by an absence of such discernment and this is the luminosity of deep sleep. The latter is superior to the former. Because it is the moment when all the thoughts and hallucinatory visions of sleep subside in the state of awareness, the dharmadhātu, it is referred to as the subsiding of the appearances of samsara into nirvana—that is, the subsiding of the hallucinatory appearances of sleep into the state of luminosity. This being so, the subsiding of dreams into the state of luminosity is important. For if this does not occur, it is through dreams that a subtle karma, a latent, diffuse habit of delusion, is accumulated. For those of the greatest diligence—and as a sign that they will gain freedom in this very life—the luminosity of the daytime merges seamlessly with the luminosity of night. For such practitioners, the pitch-black state of the first period of sleep does not occur. Generally speaking, the experience of beings of greatest, moderate, and least capacity is not the same. As the text says,

> It arises for the best; for those of moderate ability there is cessation;
> And for the least, their dreams are virtuous.

This means that for practitioners of the highest capacity, dreams arise as luminosity. For those of moderate capacity, dreams cease. And for those of least capacity, there is the experience of virtuous and excellent dreams.

* * *

The seventh section shows that sleep is a state of self-arisen primordial wisdom.

> **7. Even sleep itself is but the self-arisen**
> **Primordial expanse.**
> **Awareness's creative power is stilled,**
> **Absorbed into the ground, the ultimate expanse.**
> **All cognitions that lay hold of its display**
> **Come naturally to stillness.**
> **This is the state devoid of action,**
> **The state of self-arisen primordial wisdom.**

If dreams are recognized as luminosity, even sleep itself is no longer ordinary but mingles indivisibly in one taste with the great, primordial expanse of awareness, the self-arisen primordial wisdom of the dharmakāya. The creative power of awareness is completely stilled in this same ultimate expanse, being absorbed into the ground. And the dharmatā—that is, the ground awareness—is made manifest. Moreover, all the cognitive acts that apprehend appearing objects arising through the creative power of awareness as its display, are naturally stilled. In short, all the visions of one's dreams become inseparable from the bare, open, unimpeded state of nonaction—the self-arisen primordial wisdom that is awareness.

During the day, since through the creative power of awareness, cognition arises as the display of that same awareness, all appearing objects manifest as luminosity radiating outwardly from primordial wisdom. At night, the displayed appearances, which are assumed to be real, dissolve into the creative power of awareness. When the creative power dissolves into the ground, only the ground awareness persists. One remains in the state of luminosity where there is no cognition of anything. This is the self-arisen primordial wisdom of sleep—in other words, the luminosity of deep sleep. In the case of the lesser luminosity occurring during the state of light sleep, one knows what other people are doing even though one is asleep. But though one's vision (of luminosity) is limited, and one has a slight discernment of what is seen, one nevertheless remains in awareness. This is the oral teaching of my exalted master.

* * *

The eighth section speaks of the nail that fastens defilements to the openness and freedom of their natural condition with which they are perfectly aligned.

8. And therefore all your attitudes
Of wanting or not wanting or indifference,
As well as the three poisons that appear
Through awareness's creative power as its display—
All occur within the ultimate expanse,
All arise within the ultimate expanse.
Since they subsist within the ultimate expanse,
Not stirring from it in the slightest,
Do not fall into the meshes
Of contriving or transforming these same attitudes.

It is crucial that you recognize this ultimate expanse.
As soon as you are settled there,
These attitudes come naturally to stillness.
They naturally vanish and subside.

As was previously explained, all attitudes of wanting, which occur in dependence on the five pleasant sense objects, all attitudes of not wanting, which occur in dependence on unpleasant objects, and all states of mental indifference arising with regard to neutral objects—all such attitudes, together with the defilements (the three or five poisons and so on)—manifest as the display of awareness through the latter's creative power. Other than that, they have no existence. They have no supporting basis, no source or origin, and no destination. Since these attitudes are groundless (they are empty forms appearing to oneself), they at first arise while never stirring from their place of origin—namely, awareness—the expanse of ultimate reality. In the present moment, they arise [and remain] in awareness, the expanse of ultimate reality, which, as well as being their place of arising, is also their place of dwelling. And as for their place of subsiding, they finally sink into awareness, the expanse of ultimate reality. This being so, whatever attitudes occur—arising, dwelling, and subsiding—they do so, they come and go, within the dharmadhātu and never stir from it.

One must not wander into the meshes or traps of thoughts that cling to such deluded attitudes. One should neither mentally contrive them nor actively transform them and so on. In short, without any contrived alteration through [the action of] grasping thought, one should simply settle in the natural state. In this way, one should refrain from any kind of manipulation. For deluded perceptions are not relinquished, however much one tries to abandon them. They reappear, [following behind] like the shadow of one's body. They will never be purified, however much one tries to purify them. A clear crystal is always clear, whether you try to clean it or not.

Since the object to be cleansed is not different from agent of cleansing, there is no way to clean it! Neither can the mind's deluded perceptions be transformed. Just as there is no way to alter the blue color of a turquoise, the mind cannot change itself [into something other than it is]. It cannot free itself through the use of [extraneous] antidotes. In the same way that water is made murky by stirring it with a stick, the natural state of the dharmatā is obscured when deluded perceptions are altered and changed through the use of antidotes. It is as *The Union of the Sun and Moon Tantra* says,

> Defilement is not relinquished through relinquishing
> And likewise is not cleansed by cleansing.
> It is not changed by changing it.

And,

> Like a rock of crystal or a turquoise stone,
> You cannot cleanse or change it.

It is therefore crucial to recognize that all that occurs does not extend beyond awareness, the expanse of ultimate reality. One must then settle in the state in which it is just left as it is. In that very moment, all is naturally stilled. It is as when one pulls out a pin that is holding a knot together. Everything naturally vanishes, naturally subsides, and is naturally cleansed away. It is not that deluded perceptions subside as a result of striving, as is the case in the other vehicles. In the Great Perfection, they are purified in the ultimate expanse without their being abandoned, and this occurs thanks to the crucial point of realizing awareness, open, unimpeded, and self-cognizing. The method for realizing uncontrived naked awareness lies in the effortful cultivation of the luminous visions of thögal and in the effortless, natural openness and freedom of awareness in trekchö. It is through the realization of awareness in its naked state that defilements subside.

* * *

The ninth section speaks of the nail that fastens adoption and rejection, good and evil, to their nonexistence with which they are perfectly aligned.

> **9. Even the defilements, actions, and habitual tendencies**
> **Arise as a display through awareness's creative power.**
> **Even antidotes and virtuous acts—the path of liberation—**
> **Manifest as a display arising through creative power.**
> **Both are a display primordially arising through creative power.**
> **Recognize therefore their nature.**
> **Rest within it uncontrivedly—this is indeed a crucial point.**
> **Both are equal in rapidity and movement,**
> **Equal in their stirring in the ground.**
> **Occurring through conditions, they're compounded**
> **And are not beyond dependent origin.**
> **It is important thus to rest within the natural state,**
> **To leave them as they are,**
> **And to be certain with regard to cause and fruit.**

Moreover, in answer to the question whence all defilements, unvirtuous actions, and bad habitual tendencies arise in all their various array, it must be said that they manifest as a display through the creative power of awareness. Instead of taking these manifestations as things to be abandoned, and instead of striving in ways to rid oneself of them, if one rests in the natural state, in the state of uncontrived naked awareness, these same manifestations will subside on their own. It is important to understand this.

All the antidotes to what is to be abandoned (defilement, unvirtuous actions, and habitual tendencies), in other words, all that is referred to as the path to liberation (good deeds of pure virtue, such as the accumulation of merit and wisdom, and the purification of obscurations)—all these antidotes likewise manifest as a display arising through the creative power of awareness. Therefore if all the positive actions of the three doors, which are undertaken as remedies to the defilements, are taken to be real with respect to the three spheres [of subject, object, and action], they themselves will simply prolong samsara. On the other hand, if one disregards them and rests nakedly and without contrivance in awareness, the hold that they exert will cease.

It is important to recognize that both the [negative] thoughts, which arise in all their variety and are to be abandoned, and the positive thoughts, which act as their remedial antidotes, arise equally, and from the very first, as the display of the creative power of awareness. To recognize that their nature is awareness alone, and to rest evenly and without contrivance in this immense natural state, is indeed a crucial point.

When thoughts, both good and bad, first arise within awareness, they are equal in their rapidity and equal in their movement. Subsequently, when they apprehend the sense objects in relation to which they arise, they are likewise equal in rapidity and equal in their movement. And finally, at the moment of their cessation, they are equal in the way they vanish on their own. Similarly, good and bad thoughts are equal in the way they stir within the ground, arising as the display of its creative power.

In the deluded conventional outlook of beings, the positive thoughts that act as antidotes and the negative thoughts that are thereby to be abandoned are similar in that both arise according to conditions. They are similar in being conditioned and in the fact that they do not transcend dependent origination and causality. In truth, however, the antidotes that belong to the path (positive thoughts, the view, meditation, action, and result) and the mental states that are to be abandoned (delusion, negativity, the three and five poisons, and so on)—all such conditioned appearances, which seem to arise according to circumstances, are groundless and rootless. If, to begin with, one searches for their origins, one finds that they are unoriginate. Subsequently, even though the eighty-four thousand thoughts and so on seem to exist for as long as they are not analyzed, when they *are* analyzed, they are found to be nothing more than a state of unimpeded openness devoid of objective reference. Finally, they go nowhere—they are beyond going and coming. They cannot be found—they are free of all such extremes. They are simply an open, bare state beyond all mental elaboration. Resting naturally therefore in the fundamental condition of the mind, and leaving thoughts and mental states just as they are in the bare state of awareness, one should be confident, indeed quite certain, that in the supreme state of leaving everything as it is, there is no such thing as causality. This is extremely important. As it is said in *The Great Garuda*,

> Those who assert a path without a ground
> While wishing for its fruit
> Obscure the path to freedom by that very wish.

And,

> Those who want to find a limit
> Are like blind birds that seek the limits of the sky.
> There is no such finding.

* * *

The tenth section speaks of the nail that fastens the heritage of this sovereign vehicle to those who can uphold it and who are perfectly in line with it—keeping it secret from those of lesser aptitude.

> **10. This is the very summit of the supreme secret vehicle.**
> **It is most secret. Do not speak of it to those of lesser mind.**
> **For they will mar the quintessential teachings**

By superimposition or depreciation.
Understanding falsely, they will wander from its view.
Those who breach the door of secrecy
Will fall to lower destinies that have no end.
Therefore the heritage of the most secret sovereign vehicle
Should be entrusted and revealed
To sublime beings of excellent good fortune.

The quintessence of the supremely secret teachings of the Great Perfection, the very summit of the nine gradual vehicles, is the most secret of all the secret teachings. The marvelous heritage of this sovereign vehicle should be revealed to those of excellent good fortune. It should be entrusted to supreme vajra sons and daughters of perfect destiny. It should not be spoken of to ordinary beings who have no karmic connection with this profound doctrine or to those of lesser aptitude who have entered the common vehicles. It should be kept extremely secret, for it will not conform with their minds and they will be alarmed by it. These secret teachings should therefore be withheld from those who are not suited to receive them and even from those who are suited but for whom the proper time has not yet come.

People of lesser capacity, who are not appropriate vessels, may misinterpret the teachings through superimposition or depreciation, thereby distorting the quintessential doctrine and causing it to decline. And those who denigrate it will have to go to the lower destinies, which have no end. It is said in *The Sublime Continuum*,

Even people who repeatedly keep company with sinful friends
And thereby harbor evil will against the Buddha,
Who do evil like the slaying of their father or their mother or an arhat,
Or cause division in the supreme sangha—
All such people may be swiftly freed from this

Through their true contemplation of the dharmatā.
But how could liberation be for those
Whose minds are turned against the Dharma?

If people commit the five evil deeds of immediate retribution—that is, if with evil intention they cause the body of a buddha to bleed, if they kill their father or mother or an arhat, or cause a schism in the supreme assembly, creating dissension in the Buddhist community—they may quickly free themselves of their sin through confession endowed with the four opposing forces, and meditation on profound suchness. By contrast, how can liberation be achieved by someone who feels aversion for the Dharma and is constantly denigrating it?

Those who misinterpret the teachings, whether through overstating or understating them, will inevitably remain endlessly in the lower realms. Moreover, because they stray from the profound view, even if at a certain time they gain freedom from the lower realms, they will not encounter the profound teachings for many lives. Those who breach the door of secrecy and speak openly of the hidden teachings will fall into evil destinies without end. They will remain in the hell of Torment Unsurpassed where the field of their tongues will be plowed with a plowshare of incandescent iron. It is said in *The Lion's Perfect Power*,

For those who do not keep the secret,
A plow will dig the meadow of their speaking tongue.
Great will be their torment.
Therefore keep the teachings of true meaning secret.

The teachings are not kept secret because they have some flaw. On the contrary, if this doctrine is not concealed from those who are unsuitable vessels for it, the greatness and blessing power of these same teachings will decline and punishment will follow. As it is again said in *The Lion's Perfect Power*,

> The Secret Mantra has no fault.
> It teaches acts that correspond to beings skilled in means.
> And, skilled in means, the Great Compassionate One
> Conceals it from unsuitable recipients:
> From those whose minds are dull
> Or have a wrong karmic connection.

As it is said,

> The secret Mantrayāna has no flaw,
> But it is kept extremely secret for the sake of beings.
> If the secret is maintained, there is no fading of
>   accomplishment.
> Therefore it is called the secret Mantrayāna.

And,

> The Secret Mantra is so called
> Not because it harbors any defect.
> It is hidden from the narrow-minded,
> Those who enter lower vehicles.

Therefore, not only should this teaching be withheld from those who are unsuitable vessels, but even its name, its scriptures, its essential points, even a fragment of its wording, should be concealed. At times that are inopportune, in places where there is no interest in it, in countries that are like wild and barbarous borderlands, the Secret Mantra should not be explained even in part. When people who have some knowledge ask about it, one should say, "Oh I have no idea. I don't practice it, I really don't know." Again, as it is said in *The Lion's Perfect Power*,

> So keep definitive instructions secret.
> Do not disclose them even to the wind.

So it is that this marvelous heritage of the utterly secret sovereign vehicle should be kept secret from those who do not have the proper karmic fortune, or who have wrong views. It should be taught to those who are worthy and have such fortune. It should be entrusted to the sublime holders of the transmission lineage of realization.

But what are the people like who are suitable vessels for this teaching? We are told in *Awareness Self-Arisen*,

> They are strong in faith and have great diligence.
> They have abundant wisdom and have no clinging or
> attachment.
> They show great respect and practice secret Mantrayāna.
> Free of thoughts, their minds are undistracted.
> They keep samaya and make effort in the practice.
> They are firm and constant and affectionate.
> They are steady, calm, and strive in meditation.

Such people have great faith and diligence and are possessed of wisdom and discernment. They are without attachment and do not cling to the pleasures of the senses. They show great respect and esteem, and it is easy for them to blend their minds with the teachings of the secret Mantrayāna. They are undistracted, their minds dwell in the nonconceptual view, and they keep the samayas to which they have pledged themselves. They have the ability to strive in the practice and do not neglect it. Physically, they are able to sit still. They have constancy of mind and are very affectionate toward their Dharma siblings. In their body, they are steady and relaxed and are not over-occupied. Mentally, they are calm and are untroubled by wild thoughts. People like this are suitable vessels for this teaching. Moreover, the text just quoted goes on to say,

> They act according to their master's words.
> They do not break samaya.
> They act in harmony with others.

> They have clear, devoted minds.
> Every word explained they take to heart.

In other words, they do not contravene even a fragment of their master's instructions and do not transgress the samayas of body, speech, and mind to which they have bound themselves. They remain in harmony with others and show respect to their vajra master. They do not let his teachings go to waste but put them into practice.

The same text goes on to say,

> For their own sake, they act as has been said before.
> They are able to keep secret what has been bestowed on them.
> They do not wander from the vajra view.
> They take support of people of great learning.
> They never contravene their goal.
> Speaking gently, without arrogance,
> Their behavior is agreeable to others.
> They consider that their master and the tathāgata
> Are one, in no way different.

As this text says, vajra disciples do not behave in wild and unconventional ways. On the contrary, their conduct is peaceful, subdued, and circumspect. They are able to keep the secrets entrusted to them and in their practice they maintain the vajra view to which their master has introduced them. Thanks to the study of many scriptures, they are knowledgeable and they are able to accomplish their own objective—namely, the dharmakāya—in this very life and body. Like bulls with broken horns, they are without arrogance and pride. Any word that they speak will be conducive to harmony. Like an adjustable belt, they are pleasant company for their vajra kindred, and they behave in a way that is agreeable to others. They have a pure attitude, which enables them to see that there is no difference between their teacher and the tathāgata. It is said in *Awareness Self-Arisen*,

> Disciples who have all such qualities
> Are said to be the vessels for the Great Perfection.

Disciples should be examined before they receive the teachings to see whether or not they are suitable recipients. They should be examined to determine whether or not they will lose faith if they are entrusted with work [that seems] beyond their ability, or if they are criticized with words that pierce their hearts, or in the face of contradictory behavior on the part of the teacher. And by demands for various things, their generosity should be tested. If they are unsuitable vessels, they will lose faith and, being attached to their possessions, they will give nothing. It should be understood that such people will not be benefited by the teachings. And though the teacher has no need of them, the riches and possessions of the disciples must be accepted because, as it is said in *The All-Creating King*,

> To test the character of the disciples
> And to free them from their worldly clinging,
> The teacher accepts everything—their body and
> possessions—
> And having understood their capability,
> Bestows on them the quintessential teaching
> Of the All-Creating King.

And,

> To their own bodies,
> Children, spouses, servants, and possessions
> Disciples should not cling,
> But offer them with joy, devotedly.

> This is the sign that they have faith and keep samaya.
> To them the quintessential teachings should be given.

And,

> In order to receive the quintessential teachings,
> They should have no care for body or for life.
> They should not contravene their teacher's word.
> To people who display such signs,
> The quintessential teachings on the unborn nature should be given.

Regarding the great stature of the teachers who set forth the profound path, the following is said. They must be learned in the meaning of the scriptures. They must have great love and compassion for others. Their own minds must be free so that their blessing power can liberate the minds of others. They must be completely trained in the practice and display the signs that their own minds have gained freedom. They must feel great responsibility for the teachings. All connections with such teachers are necessarily meaningful. It is said in *Awareness Self-Arisen*,

> Masters who have realization of the vajra teachings
> Are of a noble character.
> They are skillful with regard to their disciples.
> They have received empowerments. They devote themselves
> To the instructions of the secret Mantrayāna.
> In the outer and the inner rituals they are expert
> And are inseparable from their yidam deity.
> Not distracted from their concentration,
> They possess the pith instructions of the Great Perfection.
> They are learned in the secret tantras of the Mantrayāna.
> Able to distinguish the outer and the inner methods
> Of accomplishment, they constantly remain within the view.

> They give up all activities, outer, inner, and secret,
> And enjoy a treasure that is inexhaustible.

As this text says, the masters who bestow the pith instructions should be peaceful and self-disciplined. They should be of noble character and skillful in expounding the methods to free the minds of others. They must have received empowerments themselves and have correctly observed the samayas to which they pledged themselves at the time of these empowerments. They should know all the outer and inner ritual practices, such as the approach and accomplishment phases and the four activities. They should have beheld the face of their yidam deity and have an undistracted concentration. In possession of the profound pith instructions, they should be learned in the teaching of the tantras and adept in the profound secret. They should be skilled in distinguishing the meaning of the outer, inner, and secret methods of accomplishment. Remaining constantly within the view, they should give up all activities, outer, inner, and secret. As a result, their inexhaustible qualities burst forth like a treasury of precious gems.

As for false teachers who are mere impostors, *Awareness Self-Arisen* has this to say:

> They have the talk of learned masters
> But they are ignorant and arrogant.
> Foolish and deluded, they keep just to the words,
> And do not penetrate the meaning of the Secret Mantra.
> They speak proudly, wounding others with their words.
> They have entered a wrong path
> And have not seen the mandala of the empowerment.

As this text says, such teachers pretend to have the position of learned masters. They are proud of themselves even though they are ignorant of the profound teachings. Foolish and deluded, they simply follow the words. They care only for the eight worldly concerns and do not contemplate the view, meditation, action, and result of the profound secret Mantrayāna. They speak haughtily to everyone regardless of their rank and their approach to both people and the teaching is hostile. Their minds are inflated with pride and they stray into a false path. They are destitute of empowerment, reading transmission, and instructions. And even if they have received some empowerments, they fail to keep the samaya pledges. *Awareness Self-Arisen* has even more to say:

> Degenerate in their samaya,
> They fail to answer those who come with questions.
> Small in learning, great in pride,
> These unexamined masters are but demons for disciples.
> They are not masters who can teach the Secret Mantra,
> And they are unable to set forth
> The Ati teachings of the Great Perfection.
> Do not keep company with them.

Such teachers are unable to answer questions regarding the secret key points of the Great Perfection. They are like well frogs with little learning but great pretension. One should not keep company with them.

Disciples to whom instruction should be given are described in *The Word-Transcending Tantra*:

> They uphold the view and meditation
> And have great faith and diligence.
> They are able to be generous and are devoted to their
> teacher.
> Embracing yogic discipline, they shun all sinful conduct.
> They are steadfast and hold firm to the instructions.

The meaning of this text is that disciples who have the capacity to hold in their minds the view, meditation, action, and result, which are already present in the minds of their teachers, will have the kind of faith that allows them to see their masters as true buddhas.

They have a diligence that enables them to strive powerfully in the implementation of the instructions. They are able to sacrifice even their bodies and their lives for their teachers. They honor and serve them in word and deed and are able to undertake profound yogic disciplines of secret conduct. They do not disparage ethical teachings regarding what is to be done and not done and are meticulous in avoiding negative conduct. Their minds are steadfast and they are able to hold the instructions firmly in their minds. It is to such disciples that the essential instructions should be given. *The Word-Transcending Tantra* continues,

> Tolerant, serene, their attitude
> Is easygoing and relaxed.
> They are like simple-minded folk.
> Free of many thoughts,
> Their temperament is naturally calm.
> Free of busyness in word and deed,
> They are wise and can uphold the teachings.

In other words, disciples of this stamp are noble in character. They are tolerant and gentle, peaceful, diligent, and careful. The way they act and speak is straightforward and relaxed. They are like simple-minded people, completely without guile. Easygoing in thought, word, and deed, they are mentally uncluttered and gentle. They do not take pleasure in excessive activity and talk but instead are wise and discerning. The possession of all such physical, verbal, and mental characteristics indicates an ability to uphold the teachings.

Entrusted to such people, the highest of the quintessential instructions will endure for a long time. Thus the tradition whereby countless beings may be led along the path to enlightenment will not be weakened—and this will be thanks to the extraordinary merit that these beings possess. More specifically, in addition to uncontrived and relaxed simplicity, there are other characteristics that distinguish them from others and indicate that they are vessels for the extraordinary teachings of the Great Perfection. They are described in *The Array of Studded Jewels* as follows:

> Strong in limb and with a dark complexion,
> They have white and even teeth.
> Their eyes are slightly bloodshot
> And their black abundant hair turns clockwise to the right.
> They take little care of their appearance.
> Outwardly they have an ordinary demeanor,
> And they are uninhibited in speech.

As the text says, such people have a robust constitution and a dark complexion. Their teeth are white and even, they have bloodshot eyes, and their hair curls to the right. They take little care of their appearance and have no love for personal grooming. Outwardly, they behave in an ordinary way and say whatever comes into their minds. The same text continues,

> Or else they simply repeat what others say.
> It is said that teachings of the Great Perfection
> Should be granted them.
> If all these features are gathered in a single person,
> However lowly they may be—
> A butcher, harlot, sweeper, scavenger—
> The essence of the secret pith instructions
> Should be granted them.

This text may be explained as follows. These people either say the first thing that comes into their minds or else they simply repeat what their interlocutors say. If all the characteristics just described are found to be present in a single person, he or she must be considered an authentic disciple, one to whom the secret pith instructions of the Great Perfection should be given. Regardless of their social position—for such people may be of very humble station (butcher, prostitute, cleaner, or scavenger)—it is on them that the essence of the pith instructions should be bestowed.

* * *

The eleventh section speaks of the nail that fastens the dharmatā, the definitive meaning of the pith instructions, to the great state of leaving as it is—with which it is perfectly aligned.

> **11. In short, whatever circumstances may occur—**
> **A sense object or state of mind—**
> **Do not apply an antidote.**
> **Do not strive to rid yourself of it.**
> **For the key point of awareness is the natural state,**
> **The unaltered state, the state left as it is.**

Briefly, no matter what outer or inner phenomena belonging to the world and beings may occur—in particular, whatever circumstances in the form of unwanted sense objects and states of mind, together with the suffering they may provoke—one should not apply antidotes to them. One should not strive to rid oneself of them, adopting and rejecting them as an ordinary person might do. Recognizing that they themselves constitute the yogic path to freedom, one should maintain one's awareness in its naked, fundamental condition, leaving it in the natural state, the unaltered state, the state left as it is, free of all contrivance. If one manages to do this, all these circumstances will subside naturally on their own. This is a profound and crucial point. As *The Great Garuda* tells us,

> In natural, uncontrived awareness,
> Authentic, self-cognizing,
> All things are free and open from the outset.
> By no one can they be destroyed.
> Neither are they rendered free and open.
> They are free and open in their natural condition.
> What is it that effort may achieve?

If free of any contrivance, one maintains the naked, fundamental condition of great immensity left as it is and unaltered, one will see that all phenomena are open and free from the very beginning. They are primordially the state of buddhahood in the one sole sphere of the dharmakāya, the state of primordial purity. There is no need in the present moment to strive on a path to make them free and open. For they are already open and free completely and primordially.

* * *

The twelfth section speaks of the nail that fastens happiness and suffering to a single taste, with which they are aligned, by blending them together.

> **12. All happiness and suffering**
> **Are ways in which awareness manifests.**
> **If you regard them dualistically,**
> **As things to take or to reject,**
> **Then you are bound within existence.**
> **All objects that appear are equal—**
> **They do no more than manifest to faculties of sense.**
> **All mental states are equal**
> **They are no more than thoughts that in awareness**
> **leave no trace.**
> **Both are equal in immediate presence—**
> **They do no more than bind you in acceptance and**
> **rejection.**
> **Truly in their final status they are equal—**
> **They are no more than things appearing groundlessly.**
> **In their distinctiveness the objects of the senses are**
> **all equal—**
> **They are no more than traceless when they're broken**
> **down.**
> **All mental states are equal in the way they are**
> **perceived—**

They are no more than space when they're
investigated.
Mind and objects are not two—
They're no more than the pure and intervening air.
Those who know this are the scions of
Samantabhadra.
They are vidyādharas upon the highest ground,
The supreme heirs of the Victorious Ones.

It is a mistake to make a difference between the water of the ocean and the waves that appear in it—thinking that the one is good and the other bad, accepting and rejecting accordingly. In the same way, it is wrong to think of happiness, as it appears within in the state of awareness, as something good to be indulged in, while at the same time considering suffering as something bad to be rejected. It is inappropriate to have attachment for the one and aversion for the other. Attachment and aversion, acceptance and rejection, are all equal in being the causes of the three worlds of samsara. Since happiness and suffering arise within the expanse of awareness, they are just different ways in which awareness manifests. When one distinguishes some [of these manifestations] as good and to be welcomed and some as bad and to be eschewed—that is, when one reacts to them in a dualistic manner—one is shackled to the conditioned existence of samsara. The different ways in which the dualistic apprehension of happiness and suffering appears are all the same in binding beings in samsara. Black and white clouds are the same in obscuring the sun and moon. Ropes and golden chains are equal as implements for tethering a horse. As it is said in *The Treasury of the Fundamental Nature*,

Just as ropes and golden chains bind equally,
Virtuous and unvirtuous states
Bind equally the ultimate, definitive quintessence.
Clouds black and white enshroud the sun in equal measure.
Likewise, virtue and nonvirtue equally obscure awareness.

And in *The Classification of Empowerments* it is said,

> All happiness and sorrow are awareness's display.
> It is deluded to believe that one should be accepted and the other spurned.

And *The All-Creating King* tells us,

> Happiness do not accept, and suffering do not spurn.

The reason for this is that all that appears, all the phenomena of the outer world and the beings it contains—forms, sounds, smells, tastes, and textures—which arise as external objects, are in fact groundless and rootless. They have no existence apart from awareness, which is by nature the open, unimpeded state, devoid of objective reference. They are therefore equal in its bare and empty expanse. But whereas they are empty, their ceaseless appearances manifest to one's sense faculties. If this is recognized, they are all equal in the simple fact of appearing to the sense consciousnesses.

Since they have no existence in awareness and yet are spontaneously present in it—inasmuch as awareness is able to arise as anything whatsoever—all mental states, all thoughts good and bad, all happiness and suffering that appear in the mind, do so like designs traced on water. And if this is recognized, one sees that they are all equal in their great spontaneous vanishing—that is, in their self-subsiding in the very act of their self-arising. All recollections and thoughts are equal in being simply nonexistent within the expanse of empty, luminous, unceasing awareness. Like birds in flight, they leave no trace.

In the absence of analysis and investigation, both appearing objects and mental states are, in their immediate presence, equal. To the deluded mind, they both seem truly to exist. They are equal too in that whether one accepts them or rejects them, they are both fetters—in the same way that golden chains and ropes bind equally.

In truth, objects, mental states, and so on—all the outer and inner phenomena of the world and its inhabitants—are groundless and rootless. Therefore in their final status, they are equal; they have no existence. Nevertheless, though groundless and rootless, they arise unceasingly through the creative power of awareness, like reflections in a mirror. They are equal in being no more than unceasing appearances.

The six objects of the senses and the consciousnesses that perceive them are equal in being clear and distinct appearances. Yet, when an investigation is made, the sense objects do not exist outwardly and the consciousnesses do not exist inwardly. They are empty and traceless like the flight path of a bird. They are self-vanishing, self-subsiding, and are equal in their bare emptiness.

When an examination and analysis is not made, however, all mental phenomena perceived by the deluded mind are equal in what seems to be their true existence. And yet when they are examined by the kind of reasoning that aims to establish their ultimate status, they are found to be empty from the very first. They are equal simply in being no more than space.

The so-called object of apprehension and the so-called apprehending mind are not two things. In truth, they are no more than the pure intervening air. They are primordially equal within the state of empty, open, unimpeded, naked awareness.

Those who know this are scions, holders of the lineage, of the dharmakāya Samantabhadra. They are the supreme heirs of the Victorious Ones. They are called vidyādharas with mastery over the sixteenth, and highest, ground of Unsurpassed Wisdom. It is said in *The Secret Essence*,

> The supreme holders of awareness
> Are blessed by holy beings, by all the supreme holy ones,
> Who think of them as their own children and their kin.
> The sovereigns of the world and all their retinues
> Bow down before them.
> They dwell upon the highest level of vidyādharas.

As has been explained above, practitioners who are in possession of such realization are vidyādharas, the representatives of the lineage of Samantabhadra. They are blessed as the scions of the Victorious Ones, or as their kindred and close friends. They are worthy of the homage of all the rulers of the earth—the Cakravartin king, Brahmā and Indra, the lords of the gods, and so on, and of all their retinues.

As it is said in *The Six Expanses*,

> All those yogis who are used to this
> Are fortunate, for they will look upon my body,
> The body of Samantabhadra.

And,

> They uphold the light of my cognizant power.
> They are equal to myself in fortune.

There are many detailed teachings to the same effect.

* * *

The thirteenth section speaks of the nail that fastens vast, universal equality to the natural condition of the pure dharmatā with which it is perfectly aligned.

> **13. Therefore all phenomena are equal—**
> **Equal in existing, equal in their not existing,**
> **Equal in appearing, equal in their emptiness,**
> **Equal in their truth, and equal in their falsity.**
> **Abandon therefore all fixation, all that fetters you—**
> **Things to be abandoned, their counteracting antidotes,**
> **And all concerted effort.**
> **Grow, become commensurate with great equality,**
> **Free of all objective reference.**

Grow, become commensurate with great awareness,
Free of ordinary mind.
Grow, become commensurate with great equality
and purity,
Free of any flaw.

The outer and inner phenomena of the world and beings—all of which seem to exist on the conventional level—are equal in being like magical appearances, dreams, reflections of the moon in water. In truth, they are equal in being empty, nonexistent. In like manner, all outer appearances and inner consciousnesses—all the phenomena of samsara and nirvana—have no existence at all and yet they are able to appear. They are thus equal in their manner of appearing—in their nonexistence and yet clear appearance. They are therefore equal in being beyond the fixation that binds one to things to be discarded and their corresponding antidotes, and equal in being empty by their nature, in the manner of utterly pure space devoid of objective reference. Likewise, phenomena are equal in their truth and equal in their falsity, and so on. Within the vast expanse of awareness, in which extreme positions have no place, all true and false appearances are equal. One should therefore give up all fixation, all that fetters—all the things to be discarded, their antidotes, and all effortful striving, which are posited through the imputation of real existence. One should just let them go in the expanse of great, impartial equality.

One should grow and become commensurate with this open and unimpeded equality, which is devoid of objective reference, the primordial emptiness of all phenomena in both samsara and nirvana. One should grow and become commensurate with the vast expanse of bare awareness, which is beyond all mental activity and is free from the apprehending and fixating thoughts that are characteristic of the ordinary mind. One should grow and become commensurate with the great purity and equality of phenomenal existence—the world and its inhabitants—unspoiled by the flaw of impure, deluded perception.

There exist many texts that demonstrate the fifteen points of the extraordinary supremacy of the Great Perfection, but I have not mentioned them here for fear of excessive prolixity.

* * *

This concludes the commentary on the eleventh chapter of *The Precious Treasury of the Dharmadhātu*, which shows that every kind of experience is as pure as space.

12. Phenomena Are Primordially Open and Free within the Enlightened Mind

This chapter shows that all phenomena are open and free primordially within the enlightened mind. It begins with a short summary, which is followed by an extensive exposition.

> **1a. Everything is free and open in the enlightened mind.**
> **There are no phenomena that are not free and open.**

For example, when a pebble or a stick, acting as the cause, is conjoined with a magical spell, acting as the condition, illusory men and women, horses, oxen, and so on appear. From the very beginning, however, these appearances are free and open in their illusoriness, and there is not a single thing that is not open and free. All is but the clear appearances of nonexistent things. There are no actual horses and oxen present, existing according to their characteristics.

In the same way, on the basis of a dependent arising that consists in the coming together of the cause (self-clinging) and the condition (discursive thought), the teeming ocean of all things in phenomenal existence, the world and its inhabitants, occurs simply as the manifestation of the appearances of the ground within the expanse of awareness, the ultimate enlightened mind. They are in truth and from the very beginning open and free in the expanse of primordial purity, the state of equality that is free of mental elaboration. There is not a single thing, not even a single atom, that is not free and open. It is as *The Great Garuda* says,

Phenomena are free and open from the very outset;
You cannot make them free and open.

* * *

The detailed exposition of this topic comprises fifteen sections, the first of which shows that phenomena are primordially free and open in being groundless and rootless.

1b. Samsara is free and open from the very first,
Free and open in primordial purity.
Nirvana is free and open from the very first,
Free and open in spontaneous perfection.
The appearing world is free and open from the very first,
Free and open in its groundlessness and rootlessness.
Living beings are free and open from the very first,
Free and open in the essence of enlightenment.
The elaborations of the mind are free and open from the very first,
Free and open in their lack of limits and extremes.
The absence of elaboration too is free and open from the very first,
Free and open in its unborn purity.

All the happiness and suffering appearing in last night's dreams, good and bad, are found never to have existed when one wakes up the following day. In the same way, all the appearances perceived by the deluded mind—which is what we call samsara—have never existed. They are free and open from the very first—free and open in their original purity. This is referred to as great primordial purity.

Likewise, the phenomena of nirvana—the four kāyas, the five wisdoms, and so on, and also the appearance of buddhas and buddha fields—are the ground appearances arising within the ground from which they are inseparable. Therefore, they too are free and open from the very first, free and open in their uncontrived spontaneous perfection—namely, self-arisen awareness.

The appearances of samsara, the world and the beings that it contains, which we take to be the outer objects of our senses, constitute what we call phenomenal existence. All the appearances of the outer vessel of the world, mountain ranges, cliffs, houses, and so on are themselves primordially open and free—free in the expanse of bare awareness. For they are groundless and rootless, completely without real existence.

Living beings, the inhabitants of the desire, form, and formless realms (the living contents of the world) are also primordially open and free. The experiences of happiness and suffering, the results of the karma and defilement of the beings of the six migrations, have never really existed. They are free and open in the expanse of awareness, the essence of enlightenment.

The elaborations of the mind together with all the appearances of the relative truth are also primordially open and free in the sense that they have never existed. They are open and free in the expanse of great equality beyond all conceptual extremes and the limits of existence, nonexistence, both, and neither.

The state of freedom from mental elaboration—namely, all the aspects of emptiness—is also primordially open and free in the state of unborn purity, which is devoid of arising, remaining, and ceasing and is the one sole sphere of empty awareness.

* * *

The second section shows that since the self-experience of awareness manifests in the manner of a dream or magical illusion, it follows that happiness and suffering are primordially open and free in being pure and equal in their groundlessness.

> **2. Happiness is free and open from the very first,**
> **Free and open in the all-pervading dharmatā.**
> **Suffering is free and open from the very first,**
> **Free and open in the ground's immense equality.**

Indifference is free and open from the very first,
Free and open in the spacelike dharmakāya.
Purity is free and open from the very first,
Free and open in the emptiness of the ground's purity.
Impurity is free and open from the very first,
Free and open in the supreme state of utter openness and freedom.

Whatever experiences may occur, whether of happiness, suffering, or indifference, and whatever appearances may manifest, whether pure or impure, they are all groundless—free and open from the very first.

All experiences of happiness in waking life or in dreams, occurring in past, present, or future lives, are groundless and rootless. They are empty. From the very first, they have never existed. They are primordially open and free, open and free in primordially pure awareness, the vast and all-pervading dharmatā.

Similarly, the inconceivable number of different kinds of unwanted suffering experienced by gods and humans in the higher destinies down to those of the three lower realms, are also an open, unimpeded state devoid of objective reference. From the very beginning, they have never existed. They are open and free from the first. In the primordial expanse of the ground, happiness and suffering are equal; they are primordially open and free in the vast expanse of awareness.

Likewise, all feelings of indifference and neutrality, experiences that are neither pleasant nor painful, are also primordially open and free. From the very first, they are open and free in empty awareness, in the dharmakāya vast as space.

It is thus that all the pure appearances of the buddhas and buddha fields are primordially open and free in the vast state of equality beyond the elaborations of the mind—in other words, awareness that is pure from the beginning. They are naturally free in the emptiness of the pure ground of both "purity" and "impurity," so called.

The same is true of the impure hallucinatory appearances of samsara. They have never existed from the very beginning. They are groundless and rootless. In the very moment of their birth or arising, their causes are nonexistent. They are empty, open and free from the very beginning. And in their remaining, they are like reflections in a mirror. They are simultaneously self-arising and self-subsiding. They appear and yet are empty. They are but the inseparability of appearance and emptiness. And in their ending, although they seem to cease, their cessation too is by nature free of causes and conditions. They are pervasively and primordially free and open. All phenomena, which seem to emerge within the expanse of the unborn dharmakāya; which seem to subsist as the unceasing, luminous radiance of the sambhogakāya; and which, manifesting as the nirmāṇakāya while never stirring from the dharmakāya, seem to cease in their simultaneous self-arising and self-vanishing, in fact are free of any actual arising, subsisting, and subsiding. Throughout the lapse of the three times, the phenomena of both samsara and nirvana are completely open and free. They are but the utter openness and freedom of the dharmatā. The state of openness and freedom of the primordial purity of phenomena is said to be complete because there is not a single phenomenon that is not so open and free. It is as *The Natural Openness and Freedom of Awareness* says,

> So too, all things endowed with characteristics
> Are free and open in the state devoid of all such
> characteristics.
> All things made, material phenomena,
> Are free and open in the state of emptiness devoid of action.
> All phenomena, the self-experience of awareness,
> Are free and open in the state of emptiness, completely
> pure.

All phenomena endowed with characteristics—in other words, the appearing mode of things—are in truth open and free in the state of awareness devoid of all characteristics. All material objects produced through causes and conditions are in truth open and free in the state of nonaction—that is, the state of inconceivable emptiness beyond all mental elaboration. All phenomena, which are the self-experience of awareness, which manifest within that same awareness and are beyond all fixation and effort, are free and open in the dharmatā—namely, utterly pure awareness free of fixation, effort, and mental elaboration.

* * *

The third section shows that the path to be followed is like space, primordially open and free, and is beyond all striving.

> **3. The grounds and paths are free and open from the very first,**
> **Free and open in transcending generation and perfection.**
> **View and meditation are free and open from the very first,**
> **Free and open in the absence of acceptance and rejection.**
> **Action too is free and open from the very first,**
> **Free and open in the vast space of Samantabhadra.**
> **The result is free and open from the very first,**
> **Free and open in transcending hope and fear.**
> **Samaya too is free and open from the very first,**
> **Free and open in great dharmatā.**
> **Recitation, mantra repetition**
> **Both are free and open from the very first,**
> **Free and open in transcending all expression.**
> **Concentration too is free and open from the very first,**
> **Free and open in transcending the domain of contemplation.**

Even though, in relation to awareness, we make a distinction between view, meditation, action, and result, the truth is that awareness is primordially empty and bare. It is a nonthing, devoid of all conceptual elaboration. Now, inasmuch as the view, meditation, action, and result are described as being individual, separate entities, they become conventional things. And because things and nonthings are mutually exclusive, it follows that in the great state of nonaction, which is primordially open and free, what we refer to as view, meditation, action, and result cannot be distinguished.

So it is that in awareness, in the ultimate enlightened mind, it is not possible to discern a structure of grounds and paths. The latter are open and free naturally and primordially. It is said in *The All-Creating King*,

> There is no view on which to meditate
> And no samaya to observe,
> No activity in which to strive,
> And no primordial wisdom to obtain.
> There are no grounds on which to train,
> No paths to be traversed.

It is in order to train on the grounds and paths that the ten essential factors are taught. However, regarding awareness, the dharmadhātu, there can be no training on the grounds and paths by these means. To realize that awareness is free of the so-called generation stage (the aspect of skillful means) and of the perfection stage (the aspect of wisdom)—that is, to realize that it transcends conceptually elaborated teachings involving concerted effort and the attitudes of acceptance and rejection—is the wisdom of Samantabhadra, free and open from the very beginning.

Similarly, when a clear certainty is attained regarding the all-pervading luminous expanse of the wisdom of the dharmakāya Samantabhadra, [one finds that] it is impossible to indicate the appearances arising within awareness through their corresponding apprehending cognitions. In other words, they cannot be established. From the very beginning, they are beyond all mental elaboration. So-called view and meditation cannot be individually discerned. Within the fundamental stratum of the one sole sphere of nonaction, there is no view to be viewed and no meditation to be meditated. They are both primordially open and free. The supreme dharmatā is not something to be fabricated or contrived by view and meditation. If this were possible, it would entail the consequence that the teaching that awareness transcends view and meditation is false. As it is said in *The Lion's Perfect Power*,

> It's not through thinking
> That primordial wisdom is discovered.
> If through thinking primordial wisdom were discovered,
> It would be a lie [to speak of] self-arisen primordial wisdom.
> It's not through meditation
> That dharmakāya is seen,
> If through meditation dharmakāya were seen,
> It would be a lie [to speak of] self-appearing dharmakāya.

Self-arisen primordial wisdom transcends both thought and expression. But such a statement would be falsified if primordial wisdom were discovered through reflection. Self-arisen primordial wisdom transcends both the object and the agent of meditation. It is free of both a meditating mind and a meditated object. If it were possible to behold the dharmakāya by meditating on it, it would be mendacious to speak about a so-called view of nonmeditation. This false consequence would follow. The same text continues,

> It's not through viewing of a view
> That awareness will be realized.
> If through viewing of a view awareness could be realized,
> It would be a lie [to speak of] ceaseless dharmakāya.

Awareness is beyond both the object and the agent of a view. If, therefore, it were possible to realize awareness by viewing [thanks to a view], it would be false to say that the unceasing dharmakāya is beyond an object viewed and an agent who views. Again the text continues,

> It is not through teachings
> That ignorance is rooted out.
> If ignorance were rooted out by teachings,
> It would be a lie [to speak of] wisdom's primal purity.

Primordial wisdom is beyond expression. Therefore, if the explanatory teachings were able to eradicate ignorance, it would be mendacious to say that the wisdom that is pure from the beginning is primordially free from conceptual elaboration. This erroneous consequence would follow, and the point is proven by many texts, the details of which are given in Longchenpa's autocommentary, *The Treasury of Teachings.*

In short, the view and meditation are primordially open and free in the absence of acceptance and rejection. And since awareness does not exist as anything whatsoever—for it is beyond all conceptualization and is open, unimpeded, and naked—so-called action is also primordially open and free, there being neither agent, object, nor act itself. It is open and free in the expanse of Samantabhadra, awareness that is empty, unchanging, and motionless. *The Word-Transcending Tantra* observes,

> Action leads to deviation, obscuration.
> Samsara is the fruit that it produces.

Shabkar has also said,

> Within the one sole sphere of primal wisdom self-cognizing,
> The object and the agent of an action are not two.

And,

> Supreme action is beyond all striving.

And,

> You don't accomplish it through acting.
> Take it as a magical illusion and let it go!

And,

> If you're free of taking and rejecting,
> This is the supreme and sovereign action.

And,

> You cannot act on it.
> Abandon all assertion and negation,
> Adopting and rejecting.

Generally speaking, the twelfth and thirteenth chapters are devoted to an explanation of the result. On earlier occasions when the view, meditation, action, and result were being individually explained, it was already pointed out that the ten essential factors of tantra have no existence. This being so, is it not a fault to mention them again here? In fact, no fault is incurred. Admittedly, the same point is being explained on both occasions but when previously the view, meditation, action, and result were distinguished, it was necessary to grasp their conceptual aspects without mixing them up. Regarding the view, it was taught that one must realize, and be convinced, that the fundamental nature is as it was explained. Regarding the meditation, it was taught that since the fundamental nature is as it was explained, there is no need for effortful striving. Finally, regarding the result, it was taught that since one is enlightened from the very first, there should be no doubt or expectation of realizing it now.

Likewise, all the phenomena of both samsara and nirvana, the whole of phenomenal existence, are primordially open and free. None lies outside the one sole sphere of primordial purity. Phenomena are already buddha in the great state of primordial openness and freedom. There is no need to attain the goal or result anew. Therefore, one should not hope to achieve it anew. One should have no doubt, thinking that one might not achieve it. One should simply understand that the result is primordially open and free. It is said in *The Necklace of Pearls*,

> Not changed through action,
> Appearances are free and open.
> Not found through meditation,
> Phenomena are free and open.
> Not examined through the view,
> Permanence, discontinuity—both are free and open.
> Not bound by the result,
> One's mind is free and open.
> On all appearances
> The primal seal is set.

As this text says, no matter what appearances may occur, they are open and free as they arise all by themselves within the expanse of dharmakāya, the primordial wisdom that dwells in the ground, unmodified by action, whether good or bad. In the expanse of self-arisen awareness, which is primordially present and cannot be found by the kind of meditation that focuses on an object, all phenomenal appearances endowed with characteristics are themselves the dharmatā, primordially open and free. In the expanse of awareness, which from the first is unconfined and impossible to examine in terms of partial views, the conceptual constructs of permanence or discontinuity of existence, nonexistence, both or neither, and so on are themselves open and free from the very beginning. In the expanse of bare, primordially pure awareness, which is not bound by hopes or doubts regarding the attainment or nonattainment of a result, all the mind's discursive thoughts are naturally free and open from the very beginning. So it is that the appearances of infinite phenomena are open and free. They bear the seal of self-cognizing primordial wisdom.

Likewise, since the samayas of nothing to keep are from the very first open and free within awareness, it follows that the myriad samayas of the Mantrayāna are also open and free primordially in the dharmatā, the expanse of awareness. All the sounds and words of recitation and the repetition of mantra are primordially open and free within the uncontrived, fundamental condition, in which all sounds are realized as mantra. And when primordial wisdom, which realizes the great state of nonaction, manifests, these sounds are open and free in transcending all expression. Since all phenomena are open and free in the primordially pure dharmatā, the state of ineffable and mind-transcending concentration—and are so from the very beginning—it follows that now, in this present moment, they are free and open in transcending the domain of contemplation. They are not the objects of thought. They are beyond all expression.

* * *

The fourth section is an essentialization of the key points.

> **4. Existence, nonexistence**
> **Both are free and open from the very first,**
> **Free and open in transcending such extremes.**
> **Permanence, discontinuity**
> **Both are free and open from the very first,**
> **Free and open in their groundlessness and**
> **rootlessness.**
> **Wholesomeness is free and open from the very first,**
> **Free and open in transcending thought and aim.**

Unwholesomeness is free and open from the very first,
Free and open in transcending thought and partiality.
Karmic deeds are free and open from the very first,
Free and open in not staining.
Defilements too are free and open from the very first,
Free and open in the absence both of bondage and of freedom.
Habitual tendencies are free and open from the very first,
Free and open in the absence of foundation.
The full ripening of acts is free and open from the very first,
Free and open in the absence of a basis of experience.

When it is realized that all the appearances of samsara and nirvana are the one sole sphere of awareness, they are seen to be open and free in this same sphere. It is impossible to find anything that is not open and free. All things in phenomenal existence, the world and its beings, are like a magical illusory display and have never existed on their own account. If one does not lose one's nerve, [one understands that] one cannot be thrown into an abyss or be destroyed by an army of phantoms. If, on the other hand, one succumbs to fear, one will be like the people of Vaiśālī in the old story. The people of Vaiśālī were being chased by a phantom army, and as they were fleeing, they fell over a cliff. In the same way, if one is deluded and takes benefit, harm, and so on to be real, an uninterrupted experience of happiness and sorrow lies ahead. But just as when one is not alarmed when one understands that the phantom army is not real, when one realizes that all phenomena are the one sole sphere of awareness, one realizes likewise that all acts, habitual tendencies, defilements, the fully ripened effects of action, and so on—as well as existence, nonexistence, both and neither, permanence and discontinuity, exclusion and inclusion, and all the rest—are utterly unreal. Not one of them is outside the one sole sphere of awareness, the primordial state of openness and freedom.

So it is that existent things and nonexistent things—things that appear and nonthings that are empty—are all primordially open and free. They are like the things and nonthings of a dream, which lie beyond the extremes of existence and nonexistence. They are open and free in the state of awareness, which from the very outset lies beyond the extremes of existence and nonexistence.

In the same vein, permanence (the grasping at the continuum of existent things as being a self) and discontinuity (the grasping at the nonexistence of things in terms of their momentariness) are both without existence. If what is referred to as time is not established, then however one may examine the continuity of time, or a sequence of earlier and later moments and so on, it will be found that it has never existed in and of itself, and that it is open and free from the very first. It is groundless and rootless, beyond the elaboration of thought. It is like the continuity of time, or the sequence of instants and so on, that is experienced in a dream and that has never existed. It is thus that all phenomena are open and free from the very beginning. They are the one sole sphere of empty awareness.

Again, wholesomeness (all the positive or "white" phenomena of the path to liberation) has likewise never existed. It is like the virtuous experiences occurring in last night's dream. It is primordially open and free, free and open in being bare awareness beyond thought and aim.

And also unwholesomeness (all evil and wrongdoing) has never existed. It is like the evil and wrongdoing experienced in a dream. It is open and free in the expanse of the primordial purity of empty awareness. If one examines and searches for it, it is not found anywhere in any of the main and intermediate directions! Beyond the reach of thought, it is open and free from the outset.

So too karmic deeds, their ripened results, and the habitual tendencies to which they give rise are, just as with the eight examples of illusion, primordially open and free. Since they are simply empty, so-called white and black actions have never existed, and it is impossible to be stained by them. Not one of them exists. All are open and free within the bare state of awareness.

Neither is it possible for the defilements (the three or five poisons and so on) to exist. It may be thought that they exist in being dependent on the mind. But if scrutinized with regard to its arising, remaining, and departing, the mind itself, their putative support, is not found. And if the mind itself does not exist, then even if one looks for them, the supposedly supported defilements are not to be found. It is certain that they do not exist. They are free and open from the very beginning. Furthermore, if defilements do not exist, it is not possible to be bound by them. And if there is no bondage, there can be no freedom from bondage. Defilements are open and free within the expanse of awareness, beyond both bondage and freedom, the state of equality beyond mental construction.

Likewise, it is impossible for so-called habitual tendencies to exist. If they are thought to be dependent on the mind, then just as previously, when they are investigated, no existence can be ascribed to either the support or the supported. If, on the other hand, it is thought that habitual tendencies are dependent on the body, the body itself is not found when dissected and analyzed into its constituent parts down to the partless particles. And even the latter are resolved into the state beyond reference. Therefore, habitual tendencies are also primordially open and free—open and free in bare and groundless awareness.

Again, the supposed fully ripened results of action exist neither in dependence on the mind nor in dependence on the body. They are open and free from the very first and do not occur outside the one sole sphere. Therefore, no existence can be ascribed to them. The fully ripened results of action are free and open from the very first. There is no basis for their being experienced. This is the message of *The Great Garuda*, which says,

> Within this mind which cannot be affirmed at all,
> There is no basis for the fully ripened fruit of actions,
> No basis for habitual tendencies.
> What is it, therefore, that supports them?
> Just as flowers cannot grow in unsupporting space,
> There being neither mind nor body,
> There is no support for tendencies.

As this text says, actions, defilements, habitual tendencies, and the fully ripened effects of action have never truly existed. They are groundless, and destitute of all support. Just as sky flowers are non-existent because there is nowhere for them to grow, all phenomena are primordially open and free. They are but the one awareness, the state of equality beyond all mental elaboration.

* * *

The fifth section shows that the fettering fixation upon the path and antidotes is transcended.

> **5. Antidotes are free and open from the very first,**
> **Free and open in there being nothing to abandon.**
> **Acceptance and rejection—neither has existence;**
> **Both are free and open in a vast spacelike immensity.**
> **Freedom too is free and open from the very first,**
> **Free and open in there being no bondage.**
> **Freedom's absence too is free and open from the very first,**
> **Free and open in there being no freedom and no bondage.**
> **Relaxation too is free and open from the very first,**
> **Free and open in there being nothing to relax.**
> **Leaving as it is is free and open from the very first,**
> **Free and open in that there is nothing to leave as it is.**

The things that we call antidotes are themselves primordially open and free. Generally speaking, antidotes are defined in relation to things that are to be abandoned. According to the approach of the Great Perfection, however, the things to be abandoned (the defilements and activities of samsara) have no existence and are open and free primordially. Consequently, the remedial antidotes—referred to as true paths—are also groundless and rootless. They are not outside awareness, which is utterly bare, like space itself.

The defilements to be discarded together with their antidotes are necessarily attributed to the mind. Now the mind is groundless and has no support. It is like space and is free of the three factors of arising, remaining, and departing. Therefore, acceptance and rejection have no real existence; they are naturally open and free in the vast, spacelike immensity of awareness, self-arisen primordial wisdom.

Moreover, freedom is also open and free. Generally speaking, freedom must be posited in relation to bondage, in the sense that to be free is to be unbound. But since bondage has no existence, being itself naturally open and free, there is no way to posit the state of freedom from it. Therefore, bondage and freedom do not exist as two counterparts. They are both equal in their primordial openness and freedom.

What is referred to as freedom's absence is also primordially open and free. If such a thing existed, it would necessarily be a phenomenon. And if it were a phenomenon, it would necessarily be empty by nature and beyond mental elaboration. Freedom's absence is therefore naked, primordially pure awareness, open and unimpeded beyond both bondage and freedom.

Similarly, relaxation is also primordially open and free. A subject of relaxation—something that could be said to be either relaxed or not relaxed—has never existed. Therefore, relaxation as such has no existence. It vanishes naturally into emptiness, the great, natural openness and freedom of awareness.

Finally, the so-called practice of leaving as it is is also primordially open and free. There is no place where something could be left as it is; there is no action of leaving, and no agent of such a leaving as it is. Therefore, such a leaving is naturally open and free; it is in no way different from naked awareness, primordially open and free. It is as we find in *The Lion's Perfect Power*,

> The final view of Great Perfection
> Does not fall into the side of virtue or of vice.
> It goes beyond extremes of being and nonbeing.
> No perfection and no imperfection can be found in it.
> Within the great perfection, nature of awareness,
> There is no delusion, no absence of delusion.

* * *

The sixth section gives a definitive summary of the key points.

> **6. In brief, then, all things that appear or can appear,**
> **And all that is beyond such things and does not or cannot appear**
> **Are free and open from the very first**
> **Within the ultimate expanse.**
> **No one therefore needs to strive**
> **To make them free and open now.**

In brief, there is on the one hand the oceanlike infinity of phenomena that appear or can appear as objects of the mind. On the other hand, there are deep and secret phenomena that are extremely difficult to realize—that is, the phenomena of nirvana, which for the time being do not appear to the dualistic minds of ordinary beings and which cannot be the objects of their minds. As Śāntideva has said,

> The ultimate is not within the reach of intellect
> For intellect is said to be the relative.[102]

Now all that appears and all that lies beyond the phenomena detected by the mind are already primordially open and free in the ultimate expanse of equality that is free of mental elaboration, the primordial purity of awareness. There is therefore no need for anyone to make them free and open now. As it is said in *The Word-Transcending Tantra*,

> Since they are free and open from the first,
> No need is there to make them free and open once again.

* * *

The seventh section shows that the validity of the preceding points means that all concerted effort is pointless.

> **7. Though you may strive therein, it is to no avail.**
> **So do not do it! Do not do it!**
> **Do not try with effort to achieve it!**
> **Do not watch them! Do not watch them!**
> **Do not watch your thoughts!**
> **Do not meditate! Do not meditate!**
> **Do not meditate on mind!**
> **Do not investigate! Do not investigate!**
> **Do not investigate the objects of the senses and the mind!**
> **Do not labor! Do not labor!**
> **Do not labor for the fruit with hope and fear!**
> **Do not reject! Do not reject!**
> **Do not reject defilements and activities!**
> **Do not adopt! Do not adopt!**
> **Do not adopt the pure phenomena!**
> **Do not fetter! Do not fetter!**
> **Do not fetter your own mind!**

Awareness is beyond the conceptual constructs of existence, nonexistence, both and neither. Therefore regarding its nature, which does not exist as anything at all, the negative injunctions are repeated twice. This is done to indicate that they are extremely meaningful and highly important. As *The Precious Source*, a manual on poetics, says,

> For things that are of high importance
> The same word should be uttered twice.

In this particular instance, the objects of refutation are the phenomena that appear and the phenomena that apprehend such appearances. Within awareness itself, neither the appearing phenomena (the objects of actions) nor the apprehending phenomena (the subjects of such actions) are to be found. Given the fact that awareness thus transcends all effort and achieving, the root text repeatedly insists that one should not make effort, trying to achieve it.

Everything in phenomenal existence, samsara and nirvana, is already—and primordially—free and open within the ultimate expanse. However much effort one may make to achieve such a state, whether through acceptance or rejection, affirmation or negation, it is all pointless.

"Do not do it! Do not do it!" Longchenpa tells us. And what is it that we should not do? We should not make effort trying to achieve it. And why? Because both the object of effort and the act of effortful achieving have no existence. Awareness, the state of equality beyond all mental elaboration, transcends both the object of effort and the action of making effort. Like space, it is primordially open and free.

"Do not watch them! Do not watch them!" And what is it that we shouldn't watch? It is our thoughts, the phenomena of our intellect. And why? Because awareness is beyond both the object and the agent of watching. It is the bare state of primordial openness and freedom.

"Do not meditate! Do not meditate!" What is it that we should not meditate on? We should not meditate on mental objects. And why? Because awareness is beyond both the object of meditation and the meditating mind. Free of both an object and an agent of meditation, awareness is free and open from the very first. It is the dharmatā, primordially pure and free of the investigating intellect. It is the state of equality, the state of spontaneous great perfection.

"Do not investigate! Do not investigate! And what is it that we should not investigate? We should not investigate the sense objects that appear to our apprehending minds. And why? Because neither the objects of the senses nor the mind have ever truly existed. In themselves, they are primordially open and free. They are devoid of change and movement in the vast expanse of all-pervading awareness.

"Do not labor! Do not labor!" And what is it that we should not labor at? We should not labor at trying to achieve the result with expectation and fear. Why is this? It is because the result is, from the very beginning, already achieved—uncontrived, spontaneous, and self-arisen. We should therefore settle in the natural state, in equality, without hope or fear—without hoping to achieve the result or fearing not to achieve it.

"Do not reject! Do not reject!" And what is that we should not reject? We should not reject either defilements or activities. And why? Because within awareness, neither defilements nor activities, good or bad, have ever existed. They are primordially open and free and have never fallen outside the one sole sphere.

"Do not adopt! Do not adopt!" And what is it that we should not adopt? We should not adopt the phenomena that we think are pure. And why? Because in awareness, the distinctive features of object and agent—that is, the pure phenomena that are the objects of adoption and the adopting mind have no existence. They are primordially open and free and never stray from the state of purity and equality.

"Do not fetter! Do not fetter!" And what is it that we should not fetter? We should not fetter our mind streams. And why? Because in awareness, objects of fettering (the objects of apprehension) and fettering agents (apprehending minds) have never truly existed. They are primordially open and free within the one sole sphere. It is said in *Awareness Self-Arisen*,

From things both existent and nonexistent it is free,
Unstained by grasped-at objects and by grasping minds.

There are indeed many such specifications, but in sum it is as we find in *The Lion's Perfect Power*,

There's no delusion and no absence of delusion
In awareness of the Great Perfection.
Thoughts in the minds of beings,
Words and scriptures cannot indicate it.
It comes to just the three points of instruction.

With regard to the fact that there is neither delusion nor the absence of delusion in the nature of awareness, if all the key points are brought together, they come down to three essential points of instruction—by which is meant the ultimate nature, luminous character, and cognizant potency. The same tantra continues,

The vision of the dharmakāya, awareness self-cognizing,
Is not to be beheld by watching.
It comes down to the threefold way
Of leaving as it is.

Because the nature of awareness is beyond both the object and the agent of watching, it cannot be beheld by watching. It can only be realized through the three ways of leaving as it is. When, through the unceasing creative power of the cognizant potency of awareness, appearances arise as outer objects, all such appearances should be simply disregarded and one should rest in naked awareness. This is referred to as "leaving outer appearance as it is." When any good or bad thoughts, the three or five poisons and so on, arise in the inner mind, they should be disregarded and one should rest naturally and without contrivance in naked awareness. This is called "leaving inner movement as it is." And if self-aware, self-knowing cognizance is stripped to its nakedness and its power brought forth, this same awareness, in which there is no boundary between outside and inside, arises as the one sole dharmatā. This is called "leaving secret awareness as it is."

The key points of action or conduct related to the Great Perfection are described in *The Lion's Perfect Power* as follows,

> The unimpeded conduct of the Great Perfection
> Does not happen through intentioned action.
> It comes down to the absence of attachment
> And threefold natural openness and freedom.

Since the action or conduct of the Great Perfection, which is unimpeded, open, and free, is not a matter of deliberate performance, this means that the conduct of nonaction must be free of attachment and endowed with the three key points of natural openness and freedom. When, without accepting or rejecting whatever appearances arise, one rests nakedly in awareness itself, these same appearances will be open and free intrinsically—where they stand. This is the naked openness and freedom of appearance. Whatever thoughts may stir, they naturally vanish all by themselves, in the same way that a knot made on a snake comes undone all by itself. This is the natural openness and freedom of inner movement. And since, in the absence of all contrivance, awareness is open and free from the very beginning, awareness is itself the state of primordial openness and freedom.

In the same vein, *The Lion's Perfect Power* describes the key points of the habituation to the view of the Great Perfection as follows:

> Habituation to the view of Great Perfection
> Is present from the very start.
> It does not come about through growing used to it.
> It comes down to the four unmoving, thought-free aspects.

Habituation to the view of the Great Perfection requires four decisive, primordial states of familiarity. These are, first, the state in which there is no clinging to outer appearances; second, the state in which there is no stirring of the inner mind; third, the state where there is no fixation upon secret awareness; and fourth, the state of never leaving the condition of suchness.

The key points of the realization of the meaning of the Great Perfection are again described in *The Lion's Perfect Power*:

> Two points of the Great Perfection
> Are difficult to realize.
> They are not found through mere description
> But come down to the two essential secret points
> Of the instruction.

These two essential and secret points of instruction, in which the mind is considered as luminosity, are as follows. When the mind is still, one should recognize it as open and unimpeded awareness. When the mind is in movement, one should recognize it also as open and unimpeded awareness.

The key point of the ultimate reach of awareness in the Great Perfection is described in *The Lion's Perfect Power* as follows:

> According to the Great Perfection,
> Awareness is beyond all ordinary cognition.
> Not through meditation is it realized.
> It comes down to one great final point.

As this text says, the one final point of the natural state of awareness, which is beyond the state of ordinary cognition, is the self-arisen, naked, unadulterated awareness experienced in the practice of trekchö.

The same tantra speaks further about the definitive key points of the profound, fundamental nature of awareness in the following terms:

> The self-arisen primordial wisdom of the Great Perfection
> Is not accomplished through practice,
> But comes down to two definitive essential points.

These two definitive essential points of spontaneously present awareness are its ultimate nature of primordial purity and its character of spontaneous presence. It is thanks to them that awareness transcends the two extremes of permanence and discontinuity and is definitively revealed as nakedly open and unimpeded.

Now regarding the key points of the result of the Great Perfection, the same text says,

> The Great Perfection's definitive result
> Is not perfected through its being brought forth.
> It comes down to three essential pith instructions
> On freedom from attachment.

These three pith instructions, which concern the result that is free from attachment and is spontaneously present, are as follows. The ultimate nature of awareness is empty like space. Its character is naturally luminous. In other words, awareness is endowed with luminosity. Its cognizant power ceaselessly arises.

There are five key points thanks to which the thoughts associated with the five poisons, as they arise for yogis of the Great Perfection, subside on meeting with their objects. This is again described in *The Lion's Perfect Power*:

> In the Great Perfection,
> The appearances encountered
> Have no hold upon the yogi.
> All comes down to the five purities.

When the five objects of sense are encountered, if thoughts marked by the five poisons become engrossed with them, one accumulates karma as ordinary beings do and one will be reborn in the lower destinies. But if naked and free awareness manifests in the encounter of thoughts of the five poisons with the objects of sense, these same five poisons will subside and will appear as the five primordial wisdoms. This is referred to as the five key points whereby the encounter [of thoughts with sense objects] dissipates there and then.

The Lion's Perfect Power goes on to describe the six kinds of limpidity associated with the empty and luminous state.

> If there is attachment to the luminous radiance,
> Free of ordinary cognition, of the Great Perfection,
> The ultimate will not be realized.
> This comes down to the six aspects of being.

When the limpid awareness, free of ordinary cognition, of the Great Perfection manifests, if one fixes on it and becomes attached to it, one will fail to realize the ultimate, fundamental nature. On the other hand, the crucial points for [the gaining of] this realization consist in six kinds of limpidity, or rather the six ways of being of the empty and luminous state. It is important to possess them and they are as follows. Because [the fundamental nature] is a state that is primordially empty, there is no unfolding or dissolving of thought. Because it is naturally empty, it rests in its natural condition. Because it is luminous at the same time as being empty, the appearance of sense objects is unceasing. Because it is intrinsically empty, it does not stir from its own state. Because it is empty of existence, it cannot be detected as a real thing endowed with characteristics. Because it is empty of nonexistence, it subsists in the state of ceaseless, limpid awareness. The possession of these six points is of great significance.

Likewise, there are eight ultimate key points that concern the final level of the exhaustion of phenomena. *The Lion's Perfect Power* has this to say:

> The aspects of the Great Perfection
> Come to their ending in the ground.

> Investigation does not bring you to this final point.
> It all comes down to eights ways of non-clinging.

All the aspects of the ground, path, and result of the Great Perfection come to an end in the ground of primordial purity, the expanse of the exhaustion of phenomena. This concluding point of the Great Perfection is not to be reached through rational investigation. Instead, one must realize the eight ultimate key points of non-clinging. This means to refrain from clinging to existence, to nonexistence, to appearances, to emptiness, to samsara, to nirvana, to bondage, and to freedom. By such means, one is brought to the vast expanse, free of all such extreme positions—to the primordial purity of the level of the exhaustion of phenomena, wherein not even the names of such phenomena exist.

Similarly, in the tradition of the Great Perfection, all appearances are understood to be the three mandalas and are thus beyond both acceptance and rejection. *The Lion's Perfect Power* says,

> The Great Perfection's five unchanging paths
> Are not traversed by dint of training.
> They come down to the three mandalas.

The five unchanging paths of the Great Perfection are primordially and at once perfectly complete within awareness. They are not to be traversed by diligent training in the present moment. They all come down to the realization that all appearances are the three mandalas. Visual appearances are the mandala of the enlightened body, sounds are the mandala of enlightened speech, and states of mind are the mandala of the enlightened mind. Thanks to this understanding, and in the absence of acceptance and rejection, whatever manifests is simply awareness itself.

There exist twenty-one skillful methods for introducing the nature of the mind, arranged according to the superior, average, and basic capacities of the practitioners of the Great Perfection. *The Lion's Perfect Power* says,

The Great Perfection's fruit, intrinsically pure,
Is not achieved through practice.
It all comes down to one and twenty skillful means.

And we find in *The Tantra Adorned with Introductions to the Nature of the Mind*,

According to capacity of mind,
Twenty-one methods are arranged.
By seven introductions to light and to primordial wisdom,
Seven kinds of beings of least capacity are freed.
Seven introductions to the kāyas and disks of light
Are for seven kinds of beings of medium capacity.
Seven introductions to awareness and the ultimate expanse
Are for those of great capacity.

As this text says, the seven kinds of introduction to the nature of the mind by means of light and through primordial wisdom are designed for persons of lesser capacity of mind. Seven skillful methods of introduction to the nature of the mind related to the kāyas and disks of light are taught as ways to introduce beings of medium capacity. Finally, seven skillful methods related to awareness and the ultimate expanse are taught as ways of introduction for beings of highest capacity. In short, twenty-one ways of introducing the nature of the mind are set forth, but for their details, other texts should be consulted.

There then follow three kinds of mastery. *The Lion's Perfect Power* says,

The Great Perfection is the essence of the Secret Mantra.
It is not achieved through making offerings
But comes down to three kinds of mastery.

Mastered appearances are [illustrated] by the eight examples of illusion. The mind, when mastered, is traceless in its natural vanishing. It is like the movement of a breeze in the air. Awareness, when mastered, is open, unimpeded, and empty like space.

The same scripture goes on to describe three kinds of essence.

> The Great Perfection is primordial wisdom, emptiness.
> Awareness self-cognizing is not seen by thinking.
> It all comes down to the three essences of doctrine.

The three essences are, first, the empty essence of naked, primordial openness and freedom; second, the luminous essence of naked, natural openness and freedom; and third, the unceasing essence of naked, ever-present openness and freedom.

The same scripture also speaks of the three visions.

> The Great Perfection's natural luminosity
> Is not seen through its being granted.
> It comes down to the ultimate three visions.

These three visions are, first, the vision of the radiance of awareness that is the vision of the five lights; second, the vision of awareness that is the vision of pristine limpidity; and the vision of the fundamental nature that is the vision of the exhaustion of phenomena beyond all apprehending and clinging.

In like manner, the five paths linked with the four visions of spontaneous presence, which in the present context of trekchö are presented in reverse order [as compared with thögal], indicate the experiences of the five primordial wisdoms. When awareness, the path of the primordial wisdom of the dharmadhātu—one's own bare nature free of mental elaboration—is directly realized, the dharmatā, the final object of realization, is also actualized. This is the vision of the exhaustion of phenomena in the dharmatā.

When familiarity with this is gained, awareness (which can arise as anything at all and is the path of mirrorlike primordial wisdom) reaches its climax. Henceforth, one no longer falls away from the limpid state of self-cognizing awareness free of all delimitation and extremes. This is the vision of the climax of awareness.

Further, familiarity with it brings the realization of the equality of samsara and nirvana. The meditative experiences of the path of primordial wisdom of equality successively intensify. This is the vision of the intensification of experiences.

Through yet further familiarity, there occurs a freedom from all clinging to, and fixation on, experiences. This is the path of all-perceiving wisdom together with the ceaseless arising of the kāyas and wisdoms, the self-experience of awareness. The final attributes of the result are actualized, and this is called the vision of the direct perception of the dharmatā.[103]

In the trekchö context, the order of the four visions is the reverse of that found in thögal. On this point, Vimalamitra says,

> They lead in reverse order
> To self-cognizing awareness, the original ground.

* * *

The eighth section shows that at the moment of realization, there arises a certainty free of doubt regarding the exhaustion of phenomena wherein not even their names remain.

> **8. All things break down together;**
> **No "object" is there found in anything.**
> **There is no plan of action and there's nothing to be done.**
> **No conceptual target is there to identify.**
> **The ground breaks down, the path breaks down,**
> **And the result breaks down.**
> **Excellence and defects, deviation and decline—**
> **The slightest trace of these cannot be found.**
> **All is even, utterly without existence,**
> **Nonexistent from the first—**

Phenomenal existence is reduced to nothing.
Samsara and nirvana both break down.
They're nonexistent in the ultimate expanse.
So what is there and what is going on?
There is nothing to be pointed out by saying "It is this."
So what is "you" and where indeed is "I"?
These are but traces of a past that is no more.
And who is there who might do anything about it?
Ha ha! It's so amazing that it makes me laugh!

Yogis who reach the state of the exhaustion of phenomena beyond the mind have a direct realization that everything in phenomenal existence, the world and the beings it contains, is without true existence. For them, the appearances, which we cling to as real, break apart all together. There is nothing objective in anything that appears to the six consciousnesses, nothing that can constitute an objective reference to be clung to and fixated upon. For them there is no change or stirring from the great expanse of primordial purity, which is like the vast abyss of immaculate space.

At that point, there is neither virtue nor sin, neither good nor bad, neither acceptance nor rejection—no plan of action for any kind of concerted effort.[104] There is no ambition; there is nothing that one would like to achieve. All concepts, all things to be done recede into awareness, the expanse of primordial purity. Nothing can be identified; all is unimpeded openness. The "view beyond conceptual extremes," which is itself based on a mental construction—in other words, the ground that hitherto had been intellectually trusted and relied upon—breaks down. For awareness, free of concepts and extremes, beyond both indication and expression, is now manifest.

Calm abiding with its focused mind, a meditation in which there is fixation on conceptual extremes and so on—in other words, the path endowed with mental fabrication—breaks down. For the dharmatā, self-arisen primordial wisdom, the state of equality beyond conceptual elaboration, has been stripped to its nakedness.

Since there is nothing to accomplish in the sense of a goal based on dualistic perception, the putative result, the object of hope and fear, breaks down. The four kāyas, the five wisdoms, and so on, which are the actual result, awareness in its fundamental stratum, are actualized, and serenity of mind arises from within.

Since good and bad, excellence and defects are perceived no more, one is delivered from danger, from faults like deviation, straying, error, and decline. Not the slightest trace of hope or fear regarding the result can be found. The ultimate result of primordial purity has been actualized.

Subject and object, the mind and appearances, cannot be divided. They are an all-pervading space of evenness, equality. All phenomena are utterly nonexistent. They are of one taste in the expanse of vivid, clear, yet nonexistent awareness. Hallucinatory appearances do not exist; they have never existed from the very first. And when one sounds the depths of the primordial unreality of all phenomena and gains a clear certainty that they are but nonexistent yet clear appearances, that they are insubstantial and evanescent optical illusions, phenomenal existence is reduced to nothing.

In awareness, the dharmadhātu, the expanse of ultimate reality, the appearances of samsara and nirvana all break down. They are as one with all-pervading dharmadhātu, the state of equality. Everything is therefore but the open and unimpeded state of awareness, the dharmadhātu. There is not even the slightest suspicion that something other than the dharmadhātu could be found, for all is groundless and rootless.

So what is there? What is going on? There is nothing to be indicated with the words "It is this." There is but a single immensity, devoid of all points of reference, a vast expanse of all-pervading awareness.

Since there are no objects to be apprehended in what appears outwardly, there is the realization of an outer emptiness. Since in what cognizes inwardly there is no apprehending mind, there is the realization of an inner emptiness. And what, Longchenpa exclaims, is meant by "you" and so on? For it is certain that all the things that appear distinct and separate from himself are nothing other than the self-experience of his own mind. All these things are but nonexistent yet appearing forms that appear to him. "What am I to do,"[105] he says, "but sit back and watch this wondrous spectacle?" All phenomena, actions and their agents, are like dreams that have been recognized as dreams. There is no clinging to them, no fixating on them. And this is actually a very pleasant experience.

The tethering stake of the inner mind—the mind that apprehends and clings to true existence—is pulled out. The rope of "I" and clinging to self is loosed. And though one may search for the stallion of open and unimpeded awareness, it is nowhere to be found. And so, Longchenpa asks, "Where is my 'I'?" The self that allows him to say "I" is nowhere to be found. Even the location or dwelling place of such an "I" is groundless and rootless. It has simply vanished into emptiness, even, pristine, and bare.

Previously, Longchenpa says, he had something marvelous to maintain: the nature of his mind, the luminous, naked dharmakāya. But now this is lost and he does not know where it went. All possible assertions such as "It is this" and "It is not that," and even the mind that watches the fundamental nature, awareness, the dharmatā, have gone. All such traces of the past cease to exist in the fundamental stratum of the dharmatā. And who is there who can do anything about it? As he watches outer appearances, he sees that they are open and unimpeded, that they are evanescent, insubstantial, fluid, and that they fall neither into the extreme of being nor into that of nonbeing. As Longchenpa watches the fundamental stratum of the inner mind, self-cognizing awareness, it vanishes into even, pristine, bare emptiness—divisionless, clear of thoughts, traceless, even. Empty by its very nature, it is nothing at all. "Ha ha," he cries, bursting into laughter at the great wonder of such an intense experience of the dharmatā. The meaning of his laughter, moreover, is explained in the commentary on the twelve vajra laughters.[106]

* * *

The ninth section shows that because, at that moment, thoughts arise without ensnaring one, they are spontaneously present as the display of the self-experience of dharmatā.

9. The delusion of phenomenal existence,
The world together with the beings it contains, breaks down.
Day and night clear naturally away, primordially away;
Into space, they clear away.
Days and dates are cleared away;
Years and months, whole kalpas, clear away.
One is cleared and all is cleared away;
Virtue and nonvirtue are all cleared away.
Samsara and nirvana, the basis of delusion,
Clear away into the ground's primordial, vast expanse.
And the so-called primordial expanse,
Convention of the ordinary mind, is likewise cleared away.
So what is to be done and what is there to strive for?
What purpose is there to pursue?
There are no ties of the desiring mind.
There is just space, a great and supreme wonder.
The nature [realized by] this beggar free of Dharma
Is like this and is nothing more!

These two stanzas, eight and nine, express the profound and secret meaning of the tantras. If these words fall upon the ears of beings endowed with fortunate karma, they will accumulate the merit and wisdom, and purify the obscurations, of entire kalpas. And certain it is that the realization of the teachers of the mind-to-mind, symbolic, and hearing transmissions of the Great Perfection will be transferred to them. Regarding these verses, therefore, I, Tenpa'i Wangchuk, beseech you to practice pure perception. Since our omniscient master composed these verses in the manner of a spontaneous vajra song, according to his own experience and realization, and since they contain words, some of which are ancient or else the uncontrived, self-arisen expressions of the Great Perfection, to unravel their essential points is not an easy matter.

According to the experience and realization of our all-knowing master, within the expanse of awareness, there is no delusion, no clinging or fixation, with regard to the appearances of phenomenal existence, the world and the beings it contains. They are broken down in awareness, the expanse of primordial purity, the dharmatā. As a result, all concepts that assume the real existence of things, as in statements like "This is a delusion; this is not a delusion" are dissipated. And everything one sees is released into the even state of open, unimpeded equality.

In awareness, open, unimpeded, and groundless, all previously held notions of day and night, of short or long duration, and so on are cleared away naturally and from the very beginning—cleared away as if into empty space. Daytime perceptions naturally clear away and there is no more apprehension of their bright vividness. Nighttime perceptions also clear away, and there is no further apprehension of their murky uncertainty. In open and unimpeded awareness, the perceptions of day and night blend together inseparably and become a state of equality.

The idea of solar days of twenty-four hours clears away into awareness, becoming a state of the even equality of the ground. The notion of lunar months and dates also clears away in the even expanse of awareness. Even the ideas of years and kalpas, which are the uninterrupted sequences of days, vanish on their own, naturally clear away, and no longer exert their entangling hold on the mind.

The idea of *one*, of individual singularity, is cleared away. It becomes groundless. Likewise that of *all*, the collectivity, is dissolved into the state beyond objective reference. No longer differentiated, spiritual and worldly experiences clear away into primordially pure awareness, stripped to its naked limpidity. Samsara, nirvana, the ground of delusion, and the ground of freedom are no more. They are cleared away into the expanse of great, primordial emptiness. Not even their names remain; they too vanish into emptiness.

Now that everything is cleared away into the primordial expanse, one may well wonder what this primordial expanse is like. But even this so-called primordial expanse is but a conventionally labeled phenomenon of the ordinary mind. And even this is cleared away into empty awareness, free of all mental elaboration, naked and unalterable. Thus there is nothing to accomplish; there is but the realm of emptiness, the buoyant impetus of the one great emptiness, the expression of the one great emptiness, the all-embracing dimension of the one great emptiness. There is nothing to strive in. There is just the range, the domain, of the dharmatā. What objectives are there to pursue? They are all exhausted. The dharmatā is like a wish-fulfilling gem whereby all desires are fulfilled. All the ties of the desiring mind have now been exhausted in the primordial purity, the expanse of the one sole sphere. There is but the one, wondrous, fundamental nature, that marvel similar to space immaculate and free of stain. The great omniscient Longchenpa concludes by declaring that if he, a beggar without Dharma,[107] is to describe his realization of the profound, fundamental nature in precise terms without concealing anything, then what he has said [in this and the previous stanza] is exactly how it is.

* * *

The tenth section shows in conclusion that awareness abides in the citadel of phenomenal exhaustion and is therefore changeless and unmoving throughout the passage of time.

> **10. The precious foundation is the citadel of space.**
> **It is without support; it's free and open from the very first**

And present of itself within awareness.
The three worlds of existence,
The world and all the beings it contains,
Are therefore open and free in that great state
That is devoid of all objective reference.

All outer and inner phenomena, the universe and the beings it contains, are beyond arising, abiding, and ceasing. They are beyond the eight conceptual extremes. Thus the precious foundation of the supporting universe with its mountain ranges, cliffs, houses, and so on, together with all that it supports—namely, the beings of the three worlds—is empty. It has no existence whatever and is referred to as the citadel of space.

This emptiness is not a mere void. Its luminous character is made manifest in the form of empty reflections, which appear and yet do not exist. This unceasing luminosity is referred to as the citadel of jewels. In truth, both these citadels are baseless and primordially open and free. They are spontaneously present in the naked state of self-arisen awareness, and this is referred to as the vajra citadel of the one sole sphere of awareness.

In very truth, therefore, the appearances of the three worlds of existence, the universe and beings, are primordially open and free in the great, bare, unimpeded state devoid of objective reference. None exceeds the confines of the vajra citadel, the one sole sphere of primordial openness and freedom.

The implication of this is that the ground transcends both freedom and delusion. This is set forth in a self-arisen manner in the twelve vajra laughters and the seven marvelous sovereign statements, which are contained in *The Heap of Jewels Tantra*. These seven crucial points are as follows. First, awareness transcends both good and evil. Second, there is no difference between meditation and nonmeditation. Third, there is no difference between the completion or noncompletion of the two accumulations. Fourth, there is no difference between training and failure to train on the path. Fifth, there is no difference between buddhas and beings.

Sixth, there is no difference between the realization of no-self and the belief in the reality of a self. And seventh, there is no difference between a yogi who is free of action and a person who is not so free. The meaning of these seven marvelous statements is explained in detail in *The Treasury of Teachings*, Longchenpa's autocommentary.

* * *

The eleventh section consists of advice to be rid of all that is incompatible with realization.

> **11. Those bound by taking sides where there are no such sides**
> **Do not know the nature of phenomena**
> **And by this they are damaged.**
> **They are confused, they are deluded, they are so deluded!**
> **Though there is no delusion,**
> **These beings are deluded**
> **And perceive [samsara's] great abyss.**

Phenomenal appearances in their oceanlike infinity are of one taste with the enlightened mind, awareness, which is unconfined and does not fall to one side or another. But those who fail to understand this—those who belong to the lower vehicles, together with ordinary beings and those that are deluded and foolish—apprehend and cling to self and consequently fragment the all-pervading vastness of awareness (which transcends all taking of sides) into friends and enemies, into self and other, into tenet systems, view, meditation, and so on. Bound to the apprehension of these contrasting aspects, they become powerfully deluded. They are damaged through their failure to understand that the nature of phenomena never stirs from the expanse of the one awareness, which is like space and is devoid of partiality and conceptual extremes. Not recognizing their own nature of awareness, they take it for something else. They are like people who are afraid of their own shadows. Deceived by the hallucinatory objects and subjects of apprehension, and failing to understand that awareness, the dharmakāya, is within them, they cut themselves off from all-pervading awareness. Taking as something other what is but the self-experience of their own minds, they deceive themselves and are confused. Deluded, they continue to wander in the realms of samsara, and are tormented by suffering. In the eyes of a yogi who has realized the ultimate mode of things, they are like children who are upset and cry when their sandcastles collapse. It is as Śāntideva says,

> Children can't help crying when
> Their sandcastles come tumbling down.

And Saraha remarks,

> Children find exhausting
> What for me is just a game.

As it has been said, all these hallucinatory appearances have never existed, yet beings who are bound by the apprehension of their reality suffer the hardships that arise from this. "They are so deluded!" exclaims Longchenpa.

Indeed, the hallucinations, the appearing yet nonexistent experiences of the three worlds, which have never existed and yet seem to do so, are like the clear yet insubstantial visions of one's dreams. They are taken to be inherently real, to have a self, and it is thanks to this assumption of self and this clinging to "I" that beings are deluded in their perception of the abyss of suffering that is samsara. It is a delusion whereby they are utterly worn down. It is said in *The Lion's Perfect Power*,

> The situation is not so,
> Yet beings are led astray
> By their distracting thoughts.

And,

Some are led astray by things deemed in the outer world,
Others led astray by the inner apprehender.
Some are led astray by cultivating states of concentration,
Others led astray by their activities and conduct.

And,

They do not behold primordial wisdom self-cognizing.
They take as real what is but an appearance
And do not see the face of supreme pure perception.

* * *

The twelfth section consists of advice to let go of the assumption of real existence and the fixation on it. For delusion arises from the belief in self—that is, the inherent existence of nonexistent things.

12. Delusion and the absence of delusion
Are but the vast expanse of the enlightened mind.
From the very first, in the enlightened mind,
There never was delusion nor the freedom from delusion.
You are fettered by your clinging
To what arises as enlightened mind's display.
But since there is no bondage and no freedom,
There is neither mind nor object.
Do not be misled by taking for existent
What does not exist.

Delusion, or the appearances of the three worlds of samsara, and the absence of delusion—namely, the appearances of the peace of nirvana—have never stirred from the expanse of awareness, the enlightened mind. Consequently, in the enlightened mind, the state of awareness, there has never been, from the very beginning, either bondage or freedom, delusion or freedom from delusion. The enlightened mind is a state of unimpeded openness. And though awareness has never existed, it naturally possesses a perfect capacity to manifest as anything at all. In the display that arises through its creative power, there is both samsara and nirvana, both delusion and freedom from delusion. Because one is fettered by clinging and fixation to that same creative power and display, the hallucinatory appearances of the three worlds unceasingly arise through the interplay of causes and conditions and in the manner of dreams and magical illusions. But the truth is that neither bondage nor freedom are real; neither the appearing object of apprehension nor the apprehending mind exist. They are nothing other than unaltered, open, and unimpeded awareness. Subject and object, self and other, good and bad, bondage and freedom, and so on have no reality within the nature of awareness. And yet, infected by their dualistic apprehension, beings take them as existent. Consequently, Longchenpa says, we should not allow our minds to be misled.

It is thus that all delusion comes down to the subject and object of apprehension. And when the one meets the other, it is important to implement the essential instruction so that this encounter of subject with object subsides into the objectless state.

Now generally speaking, although there are many methods in the sutras, the tantras, and the teachings of the Great Perfection whereby delusion is halted, they are all gathered into three methods. The first concerns the halting of delusion in the ground. This involves the identification of the ground of delusion as the object and subject of apprehension. When one points a finger at the face of someone whom one recognizes as a thief, he or she will be ashamed and will go away never to return—and one will feel secure in one's home. In the same way, when one realizes that the hallucinatory appearances of the subject and object of apprehension, and all their attendant thoughts, are—in this very moment and without any change to their form and color—the one sole awareness of the dharmakāya, all delusion will be halted in the ground. This means that appearances will naturally subside and come to an end. This method is a practice specific to the Great Perfection.

The second method is to halt delusion at the stage of the path. This means to carry delusion—namely, the five poisons—onto the path in the present moment, taking support of the profound path of the skillful means of the Secret Mantra.

The third method is to halt delusion at the stage of the result. This is the technique peculiar to the causal vehicle, wherein it is believed that delusion and its habitual tendencies cease when buddhahood is attained. It is like a king who is able to subdue the armies of his enemies once he has assumed control of his kingdom.

These methods differ according to the profundity or otherwise of their tenet systems and paths, which vary according to the differing skill and mental capacity of the people concerned. Those who are suited to the higher paths understand the methods of the lower paths, but the reverse is not the case. Those suited to the lower paths cannot grasp the methods of the higher paths. Therefore, since those who belong to the lower vehicles cannot accommodate the crucial points of the Natural Great Perfection, these teachings must be hidden from them. Otherwise they will be spoiled and the fault of proclaiming the secret will be incurred. So it is that *The Heap of Jewels Tantra* declares,

> Do not utter a single word of this in the presence of the śrāvakas, pratyekabuddhas, and the like. For they will be alarmed to hear such teachings. They will faint with fear. They will feel no devotion for the Secret Mantra. They will repudiate it, and the ripened effect of such a rejection will be the experience of the Great Hell. Far from your actually instructing them and their listening to you, you must not even speak of such teachings in the wind that blows in their direction.

* * *

The thirteenth section is divided into six parts and gives a detailed explanation of the importance of giving up all clinging and fixation. The first part speaks of primordial buddhahood as being unspoiled by delusion.

13a. Awareness, free and open,
Is the state of primal buddhahood.
Therefore do not snare it in the clinging and fixating
Of the trap of Dharma.
Pure in every way, it is the vast expanse
Devoid of objects of the senses from the very first.
It is the vast space of enlightenment,
The ground and root of great bliss, equal to the sky.
It is the primal nature where samsara is not possible.

Awareness in itself is primordially unstained by samsara. It is free of all mental elaboration. It is the state of buddhahood and as such is already open and free. Longchenpa's teaching here is that we should not bind or fetter it in the mind's trap—the fixating and clinging of adventitious thought. There are indeed many ways in which awareness is fettered in the trap of the Dharma. They may be summarized into ten kinds: the trap of fixating on conventional designations; the trap of stagnant nonconceptual states; the trap of fixating on concerted effort; the trap of believing in the reality of appearances; the trap of looking for a definitive truth that is outside [awareness]; the trap of apprehending the characteristics of empty forms; the trap of a conceptual view of emptiness through relying on discursive thought; the trap of idle talk about one's realization; the trap of meditation on emptiness that is like throwing a stone in the dark; and the trap of enduring suffering through missing the crucial point. If one manages to maintain the fundamental condition of awareness, unconfined by all such traps, there will be no others.

From the very beginning, awareness is inseparable from the primordially pure expanse free of sense objects, the state of spacelike emptiness endowed with supreme qualities. It is inseparable from the unaltered, open, unimpeded state free of mental elaboration. It is therefore free of all the traps of deviation and straying. This emptiness endowed with supreme qualities, this primordial purity, is from the very beginning, utterly free from the snares of delusion. Like space, it is beyond delimitation and falls into no direction or side. This empty awareness is great bliss. It is the expanse of the ultimate enlightened mind, which is groundless and rootless. This is the state of the one sole sphere, the final destiny of all phenomena. It is impossible to find within it even the name of something called samsara or the trap of delusion. This is the primordial fundamental nature.

If this nature, primordial buddhahood, is not found, one is trapped in the snare of delusion. Moreover, *The Heap of Jewels Tantra* mentions ten ways in which this happens and illustrates them with examples. They are cited by the great and omniscient master in his autocommentary, *The Treasury of Teachings*.

* * *

The second part of the thirteenth section gives advice on how to gain victory over the samsaric demon of the subject and object of apprehension.

13b. There are no edges and no corners in the one sole sphere.
To see identity or difference is the mind's delusion.
There are no causes and conditions that relate
To self-arisen primal wisdom.
To claim so is to go upon samsara's path:
It is a blockage to enlightenment.
Spontaneous presence is impartial and beyond extremes.
To think of it one-sidedly
In terms of ontological extremes
Is but the māra of conceit.

Unceasing emptiness is substanceless and has no features.
To label it existent, nonexistent, empty, or appearing
Is simply the distorted mind.
Forsake the snare, therefore, of your one-sided claims,
Knowing that spontaneous presence
Is like space; it has no partiality.

Awareness, the one sole sphere, is completely free of the edges and corners of conceptual constructs such as existence, nonexistence, both and neither, appearance and emptiness, view and meditation. Therefore, to consider that phenomena are either essentially identical or distinct, existent or nonexistent, inclusive or exclusive, and so on is nothing but a delusion of the mind. For phenomena are not outside the expanse of awareness, the one sole sphere. They are inseparable from it.

Self-arisen and self-cognizing primordial wisdom, free from mental elaboration, does not exist as anything at all. There is no way to produce it with effort and through causes and conditions. [If one were to make such an attempt,] straying into samsara and the pathways of samsara, and if one were to hold that hallucinatory appearances exist in one's mind, this is an obstacle that prevents the realization of the dharmatā, the state of great enlightenment.

Awareness, self-arisen spontaneous presence, is primordial wisdom, and this is free of partial one-sidedness and of all ontological extremes. To view it one-sidedly, to take an extreme position declaring it to be existent, nonexistent, both or neither, and so on has the effect of veiling the state of freedom from conceptual elaboration with the adventitious thoughts of the ordinary mind. It means straying into the web of different kinds of mental elaboration. In brief, all ideas, expressions, concepts, and beliefs are simply fallacious thought. They are what is known as the māra of conceit.

The term *mara*, or "demon," should be understood as meaning all the factors that are to be eliminated and from which one has not been freed. The māra is ignorance and deluded thoughts together with dualistic perception. It is defined as that which prevents one's liberation. Indeed, there are several categories of māra. Primarily, there are the two māras of the subject and the object of apprehension. Then, in a secondary sense, these are the māra of the aggregates (that is, of ego-clinging), the māra of death, the māra of the five poisons or defilements, and the māra child of the gods (the māra of pleasures). Then again, there are subsidiary categories corresponding to the twenty lesser defilements.[108] And if the māras are classified according to the different ways of being deluded, there are as many māras as there are innumerable mental factors, as actions in all their variety, and as defilements. Summarized, they may all be gathered into discursive thought. And if this subsides in awareness, and if one realizes awareness in all its openness and freedom, one is said to be a yogi victorious over the māras. It is said in *The Natural Openness and Freedom of Awareness*,

> If you understand that all the māras
> Are your own awareness,
> If you understand them so,
> Demonic forces then will be no more.
> They will naturally be overcome.

Moreover, in awareness, there is not even a trace of substance and characteristics. Awareness is the primordial wisdom of great emptiness and the unceasing, variegated manifestation of luminosity. To ascribe to it a one-sided extreme—existence, nonexistence, both or neither, appearance or emptiness—is nothing but the product of a distorted mind. It is the door to the darkness of samsara that impedes the realization of open, unimpeded, unaltered awareness.

If, with regard to the assertions of a one-sided tenet system, one is influenced by aversion or attachment, by thoughts of hope or fear, one will be unable to look upon the countenance of the ultimate, fundamental condition of things. All such traps should therefore be avoided, and one must understand that self-cognizing awareness is the state of spontaneous presence free of partiality. It is the state of equality—the uncontrived, naked, vast, and all-pervading expanse that like space embraces all things. As *The Great Garuda* says,

> The truth of dharmatā is veiled
> By focusing the mind,
> By alterations to one's body and one's speech.
> What greater antidote is there than this?

If one effortfully manipulates one's body and speech, and if one's mind falls under the influence of concepts and grasping, this will have the effect of veiling the dharmatā. Therefore without any grasping and conceptual activity, one should nakedly watch the face of awareness, the dharmakāya. There is no greater remedy for one's effortful striving and grasping.

* * *

The third part of the thirteenth section advises us to be convinced of the expanse of dharmatā, the enlightened mind.

> **13c. Whatever may arise in the six consciousnesses—**
> **Sights seen, sounds heard, and all the rest—**
> **They are the vast expanse of luminosity,**
> **Beyond all differentiation.**
> **They are the vast expanse, primordially free and open, of equality.**
> **Be utterly convinced of this!**

All the perceptions of the six sense consciousnesses, which manifest in the form of outwardly occurring objects—appearances seen, sounds heard, and so on—are the creative power and display of self-cognizing awareness, which is empty, luminous, and unceasing.

And given that the creative power and display of the one awareness cannot be differentiated as good or bad, they are but the unborn expanse of the dharmadhātu, which is beyond the range of thought or word. As it is said in *The Lion's Perfect Power*,

> I am beyond all talk of emptiness.
> In me there is no element of obscuration.
> I am the great and self-appearing light.

The meaning here is that since "I"—the all-creating king—am the state of freedom from mental elaboration, and fall into neither the extreme of appearance nor that of emptiness, I am devoid, or beyond, all talk of emptiness. Since I am the self-appearing light of luminous self-cognizing awareness, I am free of all the obscuring factors of ignorance. The text continues,

> Since within me nothing is contrived,
> I am, from the outset, free from birth . . .
> Since no conceptual extreme is found in me,
> I am not something, neither am I nothing.

Awareness, the all-creating king, self-arisen primordial wisdom, is like space. It is free of mental elaboration. It transcends all action and striving. It is primordially free of birth. And being free of the extremes typified by discursive thought, it is beyond phenomena, which are taken to be either something or nothing, either existent or nonexistent.

The phenomena of samsara and nirvana do not suddenly become open and free at the moment when in one's meditation, one realizes that they are empty. They are open and free from the very beginning. One should be completely convinced that they are nothing but the primordially open and free expanse of equality, awareness, the dharmadhātu.

Awareness, self-arisen primordial wisdom, the state of the exhaustion of phenomena, where not even the names of things remain, is the one sole sphere [of the dharmakāya]. To be convinced and clearly certain of this is a vitally important point.

* * *

The fourth part of the thirteenth section supplies general explanations of the terms "ultimate expanse," "ground," "vast expanse," and "enlightened mind."

> **13d. [Awareness] is the ultimate expanse,**
> **For all appearances occur**
> **Within this one state of equality.**
> **It is the ground, for it gives rise to every excellence.**
> **It is the vast expanse,**
> **For in it all arises naturally**
> **Free of differentiation.**
> **It is the enlightened mind, for it arises**
> **As the essence of everything that manifests.**
> **Understand that, like space,**
> **It is pure from the beginning.**

Since all appearances of samsara and nirvana arise within self-arisen awareness, which is the immensely vast expanse of emptiness and the single state of equality, it follows that awareness may also be called the ultimate expanse in the sense that it is their ground of arising. Moreover, awareness, the primordial wisdom of the dharmadhātu, may arise as anything at all, even though it has no existence whatever. Since it causes manifold appearances to arise, and reveals them clearly, limpidly, and without ceasing, it is also referred to as the ultimate enlightened mind. It is as *The All-Creating King* says,

> Since I reveal all things without exception,
> Ceaselessly and clearly,
> I am called the enlightened mind.

Because awareness, the dharmadhātu, gives rise to all the excellent qualities of precious spontaneous presence without exception, it acts as their foundation and is therefore referred to as their ground. Just as the earth is the basis and foundation of all things both animate and inanimate, awareness, the dharmadhātu, is the ground that gives rise to everything.

Because all phenomena are the creative power and display of the one self-arisen awareness, and because the creative power and display are not different from this same self-arisen awareness, it is impossible to make a qualitative distinction between them, saying that one is good and other bad. For they do not go beyond the vast expanse of the one sole sphere of primordial purity. All phenomena are thus a single, sole awareness, the dharmatā. As *The All-Creating King* says,

> All the teachers are the dharmatā,
> And all the teachings are the dharmatā.
> Time, place, retinue are all the dharmatā.
> There is not a single thing that is not dharmatā.

So it is that even the five perfections of place, time, teacher, teaching, and retinue are awareness, the enlightened mind. As *The All-Creating King* declares,

> I am the very heart of all that manifests.
> It is in the enlightened mind
> That the three teachers manifest
> And also the three kinds of teaching,
> Their retinues, their places, and their times.
> The enlightened mind is thus set forth
> As the very heart of all that manifests.

Since awareness, the enlightened mind, is, so to speak, the very heart or essence of all that manifests in both samsara and nirvana, it is within that same awareness that there arise three teachers: the dharmakāya, the sambhogakāya, and the nirmāṇakāya. Three kinds of teaching likewise appear within it. First, there is the outer expository causal vehicle of the vinaya, the sutras, and the abhidharma. This is the threefold outer vehicle that leads beings away from the origin of suffering and is the teaching of the nirmāṇakāya. Second, there are the Kriyā, Ubhaya, and Yoga tantras, which constitute the inner vehicle of knowledge through ascetic practice and are the teachings of the sambhogakāya. Finally, there are the Mahā, Anu, and Ati yogas, which constitute the secret vehicle of mastery through skillful means and are the teachings of the dharmakāya. And since, together with their associated retinues, places, and times, they manifest within the enlightened mind, the latter is referred to as the essence or heart of all things.

Regarding the three kinds of retinue, that of the nirmāṇakāya is fourfold: the fully ordained monks and nuns and the male and female lay practitioners. The sambhogakāya retinue consists of the bodhisattvas dwelling on the ten grounds of realization, while the dharmakāya retinue refers to all the phenomena that arise as the infinite display of the dharmatā and the five primordial wisdoms and so forth.

As for the three kinds of place, the location of the dharmakāya is the ultimate Akaniṣṭha, which is the inconceivable and inexpressible dharmadhātu. The place of the sambhogakāya comprises the fields of the five enlightened families, together with the "multistoried mansion of Akaniṣṭha"—namely, the fields that are half nirmāṇakāya and half sambhogakāya. Finally, the location of the nirmāṇakāya corresponds to the Vulture Peak and various other places.

The three times are first, the inexpressible time of the dharmakāya; second, the continuous wheel of luminosity and purity, the time of the sambhogakāya; and third, all the moments when the conditions come together for the appearance of the Dharma teachings and which is the time of the nirmāṇakāya.

The ground, therefore, from which all phenomena arise is the precious ultimate enlightened mind. And since the latter manifests as the essence or heart of all phenomena, these same phenomena are also the ultimate enlightened mind. As *The All-Creating King* declares,

> I am the essence,
> The essence of all things.

So it is that one should understand the ultimate enlightened mind to be like space, primordially pure. It is free of all mental elaboration. It does not exist in any way and is, from the very first, free of every obscuration.

* * *

The fifth part of the thirteenth section gives a specific explanation of the term "enlightened mind" or, more precisely, "the pure and all-encompassing mind."

> **13e. Primordial wisdom self-arisen,**
> **The ground's immense expanse,**
> **Is pure in being primordially unstained,**
> **Untainted by samsara.**
> **It is all-encompassing, for all its qualities**
> **Are present of themselves therein,**
> **Transcending causes and effects.**
> **And it is mind—awareness self-cognizing,**
> **The essence of pure luminosity.**
> **In this mind that's pure and all-encompassing,**
> **All things are gathered, all completely pure.**

Self-arisen, self-cognizing primordial wisdom knows no limit and falls neither to one side nor another. It is the vast expanse of the ground that pervades the whole of samsara and nirvana. This is the so-called "enlightened mind," or more precisely the "pure and all-encompassing mind" (*byang chub kyi sems*). Why is it so called?

Self-arisen, self-cognizing primordial wisdom is, from the very beginning, completely pure. It is free of the obscurations of both defilement and conceptual cognition. It is totally free from the stains of samsara and is wholly untainted by its hallucinatory perceptions. It is open and free in itself, and for this reason, it is said to be pure (*byang*). As it is said in *The All-Creating King*,

> This then is the sense of "pure."
> The essence, the enlightened mind,
> Is completely pure primordial self-arisen wisdom.
> And all that the all-creating king creates
> Is completely pure within Samantabhadra.
> This same enlightened mind, therefore,
> Is thus described as pure.

Within self-cognizing primordial wisdom, all qualities are completely and primordially present. All the appearances of the kāyas and wisdoms are uncontrived and thus are self-arisen—which is to say, spontaneously present. Therefore, self-cognizing primordial wisdom is that which makes them arise. These same qualities do not depend on effortful striving in terms of cause and effect. They are completely encompassed by a state that is utterly beyond the exertion of practice. For this reason, primordial wisdom is said to be encompassing (*chub*). As we find in *The All-Creating King*,

> The meaning of "encompassing" is this.
> The essence, primal wisdom self-arisen,
> Encompasses all things, pervading them—
> All phenomena and living beings,
> All that's gathered in the world and its inhabitants,
> As well as all the buddhas past, present, and to come,
> With the six kinds of beings who dwell in the three worlds,
> And finally their suchness.
> Primordial wisdom thus is said to be "encompassing."

In brief, since appearance and emptiness, the world and its inhabitants, buddhas and beings, are wholly encompassed by, and completely included within, the one expanse of awareness, the latter is said to be "encompassing."

Primordial wisdom, the essence of self-cognizing awareness, does not fall into a one-sided state of emptiness. It is present as an all-pervading cognizant potency. It therefore pervades the whole of samsara and nirvana and has the character of pure luminosity. And since this self-cognizing primordial wisdom—this self-aware, self-knowing cognizance—is a state of unobstructed openness, it is called "mind" (*sems*). As *The All-Creating King* says,

> The meaning of "mind" is this.
> Primordial wisdom self-arisen is the essence.
> It permeates, controls, and clearly knows
> Phenomena and living beings,
> The worlds and all that lives in them.
> Therefore it is called the "mind."

In awareness, in the pure and all-encompassing (or enlightened) mind, all the phenomena of samsara and nirvana are gathered in the manner of a single, nondual state of union. Therein, they are completely pure and primordially unstained by any kind of impurity. This mind, the ultimate enlightened mind, must be understood as being self-cognizing primordial wisdom, whereas the ordinary mind of distinct cognitive acts, as well as all mental factors, arise as the impure display of that same primordial wisdom and are therefore hallucinatory. For this reason, these two minds—the enlightened mind and the ordinary mind—are mutually exclusive.

* * *

The sixth part of the thirteenth section gives a definitive and reasoned conclusion.

13f. When you realize the nature of phenomena
That arise as the display of the creative power,
There comes a sudden "re-enlightenment."
When there is no such realization, there is ignorance
And the arising of deluded consciousness.
From the universal ground unfold
Eight consciousnesses with their objects.
But no matter what display may manifest
Of worlds and their inhabitants,
It does not stray beyond
The vast expanse of the enlightened mind.
Not stirring from this mind's expanse,
Samsara and nirvana are encompassed by equality.
They are free and open in the vast space of
awareness.

The ultimate enlightened mind, self-arisen awareness, has no existence whatever. Yet it can arise as anything at all, just as with the reflections in a mirror. Therefore, whatever pure or impure appearances there may be, arising in the manner of a display through awareness's creative power, their nature is awareness, which is not established as anything at all and is free of all mental elaboration. The result of the realization of their nature, their profound fundamental condition just as it is, is that one seems to achieve enlightenment, as it were once again, through being freed suddenly [in a specific point in time] from adventitious impurity, even though there has never been a moving away from the appearing mode of awareness. By contrast, when the fundamental condition of awareness is not realized as it is, there arises, in the perception of ignorant and deluded beings, the world and its inhabitants together with the perceptions of the eight consciousnesses—even though nothing that manifests ever stirs from the state of awareness.

Within the indeterminate universal ground, which has the nature of ignorance, there unfolds the limpid consciousness of the universal ground, which is without discernment. From this there develop the five nonconceptual sense consciousnesses: the visual consciousness that sees forms by virtue of the eye, the auditive consciousness that hears sounds through the ear, and so on. There then unfolds the mental consciousness, which is of two kinds: a conceptual mental consciousness that apprehends objects and a mental consciousness that is nonconceptual, one-pointed, and does not apprehend objects. From the mental consciousness there unfolds the defiled mind—a consciousness marked by the three or five poisons, and so on. So it is that, unfolding in this way, there are eight consciousnesses together with their objects.

In short, all that arises as the display of awareness's creative power—the whole of phenomenal existence, the world and its inhabitants—never stirs from the expanse of awareness, the enlightened mind. Not stirring therefrom, all phenomena of samsara and nirvana are fully encompassed by the state of equality. They are primordially open and free in the vast expanse of that same state of equality that is awareness.

All that arises therefore as the display of creative power is awareness. It is an illusory form manifesting to oneself, appearing yet nonexistent. Awareness, present of itself, is thus the ground for the arising of anything at all. It is said in *The Necklace of Pearls*,

> The nature of the mind is like a jewel,
> For it fulfills all needs and wants.
> It is like a treasury,
> For it has everything that one might need.
> It is like a mirror,
> For all that is displayed appears therein.
> It is like a crystal orb,
> For it is clear, immaculate.

Since all qualities are naturally present within it, awareness is said to be like a jewel. Because all that one might need is naturally and effortlessly present, awareness is like a treasury. Awareness is compared to a mirror, since as the ground of manifestation, it is an unobstructed space. And it is like an orb of crystal because it is a naked state of unimpeded openness. The same text continues:

> It is like brocade,
> For it appears in great variety.
> It is like a great garuda,
> For it is free of all discursiveness.
> It is like a lion,
> For it is mastery of the view.
> It is like the ocean,
> For it is vast and deep.
> It is like the sky,
> For it is free and open by its very nature.
> It is like the earth,
> For it is all-sustaining.
> And over every sense object
> It is supremely eminent.

As this text says, in being ceaselessly vivid and various in its appearing mode, awareness is like a piece of brocade. In being free of discursive activity and in crossing the abyss of samsara, awareness is like a great garuda. Free of hope and fear, awareness is like a lion. In being limpidly clear and all-pervading, awareness is like an ocean. In being empty and not existing as a substance endowed with characteristics, it is like space. And since it is the support for all qualities, the kāyas and the wisdoms, awareness is like the earth.

* * *

The fourteenth section of the twelfth chapter gives a twofold explanation of the fundamental nature. The first part speaks of the genuine authentic nature, the unfabricated state of the fundamental condition.

14a. In the fundamental state,
Samsara and nirvana are impossible
Because this state is natural, free of fabrication.
Good and bad, adoption and rejection are
impossible therein
Because this state is natural, free of fabrication.
Gain, rejection, apprehender, apprehended are
impossible therein
Because this state is natural, free of fabrication.
Defilements of five poisons are impossible therein
Because this state is natural, free of fabrication.
Limits and extreme positions are impossible therein
Because this state is natural, free of fabrication.
Creative power and its display are impossible therein
Because this state is natural, free of fabrication.
But there is no negation of their simple labels,
For this state is natural, free of fabrication.

Although awareness in itself has no existence whatever and is the mere, naked, unimpeded open state of freedom from mental elaboration, it can arise as anything at all—and may be appraised and designated, on the conventional level, in various ways [as samsara and nirvana and so on]. But from the very beginning, in the fundamental nature of awareness itself, it is not possible to have conditioned existence—so-called samsara, which is to be abandoned, or the peace of nirvana, which is to be achieved. For awareness in its nature and fundamental condition is free of fabrication.

In the fundamental condition of awareness, there are no white, or virtuous, actions to be performed and no black, or unvirtuous, actions to be avoided. As objects of adoption and rejection they are impossible, being simply the state of naked, unimpeded openness. For awareness in its nature and fundamental condition is free of fabrication.

[In the fundamental condition of awareness,] there is, from the very beginning, no "karma and defilement" to be rejected and no buddhahood to be gained. Thus the hallucinatory appearances of subject and object of apprehension are impossible. For awareness in its nature and fundamental condition is free of fabrication.

If there is no samsara, it necessarily follows that there is no duality of apprehender and apprehended, which is the cause of samsaric wandering. And if this does not exist, there can be no such thing as the defilements of the three or five poisons. They are simply the primordial and natural pristine state of equality free of mental elaboration. For awareness in its nature and fundamental condition is free of fabrication.

From the very beginning, there is in the fundamental condition of awareness, no delimitation and no falling into any extreme. Delimitations and extremes are therefore impossible. For awareness is the one sole sphere of primordial purity. It is a natural, unfabricated state. As it is said in *The Six Expanses*,

> It is beyond the elaborations of many words and phrases.
> It is not a thing and it transcends all labeling.
> There are no buddhas and there are no beings.

And *The Word-Transcending Tantra* says,

> No one has created dharmatā.
> Pure by nature, it is freedom from elaboration.
> It lies beyond the sphere of differentiated thought.

Although awareness is itself empty and without any existence whatever, it is spontaneously present as that which causes anything at all to arise. For this reason, it is referred to as "creative power" and "display." And yet, since awareness is primordially open and free, and since its creative power is also open and free, it follows that this same creative power and its display are impossible [they cannot exist]. For awareness is the one sole sphere of Samantabhadra; it is the natural state free of fabrication.

Therefore, all the things that now appear, all arising phenomena, are like magical illusions and dreams. They are simply dependently arising appearances. As mere designations (for example the different words for buddhas and beings), they are not negated, and when one rests in the natural state, they do no harm. The reason for this is that when the fundamental nature is realized, all such appearances arise naturally and vanish naturally, subsiding all on their own. And this is also a natural state free of fabrication.

* * *

The second part of the fourteenth stanza explains why the creative power and the ground of arising are without existence, even though their labeling is not negated.

> **14b. Self-arisen primordial wisdom**
> **Is the exhaustion of phenomena,**
> **Where even names do not exist.**
> **Its creative power and all that is displayed**
> **Are but a state of groundlessness.**
> **No bondage is there and no freedom—**
> **The fundamental nature of them both**
> **Is but the natural state devoid of fabrication.**
> **"Freedom" is no more than labeling**
> **That simply fades away and leaves no trace.**
> **"All are" and "all are not," as labels, are not contradictions,**
> **For all is free and open from the very first.**
> **And this is all that one can say.**

If what is referred to as primordial wisdom is examined and investigated, it is found to be empty, to have no existence. And also its name, if one thoroughly searches for it, is empty and not found. So it is that if the name of self-arisen primordial wisdom and self-arisen primordial wisdom itself are analyzed, both are found to be simply nonexistent. Primordial wisdom is the state of the exhaustion of phenomena beyond the ordinary mind. Consequently, not only is the name not found but neither is the thing itself. There is therefore no connection between self-arisen primordial wisdom and its name, for both are nonexistent.

Therefore, if awareness has no existence, it is impossible for its creative power to exist. And if this does not exist, then whatever arises as its display does not exist either. The appearances that arise unceasingly within it are but designations and are in fact groundless and without root.

Now if there is no such thing as awareness, there is no such thing as ignorance, the absence of awareness. And if there is no such thing as ignorance, then the subject and object of apprehension, which derive from it, have no existence either. And if they do not exist, then there is no such thing as the bondage caused by the hallucinatory subject and object of apprehension. If there is no such thing as bondage, there is no such thing as freedom from bondage—there is simply the fundamental nature devoid of fabrication.

If one searches for awareness, one finds that it does not exist as anything at all. And yet it has the power to appear as anything—its mode of appearance is unceasing. When appearances manifest, they may be designated with various names, as happens with the apparitions of a magical spectacle. All the illusory beings, men and women, horses and oxen, displayed thanks to the substances and incantations of a magician—for as long as they remain uninvestigated—are things to be marveled at. In dependence on a magician, there are the magical substances and formulas, and thanks to them, the apparitions of horses, oxen, and so on occur. The different appearances are based one on the other. Similarly, because there is awareness, there is creative power, and because of creative power, a display appears—the phenomenal existence of samsara and nirvana. For as long as no investigation is made, this is what presents itself. If, however, an investigation is made, nothing is found to exist. In terms of the example, the illusory horses and oxen can be shown to be the clear appearance of something that is nonexistent. The incantation can be shown to be no more than empty, untraceable, sound. The physical body of the magician can be reduced to atoms, and his mind—by means of the argument of neither one nor many—can be established as nonexistent, a bare state beyond mental elaboration. In like manner, the display of the world and its inhabitants, the whole of samsara and nirvana, arisen through the creative power of awareness, does not exist and yet clearly appears; the creative power is an empty luminosity; and awareness is unimpeded openness, the great exhaustion of phenomena, beyond the reach of conceptual and verbal elaboration.

Therefore, if these three things (awareness, its creative power, and display) are nonexistent, there is no such thing as bondage. And if there is no bondage, then freedom from bondage is no more than a kind of label to facilitate the understanding of those who do not investigate. In effect, it fades away by itself, leaving no trace. For awareness is an unimpeded openness where phenomena are exhausted. It transcends the extremes of one and many and is beyond the reach of conceptual and verbal elaboration.

Although awareness in itself is beyond the reach of the elaborations of thought and word, nevertheless, in terms of its mode of appearance (which, while being nonexistent manifests unceasingly), it is not a contradiction to speak of these manifestations in various ways, saying that they all are or are not [such and such]. For all phenomena are said to be primordially open and free. This is all that one can say as a means to facilitate one's understanding. Indeed one may search everywhere for freedom and delusion, but nothing will be found. It is as *The King of Concentration Sutra* says,

> When a child is born,
> Its parents give to it a name.
> But even after thorough search, this name cannot be found.
> Understand that all things are like that.

And it is also said in *The Great Mother*,

> O Subhūti, phenomena are no more than nominal ascriptions. They are just adventitious names. You may

> look for them everywhere, but they do not exist, they are not found, in the inner world. They do not exist, they are not found, in the outer world. And you will not find them somewhere in between. They do not exist. They are empty by their nature.

Now we may enlarge on this topic slightly by reflecting that those who claim that appearances are the mind say that since they manifest through the creative power [of awareness], they *are* the mind. They are consciousness. But by the same logic, this would mean that if illusory horses and oxen manifest through the display of the magician's magical power, it follows that they are the magician. And if they are the magician, it follows that, when these illusory appearances dissolve, the magician would too! It would also follow that, previously, when the illusory appearances did not exist, the magician would also be nonexistent. For the illusory appearances *are* the magician! It is for such reasons that, in our tradition, the existence or nonexistence of the magician is not said to depend on the existence or nonexistence, the vanishing or otherwise, of the magical illusion. The illusion and the magician are not the same thing, and similarly, appearances and one's mind are not the same. This amounts to saying that what appears does not depend on the presence or absence of oneself, and oneself does not depend on the presence or absence of what appears. For the two are not the same.

To this it may be objected that since appearances are the display of one's awareness, it is logical to conclude that they are contingent on one's presence or absence. This however does not follow. The hallucinatory appearances that belong to beings generally do not depend on the presence or absence of individuals. When individual beings die, the mountains and so on stay behind. On the other hand, it is the display of the mountains that appeared to them as individuals that subsides in their perception. Thus the display of private perceptions depends on the presence or absence of individuals, whereas common appearances or collective perceptions are contingent on the presence or absence of the collectivity.

It may be thought that when a person no longer exists, although the mountains that figured in his or her subjective perception are no longer present to that person, nevertheless the display of the mountains does not cease to exist. The display is left behind. However, the mountains that are left behind are the appearing object in the perception of the collectivity. It is the appearance of the mountains perceived by the rest of humanity. It is not the appearance that was perceived by the dead person.

* * *

The fifteenth section of the twelfth chapter gives a detailed explanation of what primordial openness and freedom is like. It has six parts, the first of which shows that the actual ground of arising, together with its creative power, is primordially open and free.

> **15a. There is no differentiation—all is free and open**
> **In the expanse of spontaneous presence.**
> **There is no separation—all is free and open**
> **In the expanse of the one sole sphere.**
> **Anything may manifest—free and open**
> **In the expanse free of all determination.**

All appearances, outer and inner, of the world and its inhabitants, are completely free of differentiation in terms of good or bad—as things to be adopted or rejected. From the very beginning, they are free and open in the vast expanse of uncontrived spontaneous presence—namely, awareness. Awareness and all the appearances of samsara and nirvana, which manifest through its creative power, are, without any separation, free and open in the expanse of the one sole sphere of primordially empty awareness. Whatever appearances arise, pure or impure, they are all open and free in the indeterminate expanse of awareness in which phenomena come to their exhaustion.

Generally speaking, with regard to awareness, there are two ways of speaking about openness and freedom. First, awareness is open and free in the sense of being itself the state of primordial purity.

Second, awareness is the state in which phenomena are open and free, the state in which they subside.

The nature of awareness is open and free as primordial purity in the sense that it does not exist either as an existent thing or a nonthing, either as one or manifold, as existent, nonexistent, both, or neither, and so on. In the sense of being empty of substance and characteristic features, it is said, on the conventional level, that its nature is open and free as the state of primordial purity and that it is free of all the phenomena of samsara and nirvana. The truth is however that awareness is beyond being either the subject or the object—the agent or the patient—of such openness and freedom. It is simply primordial wisdom, the state of perfect equality devoid of mental elaboration.

Regarding awareness as the state in which phenomena are open and free or as the state in which they subside, the meaning is that when bare awareness is directly and nakedly realized, phenomena are released, or vanish, into a state in which they are no longer objects of reference, and there manifests only awareness stripped to its nakedness. This, however, does not mean that there is nothing to be seen, that phenomena actually go away, that they actually disappear into the state of awareness, like objects sinking into a lake. For all things (phenomena and awareness) are by their very nature groundless and rootless.

The phenomena of samsara and nirvana, which arise through the creative power of awareness, do not exist [in the way that they appear]. They are empty. And from the very first, awareness has no real existence either. Therefore, since the place of openness and freedom, the agent of openness and freedom, and that which is open and free do not exist, the state of openness and freedom itself is impossible—just as it is impossible for the child of a barren women to be drowned in the water of a mirage. The state of openness and freedom, the state of subsiding, is consequently no more than a conventional designation.

In the present context, when one speaks of bare awareness stripped to its nakedness, only three stages can be enumerated: the recognition of the nature of awareness, the maintaining of it, and the training therein. When awareness, the primordially uncontrived, spontaneous presence, free of all differentiation, is introduced, it will become nakedly manifest for yogis of the highest capacity. This is for them their final and only goal, their ultimate destination. When they recognize it, all reference points, all clinging and fixation subside in the expanse of awareness, indivisible from the one sole sphere of luminosity. And they gain confidence in a spontaneous meditative absorption that has the nature of limpid, naked awareness. There is nothing more for them to attain. This is what is meant by the recognition and maintaining of awareness. To train in this skill means simply to train oneself in the subsiding into the primordial expanse of all appearances, which are unceasingly displayed, like the reflections in a mirror, through the limpid creative power of awareness. If this training is maintained, there arises a decisive certainty that defilements—no longer to be discarded—are naturally open and free and vanish without trace all by themselves. And uncontrived primordial wisdom manifests in all its unimpeded openness. Recognition, confidence, and decisive certainty are the three nails that fix the yogi firmly in the spacious state of spontaneous presence, the great perfection that is free of action.

* * *

The second part of the fifteenth stanza states that the appearances arising as a display through the creative power of awareness are in themselves open and free within the expanse devoid of intrinsic being.

> **15b. All appearances perceived as forms**
> **Are free and open in themselves.**
> **All that resonates as sound**
> **Is free and open in itself.**
> **All that is perceived as smell**

> **Is free and open in the ultimate expanse.**
> **Experiences of taste and touch**
> **Are free and open in themselves.**
> **Thoughts and recollections, all perceptions**
> **Are all free and open—groundless, rootless, and without support.**

Everything that appears in the world, in various forms good or bad (manifesting as a display through the creative power of awareness, the dharmatā), is but empty form, nonexistent and yet clearly appearing to perception. The visual consciousness, which apprehends form, is also primordially empty. Appearances and the consciousness [that perceives them] are open and free in the empty expanse of spacelike dharmatā, devoid of all support.

In the same way, everything in the world that resonates as sound (manifesting as a display through the creative power of awareness) is but empty sound, nonexistent and yet clearly perceived. The auditive consciousness, which apprehends sound, is also primordially empty. From the very beginning, sound and the sound-apprehending consciousness have never existed. They do not have the slightest existence as phenomena with a graspable identity. For they are in themselves open and free within the expanse of empty dharmatā.

Similarly, all the good and bad odors that manifest as a display through the creative power of awareness—in short, all the sensations of smell within the world are but empty sensations, nonexistent yet clearly perceived. Even the olfactive consciousness that detects such smells is itself primordially empty. Both the smell and the consciousness of the sensation of smell have, from the very beginning, never existed. They are empty, open and free, in the ultimate expanse.

All these experiences seem truly to exist, and yet they do not exist. Furthermore, even that which seems false has no existence as a false appearance. It must be understood that no matter what appears, be it true or false, it has no existence. In the very moment that such empty forms—nonexistent and yet appearing like moons reflected in the water—are perceived within the womb of the ultimate expanse of emptiness free of all extremes, they are but nonexistent appearances, mere empty forms. No purpose at all is served in investigating them, in adopting or rejecting them, in having hopes or fears in their regard. It is as Āryadeva has said,

> Given the true nature of all that may appear,
> Refrain from its investigation.

This shows that, since all appearances are by their nature empty and beyond the reach of conceptual elaboration, one should refrain from investigating them. One should rather settle in their nature.

Likewise, the experiences of bitter and sweet tastes or of soft and rough sensations arise as a display of the creative power of awareness, the dharmatā. They manifest as appearing objects but are the empty experiences of taste and tactile sensation. They are nonexistent, yet clearly appearing, empty forms. Furthermore, the two corresponding consciousnesses that apprehend them are also, and from the very beginning, empty in themselves. In other words, both the appearances and the apprehending consciousnesses are in themselves primordially open and free. No matter how these appearances manifest, they are empty in themselves. They are beyond the categories of true or illusory existence and occur in manifold ways. They are beyond the conceptual constructs of existence, nonexistence, both, and neither. All such indeterminate and variegated appearances arise simply by virtue of dependent origination: the coming together of nonexistent and yet clearly appearing causes and conditions that arise through the creative power of awareness.

Recollections, thoughts, perceptions—none exists intrinsically. They are groundless and rootless. They are free and open in the state of primordially empty dharmatā free of all support.

* * *

The third part of the fifteenth stanza shows that all designated things are primordially open and free, for they are empty by their nature.

> **15c. All is free and open in the one sole sphere,**
> **Free and open in the space of dharmatā.**
> **Minds and objects are not two,**
> **Free and open in equality.**
> **Free and open is the self-arisen,**
> **Free and open in the space of primal wisdom.**
> **Free and open is spontaneous presence,**
> **Free and open in the ground's immaculate expanse.**

All things in phenomenal existence, samsara and nirvana, are unborn from the very beginning. Therefore, they are free and open in the one sole sphere of empty awareness beyond mental elaboration. Since there is no differentiating that which is open and free from the location of its openness and freedom, they are both open and free within the expanse of bare awareness, the dharmatā. They do not extend beyond it.

The appearing objects of the six consciousnesses as well as the consciousnesses themselves (the subjects that apprehend these objects) seem to be two separate categories and are considered in this way. Nevertheless, in their ultimate mode of being, appearances and the mind are not two, and this is so because neither the mind nor its object extends beyond the one awareness. Mind and object are open and free in nondual equality.

Self-arisen primordial wisdom, awareness, is also said to be free and open in its own expanse, which transcends delimitation and does not fall into any extreme. Here, the words of the root text speak of the great, natural openness and freedom of awareness itself. What is being referred to here as the natural openness and freedom of awareness comes down to openness and freedom in the expanse of the dharmatā, ultimate primordial wisdom, the one sole sphere that is free of all mental elaboration.

The one sole sphere of spontaneous presence is also open and free within the ultimate expanse of unimpeded openness, which lies beyond both indication and expression. The words [of the last two lines] of the stanza reveal that both the object and the agent of openness and freedom are not two. This unimpeded openness, beyond both indication and expression, is open and free within the pure expanse of the ground, which is inseparable from the ground of freedom of Samantabhadra himself.

* * *

The fourth part of the fifteenth stanza shows that the openness and freedom of the display within the dharmatā is a crucial point.

> **15d. Phenomena in their variety are free and open,**
> **Free and open in the single sole expanse.**
> **Without orientation, they are free and open,**
> **Free and open in the vast space of spontaneous presence.**
> **Everything is free and open,**
> **Free and open in the vast expanse of the quintessence.**

Outer and inner phenomena, in all their variety and in oceanlike infinity, which make up the world and its inhabitants, are free and open. For from the very beginning, phenomena are intrinsically pure, groundless, and rootless. They are open and free in the expanse of the one sole sphere from which they are inseparable. Phenomena, which manifest everywhere and without specific orientation, vanish, free and open, in the state of unborn, empty awareness. The reason for this is that such appearances, unoriented as they are, are primordially open and free in being inseparably united with uncontrived, self-arisen awareness, spontaneous presence. The oceanlike infinity of phenomenal appearances is, without exception, open and free. Appearances are open and free in the expanse of the quintessence, in other words, the ultimate enlightened mind—empty awareness, the dharmakāya, with which they are mingled in a single taste.

Sense objects, which appear outwardly, are open and free. Inwardly, the apprehending mind is also open and free. Secretly, awareness itself is also open and free. When this is realized, one sees that there cannot be a single thing that is not open and free. It is as we find in *The Necklace of Pearls*,

> When the nature of samsara has been understood,
> There's nothing else that we may call nirvana.
> When the nature of the five defilements has been
> understood,
> There is no primal wisdom to be found elsewhere.
> When sorrow's nature has been understood,
> No need is there to search for great bliss somewhere else.

If one has the level of realization spoken of in this and other texts, obscurations are purified without being abandoned, grounds and paths are attained without being striven for, the result is reached without one's ever arriving at it. All this is accomplished. If one is able to leave all that appears just as it is in its natural state—all the pure and impure objects that appear to the six consciousnesses—one will remain in the intrinsically pure, naked, natural state of uncontrived, empty but luminous awareness. This is an unerring key point of practical instruction. *The Blazing Relics Tantra* declares,

> When empowerment, complete and perfect in the ground,
> Has been received though not bestowed,
> Instruction is imparted on how to leave all things
> Just as they are within their natural state.
> Then keep the pledge of nothing to be kept,
> Which cannot be transgressed.
> It is the very wisdom mind that dwells within you.

The self-arisen ultimate empowerment of awareness is beyond both bestowing and receiving. It is perfectly complete within oneself without ever having been given. If one knows the pith instruction on leaving everything as it is in its natural condition, one is able to realize all other pith instructions. It is as if a hundred streams were gathered under a single bridge. If one recognizes that the sovereign samayas of nothing to keep and that cannot be transgressed, are present within oneself, one will penetrate the very wisdom mind of all the buddhas past, present, and to come.

For the practical instruction itself, one should simply leave whatever appears as it is, allowing it to subside in natural openness and freedom. And in becoming itself naturally open and free, it will be simply the bare vision of naked, limpid awareness. Indeed, as it is further said in *The Self-Arisen Perfection*,

> As one acquires four kinds of understanding,
> By simply leaving everything just as it is,
> One does not stir from natural openness and freedom.

The four kinds of understanding are the realization that appearances are groundless, that consciousness is devoid of objective reference, that awareness is devoid of all support, and that phenomenal exhaustion is a state where not even the names of things remain.

* * *

The fifth part of the fifteenth stanza reveals that everything, now shown to be by nature primordially open and free, is simply unwavering luminosity, pure and empty.

> **15e. Luminosity is free and open,**
> **Free and open in the vast expanse of sun and moon.**
> **Dharmatā is free and open,**
> **Free and open in the vast expanse of space.**
> **Phenomena are free and open,**

> **Free and open in the ocean's vast expanse.**
> **The immutable is free and open,**
> **Free and open in Mount Meru's vast expanse.**

The nature of the mind is primordially open and free in the expanse of luminosity. This means that awareness is not mere emptiness; its character is luminosity. For this reason, the root verse says that luminosity is free and open in the vast expanse of the sun and moon. And just as the sun and moon ride high in the sky, [the luminous vajra essence] is the summit of the nine vehicles. And just as the sun and moon dispel darkness, so too self-cognizing primordial wisdom scatters the gloom of ignorance. This is the meaning of the poetic metaphor of sun and moon.

The dharmatā is primordially free and open in the expanse of emptiness. And since awareness, from the very beginning, is devoid of zenith and nadir and of the primary and secondary directions, it is said in the root text to be free and open in the expanse of space. Space is beyond change and movement, awareness is likewise, possessing as it does the seven attributes of a vajra. Space is immaterial and intangible and awareness is exactly the same. The metaphor of space serves to indicate the naked and unimpeded openness of awareness.

Phenomenal appearances, which have arisen through the creative power of awareness, are free and open in the vast expanse of the great primordial dharmatā. Indeed, the root verse says that they are free and open in the vast expanse of the clear and pure ocean. For just as the ocean is clear and limpid, awareness is likewise the inseparable union of clarity and emptiness. And just as the waves rise within the sea, so too creative power and display arise ceaselessly within awareness. All this is indicated through the metaphor of the ocean.

Primordially unchanging awareness is free and open in the expanse that is beyond movement and change. The root verse says that it is free and open in the expanse of Mount Meru. Just as the king of mountains is unmovable and unshakable, so too awareness is the state of the unchanging and unmoving view beyond establishment and refutation. And just as Sumeru is the king of all mountains, this resultant vehicle is the sovereign of every other. This is the meaning of the metaphor.

* * *

In conclusion, the sixth part of the fifteenth stanza subsumes all phenomena into the enlightened mind, vast as space—the one dharmatā, primordial buddhahood.

> **15f. All is free and open from the very first,**
> **Free and open in the unborn vast expanse.**
> **All is free and open, all at once,**
> **Free and open in the vast expanse primordially pure.**
> **All is free and open in an utter openness and freedom,**
> **Free and open in the vast expanse primordially in flower.**

All phenomena of samsara and nirvana are free and open primordially. But what is the expanse in which they are so? They are free and open in the one sole sphere of the unborn dharmakāya, primordial wisdom pure from the beginning, where both the object and the agent of openness and freedom—are indivisible. Though some may think that this primordially pure, unborn awareness is existent, it has no existence whatsoever. It is the great emptiness of primordial purity. And though some may say that it is nonexistent, the displayed appearances of its ceaseless, luminous character are bright and vivid like the stars and planets reflected on the sea. Transcending view and meditation, awareness is an ineffable, inconceivable, inexpressible state of unimpeded openness. By whom has this been realized? It has been realized and directly perceived by a yogi skilled in the practice of the vast expanse [Longchenpa]. Without searching, he discovered it. Without practicing, he achieved it. Without watching, he saw it. And thus he won his freedom.

So it is that all things in phenomenal existence, samsara and nirvana, are all together and without exception, open and free. Now where is it that they are open and free? They are open and free in the expanse of the ground of freedom of the dharmakāya Samantabhadra, the state of buddhahood, pure (*sangs*) and in flower (*rgyas*) from the very beginning, where there is not even the name of that which is open and free nor even the location of its openness and freedom. Empty by its nature, the primordial wisdom of buddhahood is beyond the extreme of permanence. Luminous in character, it is beyond the extreme of discontinuity. And since its cognizant potency is ceaseless, it falls neither into the extreme of both permanence and discontinuity nor into the extreme of neither. Therefore it is without journeying that the kingdom of great primordial openness and freedom is reached. It is without purifying that purity is attained. It is without training that knowledge is gained and without meditating that freedom is won.

Appearances in all their variety are without exception open and free in the utter openness and freedom of their primordial purity. What is the expanse in which they are so? It is the expanse of utterly bare, naked awareness, pure and spontaneously in flower from the very first [in other words, primordial buddhahood], where both the presence and the absence of openness and freedom are inseparably united.

By what practice is freedom to be gained? It is not gained by rejecting defilements and choosing awareness. It is not gained by meditation. It is not gained by refutation, reflection, or formulation. Freedom is gained by resting in the utterly bare, naked, fundamental nature—fresh and naturally free and open.

* * *

This concludes the commentary on the twelfth chapter of *The Precious Treasury of the Dharmadhātu*, which shows that all phenomena are by their nature primordially open and free in the enlightened mind.

13. The Regaining of Buddhahood without Effortful Practice

The thirteenth chapter explains how phenomena, which as the enlightened mind are primordially the state of buddhahood, "re-become," or become again, the state of buddhahood in the absence of effortful practice. As it has already been explained, when the result endowed with the two purities becomes manifest, the immaculate gem that is the dharmatā accomplishes all that we and others may wish. And yet simply to possess a wishing gem does not suffice. If it is not polished and placed at the top of a victory banner, and if prayers are not made before it, one's wishes will not be fulfilled. In the same way, one does not accomplish the state of freedom merely through the possession of awareness. If one fails to meditate on the profound, fundamental nature, it is impossible for the result—the four kayas, the five primordial wisdoms, and so on—to manifest. Therefore, it is not enough to be primordially enlightened, it is necessary to be enlightened again, to be re-enlightened.

When, within the ground of both samsara and nirvana (the dharmadhātu free of mental elaboration), the appearances of the ground arise without their nature being recognized, one falls victim to mistaken perception and apprehends and clings to these same appearances as having a self, as being really existent. And it is through the power of this habitual tendency that the samsaric phenomena of minds and mental factors, the eight consciousnesses, the aggregates, elements, and sense fields all arise like thick clouds veiling the sun of self-cognizing primordial wisdom, rendering it invisible.

Thanks however to the pith instructions of one's teacher, these dense clouds of adventitious obscuration are removed. The orb of the sun, one's indwelling awareness, shines out, and enlightened activities are like beams of light radiating in all directions, dispelling the darkness of ignorance in the minds of beings as infinite as space is vast. Such is the result of this profound path.

This point is the subject of the following detailed exposition, which has three sections. First, there is a general explanation of the nature of enlightenment; second, there is a specific explanation of its validity; third, there is a concluding description of the actual result itself. The first section is a general explanation of the nature of enlightenment.

> **1. If, with the crucial point of freedom from exertion,**
> **You train in the spontaneous and enlightened**
> **essence of phenomena,**
> **Already buddha from the first, you will be buddha**
> **once again.**
> **This is the summit of the vajra essence unsurpassed,**
> **The heart of the nine gradual vehicles,**
> **The vast expanse of the enlightened state.**

Self-arisen awareness is the nature of all things in phenomenal existence, samsara and nirvana. It is endowed with the kāyas and primordial wisdoms, which are spontaneously present from the very beginning. It is the essence of enlightenment. It is not visible, however, for it is veiled by adventitious obscuration. There is nevertheless a means to make it manifest: the profound path of the pith instructions, whereby the three doors are left uncontrived and natural, and the primordial wisdom of great bliss is maintained without exertion. If, as a result of long training in the key points of this instruction, one is able to bring this practice to completion, the adventitious obscurations now present will be cleared away. And even though one is buddha primordially, abiding in the dharmakāya, which is awareness utterly pure by nature, one will, as it were, become buddha again. For awareness will now be freed from the adventitious obscurations, like the sun emerging from behind the clouds. Such is the full manifestation of the ultimate result.

This ultimate result is the objective pursued by all the vehicles. It is the final goal of Atiyoga, the summit of the unsurpassed vajra essence of the supreme vehicle, and is the very quintessence of the nine vehicles of the gradual path. All phenomena are of a single taste with the one sole sphere of the dharmakāya. Hallucinatory appearances, together with all deluded thoughts, are stilled in the ultimate expanse, becoming inseparable from the vast space of the ultimate enlightened mind, the inconceivable space of dharmatā. It is thus that the nondual state of equality—the crucial point more profound than the profound, the supreme and ultimate condition greater than the great, the quintessence, the distillation of the very essence—is actualized. And this is buddhahood itself.

If one actualizes primordial wisdom, in which the naturally and utterly pure dharmakāya of primal buddhahood blends with the dharmakāya, which is free from adventitious obscuration, all the appearances that have arisen through the creative power of awareness mingle inseparably, in a single taste, with the expanse of awareness. It is like water mingling with water, oil mixing with oil, space merging with space. This is the dharmakāya in its final state. It is as we find described in *The Blazing Relics*,

> Dissolving into that which is their nature,
> They become inseparable and indistinguishable—
> Like water mixed with water, oil with oil, and space with space.
> Inseparable, they are discerned no longer.

And it is said in *Drops of Nectar: A Letter of Advice*,

> Like water into water poured,
> Like oil with more oil blended,
> Knowledge objects are not separate

From the state of non-elaboration.
They merge with primal wisdom.
This is called the dharmakāya
Of all enlightened beings.

At that point, all the appearances of the kāyas and primordial wisdoms subside into the primordially and utterly pure dharmakāya of the inner ultimate expanse—into the subtle primordial wisdom of inner luminosity, absorbed within but not obscured. This is buddhahood within the ever-youthful vase body of the inner ultimate expanse.

Certain authorities consider that, at that point, the dharmakāya is devoid of primordial wisdom. But if this is so, if the dharmakāya is so deprived, one is bound to conclude that it is like space, a pure void. According to our tradition by contrast, it is said that the dharmakāya is actually present as the subtle primordial wisdom of inner luminosity, absorbed within but not obscured. It is from this that the kāyas and wisdoms manifest as outwardly radiating luminosity, just as five-colored lights appear from a crystal when it is struck by the sun's rays.

Moreover, the moon appears to increase in size from the first to the fifteenth night of the lunar month and to decrease in size from the fifteenth till the night of the new moon, when it appears to exist no longer. In truth, however, the moon's surface neither increases nor decreases, becoming full and then dwindling to nothing. Likewise, when the kāyas and wisdoms of outwardly radiating luminosity dissolve into the subtle primordial wisdom of inner luminosity, this does not mean that the primordial wisdoms cease to exist. For the five certainties of Akaniṣṭha, the buddha field of Dense Array, manifest from it as an outer luminosity. And from this there manifest the half-sambhogakāya–half-nirmāṇakāya buddha fields of the five enlightened families, which in turn give rise to the infinite buddha fields of the nirmāṇakāya.

Therefore, when the eight consciousnesses together with the main minds and mental factors cease, awareness, the ground of cessation, is actualized. This is the kāya of primordial wisdom. From this dharmakāya, the rūpakāya then appears as an outer luminosity and works for the sake of beings until the emptying of samsara. It is as *The Introduction to the Middle Way* tells us,

> The tinder[109] of phenomena is all consumed,
> And this is peace, the dharmakāya of the Conquerors.
> There is no origin and no cessation.
> The mind is stopped, the kāya manifests.[110]

The expression "The mind is stopped" refers to cessation in the expanse of the dharmakāya. "The kāya manifests" refers to the fact that when the dharmakāya manifests, one is buddha. Manifesting as the rūpakāya from within the dharmakāya, one is able to work unhindered for the benefit of beings.

* * *

The second section is a specific explanation of the validity of the result. It is divided into three parts. The first part validly establishes the elimination of the obscurations that arise owing to the fact that self-arisen primordial wisdom is veiled by the very display that arises through its own creative power. The second part validly establishes that when one is freed from the shell of the physical body, buddhahood is attained through the recognition of the dharmakāya, naturally present within oneself. The third part validly establishes that once buddhahood has been attained, the benefit of beings arises by virtue of cognizant potency. The first part is divided into four topics. The first topic of the first part of the second section describes how the obscurations that conceal primordial wisdom are purified thanks to the key point that they arise as the display of that same wisdom.

> **2a1. Like mandalas of sun and moon**
> **That clearly shine within the vault of heaven,**
> **Enlightenment resides within, though it does not appear.**

This quintessence is completely hidden
By great clouds: the lack of realization.

The buddha nature, awareness, the sugatagarbha, the luminous nature of the mind, is compared here to the bright mandalas of the sun and moon aloft in the vastness of the sky. Just as the natural light of the sun and moon annihilates the darkness, in the same way, awareness, which is by nature luminous and unstained by impurity, and is therefore comparable to the sun and moon, scatters the darkness of ignorance. Nevertheless, for as long as the fundamental nature of awareness is not realized just as it is, the outer and inner hallucinatory appearances of the world and its inhabitants arise like thick clouds. They are provoked by the apprehension of subject and object, which manifest as a display of the creative power of awareness, and completely conceal the quintessence, self-cognizing primordial wisdom, which is like the sun. This is why this quintessence is invisible and veiled from sight. And yet, because awareness, the enlightened mind, is free of both the object and the agent of obscuration, it neither waxes nor wanes. It neither swells to the full nor shrinks to nothing. In itself, it neither increases nor diminishes. This is what one fails to realize.

* * *

The second topic of the first part of the second section shows how, through the elimination of adventitious impurity, the dharmakāya, which is present within oneself, is made manifest.

2a2. The great clouds that have gathered in the sky
Vanish into space all by themselves.
So too, when without effort
Clouds of causes and effects disperse,
There naturally appears, within the vault of heaven,
[The sun,] the essence of enlightenment.
To this end, different vehicles exist
According to the level of capacity.

Great clouds gather in the sky, but there comes a time when they naturally melt away into space. Similarly, for practitioners of highest capacity, who have understood the instruction on leaving everything as it is, and whose three doors are left uncontrived and in their natural condition, the clouds of hallucinatory appearances (causes, effects, and habitual tendencies) disappear effortlessly into the dharmadhātu, the expanse of ultimate reality. For these appearances are intrinsically pure and do not need to be rejected. And just as the bright orb of the unclouded sun appears in the vastness of a clear sky, the dharmakāya, the essence of enlightenment, free of adventitious obscuration, instantly manifests in the [practitioners'] natural and unfabricated state, together with the appearances of the kāyas and wisdoms. The self-arisen dharmakāya endowed with twofold purity is spontaneously accomplished. As it is said in *The Lion's Perfect Power*,

> When not hidden by hallucinatory appearance,
> Primordial wisdom is apparent everywhere.

Generally speaking, meditation is practiced on the path according to the varying capacities of the people concerned. The ways of training are consequently many and various in accordance with the different vehicles, which are themselves the methods for purifying obscurations. The technique mentioned here is designed for practitioners of the very highest capacity. It is a profound method for purifying obscurations into their intrinsic nature without their having to be rejected. At the beginning, in the state of sentient beings, the nature of awareness, the dharmakāya, is hidden by cognitive obscurations and the obscurations arising from defilement. When practitioners are training on the path, these same obscurations are partly purified and partly unpurified. Finally, in the enlightenment of all the buddhas past, present, and to come, there is not the slightest trace of either good or bad. This can be likened to three conditions of the sun: completely hidden by clouds, then partly hidden, and then completely revealed. Yet in all these three situations, the sun itself is unaffected. In its own nature, [it is neither hidden nor exposed]; it is beyond good and bad.

* * *

The third topic of the first part of the second section shows how awareness is obscured by the display that has arisen through its own creative power.

> **2a3. Like the sun, awareness brightly shines**
> **In the expanse of dharmadhātu.**
> **And like the sun's rays, its creative power**
> **Gives rise to everything without distinction.**
> **As these rays fill with warmth the earth, the sea, and rivers,**
> **The rising vapor forms the clouds' display**
> **That veils the sun and its creative power.**
> **Likewise the face of the quintessence**
> **Is obscured by an impure display**
> **Deriving from its own creative power:**
> **An inconceivable hallucinatory array—**
> **Appearances of phenomenal existence,**
> **The world and its inhabitants.**

Awareness is like the sun shining in the sky. It is always present in the expanse of the dharmadhātu. It is luminous and empty, neither increasing nor diminishing throughout the lapse of time. And just as with the powerful radiation of the sun's light, the entire and unlimited array of phenomenal appearances, pure and impure, arises through the creative power and display of awareness. These appearances are beyond any kind of distinction and extreme (existence, nonexistence, appearance, emptiness, and so on) and in this way they are omnipresent.

When it is said that the sun is veiled by clouds, the obscurations in question can be ascribed to the creative power of the sun itself. For when the sun's rays fall upon the earth, the seas, and rivers, filling them with warmth, vapor arises and gathers in the sky. Consequently, an array of clouds appears in the sky, and the sun and the rays that are the sun's creative power are darkened and cannot be seen.

In like manner, if there is a failure to understand that the creative power that stirs within awareness results in the appearances of the ground that are awareness itself, these same appearances are dissociated from the ground by being apprehended and clung to in terms of really existing entities or selves. When that happens, this impure display of the creative power obscures awareness, which is the face of the fundamental nature of the quintessence of the enlightened body, speech, and mind, and which is present as primordial buddhahood. Consequently, phenomenal existence, the world and its inhabitants, is apprehended as truly existent, and all the inconceivable hallucinatory appearances of the three worlds of samsara, vast and deep, arise. So it is that owing to the belief in the impurity [the true existence] of what arises as awareness's creative power and display, this same awareness is self-obscured. As *The Lion's Perfect Power* declares,

> Buddhahood is veiled by buddhahood itself.

If awareness is buddhahood, it follows that its creative power and display is likewise buddhahood. But when this is not recognized, awareness actually obscures itself.

* * *

The fourth topic of the first part of the second section explains that it is the sun [awareness itself] that dispels the obscuration of awareness brought about through its own creative power and display.

> **2a4. Through the power of the sun's rays,**
> **Winds are stirred that drive the clouds away.**
> **So too when the nature of awareness has been**
> **realized,**

Its display arises as its ornament.
Delusion, which is free and open from the first,
Then and there subsides.
Hallucinatory perceptions and appearances
Are not spurned but purified within the ultimate expansе,
And there's no knowing where they went.
The sun (the kāyas and the wisdoms
Present of themselves)
Shines in the unencumbered sky.
The kāyas and wisdoms
Are but the stainless self-experience of awareness.
They do not come from somewhere else.

Arising from the sun itself, the brilliant sunbeams shining in the sky have the power to stir up the wind that arises suddenly from a state of calm. And as the wind gathers its strength, it disperses the clouds so that the bright light of the sun can shine forth once again.

Impure obscurations, the hallucinatory appearances of phenomenal existence, the world and its inhabitants, manifest as the unceasing creative power and display of awareness, the dharmakāya. When, thanks to the wisdom that realizes their absence of self, one recognizes that they are empty and beyond all objective reference, and when one is convinced of this, everything that manifests is seen to be an empty form, groundless and rootless. And when, without accepting or rejecting anything, one relaxes and leaves everything as it is, one comes to the realization that the very nature of awareness is uncontrived, open, and unimpeded in its nakedness, just like the sun divested of clouds. And thanks to this realization, the entire display of phenomena arises as emptiness, without ground or root. Appearances and states of mind subside all by themselves. They are simply the ornament of great primordial wisdom. The realization of the primordial openness and freedom of delusion occurs simultaneously with the realization that spontaneous presence (awareness) is intrinsically one's own possession.

As delusion automatically and immediately subsides, hallucinatory appearances and deluded perceptions are purified in the ultimate expanse without being rejected. One simply has no idea where they have gone! Like the sun that arises in an immaculate sky, luminous primordial wisdom manifests with all the self-arisen and spontaneously present qualities of the kāyas and wisdoms, which are naturally and perfectly complete within it without there being any need to attain them. The entire display of the creative power of awareness arises simply and solely as an infinite purity. It is not at all that such qualities were previously absent and have now arrived from somewhere else. They are simply the pure self-experience of awareness.

For practitioners of the greatest endeavor, all material things will, in this very life, be cleansed of all substantiality, and the three kāyas will arise in their perception. The united level of the result will be achieved in the expanse of the ground of primordial purity. Within the nature of the dharmakāya, the exclusive self-experience of the sambhogakāya will manifest and the twofold benefit of self and others will be spontaneously achieved.

* * *

The second part of the second section of the thirteenth chapter validly establishes that practitioners who realize their own nature attain buddhahood when they are free of the shell of their physical bodies.

2b. Within the egg, the twice-born's full-fledged wings
Cannot be seen, enveloped by the shell.
But when the shell is broken, the garuda soars
At once into the heart of space.
Likewise, if defilements and the false cognitions
Of an apprehending subject and an apprehended object
Have been previously exhausted,

> **When finally the shell of the residual form,**
> **The product of defilement, breaks,**
> **Awareness luminous by nature**
> **Immediately arises present of itself.**
> **The kāyas and the wisdoms fill the vast expanse of space.**
> **When they recognize their nature,**
> **Yogis come to freedom**
> **In Samantabhadra's vast expanse.**

The young of the garuda, king of "twice-born" birds, has fully-fledged wings even while in the egg. But hidden within the shell, its wings and feathers cannot be seen. When the shell breaks, however, the garuda immediately soars high in the sky. Likewise, practitioners of the Great Perfection develop the wings of meditative experience and realization even while they are still within the shell of their physical bodies. In other words, they exhaust the defiled concepts of self in relation to the false cognitions of the object and subject of apprehension, even before they die. Nevertheless, for as long as they are not freed from their physical form, they are unable actually to perceive the kāyas and wisdoms. But as soon as the residual shell of their physical bodies—the defiled result which is the residue of the maturation of previous actions—breaks, it is certain that the twenty-five spontaneously present qualities of the result, the kāyas, wisdoms, and so forth—the natural luminosity of awareness—become manifest to them. And at that moment, the appearances of the kāyas and wisdoms fill the whole expanse of space. Recognizing their nature, these yogis gain freedom in the expanse of the dharmakāya Samantabhadra, the one sole sphere of awareness. It is as *The Lion's Perfect Power* declares,

> If you do not cling to "I" and to the self of things,
> You meet your mother, dharmatā.
> If the knot of elements is loosed,
> The stake of clinging is pulled out.
> If you are free of the cocoon of habits,

> You live in the expanse of dharmatā.
> If appearances are seen
> As primal wisdom's self-experience,
> The fetter of the elements is broken.
> If it is not hidden by appearance,
> Primordial wisdom manifests on every side.

And,

> Within the very bodies of all beings
> The pure light of primordial wisdom dwells.
> And yet, as though in womb or egg,
> It dwells concealed, unmanifest.
> When its power is fully grown, it shows itself.
> And once the mind relinquishes the body,
> It reaches the domain of wisdom's self-experience.
> Awareness, self-cognizing, primordially present,
> Is seen, by nature free of ordinary cognition.
> The pure light of primordial wisdom
> And the truth of buddhahood are seen.

Yogis who have such a level of realization may appear as human beings physically, but their minds are as pure as buddhas. They are known as nirmāṇakāyas whose work is complete. Although, for the moment, they are of benefit only to their immediate environment, the time will come when they will be able to benefit all beings to the furthest confines of space. It is as *The All-Creating King* declares,

> In body they are ordinary: gods or human beings.
> But their minds are buddha, dharmatā.
> They work for the benefit of beings.
> They do so without effort and remain in ease.

And it is said in *Awareness Self-Arisen*,

Nirmāṇakāyas whose work is now complete
Have freed their minds, are buddhas in reality.
Thereafter they send forth their emanations.

* * *

The third part of the second section of the thirteenth chapter validly establishes that beings are benefited once buddhahood has been achieved. It comprises three topics. The first reveals how this benefit occurs in the future.

2C1. The display of their cognizant power
Knows no bounds throughout the ten directions.
They send forth emanations that bring benefit to beings.
And till the emptying of samsara,
They perform enlightened deeds.
Within the natural fundamental state, all this is a display
Arising from cognizant potency's creative power,
Which manifests on every side
And brings abundant benefit to beings.

After death, in the bardo of ultimate reality, these yogis recognize as the self-experience of awareness all the appearances of spontaneous presence—deities, buddha fields, and other manifestations of the ground. These then dissolve into primordial purity, the expanse of the dharmakāya, and the yogis gain freedom in this one sole sphere, becoming inseparable from it. It is said in *The Blazing Relics*,

Just as sunbeams gather back into the sun itself,
They, together with their emanations,
Melt away into primordial purity—
Their very nature whence they are inseparable,
From which they cannot be divided.

When these yogis gain their freedom in this way, the display of their cognizant power becomes boundless and limitless throughout the ten directions—even though they themselves never stir from the state of dharmakāya. They send forth countless emanations that achieve the benefit of beings in the six migrations throughout the unimaginable worlds of the three-thousandfold universe, guiding them according to their need. And for as long as samsara has not been emptied, they perform their enlightened deeds with skillful methods. As it is said,

> In all the realms of six impure migrations,
> As kings, as merchants, laborers, or priests,
> As outcastes, women, children, monks . . .

And,

> As praised or as reviled,
> As sick or as religious teachers,
> As birds or beasts, as beggars in the towns—
> [In various forms they are the guides of beings
> In accordance with their needs].

It is thus that without reprieve, they manifest an enlightened action that is everlasting, all-pervading, and spontaneous.

All this is displayed through the creative power of the cognizant potency of awareness. It manifests far and wide while never stirring from the natural, fundamental condition of the state of great perfection. This display secures the perfect benefit of beings without the need of effortful action—just like the wish-granting vase, the tree of miracles, and the wishing gem.

* * *

The second topic of the third part of the second section establishes that once buddhahood has been achieved, the benefit of beings is accomplished through its cognizant potency.

2c2. Even though the impure display
In all its aspects is completely quelled,
Emanations manifest for impure beings.
They manifest—as in the case of our own Teacher—
Through natural cognizant potency
And through the stainless acts and aspirations
Of wandering beings of pure, unsullied mind.

When yogis gain freedom in the dharmakāya, the expanse of awareness, and thus accomplish buddhahood, they remain in a state of peace. At that stage, and since they are buddhas, all impure displays—hallucinatory appearances along with their different aspects—are completely quelled. For buddhas, there is not even the slightest hallucinatory appearance of the world and its beings. It is as when one wakes from sleep. All the visions of one's dreams come to an end. When the eye disease is cured, the floaters that appear in front of oneself disappear. When one is cured of jaundice, the yellowness of the conch is no more. The world and its inhabitants are, in the perception of the buddhas, pure appearances. How, therefore, does it happen that the inconceivable emanations of the buddhas can appear to impure beings, when in the experience of those same buddhas, there is no such thing as hallucinatory appearance?

As recounted in the life story of our Teacher Śākyamuni, when the rays of light projecting from his body struck the bodies of a multitude of beings, they were reborn as children of the gods in the Heaven of the Thirty-Three. Accordingly, the sutras speak of emptiness endowed with the essence of compassion. In our tradition, the buddhas are said to possess an inherent cognizant potency that is effortless and without exertion. Therefore, even though they do not stir from the expanse of ultimate reality, they emanate inconceivable embodiments of nonreferential compassion. When these embodiments meet with beings who are pure in mind, who are endowed with faith and devotion, good karma and excellent aspirations, the activity of the buddhas' cognizant power appears to them, and an immense benefit arises.

If the buddhas were devoid of cognizant potency, samsara would be down below and nirvana would be up on high and they would never meet. There would be no connection between them and no one would be benefited. But this is not the case. For as long as samsara lasts, enlightened beings bring forth the benefit of beings. It is as *The Word-Transcending Tantra* says,

> Within the empty nature of the dharmakāya,
> The perfect knowledge of primordial wisdom
> Naturally unfolds toward all beings.
> If it were not so, the navel string
> That ties samsara and nirvana would be cut.
> This perfect knowledge of primordial wisdom
> Is luminous, aware.

Now as for the way in which the buddhas look upon beings with compassion, there are some who say that it is because of the aspirations of beings and the blessing of the buddhas that the form bodies of the latter appear in the perception of the former. They say that the appearance of other beings does not in any way occur in the experience of the buddhas, who as a result do not perceive them. The buddhas are like the shrine of the garuda, which is able to cure the diseases created by the nāgas, or the wishing gem or tree of miracles, which are able to supply all the needs and wishes of beings. Neither the shrine nor the gem nor the tree actually perceive beings. In the same way, buddhas neither know nor see beings to be guided. This, however, is incorrect. Although it is right to say that buddhas only perceive pure appearances and never impure hallucinations, it does not follow that they are unaware of the appearances and the perceptions of beings to be guided. If they were unaware, the incorrect consequence would be that buddhahood is not a state of omniscience.

Others come to [opposite,] even more extreme, conclusions. They say that buddhas perceive hallucinatory appearances to exist according to their characteristics and that it is on that basis that they work for the benefit of beings. This is completely mistaken. Although such a statement would be tenable from the standpoint of their knowing [the appearance and perceptions of] beings to be guided, if the buddhas perceived hallucinations as being actually existent from their own side, the false consequence would be that they would have been unable to complete their training in the creation of pure fields. It would follow that they were unable to effect extraordinary transformations. And it would follow that there were buddhas who had not purified their own obscurations. There would be many such unwanted consequences. On the other hand, since it is taught that the transformation of hallucinatory appearances into pure fields is effected on the three pure grounds, it is needless to say that they are effected also on the level of buddhahood.

Now the teaching of our own tradition is as follows. While buddhas do not stir from the one sole expanse of the dharmakāya, their two form bodies (which unfold from the spontaneously present primordial wisdom and cognizant potency, like rays of light from the sun) work unimpededly for the sake of beings. This is how it is. Although, in the perception of the buddhas, phenomenal existence is a state of infinite purity, the buddhas see that nonexistent yet clearly appearing phenomena occur in the perception of beings in the manner of hallucinations. And it is on this basis that they teach the Dharma. For example, if one were to see with the pure divine eye, not only would one unerringly know everything that appears, but one would also know that what other beings perceive is simply an optical illusion, like floating hairs or yellow conches appearing in their visual field. One would know that one's own perceptions were true while the perceptions of beings were false.

All this is illustrated in the following story. Once two princes were living together in the same palace. One day, while one of the princes was awake, the other fell asleep and had a terrifying dream. The prince who was awake realized that his brother was having a nightmare and shouted. "Hey, brother! Don't be afraid, it's only a dream. It's not real!" The sleeping prince heard him and, thinking that it might be true, woke up and saw that there was nothing to be afraid of.

The buddhas perceive only pure appearances. This is due to the crucial point that phenomena are primordially the state of enlightenment. Their actual and primordial condition is the state of infinite purity. There is nothing impure in what the buddhas perceive, whereas in the mistaken perceptions of beings, impure appearances occur to them with the result that they suffer. Seeing this, the buddhas work for the benefit of beings. Even the impure appearances that beings perceive manifest as pure in the perceptions of the buddhas—as the previous two examples illustrate.

* * *

The third topic of the third part of the second section explains how the emanated display secures the benefit of beings without ever stirring from the ultimate expanse.

2c3. At that time, in all the buddha fields,
Unnumbered emanations
Lead beings without limit to enlightenment,
While never stirring from the ultimate expanse,
The Teacher's dharmakāya.
In the vast expanse of primal wisdom,
Not permanent or discontinuous, not falling to extremes,
The field of Dense Array arises by itself.
And here the inconceivable display of the sambhogakāya
Appears for the vidyādharas and ḍākinīs,
As also for the bodhisattvas who reside on the ten grounds.
It appears within the ultimate expanse
Through the cognizant power of the Teacher,

Together with the virtue and the aspirations
Of beings to be guided.
It is the very face of the spontaneous presence.

The manifestation of the mandalas of the three kāyas, through the cleansing away of the impurities of the three doors, is referred to as the attainment of buddhahood in Akaniṣṭha, the highest buddha field. This is the place where all buddhas attain the state of Samantabhadra, the first buddha, and is so called because it is superior to every other phenomenon and is "not below" anything (*'og min*). It is not considered to be located in one specific place. For in brief, what we call Akaniṣṭha is the state in which primordial wisdom and the ultimate expanse are of a single taste and free of the conceptually constructed ideas of zenith, nadir, center, and periphery.

Now the Akaniṣṭha in which the Teacher Samantabhadra-Vajradhara expounded many tantras is located at the summit of all other realms. Here, there dwells a great multitude of bodhisattvas on the ten grounds, ḍākinīs, and mahāsiddhas. It is not the same as the previous Akaniṣṭha.

When phenomenal appearances are exhausted in the expanse of the primordial purity of the dharmatā, practitioners achieve freedom in the one sole sphere of the dharmakāya. They actualize the ever-youthful vase body of the dharmakāya. It is then that they emanate boundless manifestations in limitless, infinite buddha fields throughout the ten directions. Specifically, they emanate according to the needs and varying perceptions of the beings of the six classes. It is as when the single moon aloft in the sky appears reflected in all the various watery surfaces of the world. These same emanations guide limitless, unnumbered beings to the state of enlightenment without ever stirring from their ground of emanation, the dharmakāya of the Teacher Samantabhadra—in other words, the dharmadhātu free of all elaboration, the one sole sphere of primordial purity.

Within the expanse of self-arisen, self-cognizing primordial wisdom beyond delimitation and extremes, the creative power and display of this same wisdom arises all on its own, spontaneously, as the buddha field of Akaniṣṭha the Dense Array,[111] endowed with the five certainties. From this there manifest the buddha fields of the half-sambhogakāya–half-nirmāṇakāya families[112] together with the buddha field of Gaṇḍavyūha, the Dense Array of Ornaments. Here, an inconceivable array, half-sambhogakāya–half-nirmāṇakāya, appears to a host of ḍākas and ḍākinīs, bodhisattvas on the ten grounds,[113] and mahāsiddhas. Thence there manifest the emanations of the three families together with their nirmāṇakāya fields and an infinite array of the terrestrial pure lands of the nirmāṇakāya.[114] Each of these appears within the ultimate expanse as "the very face" of spontaneous presence—through the interconnection of the cognizant potency of the buddhas (manifesting in their form bodies) with the faith and devotion, good karma, and aspirations of beings to be guided.

* * *

The third section of the detailed exposition of the thirteenth chapter describes the actual result. It is in four parts, the first of which speaks of the dharmakāya and the primordial wisdoms associated with it.

> **3a. The dharmakāya**
> **Is primordial wisdom self-arisen.**
> **Primordial wisdom's oceanlike omniscience is its display,**
> **Present as the one sole sphere**
> **Within the ultimate original expanse.**

When the term *dharmakāya*, the body of ultimate reality, is explained, "ultimate reality" refers to the final goal: the primordially pure dharmatā, empty and luminous. "Body" on the other hand refers to the dimension of the ground of arising for the kāyas and wisdoms. The dharmakāya is self-arisen primordial wisdom endowed with twofold purity. Free of all conceptual extremes and inseparable from the kāyas and wisdoms, it is moreover the exclusive domain of the buddhas.[115] It is said in *Naturally Luminous Awareness*,

> Unchanging and unceasing, all-pervading—
> Such is the nature of the dharmakāya.

Even though the dharmakāya transcends all conceptual extremes and is consequently beyond classification, its creative power and display permeate the whole of samsara and nirvana, and, therefore, it is indeed the ground for their arising. Accordingly, although the dharmakāya never diverges from its status as the one sole sphere, free of all mental elaboration, if it is classified according to its aspects or qualities, it is said to be omniscient primordial wisdom endowed with an oceanlike infinity of qualities.

The situation is as follows. In relation to the three aspects of ultimate nature, luminous character, and cognizant potency, the dharmakāya's five [perfections of] place, time, teacher, teaching, and retinue must be understood as belonging to one sole empty ultimate nature.

Regarding the dharmakāya aspect of the dharmakāya, the perfect teacher is the great dharmakāya free of all mental elaboration, the perfect place is the unimaginable dharmatā, the perfect time is the utterly unchanging dharmatā, the perfect teaching is motionless concentration, and the perfect retinue is none other than the dharmakāya itself.

Regarding the sambhogakāya aspect of the dharmakāya, the perfect teacher is the indivisibility of emptiness and luminosity, the place is the unsullied state free of the impurity of the obscuring veils, the time is the dharmatā beyond permanence and discontinuity, the teaching is the dharmatā beyond all expression, and the retinue is its own empty self-experience.

Regarding the nirmāṇakāya aspect of the dharmakāya, the teacher is the unceasing ground of arising of the dharmakāya's nirmāṇakāya aspect; the place is the ground of arising that has no existence whatever; the teaching is unceasing, luminous meditative absorption; the retinue is the state of awareness, which is the indivisibility of the three kāyas; and the time is that of the manifest appearance of the fundamental nature, the very quintessence.

In similar fashion, the dharmakāya may be classified according to the five aspects of enlightened body, speech, mind, qualities, and activities.[116] The body of the dharmakāya is luminous emptiness, free of all conceptual characteristics; the speech of the dharmakāya is beyond communication by voice and word; the mind of the dharmakāya is the ineffable, inconceivable, inexpressible primordial wisdom beyond thought and movements of the mind; the qualities of the dharmakāya are constant and pervaded by the ultimate expanse and primordial wisdom; and the unceasing activities of the dharmakāya are unborn—they manifest from nowhere and yet they naturally and effortlessly accomplish the benefit of beings to be guided. These points are an explanation of the dharmakāya in the sense of a support.

For the primordial wisdoms, understood as that which is supported [by the three kāyas], the general explanation is as follows. When freedom is gained within the expanse of the one sole primordially pure dharmatā, the three aspects of ultimate nature, luminous character, and cognizant potency, immanent within the ground, provide the basis for the arising of the kāyas and wisdoms of the outwardly radiating luminosity. The primordial wisdoms that are endowed with attributes reveal their appearance [as buddhas] to beings who are pure, whereas the primordial wisdoms related to objects of knowledge (phenomena) fulfill the hopes of beings to be guided who are impure.

The specific explanation of the primordial wisdoms of the dharmakāya is as follows. The primordial wisdom of the primordial purity of the ultimate nature is the one sole sphere, free of all mental construction; the primordial wisdom of the spontaneous presence of luminous character is the foundation of enlightened qualities; and the primordial wisdom of all-pervading cognizant potency is what makes unceasing manifestation possible.[117]

For a detailed explanation of the five perfections, the five aspects of the enlightened body, speech, mind, qualities, and activities, together with the different kinds of primordial wisdom viewed from the standpoint of the qualities of the dharmakāya, one should refer to *The Treasury of Teachings*, Longchenpa's autocommentary, where all is supported by scriptural quotations.

All these aspects are present though undifferentiated in the primordial expanse, free of mental elaboration, as the one sole sphere of the dharmakāya.

* * *

The second part of the third section of the thirteenth chapter speaks of the sambhogakāya and its associated primordial wisdoms.

> **3b. The sambhogakāya is the luminous character,**
> **Spontaneously present.**
> **Its display is the five families**
> **Together with the five primordial wisdoms,**
> **Which manifest and fill**
> **The vast expanse of space.**

The term *sambhogakāya*, the body of the perfect enjoyment of riches, is explained as follows. Since the sambhogakāya is luminous in nature, distinct by character, and all-pervasive in its cognizant potency, one speaks of it in terms of riches. Since it enjoys the appearances of the five kinds of sense objects without apprehending their attributes, one speaks of enjoyment. Since whatever appears is perfectly encompassed by the state of freedom from objective reference and mental elaboration, it is perfect. And since the appearances of its luminous character, which has no existence and yet manifests in any form, are endowed with individual features, it is referred to in terms of a body.[118]

Since the ultimate nature of awareness, its empty aspect, is the dharmakāya, and since the luminous character of awareness, its aspect of spontaneous presence, is the sambhogakāya, it follows that the sambhogakāya and the ultimate nature, the dharmakāya, are one. They are inseparable from each other. When one speaks of the luminous character of awareness, the sambhogakāya, this refers to its spontaneously present, unceasing radiance. Although it is one with the ultimate nature, the dharmakāya, when the creative power and display of awareness manifest as outwardly radiating luminosity, the five buddha families and the five kinds of primordial wisdom appear and fill the whole expanse of space—above and below and in all the primary and secondary directions.

In the case of the dharmakāya aspect of the sambhogakāya, the teacher is the buddha Vairocana Mahāsāgara, the sovereign of all mandalas, for whom there is neither out nor in, neither front nor behind, and whose face looks [simultaneously and] without impediment in all the ten directions. He presides over the pure fields of twenty-five universal systems, supported on the palms of his hands. His place is the utterly pure Dense Array, his retinue is not different from himself, his teaching is the primordial wisdom that is experienced by him, and his time is the time of actual realization.

In the case of the sambhogakāya aspect of the sambhogakāya, the teacher is the main buddha of the family of whichever tantra is being expounded, the place is the Dense Array of Akaniṣṭha, the retinue is the corresponding family, the teaching comprises the five kinds of primordial wisdom, and the time is the unfolding and gathering back of luminous appearances.

In the case of the nirmāṇakāya aspect of the sambhogakaya, the teachers are the five principal buddhas of the five families, whose characteristics appear although they are without intrinsic being. They are luminous and beyond dualistic cognition. They are surrounded by inconceivable numbers of male and female deities, all of whom enjoy the self-experience of awareness.[119] The place is Alakāvatī, the blissful, utterly uncompounded field of Willow Trees. This, however, indicates the specific location of each of the five families. It is not the buddha field of Vajrapāṇi. The retinue consists of the buddhas' own exclusive self-experience and the assemblies of the buddhas within their mandalas. The time is the time of the self-experience of awareness.

Similarly, the sambhogakāya may be classified in terms of enlightened body, speech, mind, qualities, and activities. The body of the sambhogakāya, appearing yet without intrinsic being, is luminous and illuminating and is completely pervaded by awareness. The speech of the sambhogakāya is self-arisen and is the self-experience of awareness. The mind of the sambhogakāya is an uninterrupted state of knowledge arising through the power of wisdom. The qualities of the sambhogakāya consist of the display of the major and minor marks of enlightenment, which appear according to need, and the perfect capacity of supernatural knowledge. The activities of the sambhogakāya consist of teachings through symbols, imparted to the retinue through the rays of light issuing from the tongues of the sambhogakāya buddhas.

The primordial wisdoms, for which the sambhogakāya is a support, may be briefly explained as the primordial wisdom of the dharmadhātu, the mirrorlike primordial wisdom, the primordial wisdom of equality, the all-perceiving primordial wisdom, and the all-accomplishing primordial wisdom. Longchenpa's autocommentary should be consulted for a more detailed account of these matters.

In short, the qualities of the sambhogakāya, the five perfections, the enlightened body, speech, mind, qualities, and activities, together with the five primordial wisdoms, all manifest and pervade the whole of space.

* * *

The third part of the third section of the thirteenth chapter discusses the nirmāṇakāya and its associated primordial wisdoms.

> **3c. The nirmāṇakāya is cognizant potency,**
> **The ground and basis for arising.**
> **Its displays occur according to the needs**

> **Of beings to be guided.**
> **It has mastery of great enlightened action.**

Generally speaking, the dharmakāya is emptiness. The sambhogakāya is luminosity. The nirmāṇakāya is unceasing cognizant potency, which is the ground for the arising of its various emanations. This is what is meant by "nirmāṇakāya." The emanations arising as the display of the creative power of the nirmāṇakāya manifest in manifold ways as teachers who guide beings, pure and impure, according to their need, and in forms suitable to the purpose. They appear for example as the six munis, guides of beings, as persons belonging to the royal or merchant caste, and so forth—and even in the form of various animals, such as birds, deer, insects, or snakes. Thanks to their supreme activities of enlightenment, they are masters in their work for the benefit of beings, which lasts until the very emptying of samsara. As it is said in *Awareness Self-Arisen*,

> Appearing in whatever form appropriate for guiding beings,
> They manifest in harmony with others—
> They know what brings them benefit.
> At need, they have the power of transformation.

The same text goes on to say,

> O Lord of Secrets! You should understand the meaning of the nirmāṇakāya, the body of manifestation. It is the nirmāṇakāya because it appears in forms that accord with the beings of all the realms in the universe. It is the nirmāṇakāya because it is able to secure the benefit of beings. It is the nirmāṇakāya because it performs all activities. It is the nirmāṇakāya because it liberates countless beings. It is the nirmāṇakāya because in any given buddha field, it is transitory. It is the nirmāṇakāya because its compassion manifests without partiality.

The nirmāṇakāya may be classified in three ways. First there are "nirmāṇakāyas [or *tulkus*] who have completed their work." This means that their minds have ripened into the dharmakāya and that they strive for the benefit of beings but are not yet released from the physical body, the result of the full ripening of their karma. They are vidyādharas endowed with a karmic body. Second, there are "nirmāṇakāyas who perform activities." These arise directly from the ultimate expanse. They are vidyādharas with power over life and are untouched by birth, death, old age and decline. Finally, there are the fabricated or inanimate nirmāṇakāyas, the born or animate nirmāṇakāyas, and the supreme nirmāṇakāyas [thus classified according to their enlightened activity].

Again, the nirmāṇakāya may be classified according to the five perfections. In the case of the dharmakāya aspect of the nirmāṇakāya, the teacher is the supreme Vajradhara; the place is the countless billions of three-thousandfold universes; the retinue comprises all beings born in the four ways; the teaching is *The Word-Transcending Tantra*, the root of all the collections of teachings; and the time is the epoch when beings lived for unnumbered years.

In the case of the sambhogakāya aspect of the nirmāṇakāya, the teacher is Vajrasattva; the place and buddha field consist of a billion three-thousandfold universes; the retinue is made up of the bodhisattvas on the three pure grounds of realization; the teaching is that of the vehicle of definitive meaning; and the time is beyond specification.

In the case of the nirmāṇakāya aspect of the nirmāṇakāya, the teacher is Śākyamuni; the buddha field comprises the billion worlds of the Saha universe; the place consists of the Vulture Peak, the summit of Mount Meru, Vaiśālī and so on; the retinue consists of gods, human beings, gandharvas, kumbhandas, and so on; the teaching is that of the causal and resultant vehicles; and the time is the moment when doubts are severed with complete certainty.

The nirmāṇakāya may again be classified according to the enlightened body, speech, mind, qualities, and activities. The body of the nirmāṇakāya is adorned with the major and minor marks and manifests in various forms according to need. The speech of the nirmāṇakāya sets forth the Dharma with all the sixty melodious intonations of the voice of Brahmā. The mind of the nirmāṇakāya cognizes all knowable phenomena simultaneously. The qualities of the nirmāṇakāya are the inconceivable qualities of elimination and realization. The activities of the nirmāṇakāya perfectly encompass without exception all the outer, inner, and secret deeds of enlightenment.

Primordial wisdom—namely, that which is supported [by the nirmāṇakāya]—is of two kinds. The primordial wisdom of the unmistaken knowledge of the nature of things cognizes the fundamental nature of all phenomena, while the primordial wisdom that beholds all things in their multiplicity knows all phenomena and their limitless causes and effects.

In short, the nirmāṇakāya is endowed with the qualities of the five perfections, the enlightened body, speech, mind, qualities, and activities, together with the two kinds of primordial wisdom.

* * *

The fourth part of the third section of the thirteenth chapter explains the source of the resultant kāyas and wisdoms.

> **3d. These three kāyas are not gained**
> **Through striving and in causal sequence.**
> **They are present of themselves primordially**
> **And manifest when all is left just as it is.**
> **To those most adept in the supreme secret,**
> **They manifest within this very life,**
> **And also they appear to those**
> **Who in the bardo state are not misled.**
> **The vajra essence, summit of all vehicles,**
> **Is thus exalted over all the causal and resultant vehicles.**

The perfect result of the kāyas and wisdoms is not something to be achieved anew through effort and through the causal processes of gathering the accumulations and purifying obscurations in difficult practices on the conventional path marked by mental elaboration. They are unconditioned, uncompounded, and primordially present of themselves. It is as *The Sublime Continuum* has declared,

> Uncompounded and spontaneous,
> Not realized through extraneous conditions,
> Possessing knowledge, love, and power—
> This is buddhahood endowed with twofold benefit.

And *The Six Expanses Tantra* says,

> Primordial buddhahood, present from the first,
> Is found through the essential teaching
> On resting without searching,
> Which derives from nonconceptual primal wisdom.

When now, in the present moment, yogis rest in the natural state in which everything is left just as it is—a state outside the causal sequence—primordial wisdom actually appears. It dwells within and is present as the fundamental stratum [of the mind]. For yogis of the supremely secret Great Perfection—that is, practitioners of the highest capacity—conventional appearances are exhausted in this very life in the expanse of dharmatā. Primordial purity, wherein all phenomena are exhausted, appears to them directly. They gain buddhahood in this very life. For practitioners of moderate capacity, the luminous dharmatā, the wisdom of primordial purity, appears to them at the moment of death, and they find freedom. Finally, if, in the bardo of pure ultimate reality, practitioners of basic capacity are not misled by the appearances of deities and buddha fields but recognize them as the self-experience of awareness, they are certain to gain freedom—like children climbing into their mother's lap.

The summit of the nine vehicles, the profound teaching of the vajra essence of the Secret Mantra, is thus exalted above every other causal and resultant vehicle.

* * *

This concludes the word commentary on the thirteenth chapter of *The Precious Treasury of the Dharmadhātu*, which shows that the regaining of buddhahood occurs without effortful practice.

Conclusion

The conclusion of Longchenpa's treatise consists of seven sections. The first section reveals the place where the text was perfectly composed.

> **1. This song of ultimate reality, the vajra essence,**
> **Spacelike nature pure from the beginning,**
> **Arose all by itself within the groundless,**
> **Rootless, and unchanging place.**
> **It is the play of what is free of movement and of change.**

As it was explained above, this profound and secret song reveals, without concealing anything, the ultimate reality of all phenomena—their uncontrived, fundamental nature beyond the elaborations of the mind—the indestructible vajra essence. It shows that phenomena, of both samsara and nirvana, are primordially empty and beyond all mental elaboration. This ultimate reality, the spacelike and primordial state of buddhahood, is the nature [of the mind] pure from the beginning.

Conventionally speaking, the place where this song was made is the abode of many powerful siddhas. It is a place where the qualities of spiritual experience and realization arise naturally like jewels within the mind. It is the mountain peak blessed by the self-arisen Lotus King, a high place where the panoramic vision of a hundred views brings rest to the mind.

In truth, however, the word "place"—the place where this treatise was set forth—refers to ultimate, self-arisen primordial wisdom, which from the very beginning is pure, unchanging, and without ground or root. The treatise arose naturally within the expanse of self-arisen primordial wisdom as a nonexistent and yet appearing empty form. In truth, *this very text* is none other than the creative power and display of the expanse of awareness beyond all movement and change.

* * *

The second section identifies the subject of this treatise, which is to be realized.

> **2. Its meaning is the vast state, all-pervasive,**
> **Of primordial equality.**
> **Without arriving anywhere,**
> **I stay in my primordial nature—**
> **The unmoving dharmatā, spontaneously present,**
> **Limitless, not falling to extremes.**

Everything within phenomenal existence, the world and its inhabitants, is but the vast immensity, the all-pervasive state of primordial equality. If this is realized, then whatever arises is simply the manifestation of the dharmatā. Whatever appears is understood as self-arisen primordial wisdom. The dharmatā, which is beyond going and coming, becomes manifest.

Since effort and exertion simply ceased where they stood, Longchenpa did not go, did not arrive, anywhere. He rests in the fundamental stratum, his own primordial nature, unmoving in the unaltered, naked dharmakāya. He has himself recognized the dharmatā, spontaneously present of itself, which is the subject matter of this treatise and is what is to be realized. His text constitutes an empowering blessing. It creates the auspicious circumstance whereby the uncontrived, original purity, the ultimate primordial wisdom, which is beyond delimitation and falls to no extreme, arises in the minds of fortunate beings who implement it.

* * *

The third section shows that, since Longchenpa has attained the vast expanse of spontaneous presence, he has perfect mastery of the words and meanings of his treatise.

> **3. In themselves, these teachings**
> **Are a vast immensity that equals space itself.**
> **Here, unmoving is the sovereign**
> **Of the self-arisen vast expanse.**
> **Here, all manifold appearances subside just where they stand.**
> **I have gone into the vast womb of the ultimate expanse,**
> **Which is not to be pointed out by saying "this."**

The omniscient Longchenpa, lord among Victorious Ones, well understood the teachings of all the vajra topics of the Natural Great Perfection. His mind transformed into the supreme ultimate state of wisdom, the vast immensity that is the equal of space itself and he gained dominion over the ultimate realm of self-arisen awareness, the sovereign of the vast expanse that never stirs from the profound, fundamental nature of things. It is there that phenomenal appearance in all its variety subsides naturally and automatically in the moment of its self-arising. In his very life, Longchenpa entered this state—the vast womb of the ultimate expanse of the primordially pure, unchanging dharmatā, which cannot be pointed out by the dualistic, discursive mind with the word "this." And he composed his treatise in full sovereign possession of an ultimate wisdom that is infallible in its words and meanings. Fortunate beings who have an interest in the supreme vehicle should cherish it like their hearts and eyes.

* * *

The fourth section describes how the treatise was composed.

> **4. In the certainty of realization,**
> **I, a yogi similar to space itself,**

Set forth, in sum, my own experience
In concord with the scriptural tradition:
The twenty-one root scriptures of the mind class,
The three series of the space class,
And the four sections of the pith instruction class.

The composer of this text, Longchen Rabjam, lord among Victorious Ones, was a true emanation of the great paṇḍita Vimalamitra. There is a prophecy in *The Word-Transcending Tantra*, the root [of all the Great Perfection scriptures], that an emanation of Vimalamitra will appear every hundred years. And it is said that the line of the text "Later [the lineage] will be upheld by one known as the glory of those learned in the [Sanskrit] tongue" refers to Longchenpa himself.

Longchenpa touched with his head the feet of his holy teacher, Kumaradza, glorious lord of Dharma, and through his blessings realized without error all the secret and profound points of the luminous Great Perfection. He assimilated all its teachings, the deep meaning of which is hard for ordinary beings to fathom. Thus he was able to compose his text without impediment, for the lotus of his understanding blossomed into full flower. He became a yogi of the luminous vajra essence. The moment of certainty came to him and he achieved for his own sake the state of dharmakāya and, for the sake of others, the capacity to perform enlightened activities. As his realization welled up from within, he became a glorious yogi similar to space itself. As such, he composed this text as a summary account of his own experience and realization.

Condensing the teachings bestowed on him by the second Samantabhadra, his peerless teacher Kumaradza, he set them down in writing, intending to bring benefit to later generations and to preserve Kumaradza's tradition from decline. For those who are unable to bring together the countless teachings of the tantras and pith instructions, he composed this text in accordance with scriptural tradition thus allowing them to implement these teachings easily as though they were enjoying a well-cooked meal. Spurning any kind of personal inventiveness or arbitrary contrivance, he took the words of scripture as his witness and rendered his text trustworthy by composing it in line with the tantras of the root or outer mind class, the inner space class, and the secret pith instruction class of the Great Perfection.

Of these, the mind class contains twenty-one tantras. This collection includes the five texts translated first—namely, *The Cuckoo of Awareness*, *The Stirring of Supreme Creative Power*, *The Soaring Flight of the Great Garuda*, *Smelting Gold from Ore*, and *The Victory Banner Never to Be Lowered*.[120] These are followed by thirteen texts translated later—namely, *The Peak of Spontaneity*, *The King of Space*, *The Blissful Magical Array*, *The General Principles of Perfection*, *An Explanation of the Enlightened Mind*, *The Infinite Bliss*, *The Wheel of Life*, *The Six Spheres*, *The General Definition of Perfection*, *The Wish-Fulfilling Jewel*, *All-Embracing Awareness*, *The Venerable Sublimity*, and *The Accomplishment of the Goal of Meditation*.[121] These thirteen tantras and the five previous texts taken together are known as the eighteen lower tantras or the eighteen mother and child tantras of the mind class. To these are added *The All-Creating King*, *The Wondrous King*, and *The Ten Scriptures*.[122] The last of these titles comprises the ten scriptures of *The Gathering of the Great Assembly* and are in the Kangyur.[123] Taken together, these are the twenty-one tantras of the mind class teachings.

The many teachings of the space class are arranged into three series: the white space, the black space, and multicolored space. The white series is subdivided into the "sky-space," the "ocean-space," and the "jewel-space." The black series consists of three groups: the "black space of compassion," the "black space of enlightened activities," and the "black space of emanations." The multicolored series is divided into, first, the multicolored space class that accords with the mind class in asserting existence; second, the multicolored space class that accords with its own [that is the space] class in asserting nonexistence; and third, the multicolored space class that accords with the pith instruction class in asserting neither existence nor nonexistence. Within these nine spaces are gathered the teachings of the space class.

The pith instruction class has four cycles: outer, inner, secret, and unsurpassed secret. Although this class covers an inconceivable number of topics drawn from the various tantra classes, they are all gathered in the seventeen tantras of the definitive great secret. These are, as *The Word-Transcending Tantra* says,

> *The Self-Arisen* and *The Naturally Free and Open*,
> *The Self-Occurring* and *The Perfect Power*,
> *The Beauty* and *The Studded Array*,
> *The Pearl Necklace* and *The Unwritten*,
> *The Mirrors of the Heart and Mind*,
> *The Union of the Sun and Moon*,
> *The Adornment of the Introductions*,
> *The Blazing Relics* and *The Heap of Jewels*,
> *The Burning Lamp* together with *The Six Expanses*—
> The sequence of these sixteen texts
> Is surely taken from *The Word-Transcending*
> And appears for beings to be guided.

This text thus refers to *The Tantra of Awareness Self-Arisen*, *The Tantra of the Natural Openness and Freedom of Awareness*, *The Tantra of Self-Occurring Awareness*, *The Tantra of the Lion's Perfect Power*, *The Tantra of Auspicious Beauty*, *The Tantra of the Array of Studded Jewels*, *The Necklace of Pearls Tantra*, *The Unwritten Tantra*, *The Tantra of the Mirror of Vajrasattva's Heart*, *The Tantra of the Mirror of Samantabhadra's Mind*, *The Tantra of the Union of the Sun and Moon*, *The Tantra Adorned with Introductions to the Mind's Nature*, *The Tantra of the Blazing Relics*, *The Tantra of the Heap of Jewels*, *The Tantra of the Blazing Lamp*, and *The Tantra of the Six Expanses*. The list concludes with the root tantra—namely, *The Word-Transcending Tantra*. These then are the seventeen tantras of the Heart Essence. It should be noted that there are eighteen tantras if one adds *The Tantra of the Wrathful Protectress of Mantra*.[124]

Broadly speaking, the teachings of the mind, space, and pith instruction classes of the Great Perfection may be summed up as follows. Of the teachings of the Secret Mantra belonging to the two stages of generation and perfection, which were set forth by Samantabhadra in the form of Vajradhara, the perfection stage is divided into great and small. The [teachings of the] great perfection stage comprise six million four hundred thousand *ślokas*, thirty-five thousand chapters, twenty-one thousand śloka divisions, one hundred and eighty nail-like instructions, fifteen hundred teachings related to obstacles, three thousand summaries of crucial points, and four hundred thousand topics related to the differentiation and certain identification of deviations and obscurations. All these are contained in twenty thousand tantras all with different names. The root of all scriptural collections, *The Word-Transcending Tantra*, has this to say:

> From the Natural Great Perfection
> Different words pour forth.
> From the three classes there derive nine spaces.
> Their words are all contained
> In six million and four hundred thousand ślokas,
> In thirty-five thousand chapters,
> And twenty one thousand volumes.
> Their import equals the extent of space,
> Cutting through the thoughts
> Of beings to be guided.
> Their subjects may be summarized
> In a hundred and eighty nail-like teachings,
> Fifteen hundred teachings that relate to obstacles,
> Three thousand summaries of crucial points,
> Four hundred thousand teachings that relate
> To deviations and obscuring veils.
> All are found in twenty thousand tantras

All with different names,
In which the order of their contents is explained with clarity.

Longchenpa's text was composed in accordance with all these teachings.

* * *

The fifth section is the dedication of virtue to the attainment of enlightenment.

5. Through this virtue,
May all beings, leaving none aside,
Attain without exertion the primordial ground.
May they, upon Samantabhadra's level,
Free of movement and of change,
Be sovereigns of the Dharma,
Spontaneously accomplishing
The twofold goal.

The Precious Treasury of the Dharmadhātu is the quintessence of all the texts of Dharma that the world contains. And from the perfect composition of this marvelous teaching, virtue was obtained on a prodigious scale. On this basis, may all beings, leaving none aside, as infinite in number as space is vast, come, without the need of effortful practice, to perfect enlightenment. Attaining the primordial ground, may they be inseparable from Samantabhadra, the dharmakāya. Within the one sole, all-embracing sphere, the level of Samantabhadra beyond all change and movement, may all beings, becoming of one taste with it, actualize the state of the Bhagavan Buddha and thus become sovereigns of the Dharma, spontaneously accomplishing the twofold goal.

* * *

The sixth section is a dedication of virtue to the good fortune of all beings, and to a vast increase of their well-being and prosperity.

6. In all directions may there be
Glory, wealth, and happiness,
And may all wishes, just as in a buddha field,
Be spontaneously fulfilled.
Through the sounding of the Dharma drum
May liberation's flag of victory be raised.
And, never waning, may the sacred teaching spread and flourish.

May the light of the immense merit accruing through the words and meanings of this excellent composition radiate in all directions, bringing perfect splendor and happiness, all glory and wealth! May all the beings in the three worlds be contented and free of sorrow! And through their wonderful joy in the teachings that lead them to liberation, may beings be endowed in mind and body with glory and good fortune day and night! And as if they were dwelling in pure fields such as Sukhāvatī, Abhirati, and Padmakūta, may their every wish for perfect and glorious excellence be spontaneously fulfilled! May the drum of the Dharma, whereby this profound teaching is upheld, preserved, and propagated, resound on all sides! May every being who sees, hears, touches, or recalls this teaching reach the state of liberation and the attainment of omniscience! May the teachings of the unsurpassed essence ever expand and increase like the miraculous tree of the gods and the victory banner crowned with the wish-fulfilling jewel! May the profound and holy Dharma never wane but spread and flourish in the ten directions to the very confines of space!

* * *

The seventh section is an explanation of the text's colophon, which reads,

This completes *The Precious Treasury of the Dharmadhātu*, well composed upon the slopes of Kangri Thökar, by Longchen Rabjam, a yogi of the supreme vehicle.

The nature of the mind, which is intrinsically free of all the extremes of conceptual elaboration, is called the dharmadhātu, the expanse of ultimate reality. The dharmadhātu is uncontrived. It is self-arisen and present of itself and is therefore likened to a precious jewel. And since it is the source of all phenomena without exception, of both samsara and nirvana, it is compared to a treasury. This then is the explanation of the meaning of the title of the text.

As far as concerns its subject matter, this text is a detailed presentation of the ground, path, and result according to the teaching of the luminous Natural Great Perfection. It is a clear exposition consisting of thirteen chapters and is enriched with numerous points related to the profound and vast meaning and terminology of the Dharma. This is why the title refers to *dhātu* or profusion.[125] Spontaneously endowed with a wealth of excellent words and meanings, [the text] is described as *precious* and as a *treasury* of profound and vast *teachings*. And since it is a treasury of such precious substances—for it is indeed a perfect exposition of the nature of the ground, path, and result—we arrive at an alternative interpretation resulting in the title *The Precious Treasury of a Profusion of Teachings.* Given the perfection of its words, and the meaning they express, this is indeed a perfect treatise.

Regarding the [description of Longchenpa as a] yogi of the supreme vehicle, the following may be said. Generally speaking, the highest of all vehicles is the resultant vehicle of Vajrayāna. And of the doctrines of the Vajrayāna, the luminous Great Perfection is, so to speak, the heart or essence. To take the matter yet further, we may say that, of the subdivisions of the Great Perfection, emphasis is placed on the unsurpassed and most secret cycle of the secret pith instruction class, which is more profound than the profound, the essence of the essence. This then is what is known as the supreme vehicle. And since Longchenpa was one who realized truly and without error the meaning of its teachings, he is referred as a yogi of the supreme vehicle.

Moreover, his very name, Longchen Rabjam, itself reveals the subject of this text. For in the vast and spacelike expanse (longchen, *klong chen*) of his realization, the continuity of the dharmatā—namely his awareness—is infinite (rabjam, *rab 'byams*) and at all times free of dullness and agitation, hope and fear. Therefore, he is indeed Longchen Rabjam.

All the various authorial names that Longchenpa attached to his different compositions are indicators of their contents. For texts that deal principally with the teachings of expedient meaning and that correspond to the various common fields of knowledge and science, such as poetry, prose, and rhetoric, he would sign himself Ngaki Wangpo or Tsultrim Lodrö from Samye. For works that discuss the inner principles of the secret Mantrayāna, he would use the name Dorje Ziji. In the case of treatises that expound profound topics of the gradual vehicles or those that principally set forth meditative concentration, either directly or by implication, he would sign himself Drimé Özer. For texts that reveal the vast expanse of the inconceivable fundamental nature, he used the name Longchen Rabjam. Finally, for texts that treat extensively of the different vehicles, philosophical tenets, suchness and so forth, he would sign himself as All-Knowing Ngaki Wangpo.

This treatise was perfectly composed upon the slope of Kangri Thökar, the supreme place of accomplishment.

Hard it is indeed to understand
The Dharma so profound of final meaning,
And to discern it properly I am of poor intelligence.
And yet for certain persons
Who enjoy a fortune equal to my own,
With pure intention I composed these words,
Desiring that they be of some slight help to them.

Profound and supreme distillation
Of the mind, the space, and pith instruction classes,
The teaching of this text is very deep.
And so, my lack of understanding,
All my faults and errors and confusion,

In the presence of the teachers of the three transmissions
And the guardians of the Doctrine, I confess.

Through the virtue of my efforts here,
May all beings without limit
See in truth the face of the primordial wisdom
That within them dwells.
And without effort and exertion,
May they gain, within the inner and primordial expanse,
The everlasting state,
The vase body of perpetual youth.

From now until the essence of enlightenment,
Relying on my supreme teacher
And the deep and secret Doctrine,
Through the power of my meditation
And the teachings that I give to others,
May I be a guide for beings without end.

May this teaching, like the sun that rises in the sky,
Spread throughout the ten directions, filling all the world.
May it drive away the gloom of ignorance
From the minds of beings as infinite as space is vast.
May all enjoy the glory and magnificence of the four kāyas.

In answer to the repeated requests and many accompanying gifts, principally on the part of Tertön Chönyi Lingpa, Zurwa Akhu Palzang Rinpoche, abbot of my own monastery, and his many disciples, and at the behest also of the supreme Tulku Dorje, the foretold speech emanation of Garlong Terchen, and of my own nephew, the noble Tsultrim Zangpo, and others, I, Öntrul Tenpa'i Wangchuk, composed this commentary as my Dharma legacy to all who have an interest in it. It was completed on the eighth day of the Saga month (May 25) of the fire male mouse year (1996)—the tenth year of the seventeenth rabjung (sixty-year cycle) according to Tibetan reckoning, called in Sanskrit *dhātu* and in Tibetan *dzinche* (*'dzin byed*). It was composed while I was staying in strict retreat in Ösel Chönyi Ling, the retreat center of the great monastery of Kadak Trödrel Ling, in the periods between my meditation sessions. Virtue! *Sarva Mangalam.*

Glossary

action (conduct)	*spyod pa*
all-embracing dimension	*khor yug*
all-encompassing (embracing, inclusive) sphere	*kun zlum thig le*
apprehender (subject of apprehension)	*'dzin pa*
apprehensible (object of apprehension)	*gzung ba*
arising-subsiding	*shar grol*
array (display)	*cho 'phrul (bkod pa)*
awareness (knowledge)	*rig pa*
awareness (wisdom, state, realization, view, teaching)	*dgongs pa*
awareness in the present moment	*da lta'i rig pa*
bliss	*bde ba*
bondage and freedom	*'ching grol*
buddha element	*khams*
buoyant impetus	*yo lang*
coemergent ignorance	*lhan skyes kyi ma rig pa*
cognitive act, cognition (ordinary, dualistic)	*rtog pa*
cognizant creative power	*rig byed rtsal*
cognizant potency (power)	*thugs rje*
complete (utter) openness and freedom	*yongs grol*
complete (perfect)	*rdzogs pa*
concentration	*ting nge 'dzin*
conceptual ignorance	*kun tu brtags pa'i ma rig pa*
creative power	*rtsal*

delusion (delusive, hallucination, mistake)	*'khrul pa*
dharmadhātu, expanse of ultimate reality	*chos dbyings*
dharmatā, ultimate reality, nature of phenomena	*chos nyid*
direct and instantaneous	*spyi blugs*
direct concentration	*thog babs chen po'i ting nge 'dzin*
direct empowerment in the manner of a king	*rgyal thabs spyi blugs*
display	*rol pa, cho 'phrul*
dualistic apprehension (perception)	*gnyis 'dzin*
edges and corners	*grva zur*
enlightened mind (pure and all-encompassing mind)	*byang chub kyi sems*
emptiness endowed with supreme aspects	*rnam kun mchog ldan stong pa nyid*
equal, equality	*mnyam pa, mnyam pa nyid*
even, evenness	*phyal ba, mnyam pa*
ever-youthful vase body	*gzhon nu bum pa'i sku*
exhaustion (of phenomena) in the dharmatā	*chos nyid zad pa'i sa*
expanse of ultimate reality	*chos dbyings*
expository causal vehicle	*mtshan nyid rgyu'i theg pa*
figurative emptiness	*rnam grangs pa'i stong nyid*
fixation and clinging	*'dzin zhen*
fourth state free of the other three	*bzhi cha gsum bral*
freedom from mental (conceptual) elaboration	*spros bral*
fundamental nature	*gnas lugs*
fundamental stratum (of awareness)	*rang mal*
ground in its natural state	*gzhi gzhag*
hallucination, hallucinatory	*'khrul pa*

ignorance, lack of awareness	*ma rig pa*
immediate and unmediated	*spyi blugs*
indwelling concentration	*rang gnas chen po'i ting nge 'dzin*
indwelling (immanent) meditative absorption	*rang gnas kyi bsam gtan*
infinite purity	*dag pa rab 'byams*
inner luminosity	*nang gsal*
instantaneous openness and freedom	*skad cig mar grol ba*
instantaneous subsiding	*skad cig mar grol ba*
key (crucial) point	*gnad*
leaving appearances nakedly as they are	*snang ba cer gzhag*
leaving as it is that is mountainlike	*ri bo cog bzhag*
leaving as it is that is oceanlike	*rgya mtsho cog gzhag*
leaving awareness as it is	*rig pa cog gzhag*
luminosity	*'od gsal*
luminosity of deep sleep	*gnyid 'thug gi 'od gsal*
luminosity of light sleep	*gnyid srab mo'i 'od gsal*
luminous character	*rang bzhin*
manifestation (display, array)	*cho 'phrul*
māra (demon)	*bdud*
meditative absorption	*bsam gtan*
meeting (of subject and object)	*thug phrad*
mere perceived appearance	*snang tsam*
metaphor, referent, sign (evidence)	*dpe don rtags*
movement and change	*'pho 'gyur*
nail	*gzer*
naked, direct openness and freedom	*cer grol*
naked, direct subsiding	*cer grol*
natural meditative absorption	*rang bzhin (rang babs kyi) bsam gtan*
natural openness and freedom	*rang grol*

natural (uncontrived) state	*rang gzhag*
natural state free of fabrication	*rang bzhin babs*
natural (self) subsiding	*rang grol*
nature	*ngo bo, rang bzhin*
nonaffirming negation	*med dgag*
nondual (nonduality)	*gnyis med*
object (sense object)	*yul*
objectless (without objective reference)	*yul med*
one sole openness and freedom	*gcig grol*
one sole sphere	*thig le nyag gcig*
open and unimpeded	*zang thal*
open(ness) and free(dom)	*grol ba*
openness and freedom of the ground	*gzhi grol*
original common ground	*thog ma'i spyi gzhi*
outwardly radiating (outer) luminosity	*phyi gsal*
perfect (complete)	*rdzogs pa*
perfectly included	*rdzogs pa*
primordial (dualistic) knowing	*ye shes*
primordial openness and freedom	*ye grol*
primordial subsiding	*ye grol*
primordial (primal) wisdom	*ye shes*
primordial wisdom absorbed within yet not obscured	*ye shes thim la ma rmugs*
pure and all-encompassing mind	*byang chub kyi sems*
purity and equality	*dag mnyam*
radiance	*gdangs*
reference point	*dmigs gtad*
samayas of nothing to keep (observe)	*bsrung du med pa'i dam tshig*
sealing concentration	*rgyas 'debs chen po'i ting nge 'dzin*
seamless	*bar med*
self-arising	*rang shar*

self-arisen primordial wisdom	*rang byung ye shes*
self-aware, self-knowing cognizance	*rang rig rang shes*
self-cognizing awareness	*rang rig*
self-cognizing primordial wisdom	*rig pa'i ye shes*
self-experience (display) of awareness	*rang snang*
self-subsiding	*rang grol*
sphere (one sole)	*thig le (nyag gcig)*
spontaneous presence	*lhun grub*
subsiding upon seeing	*mthong grol*
ten elements of tantra	*rgyud kyi dngos po bcu*
ten essential factors	*rang bzhin bcu*
to be free and open	*grol ba*
to break down	*log pa*
to distill the essence (essentialize)	*'gag bsdams pa ('gag bcing ba)*
to gain decisive certainty (conviction)	*la bzla ba*
to fasten with a nail and perfectly align	*gnam gzer gdab pa*
to resolve difficulty	*'phrang bsal ba*
to subside	*grol ba*
trap (mesh)	*gzeb*
true reality	*rnal ma'i don*
ultimate expanse (space)	*dbyings*
ultimate nature	*ngo bo*
ultimate nature, luminous character, cognizant potency (power)	*ngo bo rang bzhin thugs rje*
ultimate place of freedom	*mthar thug gi grol sa*
ultimate reality	*chos nyid*
unimpeded openness	*zang thal*
uncontrived nature	*gnyug ma*
vajra essence	*rdo rje snying po*
vast expanse	*klong*
view	*lta ba*
wind (wind energy)	*rlung*

Notes

Abbreviations

TPQ, Book 1 — Jigme Lingpa and Longchen Yeshe Dorje, Kangyur Rinpoche, *Treasury of Precious Qualities, Book 1*, translated by Padmakara Translation Group (Boston: Shambhala Publications, 2010).

TPQ, Book 2 — Jigme Lingpa and Longchen Yeshe Dorje, Kangyur Rinpoche, *Treasury of Precious Qualities, Book 2*, translated by Padmakara Translation Group (Boston: Shambhala Publications, 2013).

---

1. *bsTan bcos kyi dkar chag rin po che'i mdzod khang.*
2. See Chödrak Zangpo, *Meaningful to Behold*, pp. 59–79.
3. See Nyoshul Khenpo, *A Marvelous Garland of Rare Gems*, pp. 131–44.
4. See Germano, "Poetic Thought," p. 24.
5. The text is titled *Kun mkhyen klong chen rab 'byams pa'i gsung rab mdzod bdun la blta bar bskul ba.* See *dPal sprul o rgyan 'jigs med chos kyi dbang po'i gsung 'bum*, vol. 1 (Si khron mi rigs dpe skrun khang), p. 179.
6. See *'Ju mi 'pham bka' 'bum*, vol. 9b (Si khron mi rigs dpe skrun khang), p. 540.
7. Respectively, *Yid bzhin rin po che'i mdzod* and *Grub mtha' rin po che'i mdzod.*
8. *Man ngag rin po che'i mdzod.*
9. Respectively, *Chos dbyings rin po che'i mdzod* and *gNas lugs rin po che'i mdzod.*
10. Respectively, *Theg mchog rin po che'i mdzod* and *Tshig don rin po che'i mdzod.*
11. See Tulku Thondup, *Practice of Dzogchen*, p. 145.
12. Two other translations of *The Treasury of the Dharmadhātu*, root text and autocommentary, now exist. See Richard Barron, *A Treasure Trove of Spiritual Transmission* (Junction City, CA: Padma, 2001) and Lama

Chonam and Sangye Khandro, *Jewel Treasury of the Dharmadhātu* (Ashland: Light of Berotsana, 2024).

13. See Shechen Rabjam ('Gyur med kun bzang rnam rgyal), *The Catalog of the Seven Treasuries* (*mDzod bdun dkar chag*) (Deorali Chorten Gangtok: Dodrup Sangyay Lama, 1976).
14. See Nyoshul Khenpo, *A Marvelous Garland of Rare Gems*, p. 55.
15. See p. 106.
16. See p. 428.
17. See p. 429.
18. See p. 427.
19. See p. 666.
20. See TPQ, Book 2, 390n193.
21. See TPQ, Book 2, p. xxix.
22. See p. 470.
23. See p. 621.
24. Private communication from Yingrik Drubpa Rinpoche.
25. The translation here is made according to Tenpa'i Wangchuk's commentary. It corresponds also to the root text given in the Dodrupchen version of the Adzom Chögar edition. However, the root text cited here reads *chos nyid ngang las chos can gzigs pa yang* (the vision of phenomena within the state of dharmatā).
26. The root verse reads *sems las bag chags dag par 'dod* (habitual tendencies are more pure than the mind). This is certainly a scribal error. In Tenpa'i Wangchuk's commentary and in the Adzom Chögar edition, the text reads *sems las ye shes dag par 'dod*, which is the version that we have followed here.
27. The Tibetan of both the root text and commentary used in this edition of the writings of Tenpa'i Wangchuk has the spelling *tshe* (when). In the Adzom Chögar edition of Longchenpa's works, however, the text here reads *rtse* (peak, summit) which is certainly easier to understand in the present context. It has therefore been adopted in this translation.
28. The Dodrupchen version of the Adzom Chögar edition has *sgom pa'i mchog* (supreme meditation). We have followed the wording given in Tenpa'i Wangchuk's text.
29. This is almost certainly a misspelling. Probably Mahāmudra is intended.
30. The Seven Treasuries (*mDzod bdun*) are *The Precious Treasury of Wish-Fulfilling Jewels* (*Yid bzhin rin po che'i mdzod*), *The Precious Treasury of Tenets* (*Grub mtha' rin po che'i mdzod*), *The Precious Treasury of Essential Instructions* (*Man ngag rin po che'i mdzod*), *The Precious Treasury of the*

Fundamental Nature (*gNas lugs rin po che'i mdzod*), *The Precious Treasury of the Dharmadhātu* (*Chos dbyings rin po che'i mdzod*), *The Precious Treasury of the Supreme Vehicle* (*Theg mchog rin po che'i mdzod*), and *The Precious Treasury of Words and Meanings* (*Tshig don rin po che'i mdzod*).

31. The Four Parts of the Heart Essence (*sNying thig ya bzhi*) are (1) *The Heart Essence of Vimalamitra* (*Bi ma snying tig*), (2) *The Innermost Essence of the Master* (*bLa ma yang tig*), (3) *The Heart Essence of the Ḍākinīs* (*mKha' 'gro snying tig*), (4) *The Innermost Essence of the Ḍākinīs* (*mKha' 'gro yang thig*), and (5) *The Profound Innermost Essence* (*Zab mo'i yang tig*).
32. *Ngal gso skor gsum*: (1) *Finding Rest in the Nature of the Mind* (*Sems nyid ngal gso*), (2) *Finding Rest in Meditation* (*bSam gtan ngal gso*), and (3) *Finding Rest in Illusion* (*sGyu ma ngal gso*).
33. The Trilogy of Natural Openness Freedom (*Rang grol skor gsum*) are (1) *The Natural Openness and Freedom of the Nature of the Mind* (*Sems nyid rang grol*), (2) *The Natural Openness and Freedom of the Dharmatā* (*Chos nyid rang grol*), and (3) *The Natural Openness and Freedom of the State of Equality* (*mNyams nyid rang grol*).
34. The Trilogy on Dispelling Darkness (*Mun sel skor gsum*) are (1) *Dispelling the Darkness of the Ten Directions* (*Phyogs bcu mun sel*), (2) *Dispelling the Darkness of the Mind* (*Yid kyi mun sel*), (3) *Dispelling the Darkness of Ignorance* (*Ma rig mun sel*).
35. Gyurme Dorje here refers to Terdak Lingpa (1646–1714), the great tertön and founder of the monastery of Mindroling.
36. See TPQ, Book 1, pp. 215 and 387.
37. See TPQ, Book 2, p. 461n538.
38. These well-known texts are prayers given in response to specific requests of several disciples by Guru Padmasambhava when he was on the point of leaving Tibet. The texts cited here are taken from the prayer given to Namkha'i Nyingpo.
39. *Mulamadhyamakakārikā*, chap. 7, v. 34.
40. The expression "awareness in the present moment" (*da lta'i rig pa*) refers to the fact that the mind and mental factors are, by their very nature and in this very instant, primordial wisdom.
41. See TPQ, Book 1, pp. 431–35.
42. The translation here is made according to Tenpa'i Wangchuk's commentary. It corresponds also to the root text given in Longchenpa's autocommentary. However, the version of the root text cited here reads *chos nyid ngang las chos can gzigs pa yang* (the vision of phenomena within the state of dharmatā).

43. Textual note: Suchness is as unmoving and unchanging as though it were nailed to the vast expanse which is as immense as space itself.
44. Textual note: Regarding the use of the terms "purity" and "equality," it is said in the Mahā Ati, that purity denotes phenomenal existence, while equality refers to the world and its inhabitants. In the present context, however, that of the uncommon tradition of the pith instructions of Atiyoga, purity is said to refer to awareness endowed with the character of luminosity. And because, within the state of empty, luminous, and unceasing awareness, unstained by the slightest trace of delusion, all things blend together in a single taste, one speaks of it as a state of equality.
45. Textual note: Awareness may be compared to a king and his kingdom. Just as a king is surrounded by his queen, his ministers, his children, and his many servants, so too the king-like, self-arisen awareness is accompanied by the creative power of primordial wisdom, which is like the ministers of government; it has an indwelling meditative absorption which may be compared with the queen and has the self-arisen qualities of wisdom, which are like the king's children and retainers.
46. In the autocommentary.
47. The Tibetan word *yeshe* (*ye shes*) has two meanings. First, it refers to the nondual primordial wisdom that is self-arisen, does not cognize *dualistically*, and corresponds to awareness, *rigpa* (*rig pa*). Second, it denotes a kind of knowing that, owing to coemergent and conceptual ignorance, knows objects dualistically and corresponds to the ordinary mind. This kind of knowing is primordial in the sense that it is present from beginningless time. As Tenpa'i Wangchuk explains, these two kinds of yeshe are closely related even though they are distinct.
48. It should be noted that each of these four vidyādharas passed on his own individual testament. See *Treasury of Precious Instructions, vol. 2*, pp. 15–30.
49. All phenomena of samsara and nirvana are perfectly included or contained (*rdzogs pa*) in awareness, the enlightened mind. This means that they do not in any way exist apart from awareness. According Tenpa'i Wangchuk (see *Notes on Mipham's Prayer to Mañjuśrī, the Great Perfection* [*'Jam dpal rdzogs pa chen po'i smon lam*]), Jamyang Khyentse Wangpo commented on the expression "perfectly included in awareness" in the following way. "Awareness should not be thought of as a great sack filled with things like earth, stones, mountains, and rocks. Conversely, it is also a mistake to think that awareness is something that pervades or

permeates samsara and nirvana and that the appearances of samsara and nirvana are permeated by it. The meaning is that all appearances, pure and impure, that manifest now are *in their nature* the one sole sphere of awareness without any change or impairment to their color or shape."

50. In this citation, the usual order of the terms "nature" and "character" (respectively *ngo bo* and *rang bzhin*) is reversed. *The All-Creating King* was translated in the early period and it was only later that the traditional order (*ngo bo, rang bzhin, thugs rje*) came to be generally accepted. In order to avoid confusion, we have adopted the now traditional formulation, translating (here) *rang bzhin* as "nature" and *ngo bo* as "character." It should be noted that, apart from this particular context, these two Tibetan terms are practically synonymous. For this reason, we have systematically added the qualifications "ultimate" and "luminous" respectively to "nature" and "character." They are always implicitly understood though not always expressed.
51. Textual note: Mind here means "the ultimate enlightened mind."
52. Chap. 7, v. 34.
53. Textual note: That is, the outer, inner, and secret expanses.
54. *Dbu ma rgyan gyi 'grel pa*, p. 128. See *The Adornment of the Middle Way*, p. 174.
55. This "truly perfect King" refers to awareness, Samantabhadra.
56. See *Beacon of Certainty*, chap. 4.
57. The text as quoted here is a slight variant on the *Mulamadhyamakakārikā*, chap. 24, v. 19.
58. The *Ratnakūṭa* is a collection of forty-nine important sutras and is one of the main sections of the Tibetan canon.
59. The four fearlessnesses are fearlessness in the face of hostility to four assertions with regard to himself and others. See TPQ, Book 1, p. 388.
60. See chap. 10, v. 6p, p. 492.
61. *spyi blugs*. Textual note: This term was explained to the Lord (Tenpa'i Wangchuk) by the dharma protector Yangleber, who appeared to him in a dream in the guise of a handsome monk.
62. *rgyal thabs spyi lugs kyi dbang*. See also TPQ, Book 2, 470n613.
63. *chos nyid rdzogs pa'i gnas lugs*. The "fundamental nature that is the highest dharmatā" refers to the dharmatā beyond phenomena and the nature of phenomena (*chos can* and *chos nyid*).
64. *med pa, phyal ba, lhun grub, gcig pu*. These are the four samayas "of nothing to observe" presented in Longchenpa's *Treasury of the Fundamental Nature* (*gNas lugs rin po che'i mdzod*).

65. *cho ga rnam pa lnga*. See TPQ, Book 2, p. 427n407.
66. *Yi ge med pa 'khor lo tshogs chen*. In other texts the name of this ground is given as *Yi ge 'khor lo tshogs chen*, the Great Wheel of Collections of Syllables.
67. The root verse reads *sems las bag chags dag par 'dod* (habitual tendencies are more pure than the mind). This is certainly a scribal error. In Tenpa'i Wangchuk's commentary and in the Derge and Adzom Chögar editions, the text reads *sems las ye shes dag par 'dod*, which is the version that we have following here.
68. Textual note: This refers to the way the nine vehicles are divided into two wider groups (also called vehicles), higher and lower. Of these two vehicles, the lower one comprises six vehicles up to and including Anuyoga. These are the vehicles of śrāvakas, pratyekabuddhas, and bodhisattvas (counted together as a single vehicle), the three vehicles of the outer tantras or mantras, followed by the vehicles of Mahāyoga and Anuyoga. All these six are counted together as the lower vehicle of effortful practice. By contrast, the higher vehicle, Atiyoga, is referred to as the vehicle that is free of exertion.
69. Textual note: The Tibetan word *lo* (like *grags* and *zer*) [the text reads *byang chub sems yin lo*] is an expression of astonished incredulity: "they actually allege."
70. See also the discussion on the three kinds of awareness, p. 239.
71. See note 70. Primordial wisdom and awareness are synonyms.
72. Textual note: Of all the phenomena of both samsara and nirvana, there is not a single one that is not empty. Since all phenomena are empty in the expanse of suchness, their ultimate nature, they are all alike and of the same kind. As Āryadeva has said, "He who sees the voidness of a single thing, beholds the suchness of all things," and similarly, "Emptiness of one thing is the emptiness of all." As this indicates, the ultimate nature of all phenomena is one. Therefore if the ultimate nature of awareness, the enlightened mind, is realized, the ultimate nature of all phenomena of samsara and nirvana is likewise realized.
73. The text reads *gang las*, but all consulted authorities agree that the text should read *gang la*.
74. The identity of this author is uncertain. Tenpa'i Wangchuk cites "the glorious Candrakīrti" (dPal ldan zla ba grags pa). Longchenpa, in this same context, refers to an authority named Dawa Gyaltsan (Zla ba rgyal mtshan). In any case, the text cited is taken from *The Samādhirāja Sutra*.
75. See *The Root Stanzas of the Middle Way*, chap. xv, v. 7.

76. See TPQ, Book 2, p. 101.
77. For these different kinds of view, see TPQ, Book 2, p. 341–50.
78. The Tibetan of both the root text and commentary used in this edition of the writings of Tenpa'i Wangchuk has the spelling *tshe* (when). In both the Derge and Adzom editions of Longchenpa's works, however, the text here reads *rtse* (peak, summit), which is certainly easier to understand in the present context. It has therefore been adopted in this translation.
79. Textual note: This interpretation of the root text here was revealed in a dream to Tenpa'i Wangchuk by the dharma protector Tsiu Marpo.
80. *gzhi grol.* This is synonymous with the primordially present natural purity (*rang bzhin rnam dag*).
81. *rgya grol.* This refers to the purity acquired through the removal of adventitious stains, *glo bur rnam dag pa.*
82. As Tenpa'i Wangchuk subsequently explains, this refers to the dissolution of the body (like mist into space) achieved in the bardo of the present life—that is, before the actual occurrence of physical death.
83. See TPQ, Book 2, 436n454.
84. Textual note: Meditation endowed with a conceptual target (as in the generation and perfection stages) and the rejection of defilement, the transformation of defilement, and the bringing of defilement onto the path (respectively the characteristics of the prātimokṣa, bodhichitta, and mantra vows) are all marked by striving. They therefore do not constitute the authentic path of the Great Perfection. According to the Ati teachings, if the nature of open and unimpeded awareness is maintained, one is naturally in possession of an infinite, oceanlike accumulation of merit and wisdom.
85. See *Root Stanzas on the Middle Way*, chap. 25, v. 19.
86. Textual note: Around the time that Khenpo Tenpa'i Wangchuk was reflecting on how to interpret this stanza, which is not elucidated in Longchenpa's autocommentary, he had a dream in which he saw the Dharma Protector Tsiu Marpo appearing in the form of a young man with red cheeks engaged in conversation with the Protectress of Mantra, the Lady of the Single Tress [Ekajaṭī], who had taken the form of a very beautiful lady. Tenpa'i Wangchuk asked the young man about the meaning of this stanza. In reply, the protector told him to put his question directly to the lady while he would to go to the sign of the retreat boundary and stand guard against obstacle makers. The lady explained the stanza at great length and, in conclusion, asked Tenpa'i Wangchuk whether he had understood. The latter replied in the affirmative but

declared that he would forget everything on waking up. Thereupon, from a precious tube extending from the tip of the lady's tongue, there came the sound "Ha," which melted softly into the Khenpo's heart. In the morning, Tenpa'i Wangchuk was able to commit the whole instruction to writing without forgetting anything. This is the testimony of Khenpo Tenpa'i Wangchuk given in secret to Abu Karlo.

87. *bar med du grol yang gshis mi bskyod.* This expression has been translated in light of Longchenpa's autocommentary where the text reads *gshis mi skyong.*
88. See *Tshig gsum gnad brdegs, The Three Statements That Strike Upon the Vital Points.* It should be noted that the text of Patrul Rinpoche says "dharmakāya without meditation."
89. The additions to the text here are taken from Longchenpa's autocommentary.
90. The autocommentaries on the Trilogy of Rest.
91. Despite this attribution, we have been unable to locate this citation either in *The Treasury of the Fundamental Nature* or elsewhere.
92. Vimalamitra, *Yi ge med pa'i rgyud kyi 'grel pa padma kha 'byed* (Chengdu: Ka' thog mkhan po 'Jam dbyangs, 1999).
93. *sNang ba rin po che'i pra khrid.* This appears to be a reference to a tantric text authored by Vimalamitra and translated by him into Tibetan.
94. It should be noted that *The Unwritten Tantra* is itself one of the seventeen tantras.
95. *Nges shes sgron me, The Beacon of Certainty.*
96. The Dodrupchen version (f. 111b), which is a print of the Adzom Chögar edition, has *sgom pa'i mchog* (supreme meditation). We have followed the wording given in Tenpa'i Wangchuk's text.
97. There is a slight difference of wording here between the root text and the commentary. In the root text, "awareness self-cognizing" is marked with the instrumental particle. In the commentary, it is treated as the object of the sentence.
98. See p. 424, where only four ways were explained. The fifth way is mentioned on p. 477 in the seventh key point.
99. The fact that all things, pure or impure, are primordial wisdom is not self-evident and may be doubted by others.
100. See *Root Stanzas of the Middle Way*, chap. 24, v. 19.
101. This is a rendering of the Tibetan *gnam thig gi gzer*, an expression composed of two parts. The first element, *gnam thig*, is a reference to the preliminary lines (*thig*) drawn on a support upon which a mandala is to be created. They divide the space (*gnam*) so that the various components

of the mandala can be precisely positioned and coordinated. In the general context of the teachings, Dilgo Khyentse Rinpoche explained (in his exposition of *The Flight of the Garuda*) that *gnam thig* are simply directives or guiding lines that serve to align the various aspects and elements of the instructions, showing the relationship between them. The second element *gzer* means "nail" and has the connotation of fixing or rendering inseparable and unchanging.

102. See *The Way of the Bodhisattva*, chap. 9, v. 2.

103. Tenpa'i Wangchuk has apparently omitted the fifth path. In the autocommentary (p. 160, line 3), however, Longchenpa says, "It is then that the path of all-accomplishing primordial wisdom is experienced. Freedom in the primordial purity of awareness is gained and one remains in the open, unimpeded, naked dharmatā, which is one's own nature."

104. Textual note: "*khrigs* means 'arrangement' or 'preparation'—as when one makes preparations for a journey." It has been translated here it as "plan of action."

105. There is a discrepancy here between the root text, which reads *khyed cag ci bya* (What is "you"?) and the wording of the commentary, which reads *ci zhig byed* (What am I to do?).

106. The description is found in *The Heap of Jewels Tantra* and is referenced in the autocommentary.

107. Here and in the root text, the expression *chos med* is used. This may be interpreted in three ways. If taken as an expression of humility, it would mean "Dharma-less" and Longchenpa would be referring to himself as an irreligious beggar. On the other hand, *chos med* could be understood in the sense of "free of Dharma," in other words that Longchenpa is describing himself as someone who has transcended the limits and fetters of religious concepts. Finally, "dharma" could be taken in the sense of "phenomenon" with the result that *chos med* would imply that for Longchenpa, who has now reached the level of phenomenal exhaustion, the experience of phenomena is at an end.

108. See TPQ, Book 1, p. 382.

109. Textual note: The "tinder of phenomena" means the obscurations of defilement and cognitive obscurations (*nyon shes kyi sgrib pa*).

110. See *Introduction to the Middle Way*, chap. 11, v. 17.

111. See TPQ, Book 2, p. 282.

112. See TPQ, Book 2, p. 294.

113. According to another tradition, this refers to the bodhisattvas on the tenth ground.

114. See TPQ, Book 2, p. 304.

115. Textual note: It must be understood that the kāyas and wisdoms are distinguished on the basis of a single empty nature.
116. Textual note: Since the five perfections, together with the enlightened body, speech, mind, qualities, and activities are designated in relation to emptiness, they are perfections only in name.
117. Textual note: These explanations of the dharmakāya must be understood as referring to the ceaseless radiance of inner luminosity, which is able to manifest as outwardly radiating luminosity. They refer only to the inner luminosity. They must not be understood as referring to the outwardly radiating luminosity.
118. Textual note: It should be understood that, since the sambhogakāya state refers to what is called the exclusively self-experiencing sambhogakāya, it is not perceptible to others. See also TPQ, Book 2, p. 293.
119. According to Longchenpa's autocommentary, the self-experience of awareness refers to the pure field enjoyed by the deities. Note that here, both in Tenpa'i Wangchuk's commentary and in Longchenpa's autocommentary, the aspect of the teaching is not mentioned.
120. Respectively, *Rig pa'i khu byug*, *rTsal chen sprug pa*, *Khyung chen lding ba*, *rDo la gser zhun*, and *Mi nub rgyal mtshan*.
121. Respectively, *rTse mo byung rgyal*, *Nam mkha'i rgyal po*, *bDe ba 'phrul bkod*, *rDzogs pa spyi chings*, *Byang chub sems tig*, *bDe ba rab 'byams*, *Srog gi 'khor lo*, *Thig le drug pa*, *rDzogs pa spyi gcod*, *Yid bzhin nor bu*, *Kun 'dus rig pa*, *rJe btsun dam pa*, and *bsGom pa don grub*.
122. Respectively, *Kun byed rgyal po*, *rMad byung rgyal po*, and *mDo bcu*.
123. The ten scriptures of *The Gathering of the Great Assembly* (*Tshogs chen 'dus pa*) are usually regarded as Anuyoga tantras.
124. Respectively, *Rig pa rang shar gyi rgyud*, *Rig pa rang grol gyi rgyud*, *Rig pa rang byung gi rgyud*, *Seng ge rtsal rdzogs kyi rgyud*, *bKra shis mdzes ldan gyi rgyud*, *Nor bu phra bkod kyi rgyud*, *Mu tig phreng ba'i rgyud*, *Yi ge med pa'i rgyud*, *Kun tu bzang po snying gi me long gi rgyud*, *rDo rje sems dpa' thugs kyi me long gi rgyud*, *Nyi zla kha 'byor gyi rgyud*, *Ngo sprod spras pa'i rgyud*, *sKu gdung 'bar ba'i rgyud*, *Rin chen spungs pa'i rgyud*, *sGron ma 'bar ba'i rgyud*, *kLong drug pa'i rgyud*, *sGra thal 'gyur rtsa ba'i rgyud*, and *sNgags srung khros ma'i rgyud*.
125. According to Franklin Edgerton's *Dictionary of Buddhist Hybrid Sanskrit*, the term *dhātu* has a number of acceptations, including "mass," "abundance," and "large quantity." Clearly, this is the meaning intended by Tenpa'i Wangchuk.

Texts Cited in Khangsar Tenpa'i Wangchuk's Commentary

Sutras and Vinaya

Great Mother, *Yum chen mo*, Śatasāhasrikāprajñāpāramitā-sūtra
Jewel Mound Sutra, *dKon mchog brtsegs pa'i mdo*, Ratnakūta-sūtra
King of Concentration Sutra, *Ting 'dzin rgyal po*, Samādhirāja-sūtra
Namtsing Vinaya, *'Dul ba gnam tsing*
Prajñāpāramitā Sutra in Eight Thousand Lines, *brGyas stong*, Aṣṭasāhasrikāprajñāpāramitā-sūtra
Prajñāpāramitā Sutra in One Hundred Thousand Lines, *'Bum*, Śatasāhasrikāprajñāpāramitā-sūtra
Precious Lamp Sutra, *dKon mchog ta la'i mdo*, Ratnolkā-sūtra
Sutra Decisively Revealing the Wisdom Intention, *dGongs pa nges 'grel gyi mdo*, Saṇdhinirmocāna-sūtra
Sutra in Response to the Questions of Tigresses, *sTag mos zhus pa'i mdo*
Sutra in Response to the Questions of Devaputra Suṣukla, *Lha bu rab dkar gyis zhus pa'i mdo*
Sutra in Response to the Questions of an Old Lady, *bsGres mos zhus pa'i mdo*, Mahālalikāparipṛcchā-sūtra
Sutra of Śrīmālādevi, *dPal phreng gyi mdo*, Śrīmālādevīsiṁhanāda-sūtra
Sutra of the Buddha's Ornaments, *Phal po che*, Buddhāvataṃsaka
Sutra of the Questions of the Girl Ratna, *Bu mo rin chen gyis zhus pa'i mdo*, Ratnadārikāparivarta-sūtra
Vajra Cutter Sutra, *rDo rje gcod pa*, Vajracchedicāprajñāpāramitā-sūtra
Visit to Laṅkā Sutra, *Lang kar gshegs pa'i mdo*, Laṇkāvatāra-sūtra
Wisdom at the Hour of Death Sutra, *'Da' ka ye shes kyi mdo*, Atyayajñāna-sūtra

Tantras

Accomplishment of the Goal of Meditation Tantra, *bsGom pa don grub*
All-Creating King Tantra, *Kun byed rgyal po*

All-Embracing Awareness, *Kun 'dus rig pa*
Array of Studded Jewels Tantra, *Nor bu 'phra bkod*
Awareness Self-Arisen, *Rig pa rang shar*
Blazing Relics, *sKu gdung 'bar ba'i rgyud*
Blissful Magical Array, *bDe ba 'phrul bkod*
Classification of Empowerments, *dBang rnam par phye ba*
Cuckoo of Awareness, *Rig pa'i khu bhyug*
Explanation of the Enlightened Mind Tantra, *Byang chub sems tig*
Exposition of the Utterly Perfect Qualities of the Great Creative Power, *rTsal chen yon tan rdzogs pa'i lung*
General Definition of Perfection, *rDzogs pa spyi gcod*
General Principles of Perfection, *rDzogs pa phyi chings*
Great Array of Ati Tantra, *A ti bkod pa chen po*
Great Garuda Tantra or Soaring Flight of the Great Garuda, *Khyung chen gyi rgyud*
Heap of Jewels Tantra, *Rin chen spungs pa*
Hevajra Tantra, *Kye rdo rje'i rgyud*
Illusory Net of Manifestation Tantra, *sGyu 'phrul drva ba*, Māyājāla-tantra
Infinite Bliss Tantra, *bDe ba rab 'byams*
King of Space Tantra, *Nam kha'i rgyal po*
Lion's Perfect Power Tantra, *Seng nge rtsal rdzogs kyi rgyud*
Mirror of Samantabhadra's Mind Tantra, *Kun tu bzang po thugs kyi me long*
Mirror of the Vajrasattva Heart Tantra, *rDo rje sems dpa' snying gi me long gi rgyud*
Natural Openness and Freedom of Awareness Tantra, *Rig pa rang grol gyi rgyud*
Naturally Luminous Awareness Tantra, *Rig pa rang gsal gyi rgyud*
Necklace of Pearls Tantra, *Mu tig phreng ba'i rgyud*
Only Child of the Self-Arisen Teachings Tantra, *Rang byung bstan pa bu gcig gi rgyud*
Peak of Spontaneity Tantra, *rTse mo byung rgyal*
Scripture of the Great Assembly, *mDo tshogs chen 'dus pa*
Scripture of the Summarized Wisdom of All the Buddhas, *Sangs rgyas thams cad kyi dgongs pa 'dus pa'i mdo*
Secret Essence Tantra, *gSang ba snying po*, Guhyagarbha
Secret Magical Manifestation Tantra, *sGyu 'phrul gsang ba*, Guhyamāyājāla-tantra
Seed of Secret Activity Tantra, *gSang ba spyod pa sa bon gyi rgyud*; also known as the Only Child of the Teachings Tantra, *bsTan pa bu gcig gi rgyud*

Self-Arisen Perfection Tantra, *rDzogs pa rang byung gi rgyud*
Six Expanses Tantra, *kLong drug*
Six Spheres Tantra, *Thig le drug pa*
Smelting Gold from Ore Tantra, *rDo la gser zhun*
Soaring Flight of the Great Garuda or Great Garuda, *Khyung chen lding ba*
Stirring of Supreme Creative Power Tantra, *rTsal chen sprug pa*
Tantra Adorned with Introductions to the Nature of the Mind, *Ngo sprod spras pa'i rgyud*
Tantra of Auspicious Beauty, *bKra shis mdzes ldan*
Tantra of Self-Occurring Awareness, *Rig pa rang byung*
Tantra of the Blazing Lamp, *sGron ma 'bar ba*
Tantra of the Victory Banner Never to Be Lowered, *Mi nub rgyal mtshan*
Tantra without Letters, *Yi ge med pa'i rgyud*
Two-Chapter Hevajra Tantra, *brTag gnyis*
Unimpeded Openness of Samantabhadra's Wisdom, *dGongs pa zang thal gyi rgyud*
Union of the Sun and Moon Tantra, *Nyi zla kha sbyor gyi rgyud*
Vajra Tent Tantra, *rDo rje gur gyi rgyud*, Vajrapañjara
Venerable Sublimity Tantra, *rJe btsun dam pa*
Wheel of Life Tantra, *Srog gi 'khor lo*
Wish-Fulfilling Jewel Tantra, *Yid bzhin nor bu*
Wondrous King Tantra, *rMad byung rgyal po'i rgyud*
Word-Transcending Tantra, *sGra thal 'gyur rgyud rtsa ba'i rgyud*

Sanskrit Scriptures

Adornment of the Middle Way, *dBu ma rgyan*, Madhyamakālaṃkara by Śāntarakṣita
Buddhapālita, *dBu ma sangs rgyas bskyangs* by Buddhapālita
Commentary on Bodhicitta, *Byang chub sems 'grel*, Bodhicittavivārana by Nāgārjuna
Commentary on Valid Cognition, *rNam 'grel*, Pramāṇavārttika by Dharmakīrti
Distinguishing the Two Truths, *bDen gnyis*, Satyadvayavibhaga by Jñānagarbha
Dohas, *Do ha skor gsum*, Dohākośa by Saraha
Introduction to the Middle Way, *dBu ma la 'jug pa*, Madhyamakāvatāra by Candrakīrti
Ornament of Clear Realization, *mNgon rtogs rgyan*, Abhisamayālaṃkāra by Maitreya and Asaṅga

Precious Source, Manual on Poetics, *sDeb sbyor rin chen 'byung gnas*, Candoratnākara by Ratnākaraśānti

Root Stanzas of the Middle Way, *dBu ma rtsa ba shes rab*, Mūlamadhyamakakārikā by Nāgārjuna

Sublime Continuum, *rGyud bla ma*, Uttaratantraśāstra by Maitreya and Asaṅga

Treasury of Abhidharma, *Chos mngon mdzod*, Abhidharmakośa by Vasubandhu

Unborn Precious Treasury, *sKye med rin po che'i mdzod*, by Nāgārjuna

Way of the Bodhisattva, *sPyod 'jug*, Bodhicaryāvatāra by Śāntideva

Tibetan Scriptures

Beacon of Certainty, *Nges shes sgron me* by Mipham

Blossoming Lotus, *Pad ma kha 'byed* by Vimalamitra

Distinction of the Three Crucial Points, *gNad gsum shan 'byed* by Jigma Lingpa

Essence of Luminosity, *sPyi don 'od gsal snying po* by Mipham

Father Teachings and the Son Teachings, *bKa' gdams pha chos bu chos*, by Atiśa and Dromtönpa

Finding Rest in the Nature of the Mind, *Sems nyid ngal gso* by Longchen Rabjam

Four Parts of the Heart Essence, *sNying thig ya bzhi* by Longchen Rabjam

Heart Essence of Chetsun, *lCe btsun snying thig* by Adzom Drukpa

Instruction Concerning Precious Appearances, *sNang ba rin po che'i pra khrid*, by Vimalamitra

Letter of Advice Called Drops of Nectar, *sPring yig bdud rtsi'i thigs pa* by Ngok Lotsawa Loden Sherab

Parting Testament, *'Das rjes*, by Garab Dorje

Prayer in Seven Chapters, *Le'u bdun ma* by Guru Padmasambhava

Seven Treasuries, *mDzod bdun* by Longchen Rabjam

Treasury of Knowledge, *Shes bya mdzod* by Jamgön Kongtrul

Treasury of Teachings, *Lung gi gter mdzod* by Longchen Rabjam

Treasury of the Fundamental Nature, *gNas lugs mdzod*, by Longchen Rabjam

Treasury of Wish-Fulfilling Jewels, *Yid bzhin rin po che'i mdzod* by Longchen Rabjam

Treasury of Words and Meanings, *Tshig don rin po che'i mdzod* by Longchen Rabjam

Trilogy of Chariots, *Shing rta skor gsum* by Longchen Rabjam
Trilogy of Natural Openness and Freedom, *Rang grol skor gsum* by Longchen Rabjam
Trilogy of Rest, *Ngal gso skor gsum* by Longchen Rabjam
Trilogy of Secret Essence, *sNying po skor gsum* by Longchen Rabjam
Trilogy of the Uncontrived Mind, *gNyug sems skor gsum* by Mipham
Trilogy on Dispelling Darkness, *Mun sel skor gsum* by Longchen Rabjam

Bibliography

Chödrak Zangpo. *Meaningful to Behold: A Critical Edition and Annotated Translation of Longchenpa's Biography.* Translated and commented by Shinichi Tsumagari. San Bernadino, CA: CreateSpace, 2017.

Germano, David. "Poetic Thought, the Intelligent Universe, and the Mystery of Self: The Tantric Synthesis of Rdzogs Chen in Fourteenth Century Tibet." PhD diss., University of Wisconsin, 1992.

Jigme Lingpa and Longchen Yeshe Dorje, Kangyur Rinpoche. *Treasury of Precious Qualities, Book 2.* Translated by Padmakara Translation Group. Boston: Shambhala, 2013; Boulder: 2020.

Khangsar Tenpa'i Wangchuk. *Chos dbyings rin po che'i mdzod kyi 'bru 'grel 'od gsal thig le nyag gcig.* In Khang sar bstan pa'i dbang phyug gi gsung 'bum, vol. 4. Beijing: Mi rigs dpe skrun khang, 2005.

Longchen Rabjam. *Chos dbyings rin po che'i mdzod.* Collected Works of Longchenpa. Varanasi: Dodrupchen, 1965.

———. *Chos dbyings rin po che'i 'grel ba lung gi gter mdzod.* Collected Works of Longchenpa. Varanasi: Dodrupchen, 1965.

———. *Jewel Treasure of the Dharmadhātu with the Autocommentary "A Treasury of Citations."* Translated by Lama Chönam and Sangye Khandro. Ashland, OR: Berotsana, 2024.

———. *A Treasure Trove of Scriptural Transmission: A Commentary on the Precious Treasury of the Basic Space of Phenomena.* Translated by Richard Barron. Junction City, CA: Padma, 2001.

Nyoshul Khenpo. *A Marvelous Garland of Rare Gems.* Translated by Richard Barron. Junction City, CA: Padma, 2005.

Shechen Rabjam ('Gyur med kun bzang rnam rgyal). *The Catalog to the Seven Treasuries (mDzod bdun dkar chag).* Gangtok, Sikkim: Dodrup Sangye Lama, 1976.

Tulku Thondup. *The Practice of Dzogchen.* Boston: Snow Lion, 2014.

The Padmakara Translation Group Translations Into English

The Adornment of the Middle Way, Shantarakshita and Mipham Rinpoche. Boston: Shambhala, 2005, 2010.

Counsels from My Heart, Dudjom Rinpoche. Boston: Shambhala, 2001, 2003.

Enlightened Courage, Dilgo Khyentse Rinpoche. Dordogne: Editions Padmakara, 1992; Ithaca, NY: Snow Lion, 1994, 2006.

The Excellent Path to Enlightenment, Dilgo Khyentse. Dordogne: Editions Padmakara, 1987; Ithaca, NY: Snow Lion, 1996.

A Feast of the Nectar of the Supreme Vehicle, Maitreya and Jamgön Mipham. Boulder: Shambhala, 2018.

Finding Rest in Illusion, Longchenpa. Boulder: Shambhala, 2018.

Finding Rest in Meditation, Longchenpa. Boulder: Shambhala, 2018, 2020.

Finding Rest in the Nature of the Mind, Longchenpa. Boulder: Shambhala, 2017, 2020.

A Flash of Lightning in the Dark of the Night, The Dalai Lama. Shambhala, 1993. Republished as For the Benefit of All Beings. Boston: Shambhala, 2009.

Food of Bodhisattvas, Shabkar Tsogdruk Rangdrol. Boston: Shambhala, 2004.

A Garland of Views: A Guide to View, Meditation, and Result in the Nine Vehicles, Padmasambhava and Mipham Rinpoche. Boston: Shambhala, 2015.

A Guide to the Words of My Perfect Teacher, Khenpo Ngawang Pelzang. Translated with Dipamkara. Boston: Shambhala, 2004.

The Heart of Compassion, Dilgo Khyentse. Boston: Shambhala, 2007.

The Heart Treasure of the Enlightened Ones, Dilgo Khyentse and Patrul Rinpoche. Boston: Shambhala, 1992.

The Hundred Verses of Advice, Dilgo Khyentse and Padampa Sangye. Boston: Shambhala, 2005.

Introduction to the Middle Way, Chandrakirti and Mipham Rinpoche. Boston: Shambhala, 2002, 2004.

Journey to Enlightenment, Matthieu Ricard. New York: Aperture Foundation, 1996.

Lady of the Lotus Born, Gyalwa Changchub and Namkhai Nyingpo. Boston: Shambhala, 1999, 2002.

Lion of Speech: The Life of Mipham Rinpoche, Dilgo Khyentse. Boulder: Shambhala, 2020.

The Life of Shabkar: The Autobiography of a Tibetan Yogin. Albany, NY: SUNY Press, 1994; Ithaca, New York: Snow Lion, 2001.

Nagarjuna's Letter to a Friend, Yeshe Dorje, Kangyur Rinpoche. Ithaca, NY: Snow Lion, 2005.

The Natural Openness and Freedom of the Mind, Deshek Lingpa and Khangsar Tenpa'i Wangchuk. Boulder: Shambhala, 2024.

The Nectar of Manjushri's Speech, Kunzang Pelden. Boston: Shambhala, 2007, 2010.

Practicing the Great Perfection: Instructions on the Crucial Points, Shechen Gyaltsap Gyurme Pema Namgyal. Boulder: Shambhala, 2020.

The Precious Treasury of the Fundamental Nature, Longchenpa and Khangsar Tenpa'i Wangchuk. Boulder: Shambhala, 2021.

The Root Stanzas on the Middle Way, Nagarjuna. Dordogne: Edition Padmakara, 2008; Boulder: Shambhala, 2016.

A Torch Lighting the Way to Freedom, Dudjom Rinpoche, Jigdrel Yeshe Dorje. Boston: Shambhala, 2011.

The Treasury of Precious Instructions, vol. 2: Nyingma, Part 2. Compiled by Jamgön Kongtrul Lodrö Taye. Boulder: Snow Lion, 2024.

Treasury of Precious Qualities, Book One. Longchen Yeshe Dorje, Kangyur Rinpoche. Boston: Shambhala, 2001. Revised version with root text by Jigme Lingpa, 2010.

Treasury of Precious Qualities, Book Two. Longchen Yeshe Dorje, Kangyur Rinpoche. Boston: Shambhala, 2013, 2020.

The Way of the Bodhisattva (Bodhicharyavatara), Shantideva. Boston: Shambhala, 1997, 2006, 2008.

White Lotus, Jamgön Mipham. Boston: Shambhala, 2007.

The Wisdom Chapter: Jamgön Mipham's Commentary on the Ninth Chapter of the Way of the Bodhisattva. Jamgön Mipham. Boulder: Shambhala, 2017.

Wisdom: Two Buddhist Commentaries. Khenchen Kunzang Pelden and Minyak Kunzang Sonam. Dordogne: Editions Padmakara, 1993, 1999.

The Wish-Fulfilling Jewel, Dilgo Khyentse. Boston: Shambhala, 1988.
The Words of My Perfect Teacher, Patrul Rinpoche. Sacred Literature Series of the International Sacred Literature Trust. New York: HarperCollins, 1994; 2nd ed. Lanham, MD: AltaMira Press, 1998; Boston: Shambhala, 1998; New Haven, CT: Yale University Press, 2010.
Zurchungpa's Testament, Zurchungpa and Dilgo Khyentse. Ithaca, NY: Snow Lion, 2006.

Khangsar Tenpa'i Wangchuk's Collected Works

In 2019, the Padmakara Translation Group began the project of translating the entire Collected Works of the Nyingma master Khangsar Tenpa'i Wangchuk under the guidance of Pema Wangyal Rinpoche and Jigme Khyentse Rinpoche, having received the transmission from Tenpa'i Wangchuk's nephew, Tsultrim Zangpo Rinpoche. The following is a list of volumes published to date. Several more are forthcoming.

The Natural Openness and Freedom of the Mind: A Treasure Tantra of the Great Perfection, by Deshek Lingpa and Khangsar Tenpa'i Wangchuk.

The Precious Treasury of the Dharmadhātu, by Longchenpa and Khangsar Tenpa'i Wangchuk.

The Precious Treasury of the Fundamental Nature, by Longchenpa and Khangsar Tenpa'i Wangchuk.

Index